AMERICAN NOVEL

American Novel
Brown to James

Edited by
FRANK N. MAGILL

Derived from Library Editions
Published by Salem Press, Inc.

SALEM SOFTBACKS
Pasadena, California

LIBRARY OF CONGRESS CATALOG CARD NUMBER: 80-54247

ISBN 0-89356-302-1

Some of this material has appeared previously in
works published under the titles *Masterplots*: Revised Edition, *Cyclopedia of World Authors*, *Cyclopedia of Literary Characters*, and *Magill's Bibliography of Literary Criticism*.

First Printing

PRINTED IN THE UNITED STATES OF AMERICA

PUBLISHER'S NOTE

MAGILL SURVEYS form a series of integrated study guides designed to provide sources for augmenting classroom work in the Humanities. These guides offer ready-reference information about authors and their works and are structured with classroom requirements strictly in mind. Articles include biographical information about authors and their total canon, and, where appropriate, they provide plot summaries, character studies, critical evaluations, and extensive bibliographical references.

Magill Surveys are intended to take the student far beyond the immediate assignment. For example, if the program calls for the study of "a Dickens novel," the appropriate Survey will present to the student half a dozen or more pages on each of several Dickens novels, including a critical biography of Dickens, plot summaries and critical evaluations of the novels, individual character analyses of scores of the characters appearing in these novels, and finally an average of about twenty bibliographical references for *each* of the novels—the latter element a highly valuable resource whether for class work or term papers. Thus, the student may gain extensive background information about the author and his canon while concentrating on in-depth study of a particular work.

The text for this Survey derives from a series of extensive library references in world literature edited by Frank N. Magill, including the following sources: *Masterplots*, *Cyclopedia of World Authors*, *Cyclopedia of Literary Characters*, and *Magill's Bibliography of Literary Criticism*.

All the material drawn from the above sources has been revised and supplemented where necessary to reflect current critical opinion. The text has been arranged to provide convenient access to a great amount of basic information condensed in one handy volume. Elaborate indexing techniques have been employed to assure information retrieval with a minimum of time and effort.

The original material reproduced in *Magill Surveys* has been developed through consultations with and contributions by hundreds of professors and scholars throughout the United States and abroad over a period of years. Its authoritativeness is attested by the thousands of academic and public libraries where the basic works from which this material is drawn will be found. The student who wishes to go beyond his assignment will find here ample means to satisfy his desire.

This collection on the American novel deals with thirty-two authors and seventy-five representative nineteenth century novels. It provides an overview of important works of American long fiction from Charles Brockden Brown to Henry James. Hawthorne, Melville, and Twain are well represented. An examination of the influence of these early writers on later American fiction will enhance the students' appreciation of twentieth century American literature.

CONTENTS

CONTENTS

CONTENTS

Special Consultant

Mary Rohrberger

List of Contributors

Gay Wilson Allen
Kenneth John Atchity
James F. Beard, Jr.
Sally Buckner
Kenneth W. Cameron
Richard Chase
Glenda Louise Hicks
Farhat M. Iftekharrudin
Thomas H. Johnson

Geraldene Jones
Jennifer Kidney
Henderson Kincheloe
Betty Jo Knight
Chapel Louise Petty
James B. Sanderson
Randall Stewart
Jeffrey Walker
James Southall Wilson

AMERICAN NOVEL

LOUISA MAY ALCOTT

Born: Germantown, Pennsylvania (November 29, 1832)
Died: Boston, Massachusetts (March 6, 1888)

Principal Works

NOVELS: *Little Women*, 1868; *An Old-Fashioned Girl*, 1870; *Little Men*, 1871; *Eight Cousins*, 1875; *Rose in Bloom*, 1876; *Under the Lilacs*, 1878; *Jack and Jill*, 1880; *Jo's Boys*, 1886.
MISCELLANEOUS: *Flower Fables*, 1854; *Hospital Sketches*, 1863.

Louisa May Alcott, the famous daughter of a famous father, was born in Germantown, Pennsylvania, on November 29, 1832; but her early life was spent in the vicinity of Concord and Boston, where she grew up under the influence of Ralph Waldo Emerson and Henry David Thoreau. Her father, Bronson Alcott, was a transcendentalist, a non-resident member of Brook Farm. Reformer, scholar, and educator, he founded the well-known Temple School in Boston.

Early in life she realized that her impractical father needed financial assistance to run his household. Accordingly she worked as a domestic, as a seamstress, and as a teacher. Her first attempts at writing were the popular melodramas of the period, in which métier she attracted some attention with such early and now forgotten plays as *The Bandit's Bride*, and *The Moorish Maiden's Vow*. Next she wrote poems and stories, some of which were published in *The Atlantic Monthly*. In 1854 appeared her first book, *Flower Fables*, a series of stories written for Ralph Waldo Emerson's daughter Ellen.

During the Civil War she served as a nurse in the Union Hospital in Georgetown. As a result of this experience her health was impaired. The letters she wrote home to her family were later revised and published as *Hospital Sketches* in 1863.

In 1864 her first novel, *Moods*, was published. In 1867 she became editor of a children's magazine, *Merry's Museum*. In the next year *Little Women* appeared, an immediate success both in English and translation. This perennially popular volume described a normal, pleasant American family life. The March family of the novel is drawn from her own family. Jo March is Louisa herself, and the March sisters represent the girls of the Alcott family. Theodore Lawrence (Laurie) is modeled after a young man whom she met in Poland during a trip abroad.

The popularity of *Little Women* was such that at last the family could live without financial worries. But Alcott continued to write other children's stories which attracted an enthusiastic and adoring audience: *An Old-Fashioned Girl*, *Little Men*, *Eight Cousins*, *Rose in Bloom*, *Under the Lilacs*, *Jack and Jill*, and *Jo's Boys*. All had their avid readers.

Her last years were spent in Boston, where she died two days after her father, on March 6, 1888. An ardent abolitionist and advocate of women's suffrage, Louisa May Alcott still has a host of admirers, for her sentimental novels continue to attract readers among each new generation of children all over the world. *Little Women*, called the most popular girls' book ever written, is her chief claim to fame.

Bibliography

Most of the books about Louisa May Alcott are intended primarily for children. The standard biography for source material is Ednah D. Cheney, *Louisa May Alcott: Her Life, Letters and Journals*, 1889. Katherine Anthony, *Louisa May Alcott*, 1938, and Marjorie Worthington, *Miss Alcott of Concord*, 1958, are more recent and perceptive studies. See also Maria S. Porter, *Recollections of Louisa May Alcott*, 1893; and Lucile Gulliver, *Louisa May Alcott: A Bibliography*, 1932.

LITTLE WOMEN

Type of work: Novel
Author: Louisa May Alcott (1832–1888)
Type of plot: Sentimental romance
Time of plot: Nineteenth century
Locale: A New England village; New York City; Italy
First published: 1868

This largely autobiographical story of four sisters growing up during and after the Civil War has remained popular for generations because of its realism and humor, its tough-minded heroine, and its innate honesty and compassion. The book is far less sentimental than is supposed by people who have not read it. There are more than a few hints in the novel of Alcott's concerns with equal opportunities for women in society.

Principal Characters

Meg, the oldest of the March girls, a plump governess to unruly neighborhood children. She marries John Brooke.

Jo, a tall, awkward, tomboyish girl who likes to write and to devise plays and entertainments for her sisters. In character and personality she corresponds to the author. She resents Meg's interest in John but later is happy to have him as a brother-in-law. She writes and sells stories and becomes a governess for Mrs. Kirke in New York. Proposed to by Laurie, she rejects him. She later marries Professor Bhaer with whom she establishes a boys' school at Plumfield, Aunt March's old home.

Beth, a gentle homebody helpful to Mrs. March in keeping house. She contracts scarlet fever from which she never fully recovers. She dies during the spring after Jo's return from New York.

Amy, a curly-haired dreamer who aspires to be a famous artist. She is a companion of Aunt Carrol on a European trip. She marries Laurie.

Mrs. March (Marmee), the kindly, un-derstanding, lovable mother of the four March girls.

Mr. March, her husband, an army chaplain in the Civil War who becomes ill while away but who later returns well and happy.

Theodore Lawrence (Laurie), a young neighbor who joins the March family circle. He falls in love with Jo, but after his rejection by her he transfers his feelings to Amy, whom he marries.

Professor Bhaer, a tutor in love with Jo, whom he marries.

Mr. Lawrence, the wealthy, indulgent grandfather of Laurie.

Aunt March, a wealthy, irascible relative who wills her home to Jo.

John Brooke, Laurie's tutor, who falls in love with and marries Meg.

Aunt Carrol, a relative of the Marches.

Mrs. Kirke, a New York boarding-house keeper.

Daisy and Demi, Meg's children.

LITTLE WOMEN by Louisa May Alcott. Published by Little, Brown & Co.

The Story

The March family lived in a small house next door to the Lawrence mansion, where young Theodore Lawrence and his aged grandfather had only each other for company in the great house. Old Mr. Lawrence was wealthy and he indulged every wish of his grandson, but often Laurie was lonely. When the lamp was lit and the shades were up in the March house, he could see the four March girls with their mother in the center seated around a cheerful fire. He learned to know them by name before he met them, and in his imagination he almost felt himself a member of the family.

The oldest was plump Meg, who had to earn her living as governess of a group of unruly youngsters in the neighborhood. Next was Jo, tall, awkward, and tomboyish, who liked to write, and who spent all her spare time devising plays and entertainments for her sisters. Then there was gentle Beth, the homebody, content to sit knitting by the fire, or to help her mother take care of the house. The youngest was curly-haired Amy, a schoolgirl who dreamed of someday becoming a famous artist like Michelangelo or Leonardo da Vinci.

At Christmas time the girls were confronted with the problem of what to do with the dollar Marmee, as they called their mother, had said they might spend. At first each thought only of her own pleasure, but all ended by buying a gift for Marmee instead. On Christmas morning they insisted on sharing their breakfast with the Hummels, a poor family in the neighborhood, and for this unselfishness they were rewarded when rich Mr. Lawrence sent over a surprise Christmas feast consisting of ice cream, bonbons, and four bouquets of flowers for the table.

Many happy days followed, with Laurie, who had met Jo at a fashionable New Year's Eve dance, becoming a part of the March family circle. But in November of that same year a telegram brought a message that their father, an army chaplain in the Civil War, was critically ill. Mrs. March did not know what to do. She felt that she should go to her husband at once, but she had barely five dollars in her purse. She was hesitant about going to wealthy, irascible Aunt March for help. Jo solved the problem by selling her beautiful, long, chestnut hair, which was her only vanity, for twenty-five dollars. She made the sacrifice willingly, but that night, after the others had gone to bed, Meg, who thought Jo was asleep, heard her weeping softly. Gently, Meg asked if Jo were crying over her father's illness, and Jo sobbed that it was not her father she was crying for now, but for her hair.

During Marmee's absence dark days fell upon the little women. Beth, who had never been strong at best, contracted scarlet fever, and for a time it looked as if Jo were going to lose her dearest sister. Marmee was sent for, but by the time she arrived the crisis had passed and her little daughter was better. By the next Christmas, Beth was her old contented self again. Mr. March surprised them all when he returned home from the front well and happy. The little family was together once more.

Then John Brooke, Laurie's tutor, fell in love with Meg. This fact was disclosed when Mr. Brooke surreptitiously stole one of Meg's gloves and kept it in his pocket as a memento. Laurie discovered the glove and informed Jo. To his great surprise, she was infuriated at the idea that the family circle might be disturbed. But she was quite reconciled when, three years later, Meg became Mrs. Brooke.

In the meantime, Jo herself had grown up. She began to take her writing seriously, and even sold a few stories which helped with the family budget.

Her greatest disappointment came when Aunt Carrol, a relative of the Marches, decided she needed a companion on a European trip, and asked not Jo but the more ladylike Amy to accompany her. Then Jo, with Marmee's permission, decided to go to New York. She took a job as governess for a Mrs. Kirke, who ran a large boardinghouse. There she met Professor Bhaer, a lovable and eccentric German tutor, who proved to be a good friend and companion.

Upon her return home, Laurie, who had always loved Jo, asked her to marry him. Jo, who imagined that she would always remain an old maid, devoting herself exclusively to her writing, tried to convince Laurie that they were not made for each other. He persisted, pointing out that his grandfather and her family both expected them to marry. When she made him realize that her refusal was final, he stamped off and shortly afterward went to Europe with his grandfather. In Europe he saw a great deal of Amy, and the two became close friends, so that Laurie was able to transfer to her younger sister a great deal of the feeling he previously had for Jo.

In the meantime Jo was at home caring for Beth, who had never fully recovered from her first illness. In the spring, Beth died, practically in Jo's arms, and after the loss of her gentle sister Jo was lonely indeed. She tried to comfort herself with her writing, and with Meg's two babies, Daisy and Demi, but not until the return of Amy, now married to Laurie, did she begin to feel her old self again. When Professor Bhaer stopped off on his way to a university appointment in the Midwest, Jo was delighted. One day, under an umbrella he had supplied to shield her from a pouring rain, he asked her to marry him, and Jo accepted. Within a year old Aunt March died and willed her home, Plumfield, to Jo. She decided to open a boys' school, where she and her professor could devote their lives to instructing the young.

So the little women reached maturity, and on their mother's sixtieth birthday they all had a great celebration at Plumfield. Around the table, at which there was but one empty chair, sat Marmee, her children and her grandchildren. When Laurie proposed a toast to her, she replied by stretching out her arms to them all and saying that she could wish nothing better for them than this present happiness for the rest of their lives.

Critical Evaluation

Little Women long has been unfairly characterized as a sentimental children's novel. Actually, it is a surprisingly tough-minded and realistic book dealing with strong and resilient people and their efforts to survive in an often bleak world. In large part it is concerned with ideals, but these ideals are integrated as part of the lives of the characters. It would have been impossible for the daughter of Bronson Alcott not to incorporate certain ideals of living in her fiction. But Louisa May Alcott possessed a much stronger character than her father, and this is evident in her powerful and at times angry picture of the place of women in mid-nineteenth century America. Any reader who approaches the book objectively will note this continuous theme. The restless Jo, not surprisingly, bears most of the weight of this important theme. In her later novels, notably in *Jo's Boys,* Alcott was to carry on and intensify her concern with women's rights. The mature Jo, in that later novel, would actively encourage young women to study medicine and other previously unacceptable occupations for women. These aspects of Jo's character and Alcott's radical preoccupations are visible in this early, excellent novel.

The importance of the family unit was vital to all of the Alcotts and this conviction gives *Little Women* much of its power. The family circle is shown as a force which can help individuals survive against all odds, against war, poverty, narrow-minded self-interest, and social change. Individuals suffer, struggle, and die, but the family endures. At the center of this family unit stands the mother. But Mrs. March is not the saccharine figure which she often is supposed. In the novel, she is a tough and courageous woman with a temper which she has had to struggle to control and a character strong enough to hold together her family even when it is divided by war and other trials.

Above all, *Little Women* is a novel rich with fine characterizations. The portraits of Aunt March, of Professor Bhaer, of old Mr. Lawrence, and so many other individuals, as well as the March clan, have endeared the book to millions of readers. These people are not sweet, idealized figures, but genuine human beings, with faults and foibles and tremendous vitality. Louisa May Alcott's artistry was so unself-conscious and natural as to seem almost nonexistent, but it was this skill which created such memorable and real characters. *Little Women* has survived the patronizing of many critics and will continue to be a popular and loved book, because it is an extraordinary and vigorous piece of writing and because it presents a picture of human endurance that is both touching and inspiring.

Bibliography

Auerbach, Nina. "Austen and Alcott on Matriarchy: New Women or New Wives?," in *Novel, a Forum on Fiction.* X (Fall, 1976), pp. 6–26.

Brophy, Brigid. *Don't Never Forget: Collected Views and Reviews.* New York: Holt, Rinehart, 1966, pp. 113–120.

Crompton, Margaret. "*Little Women*: The Making of a Classic," in *Contemporary Review*. CCXVIII (February, 1971), pp. 99–104.

Janeway, Elizabeth. "Meg, Jo, Beth, Amy and Louisa," in *New York Times Book Review*. LXXIII (September 29, 1968), p. 42.

EDWARD BELLAMY

Born: Chicopee Falls, Massachusetts (March 26, 1850)
Died: Chicopee Falls (May 22, 1898)

Principal Works

NOVELS: *Six to One: A Nantucket Idyl*, 1878; *Dr. Heidenhoff's Process*, 1880; *Miss Ludington's Sister: A Romance of Immortality*, 1884; *Looking Backward: 2000–1887*, 1888; *Equality*, 1897; *The Duke of Stockbridge: A Romance of Shays' Rebellion*, 1900.

SHORT STORIES: *The Blindman's World and Other Stories*, 1898.

Edward Bellamy, the son of a New England Baptist minister, was born at Chicopee Falls, Massachusetts, March 26, 1850. He was largely self-educated. Although he attended Union College for only a year as a special student, he read widely in history, politics, economics, and literature. As a young man, he wrote editorials for the *Springfield Union* and later helped establish the *Daily News*. For a year or so he wrote book reviews for the New York *Evening Post*.

While working as a newspaperman in Springfield, Bellamy began to write novels. His first work, *Six to One*, was light and romantic, but his second novel, *Dr. Heidenhoff's Process*, a work dealing with sin and a sense of guilt, was impressive enough to have William Dean Howells hail Bellamy as the literary successor to Hawthorne. But Bellamy did not find a wide public or general acclaim until the publication of *Looking Backward* in January, 1888.

Begun simply as a literary fantasy, *Looking Backward* presented a picture of a humane, scientific, and socialistic Utopia in the year 2000. The book sold fewer than 10,000 copies its first year, but then became enormously popular. Others, such as Cyrus Field Willard, a Boston newspaperman, formed clubs to promote Bellamy's social ideas, clubs that soon joined in the "Nationalist Movement." Before long Bellamy became a leader in this movement, editing first the *Nationalist*, then the *New Nation*, and crusading for economic equality, human brotherhood, and the progressive nationalization of industry. Bellamy spoke and wrote frequently for his cause, at the same time working on *Equality*, a sequel to *Looking Backward* which developed more fully the socialistic institutions of the Utopia. In the meantime the movement was enormously popular, its ideas forming a large portion of the platform of the People's Party in the 1892 election.

By the time of Bellamy's death, at Chicopee Falls on May 22, 1898, the "Nationalist Movement" as a political organization had disappeared, and the People's Party had been absorbed by William Jennings Bryan and "Free Silver" in 1896. Yet Bellamy's Utopian concepts, always tinged with fantasy and human values, maintained a romantic influence on thinking young men in both America and Europe. Numerous critics complained about his lack of originality, but his ideas formed the basis of "The League for the Organization of Progress" in Europe (a group which claimed Eduard Beneš, Ramsay MacDonald, Aristide Briand, and Karl Renner as members), and Americans as diverse as Thorstein Veblen, John Dewey, and A. A. Berle, Jr., have acknowledged his influence. It is as the humane and romantic Utopian, campaigning for equality and social justice, rather than as a novelist or profound political thinker, that Bellamy is remembered and read today.

Bibliography

The chief source is Arthur E. Morgan, *Edward Bellamy*, 1944, which includes a bibliography. Morgan is the editor of *The Philosophy of Edward Bellamy*, 1945, a collection of selections from Bellamy's writings together with commentary. Two useful studies appear in Vernon L. Parrington, *Main Currents in American Thought*, Vol. III, 1930; and W. F. Taylor, *The Economic Novel in America*, 1942. See also Robert L. Shurter, "The Literary Work of Edward Bellamy," *American Literature*, V (1933), 229–234; Sylvia E. Bowman, et al., *Edward Bellamy Abroad: An American Prophet's Influence*, (Essays by various hands), 1962; and Daniel Aaron and Harry Levin, *Edward Bellamy, Novelist and Reformer*, 1968.

LOOKING BACKWARD

Type of work: Novel
Author: Edward Bellamy (1850–1898)
Type of work: Utopian romance
Time of plot: A.D. 2000
Locale: Boston, Massachusetts
First published: 1888

The main interest of Looking Backward: 2000–1887 *lies in its credible presentation of a socialist Utopia; the book has served to introduce many people to the theory of socialism. Its prophecies for the world by the year 2000 are sometimes strikingly shrewd, and the judgments made of modern society are pointed and witty.*

Principal Characters

Julian West, a young Bostonian who, sleeping under hypnosis in his sound-proofed cellar, goes forward into the year 2000 to find himself in a socialistic United States where government controls everything and everyone is happy, healthy, and well-off. Julian is delighted with this new world and falls in love with a young woman of the time. They marry and plan a secure, happy life in the twenty-first century.

Dr. Leete, Julian's host in the year 2000. He is a doctor who, like everyone else at the time, has retired at forty-five. He likes Julian and enjoys telling him of and showing him the brave new world of the year 2000.

Edith Leete, the great-granddaughter of Julian's nineteenth century sweetheart.

She falls in love with Julian through the love letters he wrote to his sweetheart in the 1880's. She readily agrees to marry Julian, who has found security as a college lecturer in history.

Edith Bartlett, Julian's sweetheart in the nineteenth century. She saved his letters and passed them on to posterity after his mysterious disappearance.

Dr. Pillsbury, a quack who performs the hypnosis that allows Julian to sleep from 1887 to 2000. He administers the treatment to relieve the young man's chronic insomnia.

Mr. Bartlett, Edith Bartlett's father and Julian's host during his last evening spent in the year 1887.

The Story

Julian West had a hard time sleeping. In order to have complete quiet he had built a sound-proof room with thick cement walls in the cellar of his house. He was also in the habit of having a quack doctor named Pillsbury put him to sleep by hypnosis.

One night he went to dinner with his fiancée's family and spent an enjoyable evening with Edith and her father, Mr. Bartlett. He went home, had the doctor give him a treatment, and went to sleep. He awoke to find strange people in the room. They asked him who he was, and when he had gone to sleep. Julian was amazed when he realized that he had been asleep one hundred and thirteen years, three months, and eleven days.

From much questioning, Julian learned what must have happened. During the night that he last remembered, his house had burned down except for the sealed room in which he slept; and apparently everyone assumed that he had died in the fire. Because of his hypnotic state, his body had remained the same. He was still a young man of thirty when he was discovered by Dr. Leete in the year 2000. Dr. Leete and his daughter, Edith, were very kind to their guest from the past and tried to explain the changes in the world since he had last seen it.

Boston was a new city with only the bay and the inlets as he remembered them. The city was beautiful, with attractive buildings and spacious parks. The strikes and labor troubles of the nineteenth century had resulted in a bloodless revolution, and now a socialized government controlled all business. There was no smoke because all heating was done by electricity. All the people were healthy and happy.

Dr. Leete tried to explain the world of A.D. 2000. There was no money. The state gave everyone, no matter what his job, a card which contained the same amount of credit for a year's expenses. There was no chance, however, for anyone to spend his credit foolishly and starve. If a person proved incapable of handling his credit card intelligently, the government took care to see that he was supervised. Julian was taken to one of the big stores to see how goods were sold. The store had nothing but samples, representing every type of material made in or imported by the United States. The buyer picked out the items he wanted, called a clerk, gave the order, and the clerk relayed the order to the central warehouse from which the item was delivered to the buyer's home before he returned from the store. Julian was much impressed with this system.

He learned from Dr. Leete how education was handled. Everyone was given a full education until he was twenty-one. A broad cultural course was taught so that there was no intellectual snobbery among the people. At twenty-one, the student went into menial service for three years. During this time he waited on tables in the large public eating houses, or did some other simple task. After three years, he was given an examination to qualify him for one of the government professional schools. If he failed, he was helped to find the job for which he was best suited and which he would most enjoy. If this job proved to be the wrong one, he could change his position. In order that all necessary jobs would be chosen by enough people to do the essential work, the jobs were arranged so as to be equally attractive. If one job was so boring that few people would want to choose it, the hours were made shorter so that enough applicants could be found. Whether a citizen was a doctor or a bricklayer, he was given the same amount of credit for his work.

Crime was treated as a mental disease; criminals were put in hospitals and treated as mental cases. Julian learned that crime had been cut down amazingly as soon as money was abolished. Theft became silly when everyone had the right and power to own the same things. At the head of the government was the President, who was controlled by Congress. Education and medicine were controlled by boards made up of older professional advisers to the President. A woman chosen by the women of the country had the power to veto any bill concerning the rights of the female population. There was no public discontent with government, and there was wonderful international cooperation.

Julian asked Dr. Leete what he had done in life, and learned that the doctor had practiced medicine until he was forty-five years old. At that time he had retired. Now he studied and enjoyed various kinds of recreation.

Edith Leete took great pleasure in showing Julian the various advances the world had made in culture since his day. She showed him how music was carried into all the homes in the country by telephone. She showed him the public libraries in which Julian learned that his old favorites were still read. Dickens was especially popular, as the new world thought him one of the wisest men in judging the sadness of the old capitalistic system. When an author wrote a book, it was published at his own expense by the government. If it proved a success, he received royalties in additional credit cards. Works of art were voted on by the public in the same way. When Julian commented that this plan would not have worked in his day because of the lack of public taste, Edith told him that with general education the taste of the people had developed greatly. Julian became very fond of Edith, and thought how strange it was that she should have the same name as his long-dead fiancée.

When Julian became worried about a means of support, Dr. Leete told him that he had arranged for him to take a college lectureship in history, as Julian knew much about the past which even historians would be delighted to learn. Knowing that he was secure in this new world, Julian asked Edith to marry him. She told him that she had always loved him.

When Julian asked how this was possible, she explained that she was the great-granddaughter of Edith Bartlett. She had found some of Julian's old love letters to the other Edith, and had been charmed by them. She had always told her parents that she would marry only a man like the lover who had written them. Julian was pleased at this unexpected turn of affairs, and the two planned to marry and live happily in the wonderful world of the twenty-first century.

Critical Evaluation

Not even Skinner's renowned *Walden Two* promises to replace *Looking Backward* as America's premier utopian novel. Commonly judged one of the most influential American publications of the period 1885-1935, *Looking Backward* inspired the formation of 150 "Nationalist" clubs and strengthened the Populist cause. Its success derived from its having presented socialism in a way which made the idea uniquely appealing to Americans.

Bellamy disarmed his skeptical readers by viewing socialism as the natural outcome of capitalism. The tendency towards monopoly has its logical conclusion in the dominance of a single corporation which essentially employs the whole nation. From this point, said Bellamy, the conversion of this "Great Trust" into a public interest firm would be easy and obvious. He thus joined with economic conservatives in praising the productivity and efficiency of Big Business, defending it against all forms of "trust busting." He further pleased his readers by denying Marx's predictions of catastrophic class warfare.

But the greatest appeal of the utopia is its promise of minimal government and liberty. Here Bellamy nourishes several illusions. He places all economic and political power in the government's hands, but expects nonconformity and dissent to flourish. He prohibits all private trade and assumes that a small, innocuous police authority can enforce this rule. He implies that the involuntary conscription of workers into the Industrial Army for twenty-four years poses no threat to liberty. (The revelation that lazy workers get "solitary imprisonment on bread and water" is very chilling.) He eliminates federalism, judicial review, and congressional co-equality without providing fresh safeguards against presidential tyranny. In truth, the freedoms Dr. Leete boasts of presuppose a marked improvement in human nature.

Yet *Looking Backward* remains relevant, both for its clear statement of a particular socialist ideal and for its superb satire on capitalism's absurdities. That education should be more closely related to industrial realities; that the retired worker needs more social power; that civic beauty and a vibrant common life should be the first fruits of abundance—these are Bellamy's ideas whose time has come.

Bibliography

Aaron, Daniel. "Edward Bellamy: Village Utopian," in *Men of Good Hope: A Story of American Progressives*. New York: Oxford University Press, 1951, pp. 92–132.

Becker, George J. "Edward Bellamy: Utopia, American Plan," in *Antioch Review*. XIV (June, 1954), pp. 181–194.

Berneri, Marie L. "Utopias of the Nineteenth Century," in her *Journey Through Utopia*. Boston: Beacon, 1951, pp. 207–292.

Bleich, David. "Eros and Bellamy," in *American Quarterly*. XVI (Fall, 1964), pp. 445–459.

Boggs, W. Arthur. "*Looking Backward* at the Utopian Novel, 1888–1900," in *Bulletin of the New York Public Library*. LXIV (June, 1960), pp. 329–336.

Bowman, Sylvia E. *The Year 2000: A Critical Biography of Edward Bellamy.* New York: Bookman, 1958, pp. 112–122.

Downs, Robert B. "American Utopia," in *Books That Changed America.* New York: Macmillan, 1970, pp. 100–109.

Eastman, Max F., Jacques Barzun and Mark Van Doren. "Bellamy: *Looking Backward*," in *New Invitation to Learning.* Edited by Mark Van Doren. New York: Random House, 1942, pp. 414–427.

Harris, W.T. "Edward Bellamy's Vision," in *The American Hegelians: An Intellectual Episode in the History of Western America.* Edited by William H. Goetzmann. New York: Knopf, 1973, pp. 193–201.

Hicks, Granville. "Struggle and Flight," in *The Great Tradition: An Interpretation of American Literature Since the Civil War.* New York: Macmillan, 1935, pp. 131–163.

Howells, William Dean. "Edward Bellamy," in *Criticism and Fiction and Other Essays.* Edited by Clara Marburg Kirk and Rudolph Kirk. New York: New York University Press, 1959, pp. 246–255.

Ketterer, David. "Utopian Fantasy as Millennial Motive and Science-Fictional Motif," in *New Worlds for Old: The Apocalyptic Imagination, Science Fiction, and American Literature.* Bloomington: Indiana University Press, 1974, pp. 96–122.

Martin, Jay. *Harvests of Change: American Literature, 1865–1914.* Englewood Cliffs, N.J.: Prentice-Hall, 1967, pp. 220–223.

Morgan, Arthur E. *Edward Bellamy.* New York: Columbia University Press, 1944, pp. 204–244.

Mott, Frank. L. "Crusaders Four," in *Golden Multitudes: The Story of Best Sellers in the United States.* New York: Macmillan, 1947, pp. 165–171.

Parrington, Vernon L. "Bellamy and His Critics," in *American Dreams: A Study of American Utopias.* Providence, R.I.: Brown University Press, 1947, pp. 69–97.

Sadler, Elizabeth. "One Book's Influence: Edward Bellamy's *Looking Backward*," in *New England Quarterly.* XVII (December, 1944), pp. 530–555.

Schiffman, J.H. "Edward Bellamy and the Social Gospel," in *Intellectual History in America*, Volume II. Edited by Cushing Strout. New York: Harper, 1968, pp. 10–27.

Seager, Allan. "Edward Bellamy," in *They Worked for a Better World.* New York: Macmillan, 1929, pp. 97–116.

Shurter, Robert L. "The Literary Work of Edward Bellamy," in *American Literature.* V (November, 1933), pp. 229–234.

————. "The Writing of *Looking Backward*," in *South Atlantic Quarterly.* XXXVIII (1939), pp. 255–261.

Taylor, Walter F. "Edward Bellamy," in *The Economic Novel in America.* Chapel Hill: University of North Carolina Press, 1942, pp. 184–213.

Thomas, John L. "Introduction," in *Looking Backward: 2000–1887.* By Edward Bellamy. Edited by John L. Thomas. Cambridge, Mass.: Harvard University Press, 1967, pp. 1–88.

Ticknor, Caroline. "Bellamy and *Looking Backward*," in *Glimpses of Authors.* New York: Houghton Mifflin, 1922, pp. 112–121.

Westmeyer, Russell E. "Modern Literary Utopias," in *Modern Economic and Social Systems.* New York: Farrar, 1940, pp. 78–93.

ROBERT MONTGOMERY BIRD

Born: Newcastle, Delaware (February 5, 1806)
Died: Philadelphia, Pennsylvania (January 23, 1854)

Principal Works

NOVELS: *Calavar*, 1834; *The Infidel*, 1835; *The Hawks of Hawk-Hollow*, 1835; *Nick of the Woods, or The Jibbenainosay*, 1837; *Peter Pilgrim*, 1838; *The Adventures of Robin Day*, 1839.
PLAYS: *The Gladiator*, 1831; *The Broker of Bogota*, 1834.

Robert Montgomery Bird was born in Newcastle, Delaware, February 5, 1806. He took his M.D. degree from the University of Pennsylvania Medical School in 1827 and practiced briefly before being drawn to the theater. His first great stage success was *The Gladiator*, a play written for the celebrated actor, Edwin Forrest. The story of a Thracian captive in Rome, its themes are family love and personal honor. Bird's soundest play, and the most successful, was *The Broker of Bogota*, first performed in New York in 1834. This is a domestic tragedy about a money-lender whose heart is broken by a faithless son. Like other early plays, it reflects Bird's sustained interest in Latin America.

Throughout his career as a playwright Bird had a working arrangement with Forrest which did not sufficiently protect his own interests; while the actor made a fortune from the plays, Bird earned very little. Consequently, he broke with Forrest and turned to the novel. Two early books dealt with the adventures of Cortez in Mexico. Then Bird began to use frontier materials. His outstanding literary achievement was *Nick of the Woods*, the story of a revenge-mad Quaker who slinks through the Kentucky woods slaughtering Indians. In this novel Bird portrayed the Indian as a barbarian and rejected the noble savage conception of the Red Man.

In 1841 Bird became a professor at the new Pennsylvania Medical College, but he continued to engage in journalism until his health broke under the strain of his labors. He died in Philadelphia, January 23, 1954.

Bibliography

The basic study of Bird is Clement E. Foust, *The Life and Dramatic Works of Robert Montgomery Bird*, 1919. An interesting companion volume is Mary Mayer Bird, *Life of Robert Montgomery Bird, Written by his Wife*, edited by C. Seymour Thompson, 1945. The edition of *Nick of the Woods* edited by Cecil B. Williams, 1939, contains a bibliography, chronology, and an introduction on Bird as a novelist. A recent biography is Curtis Dahl, *Robert Montgomery Bird*, 1963. See also A. H. Quinn, "Dramatic Works of Robert Montgomery Bird," *Nation*, CVII (1916), 136–137.

NICK OF THE WOODS

Type of work: Novel
Author: Robert Montgomery Bird (1806–1854)
Type of plot: Adventure romance
Time of plot: 1782
Locale: Kentucky
First published: 1837

Robert Montgomery Bird combines an exciting chase-and-capture adventure-romance with a realistic presentation of frontier life in Kentucky during the 1780's. His hero, Nathan Slaughter, is both a fascinating, if extreme, psychological study and a vivid early example of the secret hero of popular literature—the man of unknown identity who simply appears to rescue the weak from danger.

Principal Characters

Nathan Slaughter, a Quaker trapper driven by the deaths of his wife and children to a career of violence against the Indians, who call him the Jibbenainosay, meaning Spirit-that-walks. The whites call the unknown avenger Nick of the Woods, not knowing the man is really the peaceful Quaker they ironically name Bloody Nathan.

Capt. Roland Forrester, a young Virginia patriot of the Revolutionary War. Disinherited by his Tory uncle, he seeks to start life afresh in the Kentucky country. He is still but twenty-three. He returns to Virginia when his cousin Edith is named the uncle's heir; he has to look after his cousin and also Telie Doe.

Roaring Ralph Stackpole, a braggart and a thief. Despite his shortcomings he is loyal to his fellow whites and proves a good fighter against the Indians. He is a frontiersman of the Mike Fink and Davy Crockett type.

Edith Forrester, Roland's cousin. She is temporarily disinherited when her uncle's second will cannot be found. After adventures in Kentucky she is named her uncle's rightful heir.

Wenonga, a Shawnee chief. He is killed by Nathan Slaughter for being the chief who led the attack which resulted in the deaths of Nathan's family.

Richard Braxley, Major Forrester's lawyer. He villainously conceals the Major's second will, hoping to marry Edith, produce the second will, and thus come into command of Edith's fortune. He is killed on the frontier after the second will is found in his possession.

Abel Doe, a white renegade who joins the Indians in their attack on the whites.

Telie Doe, Abel's daughter, given a home by the Bruce family.

Colonel Bruce, commander of Bruce's Station, an outpost in the Kentucky country.

Pardon Dodge, a pioneer who helps the Forresters in the Kentucky country.

Major Roland Forrester, Edith and young Roland's rich Tory uncle.

Mrs. Bruce, Colonel Bruce's voluble but hospitable wife.

Tom Bruce, the Bruces' eldest son, an able Indian fighter.

The Story

The sun was still high, on a sultry August afternoon in 1782, when a train of emigrants emerged from the gloom of the forest and rode slowly toward Bruce's Station, one of the principal forts in the District of Kentucky. The travelers, consisting of men, women, and children, were accompanied by loaded pack-horses, cattle, and slaves, the whole giving the appearance of a village on the march. In the position of responsibility at the end of the cavalcade rode a young man of scarce twenty-three, whose five years in the camps and battles of the Revolution showed in his military bearing and in the mature gravity of his features. The beautiful young woman at his side was sufficiently like him in appearance to suggest their kinship. They were followed by two slaves, both mounted and armed.

Captain Roland Forrester and his cousin Edith were on their way to the Falls of the Ohio. The orphaned children of twin brothers who had died early in the Revolution, they had been reared as wards of their stern, wealthy uncle, Major Roland Forrester. A stanch Tory, the major had never forgiven his younger brothers for supporting the cause of the American patriots, and to keep them from inheriting his estate, for he was unmarried, he had executed a will in favor of an illegitimate daughter. About the time that his brothers fell in battle the child burned to death in the home of her foster mother. The major then adopted his nephew and niece and repeatedly declared his intention of making them his heirs. Young Roland Forrester forfeited his share of the inheritance, however, when he enlisted in a troop of Virginia horsemen. Shortly after Yorktown he returned to find his cousin destitute. On her uncle's death no will making her his heiress could be found. Richard Braxley, the major's lawyer and agent, had produced the original will and taken possession of the estate in the name of the major's daughter, who was, he claimed, still alive and soon to appear and claim her heritage. Having no funds to contest the will, Roland decided to move to Kentucky, his plan being to place Edith in the care of a distant pioneer relative at the Falls while he himself carved from the wilderness a fortune which would allow him to marry his lovely cousin.

Colonel Bruce, the commander of the station, welcomed the emigrants with hearty frontier hospitality, greeting the Forresters with special warmth and insisting that they share his cabin. Having served under Major Forrester in earlier Indian wars, he told many stories of those border campaigns. Mrs. Bruce, equally voluble, bustled about giving orders to her daughters and telling them to be as circumspect as Telie Doe, who remained quietly at her loom after a startled glance up from her work when she heard the name of Roland Forrester mentioned. When the others escorted Edith into the cabin she remained on the porch, where Roland was explaining his intention of pushing on toward the Falls the next day. The colonel, while deploring his guest's haste, said that there was no danger from Indians on the trace. At last the colonel noticed Telie and ordered her into the house. She was, he said, the daughter of a white renegade named Abel Doe. Out of pity the Bruces had taken her into their own home.

At that moment Tom Bruce, the colonel's oldest son, appeared with news that the Jibbenainosay had been active again; some hunters had found an Indian with a split skull and a slashed cross on his breast. The colonel explained. The Jibbenainosay, whom the settlers also called Nick of the Woods, was a mysterious avenger who had killed many Indians and marked them thus. The Shawnees, believing that he was either a ghost or a devil, had given him his name, which meant Spirit-that-walks. Some claimed to have seen him, a giant with horns and matted hair, always accompanied by a devil that looked like a small black bear.

The news of the Jibbenainosay's latest killing had been brought to the station by Roaring Ralph Stackpole, a swaggering braggart calling himself a ringtailed squealer whose middle name was Fight. When he challenged anyone in the settlement to a trial of strength, the tough frontiersmen decided to match him with Nathan Slaughter, a Quaker trapper derisively nicknamed Bloody Nathan because of his peaceful ways and gentle speech. Nathan, as thin as his horse and as meek-looking as his dog, finally consented to try a friendly fall. Much to the surprise of the crowd, he lifted the bully and threw him to the ground. Roaring Ralph, admitting that he had been fairly beaten, asked to borrow a horse so that he could continue his journey to Logan's Station. The Quaker trapper told the settlers that the Miami Indians were gathering, a threat of trouble on the frontier. When the others refused to take his news seriously, he exchanged his furs for lead and powder and quietly left the station.

That night Telie Doe begged Edith to let her go with the emigrants as a servant. When Edith refused, the girl crept sadly away. Roland slept with Bruce's sons on the porch of the cabin. Aroused from sleep during the night, he thought he heard a whispering voice telling him he was to cross Salt River by the lower ford. Only half awake, he decided that he was still dreaming.

The next morning there was great confusion at the station. Roaring Ralph had sneaked back into the settlement and stolen Roland's blooded brown horse. Knowing that the fugitive could not get far on the tired animal, Bruce's sons had ridden in pursuit. While the emigrant train started on ahead, Roland, Edith, and one of the slaves stayed at the station to await the return of the horse. The animal was found, wandering loose along the trail, and brought back by one of the boys. He said that the others were tracking the thief, intending to make him an object of frontier justice. As the travelers were about to set out to overtake the emigrant party, a horseman arrived with word that Indians had attacked Bryant's Station. The need to muster every fighting man in the settlement left Roland and his cousin without an escort; nevertheless, they announced their intention of starting with only one surly frontiersman to guide them. On the way their guide deserted them to return and join in the fighting. The travelers were relieved from their predicament when Telie Doe appeared and offered to act as their guide.

When they came to the branch in the two fords, Roland insisted on following the road to the upper ford, in spite of Telie Doe's pleadings. On the way they were startled by an unearthly yelling, and they found Roaring Ralph, his arms bound and a noose around his neck, astride a horse in such fashion that one movement of the animal would hang the rider from a limb overhead. Left to perish in that manner after the pursuers from Bruce's Station had overtaken him, he was grateful to his rescuers and offered to devote his life to Edith's service. Roland curtly sent the braggart and thief on his way.

Not far from the upper ford they met a fleeing settler named Pardon Dodge, who told them that Indians on the warpath blocked the road ahead. In their attempt to reach the lower ford they became lost. Riding in a circle, they found a dead Indian with a cross gashed on his breast. While they waited for the dread Jibbenainosay to appear, they saw harmless Nathan Slaughter, his faithful hound at his heels, coming through the forest. Hearing that Indians were close by, the Quaker became terrified. He promised to guide the party only if he were not called upon to fight.

The travelers took refuge at last in a ruined cabin near the flooded river. Indians attacked the cabin during the night, but after a savage hand-to-hand struggle they were repulsed. During the lull the Quaker suggested that he should try to evade the warriors and bring help to the besieged. Roland agreed. Shortly before daylight Roaring Ralph came down the river in a small dugout. It was desperately decided that the braggart was to take Edith and Telie across the flooded stream in his canoe, while Roland, Dodge, and the slave would try to follow on horseback. When Dodge's mount came ashore without his rider, the others decided that he had been washed from the saddle and drowned.

Later that morning the fugitives encountered another band of Indians. Edith was captured. Roarding Ralph escaped by rolling down the bank to the river; the slave was killed. Roland, knocked unconscious during the fight, awoke to find himself wounded and tightly bound. While he was wondering what had happened to Edith, a band of Kentuckians, led by young Tom Bruce, appeared and engaged the savages. When Roaring Ralph climbed the bank and joined in the fight, the Kentuckians, believing that they were seeing the ghost of the man they had hanged, scattered in confusion. Roaring Ralph, throwing wounded Tom Bruce over the saddle, rode away on Roland's horse.

The victorious Indians proceeded to divide a store of arms, cloth, and various trinkets, the distribution being made under the directions of an old chief by a brave whom Roland thought a half-breed. He learned the man's identity when Telie ran up to protest because Roland himself had been given to a Piankeshaw warrior. The light-skinned savage was Abel Doe, the renegade.

His arms bound, Roland was tethered to the Piankeshaw's saddle and, restrained on both sides by two younger warriors, forced to make a long, wearying march before his captors decided to camp for the night. Unable to sleep because of his cramped limbs, he was startled to hear an explosion close at hand, followed by crashing and the sounds of pursuit. Horrified when one of the Piankeshaws, his face shot away, fell across his prostrate body and died, Roland lost consciousness. He revived to find Nathan Slaughter bending over him, rubbing his chafted limbs. Another dead Piankeshaw lay nearby.

The Quaker, lurking in the forest while the Indians divided the spoils, had overheard the renegade and another white man discussing the price to be paid for the capture of Roland and Edith. Convinced by Nathan's account that his cousin had fallen into Braxley's hands, Roland wished to start at once to the main Indian village after the Quaker told him that the old chief must have been Wenonga, a Shawnee chieftain notorious for his brutality and the atrocities he had committed. On their way to the Shawnee camp Roland and the Quaker found five Indians capering about a white prisoner bound to a tree. While they struggled with the savages, the prisoner broke his bonds and aided them in killing the warriors. He was Roaring Ralph, the horse thief.

When they reached the Indian village, the Quaker daubed himself like a brave and went stealthily among the houses to find Edith. Peering through the chinks in one cabin, he saw Braxley and Abel Doe, and from the conversation he learned that Braxley had in his possession Major Forrester's second will. Having disposed of Roland, the lawyer was now planning to marry Edith and get her wealth. While he searched for Edith's place of imprisonment, Nathan found old Chief Wenonga lying drunk in the grass. He was about to plunge his knife in the savage's breast when he heard Edith's voice nearby. Leaving the chief, he went to a skin tent where he found Braxley and his prisoner. Taking the other man by surprise, the Quaker seized and bound him. With the will safe on his own person, Nathan was carrying Edith to safety when a clamor broke out in the Indian encampment.

Roaring Ralph, ordered to steal four horses upon which Edith and her rescuers could make their escape, had attempted to drive off the whole heard, and the stampeding horses ran through the village, arousing the warriors. Unable to escape, the party was captured. Roland and Roaring Ralph were bound and taken to separate wigwams. Nathan, dragged before the drunken old chief, defied Wenonga with such ferocity that the Quaker worked himself into an epileptic fit. The spasm, together with his fantastic disguise, convinced the Shawnee that his white prisoner was a great medicine man.

Doe and Braxley still had not reached an agreement over the renegade's pay. What Braxley did not know was that Doe had taken the will when he had searched the Quaker after his capture. The next day the renegade went to Roland and offered him his freedom and the estate if he would consent to marry Telie. Roland refused, but offered Doe half the estate if he would save Edith. The man left sullenly.

That night old Wenonga had the Quaker brought before him. After bragging of the white women and children he had killed and the scalps he had taken, the chief offered the prisoner his freedom if he would use his powers as a medicine man to put the Jibbenainosay in the power of the Shawnee. Nathan promised to do so if his bonds were cut. Freed, he revealed himself as the Jibbenainosay, a friendly settler whose wife and children Wenonga had treacherously killed years before. Seizing the chief's ax, he sank it into the savage's head. Then, after cutting away Wenonga's scalp lock and gashing the dead man's chest, the Quaker retrieved the scalps of his children and with a triumphant cry disappeared into the night.

The next morning, finding the Jibbenainosay's mark on their dead chief, the Shawnees were roused to wild fury. Roland and Roaring Ralph were tied to the stake, timber heaped about them. The fires were lighted, but before the flames could reach them the sound of gunfire echoed above the yells of the savages and a bank of Kentuckians rode through the smoke to set the prisoners free. Braxley struck spurs into his horse and rode away with Edith in his arms. The resistance ended when Nathan, with Wenonga's scalp at his belt, appeared striking right and left with his steel ax. The Indians scattered and ran, but the rejoicing of the Kentuckians was dimmed by the death of heroic Tom Bruce, who in spite of wounds he had suffered earlier had insisted on joining the attacking party.

During the confusion Pardon Dodge rode up with Edith on the saddle before him. Washed downstream in the flooded river, he had escaped on a raft and arrived back at Bruce's Station in time to enlist in the rescue party. Seeing Braxley riding away with Edith, he had mistaken the lawyer for an Indian and had shot him. Doe, mortally wounded, gave Roland the missing will, and the young Virginian promised to look after Telie with a brother's care.

Roland and Edith, preparing to return to Virginia to claim her inheritance, asssured Nathan that they owed life as well as fortune to his bravery and daring. Although they begged him to return with them, he stoutly refused. But the work of the Jibbenainosay was done, and after a time the Quaker disappeared quietly into the woods. Roaring Ralph lived to cheat the law for many years. No one in the neighborhood of Bruce's Station ever heard of Nathan Slaughter again.

Critical Evaluation

For many years after its initial publication in 1837, *Nick of the Woods* was one of the most famous and popular nineteenth century historical romances, both as a novel and as a series of dramatic adaptations. This popularity was well deserved. *Nick of the Woods* is above all a superb adventure novel. Utilizing the chase-capture-escape pattern developed by James Fenimore Cooper and others, Bird tells an exciting story of Indian warfare, villainy, treachery, and violence in a series of vivid, suspenseful action scenes along with several moments of intense personal drama.

However, the novel also shows the characteristic flaws of the form: an insipid and improbable romance between banal lovers; an excess of melodramatic, artificial plot complexity; and an overabundance of exaggerated, sentimental language. But none of these seriously divert the force and excitement of the adventure narrative.

Nick of the Woods is, however, more than just escapist adventure fare. In the first third of the book Bird succeeds in painting a realistic picture of life on the Kentucky frontier in the late eighteenth century. And, if his aristocratic personages are stereotypes, his frontier characters are realistic and vivid.

The most fascinating and powerful character in the novel is Nathan Slaughter, a supposedly nonviolent Quaker who is revealed in the end to be the "Jibbenainosay." The idea of a pacifist who, unknown even to himself, is periodically transformed into a bloodthirsty and invincible avenger may strike modern readers as trite. But the author's skill in developing and presenting the character makes him understandable and impressive.

Bird, a medical doctor with a serious interest in abnormal psychology, bases the split in his hero's personality on Nathan's inability to reconcile his deeply rooted nonviolent convictions with the experience of seeing his entire family murdered by Indians. Thus, Bird provides both an organic (he was scalped in the attack) and a psychological explanation for the Quaker's double nature.

This split in Slaughter's personality was, to Bird, an extreme example of man's basic duality. To the nonromantic doctor, proximity to nature, far from bringing out any innate nobility, provokes man's worst qualities and excesses. Therefore, since the Indian was closest to nature, he was the most animal-like of humans, with a basic savagery that not only delighted in unprovoked attacks on innocent settlers, but even took pleasure in the killing of women and children.

It is this aspect of the novel that has been most criticized, and Bird, himself, conceded his view to be an extreme one. But he felt it a necessary corrective to the "noble savage" sentiments of Cooper and others, and one that was much closer to the real experience of the American frontier.

Bibliography

Bryant, James C. "The Fallen World in *Nick of the Woods*," in *American Literature*. XXXVIII (November, 1966), pp. 352–364.

Dahl, Curtis. *Robert Montgomery Bird*. New York: Twayne, 1963, pp. 91–102.

Dibble, R.F. "Reborn Youth; Criticism of *Nick of the Woods*," in *Sewanee Review*. XXVII (October, 1919), pp. 496–499.

Gilman, William H. "Hero and the Heroic in American Literature," in *Patterns of Commitment in American Literature*. Edited by Marston La France. Toronto: University of Toronto Press, 1967, p. 5.

Hall, Joan Joffe. "*Nick of the Woods*: An Interpretation of the American Wilderness," in *American Literature*. XXXV (May, 1963), pp. 173–182.

Richardson, Charles F. *American Literature, 1607–1885*, Volume II. New York: G.P. Putnam, 1889, pp. 394–396.

Van Doren, Carl.   *The American Novel.* New York: Macmillan, 1922, p. 66.

Williams, Cecil B.   "R.M. Bird's Plans for Novels of the Frontier," in *American Literature.* XXI (November, 1949), pp. 321–324.

HUGH HENRY BRACKENRIDGE

Born: Near Campbeltown, Scotland (1748)
Died: Carlisle, Pennsylvania (June 25, 1816)

Principal Works

NOVEL: *Modern Chivalry*, 1792–1815.

PLAYS: *The Battle of Bunker's Hill*, 1776; *The Death of General Montgomery*, 1777.

MISCELLANEOUS: *A Poem on the Rising Glory of America*, 1772 (with Philip Freneau); *Law Miscellanies*, 1814.

Hugh Henry Brackenridge, born in 1748, at Cambeltown, Scotland, was brought to this country at the age of five. The family settled in western Pennsylvania where Brackenridge grew up on the frontier. He entered Princeton in 1768. At his graduation in 1771 he receited a poem, "The Rising Glory of America," which he had written with Philip Freneau. Epic in intention, the poem is an important contribution to early nationalism. For a brief period he was the head of an academy in Maryland. During the Revolution, in addition to serving as a chaplain, he published two plays, designed for private performance, which praised the heroism of American troops, and also a group of sermons exhorting the troops to carry on bravely.

After studying law in Annapolis, he moved to Pittsburgh in 1781. He made many contributions to the cultural life of that frontier community, and there he wrote *Modern Chivalry*, the book by which he is best remembered. It is a picaresque novel, fashioned after *Don Quixote*, which satirizes incompetence and corruption in the workings of democratic government. By ridiculing the weaknesses of democracy, Brackenridge hoped eventually to strengthen it.

Despite the fact that he satisfied neither side during the Whiskey Rebellion, he was sufficiently well thought of politically to win an appointment to the Supreme Court of Pennsylvania in 1799. He moved to Carlisle in 1801. There he wrote *Law Miscellanies*, his principal contribution to legal literature, and there he died, June 25, 1816.

Bibliography

The biography of Brackenridge is Claude M. Newlin, *The Life and Writings of Hugh Henry Brackenridge*, 1932. A recent study is Daniel Marder, *Hugh Henry Brackenridge*, 1967. There is a bibliography by Charles F. Heartman, *A Bibliography of the Writings of Hugh Henry Brackenridge*, 1932. See also C. M. Newlin, "Hugh Henry Brackenridge: Writer," *Western Pennsylvania Historical Magazine*, X (1928), 224–256; and William W. Edel, "Hugh Brackenridge's Ride," *Boyd Lee Spahr Lectures in America*, I (1950), 115–145.

MODERN CHIVALRY

Type of work: Novel
Author: Hugh Henry Brackenridge (1748–1816)
Type of plot: Picaresque satire
Time of plot: First years of the United States
Locale: Pennsylvania
First published: 1792–1815

   Modern Chivalry *was the direct, immediate artistic expression of Hugh Henry Brackenridge's experiences as a political figure during America's formative years. Captain John Farrago is the sensible new American citizen; Teague O'Regan represents the potential excesses of the new political system.*

Principal Characters

Captain John Farrago, a man from colonial Western Pennsylvania. He takes his horse and his Irish servant, Teague, to go about seeing the country and observing human conduct. Eventually the Captain, after many adventures that point out the foibles of human nature, becomes, because of his learning and good sense, the governor of a new western territory. Being a rational man, he governs in the best Greek and Roman political traditions.

Teague O'Regan, the captain's cowardly but cunning rascal of a servant. He is proposed as a candidate for the legislature, has many amorous adventures, tries his luck at being an excise officer, goes on the stage as an Irish comedian, and serves as a newspaper editor, among other things. He is one of those literary rascals who always land on their feet. The author's satire revolves around the absurdities that elevate the ignorant and roguish Teague to positions of authority and respectability.

Miss Fog, a young heiress courted by Captain Farrago. Though he tries to please her, he finds whatever he does insults the woman.

Jacko, Miss Fog's other suitor, Captain Farrago's rival. When Jacko sends a second to challenge the Captain to a duel, the Captain kicks the man out after telling him duelling is unlawful.

Duncan Ferguson, a Scots emigrant who takes Teague's place as Captain Farrago's servant.

The Story

   Captain John Farrago, a Pennsylvanian in his fifties, decided to get on his horse and, accompanied by his servant Teague O'Regan, to travel about the country. He wanted to see how things were getting on and to observe human nature.

   His first adventure was at a horse-race. After the race the crowd became embroiled in arguments. When the captain tried to calm them, in the name of reason, he had his head broken for his pains. Starting out again the next morning, Captain Farrago came to a village where the election of a legislator was taking place. The candidate, a weaver, was not, in the captain's opinion, worthy of the office, and so he spoke out against the backwoods politician. Much to his dismay, the villagers wanted to send Teague, Captain Farrago's servant, as their elected representative. The captain finally convinced his Irish servant, who had far more brawn than brains, that he was better off as a servant of one man than as the servant of many.

A short time later the captain found the carcass of a very large owl. Upon taking it to a town, he met a philosopher who offered to have him made a member of the philosophical society on the basis of his discovery. When Captain Farrago refused, the philosopher asked if the servant Teague might be made a member. Once again the captain had to convince simple Teague that he was better off as a private servant than he would be chasing over the country after dangerous animals.

That same night Teague got into a scrape at an inn, where he tried to get into bed with a girl who raised a great hue and cry. Teague, a cunning chap, shifted the blame to a young clergyman by claiming that the clergyman had attempted to molest the girl and that he, Teague, had been her rescuer. The tale got out, and Captain Farrago finally had to bribe Teague with half a crown to tell the truth to the presbytery in order to clear the innocent preacher's good name. Teague, by means of blarney and flattery, convinced the presbytery that he wished to be a candidate for the ministry; only the captain's intercession with an explanation that Teague would have to give up his vices and enter into a war with the devil himself prevented the gullible clergymen from taking Teague, ignorant as he was, into the ministry.

Sometime later Captain Farrago met a Miss Fog. In his efforts to court the young lady, who had a considerable fortune, Captain Farrago only managed to insult her. Miss Fog's other suitor, Jacko, then challenged the captain to a duel. Captain Farrago, after warning the man who delivered the challenge that such conduct was against the law, kicked him out of his quarters. Calling in Teague, the captain offered to let him fight the duel if he wished; Teague, a coward, refused to do so, whereupon Captain Farrago sent a letter telling Jacko that he would not duel because one of them might be hurt or killed for no reason at all. That was the end of the matter.

Not long afterward a man approached Captain Farrago and asked to hire Teague from the captain. The man, a maker of treaties with the Indians, wanted to use Teague as a bogus chief of the Kickapoo tribe. He pointed out that the government wanted treaties and that he was going to provide treaties; he received a good salary for his work, in addition to making money from the gifts that were given to his bogus chieftains. Captain Farrago, an honest man, refused to be a party to the scheme. Fearing that Teague might take to the idea of easy money, Captain Farrago told him to stay away from the maker of treaties, lest the latter take Teague's scalp. Simpleminded Teague, fearful for his life, stayed his distance, and the man gave up his fraudulent plan.

Having kept his servant from becoming everything thus far, the captain soon faced a new problem. Teague imagined himself in love with a beautiful young woman considerably above his station, and nothing Captain Farrago could say swayed him from his illusion. In a final effort to bring Teague to his senses, Captain Farrago told the girl's brother what was happening. The brother, by a judicious and heavy application of a horsewhip, cured Teague of his matrimonial aspirations for the time being.

Later in their wanderings the captain and Teague stopped overnight at the home of a widow who took a fancy to Teague. Teague, anxious to improve his lot, flattered the woman, and the two quickly decided to get married, much to Captain Farrago's disgust. Only the captain's friendly warning to Teague that the widow might prove to be a witch or sorceress, so quickly had she won his affection, turned the servant away from the probability of marriage. As it was, he was anxious to be gone, lest some spell be cast upon him.

Shortly afterward Teague disappeared while he and Captain Farrago were in a city. All the captain's efforts, including a visit to a house of prostitution, were in vain so far as locating Teague was concerned. At last the Irishman was discovered by the captain in a theater, where Teague was being used in place of a comedian who imitated the Irish. Teague was anxious to keep his place, until the theater manager gave him a cudgeling for paying attention to the manager's mistress.

Captain Farrago determined to make something better of his servant while they were in the city. Dressing him smartly and impressing on him some semblance of manners improved Teague so much that the Irishman was given the post of exciseman in the customs service. Having lost Teague, Captain Farrago found himself a new servant, a Scot named Duncan Ferguson, who had recently arrived in America.

Teague, acting as an excise officer, was badly treated by the populace, who tarred and feathered him when he tried to collect duties in outlying towns. He returned hastily to Captain Farrago. Then the captain, upon the advice of a French friend, sent Teague to France. Arriving in France, Teague was taken up as a great common citizen, since there was no taint of the nobility about him. But Teague soon tired of France and returned to Captain Farrago's employ in America. Accompanied by his servant, the captain once again began his travels to observe human nature.

One day the captain arrived at a town where there was considerable discussion over the local newspaper. The citizens, dissatisfied with the editor, decifed to let Teague write the editorials. When he proved unsatisfactory and was quickly dismissed, the town was glad to have the original editor return. Shortly afterward, with the captain's help, Teague wrote his memoirs. So successful was the volume that Teague was suggested for the professorship of rhetoric at the local college. Only the outrage of the faculty kept the plan from going through.

Teague's adventures finally proved too much for the Pennsylvania viliage, and so the captain, accompanied by Teague and a retinue of hangers-on, moved westward. Because of his learning and good sense, Captain Farrago soon became governor of a new territory, which he attempted to set to rights according to Greek and Roman tradition. Thus ended his travels, for he now found himself in such a position of responsibility that he had to cease his aimless wanderings in favor of a settled life.

Critical Evaluation

Hugh Henry Brackenridge was neither a writer who participated in politics nor a politician who wrote as an avocation; his writing and his politics were two sides of the same coin, a passionate involvement in the affairs of his time. Brackenridge sought nothing less than the creation of the new American democracy, and, along with it, the new American literature.

Loosely modeled after *Don Quixote, Modern Chivalry* provides a satirical record of Brackenridge's political and social attitudes. The almost haphazard plot sequences and general unevenness in quality reflect the casual, off-and-on method of its composition. The book had first been provoked by a political defeat and became a running commentary on Brackenridge's experiences in public affairs, as well as an expression of his irritation at the follies he found in American society. Therefore, it appeared irregularly and unevenly over a twenty-three-year period, corresponding to the vicissitudes of Brackenridge's political fortunes.

This is not to say, however, that the book is arbitrary or ambiguous. The central themes of the novel are perfectly clear, the intellectual viewpoint is constant, and, although the book lacks specific direction, sooner or later Brackenridge turns his attention to most important American institutions and customs.

To Brackenridge the problem of the United States, once it freed itself from British rule, was how to build a democracy based upon a qualified, knowledgeable electorate. Always the moderate, Brackenridge denied the Federalist notion that the common man was incapable of functioning in a democratic society. But he was too familiar with frontier excesses and mob emotionalism to believe in the innate wisdom of the ordinary person. So he dramatized the problem in *Modern Chivalry*.

Captain John Farrago's frustrating attempts to keep track of his servant Teague O'Regan and to keep O'Regan—and those he meets—out of trouble provides the thinnest of plot lines. O'Regan is the ignorant, "innocent," common man, whose greed and capacity for self-deception are fed by the freedom, fluidity, and crudity of the frontier. Once his ambitions are ignited, he believes himself capable of accomplishing any feat or holding any office. The selfishness, foolishness, and volatility of the crowd reinforce these delusions, and O'Regan's vigorous identification with the worst attitudes and emotions of the mob wins him instant adulation. Thus he becomes, in short order, a political candidate, a clergyman, a lover, a philosopher, a university professor, a revenue collector, and so on. Few institutions or public types are spared as Brackenridge exposes the pretensions of the rich as well as the poor, the educated as well as the ignorant, the Eastern sophisticate as well as the Western backwoodsman. However, the author makes it clear, as he does so, that *education* is the answer to the excesses he pictures. Democracy is workable only if the so-called common man can be educated to understand and carry out his role as a citizen. Failing that, Brackenridge suggests, the future belongs to the O'Regans.

Bibliography

Brennecke, Ernest. "Introduction," in *Modern Chivalry*. New York: Greenberg, 1926, p. xviii.

Cowie, Alexander. "Early Satire and Realism: Hugh Henry Brackenridge," in *The Rise of the American Novel*. New York: American Book Company, 1948, pp. 43–60.

Hemenway, Robert. "Fiction in the Age of Jefferson: The Early American Novel as Intellectual Document," in *Midcontinent American Studies Journal*. IX (Spring, 1968), pp. 91–102.

Marder, Daniel. *Hugh Henry Brackenridge*. New York: Twayne, 1967, pp. 83–98.

Nance, William L. "Satiric Elements in Brackenridge's *Modern Chivalry*," in *Texas Studies in Literature and Language*. IX (Autumn, 1967), pp. 381–389.

Newlin, Claude M. "Introduction," in *Modern Chivalry*. By Hugh Henry Brackenridge. New York: American Books, 1937, p. xiv.

Spiller, Robert. *Literary History of the United States*. New York: Macmillan, 1957, pp. 178–180.

Trent, William. *Cambridge History of American Literature*, Volume I. New York: G.P. Putnam, 1917, p. 186.

Van Doren, Carl. *The American Novel*. New York: Macmillan, 1922, pp. 4–6.

Wagenknecht, Edward. *Cavalcade of the American Novel*. New York: Holt, 1952, pp. 6–9.

CHARLES BROCKDEN BROWN

Born: Philadelphia, Pennsylvania (January 17, 1771)
Died: Philadelphia (February 22, 1810)

Principal Works

NOVELS: *Wieland*, 1798; *Ormond*, 1799; *Edgar Huntly*, 1799; *Arthur Mervyn*, 1799–1800; *Clara Howard*, 1801; *Jane Talbot*, 1801.
SOCIAL TRACT: *Alcuin: A Dialogue*, 1798.

Charles Brockden Brown is given credit for being the first American to earn a living as a professional author, although he did so for only a few years of his life. He was born on January 17, 1771, into a Philadelphia Quaker family and even as a youngster was addicted to reading voluminously. Because of his constant reading, he earned for himself a reputation as a scholar and genius in Philadelphia. Early in life, too, he began to write, planning three epic poems on Columbus, Pizarro, and Cortez—all notably American rather than European themes. His first published work, entitled "The Rhapsodist" (1789), a glorification of the romantic rebel, appeared in *The Columbian Magazine*, a Philadelphia publication.

Despite his literary bent, Brown's family set him to studying law in 1787, but in 1793 he gave up law and announced that he was henceforth to be a professional writer. After several visits to New York, Brown took up residence in that city, apparently finding, especially in the Friendly Society, the stimulation he needed as a writer. Brown was an ardent admirer of William Godwin, the British radical, who was also a novelist, and Brown's fiction reflects that enthusiasm. *Alcuin: A Dialogue* is really a treatise on the rights of women, using fiction as the bearer of a message. Following that work, Brown turned to writing fiction that more nearly can be called novels, but in which he hoped to teach as well as entertain. Writing at a furious rate, within a few years he wrote and published a number of novels. His best work, *Wieland*, was based on an actual murder case in Pennsylvania. The book is a study in religious psychosis, with the novelty of ventriloquism added. The story is melodramatic and uses many of the devices of the English Gothic fiction of the time, but it is original in that it uses American materials and presents a serious study of a human mind under pressures it does not understand.

In a later novel, *Arthur Mervyn*, Brown made further use of native materials. In 1793 he and his family had fled from Philadelphia, along with hundreds of others, to escape an epidemic of yellow fever. In New York, in 1798, another epidemic of the same disease had killed his close friend, Dr. Elihu Hubbard Smith. In *Arthur Mervyn*, Brown wrote a highly realistic account of the horrors of such an epidemic, describing the effects of the Philadelphia epidemic in 1793 in a manner comparable to Daniel Defoe's description of the London plague of

1665 in his *Journal of the Plague Year*. Other of Brown's novels also made use of American subject matter. Indians and the frontier were introduced into the American novel in *Edgar Huntly*, a work which is also usually considered the first American detective story. Unfortunately, Brown knew little about Indians or the frontier and was unable to present them very realistically. The outstanding characteristic of the novel is the presentation, as in *Wieland*, of a human mind under torment.

There is no doubt that Brown's novels were influenced by European fiction. They had to be, for there were almost no American novels at the time. Scholars usually consider William Hill Brown's *The Power of Sympathy* the first American novel, and it appeared less than a decade before *Wieland*. Brown's greatness comes from the fact that he was willing to use native materials and themes in his work. Too often critics have overemphasized the similarity of Brown's work to that of William Godwin, without giving credit to the American for his own originality.

Despite his output of fiction from 1798 to 1801, Brown made very little money, too little to continue indefinitely as a professional author. To support himself he also edited the *Monthly Magazine and North American Review* in 1799–1800. When the magazine failed, he returned to Philadelphia in 1801 and became a partner in his brothers' mercantile firm. He was married in 1804 to a New York girl, Elizabeth Linn, and they had four children. Following the failure of the family firm in 1806, Brown became an independent merchant. During the last three years of his life he continued to write, but mostly hack work for various periodicals. He died in Philadelphia on February 22, 1810.

Bibliography

Of the biographical studies, William Dunlap, *The Life of Charles Brockden Brown*, 1815, remains an important source book, though often inaccurate. See also Harry R. Warfel, *Charles Brockden Brown, American Gothic Novelist*, 1949; Alexander Cowie, *The Rise of the American Novel*, 1948; George Snell, *The Shapers of American Fiction, 1798–1947*, 1947; David Lee Clark, *Charles Brockden Brown: Pioneer Voice of America*, 1952; Donald A. Ringe, *Charles Brockden Brown*, 1966; Richard Chase, *The American Novel and its Tradition*, 1957; R.W.B. Lewis, *The American Adam*, 1955; William L. Hedges, "Charles Brockden Brown and the Culture of Contradictions," *Early American Literature*, IX (1974), 107–142; Michael D. Bell, " 'The Double-Tongued Deceiver': Sincerity and Duplicity in the Novels of Charles Brockden Brown," *Early American Literature*, IX (1974), 143–163; Warner Berthoff, "Adventures of the Young Man: An Approach to Charles Brockden Brown," *American Quarterly*, IX (1957), 421–434; and Larzer Ziff, "A Reading of Wieland," *Publications of the Modern Language Association*, LXXVII (1962), 51–57.

ARTHUR MERVYN

Type of work: Novel
Author: Charles Brockden Brown
Type of plot: Confessional & reflective
Time of plot: Late eighteenth century (1793)
Locale: In and near Philadelphia and Baltimore
First published: 1798

"Memoirs of the Year 1783," Arthur Mervyn *establishes the horror of an epidemic in an American city while studying the interplay of sensuality and virtue, yet leaves the modern reader questioning Brown's unresolved story.*

Principal Characters

Arthur Mervyn, a virtuous youth who narrates much of the story to Stevens and his wife and interprets what others tell him. The opinions of the others threaten his credibility for both the reader and Dr. and Mrs. Stevens. After experiencing the plague in Philadelphia and becoming involved in all manners of intrigue, he eventually attempts to set everything right for the many people involved. He leaves many questions about his affairs unanswered in his account, but he does finally realize his love for Achsa Fielding and anticipates marrying her.

Dr. Stevens, a Philadelphia physician who takes Mervyn into his home when he has resigned himself to death. He and his wife nurse Mervyn back to health and he narrates his tale to them. Volume two of the novel contains Steven's record of an alternate version of Mervyn's story, which both qualifies and corroborates the account.

Thomas Welbeck, a profligate and forger. He meets Mervyn and employs him, involving him in the mysterious intrigue of the Lodi manuscript and money. When he flees the city, the extent of his debts becomes apparent. Before dying, he gives Mervyn money he had stolen.

Clemenza Lodi, an Italian heiress. Mervyn first sees her at Welbeck's house. Her brother had given Welbeck in trust her money and a manuscript which their father had hoped to publish. Mervyn finds her living at the infamous Villars' household.

William Hadwin, a Quaker farmer. Mervyn lives in his home while working on the translation of the Lodi manuscript. He dies of the plague.

Susan Hadwin, his oldest daughter. She follows her lover, Wallace, to Philadelphia. She dies of the plague.

Eliza Hadwin, her younger sister. She thinks she is in love with Mervyn. He makes sure that she is well taken care of. Through his mediation, she goes to live with Achsa Fielding.

Mrs. Wentworth, a Philadelphia matron in whose home Mervyn sees his portrait of Clavering. She thinks Clavering is still alive, which causes Dr. Stevens and his wife to question Mervyn's story. She later becomes Mervyn's friend.

Achsa Fielding, a wealthy English widow. Mervyn meets her at the Villars' household and warns her of the mother and her daughters. She later helps Eliza Hadwin. She falls in love with Mervyn, and they plan to marry.

Wortley, a friend of Stevens' who tells him that Amos Watson was missing a large sum of money. Welbeck and Mervyn were suspected of stealing it.

Wallace, a Philadelphia clerk. He is the lover of Susan Hadwin. He contacts the plague but recovers. Mervyn recognizes him as the youth who had once tricked him.

The Story

During the 1793 yellow fever epidemic in Philadelphia, Dr. Stevens and his wife took Arthur Mervyn into their home and nursed him to health. Their friend Wortley accused Mervyn of criminal activities and of concealing the whereabouts of Thomas Welbeck, whose flight from the city had revealed the extent of his debts. Mervyn told the Stevens his story. Driven from his rural home by his father's marriage to a milkmaid, Mervyn, in his inexperience, soon lost his money and his possessions, including a portrait of his dead friend Clavering, an eccentric Arthur's mother thought resembled her son.

Destitute, Arthur accepted dinner and an offer of lodgings from a young man who capriciously locked him in an upper room where he had to hide when a couple came to bed. From a closet, he overheard all they said including details of the man's plan to cheat a "nabob." Escaping, Mervyn met Welbeck, who stared at him, employed him as a copyist, and gave him a room and a rich array of clothes. The clothes reminded Mervyn of Clavering's wardrobe. A woman Mervyn took to be Welbeck's daughter seemed startled to see Mervyn.

Delivering a letter to Mrs. Wentworth, Mervyn saw his lost portrait in her home and asked for its return. When Mrs. Wentworth asked what he knew of Clavering, Mervyn recalled his promise to Welbeck to say nothing of his previous life. Consequently, he told her that Clavering was dead, but he refused all details, thus angering her.

Seeing Welbeck leave Clemenza's room late at night made Mervyn question their relationship; soon after, Welbeck said that she had been sent to the country. At a counting house, Mervyn heard Thetford use the word "nabob" in reference to Welbeck. He suspected Thetfort of plotting to cheat Welbeck. Eager to warn his employer, Mervyn returned to Welbeck's mansion, where he heard a shot and found Welbeck standing over a corpse. Welbeck told Mervyn his story: the dead man was Amos Watson, his former benefactor, whose sister Welbeck had seduced; Watson had found him accidentally when he had come to Philadelphia with news of the loss of a ship in which all Welbeck's fortune had been invested. Welbeck confessed that all his money belonged rightfully to Clemenza Lodi, from whose dying brother Welbeck had received it in trust. He showed Mervyn a manuscript of Clemenza's father which he said he hoped to translate and publish.

Mervyn helped bury Watson in the cellar. Welbeck gave Mervyn the dead man's pocketbook, and they started to row across the river. Welbeck fell, or leapt, into the water and disappeared. Arthur found money and an unmailed letter (to

Mrs. Watson) in the pocketbook; he mailed the letter and money. He secured the Lodi manuscript and took it with him into the country.

Dr. Stevens interrupted with corroborating details, and asked Mervyn what had made him return to the city. Mervyn told of living and working with the Hadwin family. To avoid possible emotional involvement with the younger of their daughters, Eliza, he had devoted all his leisure to translating the Lodi manuscript, in which he found money concealed. He decided that he must give the money to Clemenza.

The plague started in Philadelphia, and the older Hadwin daughter, Susan, feared that her lover, Wallace, was ill. To relieve her fears, Mervyn went secretly to Philadelphia, where he intended to find Clemenza as well. The address at which he sought Wallace was the house where Thetford had lived earlier. In an upper room, he surprised a plunderer who struck him down. He awakened as he was about to be placed in a coffin. Mr. Estwick told him Thetford's new address. There, he learned that Thetford had sent Wallace to the hospital and Thetford himself was dead. Old Hadwin appeared, and Mervyn sent him home thinking that Wallace was dead.

Wallace returned from hospital and Mervyn recognized the youth who had tricked him into the Thetford's bedroom. He put Wallace in a carriage and went for refuge to Welbeck's mansion, where he found his former employer looking for the Lodi manuscript. Welbeck said that the bills in the book were forged, and, to Welbeck's horror, the youth destroyed them. Welbeck left in fury; the bills were authentic. Mervyn wandered alone in the city, and resigned himself to death outside Stevens' house, where he was found and cared for.

Volume two opens with Stevens relating information about Clemenza Lodi, who was living with an infamous woman named Villars and her daughters. Mervyn wished to save Clemenza from the Villars' evil influence, but, first, he went to the Hadwin farm looking for Wallace. While Mervyn was away, Stevens learned an alternate version of Mervyn's life. Mrs. Althorpe reported that Mervyn had seduced the girl his father later married, and that he had stolen money from his father. Further, the girl, Betty Lawrence, had apparently followed her evil lover to the city, with additional money stolen from the old man.

Wortley told Stevens that Amos Watson was missing with a large sum of money belonging to a Mrs. Maurice concealed on his person. Welbeck and Mervyn were suspected in the case. Mrs. Wentworth had received information convincing her that Clavering was living. Dr. and Mrs. Stevens feared Mervyn had lied to them.

Summoned to debtor's prison, Stevens arranged for the comfort of his friend Carlton and found Mervyn assisting Welbeck. Mervyn, who had summoned Stevens, gladly related his latest adventures. Wallace never had returned to the Hadwin farm, though Mervyn learned that he had recovered from the fever. Hadwin himself had contracted fever and died, and Susan had died soon after Arthur's return. Failing to get anyone to care for Eliza, Mervyn suggested she go to her uncle's house. The girl refused and destroyed her father's will which named her uncle as executor of his estate. Mervyn escorted Eliza toward a house where he thought she might have lived, but her horse threw her, and Mr. and Mrs. Curling gave her refuge. Mervyn went to Philip Hadwin's tavern and learned that Eliza's uncle held a mortgage on the farm.

Leaving Eliza with the Curlings, Mervyn stopped at Mrs. Villars' house and was present when Clemenza's infant died. He warned another young woman he met there about the nature of the Villars household, and she gave him her card. She was Achsa Fielding. At Clemenza's request, he sought Welbeck at debtor's prison.

Before dying, Welbeck gave Mervyn the money he had taken from Amos Watson's decaying body. Mervyn asked Mrs. Wentworth and her friend Mrs. Fielding, whom Mervyn had met at Mrs. Villars', to assist Clemenza. He took a stage coach to Baltimore to return the money to its rightful owners. He saw Mrs. Watson, told her of her husband's death, and left money for her. At the Maurice estate, he gave money to Mrs. Maurice, who reacted suspiciously. Watson's brother-in-law Williams, helped Mervyn get the thousand-dollar reward advertised for the money's return. Back in Philadelphia, Mervyn decided to see about his father and about Eliza Hadwin before beginning medical studies with Dr. Stevens.

Mervyn arrived at the village of Newton shortly after his father's death. Eliza, however, seemed in good spirits and imposed fewer and more realistic demands on Mervyn. Studying with Stevens, Mervyn saw his new friends the Carltons, Mrs. Wentworth, and especially Mrs. Fielding whom he wished to be an "older sister" to Eliza. Mrs. Wentworth asked Mervyn to write his story, and he discovered that Dr. Stevens had already begun the account. They combined their work to form the novel.

Achsa Fielding overcame her reluctance to help Eliza Hadwin when she realized Mervyn did not wish to marry the girl but to protect her as a brother would. Achsa told Mervyn her lifestory, and, after Eliza came to live with Mrs. Fielding, Mervyn realized that he loved Achsa and that she loved him. The book ends with anticipations of their marriage.

Critical Evaluation

Charles Brockden Brown lived through the horrors of the plague of 1793, and the psychological and emotional reactions to the yellow fever epidemic provide the core of *Arthur Mervyn*. Only to a slightly lesser degree than Defoe's *Journal of the Plague Year* does *Arthur Mervyn* capture "the influences of hope and fear, the trials of fortitude and constancy" in a plague-stricken city. The novel, and its preface, make clear that Brown remains interested in social reform; Mervyn, after he recovers from the fever, wishes to supervise the attendants at the dreaded hospital to assure compassionate and efficient relief for all patients.

The chapters of the novel devoted to plague-stricken Philadelphia are painfully unrelieved from horror. The callous language and behavior of the coffin-men, charged with collection of bodies, contrast powerfully with the quiet resignation of old Mr. Medlicote who remains in the city because he is indifferent to death. The report of Thetford's irrational and ungrateful treatment of Wallace seems precisely to capture the cowardice of an indecisive man. Dr. Stevens' disinterested and generous treatment of Mervyn sets an example against which the instances of fear and suspicion, cruelty and unconcern stand out forcefully.

Important though they are, the plague chapters amount to a small portion of the total book. Though other action is dramatic and moving, few of the book's scenes qualify as gothic. When Mervyn assists Welbeck in burying Amos Watson, the gloomy terrors of the cellar prove wholly illusory. Mervyn's unwarranted fears, once relieved, lighten the scene. Brown avoids dramatizing a second cellar scene; Welbeck produces the money concealed on Watson's body without detailing the disinterment.

Brown's accomplishments in *Arthur Mervyn* would clearly prove useful to a writer like Poe, but the book's gothic impulse does not tell the whole story. The novel takes one back to the early fictional preoccupation with questions of appearance and reality. Like many another product of the Enlightenment, *Arthur Mervyn* is as much about epistemology—the process of thinking—as it is about anything else. The better-known *Wieland* provides multiple misinterpretations of the same evidence, and *Arthur Mervyn* shows that actions, no less than motives, often prove susceptible to contrary assessments.

Brown creates an almost unbelievably virtuous hero, but even as he establishes Mervyn's virtue, he allows other opinions to threaten his hero's credibility. Sensitive to the possibility that Mervyn is not what he claims to be, the contemporary reader responds to the possibility of Mervyn's actions arising from selfish motives. In short, Brown's narrative method invests his central characters with complex, even ambiguous dimensions.

Many voices tell the story in *Arthur Mervyn*, and, at the end, Mervyn tells the reader that he has produced his written account of his experiences to combine with what his friend Dr. Stevens has already written down. Much of the story appears as Mervyn narrated it to Stevens and his wife; when Stevens picks up the story, his information both qualifies and coroborates what Mervyn has told. Meantime, Mervyn's story combines his interpretation of events with what other people have told him.

Mounting evidence against Mervyn's truthfulness gradually makes even Stevens doubt his young friend, but subsequent revelations prove that what looked like evidence was actually false inference. Mrs. Althorpe, for instance, gives an account of Mervyn's character quite at odds with what he has told Stevens. She claims that Mervyn robbed his father before setting out for Philadelphia, and to support her case, she says that Arthur was seen dressed in fine clothes the day after his arrival in the city. Mervyn's claim that Welbeck provided him a wardrobe as well as lodging seems a plausible explanation.

Mervyn's personality does not lack the self-serving, fully human urge. When he finds a large sum of money hidden in the Lodi manuscript, he must talk himself into doing what he knows is right. At first, he allows himself to think that the fortune is rightfully his. Employed at the Hadwin farm, Mervyn resists entanglement with Eliza, for he recognizes that the farm will not adequately support both Eliza and her sister Susan and their husbands. After the elder Hadwin and Susan are dead, his ardor for Eliza increases, only to diminish after he learns that Philip Hadwin holds a mortgage on the farm.

Few of Brown's characters in *Arthur Mervyn* achieve anything like reality, for their characters and voices betray their hasty composition to serve a fictional purpose. The villain Welbeck haunts the reader's memory, but his intentions in hiring Mervyn as copyist remain vague—to the detriment of the story. Influenced by William Godwin, Brown wished to develop a story depending upon a character's resemblance to other characters, but the reader wonders if Arthur Mervyn's resemblance to a dead, and eccentric if not crazy, person really furthers the story.

Too often, characters and conflicts enter Brown's story without leading anywhere. Mrs. Wentworth, for instance, prompts Mervyn to record his adventures, but never does Brown satisfy the reader's curiosity about her interest in the dead youth Clavering—of whom she has had reports conflicting with Mervyn's accounts. Other stories are left hanging, most notably that of the clerk Wallace. Though beloved by Susan Hadwin, Wallace proves himself capricious on more than one occasion and disappears from the story. Similarly, Eliza Hadwin, though apparently in love with Mervyn, slips into the background at the opportune moment to allow Mervyn to marry his affluent widow, Mrs. Fielding. What happens to Clemenza Lodi seems even more to the point, for Arthur Mervyn's concern for her controlled his actions throughout a great part of the novel.

Arthur Mervyn leaves the contemporary reader grateful that Charles Brockden Brown brought to the novel his interest in social and psychological concerns, but that same reader may wonder if the novelist consciously left his story unresolved, or if Brown recognized that unfinished stories are a part of the larger question he addressed.

Bibliography

Bernard, Kenneth. "Arthur Mervyn: The Ordeal of Innocence," in *Texas Studies in Literature and Language.* VI (Winter, 1965), pp. 441–459.

————. "Charles Brockden Brown," in *Minor American Novelists.* Edited by Charles Hoyt. Carbondale: Southern Illinois University Press, 1970, pp. 1–9.

Btanaccio, P. "Studied Ambiguities: *Arthur Mervyn* and the Problem of the Unreliable Narrator," in *American Literature.* XLII (March, 1970), pp. 18–27.

Clark, David Lee. *Charles Brockden Brown: Pioneer Voice.* Durham, N.C.: Duke University Press, 1952, pp. 177–181.

Erskine, John. *Leading American Novelists.* New York: Holt, 1910, pp. 26–31.

Fiedler, Leslie A. *Love and Death in the American Novel.* New York: Stein and Day, 1960, pp. 148–161.

Justus, J.H. "Arthur Mervyn, American," in *American Literature.* XLII (November, 1970), pp. 304–324.

Kimball, Arthur. *Rational Fictions: A Study of Charles Brockden Brown.* McMinnville, Ore.: Linfield Research Institute, 1968, pp. 154–157, 171–185.

Marble, Annie Russell. *Heralds of American Literature.* Chicago: University of Chicago Press, 1907, pp. 297–301.

Spingemann, W.C. "The Poetics of Domesticity," in his *The Adventurous Muse.* New Haven, Conn.: Yale University Press, 1977, pp. 68–118.

Vilas, Martin S. *Charles Brockden Brown.* Burlington, Vt.: Free Press Association, 1904, pp. 31–33.

Warfel, Harry R. *Charles Brockden Brown.* Gainesville: University of Florida Press, 1949, pp. 141–148.

Wiley, Lulu Rumsey. *The Sources and Influence of the Novels of Charles Brockden Brown.* New York: Vantage, 1950, pp. 141–154.

ORMOND

Type of work: Novel
Author: Charles Brockden Brown (1771–1810)
Type of plot: Gothic romance
Time of plot: Late eighteenth century
Locale: Philadelphia
First published: 1799

An intriguing but seriously flawed novel, Ormond *reveals Brown's interest in eighteenth century radical ideas about the rights and capacities of women, the supremacy of reason, and human perfectability, resulting in a novel of ideas with a Gothic patina overlaid.*

Principal Characters

Constantia Dudley, the only daughter of a New York shopkeeper. She is reared to be useful and knowledgeable. Her education includes both classical languages and eighteenth century philosophy and science. Through all her family's woes she demonstrates the highest courage, resourcefulness, and calm, but these attributes are particularly evident during a plague in Philadelphia when she attends to several sick friends while cheerfully managing her own household. Nearly destitute at this time, she manages to feed her father, a maid, and herself for three months on three dollars by serving only hasty pudding—a combination of Indian meal, salt, and water. The great test of her character and background is Ormond, who is also steeped in Enlightenment thought and who tries to reason her into becoming his mistress. Because she has not been taught religion and values reason, she is somewhat susceptible to his sophistries, particularly to his rejection of conventional marriage. Ultimately she defeats Ormond, not by outreasoning him, but by instinctively stabbing him to death, even though the act goes against her scruples about bloodshed.

Ormond, a wealthy, brilliant, totally self-reliant man of the world living in Philadelphia. He has imbibed most of the radical ideology of his day, and, in particular, is totally at odds with social conventions. He was educated in Europe, lived a brutal life as a soldier, and belongs to a secret organization dedicated to the overthrow of the existing powers of Europe. The most evident feature of his personality is his disdain for social amenities, a sort of fierce insistence on honest, straightforward discourse and social relationships. In fact, so fierce has this insistence been that he once used disguise to learn what an acquaintance really was thinking of him, and thus, oddly enough, his passion for honesty has led him to be a master of concealment. His intellectuality and forthrightness attract, or, at least, interest Constantia, but despite his personal appeal and theories of benevolence, he is depraved and ultimately mad. To get Constantia he has her father killed and then kills the murderer, Thomas Craig, justifying both as acts of benevolence. In the final scenes he not only threatens rape and murder, but even necrophilia, so monomaniacal is his desire to have his way with Constantia.

Stephen Dudley, Constantia's father, who takes over and does well at his father's apothecary business, but always longs to be an artist. In that sense, he is a bit effete and never entirely satisfied with his circumstances. Thus, when Thomas Craig embezzles money from the business, Dudley is ruined, and he becomes a scrivener in order to survive. However, the new work and a move to Philadelphia lead him into a much coarser and more depressing environment than he has been used to, and he turns to drink. After his wife dies, he goes blind, and is thus wholly dependent on his daughter until their fortunes are recouped and an operation restores his sight. Because he sees through and rejects Ormond, Ormond has him killed.

Thomas Craig, an enterprising and unscrupulous young man, who joins Stephen Dudley first as an apprentice and then as a partner. He appears industrious and agreeable, but is, in fact, wholly corrupt. He embezzles money from Dudley and indebts him further beyond his ability to pay. When Constantia happens to find him years later and appeals for sympathy and minimal restitution, he buys her off cheaply with a forged fifty dollar note and lies to Ormond about his part in the Dudleys' woes. Threatened by Ormond with exposure and prosecution, Craig kills Dudley and is then himself killed when Ormond tries to win Constantia's favor by avenging her father's death.

Helena Cleves, Ormond's mistress. She is weak and dependent, skilled only in the arts—music, painting, fashion—thought appropriate to refined women of the time. When Ormond refuses to marry her, she commits suicide.

Martinette Beauvais, Ormond's sister. Like Constantia she is intelligent, strong, self-reliant, and courageous, but unlike her she is unmoved by bloodshed. She was reared in Europe and fought as a soldier in the French Revolution.

Sofia Westwyn Courtland, the narrator and Constantia's friend. When she appears toward the end of the novel, she is able to comfort Constantia after the death of her father and provide the moral guidance she needs in coping with Ormond.

Mr. Melbourne, a merchant and magistrate. Because he knew Thomas Dudley before disaster overtook him and

Mary Whiston, Constantia's neighbor. She dies during the plague after prolonged suffering. When Mary's brother abandons her, fleeing to save his own life, Constantia enters the house and comforts her as best she can. The brother subsequently dies in the countryside but is left unburied and thereby infects and destroys the family that had given him only so much aid as to house him in their barn.

Lucy, the Dudleys' maid. She is hired after the Dudleys' move to Philadelphia to help with the heavier housework, but because of her poverty, she becomes a dependent member of the Dudley household from then on.

M'Crea, the Dudleys' flinthearted landlord in Philadelphia. He extends no sympathy to the Dudleys, and is on the point of driving them into the streets or debtor's prison when Melbourne intervenes.

Balfour, a middle-aged, well-to-do businessman with a torpid intellect. After he saves Constantia from some ruffians bent on rape, his sympathy turns to love and he proposes marriage. Constantia rejects him because of his inferior intellect, because she does not love him, and because the marriage vows are too restrictive to her.
because he seemed kindly, Constantia seeks him out when charity is her only recourse. He rescues Dudley from eviction and prison, and remains one of Constantia's most trusted friends.

Mrs. Melbourne, the magistrate's wife. She helps Constantia by providing her with a job in needlework and then encourages Ormond to think of marrying Constantia.

Sarah Baxter, Constantia's friend and neighbor. When Sarah loses her husband and two daughters to yellow fever, Constantia helps her cope.

The Story

Until his father died, Stephen Dudley lived an indulgent, enriching life as an artist, first in Europe, especially Italy, and then in New York. But, the father's death required that Stephen for the first time attend to the matter of earning a living by taking over the family apothecary shop. Industrious and intelligent, Stephen actually improved the business and began to envision a time when he would be able to return to his former aesthetic life. This dream seemed even more plausible when he accepted Thomas Craig into the concern, first as an apprentice and then, because the young man had been so devoted, hard-working, and trustworthy, as a partner. Craig shattered the dream, however, by embezzling a large share of the stock, indebting Dudley for more than the rest, and running off. Thus ruined, Stephen moved to Philadelphia, changed his name to Acworth, and became a scrivener, but the occupation was dispiriting and the gloom of the reduced circumstances defeated his wife's will to live. For a time after her death Stephen turned to drink but when a cataract blinded him, he was left both chastened and entirely dependent.

In the midst of this sorrow, Constantia Dudley, Stephen's daughter and the novel's central character, reacted serenely, courageously, and resourcefully. She had been reared to both utility and reason, and was, therefore, able to meet the various setbacks with positive action and without debilitating sorrow or recrimination. Only sixteen when Craig absconded with her father's fortune, she first demonstrated her strength by refusing to marry a wealthy young man because to do so would have bound her for life at too early an age. Instead, she assumed many of the household chores, earned extra money by millinery work, and, perhaps most important, soothed her father's distress by her own calm. When her father went blind, Constantia alone was forced to support him and Lucy, a dependent young girl brought in to help with the heavier housework. Constantia found cheaper dwelling in another, humbler part of town and superintended their move there, all the while keeping a cheerful voice for her father.

Soon after the move, yellow fever struck the city and particularly ravaged the poorer sections where sanitation was less careful and the people less able to leave. With the flight of the wealthy went many of the customers for Constantia's needlework. She remained undaunted, however, and managed to survive by extreme frugality. The rent was temporarily forestalled when the landlord died in the plague. She was able to feed her father, Lucy, and herself for three months on a diet of Indian meal, salt, and water.

All around, the sights and sounds of the disease were oppressive. In the Dudleys' neighborhood, two out of three died by the plague. The air became fetid with the smells of vomit and vinegar, people died ranting in the streets, and the rumbling of the hearses was nearly constant. When a neighbor, Mary Whiston, became sick, her brother abandoned her, and Constantia assumed her care at great risk to her own life. She risked further harm by helping a former neighbor, Sarah Baxter, when the fever took Sarah's husband and two daughters. In fact, Constantia twice suffered mild attacks of the disease, but she recovered.

The return of health to the city was actually a bad omen for Constantia, since it meant her new landlord would return seeking the unpaid rent. When he did, the Dudleys were once again forced to move and to sell some of their few remaining possessions. They parted most painfully with a lute and a framed miniature portrait of Constantia's dearest friend. Constantia resumed her needlework and was thus, once again, able meagerly to survive.

About that time, Constantia was offered another chance to change her circumstances through marriage. While she was walking one evening, a wealthy, middle-aged merchant named Balfour saved her from a group of ruffians who tried to rape her. Balfour was plain, stolid, and ledger-minded, but the sympathy she aroused in him carried over into a form of love and he proposed. Once again, however, Constantia refused, recognizing that she did not love him, that he was not her intellectual-moral equal, and that because of the nature of the marriage vows, he offered to substitute a gilded prison for her unadorned freedom. Dudley disagreed with his daughter, but accepted her decision. Balfour was angered, but did not retaliate. Balfour's sister, however, maliciously spread rumors about Constantia with the result that soon no one would hire her to do needlework.

Faced with absolute poverty, Constantia overcame her scruples about charity and decided to ask for aid on her father's behalf from a former business acquaintance, Melbourne. On the way to his house she coincidentally saw Craig and learned where he lived. Rather than have him arrested, she wrote a letter to him appealing to his sympathy but avoiding acrimony or accusation. She delivered the letter in person and, in so doing, met Craig in the sumptuous home of Ormond. Craig realized that he must deal with her or risk exposure, and so he gave her a fifty dollar note. As she left the house she passed by Ormond, and his interest was immediately piqued.

Although Craig disguised his own role in the Dudleys' misfortunes, Ormond learned something of Constantia's history when he subsequently questioned Craig about his visitor. Ormond's general principles of benevolence prompted him to give Craig money to convey anonymously to Constantia, and he became even more involved in her life a few days later when he visited Melbourne's house and learned that Constantia, once again, had preceded him. She had sought relief from Melbourne because Craig's fifty dollar note turned out to be forged, and this had led to her landlord's, to whom she gave the note, seeking to have Dudley evicted and imprisoned. Melbourne was the magistrate who had authorized the arrest papers, and when he discovered who was to be the victim, he remembered his former friend and halted the arrest. Mrs. Melbourne offered Constantia sufficient work and remuneration so that the Dudleys were once more rescued from poverty. When Ormond arrived, Mrs. Melbourne told him Constantia's story and praised her beauty. She suggested that a man of Ormond's wealth might very well become here benefactor and husband.

Steeped in the radical opinions of his day and by disposition drawn to freedom for himself and dominance over others, Ormond was not the marrying kind. For some time he had kept a mistress, Helena Cleves, who was precisely the opposite of Constantia in temperament, training, and accomplishments. Whereas Constantia was strong-willed, intellectual, self-sufficient, and educated in the classical languages, modern science, and philosophy, Helena was weak, passionate, dependent, and accomplished only at "lady skills"—singing, painting, and decorating herself. Already sensing her superior intellectual attainments, Ormond was intrigued by Constantia, but Craig's account of her had cast doubt on her character, so he decided to learn more about her by disguising himself as a messenger and visiting her home. What he saw there of strength defying adversity satisfied him that she was indeed admirable. Still disguised he provided enough money to pay off Dudley's debts and to maintain the household in perpetuity at their present level. He also persuaded Helena to hire Constantia for needlework, and this act led to Constantia's finally meeting Ormond.

Helena confided in Constantia about her relationship with Ormond and of her desire to marry him. Recognizing Helena's weakness and confident of her own strength, Constantia agreed to intercede and requested an interview with Ormond. She was completely baffled by the man she met, but not altogether displeased. One of Ormond's chief traits was disdain of convention and social amenity, a rigid and sometimes brutal straightforwardness and honesty. He summarily dispensed with her arguments for his marrying Helena, but this issue of marriage, first in the abstract and then between him and Constantia, was not dropped. Their first meeting led to a series of others which were mostly high-minded debates about the role of women in society but which convinced Ormond that he must have Constantia, even if he must marry her as a last resort. Because Constantia had been reared to reason and not religion, she was particularly susceptible to his sophistries.

His first step was to drop Helena. He provided generously for her support, but did not spare her feelings in telling her his plans. Without Ormond to center her life, Helena was crushed, and she committed suicide. Because of Ormond's generosity, she left a considerable estate which went to the Dudleys and restored them to their former affluence. Even Mr. Dudley's sight was regained when Ormond commissioned a doctor friend to examine and than operate on him. With Constantia now more nearly his equal, Ormond could pursue her in earnest, although until the very end this pursuit was primarily intellectual. In fact, a few months after Helena's death and the Dudleys' restoration, Ormond left Philadelphia but carried on his debate with Constantia by mail.

While Ormond was absent, Constantia met Martinette Beauvais. Constantia first had been acquainted with her without knowing her name when during the plague Sarah Baxter had described the plight of a neighbor girl who had to assume responsibility for burying her own father. Coincidentally, that girl had bought Stephen Dudley's lute, and Constantia's hearing it played while she was visiting Mrs. Melbourne, led to her meeting its owner. Martinette was Ormond's sister and was a rebel soldier in the French Revolution. She shared many radical beliefs with Constantia, and like her, she had faced adversity with strength and courage. But Martinette had been made mannish by her experiences. In particular, she had become inured to bloodshed, even seemed to delight in it, and when Constantia learned this of her, their friendship cooled. About the same time Mr. Dudley conceived the idea of returning to the scenes of his early aesthetic life in Italy. Constantia, of course, would accompany him, reluctant only because of her lingering interest in Ormond. Dudley had seen through Ormond's sophistries about the marriage state and opposed him, but before Dudley could take his daughter to Europe, Ormond induced Craig to murder him.

Constantia was nearly devastated by the loss, but she sought out her girlhood chum, Sophia Westwyn, for solace and companionship. Sophia had lived with the Dudleys for many years but left to follow her dissipated mother to Europe. There Sophia met and married Courtland, but she had been unable to forget her friend and had returned to America to find Constantia at the same time that Constantia was looking for her. The framed picture Constantia sold during the plague was the apparent key to their finding each other, but Ormond in disguise had, in fact, orchestrated the reunion.

Sophia soon learned of her friend's interest in Ormond, and she recognized the threat he posed. In several conversations she warned Constantia to refuse him, finally persuading her to evade him by traveling to Europe. But, just before they were to leave, Ormond returned and astounded Constantia with his knowledge of her activities, her future plans, even of her private conversations with Sophia. His skill at disguise and at clandestine eavesdropping had given him this knowledge, but as he confronted Constantia with it, he claimed the power of foresight. As a parting gesture, he predicted her imminent loss of virginity.

When Sophia learned of this prediction, she immediately suspected that Ormond planned either to seduce or rape Constantia. To prevent this, Sophia hastened the move to Europe. She booked passage to England and authorized Melbourne to sell Constantia's property and send her the money. Constantia easily consented, but wished to spend a few days at her estate in New Jersey while Sophia went on to New York to make ready for their journey. Sophia reluctantly agreed and Constantia was left alone, away from the well-traveled roads.

One evening, while Constantia was in her second-story writing closet watching the sunset, she saw a horseman approach, come to the house, and then disappear. She recognized the man as Ormond and for the first time feared his presence. After hearing a scuffle followed by silence in the next room, she mounted enough courage to investigate and discovered a man's body. She ran downstairs, trying to escape, but instead met Ormond.

Now the mast dropped. Ormond admitted that he intended to deflower her and that he had killed the man upstairs. He identified the man as Thomas Craig and told Constantia that he had induced Craig to kill her father. He tried to justify all this with radical philosophy, but he was clearly mad. He vowed to have his way with Constantia even if she took her own life.

Thus, Constantia's scruples against bloodshed were put to a severe test. She was armed with a small penknife but was uncertain whether to use it against herself, against Ormond, or not at all. At the crucial moment, she acted instinctively and killed Ormond. Sophia arrived almost immediately afterwards to comfort her friend and escort her to Europe and to a happier, more tranquil life.

Critical Evaluation

Charles Brockden Brown's first four published novels, *Wieland* (1798), *Ormond* (1799), *Arthur Mervyn* (1799, 1800), and *Edgar Huntley* (1799), continue to be studied by scholars and occasionally read by students. This interest has persisted despite the obvious flaws in his work—a dreary, latinate style, inconsistent characterization, and excessively complex plot structure—that make these novels almost inaccessible to the general reader. In part, Brown's work is interesting to scholars because it represents the efforts of the first American to try to make a living by writing fiction. Brown was a brilliant student, widely read in philosophy, interested in politics, and clearly acquainted with the more popular fiction modes of his day—the sentimental romances of Samuel Richardson, the gothic melodramas of Ann Radcliffe, and the political-gothic novels of William Godwin. That he attempted, at a time when novel writing was not encouraged in America, to fashion works of art that reflected the crosscurrents of eighteenth century thought as they bore on the American scene was indeed an admirable goal, well worth our continued study. Critics have found in Brown, particularly in his fascination with insanity and with the psychology of terror, seeds of what bloomed in many of America's greatest writers, such as Poe, Hawthorne, Melville, and Henry James. Brown also shares these writers' use of ambiguity, and it may be that quality, the fact that Brown's work is simply puzzling, that has kept scholars and critics reading his novels.

Ormond, Brown's second published novel, depends less on the machinery of terror and has a simpler plot structure than his other major works (*Clara Howard* and *Jane Talbot*, both domestic novels, are usually considered secondary and feebler attempts by Brown). However, those features are not absent from *Ormond*, and like the others it can be read as a testing of certain eighteenth century ideas. The main concern in Ormond is the value of an enlightened education for a woman, an education that strengthens her mind with reason, reduces her dependence on emotions, and equips her with the same knowledge and even some of the same skills as those of a man. That value is tested in the career of Constantia Dudley and in the contrasts between her, Helena Cleves, and Martinette Beauvais.

The key to Constantia's strength and the value of her education is in equanimity. Despite all that befalls her and her family, she remains calm and resourceful. While her father broods himself into dissipation and her mother "dies of regret," Constantia applies her reason to solve the problem of survival. Moreover, because she has been taught useful skills and is intelligent, she is self-reliant. Unlike Helena Cleves, who is destroyed when Ormond rejects her, Constantia twice refuses marriage even though the men were wealthy and could have provided for her and her father.

Constantia has her flaws, however. At times, she displays emotion, or sensibility (to use the age's cult term), and to some degree these lapses cost her: during the plague she becomes ill, and in the final scenes she loses her scruples against bloodshed. On the other Hand, this sensibility distinguishes her from Martinette, who shares many of Constantia's attributes but has become hardened, mannish, and brutal. A more serious flaw in Constantia's character is her lack of religion. She has reason, but without the moral force that religion supplies, and that reason makes her vulnerable to Ormond's sophistries. Thus, Sophia Westwyn, who has religion, is able to see through Ormond and ultimately protect Constantia from him.

If Constantia's virtues are qualified with some failings, Ormond's considerable vices are qualified by virtues. The principles he lives by include universal benevolence, forthrightness, and a radical rejection of marriage that Brown has espoused earlier in his feminist dialogue, *Alcuin*. In some ways, Ormond invites comparison with Melville's Ahab, for both are supremely self-reliant men of lofty intelligence, tremendous inward force, and transcendent idealism, whose intelligence, forced to an extreme, becomes demented, and their creative force becomes destructive.

Thus, Brown's more important concern in the novel is less rationalism *vs.* anti-rationalism, feminism *vs.* anti-feminism, but the complexities of human nature, the mixtures of virtues and vices found in Ormond and Constantia and, to lesser degrees, in some of the other characters as well. Even more, the emphasis on mystery, false appearance, and hidden identity suggests that human events are not explained by single-minded theories, but must remain essentially baffling.

Bibliography

Bernard, Kenneth. "Charles Brockden Brown," in *Minor American Novelists*. Edited by Charles Hoyt. Carbondale: Southern Illinois University Press, 1970, pp. 1–9.

Clark, David Lee. *Charles Brockden Brown: Pioneer Voice of America*. Durham, N.C.: Duke University Press, 1952, pp. 171–174.

Davies, R.R. "Charles Brockden Brown's *Ormond*: A Possible Influence upon Shelley's Conduct," in *Philological Quarterly*. XLIII (January, 1964), pp. 133–137.

Erskine, John. *Leading American Novelists*. New York: Holt, 1910, pp. 22–24.

Fiedler, Leslie A. *Love and Death in the American Novel.* New York: Stein and Day, 1966, pp. 148–161.

Kimball, Arthur. *Rational Fictions: A Study of Charles Brockden Brown.* McMinnville, Ore.: Linfield Research Institute, 1968, pp. 115–124.

Krause, S.J. "Ormond: Seduction in a New Key," in *American Literature.* XLIV (January, 1973), pp. 570–584.

Marble, Annie Russell. *Heralds of American Literature.* Chicago: University of Chicago Press, 1907, p. 297.

Ringe, Donald A. *Charles Brockden Brown.* New York: Twayne, 1966, pp. 49–64.

Rodgers, P.C. "Brown's *Ormond*: The Fruits of Improvisation," in *American Quarterly.* XXVI (March, 1974), pp. 4–22.

Van Doren, Carl. *American Novel.* New York: Macmillan, 1922, p. 11.

Vilas, Martin S. *Charles Brockden Brown.* Burlington, Vt.: Free Press Association, 1904, pp. 27–30.

Warfel, Harry R. *Charles Brockden Brown.* Gainesville: University of Florida Press, 1949, pp. 125–140.

Wiley, Lulu Rumsey. *The Sources and Influence of the Novels of Charles Brockden Brown.* New York: Vantage, 1950, pp. 122–141, 279–282.

WIELAND

Type of work: Novel
Author: Charles Brockden Brown (1771–1810)
Type of plot: Mystery romance
Time of plot: Eighteenth century
Locale: Pennsylvania
First published: 1798

Wieland, *the best of Brown's works, is a romantic tragedy in the genre of horror and remorse which Poe was to cultivate later on. In spite of many flaws of carelessness, the book features macabre effects that can still stir readers partial to gothic stories of grotesque terror.*

Principal Characters

Mr. Wieland, a religious fanatic. He fears a dreadful punishment because he has not answered a "call" to become a missionary. He dies by what seems spontaneous combustion, for his clothes suddenly burst into flames one night as he meditates. He is Clara and young Wieland's father.

Clara Wieland, the narrator, who writes a long letter telling of the tragedy that is visited upon her family. She is attracted to Carwin, but when he defames her character to drive off a rival suitor, her love ends. Eventually she marries Henry Pleyel, brother of her childhood friend.

Mrs. Wieland, Clara's mother. She dies shortly after her husband, leaving Clara and young Wieland to be reared by an aunt.

Wieland, Clara's brother. He, Clara, and his wife Catharine live together as friends. He is a somber, melancholy man of a religious turn. When he hears strange voices he believes he is in communication with some supernatural power. Thinking he is guided by heaven, he sacrifices his wife and their children. Regaining his sanity later, and crushed by remorse, he commits suicide by stabbing himself.

Catharine Pleyel, childhood friend of the Wielands. She marries Wieland and has four children by him. She is killed, along with their children, by her husband, while he is in a fit of madness.

Henry Pleyel, Catharine's brother, a lively young man. Eventually he and Clara marry, after the death of his first wife, a European baroness.

Carwin, a stranger who appears dressed like a humorous beggar. He loves Clara, but defames her to Henry, out of jealousy. He is accused by Clara of being the "voice" which guided Wieland to kill, as he is a ventriloquist. He assures Clara of his innocence and disappears from the area to become a farmer.

The Story

In a long letter to a friend, Clara Wieland told the story of the tragedy of her family. Her father had been almost a religious fanatic, a strange man who feared some dreadful punishment because he had not answered a call to the mission

field. He became more and more depressed and withdrawn until his life ended in
a horrible fashion. One night he visited a temple he had built for solitary meditation. His wife, fearing the appearance and manner of her husband, followed him
and saw his clothing suddenly go up in flames. She found him insensible, mutter-
ing incoherently about having been struck down by an unseen hand. Soon afterward he died. Within a few months the mother followed her husband to the
grave, leaving Clara and her brother orphaned but wealthy. They were happily
reared by an aunt who gave them love and comfort and a good education.

One of their companions was Catharine Pleyel, a rich and beautiful girl with
whom Wieland fell in love when he reached young manhood. Catharine returned
his love, and when Wieland came of age they were married. Wieland took possession of the family house and half of the fortune, Clara the other half of their
inheritance. Since she and Catharine and Wieland were beloved friends as well as
relatives, Clara took a house only a short distance from her brother and sister-in-
law. The three spent much time together. Clara and Catharine were frank and
cheerful, but Wieland was more somber and thoughtful in disposition. But he was
always considerate of their happiness and nobly devoted his life to it. His melancholy was not morbid, only sober. The temple in which their father had met his
strange fate was used by the three as a setting for long and delightful conversations, although Wieland's talk dwelt too often on death to suit Clara and
Catharine.

Their circle was soon augmented by the addition of Catharine's beloved
brother Henry, who had been for some time in Europe. His boisterous mirth en-
livened the little group. Henry and Wieland found one great difference in their
beliefs: Wieland built his life on religious necessity; Henry, on intellectual liberty.
But their fondness for each other allowed them to differ without altering their
mutual affection.

Wieland's family was enlarged during the next six years by four natural children and a foster child whose mother had died while under his aunt's protection.
About that time another strange occurrence took place in the Wieland family.
One day Wieland went to the temple to pick up a letter which would settle a
minor dispute. Before he reached the temple he was stopped by his wife's voice,
telling him that danger lay in his path. Returning quickly to the house, he found
his wife there. Clara and Henry verified her statement that she had not left the
room. Although the others soon dismissed the incident from their minds, it
preyed on the already melancholy Wieland to the exclusion of everything else.

Not long after that incident Henry Pleyel learned that Wieland had inherited
some large estates in Europe and he wanted Wieland to go abroad to claim them.
Henry would accompany his friend because he had left his heart with a baroness,
now widowed and willing to accept his suit. When Wieland seemed reluctant to
make the journey, Henry, in an effort to persuade him, asked him one night to go
for a walk. Their walk was interrupted by a voice telling them that the baroness
was dead. Again the voice was Catharine's, but again Catharine had been nowhere near the men when the voice was heard. More frightening was the verifica-

tion of the baroness' death given to Henry a few days later. Some dread supernatural power, Wieland believed, had spoken to them.

Shortly after these two mysterious occurrences, a stranger appeared in the neighborhood. He was dressed like a clown or a pathetically humorous beggar, but his voice had the musical ring of an actor. Clara, who saw him before the others knew of his existence, was strangely drawn to him.

She forgot him, however, because of another frightening incident. One night, alone in her room, she heard two voices in the closet planning her murder. One voice advised shooting; the other, choking. She fled to her brother's house and fell at his door in a faint. Wieland and Henry came to her rescue in answer to a summons from an unknown source, a voice calling that a loved one lay dying at the door.

Henry insisted upon occupying a vacant apartment in Clara's home in order to protect her from her unknown enemies. Clara was beset with nightmares, the mystifying voice having warned her of danger from her brother. Soon after the affair of the voices in the closet, she met the stranger she had seen and to whom she had been unaccountably drawn. His name was Carwin, and he had known Henry in Spain. His intelligent conversation and his wide travels making him welcome in the little group, he joined them frequently. When they discussed the supernatural voices they had all heard, Carwin dismissed the voices as fancy or pranks.

Clara, beginning to feel herself in love with Henry, believed that he returned her love but feared to tell her of it because he did not know her feelings. Then he confronted her with the accusation that she was a wanton. He said that he had heard her and a lover, Carwin, talking and that her words made her a sinner and a fallen woman. Henry had also learned that Carwin was wanted for murder, and he heaped abuses on the innocent Clara for consorting with such a man. All her pleas of innocence went unheeded, and she was thrown into despair. Thinking that Carwin had set out to ruin her, she was enraged when she received a note in which he asked for an interview. Reluctantly she agreed to meet him and hear his story. He was to come to her home, but when she arrived there she found only a note warning her of a horrible sight awaiting her. In her room, she found Catharine on the bed. She had been murdered.

Wieland entered her room, his manner strange and exulted, and begged that this sacrifice not be demanded of him. Before he reached Clara, however, others came into the house. From them she learned that her brother's children were also dead, killed by the same hand that had murdered their mother.

Clara was taken by friends to the city. There, after a time, she learned the tragic story. The murderer had been Wieland, his hand guided, he said, by a voice from heaven demanding that he sacrifice his loved ones to God. But he felt no guilt, only glory at having been the instrument through whom God worked. Twice Wieland had broken out of prison, his belief being that he must also kill Clara and Henry. Clara suspected that Carwin had somehow influenced Wieland to kill.

Carwin went to Clara and protested his innocence of the crime. He admitted that his had been the other voices heard. He was a ventriloquist who had used his tricks either to play some prank or to escape detection while prying into other people's affairs. Clara refused to believe him. While they talked, Wieland entered the apartment. Prepared to kill Clara, he had again broken out of prison to fulfill his bloody destiny. But this time Carwin, using his skill to save Clara, called out to Wieland that no voice had told him to kill, that only his own lunatic brain had guided him. At his words Wieland, regained his sanity and seemed to understand for the first time what he had done. Picking up a knife, he plunged it into his throat.

Three years passed before Clara knew peace. Her uncle cared for her and arranged a meeting between Carwin and Henry so that Carwin might confess his part in the defamation of Clara's character. Carwin had been jealous and thus tried to destroy Henry's affection for her. Henry learned also that his baroness was not dead; the report had been another of Carwin's tricks. Henry married the baroness and settled down near Boston. Carwin, not a murderer but the victim of a plot, escaped to the country and became a farmer. Henry's wife died soon after their marriage, and he and Clara renewed their love. Their later happiness was marred only by sad and tragic memories.

Critical Evaluation

Though badly flawed in plot and characterization, *Wieland* deserves a higher place in American literature than that accorded a historical curiosity. In this novel, Brown initiates the characteristically American use of the fantastic and grotesque Gothic tale to explore the moral and psychological dimensions of experience. Poe, Hawthorne, and Melville would refine the Gothic mode into the American romance, but it was Brown and *Wieland* that first introduced the genre into our literature and demonstrated its possibilities.

Like most romancers, Brown had little interest in such concrete details as time and place. His locales are generalized, and he offers little in the way of observation about manners in Pennsylvania society of the eighteenth century. Rather, his characters occupy a landscape of the mind, more symbolic than real, in which their actions dramatize basic human hopes, fears, and passions rather than realistic situations. But the Gothic horrors which abound in *Wieland* are not introduced for the sake of sensationalism. They represent symbolic dramatizations of aspects of the human condition and the American experience.

The two most memorable characters to emerge in *Wieland* are the religious fanatic, Wieland, and the mysterious Carwin. The latter character is only partly responsible for Wieland's dimentia. Driven by the madness of a monomaniacal religious obsession to commit unspeakable crimes upon his loved one, Wieland anticipates the obsessed characters of Poe, Hawthorne, and

Melville. Carwin, on the other hand, represents the man whose cold, scientific curiosity impairs his humanity, so he experiments with human subjects without regard to the consequences. Frequently in later writers, these two figures merge into one to create such monomaniacal seekers after knowledge as Hawthorne's Ethan Brand or Melville's Ahab.

Others would take the American romance to greater heights than Brown could achieve, but they would do so within the tradition he established on American soil.

Bibliography

Bernard, Kenneth. "Charles Brockden Brown," in *Minor American Novelists.* Edited by Charles Hoyt. Carbondale: Southern Illinois University Press, 1970, pp. 1–9.

Berthoff, W.B. "Lesson on Concealment: Brockden Brown's Method in Fiction," in *Philological Quarterly.* XXXVII (January, 1958), pp. 45–57.

Chase, Richard. *The American Novel and Its Tradition.* New York: Doubleday, 1957, pp. 29–35.

Clark, David Lee. *Charles Brockden Brown: Pioneer Voice of America.* Durham, N.C.: Duke University Press, 1952, pp. 162–169, 297–302.

Erskine, John. *Leading American Novelists.* New York: Holt, 1910, pp. 14–22.

Fiedler, Leslie A. *Love and Death in the American Novel.* New York: Stein and Day, 1966, pp. 148–161.

Frank, J.G. "The Wieland Family in Charles Brockden Brown," in *Monatshefte.* XLII (November, 1950), pp. 347–353.

Garrow, Scott. "Character Transformation in *Wieland*," in *Southern Quarterly.* IV (April, 1966), pp. 308–318.

Gilmore, M.T. "Calvinism and Gothicism: The Example of Brown's *Wieland*," in *Studies in the Novel.* IX (Summer, 1977), pp. 107–118.

Hendrickson, J.C. "Note on *Weiland*," in *American Literature.* XIII (November, 1936), pp. 305–306.

Kerlin, R.T. "*Weiland* and the *Raven*," in *Modern Language Notes.* XXXI (December, 1916), pp. 503–505.

Ketterer, David. "The Transformed World of Charles Brockden Brown's *Wieland*," in *New Worlds for Old.* Bloomington: Indiana University Press, 1974, pp. 167–181.

Kimball, Arthur. *Rational Fictions: A Study of Charles Brockden Brown.* McMinnville, Ore.: Linfield Research Institute, 1968, pp. 44–74.

Krause, S.J. "Romanticism in *Wieland*: Brown and the Reconcilation of Opposites," in *Artful Thunder*. Edited by Robert J. DeMott. Kent, Oh.: Kent State University Press, 1975, pp. 13–24.

Manly, W.M.   "Importance of Point of View in Brockden Brown's *Wieland*," in *American Literature*. XXXV (November, 1963), pp. 311–321.

Marble, Annie Russell.   *Heralds of American Literature*. Chicago: University of Chicago Press, 1907, pp. 294–296.

Prescott, F.C.   "*Wieland* and *Frankenstein*," in *American Literature*. II (May, 1930), pp. 172–173.

Ridgely, J.V.   "The Empty World of *Wieland*," in *Individual and Community*. Edited by Kenneth H. Baldwin. Durham, N.C.: Duke University Press, 1975, pp. 3–16.

Ringe, Donald A.   *Charles Brockden Brown*. New York: Twayne, 1966, pp. 24–52.

Van Doren, Carl.   *American Novel*. New York: Macmillan, 1922, pp. 13–14.

Wagenknecht, Edward C.   "Brockden Brown and the Pioneers," in *Cavalcade of the American Novel*. New York: Holt, 1952, pp. 9–13.

Wiley, Lulu Rumsey.   *The Sources and Influence of the Novels of Charles Brockden Brown*. New York: Vantage, 1950, pp. 84–87, 96–121.

Witherington, P.   "Benevolence and the Utmost Stretch: Charles Brockden Brown's Narrative Dilemma," in *Criticism*. XIV (Spring, 1972), pp. 175–191.

Ziff, L.   "Reading of *Wieland*," in *PMLA*. LXXVII (March, 1962), pp. 51–57.

WILLIAM HILL BROWN

Born: Boston, Massachusetts (1765)
Died: Murfreesborough, North Carolina (September 2, 1793)

Principal Works

NOVELS: *The Power of Sympathy*, 1789; *Ira and Isabella*, 1807.

William Hill Brown, the author of America's first novel, was born in Boston in 1765 to a noted clockmaker, Gawen Brown, and his third wife, Elizabeth Hill Brown. Catherine Byles, the half sister of Gawen Brown's second wife, Elizabeth Byles Brown (a great-granddaughter of Increase Mather), helped foster William's early interest in literature. She also recorded about all we know of his childhood—that he was a happy boy and helpful to his father.

The Power of Sympathy was published in 1789 when Brown was twenty-four. It was his first published work and also was advertised as the first American novel. The latter claim has been disputed from time to time, but considering all the criteria—that it be both a narrative and fiction, that it make significant use of the American scene, that it be written by an American citizen, and that it be published in America—Brown's novel certainly qualifies. However, since it appeared anonymously, he gained little fame for its precedence. Other examples of his work—essays, prose tales, poetry—appearing about this time in periodicals such as the *Massachusetts Magazine* and *Columbian Centinel*, were written under a pen name, either "The Yankee" or "Pollio."

In 1792 Brown went south to Murfreesborough, North Carolina, following his younger sister Eliza, who had married John Hinchborne, and moved to the Hinchborne plantation there. Brown began to study law but did not give up writing. He published poems and essays in *The North Carolina Journal* under the pseudonym "Columbus." In August, 1793, a malaria epidemic struck the region, and Brown was one of its victims. He died September 2, 1793. His obituary in the *Journal* described his "uncommon genius", studiousness, and a "richness of fancy and copiousness of expression" which made him both a pleasing writer and good company.

After his death, a tragedy, "West Point Preserved or the Treason of Arnold," was performed in Boston based on Brown's manuscript play, "The Tragedy of Major Andre." This manuscript was also the basis of William Dunlap's *Andre*. Then, between 1805 and 1807 the *Boston Magazine* and the *Emerald* published a number of Brown's works. His only other novel, *Ira and Isabella: or the Natural Children*, appeared in 1807. It is a retelling of *The Power of Sympathy* but with a happy ending, and since the title page gives his name, it is one of the bits of evidence that he wrote the first novel.

Brown's sole claim on the modern reader's interest has been *The Power of*

Sympathy and its status as the first American novel. The work itself, although set in America, mixes several European traditions, particularly the sentimental novel of seduction and the cult of sensibility. It is sententious, lurid, ornately styled, thinly and chaotically plotted, but does show the author's erudition and does spark some interest through its incest theme. However, that it was "first" is its main achievement, and Brown's share of that honor has not always been secure. Until late in the nineteenth century, Mrs. Sarah Wentworth Apthorp Morton, a minor New England poet, was often credited with the novel, perhaps because the Ophelia story, a scene from which was featured in the engraved frontispiece, was based on the seduction of her sister, Fanny Apthorp, by her own husband, Perez Morton. It is unlikely, however, that a woman such as Mrs. Morton would exploit the scandal in her own family. Moreover, in 1894, Brown's niece claimed that her uncle had written *The Power of Sympathy*, and such evidence as has been discovered since points consistently to William Hill Brown as the first American novelist.

Bibliography

Little has been written about Brown or his work, but William S. Kable's "Introduction" to *The Power of Sympathy*, 1969, provides much useful information. For biography consult the *Dictionary of American Biography*, Supplement One, 125–126. See also: Herbert Ross Brown, "Introduction," *The Power of Sympathy*, 1961, and *The Sentimental Novel in America 1789–1860*, 1940; Alexander Cowie, *The Rise of the American Novel*, 1948; Cathy N. Davidson, "*The Power of Sympathy* Reconsidered: William Hill Brown as Literary Craftsman," *Early American Literature*, X, 14–29; Leslie Fiedler, *Love and Death in the American Novel*, 1960; Henri Petter, *The Early American Novel*, 1971.

THE POWER OF SYMPATHY

Type of work: Novel
Author: William Hill Brown (1765–1793)
Type of plot: Sentimental romance
Time of plot: Late eighteenth century
Locale: Principally Boston and New York
First published: 1789

Generally considered the first American novel, The Power of Sympathy *is an epistolary novel in the mode of Richardson characterized by an inflated style, moralizing tone, and weak plotting, yet remaining interesting for its historical importance in American literature and its theme of incest.*

Principal Characters

Tom Harrington, a young upper-class gentleman. He is first presented as a seducer, but quickly transforms into the devoted and virtuous admirer of Harriot Fawcet. Thwarted by his father's ban against an early marriage, especailly to someone without wealth, family, or position, he plans to elope with Harriot. At the eleventh hour he learns she is his half sister, and when the same news destroys Harriot's mind and life, he shoots himself. Thus, he becomes the victim of his father's sins. Tom is initially impetuous, ardent, a man of strong but not necessarily well-guided feelings. These overly exuberant feelings, had they not been stopped, would have made incest of his elopement, and when they as intensely turn to sorrow, lead to despair and suicide.

Harriot Fawcet, the illigitimate child of Tom Harrington's father. She has been reared by Mrs. Francis, but her position in the household is more as menial than daughter. She falls in love with Tom as easily as he does with her, but is saved from seduction by "the power of sympathy" which silently pleads that her honor not be sacrificed to rescue her from deprivation. The news that Tom is her half brother de-

stroys her mind for she cannot reconcile her mixed feelings about him.

Myra Harrington, Tom's sister and confidante to Harriot. Myra is engaged to Tom's friend Jack Worthy, and their relationship illustrates the virtuous side of the sensibility that brought Tom and Harriot together. She is also the chief recipient of Mrs. Holmes' preaching about the education of women; the one who then tries to separate them without knowing why; and the bearer of the glad-sad news to Harriot. In all these actions, she is less character than device.

Jack Worthy, Tom's friend, future brother-in-law, and chief correspondent. Worthy's role is to counterpoise a more refined, rational, and moral sensibility to Tom's ruinous sentimentality. In the conversations at Belleview, he defends Sterne and La Rochefoucauld and warns against reading the wrong kinds of novels. When Tom broods over Harriot's loss, Worthy argues that he should not dwell on his sorrows, but "take the light of facts, and reason from them."

J. Harrington, Tom's, Myra's, and Harriot's father. He seduced Maria Fawcet while married to Amelia, but defended himself as misguidedly prone to dissipation then and since reformed. Maria was sacrificed to preserve the marriage with Amelia. However, added to the crime of seduction, are his obdurate resistance to young marriage, which forces Tom to be secretive, and his cowardice in not telling Tom himself that Harriot is his half sister.

Mrs. Eliza Holmes, a widow and friend of the Harrington's, a woman of sensibility. She provides moral instruction for Myra and others and is ultimately responsible for revealing Harriot's parentage.

Maria Fawcet, Harriot's mother. Hers is the often heard, sad tale of the young girl reduced in circumstances and therefore susceptible to a seducer's advances.

Reverend Holmes, Eliza Holmes' father-in-law. A kindly country preacher, he prefers looking mostly on the bright side of human nature and is therefore more narrow in his views than Worthy. He provides for placing Harriot and chides her father for the harm he has caused.

Mrs. Francis, the guardian of Harriot. Little is revealed of her, although Tom dislikes her, and Harriot at one point suggests she prefers to flee her cousin Martin's sorrow rather than try to ease it.

Mrs. Holmes, Eliza's mother-in-law, a kindly, generous woman.

Amelia Harrington, J. Harrington's wife.

Mrs. Martin, Mrs. Francis' cousin.

Mr. Martin, who cruelly seduces his sister-in-law and then abandons her when she is pregnant and he is forced to confront her angry father.

Ophelia, Mrs. Martin's sister. She bears Martin's child and then poisons herself because of her father's forcing a confrontation with Martin and because Martin's love has turned to hate. Her story is based on the real life of Frances Apthrop. Mrs. Martin in the story was Sarah Wentworth Morton, a prominent pre-Revolutionary War poet, who was first thought to have written *The Power of Sympathy*.

Shepherd, Ophelia's father. He is stubborn, prideful, unforgiving, vengeful.

Fidelia, a pretty young country girl. When her true love drowns himself, she loses her mind. Her fate is to wander the fields near Belleview, melancholy and distractedly incoherent.

Henry, a simple, somewhat retiring country boy. Fidelia's true love, he drowns himself when he sees her abducted and believes she is gone forever.

Williams, a more dashing, assertive, and citified outsider. Failing to seduce Fidelia, he tries to carry her away, but he is pursued, wounded, and driven off.

Miss Whitman, a real life seduction victim whose story is recounted in a footnote. Her fault was to read too many novels and shape her view of life by them. The honorable young beaux could not meet this standard. She grew older and less demanding, but the successful beau was not honorable. Her end, too, is death.

Mrs. Bourn and Miss Bourn, mother and daughter, *nouveau riche* guests of Mrs. Holmes at Belleview. Mrs. Bourn's query about the proper reading for her daughter sets off the discussion Mrs. Holmes reports to Myra. They are anti-sentimentalists.

The Story

Tom Harrington declared his love to beautiful Harriot Fawcet and finding her responsive began to plot her seduction. In a letter to his friend Jack Worthy, Harrington explained that since Harriot had no wealth or family, living instead with a Mrs. Francis, he was not enough of a democrat to marry beneath his class. Moreover, at the time he was somewhat of an idolator at the temple of Love. Against Worthy's admonition that he not misuse her, Harrington defended his generosity by proposing to establish Harriot comfortably in a fine apartment.

However, at the moment when Harrington began to proposition Harriot directly, he faltered. Convinced, he said, by the reason of her beauty and goodness, which silently pleaded that her poverty not be relieved by loss of virtue, he forgot about seduction and vowed to himself to marry her. He later went further and changed his politics after attending a party where the genial atmosphere was ruined by some thoughtless snob's too loud reference to another guest's lowly origins. A final barrier remained, however, when he realized his father's obstinate objection to an early marriage. The only course left for him was to elope.

Meanwhile, Worthy was engaged to Harrington's sister, Myra, who was, in turn, a close friend and correspondent of Harriot. Myra Harrington also exchanged letters with Mrs. Holmes, a widow living in an idyllic rural retreat called Belleview. While Worthy visited Mrs. Holmes, she kept Myra abreast of her fianceé's doings and of the general conversation at Belleview, most of which centered on the dangers and virtues of various kinds of reading in the education of young girls. Myra in turn had written Mrs. Holmes that she suspected her brother was in love, but she did not know with whom. Harriot similarly had described to Myra the interest of a young man, but had not named him. All of this mystery lingered while Harrington more insistently and more exaltedly urged his love on Harriot.

The mystery was solved as a result of Harriot's journey to Rhode Island with Mrs. Francis to visit one of the older woman's cousins. Mooning over his lover's absence, Harrington sent her a letter containing an original poem. Harriot sent the poem to Myra who recognized the handwriting, coyly confronted her brother with the evidence and then told all to Mrs. Holmes. Surprisingly Mrs. Holmes urged Myra to prevent her brother's marriage to Harriot at all costs but she did not say why, only alluding to a tale to tell. However, when Myra tried somewhat imperatively to dissuade Tom from his wedding plans, the pressure backfired. He became more worked up and more determined. He gave evidence of his distraction when he found himself not invited to a party because he was bad company. Also, he was enraged and urged even closer to action when Mrs. Francis reprimanded Harriot in his presence.

When Myra reported the imminence of Tom and Harriot's elopement to Mrs. Holmes, the widow revealed that Harriot was Tom and Myra's half sister. Maria Fawcet, Harriot's mother, had found herself reduced in social and economic status when her father died, and this had made her susceptible to Mr. Harrington's advances since she had already fancied him. Harriot was born of their adulterous affair, and, soon after, Harrington had become moody, distant, and ultimately estranged. Left on her own, Maria had wandered with her child and happened on Belleview where Mrs. Holmes' mother-in-law found her and had taken her in. Maria soon died, and her child had been entrusted to Mrs. Francis. Mrs. Holmes' father-in-law had written to Harrington reprimanding him for seducing and leaving Maria. Harrington in turn had admitted his guilt but justified his abandoning Maria as the only way to rectify his life and preserve his marriage with Amelia. His secret had been kept for sixteen years, but Tom's marriage plans forced disclosure.

Harrington assumed responsibility for telling his son, but, unable to carry through, he hired someone to write an anonymous letter, and thus Tom Harrington learned that he was planning incest. Of course, Tom was distraught, but when Harriot learned the secret from Myra, she was even more devastated. Unable to reconcile the fact that she still felt unbrotherly passion for her brother, Harriot lost her sanity and quickly died. Even before her death Tom had begun to hint at suicide in his letters to Worthy, but after she died that note was struck repeatedly. He soured on humanity and life in general, and Worthy's counterarguments failed to influence him. Finally, on a night when Worthy had come to see him but had been prevented by the family for fear of disturbing his sleep, Tom Harrington shot himself in the head and died. He was buried next to Harriot, leaving a Monumental Inscription which attested to their undying and now sanctified love and warned against the dangers of seduction.

The novel contains three other brief narratives that are relevant, but not directly a part of the main story. The first of these, mentioned in one of the conversations at Belleview and elaborated in a footnote, is the true story of Miss Whitman, a beautiful and respectable young lady from Connecticut. She had good sense but read too many novels and based her ideas of love on them. Unsatisfied by the real young men who courted her, she turned them all down until she was no longer so youthful and no longer so heavily sought after. The men's overtures also became less respectable, and she eventually succumbed. When she found herself pregnant, an attempt was made to buy a husband, but he disappeared when he received his money. Her baby was dead at birth, and she soon died of puerperal fever.

The second tale is related by Harriot. When she visited Mrs. Martin, Mrs. Francis' cousin, in Rhode Island, she found the household obviously upset. The source of the sorrow was Mr. Martin's recently discovered affair with his sister-in-law Ophelia and her subsequent suicide. Martin, it had been discovered, had become enamored of Ophelia after his marriage and after her return from a European visit. On her arrival, he offered to set her up in an apartment in his house. When she accepted, he had the opportunity to ply his wiles and eventually he had seduced her. They maintained their affair for some time, but her pregnancy forced her home to the country where a son was born, much to the embarrassment and anger of her father, Shepherd. His resentment of his daughter and vengeful attitude toward Martin, soon turned her lover's feelings to hatred. Shepherd tried to force a confrontation with Martin and Ophelia, by bringing them before him in his home, but the prospect of that was too much for Ophelia and she poisoned herself. When Harriot and Mrs. Francis were there, the debate still raged whether Martin was responsible for Ophelia's death because he had seduced her, or Shepherd was responsible because he had forced the confrontation and would not forgive his daughter her sin.

The third disconnected narrative is Worthy's. While walking with Mrs. Holmes in Belleview one day, he heard someone singing a melancholy tune. That someone was Fidelia, a beautiful and pure farm girl who had been engaged to marry Henry, a local boy she had known and been attached to nearly all her life. Their bright hopes for the future had been destroyed when a more worldly rival, Williams, appeared. Williams tried to win Fidelia, and for a time she had been pleased with his attentions, but her heart was Henry's, and they had pledged their love and faith to each other. Not to be thwarted, Williams simply grabbed Fidelia and tried to run off with her. He had been stopped by the young men of the village, and Fidelia was rescued. But Henry, knowing only that his love was gone, had despaired of life and drowned himself in the river. When Fidelia learned of her true love's fate, her mind had been destroyed. Ever since, she had wandered the fields sadly distracted, just as she appeared to Mrs. Holmes and Worthy.

Critical Evaluation

According to rumor and some documentable evidence, soon after *The Power of Sympathy* was published an attempt was made to suppress it by buying and destroying whatever copies were available. The author (generally, but not incontestably recognized to be William Hill Brown) had learned that his thinly fictionalized account of the seduction of Frances Apthrop (the novel's Ophelia) was distressing her family, and he, therefore, initiated the suppression himself. However, if true, this alleged suppression was apparently unsuccessful. It did not, on the other hand, encourage sales with the sniff of scandal. America's first novel was not a great publishing success, and is, therefore, a limited reflector of eighteenth century American reading tastes.

Nevertheless, *The Power of Sympathy* does draw from the literary fashions of its time in several key respects. The epistolary mode, didacticism, and the seduction theme are sentimental romance conventions *à la* Samuel Richardson's *Clarissa* and *Pamela*, and the focus on sensibility owes much to Laurence Sterne's *A Sentimental Journey* and Alexander McKenzie's *The Man of Feeling*. Brown directly pays respect to Goethe by having a copy of *The Sorrows of Young Werther* by Harrington's side when he commits suicide.

In fact, the evidence of Brown's wide reading signals perhaps the novel's main strength—its seriousness. Although clumsily introduced and inadequately dramatized, Brown does struggle with ideas, does try to account for mysteries of human behavior and the possibilities of virtue on a fairly high plain. He even evidences some originality insofar as he tries to write something "applicable to the situation of an *American* lady."

The central theme of the novel is not only the evils of seduction, although warning against that vice is the objective stated on the dedication page, but also the roles of the rational and the irrational, of education and nature, in creating the good and happy life. Some of these issues, or more specifically the effects of certain kinds of reading on young women, is the subject of a prolonged discussion at Belleview reported by Mrs. Holmes. The more reliable spokespersons, Worthy, Mrs. Holmes, and her father-in-law, Reverend Holmes, all urge that reading is necessary for the young female mind but that the reading must be carefully selected. Novels can be dangerous if they become the only window on life. The young girl will have either an overheated imagination by too much emphasis on love, a weakened intellect by too much emphasis on fashion and meretricious beauty, or a dangerous naïveté by an unrealistic representation of human behavior. However, these genteel souls are not prudes. Worthy and Mrs. Holmes defend La Rochefoucauld's maxims against the charge that they "degrade human nature" by insisting they provide a true picture of humanity and thereby better enable the young lady to deal with real life. Sterne's *A Sentimental Journey* is also defended, as is satire, including Swift's. A kind of composite point of view emerges which strives for a balance between reason and feeling, too much reading and not enough, unguided and overly restricted education. Mrs. Holmes, in particular, forsees that the American young girl will rise above her English counterpart by being better, more solidly educated, her learning founded on "virtue and religion."

Belleview is the perfect setting for this celebration of the Golden Mean. The Reverend Holmes has designed his garden to provide the most sublime prospects of the surrounding countryside, and although away from the sordid and tawdry cares of the city, it provides many occasions for the best company and stimulating conversations. In the midst of this deist's paradise a Temple of Apollo has been built, complete with library and dedicated to contentment. It is the central image that explains the novel's subtitle, "The Triumph of Nature": not a nature of unruly passions or amorality, but God's nature, the perfect harmony of reason, emotion, and virtue.

At this point, however, the novel clouds but also becomes interesting. The "power of sympathy" or sensibility which binds Worthy to Myra and which is evidenced in their parallel responses to the scenes of Belleview, also binds Tom to Harriot. To be sure, Worthy is a man of true sensibility, his feelings checked by reason, and Harrington is excitable and impetuous, his passions ungoverned. Yet, Tom and Harriot's falling in love was not merely passion, but this subliminal sympathy in the form of sibling affection operating on them both without their knowledge. That is why Tom so quickly foregoes seduction and why her eyes can speak to him without words. The problem is that this power of sympathy in Tom and Harriot's case is too plainly incestuous and leads to tragedy. The lovers can redirect their feelings from illicit to licit love, but the next step, from husband-wife to brother-sister love, is only possible in death. Harriot in particular is driven mad because she cannot stop wanting Tom as a husband. Brown tries to sanctify their relationship in the final vision of their lying together, cleansed by the grave, but the attempt does not work. In the world in which all his characters live, incest is still incest, just as much as seduction is seduction. Brown's interest in this unreconciled, shady side of nature has prompted one critic to describe him as a precursor to America's "dark Romantics"—Poe, Hawthorne, Melville, and Faulkner. Such an association is slight and honors Brown's novel far beyond its worth, but the incest theme remains a spark of interest in an otherwise undistinguished performance.

Bibliography

Byers, J.R.   "Further Verification of the Authorship of *Power of Sympathy,*" XLIII (November, 1971), pp. 421–427.

Ellis, M.   "Author of the First American Novel," in *American Literature*. IV (January, 1933), pp. 359–368.

McDowell, Tremaine.   "The First American Novel," in *American Review*. II (November, 1933), pp. 73–81.

Marble, Annie Russell.   *Heralds of American Literature*. Chicago: University of Chicago Press, 1907, p. 280.

Spiller, Robert.   *Literary History of the United States*. New York: Macmillan Company, 1957, p. 177.

Wagenknecht, Edward.   *Cavalcade of the American Novel*. New York: Holt, 1952, p. 2–5.

Walser, Richard.   "More About the First American Novel," in *American Literature*. XXIV (November, 1952), pp. 352–357.

JAMES BRANCH CABELL

Born: Richmond, Virginia (April 14, 1879)
Died: Richmond (May 5, 1958)

Principal Works

NOVELS: *The Eagle's Shadow*, 1904; *The Cords of Vanity*, 1909; *The Rivet in Grandfather's Neck*, 1915; *The Cream of the Jest*, 1917; *Jurgen*, 1919; *Domnei*, 1920; *Figures of Earth*, 1921; *The High Place*, 1923; *The Silver Stallion*, 1926; *Something about Eve*, 1927; *The Way of Ecben*, 1929; *Smirt*, 1934; *Smith*, 1935; *Smire*, 1937; *The King Was in His Counting-House*, 1938; *Hamlet Had an Uncle*, 1940; *The First Gentleman of America*, 1942; *There Were Two Pirates*, 1946; *The Devil's Own Dear Son*, 1949.

SHORT STORIES: *The Line of Love*, 1905; *Gallantry*, 1907; *Chivalry*, 1909; *The Certain Hour*, 1916; *The Music from behind the Moon*, 1926; *The White Robe*, 1928.

ESSAYS AND CRITICISM: *Beyond Life*, 1919; *Straws and Prayer-Books*, 1924; *Some of Us*, 1930; *These Restless Heads*, 1932; *Special Delivery*, 1933; *Ladies and Gentlemen*, 1934; *Let Me Lie*, 1947; *Quiet, Please*, 1952.

AUTOBIOGRAPHY: *As I Remember It*, 1955.

James Branch Cabell was born in Richmond, Virginia, on April 14, 1879. He attended the College of William and Mary, graduating with high honors in 1898, and entered journalism in Richmond. After two years (1899–1901) with the New York *Herald*, he returned and, while working on the Richmond *News*, began the publication of his fictional writings in short stories and novels. Cabell's first major popular success was delayed until the publication of *Jurgen* in 1919; then, ironically, popular attention came largely because the book was banned in several cities through censorship. The publicity attracted both critical and popular attention, and James Branch Cabell enjoyed a huge success throughout the 1920's. By 1929 Cabell believed that a distinct phase of his writing had been completed, and he prepared the Storisende Edition of his collected works under the title *The Biography of the Life of Manuel*. The whole series of eighteen volumes is an interrelated saga of Dom Manuel of Poictesme and tells of characteristic traits passed by him to his descendants. The *Biography* covers centuries in time and has settings in both Europe and America. After 1929 further books by the author were to appear over the signature of Branch Cabell, until in 1942 he resumed his full name.

Cabell was a romanticist with a difference; he was romantic in his subject matter but ironical in his conclusions. His style was polished to brilliancy, frequently teeming with archaisms selected for piquant flavor. He was witty and erudite in his literary background.

Rearranged in time sequence, the books that make up *The Biography of the Life of Manuel* integrate the richly involved story of a swineherd, Manuel, who during the medieval period becomes ruler of the mythical kingdom of Poictesme in what is now the south of France. Progenitor of numerous descendants and characteristics, Manuel after death is legendized into a cultural faith and eventually reappears on earth. Making up the *Biography* are novels, short stories, poems, plays, essays. Among the most significant novels are these: *Figures of Earth* presents the story of Manuel's origin in mythic Poictesme, his rule, and his death; *The Silver Stallion* traces the legendary growth of Manuel as a "Redeemer" who is worshiped by later generations; *Jurgen*, most famous individual novel by Cabell, tells the story of a middle-aged pawnbroker who, seeking his wife Lisa, dons a magic shirt which allows him to return to his youth and enjoy associations with famous beauties of fiction and myth, but who returns to his commonplace life as he knows it and to his wife as he knows her. *The High Place* tells the story of Florian de Puysange, who grasps the ideal romantic goal only to renounce it. *The Rivet in Grandfather's Neck* and *The Cream of the Jest* both tell satirically of Poictesme-like romantic ideals in the American South. Cabell's reiterated theme seems to be that ideals to strive for are more stimulating and satisfying than an ideal actually achieved.

After 1934 Cabell published three fictional trilogies, none of them adding greatly to his fame as a novelist. They include *The Nightmare Has Triplets*, made up of *Smirt*, *Smith*, and *Smire*; *Heirs and Assigns*, made up of *The King Was in His Counting-House*, *Hamlet Had an Uncle*, and *The First Gentleman of America*; *It Happened in Florida*, made up of *The St. Johns*, *There Were Two Pirates*, and *The Devil's Own Dear Son*.

In 1913 Cabell married Miss Priscilla Bradley, who bore him one son and who died in 1948; in 1950 Mr. Cabell married Miss Margaret Waller Freeman. In his later years he and his wife spent much of their time in Florida. During the late 1930's and the 1940's Cabell's popular and critical position was in eclipse, but Edmund Wilson, a perceptive critic, writing in 1956, began among many readers a revival of interest in Cabell's writings.

Bibliography

Books written before 1930 have been collected in the Storisende Edition of *The Works of James Branch Cabell*, 1927–1930. There is no extensive biographical study. For general information on the man and his work see Carl Van Doren, *James Branch Cabell*, 1925, (rev. ed., 1932); H. L. Mencken, *James Branch Cabell*, 1927 (pamphlet); more specialized studies are found in Don M. Bregenzer and Amy Loveman, eds., *A Round Table in Poictesme*, 1924; Warren A. McNeill, *Cabellian Harmonics*, 1928; James P. Cover, *Notes on "Jurgen,"* 1928; John P. Cranwell and James P. Cover, *Notes on "Figures of Earth,"* 1929. After a period of neglect studies of Cabell have resumed with Joe Lee Davis, *James Branch Cabell*, 1962; Arvin R. Wells, *Jesting Moses: A Study in Cabellian Com-*

edy, 1962; and Desmond Tarrant, *James Branch Cabell: The Dream and The Reality*, 1967. See also Padraic Colum and Margaret Freeman Cabell, *Between Friends: Letters of James Branch Cabell and Others*, 1962.

See also Percy Boynton, *Some Contemporary Americans*, 1924; Stuart P. Sherman, *The Main Stream*, 1927; Henry S. Canby, *American Estimates*, 1930; Russell Blankenship, *American Literature as an Expression of the American Mind*, 1931; Edward Wagenknecht, *Cavalcade of the American Novel*, 1951; Hugh Walpole, "The Art of James Branch Cabell," *Yale Review*, IX (1920), 684–698; Clara F. McIntyre, "Mr. Cabell's Cosmos," *Sewanee Review*, XXXVIII (1930), 278–285; Gay Wilson Allen, "Jurgen and Faust," *Sewanee Review*, XXXIX (1931), 485–492; W. R. Parker, "A Key to Cabell," *English Journal*, XXI (1932), 431–440; Edmund Wilson, "The James Branch Cabell Case Reopened," *New Yorker*, XXXII (1956), 140–168; Edd W. Parks, "Cabell's *Cream of the Jest*," *Modern Fiction Studies*, II (1956), 68–70; and Raymond Himelick, "Figures of Cabell," *Modern Fiction Studies*, II (1956–1957), 21–220.

JURGEN

Type of work: Novel
Author: James Branch Cabell (1879–1958)
Type of plot: Fantasy
Time of plot: Middle Ages
Locale: Poictesme, a land of myth
First published: 1919

Jurgen. A Comedy of Justice. *is one of a series dealing with the mythical country of Poictesme. The novel can be read on different levels—as a narrative of fantastic love and adventure, as a satire, and as a philosophic view of life.*

Principal Characters

Jurgen, a middle-aged pawnbroker who, searching for his lost wife, returns twenty years to the days of his youth, in which he thought himself a very clever fellow. After a year, during which he becomes a duke, a prince, a king, an emperor, and a pope, he asks to be returned to plain, practical, and moderately peaceful middle age with his wife, who is rather well suited, after all, to a man like him.

Adelais (Dame Lisa), his shrewish wife who, contemptuous of poetry and romance, converted a poet into a pawnbroker.

Dorothy la Désirée, his childhood sweetheart, second sister of Count Emmerick. She is Jurgen's Heart's Desire who married Heitman Michael. She also appears for a time to be Helen of Troy.

Mother Sereda (also **Aesred** and **Res Dea**), an old woman, Jurgen's godmother, who takes the color out of things and who controls Wednesdays. Her shadow follows Jurgen everywhere after she has restored to him a year of his youth, following which time she makes him the middle-aged man he is.

Queen Guenevere. Jurgen has a love affair with her before her marriage to King Arthur. She does not recognize him after he has returned to middle age.

King Gogyrvan Gawr, her father, to whom Jurgen returns her after murdering King Thragnar.

Dame Anaïtis (The Lady of the Lake and **Queen of Cocaigne),** a myth woman of lunar legend who instructs Jurgen in many varieties of pleasure and to whom he becomes for a while Prince Consort. Like Guenevere, she does not recognize the older Jurgen.

Chloris, a plump Hamadryad to whom Jurgen is husband for a time.

Queen Helen of Troy, the legendary Swan's daughter, Jurgen's (and man's) vision of supreme beauty.

Queen Dolores, Philistine ruler to whom Jurgen explains Praxagorean mathematics.

Grandfather Satan, Hell's horned and bushytailed magistrate with whom Jurgen discusses Hell as a democracy.

St. Peter, Heaven's gatekeeper, with whom Jurgen talks over pseudo-Christian beliefs.

Koshchei the Deathless (also The Prince of Darkness), the maker of things as they are. Because Jurgen once spoke a good word for him, Koshchei disencumbers him of Dame Lisa; but after a year he restores her at Jurgen's request.

Nessus, a centaur who gives Jurgen a glittering shirt and takes him to the garden between dawn and sunrise.

Azra, Jurgen's mother, loved briefly by Coth.

Coth, Jurgen's father, whom he meets and quarrels with in Hell.

Heitman Michael, the man who married Dorothy, over whom he and Jurgen duel with swords.

Felise de Puysange, one of many women loved by Jurgen, who fathered her son.

King Thragnar, the Troll King who captured and imprisoned Guenevere. He disguises himself as Dame Lisa and Jurgen slays him.

Dame Yolande. Jurgen kills a giant for her and with her he spends a most agreeable night after he blows out the candles.

King Smoit and
Queen Sylvia Tereu, ghosts of King Gogyrvan's grandfather and his ninth wife. According to King Smoit's story, he is also secretly the father of Coth and therefore Jurgen's grandfather.

Merlin Ambrosius, a sorcerer sent with Dame Anaïtis to fetch Guenevere for King Arthur.

Florimel, a seductive and humorously talkative vampire whom Jurgen meets and marries in Hell.

Steinvor, Jurgen's grandmother, an old woman with illusions about her children and grandchildren.

The God of Steinvor, created by Koshchei to satisfy the old woman.

The Story

Once in the old days a middle-aged pawnbroker named Jurgen said a good word for the Prince of Darkness. In gratitude, the Prince of Darkness removed from the earth Dame Lisa, Jurgen's shrewish wife. Some time later Jurgen heard that his wife had returned to wander on Amneran Heath; consequently the only manly thing for him to do was to look for her.

It was Walburga's Eve when Jurgen met Dame Lisa on the heath. She led him to a cave, but when he followed her inside she disappeared and Jurgen found a Centaur instead. Jurgen inquired for his wife. The Centaur replied that only Koshchei the Deathless, the maker of things as they are, could help Jurgen in his quest. The Centaur gave Jurgen a beautiful new shirt and started off with him to the Garden between Dawn and Sunrise, the first stopping place of Jurgen's journey to find Koshchei.

In the garden Jurgen found Dorothy la Désirée, his first sweetheart, who retained all the beauty he had praised in his youthful poetry. She no longer knew him, for she was in love only with Jurgen as he had been in youth, and he could not make her understand that in the real world she also had become middle-aged and commonplace. So he parted sadly from her and found himself suddenly back in his native country.

His friend the Centaur had now become an ordinary horse. Jurgen mounted and rode through a forest until he came to the house of Mother Sereda, the goddess who controlled Wednesdays and whose job it was to bleach the color out of everything in the world. By flattery Jurgen persuaded her to let him live over a certain Wednesday in his youth with Dorothy la Désirée. But when the magic Wednesday ended, Dorothy la Désirée turned into the old woman she really was, and Jurgen quickly departed.

He wandered again to Amneran Heath and entered the cave to look for Koshchei and Dame Lisa. There he found a beautiful girl who said that she was Guenevere, the daughter of King Gogyrvan. Jurgen offered to conduct her back to her home. When they arrived at the court of King Gogyrvan, Jurgen, pretending to be the Duke of Logreus, asked for the hand of Guenevere as a reward for her safe return. But she had already been promised to King Arthur. Jurgen stayed on at court. He had made the discovery that he still looked like a young man; the only trouble was that his shadow was not his shadow; it was the shadow of Mother Sereda.

King Arthur's envoys, Dame Anaïtis and Merlin, had arrived to take Guenevere to London. Jurgen watched her depart for London without feeling any sorrow because of a magic token Merlin had given him. Then Dame Anaïtis invited Jurgen to visit her palace in Cocaigne, the country where Time stood still. There Jurgen participated with her in a ceremony called the Breaking of the Veil, to learn afterwards that it had been a marriage ceremony and that Dame Anaïtis was now his wife. Dame Anaïtis, a myth woman of lunar legend, instructed Jurgen in every variety of strange pleasures she knew.

Jurgen visited a philologist, who said that Jurgen had also become a legend; consequently he could not remain long in Cocaigne. When the time came for him to leave the country, Jurgen chose to go to Leukê, the kingdom where Queen Helen and Achilles ruled. Jurgen's reason for wishing to go there was that Queen Helen resembled his first sweetheart, Dorothy la Désirée.

In Leukê, Jurgen met Chloris, a Hamadryad, and married her. He was still curious about Queen Helen, however, and one evening he entered her castle and went to her bedchamber. The sleeping queen was Dorothy la Désirée, but he dared not touch her. Her beauty, created from the dreams of his youth, was unattainable. He left the castle and returned to Chloris.

Shortly afterward the Philistines invaded Leukê and condemned all its mythical inhibitants to limbo. Jurgen protested because he was flesh and blood and he offered to prove his claim by mathematics. Queen Dolores of the Philistines agreed with him after he had demonstrated his proof to her by means of a concrete example. However, he was condemned by the great tumble-bug of the Philistines for being a poet.

After Chloris had been condemned to limbo, Jurgen went on to the hell of his fathers. There he visited Satan and learned that Koshchei had created hell to humor the pride of Jurgen's forefathers. Then he remembered that he was supposed to be looking for Dame Lisa. Learning that she was not in hell, he decided to look for her in heaven. Mistaken for a pope by means of the philologist's charm, he managed to gain entrance to heaven. Dame Lisa was not there. St. Peter returned him to Amneran Heath.

On the heath he again met Mother Sereda, who took away his youth and returned him to his middle-aged body. Actually, it was a relief to Jurgen to be old again. Then for the third time he entered the cave in search of Dame Lisa. Inside he found the Prince of Darkness who had taken her away. The Prince was really Koshchei; Jurgen was near the end of his quest. He asked Koshchei to return Dame Lisa to him.

Koshchei showed him Guenevere, Dame Anaîtis, and Dorothy la Désirée again. But Jurgen would not have them. He had had his youth to live over, and he had committed the same follies. He was content now to be Jurgen the pawnbroker.

Koshchei agreed to return Jurgen to his former life, but he asked for the Centaur's shirt to return. Jurgen gladly gave up the shirt. Koshchei walked with him form the heath into town. As they walked, Jurgen noticed that the moon was sinking in the east. Time was turning backward.

It was as if the past year had never been. For now he approached his house and saw through the window that the table was set for supper. Inside, Dame Lisa sat sewing and looking quite as if nothing had ever happened.

Critical Evaluation

Jurgen possesses the artificiality and mannered style of much of Cabell's writing. Somewhat reminiscent of the satires of Anatole France, this novel does contain scenes of humor worthy of the French master, but other sections are heavy-handed and obscure. A fairy tale for adults, *Jurgen* assumes a certain sophistication in its reader; even its humor tends to be artificial and mannered. The novel illustrates Cabell's persistent avoidance of "realism" in his work, as well as his essentially antiromantic point of view. *Jurgen* presents the full range of Cabell's skeptical vision of human nature and his biting opinion of mortal existence on earth. Nevertheless, much of Cabell's supposedly sophisticated approach to sex is little more than suggestive snickering or is borrowed from *Tristram Shandy*.

A picaresque fantasy, inspired by medieval chivalric romances, *Jurgen* follows its hero in his search for his lost shrewish wife. The plot, such as it is, reminds one of Maeterlinck's *The Bluebird,* for Jurgen finds his wife at home, the one place where he had not thought to look for her. Many of the hero's adventures are humorous, and most of them are improbable, including, as they do, figures from ancient history and mythology. Cabell does not develop his characters as much as he lets them represent certain viewpoints or symbolize particular conditions of being.

In a sense, Jurgen's search is into his own past, as well as the past history of the world, for he encounters people from his own life as well as from antiquity. His hopes are all frustrated as he wanders, and he comes to realize that time is merciless; the past cannot be recaptured. Youth, when regained, he discovers, proves to be less desirable than one would think. A dreamlike quality pervades much of the narrative, and a charm and gaiety often surfaces, despite the artificiality of the tale. A reaction against the prevailing trend of realism in American fiction at the time, *Jurgen* stands isolated with its author, a brilliant oddity in the history of American literature.

Bibliography

Aiken, Conrad. *A Reviewer's A B C: Collected Criticism of Conrad Aiken from 1916 to the Present.* New York: Meridian Books, 1958, pp. 143–148.

Allen, Gay W. "*Jurgen* and Faust," in *Sewanee Review.* XXXIX (October–December, 1931), pp. 485–492.

Brewster, Paul G. "*Jurgen* and *Figures of Earth* and the Russian Shazki," in *American Literature.* XIII (January, 1942), pp. 305–318.

Brussel, I.R. "The First Fifty Years of *Jurgen*," in *Cabellian.* I (1969), p. 74.

Davis, Joe Lee. *James Branch Cabell.* New York: Twayne, 1962, pp. 88–94, 104–106.

Flora, Joseph M. "*Jurgen* in the Classroom," in *Cabellian.* I (1969), pp. 31–34.

Gabbard, G.N. "The Dance Version of *Jurgen*," in *Kalki.* VI (1975), pp. 115–117.

Hartman, Harry. " 'The Comstock Lewd': *Jurgen* and the Law—Updated," in *Kalki.* III (1969), pp. 16–19.

Loveman, Samuel. *A Round-Table in Poictesme.* Cleveland: Colophon Club, 1924, pp. 51–53.

Schley, Margaret A. "The Demiurge in *Jurgen*," in *Cabellian.* IV (1972), pp. 85–88.

Tarrant, Desmond. *James Branch Cabell: The Dream and the Reality.* Norman: University of Oklahoma Press, 1967, pp. 26–29, 86–89, 129–145.

Van Doren, Carl. *James Branch Cabell.* New York: Robert M. McBride, 1925, pp. 41–51.

Walpole, Hugh. *The Art of James Branch Cabell.* New York: Robert M. McBride, 1924, p. 23.

Wells, Arvin R. *Jesting Moses: A Study in Cabellian Comedy.* Gainesville: University of Florida Press, 1962, pp. 108–118.

GEORGE WASHINGTON CABLE

Born: New Orleans, Louisiana (October 12, 1844)
Died: St. Petersburg, Florida (January 31, 1925)

Principal Works

NOVELS: *The Grandissimes*, 1880; *Dr. Sevier*, 1884; *Bonaventure*, 1888; *John March, Southerner*, 1894; *The Cavalier*, 1901; *Bylow Hill*, 1902; *Kincaid's Battery*, 1908; *Gideon's Band*, 1914; *The Flower of the Chapdelaines*, 1918; *Lovers of Louisiana*, 1918.

SHORT STORIES: *Old Creole Days*, 1879; *Madame Delphine*, 1881; *Strange True Stories of Louisiana*, 1889; *Strong Hearts*, 1899.

HISTORICAL AND SOCIAL STUDIES: *History and Present Condition of New Orleans*, 1881; *The Creoles of Louisiana*, 1884; *The Silent South*, 1885; *The Negro Question*, 1890.

George Washington Cable, a man of diverse and lively talents, was born in New Orleans on October 12, 1844. His father was from an old slaveholding family in Virginia, while his mother came of straitlaced Puritan stock; from this contrast may have stemmed some of the contradictions which later marked Cable's adult personality and literary career.

In 1859, on the eve of the Civil War, Cable's father died after a series of business reverses which had brought the family circumstances to the brink of poverty. During the next few years the boy, only fourteen at the time of his father's death, became the mainstay of the family. In 1863 he enlisted in the Confederate cavalry. Twice wounded, he nevertheless served until the end of the war, interspersing his activities as a trooper with self-imposed studies in mathematics, Latin, and the Bible.

For two years after the war Cable was almost completely incapacitated by malarial fever. Recovering slowly, he began to write for the New Orleans *Picayune*, doing a regular column called "Drop Shot." His journalistic career proved short-lived, however, when the paper dropped him for refusing to report theatrical performances. Next, as an accountant and correspondence clerk, he found congenial work with a firm of cotton factors. His marriage, in 1869, to Louise S. Bartlett seemed to complete the pattern by which his life would be ordered.

Suddenly, however—and almost by accident—this course was changed. His passion for self-education had led him to develop mastery of French and to dig into the city archives. Among the latter he found numerous fascinating events which he could not resist using as the basis for narratives of his own. When a literary scout, Edward King, examined his papers for *Scribner's Monthly*, the result was publication of "'Sieur George" in the October, 1873, issue of that magazine. *Old Creole Days*, a collection of seven tales, followed six years later. This

volume gained for its author instant recognition as a new and interesting interpreter of the South. When the firm for which he worked was eventually dissolved,
he seized the opportunity to turn to writing as a full-time occupation. In steady
succession appeared *The Grandissimes*, *The Creoles of Louisiana*, *Dr. Sevier*, and
The Silent South. Criticism of his views on the South led him, in 1885, to establish a home for his family in Northampton, Massachusetts. During his later years
in New England he became a close friend of Mark Twain, and he continued to
write and publish as late as 1918. He died in St. Petersburg, Florida, on January
31, 1925.

A large part of Cable's remarkable energy went into his varied activities as an
advocate of social reform. His Puritan inheritance found its outlet in untiring
work as a philanthropist, a religious leader, and a Bible-class teacher; and his
outspoken views, especially those regarding justice for the Negro, often earned
him the resentment of his native South. Nevertheless, it is as a romanticist that
the twentieth century most easily identifies George Washington Cable. His early
work, for which he is by now best remembered, has established him as a leading
exponent of the "local color" school, and his Louisiana tales have preserved an
exotic segment of American life which is fast losing its identity.

Bibliography

There is no collected edition. The official biography is Lucy L. C. Biklé, *George
W. Cable: His Life and Letters*, 1928, now superseded in many important details
by Arlin Turner, *George W. Cable: A Biography*, 1957; and *Mark Twain and
George W. Cable: The Record of a Literary Friendship*, 1960. The biographical
sketch in the *Dictionary of American Biography* is by Fred L. Pattee. A recent
study is Louis D. Rubin, Jr., *George W. Cable: The Life and Times of a Southern
Heretic*, 1969. See also Harry A. Toulmin, *Social Historians*, 1911; Fred L. Pat-
tee, *A History of American Literature since 1870*, 1915; Arthur Hobson Quinn,
American Fiction, 1936; Van Wyck Brooks, *The Times of Melville and Whitman*,
1947; Lafcadio Hearn, "The Scenes of Cable's Romances," *Century*, New Series
V (1883), 40–47; Edward L. Tinker, "Cable and the Creoles," *American Litera-
ture*, V (1934), 313–326; Richard Chase, "Cable and His *Grandissimes*," *Kenyon
Review*, XVIII (1956), 194–204; and Edmund Wilson, "The Ordeal of George
Washington Cabel," *New Yorker*, XXXIII (Nov. 9, 1957), 172–216.

THE GRANDISSIMES

Type of work: Novel
Author: George W. Cable (1884–1925)
Type of plot: Regional romance
Time of plot: 1804
Locale: New Orleans
First published: 1880

A story of love, honor, intrigue, and tragedy set in the Creole society of New Orleans, the novel re-creates a part of American life now gone. The villains of the piece are not so much the actors in the drama, but rather the institutions of slavery and the caste system. Because of these, lovers cannot marry each other, and the quadroon son of a wealthy nobleman must lead a life of humiliation. It has been said that the tragedy of the American black is more effectively and truthfully presented here than in many modern novels on the subject.

Principal Characters

Honoré Grandissime, a merchant, head of the Grandissimes. Extremely handsome and well-dressed, he is an impressive figure, the flower of the family. His egalitarian views and his opposition to slavery are viewed with suspicion and distaste by other Grandissimes. He represents the peacemaking element as his uncle, Agricola, represents the strifemaking element in the family. Conscience-stricken over his possession of and profit from Aurora's property (given him by Agricola), he returns it and thereby angers his family. He further alienates them by going into partnership with another Honoré Grandissime, a free man of color.

The Darker Honoré Grandissime, his older quadroon half brother, a rentier. (To prevent confusion, he is usually distinguished from the white Honoré by the initials f. m. c.—free man of color—after his name.) He has strong feelings about the lot of the Louisianians of mixed blood, but he is feeble of will about fighting the caste system. He hates Agricola and loves Palmyre. After going with Palmyre to Bordeaux following

Agricola's death, he vainly courts her and then drowns himself.

Agricola Fusilier, Honoré's uncle, a sturdy, bearded old lion careless of his dress. Loving all things French, he scorns Americans and their jargon. He is proud of his Creole blood, contemptuous of all people of color, and fearful of Palmyre. He is mortally stabbed by Honoré f. m. c., whom he has attacked. Dying, he affects to forgive all enemies of the Creole aristocracy, but he dies with his prejudices.

Aurora Nancanou (nee De Grapion), a beautiful young widow whose husband died in a duel after accusing Agricola of cheating at cards. She is poor but proud, and she superstitiously believes in Palmyre's spellmaking powers. In love with Honoré, she is mindful of the enmity of the Grandissimes toward her own family, the De Grapions. After Agricola, dying, admits to having, years before, promised a marriage between Honoré and Aurora, she still resists, but finally accepts her formerly diffident adorer.

Clotilde Nancanou, her lovely daughter,

who appears to be a younger sister rather than the daughter of the youthful-looking Aurora. Loved by Joseph, she finally accepts his suit.

Joseph Frowenfeld, a handsome young American immigrant of German ancestry whose family all die of yellow fever, which Joseph survives. He becomes a proprietor of an apothecary shop. A serious student, he has liberal views which are resented by the Creoles. He cannot understand why the caste system for people of varied colors is permitted to continue in Louisiana. Wounded mistakenly while attending Palmyre after she is shot, he recovers and becomes a partner in an expanded drug business supported by capital from Aurora. He falls in love with Clotilde and apparently will marry her.

Dr. Charlie Keene, Joseph's physician and friend, red-haired and freckled. Intelligent and perceptive, he acquaints Joseph with the Creole-dominated society of New Orleans.

Palmyre Philosophe, a freed quadroon slave, formerly Aurora's maid, who hates Agricola and who is wounded after stabbing him. Loved by Honoré f. m. c., she ignores him and hates all men except the white Honoré and Bras Coupé, to whom she was married before he ran away. She passionately desires the love

of Honoré, but in vain.

Bras Coupé, a giant African prince captured by slavers and brought to Louisiana. After marrying Palmyre, he strikes his master in a drunken fit and escapes. Returning to get Palmyre, he is captured, imprisoned, and mutilated, and he dies in prison after removing the curse he had put upon Don José's family and land. Bras Coupé is a symbol of the dignity, the native worth, and the tragedy of his race.

Don José Martinez, Honoré's brother-in-law and Bras Coupé's master.

Governor Claiborne, a young Virginian, governor-general of Louisiana.

Numa Grandissime, father of the two Honorés.

Raul Innerarity, an amateur artist, a cousin of Honoré. He becomes Joseph's clerk.

Achille,
Valentine,
Jean-Baptiste,
Hippolyte,
Sylvestre, and
Agamemnon, kinsmen of Honoré.

Clemence, Palmyre's voodoo accomplice, shot to death by an unknown marksman after her lynching is interrupted.

The Story

Honoré Grandissime and Aurora Nancanou, both members of the Creole aristocracy, met at a masked ball and fell in love at first sight. Each was unaware of the other's identity. Honoré was a young merchant, the head of the Grandissime family. Aurora, a young widow, was the daughter of a De Grapion. Honoré's uncle, Agricola Fusilier, had killed Aurora's husband in a duel, after he had accused Agricola of cheating at cards. Agricola won the duel, cleared his honor, and collected the gambling debt, the entire estate of Aurora's husband. Aurora and her daughter Clotilde, were left penniless. Agricola gave Aurora's estate to Honoré and made him a wealthy man.

Shortly afterward Joseph Frowenfeld, a young American immigrant, arrived in New Orleans with his parents and sisters. All were stricken with fever; only

Joseph survived. The lonely young man formed a friendship with his physician, Dr. Keene. Joseph and Honoré met by chance one day and found a common interest in their concern over the injustice of slavery and the caste system of New Orleans society. Honoré's life however depended upon these institutions. Joseph wished to have them wiped out at once.

Deciding to earn his living as a druggist, Joseph opened a small shop and soon became friendly with his aristocratic landlord. The landlord was actually Honoré's half brother and he bore the same name, but he was not acknowledged as a member of the family because he was a quadroon. He was called the darker Honoré.

Joseph found another new friend in old Agricola. He was also struck by the charm of Aurora and Clotilde when they called to make purchases. He learned more about Aurora from Dr. Keene. The physician told him about Palmyre, a freed slave who had once been Aurora's maid. The girl hated Agricola. One night Joseph was awakened by pistol shots nearby. A few minutes later Dr. Keene and several others entered the shop with the wounded Agricola; he had been stabbed, and his companions had fired upon his assailant.

Several days later Aurora called upon her landlord in order to make some arrangements about the rent she could not pay. She knew her landlord's name was Honoré Grandissime, but she did not connect this name with the man she loved. Upon learning that the two men were half brothers, Aurora was upset and her family pride caused her to be harsh with Honoré.

When Dr. Keene fell sick, he asked Joseph to attend one of his patients. The patient was Palmyre, who had been wounded as she ran away after stabbing Agricola. Joseph promised Dr. Keene to keep her trouble a secret and went to dress the wound.

Joseph paid his last visit to the wounded Palmyre, now almost recovered. Palmyre begged him to help her make the white Honoré love her. But Palmyre's maid, misunderstanding the conversation, thought that Joseph had wronged her mistress. She struck him over the head, and Joseph reeled groggily into the street. Some passing pedestrians, seeing him emerge bleeding from Palmyre's house, drew a natural inference, and soon everyone knew about Joseph's misfortune. Only Clotilde and Honoré believed him innocent.

Public feeling was running high against the Americans, and Joseph found himself despised by most of the Creoles. Both his liberal views and his trouble at Palmyre's house were against him.

Honoré's conscience bothered him. He felt that he unjustly held Aurora's property, but he also knew he could not return it to her without ruining the finances of his family. But he made his choice. He called upon Aurora and Clotilde and presented them with their property and the income from it. Now he could not declare his love for Aurora; if he did so, his family would think he had returned the property because of love instead of a sense of justice.

On his way home from Aurora's house, Honoré met the darker Honoré with

Dr. Keene. The physician had risen from his sickbed because he had heard of Honoré's call at Aurora's house. Dr. Keene, also in love with Aurora, was jealous. His exertion caused a hemorrhage of the lungs, and the two Honorés carried him home and watched over him.

While they attended the sick man, the darker Honoré proposed to his brother that they go into partnership, so that the darker Honoré's money could save the family from ruin. His brother accepted the offer. But this action turned Honoré's family against him. Agricola led an unsuccessful lynching party to find the darker Honoré. Not finding him, the mob broke the windows of Joseph's shop as a gesture against liberal views in general.

Aurora set Joseph up in business again on the ground floor of her house and made Clotilde a partner in the store. Brought together in this manner, the two young people fell in love. At the same time, the darker Honoré lay wasting away for love of Palmyre, who was trying to revenge herself upon Agricola by voodoo spells. When Agricola could no longer sleep at night, his family determined to catch Palmyre in her acts of witchcraft. They caught her accomplice, but Palmyre escaped.

Meanwhile the darker Honoré went to Joseph's store to get some medicine for himself. Meeting Agricola, who insulted him, the darker Honoré stabbed Agricola and escaped. The wounded man was carried upstairs to Aurora's house to die; there the two families were united again at his deathbed. Agricola revealed that he had once promised to Aurora's father a marriage between Aurora and Honoré.

The darker Honoré and Palmyre escaped together to France. There he committed suicide because she still would not accept his love.

Joseph finally declared his love for Clotilde. But Aurora would not accept Honoré's offer of marriage because she thought he had made it out of obligation to Agricola. Then Honoré made his offer again as a man in love. As a last gesture of family pride Aurora refused him, but at the same time she threw herself into her lover's arms.

Critical Evaluation

George Washington Cable has been best known as an early regionalist who evoked a picturesque society with an amusing variety of quaint dialects, but his best work was serious in its social and moral penetration. New Orleans gave him a fascinating stage for the interaction and conflict of cultures and values as well as dialects, and his approach was that of a linguist, sociologist, and moralist, rather than an entertainer. *The Grandissimes* is based on the true story of an African prince, Bras Coupé, captured by slavers and transported to Louisiana, a story Cable had been unable to publish separately because his publishers found it "unmitigatedly distressful." Cable, who felt that fiction should "teach without telling," therefore embodied his social criticism within a romantic plot, and succeeded in mitigating the distress sufficiently for a wide public; at the same time, he was able to convey a detailed and sweeping picture of New Orleans society that served as an indictment of race and caste prejudice. He later noted that any parallels his readers might find between the situation in the novel, that of the new American supremacy in 1803, and that of the Reconstruction period of seventy-five years later, were fully intended. Indignant reaction in New Orleans testified to the accuracy of his depiction, and his message still holds truth for modern readers.

The author analyzes in *The Grandissimes* with skill and a light although penetrating touch a complicated, if narrow, society. Each class or caste illustrated in the novel thinks itself above the others; from the African slave Prince to the Creoles and the pure whites, each refuses to bow before the others and submits only bitterly to physical, economic, or political domination. But the individuals in the book also possess a witty pride combined with a shrewd sense of self-appraisal; they know their worth and do not need to pretend to be more or less than they are. They cling to a long-standing sense of pride in family and clan as tenaciously as they cling to their old superstitions, many of which were taken from the slaves.

Cable neatly weaves a sly humor into the rich texture of his narrative, a humor that is even present in the intense discussion of deliberately narrow-minded and parochial attitudes and prejudices. Cable writes with an exquisite, graceful prose style, at once poetic and witty, realistic and fanciful. The novel introduced a new realism and breadth of vision into the literature of the South, as well as a new and highly professional standard of craftsmanship. The novel is important not only for its place in American and Southern literary history, but because it is a superbly written and deeply felt document and a work of fiction of the highest quality.

MADAME DELPHINE

Type of work: Novel
Author: George W. Cable (1844–1925)
Type of plot: Regional romance
Time of plot: 1821–1822
Locale: New Orleans
First published: 1881

In Madame Delphine, *Cable reveals his ability to write a regional romance, an ability for which he is widely praised. In addition, this novel supports the critical attitude that he is also a facile social critic with a pungent wit.*

Principal Characters

Delphine Carraze (Madame Delphine), a widowed quadroon woman. She asks Ursin to be her daughters guardian, which results in his marriage to the girl. However, when Ursin's friends object to his marriage to a quadroon, Madame Delphine claims that the girl is the daughter of white parents. After the marriage, she confesses her lie to Pere Jerome and dies immediately thereafter. His final words, requesting her absolution, contain the message of the novel. While not the major figure in the novel, her interaction with Pere Jerome provides a means for Cable to express his views on racial and social injustice.

Pere Jerome, a kindly parish priest who gains Madame Delphine's confidence after she hears a stirring sermon he delivers. He becomes confidante to both Ursin and Madame Delphine and presides at the wedding between Ursin and Olive. His position as cleric provides him with an all-inclusive view of the world depicted in the novel. It is Pere Jerome through whom Cable castigates his readers for the way they treat their fellow human beings. His understanding and love is shown in his repeated prayer that man not be held responsible for sins resulting from society's racial injustice.

Captaine Ursin Lemaitre-Vignevielle, a privateer and soldier of fortune turned gentleman banker. When he is given a missal by a beautiful woman and told to leave the ship she is on, he abandons his life as a pirate, claims Lemaitre is dead, and opens a bank. Due to his kindness to Madame Delphine, she asks him to be her daughter's guardian. He wanders the streets at night searching for the woman who brought about his reformation, only to discover that she is Madame Delphine's daughter, Olive. His friends try to prevent his marriage to her because she is a quadroon. Only when Madame Delphine lies to them about Olive's parentage will they allow the marriage.

Olive Carraze, the beautiful young daughter of Madame Delphine. Although she is a quadroon, she is so light skinned that she can pass for white. When Ursin discovers that she is the woman who caused him to change his ways, he wants to marry her. Only through Madame Delphine's lies are the lovers able to marry.

Evariste Vairillat, and **Jean Thompson,** Creole aristocratic friends of Ursin. They hide Ursin when the government searches for him because of his piracy. They use this situation to blackmail

Madame Delphine and Olive, saying they will turn him over to the government if the women do not renounce the marriage agreement. The friends agree to the marriage only when Madame Delphine convinces them that Olive is white. They represent the racial attitudes against which the novel speaks.

The Story

Madame Delphine and Pere Jerome first met after Pere Jerome delivered a stirring sermon in the cathedral. The content of the sermon included a story which had as its principals, Madame Delphine's daughter, Olive, and one of Pere Jerome's boyhood friends turned pirate, Ursin Lemaitre-Vignevielle. Pere Jerome was unaware of Olive's part in the story, but became Madame Delphine's confessor and confidante when she came to him for advice concerning her daughter, a quadroon like herself, but one who easily passed for white. On the night Madame Delphine first visited Pere Jerome, Ursin Lemaitre-Vignevielle also visited him.

Shortly after the two visits, Ursin, swearing "Capitaine Lemaitre" was dead, opened a bank in New Orleans and had the opportunity to treat Madame Delphine kindly when she came in for change. As a result of his kindness and Pere Jerome's urgings, Madame Delphine asked Ursin to become Olive's guardian.

Ursin, having given up his life as a pirate, searched New Orleans, discreetly, for the girl who turned him from piracy by giving him a missal and ordering him to leave the ship she was on. These events comprised the gist of the story which Pere Jerome told in his sermon in the cathedral. Ursin's nightly wanderings earned him a reputation for eccentricity and caused his friends, Evariste and Jean, to worry for his mental health. Eventually, however, Ursin happened into Madame Delphine's garden and saw, from afar, Olive, who was the woman he had met and fallen in love with on the high seas. He did not discontinue his nightly prowling, but now it had purpose, and he no longer searched.

Ursin arranged to meet Madame Delphine on the pretense, as Olive's guardian, of finding Olive a husband. When Olive saw Ursin, she realized who he was and that she loved him. It was only a matter of time before a wedding had been arranged.

However, before the wedding could occur, the government began to seek Ursin for his acts of piracy. Evariste and Jean hid him, but hearing of the coming wedding, they blackmailed Madame Delphine and Olive with the threat of turning Ursin over to the government if the two women did not renounce the agreement. Being members of the old Creole aristocracy, they did not wish to see their friend discredit himself by marrying a quadroon woman. Madame Delphine related all this to Pere Jerome, who was aghast but tried to settle Madame Delphine before seeking out Evariste and Jean. However, Madame Delphine met the two friends before Pere Jerome reached them.

In the meeting with Jean and Evariste, Madame Delphine shocked all present by declaring that she was not Olive's mother, but rather her quadroon nurse and showed pictures of a white woman and man to prove her claim. She succeeded in convincing the two friends. After she signed legal disclaimers of parenthood, Evariste and Jean allowed the wedding to take place, convinced the government agents that Capitaine Lemaitre was dead, and Ursin and Olive began their life together free from cares.

After the wedding, at which Pere Jerome presided, Madame Delphine called Pere Jerome to hear her confession. During the confession, she admitted that she had duped all parties with pictures of her husband's relatives, to whom Olive bore a remarkable resemblance; Olive was, indeed, her daughter. Immediately on confessing the noble fraud, she collapsed in grief on the floor of the confessional and died in Pere Jerome's arms as he intoned the lesson of the sermon which precipitated their relationship—"Lord, lay not this sin to her charge."

Critical Evaluation

George Washington Cable's knowledge of the Creole way of life is explored completely in *Madame Delphine*. However, his reputation as a regional colorist, earned for this skill, does him a disservice by placing him on a lower literary level than that of the best writers. This novel goes beyond the quaint dialects and manners of a vanished society. Cable does not condemn, but questions the treatment of the neither white nor negro quadroons, the morality of "proper" people, and the responsibility of every man for his fellow beings. Cable's deep and clear understanding of Creole society warrants the label regional colorist; but his deeper significance, his social criticism, and his pungent wit demand that his works be read for something beyond their surface level.

Madame Delphine, unlike his acknowledged masterpiece, *The Grandissimes*, is a diffuse work which touches on the foibles of an entire society. He criticizes the clergy, the laity, the gentry, the blacks, the quadroon, but all with a tenderness which betrays his real affection for the decadent society.

The center of the novel is not the quadroon woman, Madame Delphine, but is Pere Jerome who, from the all-inclusive view of his clerical position, listens to, loves, manipulates, criticizes, and comments on all the players of the work. The melodramatic plot of the romance of Olive and Ursin only allows Cable, through Pere Jerome, to castigate a smug readership for their treatment of fellow human beings. The theme of the novel is clearly laid out in Pere Jerome's sermon in the cathedral, "Lord, lay not this sin to their charge," It permeates the action surrounding the pirates, the doctors, the lawyers, the bankers, and the faceless populace of the entire society; and it resounds clearly through the last line of the novel.

Madame Delphine is unkindly used if read only as a quaint regional romance. It is a bold criticism of the accepted standards of a time when blacks and half-castes were second (or worse) class citizens, and Cable's off-hand commentary on the major institutions of that society only heightens the strength of the lesson which still strikes home for modern readers.

Cable's skillful masking of the criticism with a reasonably vapid, romantic plot is a tribute to his literary facility and to his clear understanding not only of the problems he confronts, but of his audience. His humor hides the raging of a patient man willing to chip away at the walls of ignorance instead of, quixotically, confronting them head-on. Cable's novel, though less highly regarded than *The Grandissimes*, is a more valuable book in that it encompasses an entire society and attempts to prove to mankind that it is responsible for itself to itself.

KATE CHOPIN

Born: St. Louis, Missouri (February 8, 1851)
Died: St. Louis (August 22, 1904)

Principal Works

NOVELS: *At Fault*, 1890; *The Awakening*, 1898.
SHORT STORIES: *Bayou Folk*, 1894; *A Night in Acadie*, 1897.

Katherine O'Flaherty was born February 8, 1851, in St. Louis, Missouri, the gateway to the West, at the beginning of its incredible boom. She was under the influence of French culture and of women all her life. Her Irish father died when she was only four, and she was raised in a household of women: her Creole mother from an established French Catholic family; her grandmother; and her storytelling great grandmother, Mme. Charleville, who influenced her the most. She was also educated by women at the convent school, where the nuns exposed her to Catholic teachings, set rigorous academic standards, emphasized intellectual vigor, and provided a solid background in the French classics.

Kate married twenty-five-year-old Oscar Chopin, son of a French father and a Creole mother, in 1870. They lived for ten years in New Orleans, then in rural Louisiana—in Cloutierville, a hamlet in Natchitoches—where Oscar managed part of the family plantation. Here Kate Chopin became intimately acquainted with the Creoles (the French-speaking, American-born, pure-blooded descendants of French or Spanish colonists), the Cajuns or Acadians (descendants of French settlers the British expelled from Nova Scotia in the eighteenth century), Negroes, and mulattoes who were to be the subject of her work.

The couple enjoyed their marriage and their growing family until Oscar died suddenly in 1883. A widow with six children, she returned to her mother's home in St. Louis. When her mother died in 1885, she was left with no relatives. Both her husband's and her mother's estates had dwindled by this time. Left with six children to support, she turned seriously to writing partially because of the necessity to earn a living.

By 1897, she had written three novels and nearly a hundred stories and sketches, many set in Natchitoches, and she was enthusiastically hailed as a local colorist and regional writer. However, when her novel *The Awakening* was published on April 22, 1899, it was immediately condemned all over America on moral grounds. It was banned from the St. Louis library, among others, Kate Chopin was denied membership in a local arts club, and she was shunned by some of her friends. This persecution crushed her personally. When her third collection of stories was turned down by her publisher a few months later, she evidently considered herself a literary outcast and soon ceased to write.

Her premature silence as a writer is a loss to the world comparable to the early death of her contemporary Stephen Crane. She died August 22, 1904, already practically forgotten. Not until recently have critics noted the real value of her work and hailed her as not only a masterful local colorist but also a pioneer American realist. She is now included in the group of important American authors of the period.

Bibliography

The complete works were collected and published in two volumes in 1967. Also, a recent edition, *The Storm and Other Stories, with The Awakening* appeared in 1974. Further sources on Chopin's life and works are *Encyclopedia of St. Louis: A Compendium of History and Biography for Ready Reference*, edited by William Hyde and Howard L. Conrad, 1899; Per Seyersted, *Kate Chopin: A Critical Biography*, 1969; and Leonidas Rutledge Whipple, "Kate Chopin," in *Library of Southern Literature*, edited by Edwin Anderson Alderman and Joel Chandler Harris, 1907.

THE AWAKENING

Type of work: Novel
Author: Kate Chopin (1851–1904)
Type of plot: Psychological romance
Time of plot: The nineteenth century
Locale: Louisiana
First published: 1899

A novel which shocked the contemporary reading public, The Awakening *is now praised for sensitively capturing a woman's struggle to reach her potential in a society unwilling to grant her the freedom to be an individual.*

Principal Characters

Edna Pontellier, a Creole woman who experiences an awakening. While vacationing on Grand Isle, she discovers her need to be an individual rather than merely a wife and mother. The people she meets and the ocean expose her to aspects of her nature which have been unexpressed. When her husband and children are away, she is able to enjoy the freedom she longs for. She is reunited with Robert, a young man she fell in love with during her vacation; but he leaves her, not wanting to destroy her life. Realizing that she will never find the freedom she desires, she ends her life in the ocean, which had first made her aware of the physical world.

Léonce Pontellier, her husband. He treats his wife as if she were a possession. Edna's awakening individuality leads to increased bickering between them.

Robert Lebrun, a gentle, soft-spoken young man, the eldest son of Madame Lebrun, from whom the Pontelliers rent a vacation cottage on Grand Isle.

He befriends Mrs. Pontellier and they fall in love. He leaves abruptly for Mexico, but they are reunited, only for Robert to leave again.

Madame Adèle Ratignolle, a beautiful Creole woman devoted to her husband and children. She becomes a close friend of Mrs. Pontellier, who tells of her dissatisfaction with her role as a wife and mother. Madame Ratignolle is the quintessence of motherhood. She dresses in lace and white ruffles.

Mademoiselle Reisz, an eccentric, accomplished musician who plays Chopin's preludes one evening at the Lebrun's. The music contributes to Edna's awakening. Mlle. Reisz is unmarried and artistic; she scorns the company of most people. In contrast to Mme. Ratignolle, she dresses in black. She represents courage and freedom.

Alcée Arobin, a man whom Edna meets when her husband is away. They become sexually involved before Edna moves out of the large house.

The Story

Mr. and Mrs. Pontellier were vacationing with their children on Grand Isle in the Gulf of Mexico. Here, a number of Creole families came for the summer, renting a group of cottages from Madame Lebrun, a widow who lived on the island with her two sons Robert and Victor. Robert, the eldest son, was gentle and soft-spoken, a particular favorite with the Creoles. Acting as a guide and companion, he often attached himself to one of the attractive women staying on the isle; this summer, he singled out Edna Pontellier.

One afternoon, Mr. Pontellier watched his wife and Robert bathing in the Gulf of Mexico. On their return, Léonce Pontellier chided his wife for burning herself in the sun; he regarded her as he would one of his personal belongings. Growing bored with their company, he excused himself to play cards at the local club, leaving them to enjoy the afternoon on the beach.

Mr. Pontellier returned late that night to find his wife fast asleep. He awakened her, complaining that their son had a fever and accusing her of being an inattentive mother. They argued, and Edna checked on her son; he was healthy and sleeping soundly. Edna returned to her bedroom only to find her husband asleep, as well. Although such scenes had been common in their marriage, that night, she cried.

Early the next morning, Mr. Pontellier left on a business trip. Edna spent her time with Madame Ratignolle, a Creole woman of classical beauty and charm. Adèle Ratignolle, devoted completely to her husband and children, was considered a model wife and mother. Although the two women were quite different, they developed a close friendship. As they walked along the beach, Edna confided in her friend, telling her childhood home in the Kentucky blue grass country and of her life with her father on a Mississippi plantation. Edna found herself telling Adèle about her early infatuations, her dissapointments, and her hasty decision to marry Léonce Pontellier, a man she did not love. Madame Ratignolle rested Edna's head on her shoulder with a comforting gesture. Edna reflected that she had never felt close to another human being before. The two women spoke of their children, and Mrs. Pontellier asserted that, although she would give her life for her children, she would never surrender her individuality. Neither woman fully understood the meaning of Mrs. Pontellier's words, yet these words turned out to be prophetic.

Several days later, there was a party at the Lebrun's highlighted by a performance of Chopin's preludes by Mademoiselle Reisz, an eccentric but accomplished musician. After the party, the guests strolled along the beach. As they entered the water, Mrs. Pontellier, for the first time in her life, was able to swim. She was delighted with her accomplishment and strode home ahead of her friends. The memory of Chopin, her swim, the stroll along the ocean, and the full moon awakened mysterious emotions within her. Robert caught up with her and shared her mood, telling her that the spirit of the sea had found her worthy and would transport here to a celestial haven. When they reached her cottage, she lay down in the hammock. For the first time, she desired Robert. Letting him leave, however, she awaited her husband's return.

Edna sent word the next morning to Robert, asking him to accompany her to Mass across the bay to Chêniére. They crossed the bay by ferry and reached the quaint Gothic church. During the service, Edna felt faint, and Robert escorted her out, taking her to the home of a local woman to rest and recover. After a long sleep, Mrs. Pontellier awoke with a hearty appetite: she ate a loaf of bread and drank a bottle of wine before finding Robert. When he saw her, he was elated and began to tease her, accusing her of sleeping for a hundred years. They lay side by side as their hostess told them the colorful legends of the region. They waited until the sun went down before returning across the water to Grand Isle.

When Mrs. Pontellier inquired about Robert the next morning, she learned that he quite unexpectedly had decided to leave for Mexico. Everyone was surprised and dismayed; nevertheless, Robert departed, taking a hasty farewell. Mrs. Pontellier was left confused and despairing. The rest of the summer seemed lonely and bare.

At the end of their vacation, the Pontelliers moved back to their home in New Orleans. Domestic life resumed, as usual, but the Pontelliers bickered frequently. Mrs. Pontellier no longer submitted to her husband's whims, and after one particular scene, she threw her wedding ring across the carpet. Léonce noticed other changes in his wife. She spent little time at home receiving callers; she had also resumed her hobby of painting, and she had sold several pieces of her work.

Edna had also taken to visiting the friends that she had met on Grand Isle. She felt a particular urge to visit Mademoiselle Reisz and to listen to her play. During the visit, Mademoiselle Reisz admitted that Robert had written her. After much persuading, she agreed to show the letter to Edna: the letter was written almost exclusively about Mrs. Pontellier. After reading the letter, Edna left the apartment, crying.

Soon after, Mr. Pontellier had to leave on a business trip. The children were sent to their grandmother. Edna, left alone for the first time, was delighted with her new freedom. She made several new friends, including Alcée Arobin. Mr. Arobin courted Edna for several weeks, and while she did not encourage his advances, she did not repel them either.

Edna also took advantage of her time alone to move out of the large house to a small cottage located on the same property. She had a last supper at her old home to celebrate her move. Alcée Arobin lingered after the party was over. Edna allowed him to spend the night with her.

Soon after her party, Edna visited Mademoiselle Reisz, hoping that Robert had sent another letter. She was shocked when she arrived and found Robert there. The reunion was awkward; however, they were destined to meet again at a small restaurant. This time, their reserve dropped, and they confessed their love for each other. Robert admitted that he had left for Mexico, originally, so that he would not have to burden Edna with his love, knowing that she belonged to Léonce. She asserted that no one could possess her. They retired to her cottage where they were interrupted by a message saying that Madame Ratignolle was sick and about to give birth. Edna left Robert reluctantly, promising to return quickly. When she came home, Robert was gone; a short note explained that he had to leave her because he loved her.

Realizing that she could not have Robert, she escaped to the sea, her final refuge. Here she felt acutely her own isolation, and she despaired of ever finding the freedom she so desired. She entered the water, for the last time, and took her life.

Critical Evaluation

Kate Chopin, in 1899, released *The Awakening*, a novel which shocked readers and critics alike. The book was immediately banned from public libraries, and Chopin herself was barred from art and literary societies. *The Awakening*, likened to such French works as *Madame Bovary*, preempted D. H. Lawrence's novels in its frank treatment of women and human sexuality. If the novel was found shocking, however, it was not so much for its candid but discreet discussion of human relations, but rather for its portrayal of a woman who rejects her traditional roles as a mother and wife. *The Awakening* is a story about Edna Pontellier's struggle to become an individual capable of independence, artistic achievement, and love. Kate Chopin's syle is neither pointed nor pedantic. She does not preach; she simply offers her reader a sympathetic but objective portrayal of a woman in transformation.

Kate Chopin's depiction of the warm Creole society found in New Orleans provides the rich, colorful environment so appropriate for Edna Pontellier's sensual awakening. The ambience of this society created by the beautiful French-speaking women who drink wine with dinner, sip brandy while listening to Chopin, and who tell titilating tales at first frightens Edna Pontellier. However, as the story develops, Edna is excited by her surroundings; the ocean, the music played by Mademoiselle Reisz, the moonlight, and the attention of Robert Lebrun arouse her.

As Edna Pontellier becomes more aware of her physical world, she begins also to respond to her internal environment. The song "Ah, if you knew" stirs her heart and later brings back painful memories of Robert Lebrun. The sea brings out a thousand feelings in Mrs. Pontellier: the pounding of the waves against her body arouses her passions and desires. Her first swim in the ocean leaves her intoxicated, thrilled with her newly acquired power, and desirous of solitude. It is this desire for solitude, however, that eventually leads to her demise.

Kate Chopin fills the novel with beautiful images: the sea, a wounded bird, and children scampering across the beach. Many of these images recur throughout the novel and become potent symbols. The characters themselves can be seen as archetypes representing essential human qualities. In the novel, Chopin surrounds Edna with female characters who portray specific feminine types. Madame Ratignolle is the quintessence of motherhood. Dressed in lace and white ruffles, she flutters about her children, worshipping them and her husband, ministering to their real and imagined needs. Mademoiselle Reisz, in contrast, dresses in black, never marries, and scorns the company of most people. She is fiercely independent, eccentric, and a brilliant and accomplished musician. For Edna, she symbolizes courage and freedom, for she seems to have escaped the constraints of her society. Mariequita symbolizes a different type of freedom. This Spanish girl, young, beautiful, and sensuous, has avoided the ties of marriage. Edna envies her freedom to flirt so casually with men. Edna, herself, however, contains the qualities of these women: she possesses the sensuality of the young girl, the independent and creative nature of Mademoiselle Reisz, and the loyal and affectionate qualities of Adéle Ratignolle.

While many of Chopin's characters are prototypes whose lives the reader sees only briefly, Edna herself is a complex human being whose conflicting needs, strengths, and desires make her a difficult but compelling character. In addition, Edna has a unique spiritual quality which sets her apart from the other characters. Robert recognizes this spiritual nature when they walk along the beach together after her first swim. He tells the story of the spirit who rises from the Gulf once a year searching for a worthy mortal to take with him to a celestial realm. Robert insists that in Edna, the spirit has found a worthy mortal. He promises that Edna will never be the same. Robert's promise is prophetic: Edna does have a spiritual awakening, as she walks along the ocean, which changes the fate of her life.

It is the ocean that speaks to the soul of Edna Pontellier, and it is thus the most potent symbol in *The Awakening* . For Kate Chopin, the sea symbolizes the mystery of the individual's relationship to the universe and to a divine presence. For Edna, the ocean is seductive, and it awakens a hundred questions and yearnings that she has never felt before. The closer she is to the sea, the more fully she realizes her own nature. As Chopin explains earlier in the novel, Edna has blindly taken on the responsibilities of marriage for which the fates have not intended her. And so, as Edna discovers the personality hidden behind her mask of day-to-day existence, the desire for independence, solitude, and artistic expression, she drifts further and further from her marital bonds. Yet these discoveries do not bring Mrs. Pontellier happiness. Although she achieves some success as an artist and gains a measure of independence, she is unable to fulfill her greatest need: the need to form a close physical and emotional bond with another human being. She cannot find this type of bond within her own marriage or in her casual affair with Alcée Arobin. Robert, the one man who can fulfill her, refuses her, for he is, after all, a traditional young man. Edna's suicide at the end of the novel follows from the realization that her quest for freedom can ultimately only isolate her from the world she has known.

Edna's last days invite some parallels with Christ's own death. On the last evening at her home in New Orleans, Edna invites her twelve closest friends to a last supper, offering them bread and wine. When one of the guests playfully makes a crown of roses and thorns, she discards it angrily, perhaps sensing her own near death. It is at the end of *The Awakening* that Edna is betrayed by Robert, who rejects her after a passionate kiss. Ultimately, Chopin does not intend to make Edna into a Christ figure, for Edna dies for her own sins and weaknesses. Yet, like Christ, she cannot fit into the world to which she is born, and because of her visions, she must die. With an overpowering sense of her isolation, she enters the sea, seeking to merge herself with the primal forces of the universe. Although Edna is not a heroine, she is heroic. Her battle for freedom and love is a universal battle. *The Awakening* is about a woman's personal attempt to reach her potential, yet her conflicts are the conflicts that all men and women have struggled with in her century and our own.

WINSTON CHURCHILL

Born: St. Louis, Missouri (November 10, 1871)
Died: Winter Park, Florida (March 12, 1947)

Principal Works

NOVELS: *The Celebrity,* 1898; *Richard Carvel,* 1899; *The Crisis,* 1901; *The Crossing,* 1904; *Coniston,* 1906; *Mr. Crewe's Career,* 1908; *A Modern Chronicle,* 1910; *The Inside of the Cup,* 1913; *A Far Country,* 1915; *The Dwelling-Place of Light,* 1917.

SHORT STORIES: *Mr. Keegan's Elopement,* 1903; *The Faith of Frances Craniford,* 1917.

PLAYS: *The Title Mart,* 1905; *Dr. Jonathan,* 1919.

Winston Churchill was regarded, in many of his novels, as an earnest critic of American society in the first two decades of the twentieth century; on these grounds alone he remains permanently interesting, though newer and more penetrating social insights have superseded his.

Churchill was born in St. Louis, Missouri, on November 10, 1871. His education was completed at the U.S. Naval Academy, although he never served in the Navy. Private means, instead, made it possible for him to devote his life to writing. Inspired by the American past, he began as a writer of historical novels; *The Crisis* and *Richard Carvel* were immediate successes. Churchill was read by virtually everyone until the 1920's, when new literary fashions made him seem cumbrous and old-fashioned.

In 1895, Churchill moved to New Hampshire and married. Active in the political life of his state, he was a member of the legislature from 1903 to 1905, and he ran unsuccessfully on the Progressive ticket as a candidate for governor. Perhaps his political activity is indicative of the subject matter he chose to present in his later novels. Even in 1924, his rank was fourth in a list of ten "greatest" writers since 1900. He had, in his later novels, a tone of moral earnestness which gave real substance to the questions he chose to present. Yet when he tried to resolve the dilemmas he set himself, he fell back upon the genteel and the romantic. His attitude toward the American democratic tradition was dualistic; the wealthy in his novels were usually superior in taste and even in morals. Actually, Churchill was too much a man of his own era to separate his novels from rather full approval of it. His novels became a reflection of the intoxicating growth and wealth which indicated a solution for the old dilemmas. Man had the "new science"; man could control his environment and foresee new ethics. Thus, though in his own time Churchill was regarded as a reformer, his books now gather dust on the shelf. His is a voice from long ago. He concerned himself, with the exception of his early and interesting historical novels, with current problems of divorce, religion, and class relationships; but to these problems he, as a product and endorser of the status quo, had no very compelling answer. In the opinion of Carl Van Doren, Churchill was a romancer first and a critic afterwards, a kind of politician among novelists, morally eager but intellectually naïve. Yet he was both honest and factual in his research and served the truth as he saw it. He died at Winter Park, Florida, on March 12, 1947.

Bibliography

There is no authorized biography, but Warren I. Titus, *Winston Churchill,* 1963, is a recent study. See C. C. Walcutt, *Romantic Compromise in the Novels of Winston Churchill,* 1951; Morris E. Speare, *The Political Novel,* 1924; Arthur H. Quinn, *American Fiction,* 1936; Cyril Clemens, "Visit with the American Winston Churchill," *Hobbies,* LII (1947), 144–145; and Robert W. Schneider, *Five Novelists of the Progressive Era,* 1965. See also Upton Sinclair, "American Churchill," *Saturday Review of Literature,* XXXIV (June 9, 1951), 24, and the reply by H. O. Lokensgard, *ibid.,* XXXIV (August 25, 151), 21.

THE CRISIS

Type of work: Novel
Author: Winston Churchill (1871–1947)
Type of plot: Historical romance
Time of plot: Civil War period
Locale: Missouri and Virginia
First published: 1901

Churchill chose St. Louis as his setting in The Crisis *because the historical personages who appear in the novel—General Sherman, General Grant, and Abraham Lincoln—all came from that city or neighboring Illinois; and because the two streams of emigration which met in St. Louis gave him the opportunity to contrast the two cultures. Churchill's natural treatment of legendary figures such as Lincoln lend an atmosphere of reality to the story.*

Principal Characters

Stephen Brice, a young Boston lawyer who migrates to St. Louis in 1858. He falls in love with Virginia Carvel and, influenced by Lincoln, becomes an active Republican. Enlisting in the Union Army, he serves in the Civil War. His saving of Clarence Colfax's life and his outstanding qualities enable him to marry Virginia despite the fact that she is an ardent Southerner.

Judge Whipple, Stephen's friend. He helps the young man get started in a political career.

Mrs. Brice, Stephen's widowed mother, who migrates with him to St. Louis.

Virginia Carvel, an ardent Southerner. Though her partisan loyalties conflict with Stephen's, she comes to love him and, eventually, marries him.

Colonel Carvel, Virginia's father. He serves in the Confederate forces.

Abraham Lincoln, who is an influence in Stephen's life. He makes Stephen and Virginia realize they must forgive and forget their sectional loyalties.

Clarence Colfax, a young Southerner, a rival for Virginia's love. His life is twice saved by the intervention of Stephen.

Ulysses S. Grant, the famous Union general. Stephen meets him at the outbreak of the war before Grant gets a command. Near the end of the war Stephen, now a major, is sent to Virginia to report to General Grant on Sherman's campaigns.

William T. Sherman, famous Union general. Stephen meets him early in the Civil War and later serves as a member of the General's staff.

Eliphalit Hopper, an unscrupulous carpetbagger.

The Story

In 1858 Stephen Brice emigrated from Boston to St. Louis with his widowed mother. He went to accept the offer of Judge Whipple, his father's friend, who had promised Stephen an opportunity to enter his law firm. Being a personable young man, Stephen Brice found favor among the people of St. Louis, including Colonel Carvel, and the colonel's daughter, Virginia. Stephen promptly fell in love with Virginia Carvel. He was not encouraged by the girl at first because he was a New Englander.

One day Judge Whipple sent Stephen to Springfield, Illinois, with a message for the man who was running for senator against Stephen A. Douglas. When Stephen Brice finally found his man, Abraham Lincoln, he was in time to hear the famous Freeport debate between Lincoln and Douglas. Lincoln made a deep impression on Stephen, who went back to St. Louis a confirmed Republican, as Judge Whipple had hoped. Feeling that Stephen would some day be a great politician, the judge had sent him to Lincoln to catch some of Lincoln's idealism and practical politics.

Convinced by Lincoln that no country could exist half-slave and half-free, Stephen Brice became active in Missouri politics on behalf of the Republicans; a dangerous course to take in St. Louis because of the many Southerners living in the city. His anti-slavery views soon alienated Stephen from the girl he wanted to marry, who then promised to marry Stephen's rival, her cousin and fellow Southerner, Clarence Colfax.

Lincoln lost the election for the senate, but in doing so won for himself the presidency of the United States in 1860. During both campaigns, Stephen Brice worked for the Republican party. An able orator, he became known as a rising young lawyer of exceptional abilities.

The guns at Fort Sumter reverberated loudly in St. Louis in 1861. The city was divided into two factions, pro-slavery Southerners and anti-slavery Northerners. Friends of long standing no longer spoke to each other and members of the same family found themselves at odds over the question of which side Missouri should favor, the Union or the Confederacy. It was a trying time for Stephen Brice. Because of his widowed mother and his political activities, he was unable to join the army. Judge Whipple convinced him that, for the time being, he could do more for his country as a civilian. It was hard for the young man to believe the judge when all of Stephen's friends and acquaintances were going about the city in uniform.

When war was declared, Missouri had a little campaign of its own, for the state militia under the direction of the governor attempted to seize the state. This action was defeated by the prompt action of Federal forces in capturing the militia training camp without firing a shot. A spectator at this minor engagement, Stephen made the acquaintance of an ex-army officer named Sherman and of another shambling man who claimed he should be given a regiment. The young officers laughed at him; his name was Ulysses S. Grant.

Among those captured when Federal troops overcame the Missouri militia was Clarence Colfax, Stephen's rival. Clarence refused to give his oath and go on parole, and he soon escaped from prison and disappeared into the South. Virginia Carvel thought him more of a hero than ever.

Because communications with the South and the Southwest had been cut by the Union armies, Colonel Carvel went bankrupt. He and his daughter aided Southern sympathizers attempting to join the Confederate Army. At last the colonel himself felt that it was his duty to leave St. Louis and take an active part in the hostilities.

The war continued, putting the lie to those optimists who had prophesied that hostilities would end in a few months. By the time of the battle at Vicksburg, Stephen had become a lieutenant in the Union Army. He distinguished himself in that battle and came once more to the attention of Sherman. When the city fell, Stephen found Clarence Colfax, now a lieutenant-colonel in the Confederate Army. The Southerner had received a severe wound. To save Clarence's life, Stephen arranged for him to be sent to St. Louis on a hospital ship. Stephen knew that he was probably sending his rival back to marry Virginia Carvel. Young Colfax realized what Stephen had done, and told Virginia as much while he was convalescing in St. Louis. The girl vowed that she would never marry a Yankee, even if Colfax were killed.

Judge Whipple had fallen ill, and he was nursed by Virginia and by Stephen's mother. While the judge was sinking fast, Colonel Carvel appeared. At the risk of his life, he had come through the lines in civilian clothes to see his daughter and his old friend. There was a strange meeting at Judge Whipple's deathbed. Clarence Colfax, Colonel Carvel, and Stephen Brice were all there. They all risked their lives, for the Confederates could have been arrested as spies, and Stephen, because he was with them, could have been convicted of treason. That night Virginia realized that she was in love with Stephen.

After the judge's death Stephen returned to the army. Ordered to General Sherman's staff, he accompanied the general on the march through Georgia. At the battle of Bentonville, Stephen again met Clarence Colfax, who had been captured by Union soldiers while in civilian clothes and brought to Sherman's headquarters as a spy. Once again Stephen interceded with Sherman and saved the Southerner's life. Soon afterward Stephen, promoted to the rank of major, was sent by Sherman with some dispatches to General Grant at City Point, in Virginia. Stephen recognized Grant as the man he had seen at the engagement of the militia camp back in St. Louis.

During the conference with the general an officer appeared to summon Stephen to meet another old acquaintance, Abraham Lincoln. The president, like Grant, wished to hear Stephen's first-hand account of the march through Georgia to the sea. When Stephen asked for a pardon for Clarence Colfax, Lincoln said he would consider the matter. Stephen went with Lincoln to Richmond for an inspection of that city after it had fallen to Grant's armies.

Virginia Carvel, not knowing of Stephen's intercession on behalf of Clarence Colfax, traveled to Washington to ask Lincoln for a pardon. She gained an audience with the president, during which she met Stephen once again. Lincoln granted them the pardon, saying that with the war soon to end the time to show clemency had come. He left Virginia and Stephen alone when he hurried to keep another appointment. The young people had realized during their talk with Lincoln that there was much to be forgiven and forgotten by both sides in the struggle which was drawing to a close. The emotion of the moment overcame their reticence at last, and they declared their love for each other. They were married the following day.

After the wedding, they went to visit Virginia's ancestral home in Annapolis. A few days later word came to them that Lincoln had died from an assassin's bullet.

Critical Evaluation

Judged on the basis of his later novels dealing with problems such as class relationships and divorce, Winston Churchill must be considered outmoded in his attitudes and ideas. His own conservative and wealthy background biased him in favor of genteel, romantic, or impractical solutions to tough modern questions, although his thought was often enhanced by its sincerity and moral seriousness. But as a historical novelist, his reputation is secure; his early works about events in the Revolutionary and Civil Wars are excellent examples of vivid historical fiction. One of the most popular of these novels was *The Crisis,* a novel about people whose loves, loyalties, and friendships are threatened by the divisive influences of the Civil War.

Churchill's choice of the city of St. Louis as the setting for the novel's action is crucial, since that city was a crossroads between North and South when hostilities began. St. Louis had its old established families who had emigrated both from Northern and Southern states, and after 1861 the city suffered a painful division in popular sentiment between sympathizers of the Union and the Confederate causes; at one point in the narrative, Clarence Colfax is taken prisoner by Federal troops for his involvement in the Missouri militia's attempt to seize the state. St. Louis is thus the ideal setting in which to play out characters' conflicting personal beliefs and emotions against a backdrop of factual political and social history. Families which had been friends for decades cease to speak to one another, and when Missouri is finally established on the Union side, the city becomes dangerous for its own families of Southern background who have lived there for years.

Likewise, central to the plot is the love relationship of Stephen Brice and Virginia Carvel, which is threatened by the war; Stephen becomes a Union Army lieutenant, while Virginia, whose father is a Colonel in the Confederate Army, vows that she will never marry a Yankee. The two are reconciled in a dramatic scene in Abraham Lincoln's office, where Virginia has come to beg for a pardon for her old suitor Clarence Colfax, unaware that Stephen has already interceded with the president on his rival's behalf. The believable portraits of Lincoln, General Grant, General Sherman, and other historical figures are feats in themselves; and the successful fusing within a single story of personal, everyday happenings with events and characters of great historical import makes *The Crisis* succeed where so many novels of this type have failed.

Bibliography

Hofstadter, Richard and Beatrice Hofstadter.   "Winston Churchill: A Study in the Popular Novel," in *American Quarterly.* II (Spring, 1950), pp. 12–28. Reprinted in *The American Experience: Approaches to the Study of the United States.* Edited by Hennig Cohen. Boston: Houghton Mifflin, 1968, pp. 226–242.

Knight, Grant C.   *The Strenuous Age in American Literature.* Chapel Hill: University of North Carolina Press, 1954, pp. 19–20.

Quinn, Arthur Hobson.   *American Fiction: An Historical and Critical Survey.* New York: Appleton-Century, 1936, p. 497.

Schneider, Robert W.   *Novelist to a Generation: The Life and Thought of Winston Churchill.* Bowling Green, Oh.: Bowling Green University Popular Press, 1976, pp. 45–55.

Titus, Warren I.   *Winston Churchill.* New York: Twayne, 1963, pp. 46–52.

Underwood, John.   "Winston Churchill and Civic Righteousness," in *Literature and Insurgency.* New York: Mitchell Kennerley, 1914, pp. 317–322.

Van Doren, Carl.   *Contemporary American Novelists, 1900–1920.* New York: Macmillan, 1923, pp. 47–56.

JOHN ESTEN COOKE

Born: Winchester, Virginia (November 3, 1830)
Died: Clarke County, Virginia (September 27, 1886)

Principal Works

NOVELS: *Leather Stocking and Silk*, 1854; *The Virginia Comedians*, 1854; *Henry St. John, Gentleman*, 1859; *Surry of Eagle's-Nest*, 1866; *Fairfax*, 1868; *Mohun*, 1869; *The Heir of Greymount*, 1870; *Her Majesty the Queen*, 1873; *My Lady Pokahontas*, 1885.

BIOGRAPHY: *A Life of Stonewall Jackson*, 1863; *A Life of General Robert E. Lee*, 1871.

ESSAYS: *Hammer and Rapier*, 1870.

HISTORY: *Virginia: A History of the People*, 1883.

John Esten Cooke, born in Winchester, Virginia, November 3, 1830, is an almost-forgotten American novelist whose books have deserved better reputation and greater popularity. His older brother was Philip Pendleton Cooke, noted as a poet and story writer of the antebellum South. John Esten Cooke spent his early boyhood on a farm near Winchester, Virginia, but his family moved to Richmond when he was nine years old. In 1846, although he had wanted to attend the University of Virginia, he began to read law in his father's office. By 1848 he had published some poetry and prose, including pieces in *Harper's Monthly* and *The Southern Literary Messenger*. His first real success came with the publication of *The Virginia Comedians*, which was the first of a total of thirty-one books to be published before his death.

During the 1850's, Cooke was an ardent proponent of secession, and he served in the Confederate Army throughout the Civil War, rising from the rank of private to that of captain. During the war years he found time to write *A Life of Stonewall Jackson*, the pioneer study of the great Confederate tactician and general. After the war ended he continued to write, turning again to fiction. His war experience was woven into *Surry of Eagle's-Nest* and *Mohun*, among the earliest novels about the Civil War.

Following Lee's surrender at Appomattox, Cooke returned to civilian life in Virginia. In 1867 he married Mary Francis Page and settled at "The Briers," in Clarke County, Virginia, where he divided his time between writing and farming. Work of this later period in his career is varied. *The Heir of Greymount* carries the theme that the best answer to the South's postwar problems is agriculture. *My Lady Pokahontas* is a novel about the early days of Virginia as a British colony. *Virginia* is a history of colonial times. During the 1870's Cooke also wrote *A Life of General Robert E. Lee* and a volume of essays on the Civil War and related military topics, *Hammer and Rapier*. Cooke's untimely death at his home on September 27, 1886, was caused by typhoid fever.

Bibliography

There is only one biography, John O. Beaty, *John Esten Cooke, Virginian*, 1922. Oscar Wegelin, "A Bibliography of the Separate Writings of John Esten Cooke," *American Collector*, I (1925), 96–99 (separately republished, 1925, 1941), does not provide a full listing of periodical publications. Two useful brief evaluations appear in A. H. Quinn, *American Fiction*, 1936; and Jay B. Hubbell, *The South in American Literature*, 1954. For an interesting article, see Carvel Collins, "John Esten Cooke and Local Color," *Southern Literary Messenger*, NS VI (1944), 82–84; also Lucy Gaylord Starner, "Scribe of the Old Dominion," *Virginia Cavalcade*, XIII (Autumn, 1963), 32–39.

SURRY OF EAGLE'S-NEST

Type of work: Novel
Author: John Esten Cooke (1830–1886)
Type of plot: Historical romance
Time of plot: 1861–1863
Locale: Virginia
First published: 1866

Based in part upon the wartime experience of a captain in the Confederate army, Surry of Eagle's-Nest *blends a great deal of melodramatic fiction with some historical facts concerning the campaigns of General Stonewall Jackson and other prominent Confederate military figures.*

Principal Characters

Lieutenant Colonel Surry, an officer of the Confederate Army. He falls in love with May Beverley, who is already engaged. Having been involved in the feud between Mordaunt and Fenwick, and having fought under Jackson, he is able to marry May when her fiancé breaks the engagement.

May Beverley, who marries Surry when her fiancé, Frederick Baskerville, breaks their engagement.

Fenwick, a Yankee spy who has treacherously separated Mordaunt from his wife. Repeatedly escaping Mordaunt's vengeance, he is killed by Achmed.

Colonel Mordaunt, once the rival of Fenwick for the hand of Frances Carleton. Mordaunt had won her, whereupon the rejected Fenwick used forged letters to separate husband and wife. Mordaunt repeatedly seeks revenge, but Fenwick always escapes, until Achmed kills him.

Frances Carleton, Mordaunt's lost wife, who appears as the insane "White Lady." She gives Surry a paper clearing up the mystery of Fenwick's villainy.

Violet Grafton, her cousin and attendant.

Achmed, Mordaunt's Arab companion, who kills Fenwick.

Harry Saltoun, a young Confederate officer who, about to fight a duel with Mordaunt, is revealed as his son.

Mrs. Parkins, Fenwick's confederate.

General Stonewall Jackson,
General J. E. B. Stuart,
General Turner Ashby, and
Major John Pelham, officers of the Confederate Army.

Captain William D. Farley, a Confederate scout.

The Story

Cavalier Philip Surry, who rode and fought under Prince Rupert in the English Civil War, escaped to Virginia when King Charles I was beheaded. Establishing a home, which he named Eagle's-Nest, on the Rappahannock River below Port Royal, he enjoined in his will that the oldest son of the family in each generation should sign himself "Surry of Eagle's-Nest."

The present Surry, who had attended the Virginia Military Institute for one session and had studied law at the University of Virginia, was in Richmond in April, 1861, when the State Convention passed its ordinance of secession. One evening at the Capitol Square he saw with rapture a beautiful girl, whose dropped handkerchief contained the initials, M.B. On another day, in Hollywood Cemetery, he witnessed by chance a duel between a tall, bronzed stranger named Mordaunt and one Fenwick, the encounter ending when Mordaunt put a pistol bullet through Fenwick's lungs. Surry left Richmond the proud recipient of a captain's commission in the Provisional Army of Virginia, and in his new gray uniform he rode toward Harper's Ferry for duty under Colonel Jackson.

Losing his way in the Wilderness, which bordered the Rapidan River, he spent a night in a house where dwelt an insane woman in white, still possessing traces of youthful beauty, who was attended by her lovely young cousin, Violet Grafton, and by a harridan, Mrs. Parkins. Surprisingly there appeared at this house Fenwick, whose duel wound had not been fatal. In the night "the White Lady," tiptoeing into Surry's room, slipped into his coat pocket a package bearing the words, "Read these when I am dead—and remember

Your own Frances."

Further, while en route to Harper's Ferry, Surry was overtaken by a hurricane in a forest and was knocked from his horse by a large limb. He was stunned and his arm was broken. A female equestrian, whom the flying branches had spared, ordered her servant to take the injured man to her father's home, "The Oaks." There he convalesced under the eyes of Colonel Beverley and his daughter May, his rescuer and the owner of the handkerchief which he had picked up in Richmond. Surry's heart was fully captivated, but May was already bound by a between-fathers contract and a young-girl engagement to Frederick Baskerville. The fact that her new lover knew Baskerville to be a scoundrel made Surry's plight doubly bitter.

Fairly near "The Oaks" was the home of Mordaunt, which Surry visited. Its owner, who lived hermitlike with Achmed, a faithful Arab, was destined to become one of Surry's best friends. Mordaunt's air of melancholy indicated the gentleman's deeply tragic past.

After long delays, Captain Surry finally reported for duty to Colonel Thomas J. Jackson, who made him an aide-de-camp. Shortly afterward the young staff officer met Colonel J. E. B. Stuart. The two colonels, soon to become generals, would be Surry's idols to the end of his days.

Before their first battle Surry and Mordaunt, now a Confederate colonel, saw an eerie night burial in the garden of a stone house at Manassas. They observed on the scene Fenwick, the Parkins woman, and Violet Grafton. The dead person was the insane "White Lady" of the Wilderness. Again Mordaunt tried to kill Fenwick, but without success. Soon afterward Surry delivered to Violet Grafton the package which her cousin had put in his pocket.

Wounded in the Battle of First Manassas, Surry was taken to the Fitzhugh home, "Elm Cottage," where he was well nursed. Mrs. Fitzhugh, charmed by Violet Grafton, gave the orphan girl a home.

In 1862, having recovered from his wound, Surry was with Jackson throughout his spectacular Valley Campaign and held General Turner Ashby in his arms when that "Knight of the Valley" expired on the battlefield. Briefly a prisoner, he met Sir Percy Wyndham, an Englishman wearing Federal blue. Also he met and admired Captain Farley of Stuart's staff, a scout extraordinary. When Jackson joined General Lee near Richmond to defeat McClellan, Surry shared in that campaign; then he was back near Fredericksburg, in the Wilderness area.

There one night, peering through a window shutter at the house where he had first seen "the White Lady" and Violet Grafton, Surry heard Fenwick, while intoxicated, acknowledge himself to be a Yankee spy. Moreover, Fenwick reviewed to Mrs. Parkins the story of his and Mordaunt's enmity. Years before, Mordaunt and Fenwick, youthful friends, had become rivals for the love of Frances Carleton. When she married Mordaunt, Fenwick planned revenge. Still posing as a devoted friend, he utilized a trip of Mordaunt's to London to forge a letter which made Frances believe that her husband had landed in New York and was requesting her to let Fenwick escort her there to meet him. Aided by the easily bribed Mrs. Parkins, Fenwick abducted his friend's wife to Maryland, where she gave birth to a son, who was afterwards reported dead, and where she contracted a fever which permanently affected her brain. Imitating Frances Carleton Mordaunt's handwriting, Fenwick perpetrated another forgery which duped Mordaunt into believing that his wife had forsaken him. Embittered, the young husband left Virginia for a long sojourn in Arabian lands. After drunken Fenwick's remarkable disclosure Surry captured him, but the prisoner escaped after bribing a guard. At a later date, however, in a face-to-face combat, Mordaunt pinned his enemy to a tree with a thrust of his sword.

Surry, who, as the war continued, rose to be major and later lieutenant colonel, saw old Stonewall Jackson, Longstreet, and Lee defeat Pope at Second Manassas. In the Maryland campaign which followed he was captured, interviewed by McClellan, and placed aboard a prison train headed for Baltimore; but he escaped by jumping through a window while the train was in motion. In December, 1862, he was present when Lee's two corps under Longstreet and Jackson repulsed Burnside at Fredericksburg. There he saw the youthful artillery genius, Major John Pelham, mastermaneuver his guns. An ardent friendship between Surry and Pelham continued until the gallant young Alabaman was killed in battle.

The spring of 1863 brought Surry abundant joy. When Colonel Beverley's wealth at "The Oaks" was destroyed by invading armies, Frederick Baskerville lost interest in May so completely that he released her from her engagement. Consequently she married Surry, with her father's sanction.

Among Surry's friends was Harry Saltoun, a young Confederate lieutenant from Maryland. Fenwick, who repeatedly recovered from seemingly mortal wounds, by means of a lying anonymous letter provoked Saltoun to challenge Colonel Mordaunt to a duel. Tragedy was averted, however, when Violet Grafton sent Mordaunt the paper in which "the White Lady," Mrs. Frances Carleton Mordaunt, had recorded the whole truth about Fenwick and his evil deceptions. Also, through an affidavit of a Maryland woman, Harry Saltoun was proved to be Mordaunt's own son.

Fenwick's ultimate villainy was the abduction of Violet Grafton, but Mordaunt's devoted Arab companion, Achmed, trailed the knave to his hiding place. There Mordaunt and Fenwick had their final fight, but it was Achmed, not Mordaunt, who killed Fenwick with a gleaming dagger. Sadly, however, a ball from the dying villain's pistol wounded Achmed, who expired in the presence of the two persons whom he loved, Mordaunt and Violet Grafton.

"Fighting Joe" Hooker, who had succeeded Burnside as commander of the Federal army of invasion, thrust at Lee in the Wilderness, on the south side of the Rapidan and Rappahannock rivers. In a brilliantly conceived surprise movement Stonewall Jackson struck Hooker's right flank at Chancellorsville, to win a thrilling victory. This Southern triumph was dearly bought, for in the woods, on the night of May 2, 1863, Jackson was wounded by his own men, and on Sunday, May 10, that irreplaceable hero breathed his last.

Surry of Eagle's-Nest survived to tell his story and that of the war years. For him, only the ghosts of the past remained.

Critical Evaluation

Surry of Eagle's-Nest remains of interest primarily as a romanticized version of Cooke's firsthand experiences as a Confederate officer during the Civil War—an ordeal that ranged from participation in the First Manassas to the final surrender at Appomattox Court House. While Cooke served primarily as a staff officer with J. E. B. Stuart's cavalry, he numbered Stonewall Jackson, Robert E. Lee, and other high-ranking Confederates among his personal acquaintances. Cooke published military biographies of Jackson (1863 and 1866) and of Lee (1871).

On the whole, *Surry of Eagle's-Nest,* a product of six weeks' work, is an uneven attempt to blend historical fact and fiction. The novel climaxes with a romanticized account of Stonewall Jackson's death in 1863, and, in its historical aspects, draws upon the author's earlier military biographies of Jackson (just as *Mohun* [1869], the sequel to *Surry of Eagle's-Nest,* parallels Cooke's later biography of Robert E. Lee). In *Surry of Eagle's-Nest,* Cooke merely combined the fictional trappings of conventional historical romance with real wartime events and experiences. The highly melodramatic aspects of the novel, particularly the purely Gothic subplot of the antagonists Mordaunt and Fenwick and the often confusing integration of historical and fictional characters, render the work less satisfactory than *The Virginia Comedi-*

ans (1854), Cooke's most successful historical romance. Cooke's idealization of antebellum Southern society and his acceptance of the myth of Cavalier origins of the Virginia aristocracy are also more prevalent in *Surry of Eagle's-Nest* than in his previous work. The novel was one of the earliest and most important contributions to the myth of the "Lost Cause" in the postwar South.

The novel, first published in 1866, found a receptive audience among celebrants of the "Lost Cause," and it has remained one of the most popular of Cooke's historical romances. Along with *Mohun, Surry of Eagle's-Nest* ranks as the best of Cooke's war novel, but neither possesses the unity or literary quality earlier achieved in *The Virginia Comedians*.

Bibliography

Beaty, John O. *John Esten Cooke, Virginian.* New York: Columbia University Press, 1922.

Cowie, Alexander. *The Rise of the American Novel.* New York: American Book, 1948, pp. 463–472.

Holliday, Carl. "John Esten Cooke as a Novelist," in *Sewanee Review.* XIII (April, 1905), pp. 216–220.

Hubbell, Jay B. *The South in American Literature, 1607–1900.* Durham, N.C.: Duke University Press, 1954, pp. 511–521.

O'Brien, Matthew C. "John Esten Cooke, George Washington, and the Virginia Cavaliers," in *Virginia Magazine of History and Biography.* LXXXIV (1976), pp. 259–265.

Patten, Irene M. "The Civil War as Romance: Of Noble Warriors and Maidens Chaste," in *American Heritage.* XXII (1971), pp. 48–53.

Starnes, Lucy G. "Scribe of the Old Dominion," in *Virginia Cavalcade.* XIII (1963), pp. 32–37.

JAMES FENIMORE COOPER

Born: Burlington, New Jersey (September 15, 1789)
Died: Cooperstown, New York (September 14, 1851)

Principal Works

NOVELS: *The Spy*, 1821; *The Pioneers*, 1823; *The Pilot*, 1824; *Lionel Lincoln*, 1825; *The Last of the Mohicans*, 1826; *The Prairie*, 1827; *The Red Rover*, 1827; *The Wept of Wish-ton-Wish*, 1829; *The Water-Witch*, 1830; *The Bravo*, 1831; *The Heidenmauer*, 1832; *The Headsman*, 1833; *The Monikins*, 1835; *Homeward Bound*, 1838; *Home as Found*, 1838; *Mercedes of Castile*, 1840; *The Pathfinder*, 1840; *The Deerslayer*, 1841; *The Wing-and-Wing*, 1842; *The Two Admirals*, 1842; *Wyandotté*, 1843; *Ned Myers*, 1843; *Afloat and Ashore*, 1844; *Santanstoe*, 1845; *The Chainbearer*, 1845; *The Redskins*, 1846; *The Crater*, 1847; *Jack Tier*, 1848; *The Oak Openings*, 1848; *The Sea Lions*, 1849; *The Ways of the Hour*, 1850.

SOCIAL CRITICISM: *Notions of the Americans*, 1828; *Letter of J. Fenimore Cooper to General Lafayette*, 1831; *A Letter to His Countrymen*, 1834; *The American Democrat*, 1838.

TRAVEL SKETCHES: *Sketches of Switzerland*, Parts I and II, 1836; *Gleanings in Europe*, 1837–1838.

HISTORY: *The History of the Navy of the United States of America*, 1839.

Novelist, social critic, and historian, James Fenimore Cooper was perhaps the most productive and versatile American writer of his generation. In his comparatively short literary career (1820–1851), he published thirty-three substantial fictional works, three books of explicit social and political commentary, five travel works, a monumental history of the United States Navy, a book of naval biographies, and an impressive quantity of miscellaneous writing, much of it anonymous and some of it still unknown to scholars. His purpose as man and author, as he declared it, was the intellectual independence of his country, whose thought and art were, he believed, too much dominated by foreign models; and his bold experimentation with indigenous literary materials exerted a powerful formative effect on the literature of the young Republic. His interest for readers today lies mainly in his artistic triumphs in the form of the romance, at present too little understood, and in his pungent and pertinent insights into the development of American and European civilization.

Born at Burlington, New Jersey, on September 15, 1789, Cooper was reared by his wealthy, land-holding father, the Federalist leader of western New York State, in the bustling frontier community of Cooperstown at the foot of Lake Otsego. As a lad, he explored the hills, forests, and lake near his home, devoured fiction, and spun yarns of his own. From his father and his father's associates, he derived a

life-long reverence for the Constitution ("on the framing of which all the experience of the past was early brought to bear") and for the exalted ideals of the
Federalist founding fathers. Expelled from Yale for a high-spirited prank before
he was fifteen, he made an apprentice voyage before the mast and became a
midshipman in the then infant Navy, only to have his dream of glorious service
afloat shattered by relatively inactive assignments at Oswego and New York City.
In 1811, determining to resign his commission and enjoy his considerable patri-
mony as a gentleman farmer, he married Susan Augusta De Lancey of the well-
known Tory family and for the next several years devoted himself to various domestic, agricultural, military, political, religious, and cultural activities in Westchester and Otsego Counties.

When the depression of 1817–1819 swept away his inheritance, Cooper had to
seek means of paying his debts and supporting his increasing family. His first
novel *Precaution* (1820), a deliberate attempt to produce a best-seller, failed like
his other speculations; but the writing so intrigued him that he continued with
The Spy, a historical romance based on an anecdote of John Jay and on intimate
knowledge of the legends and terrain of Westchester County. Its unexpected success at home and abroad turned Cooper decisively to authorship. Moving to New
York City in 1822, he soon became a dominant literary figure, founding the Bread
and Cheese Club and rallying writers and painters to the cause of distinctively
American art. In *The Pioneers*, earliest of the Leatherstocking series, he drew
heavily on nostalgic memories of his frontier boyhood; in *The Pilot*, he initiated
the vogue of nautical romance; in *Lionel Lincoln*, he attempted in fiction an almost unprecedented exactitude of historical detail; and in *The Last of the
Mohicans*, second of the Leatherstocking Tales, he gave his first extended treatment of Indians in a wild forest setting. Though uneven artistically, these experimental romances proved the value of American literary materials and the serious
thematic potentialities of the form.

In 1826, Cooper took his family to Europe, where he wrote such favorite romances as *The Prairie*, in which Leatherstocking reappears as an aged trapper-
philosopher on the western plains, and *The Red Rover*, a second sea-tale. Friendship with Lafayette and close observation of European aristocracy led to such
strenuous efforts to expound and defend American democratic ideas as *Notions
of the Americans*, an idealized description of the United States, and *The Bravo*,
The Heidenmauer, and *The Headsman*, fictional interpretations of European history. These efforts were misunderstood at home, however; and Cooper returned to
New York in 1833 depressed and discouraged, convinced that his countrymen did
not understand their own principles. In *The Monikins*, an allegorical satire, in a
series of travel books (1836–1837), and in *The American Democrat*, he sought to
bring Americans to self-knowledge and to correct the excesses of the Jacksonian
era; but, despite the cogency of their observation, these works were almost totally
disregarded.

Cooper's return to fiction with *Homeward Bound* and *Home As Found* and
publication of his long-deferred *The History of the Navy of the United States of*

America precipitated many bitter battles with Whig editors in the press and in libel courts. Despite his numerous controversies, Cooper's final years, spent pleasantly enough in the refurbished family mansion in Cooperstown, were astonishingly productive. Concluding the Leatherstocking Tales with *The Pathfinder* and *The Deerslayer*, he reasserted and afterwards maintained his reputation as a master of romance; but, to the end, he experimented with means of fusing his imaginative materials and his specifically critical interests. These efforts, including *Afloat and Ashore*, its sequel *Miles Wallingford* (1844), the Anti-Rent trilogy— *Satanstoe, The Chainbearer, The Redskins*—and *The Crater* were not notably successful, though *Satanstoe*, the first novel of the Anti-Rent series, has been widely appreciated for its evocation of early Dutch life in New York and Albany. Cooper died at Cooperstown on September 14, 1851, after a prolonged illness.

While Cooper's stature as a social critic has been sufficiently acknowledged by twentieth-century critics, his artistic stature is still disputed. The imaginative appeal of his swift-moving narrative, graphic description, and picturesque characterization is usually conceded; but the complex symbolic structures of his better fiction have been overlooked or misrepresented, so that its intricacy and universality of meaning have been inadequately comprehended. Cooper's weaknesses (occasional turgidity of style, excessive dependence on outworn fictional convention, love of overelaboration, and careless composition) do not disappear when his works are given the strenuous reading they require; but the flaws do not essentially damage the unobtrusive brilliance of the total conceptions.

Bibliography

The *Letters and Journals* have been edited by James Franklin Beard, 1960– 1968. A new edition of Cooper in 10 vols. is in progress under the general editorship of Robert E. Spiller. The Mohawk Edition of the fiction, 33 vols., 1895–1900, is available and perhaps as satisfactory as any other. Miscellaneous selections from the family papers were published by Cooper's grandson and namesake as *The Correspondence of James Fenimore Cooper*, 1922. The most informative biographies are those by T. R. Lounsbury, 1883; H. W. Boynton, 1931; Marcel Clavel, 1938; and James Grossman, 1949. Robert E. Spiller in *Fenimore Cooper: Critic of His Times*, 1931, and in numerous articles, editions, and introductions has made the most substantial contributions to modern Cooper scholarship. Useful bibliographies are contained in Robert E. Spiller and Philip C. Blackburn, *A Descriptive Bibliography of the Writings of James Fenimore Cooper*, 1934, and in Robert E. Spiller, *James Fenimore Cooper: Representative Selections*, American Writers Series, 1936. The most recent study is George Dekker, *James Fenimore Cooper: The American Scott*, 1967.

THE DEERSLAYER

Type of work: Novel
Author: James Fenimore Cooper (1789–1851)
Type of plot: Historical romance
Time of plot: 1740
Locale: Northern New York State
First published: 1841

Though the last of The Leatherstocking Tales *to be written,* The Deerslayer *is the novel of Natty Bumppo's youth. In it, savages and the woodsman Natty Bumppo, or Deerslayer, are depicted as having codes of honor and morality, while Tom Hutter and Hurry Harry are motivated by greed and viciousness in their efforts to obtain scalps and in their murder of an innocent Indian girl. A portion of the story deals with Judith Hutter's fruitless attempts to interest Natty romantically.*

Principal Characters

Natty Bumppo, called **Deerslayer.** A skilled, modest, honorable, brave young hunter, he has been brought up by Delaware Indians and taught by Moravian pietists; he embodies a natural innocence and nobility. Arriving at Lake Glimmerglass, he allies himself with Hurry Harry March and the Hutter family, at the same time trying to help his Indian friend Chingachgook rescue his betrothed from hostile Iroquois. He is soon forced to kill his first man, an Indian. He ransoms the captured Harry and Hutter after their capture during a raid on an Iroquois camp, but he himself is caught while assisting Chingachgook. The Iroquois respect his word and give him leave to offer his friends terms of surrender. When these are rejected, he goes back to be tortured. He escapes but is recaptured. His torture is stopped only by the timely arrival of Chingachgook and Hurry Harry with British troops. Unresponsive to Judith Hutter's charms, he leaves to join the Delaware tribe.

Hurry Harry March, a ferocious, greedy, swaggering frontiersman. Captured with Hutter during a raid for Indian scalps, he is released only by Deerslayer's bargaining. His impulsive shooting of an Indian girl endangers his companions. Large and handsome, he is nevertheless refused by Judith Hutter, who favors Deerslayer. He redeems himself by leading the British soldiers to the Indian camp, thus saving Deerslayer's life.

Chingachgook (chĭn·găch′gŏŏk), the Great Serpent, a Delaware chief. A noble savage, he is as adept in woodcraft and warfare as his friend Deerslayer. He manages to escape with his beloved, Wahta!-Wah, when Deerslayer is captured. Later he saves Hurry Harry in an ambush at Hutter's "castle," and he cuts Deerslayer's bonds just before the British rout the Iroquois. Years later he revisits Lake Glimmerglass with his son Uncas and his friend Deerslayer.

Tom Hutter, a predatory former pirate who became a trapper in order to escape the law. Living with his two adopted daughters in Muskrat Castle, a hut built on a shoal, he makes his trapping rounds of the lake in a houseboat. As avaricious as Hurry Harry, he joins him on an ill-fated raid, when both are made prisoners by hostile Indians. After being ransomed he joins Harry on another raid. Returning to his hut, he is scalped in an ambush and buried in the lake by his daughters.

Judith Hutter, his gay, coquettish, shrewd young daughter, who prides herself on her clothes and appearance. Having been seduced by Captain Warley, she is cautious about men and refuses Hurry Harry. Deerslayer, however, resists her attractions and declines her offer of marriage. Having no relatives left when her sister dies, she goes to the British fort, possibly to become Warley's mistress later on.

Hetty Hutter, Judith's simple-minded sister. She embodies a pure Christian simplicity unalloyed by a sense of expediency. The Indians are in awe of her and allow her to pass unmolested as she serves as a kind of messenger between the captured and uncaptured. Her naïve love for Hurry Harry remains unrequited when she is accidentally shot in the final battle with the Indians.

Wah-ta!-Wah, Chingachgook's beloved, a Delaware maiden captured by Iroquois. A practical child of nature, she condones scalping but deplores Hurry Harry's wanton killing. Although she escapes with Chingachgook, she returns to the enemy camp with Judith and Hetty in an effort to save Deerslayer.

Captain Warley, head of the troop that saves Deerslayer and routs the Indians. A man of the world, his interest in Judith revives when he sees her in the camp in a stunning gown.

Rivenoak, the enemy Iroquois chief, a fierce foe but honorable in character. He offers to let Deerslayer live if he will marry the widow of the brave he killed.

Le Loup Cervier (lə loo sâr·vyā'), an Indian, the first person Deerslayer ever killed. In dying he names Deerslayer "Hawkeye."

Sumach, his wife, whom Deerslayer refuses.

The Panther, an Indian who attempts to kill the captured Deerslayer but is himself killed instead.

Catamount, the brave who unsuccessfully taunts captured Deerslayer.

The Story

Natty Bumppo, a young woodsman known as Deerslayer, and Hurry Harry traveled to the shores of Lake Glimmerglass together. It was a dangerous journey, for the French and their Iroquois allies were on the warpath. Deerslayer was planning to meet his friend Chingachgook, the young Delaware chief, so that they might go against the Iroquois. Hurry Harry was on his way to the lake to warn Thomas Hutter and his daughters that hostile Indians were raiding along the frontier. Harry was accustomed to hunt and trap with Hutter during the summer, and he was an admirer of Hutter's elder daughter, the spirited Judith.

Hutter and his daughters lived in a cabin built on piles in the middle of the lake. Hutter had also built a great, scowlike vessel, known among frontiersmen as the ark, on which he traveled from one shore of the lake to the other on his hunting and trapping expeditions. On their arrival at the lake the two found a hidden canoe. Having paddled out to the cabin and found it deserted, they proceeded down the lake and came upon the ark anchored to a secluded outlet. Hutter had already learned of the Indian raiders. The party decided to take refuge in the cabin, where they could be attacked only over the water. The men managed to maneuver the ark out of the narrow outlet and sail it to the cabin. They had one narrow escape. As the ark was clearing the outlet, six Indians tried to board the boat by dropping from the overhanging limbs of a tree. Each missed and fell into the water.

Under cover of darkness, Hutter, Deerslayer, and Hurry Harry took the canoe and paddled to shore to get Hutter's two remaining canoes hidden there. They found the canoes and, on their way back to the ark, sighted a party of Indians camped under some trees. While Deerslayer waited in a canoe offshore, the other two men attacked the Iroquois camp in an attempt to obtain scalps, for which they could obtain bounties. They were captured. Deerslayer, knowing that he was powerless to help them, lay down to sleep in the canoe until morning.

When Deerslayer awoke, he saw that one of the canoes had drifted close to shore. To rescue it, he was forced to shoot an Indian, the first man he had ever killed.

Returning to the fort with his prizes, Deerslayer told the girls of their father's fate. It was agreed that they should delay any attempt at rescue until the arrival of Chingachgook, whom Deerslayer was to meet that night.

Under cover of darkness, the party went in the ark and met Chingachgook at the spot where the river joined the lake. Back in the cabin, Deerslayer explained that the Delaware had come to the lake to rescue his sweetheart, Wah-ta!-Wah, who had been stolen by the Iroquois. Suddenly they discovered that Hetty Hutter had disappeared. The girl, who was somewhat feebleminded, had cast off in one of the canoes with the intention of going to the Indian camp to rescue her father and Hurry Harry.

The next morning Wah-ta!-Wah came upon Hetty wandering in the forest. She took the white girl to the Iroquois camp. Because the Indians believed deranged persons were protected by the Great Spirit, she suffered no harm.

It was Deerslayer's idea to ransom the prisoners with some rich brocades and carved ivory he and Judith found in Tom Hutter's chest. Its contents had been known only to Hutter and the simpleminded Hetty, but in this emergency, Judith did not hesitate to open the coffer. Meanwhile a young Iroquois had rowed Hetty back to the cabin on a raft. Deerslayer told him that the party in the cabin would give two ivory chessmen for the release of the captives. He was unable to drive quite the bargain he had planned. In the end, four chessmen were exchanged for the men, who were returned that night.

Hetty brought a message from Wah-ta!-Wah. Chingachgook was to meet the Indian girl at a particular place on the shore when the evening star rose above the hemlocks that night. Hurry Harry and Tom Hutter were still determined to obtain scalps, and when night closed in they and Chinachgook reconnoitered the camp. To their disappointment, they found it deserted and the Indians camped on the beach, at the spot where Wah-ta!-Wah was to wait for Chinachgook.

While Hutter and Harry slept, the Delaware and Deerslayer attempted to keep the rendezvous. Unfortunately, the girl was under such close watch that it was impossible for her to leave the camp. The two men entered the camp and boldly rescued her from her captors. Deerslayer, who remained at their rear to cover their escape, was taken prisoner.

When Judith heard from Chingachgook of Deerslayer's capture, she rowed Hetty ashore to learn what had become of the woodsman. Once more Hetty walked unharmed among the superstitious savages. Deerslayer assured her there was nothing she could do to help, that he must await the Iroquois' pleasure. She left to return to Judith.

As the girls paddled about, trying to find the ark in the darkness, they heard the report of a gun. Torches on shore showed them that an Indian girl had been mortally wounded by a shot from the ark. Soon the lights went out. Paddling to the center of the lake, they tried to get what rest they might before morning came.

When daylight returned, Hutter headed the ark toward the cabin once more. Missing his daughters, he had concluded the cabin would be the most likely meeting place. Hutter and Harry were the first to leave the ark to go into the cabin. There the Iroquois, who had come aboard in rafts under cover of darkness, were waiting in ambush. Harry managed to escape into the water, where he was saved by Chingachgook. Judith and Hetty came to the ark in their canoe. After the savages had gone ashore, those on the ark went to the cabin. They found Hutter lying dead. That evening he was buried in the lake. Hurry Harry took advantage of the occasion to propose to Judith, but she refused him.

Shortly afterward they were surprised to see Deerslayer paddling toward the ark. He had been given temporary liberty in order to bargain with the fugitives. The Iroquois sent word that Chingachgook would be allowed to return to his own people if Wah-ta!-Wah and Judith became brides of Iroquois warriors. Hetty, they promised, would go unharmed because of her mental condition. Although Deerslayer's life was to be the penalty for refusal, these terms were declined.

Deerslayer did not have to return to his captors until the next day, and that evening he and Judith examined carefully the contents of her father's chest. To the girl's wonder, she found letters indicating that Hutter had not been her real father, but a former buccaneer whom her mother had married when her first husband deserted her. Saddened by this knowledge, Judith no longer wished to live at the lake. She intimated slyly to Deerslayer that she loved him, only to find he considered her above him in education and intelligence.

When Deerslayer returned to the Iroquois the next day, he was put to torture with hatchets. Hetty, Judith, and Wah-ta!-Wah came to the camp and attempted to intercede for him, but to no avail. Suddenly Chingachgook bounded in, and cut his friend's bonds. Deerslayer's release was the signal for the regiment from the nearest fort to attack, for Hurry Harry had gone to summon help during the night.

The Iroquois were routed. Hetty was mortally wounded during the battle. The next day she was buried in the lake beside her parents. Judith joined the soldiers returning to the fort. Deerslayer departed for the Delaware camp with Chingachgook and his bride.

Fifteen years later, Deerslayer, Chingachgook, and the latter's young son, Uncas, revisited the lake. Wah-ta!-Wah was long since dead, and, though the hunter inquired at the fort about Judith Hutter, he could find no one who knew her. Rumor was that a former member of the garrison, then living in England on his paternal estates, was influenced by a woman of rare beauty who was not his wife. The ark and the cabin in the lake were falling into decay.

Critical Evaluation

The Deerslayer is the fifth and last published of the Leatherstocking Tales; when the entire series was republished in 1850 it became the first. Having written two books about Leatherstocking in middle age and two picturing him in his declining years, Cooper turned back to young Natty Bumppo before he had gained fame among the Indians as Hawkeye or Long Rifle. In *The Deerslayer* Natty is the idealized "natural man."

Deerslayer is initiated into warfare when he first kills a fellow man—in self-defense—and then comforts his dying foe, who confers upon him the new name, Hawkeye, which honors him as a fighter. He also learns of some of the evil in the world through his acquaintance with Thomas Hutter and Hurry Harry who kill Indians—including women and children—for profit only. Cooper's idealization of Indian character is brought out partly through what he himself writes about Indians and partly through what Natty says of them.

The common theme which ties the Leatherstocking Tales together is the protagonist. Although he is known by different names in the various novels, he is identified throughout the series by his qualities as a brave and honorable hero. As a character, he is developed from youth to old age. He is a loner and an individualist and has moral and ethical concerns about the environment. He commands a strong integrity in dealing with other human beings, treating both friends and enemies with courtesy and respect. Ultimately, he follows his own simple moral scheme and demonstrates unwavering dedication to the principle of self-reliance. *The Deerslayer* is one of two Leatherstocking Tales (the other was *The Pathfinder*) which Mark Twain chose to mock amusingly but rather unjustly in his "Fenimore Cooper's Literary Offenses." The defects of plot, characterization, and style are easily seen by modern readers, but the romance is a far better book than Twain's comments would lead one to believe. Some critics have seen it as perhaps the best of the five tales. Cooper in his 1850 Preface said *The Pathfinder* and *The Deerslayer* were "probably the two most worthy an enlightened and cultivated reader's notice."

Bibliography

Baym, Nina. "The Women of Cooper's Leatherstocking Tales," in *American Quarterly.* XXIII (1971), pp. 696–709.

Bowden, Edwin T. *The Dungeon of the Heart: Human Isolation and the American Novel.* New York: Macmillan, 1961, pp. 20–23.

Davis, David B. "The Deerslayer, a Democratic Knight of the Wilderness," in *Twelve Original Essays on Great American Novels.* Edited by Charles Shapiro. Detroit: Wayne State University Press, 1958, pp. 1–22.

Dekker, George. *James Fenimore Cooper: The American Scott.* New York: Barnes & Noble, 1967, pp. 170–191.

Frederick, John T. "Cooper's Eloquent Indians," in *PMLA.* LXXXI (1956), pp. 1004–1017.

House, Kay S. *Cooper's Americans.* Columbus: Ohio State University Press, 1965, pp. 315–326.

Lawrence, D.H. "Fenimore Cooper's Leatherstocking Novels," in *Studies in Classic American Literature.* New York: Doubleday, 1955, pp. 55–73.

McAleer, John J. "Biblical Analogy in the Leatherstocking Tales," in *Nineteenth-Century Fiction.* XVII (1962), pp. 217–235.

McWilliams, John P., Jr. *Political Justice in a Republic: James Fenimore Cooper's America.* Berkeley: University of California Press, 1972, pp. 238–246, 276–291.

Mizener, Arthur. *Twelve Great American Novels.* New York: World, 1969, pp. 1–8.

Noble, David W. "Cooper, Leatherstocking and the Death of the American Adam," in *American Quarterly.* XVI (1964), pp. 419–431.

Paine, Gregory L. "The Indians of the Leatherstocking Tales," in *Studies in Philology.* XXIII (1926), pp. 16–39.

Pearce, Roy H. "The Leatherstocking Tales Re-examined," in *South Atlantic Quarterly.* XLVI (1947), pp. 524–536.

Pound, Louise. "The Dialect of Cooper's Leatherstocking," in *American Speech.* II (1927), pp. 479–488.

Ringe, Donald A. *James Fenimore Cooper.* New York: Twayne, 1962, pp. 84–90.

Sandy, Alan F., Jr. "The Voices of Cooper's *The Deerslayer*," in *Emerson Society Quarterly.* LX (1970), pp. 5–9.

Smith, Henry N. "Consciousness and Social Order: The Theme of Transcendence in the Leatherstocking Tales," in *Western American Literature.* V (1970), pp. 177–194.

VanDerBeets, Richard. "Cooper and the 'Semblance of Reality': A Source for

The Deerslayer," in *American Literature*. XLII (1971), pp. 544–546.

Vlach, John M.   "Fenimore Cooper's Leatherstocking as Folk Hero," in *New York Folklore Quarterly*. XXVII (1971), pp. 323–338.

Walker, Warren S.   *James Fenimore Cooper; An Introduction and Interpretation*. New York: Holt, Rinehart and Winston, 1962, pp. 32–36, 49–53.

————. *Plots and Characters in the Works of James Fenimore Cooper*. Hamden, Conn.: Shoe String Press, 1978.

Zoellner, Robert H.   "Conceptual Ambivalence in Cooper's Leatherstocking," in *American Literature*. XXXI (January, 1960), pp. 397–420.

THE LAST OF THE MOHICANS

Type of work: Novel
Author: James Fenimore Cooper (1789–1851)
Type of plot: Historical romance
Time of plot: 1757
Locale: Northern New York State
First published: 1826

This novel remains the most popular of Cooper's Leatherstocking tales, a classic story of the French and Indian War. The battles and exciting pursuits which constitute the book's plot are rounded out by interesting Indian lore and descriptions of the wilderness.

Principal Characters

Natty Bumppo, called **Hawkeye,** the hardy, noble frontier scout in his prime during the French and Indian Wars. Traveling with his Indian companions, Chingachgook and his son Uncas, in Upper New York, he befriends an English soldier, a Connecticut singing master, and their two female charges. When the travelers are ambushed by hostile Huron warriors, he leaves the party to get help, in turn ambushes their captors with the aid of Chingachgook and Uncas, and leads the group to Fort William Henry, besieged by the French. In the massacre of English that takes place after the garrison is forced to surrender, the girls are captured again by Indians. Hawkeye assists once more in the escape of one of the girls; however, a renegade Huron chief, Magua, claims the other as his reluctant wife. In the ensuing fighting the girl and Hawkeye's friend, the noble young Uncas, are killed. Hawkeye shoots Magua in return. In the end he and Chingachgook return sorrowfully to the wilderness.

Chingachgook (chĭn·găch'gook), a courageous, loyal Mohican Chief, Hawkeye's inseparable friend. An implacable enemy of the Hurons, he is decorated like a figure of Death. Left to protect the English Colonel after the massacre, he joins the final battle with intense ferocity, only to see his son die. His grief is relieved somewhat by Hawkeye's companionship.

Uncas (ŭn'kəs), Chingachgook's stalwart son, the last of the Mohicans. A young and handsome chieftain, he falls in love with Cora Munro while protecting her and proves invaluable in tracking her after she has been captured. When a Delaware chief awards her to Uncas' rival, Magua, he follows them and is killed avenging her murder.

Major Duncan Heyward, the young English officer in charge of escorting the Munro girls from Fort Edward to Fort William Henry. Brave, good-looking and clever, he falls in love with Alice Munro and eventually succeeds in rescuing her from the Hurons. He finally marries her with Colonel Munro's blessing.

Magua (mă'gū·ə), "Le Renard Subtil," the handsome, renegade Huron chief. Both cunning and malicious, he seeks to avenge himself on Colonel Munro by turning his spirited daughter Cora into a servile squaw. Twice thwarted by Hawkeye and his companions, he wins Cora by putting his case before Tamenund, a Delaware chieftain. This victory, however, is short-lived. Cora is killed by another Huron and Magua, after killing Uncas, is shot by Hawkeye.

Cora Munro, the Colonel's beautiful older daughter. She is independent, equal to every situation, and bears up well under the strain of a capture, a massacre, and the threat of marrying Magua. Her love for Uncas, however, remains unrequited when she is carried off by Magua and then stabbed.

Alice Munro, the Colonel's younger daughter, a pale, immature, but lovely half sister of Cora. Frail and clinging, she excites Heyward's protective feelings during their adventures, and he marries her.

Colonel Munro, the able but unsuccessful defender of Fort William Henry and the affectionate father of Cora and Alice. After surrendering to the French he is forced to watch helplessly the slaughter of the men, women, and children from the fort. His sorrow is doubled when Cora is killed.

David Gamut, a mild, ungainly singing

master who accompanies Heyward and the Munro girls. His schoolbook piety contrasts with Hawkeye's natural pantheism. A rather ineffective person, he is nevertheless useful to Hawkeye, for the Hurons believe him insane and let him pass without trouble.

The Marquis de Montcalm, the skilled, enterprising general who captures Fort William Henry and then allows the defeated English to be massacred by savage Hurons.

Tamenund (tă·mə·nŭnd′), the old Delaware chief who foolishly decides to give Cora to Magua.

Hard Heart, the Delaware chief whom Magua flatters to gain Cora.

General Webb, the incompetent commander of Fort Edward. He refused to aid Colonel Munro against the French.

A Huron Chief. He calls on Heyward, who is impersonating a witch doctor, to cure a relative, and he is duped when his captives are released.

The Story

Major Duncan Heyward had been ordered to escort Cora and Alice Munro from Fort Edward to Fort William Henry, where Colonel Munro, father of the girls, was commandant. In the party was also David Gamut, a Connecticut singing-master. On their way to Fort William Henry they did not follow the military road through the wilderness. Instead, they placed themselves in the hands of a renegade Huron known as Magua, who claimed that he could lead them to their destination by a shorter trail.

It was afternoon when the little party met the woodsman, Hawkeye, and his Delaware Mohican friends, Chingachgook and his son Uncas. To their dismay, they learned they were but an hour's distance from their starting point. Hawkeye quickly decided Magua had been planning to lead the party into a trap. His Mohican comrades tried to capture the renegade, but Magua took alarm and fled into the woods.

At Heyward's urging the hunter agreed to guide the travelers to their destination. The horses were tied and hidden among some rocks along a river. Hawkeye produced a hidden canoe from among some bushes and paddled the party to a rock at the foot of Glenn's Falls. There they prepared to spend the night in a cave.

That night a band of Iroquois led by Magua surprised the party. The fight might have been a victory for Hawkeye if their supply of powder and ball had held out. Unfortunately, their ammunition had been left in the canoe which, unnoticed until it was too late, was stolen by one of the enemy who had ventured to swim the swirling river. The only hope then lay in the possibility of future rescue, for the capture of the rock and the little group was a certainty. Hawkeye, Chingachgook, and Uncas escaped by floating downstream, leaving the girls and Major Heyward to meet the savages.

Captured, Cora and Alice were allowed to ride their horses, but Heyward and David were forced by their captors to walk. Although they took a road paralleling that to Fort William Henry, Heyward could not determine the destination the Indians had in mind. Drawing close to Magua, he tried to persuade him to betray his companions and deliver the party safely to Colonel Munro. The Huron agreed, if Cora would come to live with him among his tribe as his wife. When she refused, the enraged Magua had everyone bound. He was threatening Alice with his tomahawk when Hawkeye and his friends crept silently upon the band and attacked them. The Iroquois fled, leaving several of their dead behind them. The party, under David's guidance, sang a hymn of thanksgiving, and then pushed onward.

Toward evening they stopped at a deserted blockhouse to rest. Many years before it had been the scene of a fight between the Mohicans and the Mohawks, and a mound still showed where bodies lay buried. While Chingachgook watched, the others slept.

At moonrise they continued on their way. It was dawn when Hawkeye and his charges drew near Fort William Henry. They were intercepted and challenged by a sentinel of the French under Montcalm, who was about to lay siege to the fort. Heyward was able to answer him in French and they were allowed to proceed. Chingachgook killed and scalped the French sentinel. Then, through the fog which had risen from Lake George, and through the enemy forces which thronged the plain before the fort, Hawkeye led the way to the gates of the fort.

On the fifth day of the siege, Hawkeye, who had been sent to Fort Edward to seek help, was intercepted on his way back and a letter he carried was captured. Webb, the commander of Fort Edward, refused to come to the aid of Munro.

Under a flag of truce, Montcalm and Munro held a parley. Montcalm showed Webb's letter to Munro and offered honorable terms of surrender. Colonel Munro and his men would be allowed to keep their colors, their arms, and their baggage, if they would vacate the fort the next morning. Helpless to do otherwise, Munro accepted these terms. During one of the parleys Heyward was surprised to see Magua in the camp of the French. He had not been killed during the earlier skirmish.

The following day the vanquished English started their trip back to Fort Edward. Under the eyes of the French and their Indian allies they passed across the plain and entered the forest. Suddenly an Indian grabbed at a brightly-colored shawl worn by one of the women. Terrified, she wrapped her child in it. The Indian darted to her, grabbed the child from her arms, and dashed out its brains on the ground. Then under the eyes of Montcalm, who did nothing to discourage or to hold back his savage allies, a monstrous slaughter began.

Cora and Alice, entrusted to David Gamut's protection, were in the midst of the killing when Magua swooped down upon them and carried Alice away in his arms. Cora ran after her sister, and faithful David dogged her footsteps. They were soon atop a hill, from which they watched the slaughter of the garrison.

Three days later, Hawkeye, leading Heyward, Munro, and his Indian comrades, traced the girls and David with the help of Cora's veil which had caught on a tree. Heyward was particularly concerned for the safety of Alice. The day before the massacre he had been given her father's permission to court her.

Hawkeye, knowing that hostile Indians were on their trail, decided to save time by traveling across the lake in a canoe which he discovered in its hiding place nearby. He was certain Magua had taken the girls north, where he planned to rejoin his own people. Heading their canoe in that direction, the five men paddled all day, at one point having a close escape from some of their intercepting enemies. They spent that night in the woods and next day turned west in an effort to find Magua's trail.

After much searching Uncas found the trail of the captives. That evening, as the party drew near the Huron camp, they met David Gamut wandering about. He told his friends that the Indians thought him crazy because of his habit of breaking into song, and they allowed him to roam the woods unguarded. Alice, he said, was being held at the Huron camp. Cora had been entrusted to the care of a tribe of peaceful Delawares a short distance away.

Heyward, disguising his face with paint, went to the Huron camp in an attempt to rescue Alice, while the others set about helping Cora. Heyward was in the camp but a short time, posing as a French doctor, when Uncas was brought in, a captive. Called to treat an ill Indian woman, Heyward found Alice in the cave with his patient. He was able to rescue the girl by wrapping her in a blanket and declaring to the Hurons that she was his patient, whom he was carrying off to the woods for treatment. Hawkeye, attempting to rescue Uncas, entered the camp disguised in a medicine man's bearskin he had stolen. Uncas was cut loose and given the disguise, while the woodsman borrowed David Gamut's clothes. The singer was left to take Uncas' place while the others escaped, for Hawkeye was certain the Indians would not harm David because of his supposed mental condition. Uncas and Hawkeye fled to the Delaware camp.

The following day Magua and a group of his warriors visited the Delawares in search of their prisoners. The chief of that tribe decided the Hurons had a just claim to Cora because Magua wished to make her his wife.

Under inviolable Indian custom, the Huron was permitted to leave the camp unmolested, but Uncas warned him that in a few hours he and the Delawares would follow his trail.

During a bloody battle Magua fled with Cora to the top of a cliff. There, pursued by Uncas, he stabbed and killed the young Mohican, and was in his turn sent to his death by a bullet from Hawkeye's long rifle. Cora, too, was killed by a Huron. Amid deep mourning by the Delawares, she and Uncas were laid in their graves in the forest. Colonel Munro and Heyward conducted Alice to English territory and safety. Hawkeye returned to the forest. He had promised to remain with his sorrowing friend Chingachgook forever.

Critical Evaluation

The Last of the Mohicans is the second title published in what was to become a series of five entitled collectively The Leatherstocking Tales. When Cooper published the first of these "romances," as he called them to distinguish them from the somewhat more realistic contemporary novels, he had no plan for a series with a hero whose life would be shown from youth to old age and death. In *The Pioneers* (1823) Natty Bumppo or Leatherstocking is in his early seventies. Responding to a suggestion from his wife, Cooper went back, in *The Last of the Mohicans,* to Natty's early thirties when he was called Hawkeye. The great popularity of *The Last of the Mohicans* led Cooper then to move chronologically beyond *The Pioneers* and to picture in *The Prairie* (1827) the last of Natty's life when he was in his eighties, living as a trapper and finally dying on the Great Plains far from his early home. At the time, Cooper did not intend to revive Natty in further romances. One minor romance of the forest, *The Wept of Wish-ton-Wish* (1829), was followed by a stream of nautical novels, socio-political novels, and nonfictional works of social and political criticism extending until 1840, when Cooper finally answered the pleas of many literary critics and readers, and revived the hero whose death he had so touchingly portrayed at the end of *The Prairie.* In *The Pathfinder* (1840), Natty is called Pathfinder and the action shifts from land to the waters of Lake Ontario and back again. Pleased by the resounding praise he gained for having brought back his famed hero, Cooper now decided to write one final romance about him in which Natty would be younger than in any of the earlier books. In *The Deerslayer* (1841), Natty is in his early twenties and goes by the nickname Deerslayer. In 1850, Cooper brought out a new edition of all five Leatherstocking Tales arranged according to the order of events in Natty Bumppo's life: *The Deerslayer, The Last of the Mohicans, The Pathfinder, The Pioneers, The Prairie.* For this edition he wrote a Preface in which he remarked (prophetically, as it turned out): "If anything from the pen of the writer of these romances is at all to outlive himself, it is, unquestionably, the series of *The Leather-Stocking Tales.*" Despite the many complaints, particularly from Mark Twain and later critics, about

Cooper's style, plots, structure, characterization, and dialogue, the Leather-stocking Tales continue to be read, both in the United States and in many foreign countries, and they seem assured of a long life to come.

In Cooper's day, *The Last of the Mohicans* was the most popular of the five tales and it has continued to be so. It has been filmed by American and British companies, and the British version was serialized on American television. Structurally, the novel is superior to the other tales, with three major plot actions and a transitional though bloody interlude (the massacre after the surrender of Fort William Henry). Cooper's chase-type plot, with bad characters chasing good ones or good characters chasing bad ones, has since become standard in many action novels as well as motion pictures and television dramas.

Romantic love was conventional in the plots of novels in Cooper's day. His portrayal of Duncan Heyward and the Munro sisters, Cora and Alice—who carry most of the love interest in *The Last of the Mohicans*—shows no originality. They are all genteel characters and they speak in a stiff, formalized manner that seems unreal to present-day readers. Duncan is gentlemanly and the two "females" (as Cooper repeatedly calls them) are ladylike. Cooper contrasts Cora and Alice as he does the pairs of women who keep turning up in his books. Cora, the dark one, is passionate, independent, and unafraid, even defiant; blond Alice is timid and easily frightened into faints—she resembles the sentimentalized helpless girls of popular early nineteenth century fiction.

Cooper does much better with his forest characters. Hawkeye is talkative, boastful, superstitious, scornful of the book learning he does not possess, and inclined to be sententious at times. Yet he is brave, resourceful, and loyal to his two Indian friends. His French nickname, La Longue Carabine, attests to his shooting skill. He is religious but sometimes seems more pantheistic than Christian in any formal sense. Hawkeye's arguments with David Gamut oppose his generalized beliefs and Gamut's narrow Calvinism. With his dual background of white birth and early education by Moravian missionaries on the one side and his long experience of living with the Indians on the other, he is, as Balzac called him, "a moral hermaphrodite, a child of savagery and civilization."

Chingachgook and Uncas are idealized representatives of their race. As "good" Indians, they are dignified, taciturn, even noble despite their savage ways, which Hawkeye excuses as being simply their native "gifts." Uncas is lithe, strong, handsome, and he reminds the Munro sisters of a Greek statue. Magua is the "bad" Indian, sullen, fierce, cunning, and treacherous. His desire for Cora as his squaw is motivated by his wish to avenge a former whipping ordered by Colonel Munro.

In addition to the love theme, which provides for the marriage of Heyward and Alice, Cooper includes others. Related to the love theme is miscegenation, which Cooper has been accused of evading by killing off both Cora, who is part Negro, and Uncas, who had wanted to marry her. Another theme is suggested by the title of the romance. Chingachgook is left mourning for his son, the last of the Mohican sagamores. He grieves also because he foresees the eventual vanishing of his race. Both he and Hawkeye despair as they envision the end of their way of life in the great American wilderness, which will gradually disappear. Implicit in much of the novel is the opposition of savagism and civilization, with Hawkeye realizing that civilization will triumph.

It is easy to complain of Cooper's faulty style, his verbosity, his heavy-handed humor (with David Gamut), his improbable actions, the insufficient motivation of his characters, the inconsistency and inaccuracy of his dialogue, yet many readers willingly suspend their disbelief or modify their critical objections in order to enjoy the rush of action which makes up so much of *The Last of the Mohicans*. They sorrow over the deaths of Cora and Uncas, and their sympaties go out to Chingachgook and Hawkeye in the loss of what had meant so much in their lives. Also, especially in a time when ecologists are fighting to preserve some of the natural beauty of our country, they enjoy Cooper's relishing of that beauty in his descriptions of the northeastern wilderness as it was in the eighteenth century.

Bibliography

Baym, Nina. "The Women of Cooper's Leatherstocking Tales," in *American Quarterly*. XXIII (1971), pp. 696–709.

Butler, M.D. "Narrative Structure and Historical Process in *The Last of the Mohicans*," in *American Literature*. XLVIII (May, 1976), pp. 117–139.

Darnell, Donald. "Uncas as Hero: The Ubi Sunt Formula in *The Last of the Mohicans*," in *American Literature*. XXXVII (November, 1965), pp. 259–266.

Fiedler, Leslie A. *Love and Death in the American Novel*. New York: Criterion, 1960, pp. 197–206.

Frederick, John T. "Cooper's Eloquent Indians," in *PMLA*. LXXXI (1956), pp. 1004–1017.

French, David P. "James Fenimore Cooper and Fort William Henry," in *American Literature*. XXXII (March, 1960), pp. 28–38.

Haberly, D.T. "Women and Indians: *The Last of the Mohicans* and the Captivity Traditions," in *American Quarterly*. XXVIII (Fall, 1976), pp. 431–443.

House, Kay S. *Cooper's Americans*. Columbus: Ohio State University Press, 1965, pp. 277–293.

McAleer, John J. "Biblical Analogy in the Leatherstocking Tales," in *Nineteenth-Century Fiction*. XVII (1962), pp. 217–235.

McWilliams, John P., Jr.   *Political Justice in a Republic: James Fenimore Cooper's America.* Berkeley: University of California Press, 1972, pp. 238–246, 287–291.

Martin, Terence.   "From the Ruins of History: *The Last of the Mohicans*," in *Novel: A Forum on Fiction.* II (1969), pp. 221–229.

Maxwell, Desmond E.S.   *American Fiction: The Intellectual Background.* New York: Columbia University Press, 1963, pp. 97–140.

Noble, David W.   "Cooper, Leatherstocking and the Death of the American Adam," in *American Quarterly.* XVI (1964), pp. 419–431.

Paine, Gregory L.   "The Indians of the Leatherstocking Tales," in *Studies in Philology.* XXIII (1926), pp. 16–39.

Pearce, Roy H.   "The Leatherstocking Tales Re-examined," in *South Atlantic Quarterly.* XLVI (1947), pp. 524–536.

Philbrick, Thomas.   "*The Last of the Mohicans* and the Sounds of Discord," in *American Literature.* XLIII (1971), pp. 25–41.

Pound, Louise.   "The Dialect of Cooper's Leatherstocking," in *American Speech.* II (1927), pp. 479–488.

Smith, Henry N.   "Consciousness and Social Order: The Theme of Transcendence in the Leatherstocking Tales," in *Western American Literature.* V (1970), pp. 177–194.

Vlach, John M.   "Fenimore Cooper's Leatherstocking as Folk Hero," in *New York Folklore Quarterly.* XXVII (1971), pp. 323–338.

Walker, Warren S.   *James Fenimore Cooper; An Introduction and Interpretation.* New York: Holt, Rinehart and Winston, 1962, pp. 53–57, 105–106.

————.   *Plots and Characters in the Works of James Fenimore Cooper.* Hamden, Conn.: Shoe String Press, 1978.

Zoellner, Robert H.   "Conceptual Ambivalence in Cooper's Leatherstocking," in *American Literature.* XXXI (January, 1960), pp. 397–420.

THE PATHFINDER

Type of work: Novel
Author: James Fenimore Cooper (1789–1851)
Type of plot: Historical romance
Time of plot: 1756
Locale: Lake Ontario and surrounding territory
First published: 1840

The Pathfinder, *the third in the* Leatherstocking *series, portrays wilderness scout Natty Bumppo at the height of his powers; in this novel, Natty falls in love for the first and only time, but relinquishes his claim in deference to the man his beloved really loves. Typical of Cooper's novels,* The Pathfinder *freely blends fact and fiction; descriptions of places, such as the British fort at Oswego, are often historical, but the plotline is pure fiction.*

Principal Characters

Thomas Dunham, a sergeant of the Fort Oswego garrison in the western New York territory during the French and Indian Wars. He has his daughter Mabel brought to the fort in order to promote a marriage between her and his friend Natty Bumppo, the wilderness scout called Pathfinder by the English. On a tour of duty among the Thousand Islands his party captures and sinks three French ships, but when they return to an island blockhouse his men are ambushed by Iroquois Indians and he is mortally wounded. Attended by his daughter, he dies blessing her and Jasper Western, whom he believes to be Pathfinder.

Mabel Dunham, his young, warm, frank, and pretty daughter. After Pathfinder has saved the party with which she travels from hostile Indians, she comes to respect Pathfinder's courage and skill in the woods, but the man she truly loves is his friend, Jasper Western. At Fort Oswego she finds herself courted by Jasper, Pathfinder, and Davy Muir, each of whom accompanies her father on a tour of duty. During an Indian ambush she is saved by the warnings of an In-

dian girl and the resolute defense of Pathfinder and her uncle. In the end Pathfinder relinquishes her to Jasper, whom she marries.

Charles Cap, Mabel Dunham's crusty uncle, a hardy fellow who accompanies his niece to Fort Oswego and later goes with Sergeant Dunham on his tour of duty to relieve a garrison in the Thousand Islands. A seagoing sailor, he suspects and derides Jasper Western, a fresh-water sailor, but learns to respect the young seaman when Jasper saves the cutter "Scud" after Cap had almost wrecked it during a storm. After barely escaping an Indian ambush, he ably assists Pathfinder in the defense of a beleaguered blockhouse until help arrives. He sees his niece married to Jasper and returns to the sea.

Natty Bumppo, called **Pathfinder,** the frontier scout in his prime. A man of great courage, resourcefulness, and honesty, he falls in love for the only time in his life, but in return he receives little more than Mabel Dunham's esteem. After protecting her in many perils, Pathfinder learns of Jasper Western's and

Mabel's mutual love and defers to his friend. His personal integrity remains pure as he moves on with his Indian friend, of many years, the Mohican chief Chingachgook.

Jasper Western, called "Eau-douce" because he is a fresh-water sailor, Pathfinder's younger companion and the more successful rival for Mabel Dunham's hand. A skilled and honorable man, he is nevertheless under suspicion of being a French spy. When circumstances seem to prove his guilt, his command of a cutter is temporarily taken away from him. After he has aided in relieving the besieged blockhouse, the real spy is revealed. The discovery clears his name, and Pathfinder's relinquishment of Mabel leaves him free to marry his love.

Lieutenant Davy Muir, the glib quartermaster at Fort Oswego, a thrice-wed, middle-aged suitor of Mabel Dunham. Resentful of his subordinate position, he secretly spies for the French, puts the blame for his treachery on Jasper Western, and survives an Indian ambush. His successes are cut short when Arrowhead, a resentful Tuscarora Indian, mortally stabs him.

Arrowhead, the bold, ambitious Tuscarora chief who tries to lead Mabel and her uncle into an ambush; he falls in love with the white girl. He is later caught by the party aboard the cutter but escapes to lead the two ambushes that almost prove fatal to Sergeant Dunham's party. Thinking that Muir has betrayed him, he kills the spy and is killed by Chingachgook in turn.

Dew-of-June, the submissive, gentle wife of Arrowhead. Although she saves Mabel Dunham by warning her of danger from hostile Indians and whites, she remains loyal to her husband. Mourning his death, she goes to live with Mabel, but dies soon afterward.

Chingachgook, whose name means "the Great Serpent," a Mohican chief and Pathfinder's loyal friend. A lifelong foe of the Iroquois, he aids his friend Pathfinder in many encounters with hostile Indians and the French.

Major Duncan, of Lundie, the generous, considerate commanding officer of Fort Oswego. Warned by an anonymous letter that Jasper Western is a spy for the French, he is forced to advise Sergeant Dunham to watch the young man carefully.

Captain Sanglier, the audacious French leader of the Iroquois. Captured after the siege of the blockhouse, he contemptuously reveals that Lieutenant Muir, not Jasper Western, has spied for the French.

Corporal McNab, the stubborn soldier who hesitates to believe Mabel Dunham's warning of an impending Indian ambush. He is shot during the skirmishing.

Jenny McNab, his wife. She is killed while trying to pull her husband into the blockhouse when the Indians attack.

The Story

Mabel Dunham and Charles Cap, her seaman uncle, were on their way to the home of her father, Sergeant Dunham. They were accompanied by Arrowhead, a Tuscarora Indian, and his wife, Dew-of-June. When they reached the Oswego River, they were met by Jasper Western and Natty Bumppo, the wilderness scout known as Pathfinder among the English and as Hawkeye among the Mohican Indians. Pathfinder led the party down the Oswego on the first step of the journey under his guidance. Chingachgook, Pathfinder's Mohican friend, warned the party of the presence of hostile Indians in the neighborhood. They hid from the Indians and had a narrow escape when they were discovered. Arrowhead and Dew-of-June disappeared; it was feared they had been taken captives. Chingachgook was captured by the Iroquois but escaped. On the lookout for more hostile war parties, they continued their journey to the fort, where Mabel was joyfully greeted by her father after her dangerous trip through the wilderness.

The sergeant tried to promote a feeling of love between Mabel and Pathfinder—his real purpose in bringing Mabel to the frontier. When Major Duncan, commander of the post, proposed Lieutenant Davy Muir as a possible mate for Mabel, the sergeant informed the major that Mabel was already betrothed to Pathfinder. Muir came to the major and learned that he had been refused, but he did not give up hope. Actually Mabel and Jasper were in love with each other.

A passage of arms was proposed to test the shooting ability of the men at the post. Jasper scored a bull's-eye. Muir shot from a strange position and it was believed by all that he had missed, but he said he had hit Jasper's bullet. Pathfinder used Jasper's rifle and also struck the bullet in the bull's-eye. The next test of marksmanship was to drive a nail into a tree with a bullet. Jasper almost drove the nail into the tree; Pathfinder did. The next test was shooting at a potato tossed into the air. Muir failed, but Jasper hit the potato in the center. A silken calash was the prize, and Jasper wanted it greatly as a present for Mabel. When he mentioned the desire to Pathfinder, the scout was able only to cut the skin of the potato. After he had lost the match, Pathfinder could not resist killing two gulls with one bullet. Then Mabel knew how Jasper had won the calash. In appreciation she gave Pathfinder a silver brooch.

An expedition was sent to one of the Thousand Islands to relieve the garrison there. The party was to leave in the *Scud*, a boat captured by Jasper. Before departing, however, Major Duncan had received a letter which caused him to suspect that Jasper was a French spy. Pathfinder refused to believe the charge against his friend, but when the *Scud* sailed under the command of Jasper he was kept under strict surveillance by Sergeant Dunham and Charles Cap. On the way, the *Scud* overtook Arrowhead and his wife and they were taken aboard. When Pathfinder began to question the Tuscarora, Arrowhead escaped in a canoe the *Scud* was towing astern. Becoming suspicious, Sergeant Dunham removed Jasper from his command and sent him below, and Charles Cap took over the management of the boat. But Cap, being a salt-water sailor, was unfamiliar with freshwater navigation. When a storm came up, it was necessary to call upon Jasper to save the ship. The *Scud* escaped from *Le Montcalm*, a French ship, and Jasper brought the *Scud* safely to port.

Pathfinder had really fallen in love with Mabel, but when he proposed to her she refused him. Muir had not given up his own suit. He admitted to Mabel that he had had three previous wives.

Sergeant Dunham decided to take some of his men and harass a French supply boat. Starting out with his detachment, he left six men at the post, Muir among them, with orders to look after the women. Soon after her father's departure, Mabel went for a walk and met Dew-of-June, who warned her of danger from Indians led by white men. Muir was unmoved by this intelligence when Mabel informed him. Mabel then went to MacNab, a corporal, and told her story, but he treated Dew-of-June's warning lightly. While they talked, a rifle cracked in the nearby forest and MacNab fell dead at her feet. Mabel ran to the blockhouse. The attacking party was composed of twenty Indians led by the Tuscarora renegade, Arrowhead. Those who escaped the ambush were Mabel, Cap, and Muir, all of whom survived through the help of Dew-of-June. Cap and Muir were captured a little later. Mabel discovered Chingachgook, who had been spying about the fort. She acquainted him with all the details of the situation.

Pathfinder arrived secretly at the blockhouse. He had not been fooled by dead bodies of the massacred people that had been placed in lifelike manner along the river bank by the Indians. Then the relief party of soldiers under Sergeant Dunham was ambushed, but the sergeant, seriously wounded, managed to reach the blockhouse. Cap escaped from the Indians and also gained the protection of the blockhouse. The small group then fought off the Indians during the night. Jasper arrived with men in time to relieve the situation. But Muir ordered Jasper bound, basing his action on the suspicion that Jasper was a spy. Arrowhead stabbed Muir and disappeared into the bushes, hotly pursued by Chingachgook, who later killed him. Muir died and Captain Sanglier, the white leader of the Indians, admitted that Muir had been the French spy, not Jasper. On his deathbed Sergeant Dunham, thinking Jasper to be Pathfinder, took Jasper's hand, placed it in that of Mabel, and gave the two his blessing. He died before the surprised witnesses could correct his error. Deciding that Mabel really loved Jasper, Pathfinder relinquished his claim on her. Pathfinder disappeared into the wilderness with his Indian friend Chingachgook, and was seen no more by Jasper and Mabel. From time to time Indian messengers came to the settlement with gifts of furs for Mrs. Jasper Western, but no name ever accompanied these gifts.

Critical Evaluation

Of the five novels in James Fenimore Cooper's Leatherstocking series, *The Pathfinder* was the fourth to be written; but in the chronology of the hero Natty Bumppo's life it is the third tale, since it finds Natty resurrected and rejuvenated following his old age and death in *The Prairie,* written thirteen years earlier. *The Pathfinder* is distinguished by being the first and only Leatherstocking story in which the celibate and thoroughly independent frontier scout falls in love with a woman.

Cooper was an essentially romantic writer, and although as a thorough and competent historian he was easily able to back up his fictional narrative with factual information, his primary purpose was to stir the reader's imagination through idealized portraits of frontier life. Cooper's most lasting appeal lies in his gift for storytelling. Working with even the simplest and least original plot, he was able to capture and sustain reader interest by employing ambushes and chases, hairbreadth escapes, and harrowing violence, as well as sentiment, chivalry, and romance. Linked inextricably with such a colorful and adventure-filled storyline is the familiar Cooper setting; the primal beauty of forest and sea, the grandeur and rich abundance of unspoiled nature, provide an appropriate backdrop for courageous and manly deeds. The author was intimately familiar with the area around the mouth of the Oswego River, since he had spent the winter of 1808 there as a midshipman in the American Navy, and both his knowledge and love of the land are apparent in the descriptive passages of *The Pathfinder*.

Unfortunately, however, Cooper's talents as a storyteller and descriptive writer have obscured his merits as a serious artist whose works illustrate important social and religious concerns. One recurrent theme, for example, which comes through strongly in *The Pathfinder,* is the idea that to achieve happiness and self-fulfillment, a man must live according to his "gifts," or talents, be they great or limited. Cooper believed strongly in democracy, but in a conservative way. He felt that the American continent was the perfect environment in which men could develop fresh and individualistic forms of society, but he feared that people in the frontier were moving too close to anarchy. The key to success was every individual's recognition and willing acceptance of his place within the scheme of things—a place which was determined not by heredity but by natural talent, but which nevertheless still located each person in a "class." Thus, much of the interest in *The Pathfinder* stems from the question of Mabel Dunham's marriage, since it involves discoveries about talent and appropriate courses of action on the part not only of Mabel, but of Natty, Lieutenant Muir, Jasper Western, and Sergeant Dunham.

Besides his important awareness about his true talents and calling and proper relationship to society, Natty Bumppo in *The Pathfinder* has also reached a high level of consciousness in the religious area which reflects another crucial Cooper theme. Through his self-sufficient hero, the author conveys his conviction, which grew stronger as he grew older, that Divine Providence was involved in human destiny. Natty's is a natural piety, a faith taught him by nature, which he calls "the temple of the Lord;" as he explains simply, "It is not easy to dwell always in the presence of God, and not feel the power of his goodness."

Bibliography

Baym, Nina. "The Women of Cooper's Leatherstocking Tales," in *American Quarterly*. XXIII (1971), pp. 696–709.

Bush, Sargent, Jr. "Charles Cap of *The Pathfinder*: A Foil to Cooper's Views on the American Character in the 1840's," in *Nineteenth-Century Fiction*. XX (December, 1965), pp. 267–273.

Dekker, George. *James Fenimore Cooper: The American Scott*. New York: Barnes & Noble, 1967, pp. 161–169.

Frederick, John T. "Cooper's Eloquent Indians," in *PMLA*. LXXXI (1956), pp. 1004–1017.

House, Kay S. *Cooper's Americans*. Columbus: Ohio State University Press, 1965, pp. 306–315.

McAleer, John J. "Biblical Analogy in the Leatherstocking Tales," in *Nineteenth-Century Fiction*. XVII (1962), pp. 217–235.

McWilliams, John P., Jr. *Political Justice in a Republic: James Fenimore Cooper's America*. Berkeley: University of California Press, 1972, pp. 238–246, 261, 288–291.

Noble, David W. "Cooper, Leatherstocking and the Death of the American Adam," in *American Quarterly*. XVI (1964), pp. 419–431.

Paine, Gregory L. "The Indians of the Leatherstocking Tales," in *Studies in Philology*. XXIII (1926), pp. 16–39.

Pearce, Roy H. "The Leatherstocking Tales Re-examined," in *South Atlantic Quarterly*. XLVI (1947), pp. 524–536.

Pound, Louise. "The Dialect of Cooper's Leatherstocking," in *American Speech*. II (1927), pp. 479–488.

Smith, Henry N. "Consciousness and Social Order: The Theme of Transcendence in the Leatherstocking Tales," in *Western American Literature*. V (1970), pp. 177–194.

Vlach, John M. "Fenimore Cooper's Leatherstocking as Folk Hero," in *New York Folklore Quarterly*. XXVII (1971), pp. 323–338.

Walker, Warren S. *James Fenimore Cooper; An Introduction and Interpretation*. New York: Holt, Rinehart and Winston, 1962, pp. 41–44, 57–58.

————. *Plots and Characters in the Works of James Fenimore Cooper*. Hamden, Conn.: Shoe String Press, 1978.

Zoellner, Robert H. "Conceptual Ambivalence in Cooper's Leatherstocking," in *American Literature*. XXXI (January, 1960), pp. 397–420.

THE PIONEERS

Type of work: Novel
Author: James Fenimore Cooper (1789–1851)
Type of plot: Historical romance
Time of plot: 1793
Locale: New York State
First published: 1823

The Pioneers, the first of the Leatherstocking Tales, is a romantic story of life in Upstate New York ten years after the Revolutionary War. The novel is filled with scenes of hunting and trapping life, and the description of Templeton is based upon the author's memories of his boyhood home of Cooperstown. The portrayal of Natty Bumppo and Indian John point to the tragedy of frontiersmen and Indians in a rapidly disappearing West.

Principal Characters

Judge Marmaduke Temple, the principal citizen and landholder of Templeton, a settlement in upstate New York. He is at once shrewd and honorable, benevolent and just. While trying to kill a deer he shoots an unfamiliar, educated young hunter named Oliver Edwards, has his wound dressed, and offers him a position as a secretary. When the young man's friend, the old woodsman and hunter called Leatherstocking, is arrested for threatening to shoot an officer, the Judge sentences and fines the old man but pays the fine himself. Later he learns that Edwards is in reality Oliver Edward Effingham, the son of an old friend who had entrusted him with personal effects and family funds years before. The Judge restores the property and the money to Edwards. Meanwhile Edwards and Elizabeth Temple have fallen in love, and the Judge gives the young couple his blessing.

Elizabeth Temple, the Judge's spirited, pretty daughter. Although she respects Oliver Edwards' abilities, she maintains a feminine independence. Grateful to Leatherstocking for saving her life when a savage panther attacks her, she assists in his escape from jail after the old man has been arrested for resisting an officer. Her romance with her father's secretary develops after the young man and Leatherstocking save her from a forest fire. When Edwards' true identity is revealed and he declares his love, she readily marries him.

Natty Bumppo, called **Leatherstocking,** a hardy, simple, upright woodsman in his seventy-first year. Although disgusted by wanton killing of game, he defends his right to kill game for food. He shoots a deer out of season and is arrested for resisting the magistrate who tries to search his cabin. Sentenced to jail for a month, he escapes with the help of Oliver Edwards and Elizabeth Temple. Twice he is Elizabeth's rescuer, once from a panther and again from fire. After his jail term is suspended, stricken by the death of his Indian friend and companion, he moves on to a less civilized territory.

Oliver Edwards, later revealed as **Oliver Edward Effingham,** the impoverished young hunter who lives with Leatherstocking in a cabin near Templeton.

Believing that Judge Temple has appropriated his inheritance, he is planning to recover it when he accepts the position of secretary to the Judge. In the meantime he falls in love with Elizabeth Temple. Having quit his post when Leatherstocking is arrested and jailed, he helps the old man to escape, aids Elizabeth during the fire, and finally reveals his true identity. Judge Temple immediately restores his inheritance and the young man and Elizabeth are married.

Indian John, an old Mohican chief called **Chingachgook** in his younger days. Lonely, aged, and grieving for the old free life of the wilderness, he rejects his Moravian Christianizing during a raging forest fire and appears in his ceremonial dress. He dies, attended by Leatherstocking, Elizabeth Temple, and Oliver Edwards, in a cave where they have taken refuge from the fire.

Hiram Doolittle, the cowardly, troublemaking, greedy magistrate who informs on Leatherstocking for breaking the hunting law, gets a search warrant, and is roughly handled by the old hunter when he tries to force his way into Leatherstocking's cabin.

Richard Jones, the meddlesome, pompous sheriff, a frontier fop who indulges in the irresponsible killing of game, spreads rumors that Leatherstocking is working a secret mine, and leads a raggle-taggle posse to recapture the old woodsman after his escape from jail.

Major Edward Effingham, the senile grandfather of the young man who calls himself Oliver Edwards. Years before the Major and Judge Temple had been close friends, and Effingham had entrusted some valuable property and a

sum of money to the Judge's keeping. Leatherstocking has been caring for him. His identity revealed after the fire, the old man is taken to Judge Temple's home and nursed tenderly until his death.

Mr. Grant, a sincere, eclectic minister adept at appealing to the heterogeneous frontier faiths.

Louisa Grant, his timid daughter, Elizabeth's companion. She is inept when faced with danger.

Benjamin Penguillan, called **Ben Pump,** an ex-sailor and Judge Temple's salty major-domo. Out of sympathy he shares Leatherstocking's humiliation in the stocks and thrashes Magistrate Doolittle.

Elnathan Todd, the gigantic village doctor who dresses Oliver Edwards' wound; he is an awkward quack.

Monsieur le Quoi (mə·syœ′ lə kwȧ′), the village storekeeper, a friend of Judge Temple.

Major Hartmann, a German farmer, also a friend of Judge Temple.

Billy Kirby, a good-natured woodcutter and strong man who sympathizes with Leatherstocking but takes the side of the law.

Jotham Riddel, Magistrate Doolittle's good-for-nothing deputy.

Remarkable Pettibone, Judge Temple's housekeeper.

Squire Lippet, Leatherstocking's lawyer at the time of the old hunter's trial.

Mr. Van der School, the thick-witted prosecutor.

Agamemnon, Judge Temple's silly Negro servant.

The Story

On a cold December day in 1793, Judge Temple and his daughter Elizabeth were traveling by sleigh through a snow-covered tract of wilderness near the settlement of Templeton. Elizabeth, who had been away from her home attending a female seminary, was now returning to preside over her father's household in the community in which he had been a pioneer settler after the Revolutionary War. Hearing the baying of hounds, the judge decided that Leatherstocking, an old hunter, had started game in the hills, and he ordered his coachman to stop the sleigh so he could have a shot at the deer if it came in his direction. A few minutes later, as a great buck leaped into the road, the judge fired both barrels of his fowling piece at the animal, but apparently without effect. Then a third report and a fourth were heard, and the buck dropped dead in a snowbank.

At the same time Natty Bumppo, the old hunter, and a young companion appeared from the woodland. The judge insisted that he had shot the buck, but Leatherstocking, by accounting for all the shots fired, proved the judge could not have killed the animal. The argument ended when the young stranger revealed that he had been wounded by one of the shots fired by the judge. Elizabeth and her father then insisted that he accompany them into the village in their sleigh, so he could have his wound dressed as soon as possible.

The young man got into the sleigh with obvious reluctance and said little during the drive. In a short time the party arrived at the Temple mansion, where his wound was treated. In answer to the judge's questions, he gave his name as Oliver Edwards. His manner remained distant and reserved. After he had departed, a servant in the Temple home reported that Edwards had appeared three weeks before in the company of old Leatherstocking and that he lived in a nearby cabin with the hunter and an Indian known as Indian John.

Judge Temple, wishing to make amends for having accidentally wounded Edwards, offered him a position as his secretary. When Elizabeth added her own entreaties to those of her father, Edwards finally accepted the judge's offer, with the understanding that he would be free to terminate his employment at any time. For a while he attended faithfully and earnestly to his duties in Judge Temple's mansion during the day, but his nights he spent in Leatherstocking's cabin. So much secrecy surrounded his comings and goings, and the reserve of Leatherstocking and his Indian friend, that Richard Jones, the sheriff and a kinsman of the judge, became suspicious. Among other things, he wondered why Natty always kept his cabin closed and never allowed anyone except the Indian and Edwards to enter it. Jones and some others decided that Natty had discovered a mine and was working it. Jones also suspected that Edwards was an Indian halfbreed, his father a Delaware chief.

Hiram Doolittle, the local magistrate, prowled around the shack and set free the dogs guarding it. In the meantime Elizabeth and Louisa Grant, the minister's daughter, went walking in the woods. There they were attacked by a savage panther and were saved only by the timely arrival of Leatherstocking, who shot the animal. But Natty had also shot a deer, in defiance of Judge Temple's strict game laws. With the charge that the old hunter had killed a deer out of season as his pretext, Doolittle persuaded Judge Temple to sign a warrant so that the magistrate could gain entrance to the cabin and search it. Jones was more convinced than ever that Leatherstocking was secretly smelting ore he had mined.

But when Doolittle went to the cabin, Leatherstocking, rifle in hand, refused him entrance. Then the magistrate attempted to force his way over the threshold, but the old hunter seized him and threw him twenty feet down an embankment. As the result of his treatment of an officer, Leatherstocking was arrested. Found guilty, he was given a month's jail sentence, a fine, and placed in the stocks for a few hours. When Elizabeth went to see what assistance she could give the humiliated old woodsman, she learned he was planning to escape. Edwards, who had given up his position with the judge, was planning to flee with his aged friend——he had provided a cart in which to carry the old hunter to safety. Elizabeth promised to meet Leatherstocking the following day on the top of a nearby mountain and to bring with her a can of gunpowder he needed.

The next day Elizabeth and her friend Louisa started out on their expedition to meet Leatherstocking. On the way Louisa changed her mind and turned back, declaring that she dared not walk unprotected through the woods where they had lately been menaced by a panther. Elizabeth went on alone until she came to a clearing in which she found old Indian John, now dressed in the war costume and feathers of a great Mohican chief. When she stopped to speak to the Indian, she suddenly became aware of dense clouds of smoke drifting across the clearing and discovered that the whole mountainside was ablaze. At that moment Edwards appeared, followed by Leatherstocking, who led them to a cave in the side of the mountain. There the old Indian died of exhaustion, and Elizabeth learned that he had been in earlier days Chingachgook, a great and noble warrior of the Mohican tribe.

When danger of the fire had passed, Edwards conducted Elizabeth down the mountainside until she was within hearing of a party of men who were looking for her. Before they parted, Edwards promised he would soon reveal his true identity.

The next day the sheriff led a posse up the mountain in search of Leatherstocking and those who had aided him in his escape from jail. Leatherstocking was again prepared to defend with his rifle the cave to which he had taken Elizabeth the day before, but Edwards declared that the time had now come to let the truth be known. He and Natty brought from the depths of the cave an old man seated in a chair. The stranger's face was grave and dignified, but his vacant eyes showed that his mind was gone. Edwards announced that the old man was really the owner of the property on which they stood. Judge Temple interrupted with a shout of surprise and greeted the old man as Major Effingham.

The young man told his story. His name, he said, was Edward Oliver Effingham, and he was the grandson of the old man who sat before them. His own father had been, before the Revolutionary War, a close friend of Judge Temple.

They had gone into business together, but the outbreak of the war found them on opposite sides during the struggle. Judge Temple had some money entrusted to him by his friend, money which actually belonged to his friend's father, but when he received no reply to letters he wrote to the Effinghams he at last decided that all the family had been lost in a shipwreck off Nova Scotia. The money he had invested in his own enterprises.

The judge had never met Major Effingham; he would not have recognized him if he had seen the helpless old man who had for years been hidden in the cabin on the outskirts of Templeton. During those years he was nursed faithfully by Leatherstocking and his Indian friend—by Leatherstocking because he had served with the major on the frontier years before, by Indian John because the major was an adopted member of the Mohican tribe.

Judge Temple ordered that the old man be carried to the Temple mansion at once, where he would receive the best of care. Old Major Effingham thought himself back home once more, and his eyes gleamed with joy. He died, happy and well cared for, soon afterward.

Edward Effingham also explained his belief that Judge Temple had stolen his father's property and the money left in trust years before. In his resentment he had come to Templeton to assist his grandfather and regain in some manner the property which he believed Judge Temple had unrightfully possessed. Now the judge was happy to return that part of the property which belonged to the Effinghams, and there was a reconciliation between the two men. As it turned out, however, the property stayed in the family, for Elizabeth and Edward Effingham were married within a short time.

Eizabeth and Edward Effingham wanted to build a new cabin for Leatherstocking, but the old hunter refused their offer. He intended to go off into the woods to hunt and trap in the free wilderness until he died. Settlements and towns were not for him. He would not listen to their pleas but set out soon afterward on his long journey, pausing only long enough to view the stone tablet on Indian John's grave, a monument Edward Effingham had erected. Then he trudged off toward the woods, his long rifle over his shoulder. Elizabeth and her husband watched him go. Tears were in their eyes as they waved a last farewell to the old hunter just before he disappeared into the forest.

Critical Evaluation

When the whole Leatherstocking series was published together in 1850, *The Pioneers,* originally the first, became the fourth title. In writing *The Pioneers,* Cooper did not plan it as the first of a series with a continuing hero. Thus, Natty Bumppo—with his skinny face, scraggy neck, enormous mouth, and single yellowed tusk—contrasts sharply with the romantic character that Leatherstocking was to become in Cooper's later portrayals of him as Hawkeye, Pathfinder, and Deerslayer. Yet his skill with a rifle, his knowledge of and love for the wilderness, his loyalty to Indian John Mohegan, and his independence in speaking his mind and asserting what he believes to be his rights all foreshadow the heroic frontiersman who was to reappear in the later tales.

The Pioneers is only in part a romance of the forest. It is largely a novel of manners in which Cooper contrasts the wilderness life of Leatherstocking and old Indian John with the village life of Templeton. Cooper is sympathetic toward the aging Leatherstocking (he is over seventy), who resents having to submit to a law which prohibits his killing a deer whenever he needs one. But the natural law of survival has come into conflict with the village social law which is necessary as increasing numbers of settlers fill up the land. Leatherstocking represents a way of life that is passing. The frontiersman prepares the way for settlement of wilderness territory. He then must bow to social laws or move farther into the wilderness in order to keep the natural freedom he treasures. If he chooses this latter course, he is only continuing a process of which he has already been a part. That Cooper did not disapprove of the eventual settlement, moving ever westward, of the land, the final sentence of *The Pioneers* makes clear: "He had gone far towards the setting sun,—the foremost in that band of Pioneers, who are opening the way for the march of our nation across the continent."

Bibliography

Baym, Nina. "The Women of Cooper's Leatherstocking Tales," in *American Quarterly.* XXIII (1971), pp. 696–709.

Bercovitch, Sacvan. "Huckleberry Bumppo: A Comparison of *Tom Sawyer* and *The Pioneers*," in *Mark Twain Journal.* XIV (Summer, 1968), pp. 1–4.

Dekker, George. *James Fenimore Cooper: The American Scott.* New York: Barnes & Noble, 1967, pp. 43–63.

Frederick, John T. "Cooper's Eloquent Indians," in *PMLA.* LXXXI (1956), pp. 1004–1017.

House, Kay S. *Cooper's Americans.* Columbus: Ohio State University Press, 1965, pp. 303–317.

————. "*The Pioneers*," in *The American Novel from James Fenimore Cooper to William Faulkner.* Edited by Wallace Stegner. New York: Basic Books, 1965.

Kasson, J.S. "Templeton Revisited: Social Criticism in *The Pioneers* and *Home as Found*," in *Studies in the Novel.* IX (Spring, 1977), pp. 54–64.

Kehler, J.R. "Architectural Dialecticism in Cooper's *The Pioneers*," in *Texas Studies in Literature and Language.* XVIII (Spring, 1976), pp. 124–134.

Kraus, Sister Mary Conrad. "Civilized Law vs. Primitive Law in *The Pioneers*," in *CEA Critic.* XXXIX (March, 1977), pp. 9–10.

McAleer, John J. "Biblical Analogy in the Leatherstocking Tales," in *Nineteenth-Century Fiction*. XVII (1962), pp. 217–235.

McWilliams, John P., Jr. *Political Justice in a Republic: James Fenimore Cooper's America*. Berkeley: University of California Press, 1972.

Noble, David W. "Cooper, Leatherstocking and the Death of the American Adam," in *American Quarterly*. XVI (1964), pp. 419–431.

Otten, Kurt. "Cooper: *The Pioneers*," in *Nathanael West: The Cheaters and the Cheated*. Edited by David Madden. Deland, Fla.: Everett/Edwards, 1973, pp. 21–50.

Paine, Gregory L. "The Indians of the Leatherstocking Tales," in *Studies in Philology*. XXIII (1926), pp. 16–39.

Pearce, Roy H. "The Leatherstocking Tales Re-examined," in *South Atlantic Quarterly*. XLVI (1947), pp. 524–536.

Philbrick, Thomas. "Cooper's *The Pioneers*: Origins and Structure," in *PMLA*. LXXIX (1964), pp. 579–593.

Pound, Louise. "The Dialect of Cooper's Leatherstocking," in *American Speech*. II (1927), pp. 479–488.

Ringe, Donald A. *James Fenimore Cooper*. New York: Twayne, 1962, pp. 32–37.

Robinson, E. Arthur. "Conservation in Cooper's *The Pioneers*," in *PMLA*. LXXXII (December, 1967), pp. 564–578.

Smith, Henry N. "Consciousness and Social Order: The Theme of Transcendence in the Leatherstocking Tales," in *Western American Literature*. V (1970), pp. 177–194.

Stineback, David C. *Shifting World; Social Change and Nostalgia in the American Novel*. Cranbury, N.J.: Bucknell University Press, 1976, pp. 23–42.

Vlach, John M. "Fenimore Cooper's Leatherstocking as Folk Hero," in *New York Folklore Quarterly*. XXVII (1971), pp. 323–338.

Walker, Warren S. *James Fenimore Cooper; An Introduction and Interpretation*. New York: Holt, Rinehart and Winston, 1962, pp. 36–38, 62–63, 74, 88.

————. *Plots and Characters in the Works of James Fenimore Cooper*. Hamden, Conn.: Shoe String Press, 1978.

THE PRAIRIE

Type of work: Novel
Author: James Fenimore Cooper (1789–1851)
Type of plot: Historical romance
Time of plot: 1804
Locale: Western Plains of the United States
First published: 1827

This fifth and last volume of the Leatherstocking series closes the career of Cooper's famous frontiersman and scout, Natty Bumppo. Despite rather flat characterizations, stilted dialogue, and an overly coincidental plot, the story is acceptable, for it is action-filled and successfully captures the spirit of the old West.

Principal Characters

Natty Bumppo, the resourceful, independent old woodsman at eighty-two. While trapping on the plains soon after the Louisiana Purchase, he camps one evening with a clan of tough, suspicious squatters, the Bush family. Later, accused of killing Asa Bush and having helped two young men to rescue their sweethearts from the Bushes, he is forced to avoid the squatters. Meanwhile he and his companions are captured three times by hostile Sioux Indians. Natty serves as an interpreter, pacifies their captors, and helps the captives to escape. Finally, when the Sioux have been defeated and he has acquitted himself before the Bush clan, he decides to live with a tribe of friendly Pawnees until his death. Old and weak, he dies at sundown after rising to his feet and uttering a single word, "Here."

Ishmael Bush, the huge, ferocious head of the squatters. Though he has no respect for the law, he has a rude sense of justice and honor. Enraged by Indian attacks, the murder of his son Asa, and the abduction of his niece and a female hostage, he makes a temporary alliance with the Sioux in order to capture the fugitives. When his allies betray him, he calmly helps destroy them. In a rude court of justice he sets the two pairs of lovers free, along with an itinerant naturalist. He also frees Natty Bumppo after the old hunter reveals Abiram White, Bush's brother-in-law, as the murderer. In the end, Bush and his family move on into the unknown West.

Esther Bush, Ishmael's aging, shrewish, almost mannish wife. The only literate member of the family, she reads the Bible but has the instincts of a wolf. Protective towards her young and savage towards trespassers, she is a formidable Indian fighter.

Ellen Wade, called **Nelly,** Esther Bush's pretty, vivacious niece. A homeless girl of eighteen, she feels gratitude toward the Bushes for their care, even if she feels little affection for them. More genteel than others of the Bush clan, she attracts Paul Hover, a young bee hunter from Kentucky, meets him secretly, and deserts the Bushes to share his adventures. Three times captured by Indians, and retaken by Ishmael, she finally receives Ishmael Bush's permission to marry Paul.

Abiram White, Esther's cowardly, treacherous brother. He kidnaps Inez Middleton, the wife of a young soldier, shoots Asa Bush in the back after a quarrel, and blames the killing on Natty Bumppo. When his guilt is disclosed, Ishmael Bush exacts a terrible vengeance. White is placed, bound, on a rock ledge where he must either hang himself or starve. His body is found dangling from a rope tied to the limb of a tree.

Dr. Obed Battius, also called **Obed Bat,** a pompous naturalist who prefers to travel in Natty's company rather than with the rude squatters. He exemplifies a foolish, academic approach to nature that contrasts strongly with Natty's natural, pious attitudes. A rather useless person, he owns a donkey that saves the party from a buffalo stampede by braying.

Paul Hover, Ellen Wade's reckless, spirited sweetheart and a roaming bee hunter. Captured three times by Sioux Indians, along with Natty and Ellen, he is always ready to fight, but Natty's diplomatic efforts succeed in saving his neck until he is finally safe and free to marry Ellen.

Captain Middleton, a handsome young soldier, the bridegroom of Inez Middleton, the hostage kidnaped by Abiram White. Searching for the Bushes, he comes across Natty Bumppo, Paul Hover, and Dr. Battius, who help him rescue his wife. After being captured by Indians, he is set free by Ishmael Bush, and happily reunited with his wife. He is the grandson of a British officer whom Natty Bumppo had known in the days of the French and Indian Wars.

Inez Middleton, his wife, a wealthy young woman held prisoner by the squatters. Having been rescued by her husband and captured by Sioux, she is in danger of becoming the wife of Mahtoree, the Sioux chief. When he is killed in single-handed combat with a Pawnee warrior, she is restored to her husband by Ishmael Bush.

Hard-Heart, the noble young chief who befriends Natty Bumppo and his comrades and is finally captured with them by a band of fierce Sioux. About to be tortured, he escapes to his tribe, challenges the Sioux chief to battle, kills him, and defeats the hostile tribe. Natty chooses to make his home in Hard-Heart's Pawnee village, where he lives until his death.

Mahtoree, the bold, fierce, cunning Sioux chieftain. A dangerous foe, he captures Natty Bumppo and the old hunter's friends three times. He is about to take Inez Middleton for his wife when Hard-Heart, the Pawnee brave, challenges him to combat and kills him.

Swooping Eagle, called **Le Balafré,** an aged Sioux chieftain who wishes to adopt Hard-Heart as his son, to save the young warrior from being killed. Hard-Heart expresses respect for the old man but rejects his offer.

Weucha, a boastful, greedy Sioux brave killed by Hard-Heart.

Tachechana, Mahtoree's Indian wife, shamed when she is forced to strip herself of her finery after the chief decides to discard her and wed Inez Middleton.

Asa Bush, Ishmael's eldest son, killed by his uncle, Abiram White.

Abner,
Enoch, and
Jesse Bush, Ishmael's other strapping sons.

Hetty and
Phoebe Bush, his strong, vigorous young daughters.

The Story

Shortly after the time of the Louisiana Purchase the family of Ishmael Bush traveled westward from the Mississippi River. Ishmael was accompanied by his wife, Esther, and their sons and daughters. Also in the caravan were Ellen Wade, a niece of Esther; Abiram White, Esther's brother; and Dr. Battius, a physician and naturalist. As this company searched for a camping place one evening, they met an aged trapper, Natty Bumppo, and his dog. The trapper directed them to a nearby stream.

After night had fallen, Bumppo discovered Ellen in a secret meeting with her lover, Paul Hover, a wandering bee hunter. The three were captured by a band of Sioux. While the Indian raiders stole all the horses and cattle from Ishmael's party, the captives made their escape. Unable to proceed across the prairie, the emigrant family occupied a naturally fortified hilltop shown to them by Bumppo.

A week later, Paul, Bumppo, and Dr. Battius were gathered at Bumppo's camping ground. They were soon joined by a stranger, who introduced himself as Captain Middleton of the United States Army. Bumppo was delighted to find that Middleton was the grandson of an old friend whom he had known in the days of the French and Indian wars. The young officer had come to find his wife, Inez, who had been kidnaped by Abiram White shortly after her marriage. She was now a captive in Ishmael's camp. Paul, Bumppo, and Dr. Battius agreed to help Middleton rescue her.

On the same day Ishmael and his sons left their camp to hunt buffalo. That evening they returned with meat, but Asa, the oldest son, did not return with the rest of the hunters. In the morning the entire family set out to search for him. At last his dead body was found in a thicket; he had been shot in the back with one of Bumppo's bullets. His family buried him and returned to camp. There they found that both Ellen and Inez were gone.

The girls, who had been rescued by Middleton and his friends, were rapidly making their escape across the prairie, when their progress was interrupted by a meeting with a Pawnee warrior, Hard-Heart. After the Indian had galloped away on his horse, the travelers found themselves in the path of a stampeding herd of buffalo. The group was saved from being trampled to death at the last moment by the braying of Dr. Battius' donkey, for at the strange sound the buffalo turned aside. However, Middleton's party was soon captured by a band of Sioux pursuing the buffalo herd. They were the same Indians who had captured Bumppo, Paul, and Ellen once before. At the same time Ishmael and his sons approached on foot in search of the two girls. The Indians remounted and gave horses to their captives so that all could ride to Ishmael's camp while he and his son were away. During the Indian raid on the camp, Bumppo helped his friends escape on horseback.

They rode as far as possible before making camp for the night. But in the morning they found that the Sioux had followed them and had set fire to the prairie in order to drive them into the open. Bumppo rescued the party by burning off the nearby prairie before the larger fire reached it. As they started off, they met the lone Hard-Heart again. From him they learned that the Sioux and Ishmael's family had joined forces in order to search for them. Since Hard-Heart and the little band had a common enemy in the Sioux, he agreed to take them to his Pawnee village for protection.

In order to evade their pursuers, the fugitives crossed a nearby river. As they reached the far bank the Sioux appeared on the opposite shore. That night the fugitives remained free, but snow fell and made it impossible for them to escape without being tracked. They were captured and taken to the Sioux village.

Hard-Heart, Paul, and Middleton were bound by their savage captors. Out of respect for his age, Bumppo was allowed to roam freely, but he declined to leave his friends. The women were placed in the lodge of the Sioux chief.

Using Bummppo as an interpreter, the Sioux chief asked Inez to be his wife. At the same time Ishmael asked the chief to hand over to him Inez, Ellen, and Bumppo, as had been previously agreed. When the chief refused, Ishmael departed angrily.

The Indians then gathered in council to decide the fate of Hard-Heart, and many wished to torture him to death. But an old warrior stepped forward and declared that he wished to make the Pawnee his adopted son. Hard-Heart, however, refused to become a member of the Sioux tribe. The Sioux began their torture, but in the midst of it Hard-Heart escaped and joined a war party of his own Pawnees, who arrived on the scene at that moment.

Leaving their women to guard the prisoners, the Sioux prepared to fight. The braves of the two tribes gathered on the opposite banks of a river, neither side daring to make the first move. Then Hard-Heart challenged the Sioux chief to single combat.

Meanwhile, Bumppo helped the rest of the captives to escape. Shortly afterward they fell once more into the hands of Ishmael.

Hard-Heart was victorious in the single-handed combat, and his warriors put the Sioux to flight in the battle which followed.

The next morning Ishmael held a court of justice in order to deal with his captives. He realized his mistake in carrying Inez away from her husband and allowed the couple their freedom. He gave Ellen her choice of remaining with his family or going with Paul. She chose to go with her lover. Ishmael allowed Dr. Battius his freedom because he did not think the scientist worth bothering about. Then Bumppo came up for judgment.

Ishmael still believed that Bumppo had shot his son, Asa. Bumppo, however, revealed that it was really Abiram who had done the cowardly deed. Abiram confessed his crime and then fainted. Ishmael was reluctant to pronounce judgment on his brother-in-law, but he felt it his duty to do so. That evening he gave Abiram the choice of starving to death or hanging himself. Late that night Ishmael and Esther returned to find that Abiram had hanged himself. They buried him and continued on their way back to the frontier settlements.

Middleton, Paul, and the girls invited Bumppo to return to the settlements with them, where they would make comfortable his last days. He refused, giving as his reason his desire to die away from civilization. He chose to remain in the Pawnee village with Hard-Heart.

A year later, when Middleton's duties as an army officer brought him near the Pawnee village, he determined to pay Bumppo a visit. Arriving at the camp, Middleton found the old trapper near death. It was late afternoon. Bumppo revived enough to greet his old friend. At sundown, however, he seemed to be breathing his last. As the sun sank beneath the horizon, he made one last tremendous effort. He rose to his feet and, as if answering a roll call, he uttered a loud and firm "Here"—then fell back dead into the arms of his friends.

Critical Evaluation

The Prairie is the third title published in the Leatherstocking Tales. When the series of five tales was published together in 1850, *The Prairie* became the last. Since Cooper had never seen the Great Plains area in which the action of the tale occurs, he drew from descriptions and additional information in accounts by Lewis, Clark, and other explorers. Beyond this he used his imagination.

The Prairie is related in several ways to the two earlier Leatherstocking Tales. Two themes in *The Pioneers*—the wasting of America's natural resources and the vanishing of the American Indian as a race—continue in *The Prairie*. Leatherstocking in *The Pioneers* had condemned the wasteful cutting and burning of trees, the greater slaughter of passenger pigeons, and the seining of fish that were left to rot on the lake shore. In *The Prairie* the old trapper complains: "What the world of America is coming to, and where the machinations and inventions of its people are to have an end, tne Lord, He only knows. . . . How much has the beauty of the wilderness been deformed. . . ." The theme of the "vanishing American" had been touched on with the death of Chingachgook in *The Pioneers*. It became a leading theme in *The Last of the Mohicans* and it returns in *The Prairie* with the Pawnees and the Sioux warring as the Delawares and the Mingoes had fought in *The Last of the Mohicans,* making it easier for such white settlers as Ishmael Bush and his large family finally to take over what had been the Indians' ancient homeland.

Certain resemblances between characters and character relationships in *The Last of the Mohicans* and *The Prairie* may also be seen. The genteel Captain Duncan Uncas Middleton is a grandson of Duncan Heyward and Alice Munro, who represented gentility in *The Last of the Mohicans*. The love of the old trapper for his adopted son Hard-Heart parallels the feeling that Hawkeye had for young Uncas. The enmity of Hard-Heart and Mahtoree is as fierce as that of Uncas and Magua (but the good Indian kills the bad one in *The Prairie,* whereas the bad Indian killed the good one in *The Last of the Mohicans*.) The pedantic wordiness of Dr. Obed Battius surpasses in comic absurdity the talk and the psalm singing of David Gamut.

One may object to the complexity and many improbabilities of plot in

The Prairie, to the old trapper's long-windedness, or to Dr. Battius' ridiculous vocabulary and views, but Ishmael Bush is one of Cooper's best-drawn characters, and the old trapper is both pathetic and noble as he approaches his death. The death scene itself so impressed the English novelist Thackeray that he imitated it with the death of Colonel Newcome in *The Newcomes* (1853-1855).

Bibliography

Baym, Nina. "The Women of Cooper's Leatherstocking Tales," in *American Quarterly.* XXIII (1971), pp. 696–709.

Bewley, Marius. "*The Cage* and *The Prairie*: Two Notes on Symbolism," in *Hudson Review.* X (Autumn, 1957), pp. 408–413.

Bier, Jesse. "Lapsarians on *The Prairie*: Cooper's Novel," in *Texas Studies in Literature and Language.* IV (Spring, 1962), pp. 49–57.

Chase, Richard. *The American Novel and Its Tradition.* New York: Doubleday, 1957, pp. 52–65.

Dekker, George. *James Fenimore Cooper: The American Scott.* New York: Barnes & Noble, 1967, pp. 89–103, 169–174.

Frederick, John T. "Cooper's Eloquent Indians," in *PMLA.* LXXXI (1956), pp. 1004–1017.

Hirsch, David H. *Reality and Idea in the Early American Novel.* The Hague: Mouton, 1971, pp. 106–121.

House, Kay S. "James Fenimore Cooper: *The Prairie*," in *The American Novel from James Fenimore Cooper to William Faulkner.* Edited by Wallace Stegner. New York: Basic Books, 1965, pp. 1–12.

Lewis, Merrill. "Lost—and Found—In the Wilderness: The Desert Metaphor in Cooper's *The Prairie*," in *Western American Literature.* V (1970), pp. 195–204.

McAleer, John J. "Biblical Analogy in the Leatherstocking Tales," in *Nineteenth-Century Fiction.* XVII (1962), pp. 217–235.

McWilliams, John P., Jr. *Political Justice in a Republic: James Fenimore Cooper's America.* Berkeley: University of California Press, 1972, pp. 238–246, 259–291, 321–322.

Noble, David W. "Cooper, Leatherstocking and the Death of the American Adam," in *American Quarterly.* XVI (1964), pp. 419–431.

Paine, Gregory L. "The Indians of the Leatherstocking Tales," in *Studies in Philology.* XXIII (1926), pp. 16–39.

Pearce, Roy H. "The Leatherstocking Tales Re-examined," in *South Atlantic Quarterly.* XLVI (1947), pp. 524–536.

Pound, Louise. "The Dialect of Cooper's Leatherstocking," in *American Speech*. II (1927), pp. 479–488.

Ringe, Donald A. "Man and Nature in Cooper's *The Prairie*," in *Nineteenth-Century Fiction*. XV (1961), pp. 312–323.

Smith, Henry N. "Consciousness and Social Order: The Theme of Transcendence in the Leatherstocking Tales," in *Western American Literature*. V (1970), pp. 177–194.

Stein, William B. "*The Prairie*: The Scenario of the Wise Old Man," in *Bucknell Review*. XIX (1971), pp. 15–36.

Vance, W.L. " 'Man and Beast': The Meaning of Cooper's *The Prairie*," in *PMLA*. LXXXIX (March, 1974), pp. 323–331.

Vlach, John M. "Fenimore Cooper's Leatherstocking as Folk Hero," in *New York Folklore Quarterly*. XXVII (1971), pp. 323–338.

Walker, Warren S. *James Fenimore Cooper; An Introduction and Interpretation*. New York: Holt, Rinehart and Winston, 1962, pp. 38–40, 58–63.

————. *Plots and Characters in the Works of James Fenimore Cooper*. Hamden, Conn.: Shoe String Press, 1978.

THE SPY

Type of work: Novel
Author: James Fenimore Cooper (1789–1851)
Type of plot: Historical romance
Time of plot: 1780; 1812
Locale: New York State
First published: 1821

The Spy: A Tale of the Neutral Ground *is a historical novel that clearly advances the author's patriotic sentiments. Cooper's Peyton Dunwoodie is supposed to represent the ideal American soldier and officer; Frances Wharton, the ideal of American womanhood; and George Washington, the supreme father of his*

Principal Characters

Harvey Birch, a peddler, generally believed to be a British spy, in this novel of the American Revolution. He is, however, an American patriot spying against the British.

Mr. Harper, the assumed name of disguised General George Washington.

Mr. Wharton, a British sympathizer who extends his hospitality to "Mr. Harper" during a storm.

Frances Wharton, his daughter, an ideal American woman who is in love with Major Peyton Dunwoodie.

Sarah Wharton, another daughter, whose plans of marriage to Colonel Wellmere are interrupted by news that Wellmere already has a wife who has just crossed from England expecting to join him.

Henry Wharton, the son of Mr. Wharton. A captain in the British Army, he is wrongly sentenced to hang as a British spy, but escapes through the good offices of Harvey Birch and with the help of "Mr. Harper," who thus rewards Mr. Wharton's hospitality.

Major Peyton Dunwoodie, an ideal American officer. He wins the hand of Frances Wharton.

Colonel Wellmere, a British officer professing to be in love with Sarah Wharton, though he has a wife in England.

Captain Lawton, an American officer finally killed in combat with the British, but previously engaged in a gentlemanly pursuit of the supposed British spy Birch.

Isabella Singleton, the sister of an American officer who is recuperating at the Wharton home. Frances believes Isabella's love for Major Dunwoodie is returned until Isabella, accidentally and fatally wounded, assures her of the contrary.

Miss Jeanette Peyton, the aunt of Sarah and Frances Wharton, also a member of the Wharton household.

Caesar Thompson, the Whartons' Negro servant.

Captain Wharton Dunwoodie, the son of Major Dunwoodie and Frances, and an officer in the War of 1812. After a battle he finds on the body of Harvey Birch a letter which reveals the old man's long years of self-sacrificing patriotism.

The Story

At the beginning of the Revolutionary War, Harvey Birch, a peddler, became a spy against the British. Because of the extremely secret nature of Birch's work, few Americans were aware of his true mission. As a matter of fact, they suspected that he was a British spy, and they denounced him as a bold and shameless Tory.

At the time, Westchester County in New York was considered common ground for both the rebels and the Loyalists, and the inhabitants of the county affected a neutrality they did not feel. This was the case of Mr. Wharton, a British sympathizer, who at the outbreak of hostilities had retired to his country estate with his two daughters, Sarah and Frances, and their aunt, Miss Jeanette Peyton.

One evening as a storm was approaching a horseman rode up to the Wharton house, The Locusts. He was a tall man of powerful frame, military in his bearing but plain and sober in his dress. After being let into the house by the Whartons' Negro servant, Caesar Thompson, the traveler introduced himself as Mr. Harper and asked for shelter from the storm. Mr. Wharton courteously granted the traveler's request, and the two men were soon engaged in conversation concerning the progress of the war. Mr. Wharton expressed his views cautiously in order to determine Mr. Harper's sentiments, but the stranger remained tight-lipped and uncommunicative in his replies.

The conversation between the two men was interrupted by the arrival of Henry Wharton, Mr. Wharton's son and a captain in the British army. The young man wore a disguise because he had been compelled to cross the American lines in order to visit his home. He was disconcerted when Mr. Harper recognized him, despite the disguise.

Later Harvey Birch, the peddler believed by all in the neighborhood to be a royalist spy, came to the Wharton home, bringing with him laces for the ladies, tobacco for Mr. Wharton, and news of the war—news which included a report of the hanging of Major André. During Birch's visit, Caesar, the colored servant, remarked to his master that he had heard voices in Mr. Harper's room. There seemed to be no reason why the traveler and the peddler should have matters to talk over in private.

With the return of fair weather, Mr. Harper said goodbye to his host. Before he departed he promised to help Henry Wharton, if the latter ever needed help, in return for Mr. Wharton's hospitality. Shortly after Mr. Harper left, the Wharton home was surrounded by a troop of Virginia cavalry looking for a man answering Mr. Harper's description. When the American soldiers entered Mr. Wharton's house, they discovered Henry, whose disguise was so hastily assumed that Captain Lawton, in command of the troop, was able to discover the deception. The captain was certain that Henry was a spy because he knew that Birch, whom he believed a British spy, had recently been visiting the Whartons.

Not certain what course he should follow with Henry, Captain Lawton consulted his superior, Major Peyton Dunwoodie, who was interested not only in

Henry Wharton but also in Henry's sister, Frances. She pleaded with her lover for Henry's release, but when Henry was found to have a pass signed by General Washington, Major Dunwoodie thought that the case warranted Henry's arrest.

Further investigation by Major Dunwoodie into the matter was halted by a report that British troops were in the neighborhood. The major rushed to his command, leaving Henry guarded by two soldiers.

In the confusion Henry escaped. He reported to his superior, Colonel Wellmere, leader of the advancing British troops, who professed to be in love with Sarah Wharton. When Henry advised the colonel to be wary of Major Dunwoodie and his Americans, Wellmere scorned the advice and determined to force a fight with the rebels. In the brief engagement which followed the British were routed and Captain Lawton succeeded in recapturing Henry, who was returned under guard to his father's home. Colonel Wellmere, also taken prisoner, was slightly wounded in the action. Chagrined by his defeat and capture, he gave the impression that his injuries were mortal, much to the distress of Sarah Wharton.

Birch was watching Major Dunwoodie's success from a distant hill when he was sighted by Captain Lawton, who determined to capture the spying peddler dead or alive. In the pursuit, Captain Lawton overtook Birch, but he fell from his horse and found himself at the peddler's mercy. Birch, however, spared Captain Lawton's life, and for that act of magnanimity the captain would not allow his men to overtake the peddler.

A price was put on Birch's head. One night his house was ransacked and burned by a band of lawless men called Skinners, who surprised the peddler and his dying father. They then delivered Birch to Captain Lawton and claimed their reward. Major Dunwoodie, who was also present when the peddler was brought in, accused him of treason. Although Birch possessed a paper which would have cleared him of the charge, he swallowed it rather than betray the confidence of his secret employer. Captain Lawton paid the Skinners in gold for their captive, but he also ordered them whipped for burning, robbing, and murdering.

Birch was put in jail, but that night he escaped in the guise of a washerwoman who visited his cell. The next morning, on the outskirts of the American camp, he confronted Major Dunwoodie again. With a gun pointed at the officer, to prevent recapture, the peddler warned him to be on guard against danger to the Whartons. Major Dunwoodie was alarmed by the thought of danger threatening Frances Wharton. He was also much disturbed because he felt that he could never win Frances if her brother were executed as a spy. Major Dunwoodie's troubles were magnified when, after assuring Frances that he would try to get General Washington's help for her brother, she turned from him coldly because she believed that he was in love with Isabella Singleton, the sister of an American officer who was recuperating at The Locusts from injuries sustained in the battle.

Meanwhile Sarah Wharton had accepted Colonel Wellmere's proposal of marriage, and a date for the wedding had been set, the night when there was to be an exchange of prisoners at the Wharton house. Major Dunwoodie and Captain Lawton were among the guests during the truce arranged for the exchange and the wedding. The ceremony was suddenly interrupted, however, by the appearance of Birch, who told the colonel that the Englishman's wife had crossed the ocean to meet him. Sarah fainted. Captain Lawton challenged Colonel Wellmere to a duel. The Englishman missed his mark, but Captain Lawton was prevented from killing his adversary when the Skinners leaped upon him and overpowered him. Colonel Wellmere fled the scene, and Captain Lawton was able to escape his enemies only after a fierce struggle.

The Skinners then proceeded to burn Mr. Wharton's house. Captain Lawton returned to the scene with troops he had met on the road, and after routing the Skinners he rescued Frances from the blazing house. Birch rescued Sarah and again Captain Lawton permitted the peddler to escape. A bullet fired at Captain Lawton from the darkness, apparently by the Skinners, struck Isabella Singleton and wounded her mortally. On her deathbed she confessed to Frances her love for Major Dunwoodie but said that he thought of her only as a friend.

At his trial Henry Wharton admitted that he had used a disguise in order to pass through the American lines, but he insisted that his reason for doing so had been for the one purpose of visiting his family, especially his aged father. Major Dunwoodie himself vouched for Henry's character. Frances, however, ruined her brother's chances for acquittal when she confessed that Henry had had dealings with Birch, who, she told the court, had given her brother his disguise. Henry's fate seemed certain. He was found guilty and sentenced to be hanged on the following day.

Major Dunwoodie declared that he would go to General Washington to make an appeal for the life of his friend. His attempt was unsuccessful, however, for the commander-in-chief was not at his headquarters.

Soon afterward a tall, gaunt man in clerical dress appeared and announced himself as a minister from a nearby village, come to offer spiritual comfort to the condemned man. Admitted to Henry's cell, he revealed himself as Harvey Birch. He helped Henry to disguise himself as Caesar Thompson, the faithful black servant of the Whartons, and led the young officer past the unsuspecting sentinel with the remark that the black servant was being sent on an errand for his master.

Frances, hearing of the escape, thought that her brother and the peddler would probably hide in a cabin not far away. Stealing away from the American lines, she set out to join them. But to her surprise, she found the cabin occupied by Mr. Harper, who was poring over an outspread map. Recalling his promise to help her brother, she told him the whole story. He reassured her that all would be well and told her to return to headquarters to await Major Dunwoodie.

Orders from General Washington arrived in time to relieve Major Dunwoodie of the necessity of tracking down Henry, who was thus allowed to escape. Several days later Birch saw him safely aboard a British man-of-war in New York harbor.

Frances and Major Dunwoodie decided to be married immediately. Within a short time, however, their bliss was tempered by the news that Captain Lawton had fallen in battle with the British.

Some time later Birch appeared at the headquarters of the American army in a

New Jersey town. There he had a long interview with a grave and noble man whom the Whartons would have recognized as Mr. Harper. The peddler called him General Washington. During their talk the general attempted to reward his faithful spy by giving him money. The peddler refused to accept payment for his services to his country, but he did welcome a letter of approbation from his commander-in-chief. It was agreed that the peddler's real mission as an American spy should remain a secret which only they would share.

Thirty-two years later, in the War of 1812, a gaunt old peddler appeared on the Canadian border and carried word of British troop movements to the American lines. There he met Captain Wharton Dunwoodie, the son of Major Peyton Dunwoodie and his wife Frances. To him the peddler acknowledged his earlier acquaintanceship with the young officer's parents.

A few days later, during a battle, the old peddler threw away his pack and with a musket seized from a fallen soldier rushed into the fight. After the battle Captain Dunwoodie found the old man's body and on his person a letter, signed by George Washington, which revealed Harvey Birch, not as a despicable spy but as a loyal, heroic, and long-suffering patriot.

Critical Evaluation

The Spy is an important novel both in James Fenimore Cooper's career and in the history of American literature. For Cooper, *The Spy* represented a first success in a literary career which was to include thirty-three fictional works as well as a number of other writings over a period of thirty-one years. But *The Spy* also signifies the establishment of an independent American literature, a literature based on American life, American characters, and set in an American landscape. It is significant, then, that the novel which declared "independence" from European, and especially English, literature should take for its subject the American War for Independence.

In his Preface to *The Spy*, Cooper showed he was acutely conscious of being an American writer and of writing about American subjects. Still, there is no doubt he was influenced by the major currents in literature written abroad; and, though in his Preface he offers a tongue-in-cheek apology for not including castles and nobles, as Sir Walter Scott had done, it is certain that Scott influenced Cooper in *The Spy* and in his later career as well. Scott was a great pioneer in the art of the historical novel and *The Spy* shows that Cooper learned much from Scott.

An important aspect of the historical novel are the historical types, characters who live in a specific historical period and in a particular place. One of the key differences between an authentic historical novel and a contemporary novel in a historical setting is characterization. Though one may argue that people are, in a sense, the same everywhere and at all times, it is apparent that the differences cannot be merely overlooked if one is mainly interested in accurately portraying a specific era. Thus to capture a particular place at a particular time, the novelist must do more than merely dress his contemporaries in the clothing of days past. He must have a grasp of those human features and aspects which a historical period typically requires of men and women.

The Spy is full of historically typical men. The spy himself is a courageous and ingenious man able not only to affect the times in which he lives but permitted (and encouraged) by those times to display such qualities. Thus another difference between an ordinary novel in a historical setting and a historical novel as such is that the characters help fashion history as they are fashioned by it.

In the War for Independence, fought on political as well as military grounds, involving civilians to a great extent and always posing the problem of divided loyalties, Cooper's choice of a spy is especially effective. The spy is not only a soldier in a war, he must have a grasp of politics (and theater) as well.

Cooper discovered another advantage in the use of a spy as a central character. This advantage is connected to the subtitle of the novel, "A Tale of the Neutral Ground." Effective historical novels tend to focus on periods in which significant conflicts occur. Such conflicts as the War for Independence provide not only good dramatic material for the novelist but also offer later readers an insight into their own condition, since significant conflicts in the past have shaped their lives.

But there is an artistic problem in portraying such conflicts. To give a full picture of the clash of forces one must describe both sides in the fight (in Cooper's case both the British and the Americans). Describing only one side tends to rob the novel of drama—but how is the novelist to show both and, at the same time, focus these forces on a single, central character?

Scott solved this problem by using figures of secondary historical interest as his primary focus of dramatic action. These secondary figures are able to move from one side to another as negotiators, go-betweens, and messengers. This movement back and forth allows scope for the novelist to show in a specific, concrete fashion both sides of the conflict.

Cooper has done this in *The Spy*. Instead of choosing Washington himself as a central character, Cooper has chosen a spy, a man able (and required) to move from one side to the other and yet a man who remains in the thick of the dramatic action. The "Neutral Ground," the space between opposing forces that Birch must cross and recross in his missions, the seam between the opponents, also reflects the need for an effective historical novel to move from one side to the other.

Other aspects of the historical novel are also significant. Besides the presence of other, minor "type" characters (the doctor, the housekeeper, the servant), there are the details of the warfare, the names, dates, places, historical facts, that Cooper made a conscious effort to use; and *The Spy* reflects a degree of historical accuracy and fidelity to the facts which, despite moments of highly imaginative drama and humor, lend an air of reality to the action of the book as a whole.

Additionally, Cooper expends much print and dialogue on the arguments for and against the War for Independence. The revolutionaries argue with the counter-revolutionaries. Because he is able to show both sides dramatically, in real life, Cooper is able to describe the intellectual and political conflict of the era. In this way, Cooper avoids the trap of turning a historical novel into a mere adventure story; for in the course of history, and certainly in the course of the Revolutionary War, the battle of ideas deeply influences the physical battles. If Cooper is less successful in showing how arguments change individuals, he is still able to give a richer sense of the times and of the war than if he had concentrated entirely on physical action and adventure.

There are, of course, weaknesses in Cooper's work that are all too obvious. Cooper was, apart from being an opinionated man, one who shared many of the prejudices and preconceptions of his day. These views naturally affected the quality of his work.

One of his problems, for example, was that he seemed unable to characterize certain sorts of people in much depth. His attitude toward women and black people specifically is condescending. As a result, his portrayal of these figures is almost always superficial and unreal. Cooper's women in *The Spy* and elsewhere tend to be either precious darlings or selfish schemers.

Cooper also has a tendency to use an ironic tone rather heavy-handedly. In *The Spy* Cooper follows a long tradition in English literature by making his comic characters members of the lower class. One senses that the class characteristics of those below him were humorous to Cooper. Corresponding to this general characterization of the lower orders (not true in every case, to be sure) is a general deference to those of higher rank.

Thus, in finally evaluating *The Spy* as literature the reader is drawn to a central contradiction. On the one hand, Cooper clearly supports the American side and agrees with the arguments for independence, especially those arguments based on the God-given equality of men. In Cooper's mind, men *are* equal before God. At the same time, Cooper himself is a creature of his own time and upbringing. For him, though men may be equal under God they are by no means equal to one another.

The conflict between ideals and reality is an old one in the United States and it is no surprise that Cooper, declaring himself an authentic American novelist, should exhibit that conflict. Thus, *The Spy* is an informative historical novel both because it reflects a basic conflict in the history of a nation and because, as a work of art, it contains a basic conflict.

Bibliography

Beard, James F. "Cooper and the Revolutionary Mythos," in *Early American Literature.* XI (Spring, 1976), pp. 84–104.

Dekker, George. *James Fenimore Cooper: The American Scott.* New York: Barnes & Noble, 1967, pp. 33–37, 41–42, 113–114.

Diemer, James S. "A Model for Harvey Birch," in *American Literature.* XXVI (May, 1954), pp. 242–247.

Fink, Robert A. "Harvey Birch: The Yankee Peddler as an American Hero," in *New York Folklore Quarterly.* XXX (1974), pp. 137–152.

House, Kay S. *Cooper's Americans.* Columbus: Ohio State University Press, 1965, pp. 206–216.

Hubbell, Jay B. *Southern Life in Fiction.* Athens: University of Georgia Press, 1960, pp. 47–48.

McDowell, Tremaine. "The Identity of Harvey Birch," in *American Literature.* II (1930), pp. 111–120.

McWilliams, John P., Jr. *Political Justice in a Republic: James Fenimore Cooper's Americans.* Berkeley: University of California Press, 1972, pp. 8, 48–64, 159, 397–398.

Walker, Warren S. *James Fenimore Cooper; An Introduction and Interpretation.* New York: Holt, Rinehart and Winston, 1962, pp. 12–13, 22–29.

_____. *Plots and Characters in the Works of James Fenimore Cooper.* Hamden, Conn.: Shoe String Press, 1978.

_____. "The Prototype of Harvey Birch," in *New York History.* XXXVII (1956), pp. 399–413.

RICHARD HENRY DANA, JR.

Born: Cambridge, Massachusetts (August 1, 1815)
Died: Rome, Italy (January 6, 1882)

Principal Works

TRAVEL AND ADVENTURE: *Two Years Before the Mast*, 1840; *To Cuba and Back*, 1859.

Richard Henry Dana, Jr., was born in Cambridge, Massachusetts, August 1, 1815, the son of Richard Henry Dana, critic and editor. He enrolled at Harvard University in 1831, but bad health and failing eyesight caused him to resign. Instead of taking a pleasure trip to Europe he sailed before the mast as a common sailor on the brig *Pilgrim*. This voyage around Cape Horn to California and Oregon furnished the material for his celebrated work, *Two Years Before the Mast*. Published in 1840, this book had a wide influence on other writers about the sea, and its realistic approach was much imitated. In this volume Dana was successful in bringing to public attention the hardships of a sailor's life. Today the book is also valuable as a picture of life in California in the nineteenth century.

After returning home from his trip Dana finished Harvard in 1837 and entered the law school there. After graduation he opened his law offices, specializing in maritime law. He also published *The Seaman's Friend* (1841) dealing with the responsibilities, duties, and legal rights of the sailor, a manual which was widely recognized and used both in the United States and in England. In 1859 he published *To Cuba and Back*.

Interested in politics, he early joined the Free Soil Movement. He was also an early member of the Republican Party. In 1860 he was interested in the presidential campaign and was appointed to the office of United States District Attorney for Massachusetts by President Lincoln. Meanwhile he won the *Amy Warwick* case, which was concerned with blockading Southern ports. In 1866 he published his extensive compendium on International Law entitled *Wheaton's International Law*. Thirteen years of litigation followed. In 1866 he ran for Congress unsuccessfully. In 1876 he was nominated by President Grant as Minister to England, but the Congress did not confirm the appointment. He also achieved distinction when he was asked to prosecute Jefferson Davis. In 1877 he was a member of a commission which met in Nova Scotia concerning problems of fisheries which arose between Britain and the United States. In 1879 he retired from his distinguished duties as a lawyer to spend the rest of his life writing and traveling. His death occurred in Rome on January 6, 1882. Though he achieved his greatest fame as a lawyer, he is chiefly remembered for his famous story of life at sea, *Two Years Before the Mast*.

Bibliography

The definitive biography of Dana is Charles Francis Adams' *Richard Henry Dana*, 1890. See also *The Journal of Richard Henry Dana*, edited by Robert F. Lucid, vols. I, II and III, 1968. The most recent study is Robert L. Gale, *Richard Henry Dana*, 1969. There is also an excellent essay on this writer in Bliss Perry's *The Praise of Folly and Other Papers*, 1923.

TWO YEARS BEFORE THE MAST

Type of work: Record of travel
Author: Richard Henry Dana, Jr. (1815–1882)
Type of plot: Adventure romance
Time of plot: 1834–1836
Locale: California and the high seas
First published: 1840

Intended to make the public aware of the hardships and injustices to which American sailors were subjected, Dana's realistic narrative—chiefly in the form of a journal—is noted for its careful observation of life at sea and its accurate report on Spanish California during the early nineteenth century.

The Story

In August, 1834, Richard Henry Dana, Jr., shipped aboard the brig *Pilgrim* out of Boston for a voyage to California. He went as an ordinary seaman, hoping to relieve his eye trouble by the journey; upon his return he planned to reënter Harvard College.

Since Dana was a completely green hand, he was forced to bunk in the steerage instead of in the forecastle with the other sailors. At first his duties were confusing, doubly so during the first two days, for he was violently seasick. But he soon found his sea legs and quickly learned shipboard routine. He and his companions were kept busy all day cleaning and repairing the ship. At night they took turns standing watch.

The voyage was uneventful until October, when the *Pilgrim* passed near the mouth of the River Plate. Here Dana encountered his first real storm at sea. The weather then began to get cold, and all the crew prepared to round Cape Horn.

The seas at the Horn were high, and the crew battled snow and hail. Everyone's clothing was perpetually wet. By the middle of November the ship rounded the Horn and headed northward.

The first mishap of the voyage occurred soon afterward, when a young sailor was swept overboard. A boat lowered to search for him found no trace of the lost man. Following the custom of the sea, the captain auctioned off the dead man's clothing.

Near the end of November the brig made the island of Juan Fernandez and dropped anchor for the first time since her departure from Boston. Dana was glad to see land and managed to get on shore for a short time. As soon as the ship had taken on water, however, it weighed anchor and headed for California.

Shortly after Christmas Dana was acknowledged by the crew to be experienced enough to move into the forecastle with them. Now he was a real seaman.

By the middle of January the *Pilgrim* made her first California port at Santa Barbara. There Dana learned that his work for the next year would be loading cattle hides into the ship. The sailors carried the stiff, undressed hides out through the surf on their heads and deposited them in a boat. Then the crew of the boat took the hides to the ship and stowed them away.

The *Pilgrim* next sailed northward to Monterey with some passengers. At that port Mexican customs officers inspected the cargo. Then the company agent aboard the ship set up a store in order to trade with the townspeople. The crew was kept busy on a shuttle service between ship and shore. Because he had some knowledge of languages, Dana became the interpreter for the *Pilgrim*, and he was sent ashore on errands which required a knowledge of Spanish. In this way he became acquainted with the town and its people. He found the Spaniards to be pleasant but lazy, with most of the trade carried on by foreigners. Everyone owned horses; they were so numerous that the price of a fine animal was very low.

When business began to fall off, the *Pilgrim* returned to Santa Barbara. There the crew again began the work of collecting cattle hides from shore. At the time trouble was brewing aboard the ship. Captain, mate, and crew were all at odds. One day the captain began to flog a sailor unjustly; when one of his shipmates stood up for him, the captain flogged the second sailor also. The sailors were angry, but they had no higher power to which they could appeal, for the captain's word was law. Her hold laden with hides, the *Pilgrim* sailed for San Diego.

In San Diego, Dana got his first shore leave. After drinking for a time with the rest of the crew, he and a friend hired horses and rode to a nearby mission, where they were able to get a good Mexican meal, a welcome change from the salt beef served aboard ship.

The undressed hides were unloaded from the *Pilgrim* and placed in a large shed on the beach, where they were to be dressed and stored until enough hides had been collected for the voyage home. Just as the ship had finished unloading and was ready to set sail, a man deserted ship. After an unsuccessful search, the brig put to sea without him.

The *Pilgrim* took on more hides at San Pedro and then continued on to Santa Barbara. It was the Lenten season, and Dana saw the celebrations ashore. The ship gathered more hides at several places and returned to San Diego. After the hides had been unloaded, the captain sent Dana and another man ashore to assist with the dressing of the hides. Then the ship sailed northward on another coastal voyage.

Dana became acquainted with some Sandwich Islanders who lived on the beach and worked with him; he found them to be generous men and true friends. Some of his spare time he spent reading books and studying navigation. Each day he had to perform a certain amount of work on a certain number of hides, which had to be cleaned, soaked in brine, scraped, dried, beaten, and then stored away.

When the ship *Alert* arrived at San Diego, Dana, anxious to be at sea again, exchanged places with a boy aboard the ship. The *Alert* belonged to the same company as the *Pilgrim*; she was to take aboard the hides collected by the brig and carry them to Boston. The *Pilgrim* was not to sail for home until later. The two vessels had exchanged captains, and Dana was under the same master as before. However, the first mate of the *Alert* was a good officer, and Dana found conditions much more pleasant in his new berth.

Loading hides, the *Alert* moved up and down the coast for several months. In the middle of November, 1835, she left Santa Barbara with some passengers bound for Monterey. However, such a gale came up that the ship could not put in at Monterey but went on up the coast to San Francisco.

The ship then continued working up and down the coast until there were enough hides at San Diego to make her full cargo. In May she headed southward for Cape Horn.

Rounding the Horn on the return journey was even worse than on the way out. Dana became sick with a toothache at the time he was needed most on deck. For days everyone had to work extra hours because of the danger from icebergs. Finally, however, the *Alert* got clear of the ice and ran before a strong wind around the Horn.

Once the ship entered the Atlantic tropics, the weather was fair except for occasional violent storms. Some of the men began to come down with the scurvy, but they were soon cured after the crew obtained fresh vegetables from a passing ship.

On September 21, 1836, the *Alert* anchored in Boston harbor. Hurriedly the crew performed their last duties in bringing her to the wharf. Within five minutes after the last rope had been made fast, not one of the crew was left aboard.

Critical Evaluation

If an attack of measles had not threatened Richard Henry Dana, Jr.'s, eyesight and forced his withdrawal from Harvard, America would have lost one of the most popular travel adventure books ever written, *Two Years Before the Mast*. But this physical condition could not have been the only reason for Dana's desire to ship out as a common sailor; surely less arduous and unpredictable forms of convalescence were available to a well-born young Bostonian. His decision must have, to some extent, represented important psychological and emotional needs—to have an "adventure," to "test" himself and his "manhood," to separate himself, at least temporarily, from the narrow, stifling environment and the conservative religious atmosphere of his Brahmin social class and his illustrious, formal family.

Immediately after returning from his voyage, Dana began to record his experiences, largely from memory (his brother Frank having lost the "log" he had kept of the voyage), while he finished his studies at Harvard and then pursued a law degree. The book was published in 1840 and, to everyone's surprise, became an instant commercial success. Ten years later, following the discovery of gold in California, it enjoyed a second burst of popularity, since it was almost the only book available which dealt with the early California environment. Ironically, Dana profited little from the book in a material way since, discouraged in his attempts to find a publisher, he had sold all rights to the work to Harper's for $250.

The great and perennial popularity of *Two Years Before the Mast* probably is due to the fact that it combines two of the most popular genres in a very skillful, vivid manner—the "travel-adventure romance" and the "coming-of-age" narrative.

The travel-adventure romance, which has attracted not only commercial writers, but also some of our best literary talents—James Fenimore Cooper, Herman Melville, Henry David Thoreau, Mark Twain, and Ernest Hemingway among others—has long been a favorite American genre and was especially so in the mid-nineteenth century. It vicariously fulfills at least two emotional needs in the reader: the glorification of physical hardship and an identification with the overcoming of rugged obstacles, especially nature itself; and an escape from the confines of a narrow, dull, middle-class environment to a world of sensuous experience. *Two Years Before the Mast* combines a great deal of the former and generous hints of the latter, especially in the quaint customs and free life style of the Californians. The secret to the depiction of such an "escape" vision is, of course, to make the exotic, unknown world as real to the reader as his own bland, sedate one, and this is where Dana succeeds brilliantly.

Although *Two Years Before the Mast* is autobiographical, many readers accepted it as fiction—which is a tribute to Dana's storytelling abilities. His prose style is direct, concrete, and muted, lacking the rhetorical embellishment so characteristic of most mid-nineteenth century writing, but frequently laced with colloquial shipboard phraseology. On the whole the book does not depend on exciting adventures or bizarre situations, but rather on careful, restrained descriptions of the seamen's everyday routines and activities, punctuated by periodic crises that Dana renders in vivid, dramatic scenes. The book capitalizes on what has always been one of the primary appeals of realistic writing, the intimate description of a profession or activity that seems exotic to the reader.

Moreover, *Two Years Before the Mast* is almost the only nineteenth century narrative of life at sea—Herman Melville not excepted—that does not romanticize the common sailor. Dana clearly likes his mates, but he presents them as very flawed, distinctive human beings, who may not be heroic, but who labor at a very dangerous, difficult job with courage, endurance, and tenacity. This realism, occasionally ironic but never sentimental, is quite modern in tone and attitude, a characteristic which largely accounts for the fact that the book is as entertaining and informative today as it was in 1840.

The "coming-of-age" theme in *Two Years Before the Mast* is given a special twist by the fact that Dana, the initiate, is a young, relatively naïve, religiously conservative Boston aristocrat who thrusts himself into a trial among crude, uneducated, generally amoral sailors. Therefore, he must not only move from youth to manhood, and from innocence to experience, but also from outsider to member of this seafaring subculture.

Throughout the book there is, on his side, a constant tension between his aristocratic inclinations and sensibilities and his democratic convictions and the desire to identify with his cohorts; and, on the part of the crew, there is a resentment of Dana for his social background and intellectual pretensions coupled with an admiration for his growth and development as an efficient, hardworking seaman.

In the beginning of the book Dana is an obvious novice and the crew isolates him to the steerage. But he learns quickly and gives a good account of himself in the first bad storm. He also establishes the pattern of volunteering for every difficult and dangerous job that comes up, a trait that brings him admiration from the crew, but also a reputation for foolhardiness. Then, when a young sailor is washed overboard, Dana confronts sudden death at sea and comes to learn the "joking" attitude the men have toward danger and mortality. His view of the basic futility of their lives is also crystalized: "a sailor's life is at best but a mixture of little good with much evil, and a little pleasure with much pain. The beautiful is linked with the revolting, the sublime with the commonplace, and the solemn with the ludicrous."

His initiation into the institutional side of sailing and the "justice" of the high seas comes when Captain Thompson flogs two men for trivial reasons. Young Dana had known of the Captain's absolute power, but, not until he watched this almost demented, hysterical captain dancing about on deck ranting and swearing as he viciously flogged the men, did he realize the full meaning of the custom. It was at this point that Dana committed himself to fighting for a reform of the maritime laws that allowed such flagrant and arbitrary injustice—a commitment he pursued all his life.

The flogging scene also intensifies his desire not to spend his life as a seaman, and this leads directly to his most serious moral dilemma. Throughout the book Dana tries to identify with the sailors, but, when threatened with a possible disruption of his own career plans, Dana invokes the family name and his place is taken by a less well situated substitute. He tries to mitigate the use of family influence by giving the substitute a handsome share of his pay, but the moral onus remains.

Dana's final initiation comes on the return voyage as the *Alert* rounds the Horn through a field of dangerous icebergs. During the perilous navigation he is confined below with a toothache that almost kills him. Thus, a parallel is suggested between this disruption of nature and his own personal condition. The *Alert* survives the crisis and Dana recovers his health. Having come through this double ordeal, he has become fully initiated and is a man and a sailor.

Some critics have gone so far as to suggest that his overall "coming-of-age" development is the classical mythic quest of a hero; that is, Dana as a nineteenth century Jason or Ulysses. Such a view seems forced. If *Two Years Before the Mast* is more than a "boys' book," it is less than an epic. To claim so much for it simply obscures its very real merits.

Two Years Before the Mast is an intelligent, exciting, sensitive story of a young man's transition to maturity, a vivid, convincing description of man's struggle with the elements and with himself, an accurate account of life at sea, a colorful portrait of life in California in the early nineteenth century, and a series of colorful, dramatic vignettes. But it remains the first work of a talented beginner. Had Dana decided to devote his life to letters, his writings might very well be compared today to those of his contemporary and friend, Herman Melville. But he chose law, lecturing, and public service, where he had a moderately successful, if unspectacular, career. Although he was proud of its wide appeal, in time Dana came to consider *Two Years Before the Mast* as a "boys' book" and to recall his maritime adventures as almost a youthful fling. Little did Richard Henry Dana, Jr., realize, as he stood on the bow of the *Alert* in 1836 pondering what to do with the rest of his life, that he had already lived the most important part of it.

Bibliography

Bennett, James O'Donnell. *Much Loved Books: Best Sellers of the Ages.* New York: Liveright, 1938, pp. 386–392.

Bode, Carl. *The Half-world of American Culture: A Miscellany.* Carbondale: Southern Illinois University Press, 1965, pp. 33–53.

Cline, Walter. "Dana at the Point, Discrepancies in the Narrative," in *Historical Society of Southern California Quarterly.* XXXII (June, 1950), pp. 127–132.

Downs, Robert Bingham. *Famous American Books.* New York: McGraw-Hill, 1972, pp. 94–99.

Gallery, Daniel V. "Too Far Before the Mast," in *Colophon.* II (Autumn, 1936), pp. 60–64.

Hart, James D. "An Eyewitness of Eight Years Before the Mast," in *New Colophon.* III (1950), pp. 128–131.

Hill, Douglas B., Jr. "Richard Henry Dana, Jr., and *Two Years Before the Mast,*" in *Criticism.* IX (1967), pp. 312–325.

Lawrence, D.H. "Dana's *Two Years Before the Mast,*" in *Studies in Classic American Literature.* New York: Viking, 1923, pp. 163–192.

Lucid, Robert F. "*Two Years Before the Mast* as Propaganda," in *American Quarterly.* XII (Fall, 1960), pp. 392–403.

McWilliams, John. "Rounding Cape Horn: Melville, Dana and Literary Tradition," in *Extracts.* XXV (1976), p. 3.

Metzdorf, Robert F. "The Publishing History of Richard Henry Dana's *Two Years Before the Mast*," in *Harvard Library Bulletin*. VII (Autumn, 1953), pp. 312–332.

Powell, Lawrence Clark. *California Classics: the Creative Literature of the Golden State.* Los Angeles: Ward Ritchie Press, 1971, pp. 151–162.

Shapiro, Samuel. *Richard Henry Dana, Jr., 1815–1882.* East Lansing: Michigan State University Press, 1961, pp. 187–198.

_____. "With Dana Before the Mast," in *American Heritage*. XI (October, 1960), pp. 26–37, 94–97.

Spengemann, W.C. *The Adventurous Muse: The Poetics of American Fiction, 1789–1900.* New Haven, Conn.: Yale University Press, 1977, pp. 6–67.

Winterich, John T. "*Two Years Before the Mast* by Richard Henry Dana, Jr.," in *Georgia Review*. IX (Winter, 1955), pp. 459–461.

JOHN WILLIAM DE FOREST

Born: Seymour, Connecticut (March 31, 1826)
Died: New Haven, Connecticut (July 17, 1906)

Principal Works

NOVELS: *Seacliff,* 1859; *Miss Ravenel's Conversion from Secession to Loyalty,* 1867; *Overland,* 1871; *Kate Beaumont,* 1872; *The Wetherel Affair,* 1873; *Honest John Vane,* 1875; *Playing the Mischief,* 1875; *Irene the Missionary,* 1879; *The Bloody Chasm,* 1881; *A Lover's Revolt,* 1898.

TRAVEL SKETCHES AND IMPRESSIONS: *Oriental Acquaintance,* 1856; *European Acquaintance,* 1858.

AUTOBIOGRAPHY AND REMINISCENCE: *A Volunteer's Adventures,* 1946; *A Union Officer in the Reconstruction,* 1948.

HISTORY AND ETHNOLOGY: *History of the Indians of Connecticut,* 1851.

John William De Forest, born at Seymour, Connecticut, on March 31, 1826, was a member of a wealthy and cultured New England family. Poor health, however, prevented him from following family tradition in his education and instead of attending Yale he took a two-year trip to the Near East. On his return he assembled the *History of the Indians of Connecticut,* the first book of its kind and one which is still consulted by ethnologists for its accuracy and detail.

De Forest then spent several years abroad, traveling, collecting material for books and studying foreign languages. He returned to America, married, and was living in Charleston, South Carolina, when the Civil War broke out. With his wife and child he escaped on the last boat to leave that port before the attack on Fort Sumter.

Back in Connecticut he organized a group of volunteers and led them through a series of Civil War battles. De Forest recorded his experiences in a journal, later published as *A Volunteer's Adventures.* It remains one of the best accounts of life in the Union Army. The journal also served as an important source of material for his excellent but neglected novel, *Miss Ravenel's Conversion.*

Factual, accurate, and realistic, De Forest failed to achieve the recognition he deserved from a generation which preferred sentimentalized versions of "the irrepressible conflict." Only recently has his realism been appreciated by critics who, like William Dean Howells, admire the way in which De Forest worked, "with a sort of disdainful honesty to the effects of art."

He died at New Haven on July 17, 1906.

Bibliography

For biographical details and critical comment see Gordon S. Haight, Introduction to *Miss Ravenel's Conversion,* 1939; Stanley T. Williams, Introduction to *A*

Volunteer's Adventures, 1946; Clara F. McIntyre, *John William De Forest: Pioneer Realist, University of Wyoming Publications*, IX (1942), No. I; and Thomas O'Donnell, "De Forest, Jan Petten, and Stephen Crane," *American Literature*, XXVII (1956), 578–580. A good contemporary estimate is Clarence Gordon, "Mr. De Forest's Novels," *Atlantic Monthly*, XXXII (1873), 611–621. For more recent studies see L. Moffitt Cecil, "*Miss Ravenel's Conversion* and *Pilgrim's Progress*," *College English*, XXIII (1962), 352–357; and Albert E. Stone, "Reading, Writing, and History: Best Novel of the Civil War," *American History*, XIII (1962), 84–88. The sketch in the *Dictionary of American Biography* is brief but helpful.

MISS RAVENEL'S CONVERSION

Type of work: Novel
Author: John William De Forest (1826–1906)
Type of plot: Historical romance
Time of plot: The Civil War period
Locale: New England and Louisiana
First published: 1866

With the possible exception of Stephen Crane's The Red Badge of Courage, Miss Ravenel's Conversion *is the best and most modern nineteenth century novel written about the American Civil War. De Forest's realistic, understated, mature treatment of men and women caught up in the pains and stresses of enormous historical and cultural changes is as relevant and convincing today as it was when first published.*

Principal Characters

Lillie Ravenel, a Southern girl loyal to her section during the Civil War. Vivacious and beautiful, she marries Colonel Carter, a Union officer who helps her and her father during the Federal troops' occupation of New Orleans. Her husband takes her aunt as his mistress. An old admirer, Edward Colburne, by his love restores her happiness and marries her after the death of her husband. His influence makes her recognize the justice of the Northern cause.

Dr. Ravenel, Lillie's father, a medical doctor. He wants to rehabilitate the freed slaves of the South. He has his daughter teach some of his charges to read. Aware of Colonel Carter's moral weakness, he hopes Lillie will marry Colburne. When she decides to marry Carter, however, he does not forbid it.

Colonel Carter, Lillie's first husband. He is a man attractive to women and an opportunist. He has an affair with Mrs. Larue, Lillie's aunt. A weak man, he is given to drink and indebtedness, as well

as women. He is killed in battle during the Civil War.

Edward Colburne, a long-time admirer of Lillie. He is a captain in the Union army, a courageous and capable officer as well as a man of excellent character. Worn out and sick near the end of the war, he returns home to New England, convalesces under Dr. Ravenel's care, and successfuly woos Lillie—who had returned to New England with her father after the death of her husband.

Mrs. Larue, Lillie's aunt. An opportunist, she takes up a love affair with Colonel Carter, Lillie's first husband.

The Meurices, a New Orleans Creole family sympathetic to the Northern cause. They are friends of Captain Colburne.

Major Gazaway, the cowardly commander of a Union fort. When he fails in his duty, Captain Colburne takes command and repulses a Confederate attack.

The Story

Edward Colburne, of New Boston, met Miss Lillie Ravenel shortly after the outbreak of the Civil War and not long after she had come to New England with her father, Dr. Ravenel, who had been forced to leave Louisiana on account of his refusal to support the Confederacy. Lillie was a loyal daughter of the South, Colburne an equally adamant supporter of the North.

Among Lillie's acquaintances was Lieutenant Colonel Carter, on leave because of an injury. Colonel Carter was a general favorite with the ladies, and Colburne could find only one defect in his attractive personality; he drank too much. Carter, foreseeing that the war would be a long one, hoped to enlist more troops. Colburne, a loyal Yankee, agreed to recruit a company of his own.

Lillie's flirtation with Carter alarmed her father. He liked Colburne, instead, but his daughter did not encourage that young man's attentions.

After saying farewell to Lillie, Colonel Carter and Captain Colburne set out under orders which eventually led them to New Orleans. Some time later Dr. Ravenel and Lillie returned to their former home. Lillie found the city changed; women spoke bitterly about the Yankee soldiers. When Dr. Ravenel, having no other practice in the city, accepted a position as head of a hospital held by Union forces, he added further insult to the pride of the local citizens. Because Colonel Carter had tried to help the doctor find employment, his efforts gained him a welcome in the Ravenel house, although the doctor did not approve of the officer's attraction for Lillie.

Dr. Ravenel's kinswoman, Mrs. Larue, was attracted to Carter. When the doctor reproved her, she turned her attentions to Colburne. Because the captain innocently rebuffed her attempted flirtation, Mrs. Larue took her revenge by telling Lillie that he had dined with the Meurices, a Creole family that had aided the Northern invaders.

Colonel Carter, preparing to drive a Southern regiment from the area, declared his love to Lillie before he left. Dr. Ravenel, adamant, would not consent to Carter's proposal, for he thought the officer's character questionable. Lillie wept and her father suffered. After the engagement Carter, for his heroism, was appointed Lieutenant Governor of Louisiana and stationed in New Orleans. A constant visitor in the Ravenel house, he gradually overcame the doctor's distrust, and at last he and Lillie became engaged. Carter was again ordered to active duty. Returning to New Orleans on leave, he hurriedly married Lillie before rejoining his troops.

Dr. Ravenel left his post at the hospital in order to take charge of a plantation in nearby Taylorsville, where he hoped to rehabilitate freed slaves. To Lillie's horror, he asked her to teach his charges how to read. Letters came quite frequently from Carter, and Lillie waited for his return.

Colburne, wounded in the arm, was hospitalized for a short time. When Dr. Ravenel found Colburne in the hospital, which reeked of sickness and decay, he took his young friend to the plantation. There Colburne had to endure Lillie's constant prattle about her husband. Colburne's visit was interrupted by a Confederate raid. Taking command, the captain secured the Ravenels and the Negroes in a nearby fort. In command was Major Gazaway, a cowardly and uncertain officer who urged surrender when the Southerners attacked. Colburne literally took command while Gazaway huddled in a protected spot with Lillie. After the Confederate troops had been repulsed, Dr. Ravenel attended the wounded. Lillie had been impressed by Colburne's courage.

Reporting to Carter, Colburne found him celebrating a victory with whiskey and women. The young man felt sorry for Lillie. A few days later Carter established his wife in a local cottage, and Dr. Ravenel returned to head the hospital in New Orleans. Colburne spent much time with the Carters. Carter, however, was gradually sinking under his debts. A summons to Washington took Colonel Carter away from his wife after he had borrowed two hundred dollars from Colburne. Another passenger on the ship with Carter was Mrs. Larue. Although he berated himself for his infidelity, Carter carried on an affair with Lillie's aunt.

Carter did try, unsuccessfully, to obtain a promotion for Colburne. In Washington he himself bowed to custom and beguiled senators and officials until he was promised promotion to the rank of a brigadier general. He called on Mrs. Larue in New York. They traveled together to New Orleans on the return trip. Carter borrowed one hundred dollars from the widow.

After his return Carter sank more deeply into debt. He and Mrs. Larue met frequently in a private room behind his office. When Lillie's baby was born, however, he promised himself to have nothing more to do with Mrs. Larue.

To alleviate his indebtedness, Carter began to speculate with government funds. Shortly afterward he received his appointment as brigadier general and was recalled to active duty. At that time Dr. Ravenel found and read a letter written to him by Mrs. Larue. Heartsick, the doctor tried to hide the news from Lillie. Unfortunately, she came upon the same letter and, accustomed to reading her father's mail, read it.

When Lillie became seriously ill, her father took her and the baby on a sea voyage, his intention being to take Lillie north after her recovery. The letter he wrote to his son-in-law, informing him of that decision, was delivered on the eve of a battle in which Carter was mortally wounded. Colburne grieved for the fallen officer and for the bereaved wife.

Gradually Lillie readjusted herself and devoted her time to her child. When Colburne, worn out and sick, returned to New Boston near the end of the war, Dr. Ravenel undertook to cure him. During his convalescence, Colburne renewed his friendship with Lillie, who more and more began to display her old charm. Still in love with her, he was too hesitant to speak up boldly. When he finally asked her to marry him, Lillie realized that she truly loved him, better than she had loved any other.

Critical Evaluation

In the development of modern realistic American fiction, few nineteenth century novels are more significant than *Miss Ravenel's Conversion*. In this brilliant Civil War novel, William De Forest explores issues and problems—war, political corruption, marriage, sex—with a realism and candor that would hardly be seen again in American literature before the turn of the century.

Most immediately impressive is De Forest's presentation of the war. Writing in simple, direct, but restrained language, selecting his scenes and details carefully, he conveys the futility, horror, violence, and weariness of battle with a vividness rarely equalled in American literature at least until after World War II. Avoiding descriptions of mass combat, De Forest concentrates on those lulls in battle when the terrible effects of combat can be seen in the actions of a few sharply described individuals, such as soldiers pretending normalcy in the midst of sudden death, or medics performing assembly-line amputations.

But the novel is perhaps even more impressive as a study of individuals caught up in the sweep of historical events. As the title suggests, the book centers on the "conversion" or education of Miss Lillie Ravenel. Her father, Dr. Ravenel, a Southern gentleman and self-converted "loyalist," supplies the moral idealism requisite to her growth. But it is her involvement with two lovers, Colonel John Carter and Edward Colburne, that completes the education.

The charming, sophisticated Colonel Carter is one of the most virile and forceful characters in American fiction. But, although spectacular in battle, he cannot adjust to peace. He is a man of simple courage and combat morality who is able to deal neither with the emotional difficulties of marriage nor the complexities of modern society. He loves Lillie, but his casual sexual morality cannot withstand the seductions of Mrs. Larue; he commands men adroitly in combat, but cannot manage money under pressure. It is appropriate that he dies in battle, and in doing so, attains a bit of tragic stature.

On the other hand, De Forest's Colburne, probably an idealized self-portrait, is a citizen-soldier. His does not have the automatic animal courage of the natural soldier, but the found courage of an ordinary citizen fighting for a cause in which he believes. His trial by experience purges him of his youthful naïveté and priggishness, and makes him worthy to be Lillie's second husband. And Lillie, in her turn, by virtue of having endured the war, the love, infidelity, and death of a husband, and the birth of a son, is converted from a frivolous, shallow, "secessionist" girl to De Forest's ideal—a mature, "loyalist," Christian mother.

PAUL LAURENCE DUNBAR

Born: Dayton, Ohio (June 27, 1872)
Died: Dayton (February 9, 1906)

Principal Works

POEMS: *Oak and Ivy*, 1893; *Majors and Minors*, 1895; *Lyrics of Lowly Life*, 1896; *Lyrics of the Hearthside*, 1899; *Poems of Cabin and Field*, 1899; *Candle Lightin' Time*, 1901; *Lyrics of Love and Laughter*, 1903; *When Malindy Sings*, 1903; *Li'l Gal*, 1904; *Lyrics of Sunshine and Shadow*, 1905; *Howdy, Honey, Howdy*, 1905; *Joggin' Erlong*, 1906; *The Life and Works of Paul Laurence Dunbar*, 1907; *Chrismus Is A-Comin'*, 1907; *The Complete Poems of Paul Laurence Dunbar*, 1913; *Speakin' o' Christmas and Other Christmas and Special Poems*, 1914; *Little Brown Baby*, 1940.

NOVELS: *The Uncalled*, 1898; *The Love of Landry*, 1900; *The Fanatics*, 1902; *The Sport of the Gods*, 1902.

SHORT STORIES: *Folks from Dixie*, 1898; *The Strength of Gideon and Other Stories*, 1900; *The Heart of Happy Hollow*, 1904; *Best Stories of Paul Laurence Dunbar*, 1938.

Paul Laurence Dunbar was born in Dayton, Ohio, June 27, 1872, the child of former slaves. His mother was a domestic slave until the Emancipation Proclamation freed her, and his father escaped from slavery in Kentucky by "underground railroad" to Canada, later moved to Ohio and followed the plasterer's trade. Matilda Burton was a young widow with two sons when she married Joshua Dunbar.

Both father and mother taught themselves to read as adults. Matilda Dunbar shared her son's passion for literature. She began teaching him his letters when he was four, and he learned to read as she pieced together Bible passages propped over her washtubs. He was always scribbling and made his first attempts at verse when he was six. He recited some original verses at a Sunday school Easter service when he was twelve and never ceased to write after that.

Matilda Dunbar was probably the most important influence on Dunbar. His parents separated in 1873 and later divorced. Joshua Dunbar died when Paul was twelve. He and his mother supported themselves by washing clothes and doing other such work, relying on each other to make ends meet financially. She and her friends told the young boy the old stories of Kentucky plantation life, and she shared her love of poetry with him.

From elementary school on, Dunbar had sympathetic teachers who encouraged him in his writing and in giving readings. In consequence, he continued his formal education through high school, the only black in his class. He excelled in literary studies and was president of the Philomathean Society, a high school literary group, and editor of *The High School Times*. By his graduation in June 1891, he was well known in Dayton as a writer.

However, there were no jobs for writers in Dayton, especially if the writer were black, so he finally found a job running an elevator for four dollars a week. But in the summer of 1892, events brought the first of a series of friends who were to aid Dunbar throughout his life. The Western Writers Association met in Dayton, and one of Dunbar's former teachers arranged for him to deliver the welcome. He read an original verse prepared for the occasion and so impressed his audience that some of them sought him out at his elevator. As a result, Newton Matthews wrote an article about him that was printed throughout the Middle West, brought him to the attention and commendation of James Whitcomb Riley, introduced him to newspaper editors who invited him to submit work, and led to Dunbar's plan to print a volume of his poems privately.

In 1893, *Oak and Ivy* was printed and sold out in short order. (Oak represented his literary English poems and ivy the humorous dialect pieces, for he thought they were merely leaning on the more serious work.) In June of 1893, Dunbar moved to Chicago hoping to work in the World's Fair. He continued to write and to give recitals while he earned a living as a waiter, clerk, and latrine attendant. He met Frederick Douglass who considered him the most promising black man of his day, and Douglass gave him a job at the fair with the Haitian exhibit.

Dunbar brought out his second book, *Majors and Minors*, in 1895. Through the efforts of friends, his book was read by William Dean Howells, who made Paul Laurence Dunbar famous by introducing him to the world in a review in *Harper's Weekly*. Consequently, Dunbar's poems began to sell, and he became a popular reciter, even arranging a tour to England.

He had written to Alice Ruth Moore for two years before they met. Her parents successfully kept the two who had become lovers by correspondence apart until the eve of his trip to England. Then she ran away from Boston to see him at the gala farewell reception being given in his honor by Mrs. Victoria Earle Matthews. That night, the first time he had ever seen her, he proposed; and she accepted. They married in 1898 after his trip to England.

England welcomed him as it had Phillis Wheatley, the first black woman to have a book published and one of the first black American poets, and as it had William Wills Brown, the first American black man to write a novel: she turned out her most learned and distinguished to meet, hear, and laud him. He was to England the symbol of the black struggle in America.

The tour of England brought extremely good press notices, some successful private readings sponsored by the United States Ambassador John Hay, and allowed Dunbar to get away from the color prejudice of his own country for a more objective view; but the tour did not bring financial success. However, he wrote some of his best poems and his first novel, *The Uncalled*, while abroad.

When Dunbar returned from England to a new job as assistant in the Library of Congress, his popularity had increased. His next collection, *Lyrics of Lowly*

Life, with its introduction by William Dean Howells, brought him national fame. Though in his introduction Howells says "The world is too old . . . to care for the work of a poet because he is black," he makes his appeal on the basis of race: "Paul Dunbar was the only man of pure African blood and of American civilization to feel the Negro life aesthetically and express it lyrically." That he was the only one to do so was not true; nevertheless, Howells' endorsement brought national acclaim. His first collection of short stories, *Folks from Dixie*, 1898, showed that Dunbar had a finely tuned sense of the Negro in America.

His health was never good, and the dusty shelves of the Library aggravated his condition and a cough, so he finally resigned on January 1, 1899. In May, 1899, he took pneumonia, which proved to be the first in a chain of continuing respiratory problems that ended in his death from tuberculosis.

Between 1900 and 1905, he achieved the astonishing production of three novels, three collections of short stories, two volumes of verse, three illustrated collections, and songs for a number of musicals. However, his illness recurred time and again. His family resided for a time in Colorado for his health. His doctor recommended whiskey as a stimulant. Driving himself furiously to write and to give readings, he resorted to drinking more and more to spur himself on. This was a large part of the reason that he and his wife separated in 1902. In 1903, he and his mother returned to reside in Dayton until his death on February 9, 1906. His later works reflect a deeper note of the noble power of love and more need of the divine as well as personal anguish and reflections on death. They also reflect a refinement in technique.

Paul Laurence Dunbar was more than any other black of his time a representative of his race, one whose literary talent and behavior disproved two centuries of American racial clichés. Today schools and libraries are named after him. Those who read his work enjoy it, for above the toil and turmoil of the day, he asserted the right to live, laugh, and love. American literature would be incomplete without the fine element which Paul Laurence Dunbar supplied.

Bibliography

The complete poems were collected with an introduction by W. D. Howells from *Lyrics of Lowly Life* in 1913 and reprinted in 1950. A collection of Dunbar's best stories was edited by Benjamin Brawley and published in 1938. Other important sources on Dunbar and his works are Benjamin Brawley, *Paul Laurence Dunbar: Poet of His People*, 1936; Victor Lawson, *Dunbar Critically Examined*, 1941; J. Saunders Redding, *To Make a Poet Black*, 1939; Darwin T. Turner, "Paul Laurence Dunbar: The Rejected Symbol," in *Journal of Negro History*, 1967; Kenny J. Williams, *They Also Spoke: An Essay on Negro Literature in America, 1787–1930*, 1970. Also of interest is the biographical sketch by Bertha Rodgers, *Little Brown Baby*, 1940.

THE SPORT OF THE GODS

Type of work: Novel
Author: Paul Laurence Dunbar (1872–1906)
Type of plot: Social protest
Time of plot: Post Civil War
Locale: The rural South and Harlem, New York
First published: 1902

Written by one of the first black writers to write about black problems, The Sport of the God's *serves as a social history of post-Civil War America and the black people's struggle to live in both the North and the South.*

Principal Characters

Berry Hamilton, a former slave who finds a job as a butler in the Oakley household following the Civil War. He proves a hard-working, loyal servant. When Mr. Oakley prospers, Berry moves into a small cottage on the estate, marries, and has two children. His luck sours when he is accused of stealing money from Oakley's half brother and is sentenced to ten years in prison. When he is finally exonerated, he finds his family changed. It is not possible to recapture the happiness he once had known. He and his family represent the plight of many freed slaves in the post–Civil War society.

Fannie, his wife. Following her husband's imprisonment, she and her children are rejected by the townspeople, black and white alike. They move to New York City, where Fannie watches the values she had taught her children crumble. Finally, in order to survive, she too must compromise, and she remarries. When Berry finally returns, she is too defeated to return his love. They eventually are reunited and return to work on the Oakley estate in a condition of despair.

Joe, their son. He is impressed by the fast living in New York City and naïvely squanders the money he earns. He falls in love with Hattie Sterling, who works on the stage. After he becomes an alcoholic, Hattie rejects him. He murders her and is imprisoned.

Kitty, their daughter. Hattie gets her a job as a singer on the stage, and she rapidly loses her values. She single-mindedly pursues her new career.

Maurice Oakley, a white Southern landowner who employs Berry on his estate. When Maurice's half brother, Francis, informs him that money has been stolen from his room, Maurice suspects Berry and sees that he is tried and convicted. Oakley later learns that Francis had lied, but he attempts to keep this information secret.

Francis Oakley, his half brother, an artist. Although Francis shows little possibility of success, Maurice sends him abroad to study for five years. At a farewell party, Francis claims that money has been stolen from his room. Years later, he informs Maurice in a letter that he had lost the money gambling.

Mr. Thomas, a lodger in the house where the Hamilton's first live in New York City. Attracted to Kitty, he befriends the family and introduces Joe to the fast living which proves his downfall.

Hattie Sterling, a young woman Joe first sees on the stage. She helps Kitty get work as a singer. When she finally spurns Joe's company, he kills her.

Skaggsy, a sly newspaper reporter. He learns of Berry's imprisonment and uncovers the truth which clears him of the crime.

The Story

At the end of the Civil War, Berry Hamilton, once a slave in the deep South, was finally free to find work. After much searching, he secured a job working as a butler for Maurice Oakley, and Hamilton stood by Oakley through good and hard times. When Oakley's fortune improved, Hamilton moved into a small servant's cottage on Oakley's estate. Oakley married, and not long after, Hamilton followed suit, marrying Fannie, Oakley's housekeeper. The Hamiltons had two children, Joe and Kitty, and lived comfortably and peacefully for a time.

The Oakley's themselves did not have children; however, Maurice had a half brother Francis whom he loved as a son. For several years, Maurice had supported Francis, encouraging him in his career as an artist and providing him with the best education available. Although Francis had never been successful as an artist, Maurice had offered to send him abroad to study for five years. The Oakleys gave Francis a large farewell party, and it was a tremendous success. However, in the midst of the festivities, Francis told Maurice privately that he had suffered a terrible loss: someone had stolen almost a thousand dollars from his room. Maurice comforted his brother, quickly offering to cover the loss. Francis was thus able to leave for Europe as scheduled.

Maurice immediately called in local detectives to conduct an investigation. Although no real evidence was uncovered, circumstances pointed toward Berry Hamilton, for he was one of the few servants who would have had access to Francis' room. Police discovered that Berry had recently deposited a large sum of money in his bank account. This money was, in fact, an accumulation of Berry's savings, but Maurice Oakley still suspected Berry. He rationalized that a servant, in his belief, was never above suspicion. And so Berry, after twenty years of loyal service, was tried in a Southern court and sentenced to ten years in prison.

The Hamiltons were shattered by the news, and their situation worsened. The Oakleys, anxious to be rid of them, insisted that they leave their home immediately. As Fannie and Joe tried to procure a new house and a job, they found that the town had turned against them. Many of their poorer neighbors had envied their past good fortune and were happy to condemn the Hamiltons when their luck changed. Desperate, they decided to leave the South; the Hamiltons moved to New York City.

Initially, their move was easier than they had anticipated. They quickly found cheap lodging, and their landlady, Mrs. Jones, introduced them to her favorite lodger, Mr. Thomas. Kitty attracted Thomas, who befriended the family, bringing them to the theater so that he could be with her. Kitty was shy and reserved with Mr. Thomas. Fannie distrusted him; Joe, however, was impressed by what he considered to be Thomas' sophisticated manners, and Joe was anxious to befriend him. Once Joe found work and was earning money, Mr. Thomas condescended to show Joe around his favorite clubs, introducing him to such regulars as Skaggsy, a sly newspaper reporter, and Sadness, a parasite who lived off of other people's fortunes. The clientele had no difficulty in taking advantage of Joe's naïveté, and Joe soon spent all of his money buying himself and others drinks. For Joe, the highlight of these evenings came when Mr. Thomas introduced Joe to Hattie Sterling, one of the girls he had seen on the stage one evening when he was out with Mr. Thomas. Joe was overwhelmed when Hattie began to see him regularly, and he spent less and less time at home.

Fannie and Kitty soon ran out of money and asked Joe for help. He finally agreed to introduce Kitty to Hattie to see if she could get Kitty a job on the stage. Fannie was completely against her daughter working in this hard, competitive environment, where values such as those she had learned in the rural South had become obsolete. Kitty, however, insisted on meeting Hattie.

Mrs. Hamilton watched her two children change dramatically: Joe had taken to drinking, gambling, and carousing. He had emotionally and morally rejected his past. Kitty, closer to her mother and more sensitive, had remained, at least for a time, removed from the dark circles in which her brother moved. However, she too yearned for the excitement and glitter which she believed the city held. When Hattie offered Kitty a chance to sing on the stage, she took it. In a last futile attempt to save her daughter, Fannie threatened to remarry if her daughter worked as a singer. Her threat did not have the desired effect. Kitty congratulated her mother for her good sense and wished her the best. Brokenhearted, Fannie eventually remarried against her own better judgment. She too had to survive.

By this time, Joe had become an alcoholic. When Hattie spurned his company, he reformed for awhile, but eventually, he relapsed. She finally rejected him entirely, ordering him out of her life. In a jealous rage, Joe broke into her apartment, drunk, and strangled her. The police found him hovering around the dead body a few days later. He surrendered without a murmur, a shell of the man he once had been.

Back in Europe, Francis Oakley had a change of heart. In a drunken stupor, he wrote to his brother Maurice, confessing that he never had lost the money as he had pretended. Instead, he told his brother that he had gambled the money away, attempting to raise an even larger sum of money with which he had hoped to appease his mistress. Maurice, upon receiving the letter, suffered a profound shock. When he recovered, he hid the letter in his breast pocket, determined to keep his brother's confession from the world.

Luck finally began to turn Berry Hamilton's way. Skaggsy, a reporter for the newspaper the *Universe*, remembered the story Joe had confessed over a bottle of liquor concerning the unjust imprisonment of his father. Skaggsy decided that this story would make an excellent article, and he received permission from his editor to pursue his lead. Following his instincts, he visited the Hamilton's home town and talked with Maurice Oakley. Oakley refused to admit that Berry was innocent. Skaggsy, on a hunch, wrestled with Oakley, procuring the letter Oakley had hidden in his pocket. With this crucial piece of evidence, he returned to New York to write a sensational article for the *Universe*. After the paper exerted pressure on the Southern court system, Berry was released. No one told Berry about the changes that had occurred while he was in jail. With his wife's new address in hand, he joyfully rushed to see her.

Their reunion was hardly joyful: she told him about Kitty's work on the stage, Joe's imprisonment, and her own remarriage. Berry left brokenhearted.

Berry's bad luck again seemed to change. He was reunited with Fannie when her second husband died. By this time, however, they had lost the ability to find happiness together. Without any real alternative, they returned to the Oakley's cottage where they lived the remainder of their lives. They resumed their old jobs with a resignation that bordered on despair.

Critical Evaluation

Paul Laurence Dunbar, writing at the turn of the nineteenth century, produced the first black protest novel in America. *The Sport of the Gods*, Dunbar's fourth novel, describes the plight of the men and women freed after the Civil War. According to Dunbar, despite the Emancipation Proclamation, conditions did not change significantly for the black people in the South. The story itself centers around Berry Hamilton, a man who, like so many other black men during the post-Reconstruction period, chooses to stay close to his home, struggling to rebuild and stabilize the community in which he has worked for so long. Although Berry Hamilton and his family are hired by the Oakleys, the relationship of the Hamiltons to their employers does not differ greatly from the relationship of slave to master before the Civil War. While the Oakleys are friendly and generous to the Hamiltons, the security which the Hamiltons feel, working and living on this white man's estate, is fragile at best.

Early in the novel, Dunbar reveals the exact nature of the conditions in which the Hamiltons live. When Oakley's half brother allegedly loses a large sum of money, Oakley is quick to suspect Berry Hamilton. Despite Berry's history of honest and loyal service, Oakley is deaf to Berry's innocent protests. Because Berry is black, Oakley feels he is suspect. Although there is no solid evidence against Berry, he has little chance of winning his case in the Southern courtroom, and he is sentenced to ten years in prison. Once the court finds Berry guilty, the remaining members of the Hamilton family have little hope of surviving in their community. Instead of finding support among the other black families in the community, they are greeted with suspicion and scorn. They fall victim to the envy of their neighbors who have always resented the Hamilton's past prosperity. Thus, despite the fact that they have served as faithful employees and upstanding members of their community for over twenty years, the foundation of the security of this black Southern family depends on the whims of their white employers.

Dunbar, however, is not solely concerned with the experience of the black man in the rural South. He also writes about the fate of the people who migrated North hoping to find a land of freedom and opportunity. The Hamiltons themselves decide to move to New York City. The story of their struggle to survive mirrors the tragic fate of so many black people who have been reared in the rural South and who have then attempted to move North to an urban environment so alien to their own. Dunbar poignantly contrasts the life in the city with that of the small farming community in which the Hamiltons had once prospered. Dunbar brings out the tremendous difference in values between these two areas of the county. While the Hamiltons survive the city's harsh economic challenges, their own value systems are destroyed: Kitty, once a shy and reserved girl, deserts her mother and her brother as she pushes herself to become a successful singer. Joe, who soon loses the strength and pride of his youth, falls victim to alcohol. Having long since abandoned the morals of his past, he murders a woman, feeling nothing, not even concern for his own safety. Fannie's degeneration in the city is the most confounding. This woman who had stuck so closely to her own religious faith and beliefs finally breaks down and deserts her husband, marrying another man. When Berry finally gets out of jail, he finds that she is a victim of physical abuse, with little emotional energy to even respond to his declarations of love.

Dunbar's novel is significant in many ways. First, it serves as a social history of the American people after the Civil War, the black people's attempts to live in the South, and their migration to the North. The disillusionment that the black people experience when they move North seeking a promised land has shaped their attitudes and history in America today. Most significantly, however, Dunbar's novel was one of the first incidences of a black author writing about the problems of the black people in America. He sets an important precedent, paving the way for many other great novels in our American literary heritage.

EDWARD EGGLESTON

Born: Vevay, Indiana (December 10, 1837)
Died: Lake George, New York (September 2, 1902)

Principal Works

NOVELS: *The Hoosier Schoolmaster,* 1871; *The End of the World,* 1872; *The Mystery of Metropolisville,* 1873; *The Circuit Rider,* 1874; *Roxy,* 1878; *The Hoosier Schoolboy,* 1883; *The Graysons,* 1887; *The Faith Doctor,* 1891.

SHORT STORIES: *Book of Queer Stories and Stories Told on a Cellar Door,* 1871; *The Schoolmaster's Stories,* 1874; *Queer Stories for Boys and Girls,* 1884.

HISTORY *:Brant and Red Jacket,* 1879; *A History of the United States,* 1888; *The Beginners of a Nation,* 1896; *The Transit of Civilization from England to America in the Seventeenth Century,* 1901.

Edward Eggleston was born in Vevay, Indiana, on December 10, 1837. His childhood was a sequence of serious illnesses interrupted occasionally by brief periods of precarious health. Despite concerted efforts to give him the life of a normal child, he was able to attend only two years of public school, and the rest of his early education came from the reading he was able to do as his health allowed.

Eggleston studied for a time at the Amelia Academy in Virginia and then, in another effort to regain his health, went to the rural regions of Minnesota. Here he became a circuit rider for the Methodists. By the time he was twenty-four he was regarded as the leading minister of his faith in Minnesota.

After a period in which he wrote children's stories and achieved a reputation through his contributions to literary periodicals, Eggleston went to New York to become editor of *Hearth and Home,* a magazine which came to national prominence under his editorship. *The Hoosier Schoolmaster,* first published in the magazine, was largely responsible for the sudden fame of both the periodical and its editor. The book sold over 20,000 copies in its first year of publication, and was translated into several languages for distribution abroad.

Eggleston's later career alternated between editorial duties, religious work, creative writing and, once again, the sickbed. He retired to Lake George, New York, and built "Owl's Nest," the home of his remaining days, where he died on September 2, 1902.

Throughout his life Eggleston turned to literature only when health forced him to give up his ministerial duties. His creative output frequently reflected this fact, for moral and didactic purposes often governed the structure and tone of his fiction. In the latter part of his career he turned to historical exposition. It was his belief that he had been writing history in novels and that the new field was no radical departure from the old.

Eggleston's character, which pervades all of his writing, was best summed up by his brother: "In all his life . . . Edward Eggleston never permitted himself to do any act that his conscience forbade, or to leave undone any duty that his conscience enjoined. But while in childhood the dogmas in which he had been trained gave law to his thought, his intellect, as he grew older, asserted its right to question the authority of those dogmas, and he did so with utter fearlessness, and with the same conscientious courage that had in childhood led him to obey at whatever cost."

Bibliography

The most authoritative study is William Pierce Randel, *Edward Eggleston*, 1946, which contains an extensive bibliography. This may be supplemented by the biography written by his brother, George C. Eggleston, *The First of the Hoosiers*, 1903. The best brief biographical sketch is by Ralph L. Rusk, *Dictionary of American Biography*. See also Meredith Nicholson, *The Hoosiers*, 1900. Briefer studies include John T. Flannagan, "*The Hoosier Schoolmaster* in Minnesota," *Minnesota History*, XVIII (1937), 347–370, and "The Novels of Edward Eggleston," *College English*, V (1944), 250–258; Charles Hirschfield, "Edward Eggleston: Pioneer in Social History," in *Historiography and Urbanization: Essays in American History in Honor of W. Stull Holt*, edited by Eric F. Goldman, 1941; Spencer T. Benjamin, "The New Realism and a National Literature," *Publications of the Modern Language Association*, LVI (1941), 1116–1132; and James A. Rawley, "Edward Eggleston, Historian," *Indiana Magazine of History*, XL (1944), 341–352.

THE HOOSIER SCHOOLMASTER

Type of work: Novel
Author: Edward Eggleston (1837–1902)
Type of plot: Regional romance
Time of plot: About 1850
Locale: Indiana
First published: 1871

A regional study, this book captures the twists of phrasing, the rough frontier conduct, and the morality of its country characters. With great charm and detail, the author faithfully reconstructs a picture of Indiana in mid-nineteenth century.

Principal Characters

Ralph Hartsook, the schoolmaster at Flat Creek, Indiana. He makes a place for himself in the community until his enemies accuse him of being a thief. He escapes a mob and gives himself up to the authorities. He is tried and found innocent. Being a friendly and democratic man, he tries to help everyone. He falls in love with Hannah, a hired girl, and marries her.

Hannah Thomson, the "bound girl" at the Means home. She defeats the schoolmaster in a spelling bee. He falls in love with her and marries her.

Bud Means, one of the older pupils in Ralph's school. He becomes the schoolmaster's friend. Chagrined when he is ignored by Martha Hawkins, he falls in with evil companions, but he saves himself and tries to help the schoolmaster.

Martha Hawkins, daughter of the local squire. She is in love with bashful Bud.

Dr. Small, a thief. He is Ralph's enemy and tries to lay his crime upon the schoolmaster's head. At Ralph's trial he incriminates himself and is later hanged for his misdeeds.

Pete Jones, Dr. Small's accomplice. He tries to lay the blame for the robbery on

Mr. Pearson, an honest man. He and his brother are sent to prison as punishment for their part in the robbery.

Walter Johnson, another of Dr. Small's accomplices. He is Ralph's cousin. He turns out to be a religious man who cannot keep his crime hidden. He turns state's evidence and goes unpunished.

Shocky Thomson, Hannah's young brother.

Bill Means, Bud's brother, one of Ralph's pupils.

Granny Sander, a gossipy woman who spreads evil rumors about Ralph.

Mirandy Means, sister of Bud and Bill. Infatuated with the schoolmaster, she tries to come between Ralph and Hannah.

Mrs. Means, mother of Mirandy, Bud, and Bill. She testifies against Ralph at the robbery trial to spite him for spurning Mirandy.

Mr. Pearson, a basketmaker who took in Shocky when his blind mother went to the poorhouse. He is an honest man wrongly accused of the theft.

Mrs. Matilda White, Ralph Hartsook's

aunt. She refuses to take in the unfortunate Mrs. Thomson.

Miss Nancy Sawyer, Ralph's home-town friend who takes in Shocky to prevent his being bound out.

Mrs. Thomson, Hannah and Shocky's mother, a poor but honest widow who is blind and who is finally forced to go to the poorhouse. Later she is able to make a home for Shocky again through the kindness of Nancy Sawyer.

The Story

Ralph Hartsook had not thought schoolteachers were judged by their muscular ability when he applied for the job as schoolmaster of Flat Creek, Indiana. Before long, however, he learned his competence would be judged by his power to keep his pupils from driving him out of the schoolhouse. His first step was to make friends with Bud and Bill Means, sons of the school trustee, in whose house he was to board for a time. He was tired from the ten miles he had trudged to apply for his job, but he walked almost the same distance that evening when he went coon hunting with the boys.

Ralph Hartsook held his own against the pranks and challenges of his pupils until the night of the big spelling-bee. Then before most of the people in Flat Creek he was defeated by the Means' bound-girl, Hannah Thomson.

Finding himself strongly attracted to the girl, he escorted her home after the spelling-bee.

Kept awake by curiosity about Hannah's past, Ralph had trouble sleeping that night. At two in the morning he got up, restless, and strolled down the road toward the schoolhouse. Three horsemen passed him in the darkness, one riding a horse with white markings. A few minutes later Dr. Small rode by, returning, Ralph supposed from a night call. He went back to Pete Jones' house, where he was staying at the time. The next morning he discovered that the horse with the white markings stood in Pete's stable, and he learned from Shocky Thomson, Hannah's young brother, that there had been a robbery the night before.

He decided not to tell what he knew. He had no proof that Pete Jones was connected with the housebreaking and it would have been awkward to explain his own ramblings at an early hour. To add to his misery that day, Mirandy Means, who had been casting sheep's eyes at him, informed him that her brother Bud was fond of Hannah.

Squire Hawkins invited Ralph to spend the weekend with him. Walking toward the squire's house with Shocky, who took the same direction home from school, he learned from the boy that his father was dead and his blind mother in the poorhouse. When Hannah went to live with the Meanses, he himself had been taken in by Mr. Pearson, a basket-maker.

That evening Ralph was surprised to see Dr. Small's horse tied in front of Granny Sander's cabin. She had a reputation as a witch among the people of Flat Creek, and she was a malicious gossip. Ralph did not know that the doctor was busy planting the seeds of rumors in Granny Sander's mind, rumors that Ralph had been a philanderer at home, and that he was somehow implicated in the robbery. Small disliked Ralph, though Ralph had never been able to find any reason for it. Rumor had done its ugly work by Sunday morning. At church Ralph's neighbors had little to say to him.

On Christmas Day, which came the following week, the boys did not follow the custom of asking the teacher for a holiday. Instead Bud and others of the older pupils barricaded themselves in the schoolhouse to keep Ralph from entering and had to be forced out by sulphur thrown down the chimney. Later Bud threatened to thrash Ralph because the schoolmaster had taken the squire's niece, Martha, to church the Sunday before. Bud was jealous. Ralph immediately declared he was really inclined toward Hannah, but had avoided seeing her because of Mirandy's statement. Bud and Ralph quickly became fast friends. Now, the schoolmaster felt, he had a clear field for courting.

Before Bud and Ralph finished their talk, Shocky burst into the schoolhouse with the news that Mr. Pearson was about to be tarred and feathered by the people of Flat Creek, who had been led by Pete Jones to believe the basket-maker was guilty of the robbery. Pearson, too, had seen three men riding by on the night of the robbery, and Jones had decided the best way to divert suspicion from himself would be to accuse Shocky's benefactor.

Hoping to protect the old man, Bud Means started toward the Pearson home. On the way he met Jones to whom he gave a sound drubbing.

That night Bud helped Pearson to escape to his brother's home in the next county. To thwart Pete Jones' efforts to have Shocky Thomson bound out by declaring the Pearsons paupers, Ralph took the boy to stay with his friend, Miss Nancy Sawyer, in his home town of Lewisburg. His aunt, Mrs. Matilda White, refused to have Shocky's mother in her house because she was a pauper, and so, at Miss Sawyer's own suggestion, Mrs. Thomson was brought to the Sawyer home to spend the weekend with her son. Through Miss Sawyer's efforts, a collection was taken up at church that Sunday afternoon, and with that donation and the money she earned knitting socks, Mrs. Thompson was able to make a home of her own for Shocky.

That same Sunday Bud, intending to ask Martha to marry him, visited Squire Hawkins' house. Suddenly bashful, he told her only of the spelling-bee to take place at the schoolhouse on Tuesday night. Shortly afterward the Squire received an anonymous letter, threatening him with the burning of his barn if Martha associated with Bud, the implication being that Bud was incriminated in the robbery. The squire persuaded Martha to ignore Bud. Chagrined by her refusal to let him escort her home from the spelling-bee, Bud began to cultivate Pete Jones and his friends, among them Dr. Small and Walter Johnson, Ralph's cousin.

Bud soon proved he was still Ralph's friend. One day Hannah brought Ralph a letter Bud had sent warning him that he was suspected of the robbery and that there was a plan afoot to tar and feather him that night. Ralph saved himself from the mob by going to a nearby town and giving himself up to the authorities there. His trial was held the next day.

All of Flat Creek was present to see the schoolmaster convicted. Mrs. Means and Pete Jones, particularly, were willing to offer damaging testimony, the former because Ralph had spurned Mirandy's attentions. It was Dr. Small who vindicated Ralph, however, by overshooting the mark in his anxiety to clear himself of Ralph's testimony that the doctor had been out on the night of the robbery.

Small had Walter Johnson called to the stand to testify they had spent the evening together in the physicians's office. But Johnson, at a prayer meeting he had attended with Bud, had been deeply impressed by the minister's warning of eternal damnation for sinners. Summoned before the court, he gave way to his guilty conscience and declared that he, Small, Pete Jones, and Pete's brother had committed the robbery, and that Ralph and Mr. Pearson were innocent.

Walter Johnson went free because of his testimony, but Dr. Small, who had been the ringleader of the band, was hanged. Jones and his brother were given prison sentences.

Ralph Hartsook returned to Lewisburg to teach in a new academy there. Shortly afterward he married Hannah. At Ralph's wedding Bud found his courage at last and proposed to Martha.

Critical Evaluation

As one of America's early literary realists, Edward Eggleston was part of a movement to counter the excesses of bucolic romanticism with "truth-telling" about the bleakness of agrarian life, the bitter—and often petty—rivalries of small-town life, and the very real hatreds and resentments of class conflicts. Influenced by the French critic Hippolyte Adolphe Taine, Eggleston—like such contemporaries as Hamlin Garland and William Dean Howells—followed the dictum, "he writes best who writes about what he knows best." Thus, in *The Hoosier Schoolmaster,* Eggleston based his novel upon the experiences—with which he was intimately familiar—of his brother George, a teacher in his early years and later a noted journalist, biographer, historian, and novelist in his own right. Edward Eggleston also made a special effort, in all of his work, to capture accurately and reflect the peculiar speech and behavior patterns of the people he depicted.

A direct offshoot of this particular version of realism was Eggleston's regionalism, for in writing of what he knew best, he wrote of his native Indiana whose residents were called Hoosiers. The Hoosiers who people the novel are dour, small-town folk preoccupied with the façade of respectability. Accordingly, since pauperism is construed as a major social transgression, Pete Jones's attempt to have the Pearsons declared indigent so that Shocky Thompson could be indentured is a deliberate expression of the region's value system, as is Matilda White's refusal of shelter to Shocky's "pauperized" mother who is subsequently aided by Nancy Sawyer and other members of Miss Sawyer's church.

But Eggleston softened the rigid mores of the region with his own uncompromising morality. Tempered by his ministerial experience and his Christian commitment, Eggleston gave high priority to the didactic value of his work. Swift and sure justice was thus meted out to malefactors according to the severity of their offenses. The repentant Walter Johnson was therefore spared punishment; the guilty Jones brothers were sentenced to prison, and the nonparticipating mastermind of the robbery scheme, Dr. Small, was hanged. The implacable vengeance of a wrathful Christian God was accomplished.

One need not accept or reject the demanding moral code of Eggleston or of the characters he so vividly portrayed. It is sufficient to recognize the existential mode of life which Eggleston filtered through his own sensibility in *The Hoosier Schoolmaster,* for that lifestyle was a distinct reality as the author related it. As such, the novel contributes both to our knowledge and to the author's goal of contributing to the history of civilization in America.

HAROLD FREDERIC

Born: Utica, New York (August 19, 1856)
Died: Henley-on-Thames, England (October 19, 1898)

Principal Works

NOVELS: *Seth's Brother's Wife*, 1887; *The Lawton Girl*, 1890; *In the Valley*, 1890; *The Copperhead*, 1893; *The Damnation of Theron Ware*, 1896; *March Hares*, 1896; *Gloria Mundi*, 1898; *The Market Place*, 1899.

Harold Frederic was born in Utica, New York, August 19, 1856, the son of Henry deMotte Frederic, who died when the child was only eighteen months old. Young Frederic experienced a poverty-stricken boyhood; however, starting as an office boy for the Utica *Observer*, he progressed rapidly in the newspaper world, becoming editor-in-chief of the Albany *Evening Journal* in 1882. Two years later he joined the staff of the *New York Times* as London correspondent and never returned to America. Although Frederic remained typically American, not caring greatly for European culture and never bothering to learn a foreign language, he became an extremely efficient European reporter. He made a trip through the cholera-stricken areas of southern France and Italy, writing extensively on what he saw, and in 1891 he went to Russia to investigate the persecution of the Jews in that country. The result of that trip was *The New Exodus: A Study of Israel in Russia* (1892). The bitterness of his articles caused his virtual exclusion from Russia. Like other journalists of the period, he became interested in the personality of William II and wrote a study of that controversial monarch. Frederic died October 19, 1898, at Henley-on-Thames.

Frederic produced ten volumes of fiction, writing carelessly and hurriedly—sometimes 4,000 words a day. His early books were local color novels of the Mohawk Valley region; he then turned to historical novels of the Revolution and the Civil War (*The Copperhead*), treating his materials with more realism than was common at the time.

His one important novel, and the only one to survive, is *The Damnation of Theron Ware*, published in England as *Illumination*. This story has had considerable influence on modern American fiction, particularly upon the work of Sinclair Lewis, who refers to it in *Main Street* as a favorite of his heroine. Into this novel Frederic incorporated two themes that have been further developed by later writers: the cultural barrenness of the American small town and the hypocrisy of much of American Protestantism. The novel is thus an ancestor of both *Main Street* and *Elmer Gantry*. By making his pathetic hero a Methodist minister, Frederic shocked many readers; however, he shrewdly grasped the greatest weakness of a large segment of the American Protestantism of his time: its appalling narrow-mindedness and its lip-service to moral platitudes. Theron Ware, a product of this starved environment, catches, through the Roman Catholic members of his community, a glimpse of a world beyond that of the American small town, yet his heritage debars him from entering this world and brings him to ruin when he tries to do so. In this study of the last stages of Puritanism, Frederic took an important step away from the popular romantic fiction of his day towards the modern realistic treatment of American life.

Bibliography

There is no definitive biography. For studies see Thomas F. O'Donnell, *Frederic in the Mohawk Valley*, 1968; and Austin Briggs, *The Novels of Harold Frederic*, 1969. A good introduction to the study of Frederic is contained in A. H. Quinn, *American Fiction*, 1936. Two useful articles are Carey McWilliams, "Harold Frederic: 'A Country Boy of Genius,'" *University of California Chronicle*, XXXV (1933), 21–34; and Charles C. Walcutt, "Harold Frederic and American Naturalism," *American Literature*, X (1939), 11–22.

THE COPPERHEAD

Type of work: Novel
Author: Harold Frederic (1856–1898)
Type of plot: Regional romance
Time of plot: 1860's
Locale: Four Corners, New York
First published: 1893

   The Copperhead *is the story of a man in opposition to all his neighbors, as seen through the eyes of a young boy. The theme which finally emerges is the impossibility of purely judging a man's political views before one thoroughly understands his personal background and motivations. Frederic's vividly realistic descriptions and skillful use of regional dialects provide memorable local color.*

Principal Characters

Abner Beech, a farmer and a violent Anti-Abolitionist in the equally violent Abolitionist community of Dearborn County, New York. His political sentiments earn for him the name "Copperhead" (a Northerner with Southern sympathies) and the enmity of his neighbors, who plan to tar and feather him. When Abner's house is ignited and burned by the bonfire for the tarring, the neighbors recover their senses, ask his forgiveness, and offer to restore his property. Goodwill reigns again among the folk of Dearborn County.

Jee Hagadorn, Abner Beech's Abolitionist neighbor and enemy.

Jeff Beech, Abner Beech's son, a Union soldier in love with Esther Hagadorn.

Esther Hagadorn, Jee Hagadorn's daughter and the sweetheart of Jeff Beech.

Ni Hagadorn, Jee Hagadorn's son.

Jimmy, an orphan boy who lives with Abner Beech.

Hurley, Abner Beech's Anti-Abolitionist hired man.

Warner Pitts, Abner Beech's former hired man, now an officer in the Union Army.

Byron Truax, a fellow soldier of Jeff Beech.

M'rye, Abner Beech's wife.

Janey, a hired girl.

Avery, the local squire.

The Story

   Abner Beech was a stalwart, shaggy man, who had often been supervisor of his district. Jimmy, who was an orphan, went to live with him when he was six or seven years old. Abner was a town leader, a great reader, and he owned more books than most people did in Dearborn County, located in northern New York State.

   For some reason, Abner Beech violently hated the Abolitionists. The first Abolitionist in Dearborn County, as far as Jimmy knew, was old Jee Hagadorn, but now nearly everyone except Abner Beech shared the old man's sentiments. Because the Anti-abolitionists were attacked from the pulpit every Sunday at church meeting, Abner and Jimmy finally stopped going to church. Then someone spread the rumor that Abner's milk had not been accepted at the communal cheese factory because he had put water into it. At that time Abner's household became real outcasts in Four Corners.

One day in August, Abner came home early from the field. He was furious because he learned that Jeff, his only son, had been seen walking with Esther Hagadorn, the daughter of his enemy. Abner sent Jimmy to call Jeff home. When Jimmy found Jeff and Esther, the young man gave the boy his fishing pole and told him to tell Abner that he was going to Tecumseh to enlist in the Union Army. When Jimmy told Jeff's parents what Jeff had said, they took the news calmly. They had already guessed his intention, for on that same day an entire group of boys from the area had gone off to enlist.

Abner's hired man also enlisted, and Abner hired an Irish widower, Hurley, who had been doing odd jobs in the neighborhood. Hurley was also an Anti-abolitionist, the only one in the area besides Abner. It was understood in Abner's household that Jeff's name should never be mentioned, and Abner refused to show regret over the departure of his only son.

In late September, Hurley and Jimmy went to Octavius to buy some butter firkins; Abner refused to buy firkins from Jee Hagadorn, who lived close by. In Octavius Hurley and Jimmy learned of the terrible battle at Antietam, in which a number of the boys from Dearborn County had taken part. Hurley got into a fight when some of the citizens taunted him for being a Copperhead, a Northerner who sympathized with the Southern cause in the Civil War.

On the way home from Octavius, Jimmy went to see Jee Hagadorn. Jimmy found Esther there, worrying about Jeff. Jee came home elated because Lincoln had signed the Emancipation Proclamation.

A fortnight later the Beech household learned that Jeff Beech and Byron Truax had been reported missing after a battle in the South.

The work on the farm continued. Warner Pitts, Abner's former hired man, came home on furlough as an officer. A hero to the townspeople, one day he called Abner a Copperhead. Ni Hagadorn, Jee's son, did not like Warner Pitts, and so he went to Abner's house to tell him that he was going south to try to find Jeff. Abner refused, however, to give Ni any money to help him on his journey.

The local citizens were beginning to feel that the North was not carrying on the war as virgorously as they expected. On election day, November 4, Jimmy accompanied Abner and Hurley to the polls. Abner voted proudly, but the inspector said that Hurley's naturalization papers were not in order and that he could not vote. When a fight started, another inspector then said that Hurley could vote. A few days later it was learned that the Abolitionists had lost in that congressional district. Abner was overjoyed, believing that this defeat would lead to peace and an end of what he called murder. To celebrate, Janey, one of the hired girls, made a big bonfire.

The next day Jimmy was in bed with a cold. To the amazement of everyone, Esther Hagadorn came in and asked to speak to Abner. When Abner came home he was civil to Esther and asked her to stay to supper. Esther said that there was a rumor to the effect that Copperheads were spreading clothes that had smallpox in them and that the local citizens were fearful and angry. She said that Abner's bonfire to celebrate the voting results had made them even angrier and that they were planning to come for Abner that night. Esther then accepted Abner's invitation to remain and have supper with them.

The townspeople arrived to tar and feather Abner and Hurley and to ride them on a rail. Abner, however, stood firm, a loaded shotgun on his arm. Suddenly Jimmy realized that the house was afire. He fainted.

Jimmy regained consciousness later that night. It was snowing, and the house had been completely burned. With some of the furniture that they were able to rescue, Abner and his wife, M'rye, had improvised a home in the cold barn. Esther, still with them, had regained the friendship of M'rye, since they were both able to talk about Jeff again.

Jimmy, unable to sleep that night, overheard Esther talking to Abner. Abner said that he believed that the townspeople had started a fire for the tarring and feathering and that, because of the strong wind, his house had caught fire accidentally. Esther said that Abner was really liked and respected by the townspeople but that they could not be expected to behave reasonably because so many husbands and sons were now involved in the war.

At that point Jee Hagadorn arrived in search of his daughter. Abner pulled off Jee's wet boots and gave him some warm socks. They had breakfast in near silence. Suddenly Ni Hagadorn appeared. He told M'yre that Jeff had been only slightly hurt and was due home any day. M'yre suddenly ran out of the barn, where she found Jeff returned from the war after having lost his left arm.

While everyone was welcoming Jeff and offering condolences, an unexpected visitor arrived. He was Squire Avery, who wanted, on behalf of the townspeople, to apologize for the events of the previous night. Hoping to let bygones be bygones, he asked Abner to send milk to the cheese factory again. He also wanted to have a house-raising bee for Abner's new house and to lend him money if he needed it. Abner, filled with the spirit of forgiveness, said that all of these kindnesses were nearly worth the house burning. He and M'yre expressed the hope that Jeff and Esther would marry.

Critical Evaluation

A Copperhead was a Northerner who sympathized with the South during the Civil War. The integrity of Abner Beech, the Copperhead of the title, and the pressures upon him, are the subjects of the novel. But beyond the main theme and plot is the impact of the events on the young narrator, Jimmy, and how they change him. Jimmy matures during the course of the novel, as he learns that human motivation is not as simple or obvious as it might appear. The importance of public opinion, and its power, stands over the book like a shadow. In those days of intense and bitter political convictions and violent tempers, the gossip at the general store and post office could lead to disastrous consequences. Jimmy sees all of this, and, young though he is, understands the significance of it. In a simple, unpretentious narrative, he conveys this to the reader.

Technically, the novel is an impressive achievement, a first person narration told by a character who does not participate in the main action, and yet a book with great sweep and dramatic power. The novel is perfectly designed and flows effortlessly from beginning to end, building to a dramatic climax, and then settling into a brief denouement. The tone is controlled, with no sense of hysteria or undue passion, although the book deals with irrational and hotheaded individuals. Frederic has maintained such an even tone that perhaps the narrative might even seem too dispassionate. Certainly, he leaves the conclusions of the story to the reader.

In its modest way, this short novel is as perfect as *Ethan Frome* and *The Great Gatsby*. In less than two hundred pages, it encompasses a world, and finally transcends it. Harold Frederic is writing about honor and morality in this story of the civilian side of the Civil War, about the beauty of ordinary things in a violent world, and about the need for respect for an individual's own moral code.

THE DAMNATION OF THERON WARE

Type of work: Novel
Author: Harold Frederic (1856–1898)
Type of plot: Social criticism
Time of plot: The 1890's
Locale: New York State
First published: 1896

One of the first novels to deal with the problems of an American clergyman and to suggest the disintegration of religious orthodoxy, The Damnation of Theron Ware *created a sensational controversy at the time it was written. Intended to show that every individual needs a moral bulwark on which to lean in times of adversity, the work is an indictment of the hypocrisy of a particular denomination, as well as of Ware's ministerial training, which did not prepare him to meet and accept the beliefs of others while still holding to his own.*

Principal Characters

Theron Ware, a young Methodist minister whose religious training and faith are too frail to support the stresses of his life. Unhappy as a small-town minister, he decides to write a book about Abraham, only to find his learning is too slight on this or any intellectual subject. He learns that his Catholic acquaintances have a great deal more culture than he. As his faith totters he becomes suspicious of people and alienates his friends and his wife. He proves unfit for the ministry and becomes a real estate agent.

Alice Ware, a friendly, cheerful young woman, Theron's wife. Though she is accused by her husband of being unfaithful, she is loyal to her husband. When he falls ill, she nurses him back to health and helps him prepare for a new career.

Celia Madden, a pretty Irish-Catholic girl who becomes friendly with Theron and helps him discover that his prejudices are groundless. Her cultural interests also show him how thin the culture of his own people is. She is wrongly and

outrageously accused by Theron of being in love with Father Forbes. For a time Theron thinks he is in love with her, but he alienates her by saying that he is afraid of scandal if he is seen talking to her.

Father Forbes, a Catholic priest who becomes Theron's friend until Theron alienates him by talking slightingly about Dr. Ledsmar, the priest's friend, and by following the priest and Celia to New York.

Dr. Ledsmar, a friend of Father Forbes and Theron. He is alienated when Theron suggests that there is a scandalous relationship between Father Forbes and Celia.

Mr. Soulsby, a professional revivalist. He tries to convince the young minister that his sales approach to religion is not hypocritical. When Theron falls ill and leaves the ministry, Mr. Soulsby proves to be a true friend.

Mrs. Soulsby, Mr. Soulsby's wife, a practical woman who with her husband helps Theron make a new start in life as a real estate agent.

Mr. Gorringe, a trustee of Theron's church. He is the man whom Theron suspects of having an affair with his wife.

Michael Madden, Celia's brother. He, taking a dying man's privilege, tells Theron the truth about himself, as others see the young minister.

The Story

Theron Ware had gone to the annual statewide meeting of the Methodist Episcopal Church with great expectation of being appointed to the large church in Tecumseh. He was greatly disappointed, therefore, when he was sent to Octavius, a small rural community.

To the minister and his wife, the town and its citizens did not appear formidable at first, but a hint of what was to come occurred the first morning after their arrival. A boy who delivered milk to Mrs. Ware informed her that he could not deliver milk on Sunday because the trustees of the church would object. Shortly afterward the trustees told the new minister that his sermons were too dignified and that Mrs. Ware's Sunday bonnet was far too elaborate for a minister's wife. Theron and his wife were depressed. Unhappy in his new charge, Theron decided to write a book about Abraham.

One day Theron assisted an injured Irish-Catholic workman and went home with him to see what help he might give. At the man's deathbed Theron observed the parish priest and a pretty young red-haired girl, Celia Madden, who assisted him. Upon becoming acquainted with these two, the minister was surprised to find that his earlier hostility to Catholics and the Irish was foolish. These people were more cultured than he, as he learned a few evenings later when he went to the priest for some advice in connection with his proposed book.

At the priest's home he met Dr. Ledsmar, a retired physician interested in Biblical research. Both the priest and the doctor knew a great deal about the actual culture of Abraham and his people. They tried to be tactful, but the young minister quickly saw how wrong he had been to think himself ready to write a religious book on any topic; all he knew was the little he had been taught at his Methodist Seminary.

Upon leaving Father Forbes and the doctor, Theron walked past the Catholic church. Hearing music within, he entered to find Celia Madden at the organ. Later he walked home with her and discovered that she was interested in literature and art as well as music. Once again that evening Theron was made to realize how little he actually knew. He went home with the feeling that his own small world was not a very cultured one.

Three months later there was a revival at Theron's church. Mr. and Mrs. Soulsby, two professional exhorters, arrived to lead a week of meetings which were designed to pay off the church debt and put fervor into its members. The Wares, who entertained the Soulsbys, were surprised to find that the revival leaders were very much like insurance salesmen, employing very much the same tactics. During the revival week Theron was nonplussed to discover what he thought were the beginnings of an affair between his wife and one of the trustees of his church, Mr. Gorringe.

In a long talk with Mrs. Soulsby, Theron told her that he had almost decided to give up the Methodist ministry because of the shallowness he had discovered in his people and in his church. Mrs. Soulsby pointed out to him that Methodists were no worse than anyone else in the way of hypocrisy, and that all they lacked was an external discipline. She also reminded him that he was incapable of making a living because he lacked any worldly training.

Theron's life was further complicated when he realized that he was beginning to fall in love with Celia Madden. Because of her interest in music, he had asked her advice in buying a piano for his home, and she had, unknown to him, paid part of the bill for the instrument. He also found time to call on Dr. Ledsmar, whose peculiar views on the early church interested him. He disgusted the old doctor, however, with his insinuations of an affair between Father Forbes and Celia.

In September the Methodists of Octavius had a camp meeting. Its fervor did not appeal to Theron, after his more intellectual religious reading and his discussions with Celia and Father Forbes, and he went off quietly by himself. In the woods he came upon a picnic given by Father Forbes' church. At the picnic he met Celia and had a long talk with her, kissed her, and told her of his unhappiness in his double bondage to church and wife.

Soon afterward he alienated Celia by telling her that he was afraid of scandal if he were seen talking with her. He also offended Father Forbes by reports that Dr. Ledsmar had spoken slightingly of Celia. The priest told his housekeeper that he was no longer at home to Theron Ware.

One day Theron openly confronted his wife with his suspicions about her and Mr. Gorringe. She denied the charges, but her very denial seemed to speak against her in her husband's mind. In his unhappiness he went to see Celia. She was not at home, but her brother, who was dying slowly of tuberculosis, saw him. With the license of the dying he said that when Theron arrived in Octavius he had the face of an angel, full of innocence, but that in the eight months the minister had spent in the little town his face had taken on a look of deceit and cunning. Celia's brother continued by warning the minister that he should stay among his own people, that it was bad for him to tear himself from the support which Methodism had given him.

Leaving the Madden home, Theron learned that Celia was going to New York City. It occurred to him that Father Forbes was also going to the city that evening and perhaps they were traveling together. He went home and told his wife that urgent business called him to Albany; then he went to the station and boarded the train unseen. In New York he saw the priest and Celia meet, and he followed them to a hotel. After the priest had left the hotel, he went upstairs and knocked at Celia's door. She told him that she was busy and did not wish to see him, adding that she had noticed him following her earlier in the journey. While he pleaded with her, Father Forbes came in with some other gentlemen and informed Theron that they had come to New York to get another brother of Celia's out of a bad scrape.

Dismissed, Theron stumbled down the stairs. A few days later he arrived at the Soulsby house at dawn. He told an incoherent story of having tried to commit suicide, of stealing money from the church at Octavius, and of wandering alone about the city for hours while he tried to drink himself to death.

The Soulsbys took him in and sent for his wife. He was ill for months. After his recovery both he and his wife realized that he was never meant for the ministry. Through the Soulsbys, Theron was finally able to make a new start in a real estate office in Seattle. Theron knew he would make a successful real estate agent. Or if that failed, he could try politics. There was still time enough for him to be in Congress before he was forty.

Critical Evaluation

In the nineteenth century and the early twentieth century, a great deal of religious debunking took place in American literature, both journalistic and imaginative, fueled—at least in part—by the muckraking temperament of the times. Contributions ranged from Nathaniel Hawthorne's "The Minister's Black Veil" (1836) and *The Scarlet Letter* (1850) to Sinclair Lewis' *Elmer Gantry* (1927). Harold Frederic's *The Damnation of Theron Ware* added another example to the debate. And a debate it was: clerical ethics and integrity as well as those of institutionalized religion are, in fact, still being hotly contested. Thus, Frederic's novel was meaningful in its own time and still has contemporary relevance.

From this unique position, the novel takes on a significance not usually accorded it by critical consensus, for the book has generally been viewed as a one-of-a-kind indictment of religious hypocrisy rather than as an element in the mainstream of a literary trend. Theron Ware's confusions, for example, were and are viewed in inappropriate nineteenth century terms of self-denial and sacrifice. The emotional problems of Theron Ware have thus been wrongly analyzed: the Reverend Mr. Ware, so the conventional interpretation goes, is simply trying to assert his latent creativity by attempting to write a book and expand his cultural horizons. But, this interpretation notwithstanding, Ware does not succeed, although his attempts cost him his ministry, alienate his friends, and threaten his marriage. And questions remain: "Why did Theron Ware fail? Why was Theron Ware damned?"

First of all, Ware is an extraordinarily immature person, a condition engendered largely by the narrowness of his religious upbringing and his ministerial training which left him unequipped to cope with the realities of life. Second, Ware's understanding of sexuality is, at best, adolescent, for he cannot see beyond the virgin or whore dichotomy and hence is unable to develop a mature relationship with any woman—Alice, Celia, or Mrs. Soulsby. Third, Ware has virtually no insight into himself. He knows nothing of his capabilities, his needs, or his desires; indeed, he seems, at times, hardly to be aware of his own existence. Consequently, Theron Ware is an emotional cripple, blocked from meaningful relationships with himself, with women, and with society at large, including its cultural heritage. That religious training should prove so emotionally debilitating is a severe damnation of such training. Yet the person thus afflicted is equally damned, but in another, more profound way. For Theron Ware, even with the opportunity for a new career in real estate, shows at the end of the book no more promise of succeeding than he showed at the beginning.

Bibliography

Bluefarb, Samuel. *The Escape Motif in the Modern American Novel: Mark Twain to Richard Wright.* Columbus: Ohio State University Press, 1972, pp. 27–41.

Bredahl, A. Carl, Jr. "The Artist in *The Damnation of Theron Ware*," in *Studies in the Novel.* IV (1972), pp. 432–441.

Briggs, Austin, Jr. *The Novels of Harold Frederic.* Ithaca, N.Y.: Cornell University Press, 1969, pp. 97–139.

Carter, Everett. *Howells and the Age of Realism.* Philadelphia: Lippincott, 1954, pp. 239–245.

Coole, Samuel. "Frederic and Hawthorne: The Romantic Roots of Naturalism," in *American Literature.* XLVIII (1976), pp. 29–45.

Crowley, John. "The Nude and the Madonna in *The Damnation of Theron Ware*," in *American Literature.* XLV (November, 1973), pp. 379–389.

Davies, Horton. *A Mirror of the Ministry in Modern Novels.* New York: Oxford University Press, 1959, pp. 71–78.

Farrell, James T. "Harold Frederic's *The Damnation of Theron Ware*," in *Literary Essays, 1954–1974.* Edited by Jack Alan Robbins. Port Washington, N.Y.: Kennikat, 1976, pp. 126–129.

Garner, Stanton. *Harold Frederic.* Minneapolis: University of Minnesota Press, 1969, pp. 33–38.

Graham, Don. " 'A Degenerate Methodist': A New Review of *The Damnation of Theron Ware*," in *American Literary Realism, 1870–1910.* IX (1976), pp. 281–284.

Herron, Ima Honaker. *The Small Town in American Literature.* Durham, N.C.: Duke University Press, 1939, pp. 175–181.

Johnson, George W. "Harold Frederic's Young Goodman Ware: The Ambiguities of a Realistic Romance," in *Modern Fiction Studies.* VIII (Winter, 1962–1963), pp. 361–374.

Kane, Patricia. "Lest Darkness Come upon You: An Interpretation of *The Damnation of Theron Ware,*" in *Iowa English Yearbook.* X (Fall, 1965), pp. 55–59.

O'Donnell, Thomas F. and Hoyt C. Franchere. *Harold Frederic.* New York: Twayne, 1961, pp. 108–117.

Quinn, Arthur Hobson. *American Fiction.* New York: Appleton-Century, 1936, pp. 449–452.

Raleigh, John Henry. "*The Damnation of Theron Ware,*" in *American Literature.* XXX (May, 1958), pp. 210–227. Reprinted in his *Time, Place, and Idea: Essays on the Novel.* Carbondale: Southern Illinois University Press, 1968, pp. 75–95.

Stein, Allen F. "Evasions of an American Adam: Structure and Theme in *The Damnation of Theron Ware,*" in *American Literary Realism, 1870–1910.* V (Winter, 1972), pp. 23–36.

Suderman, Elmer F. "*The Damnation of Theron Ware* as a Criticism of American Religious Thought," in *Huntington Library Quarterly.* XXXIII (November, 1969), pp. 61–75.

Van Der Beets, Richard. "The Ending of *The Damnation of Theron Ware,*" in *American Literature.* XXXVI (November, 1964), pp. 358–359.

Walcutt, Charles C. *American Literary Naturalism, A Divided Stream.* Minneapolis: University of Minnesota Press, 1956, pp. 49–53.

Wilson, Edmund. "Two Neglected American Novelists: II Harold Frederic, the Expanding Upstater," in his *The Devil and Canon Barham: Ten Essays on Poets, Novelists, and Monsters.* New York: Farrar, Straus, 1973, pp. 48–76.

Ziff, Larzer. *The American 1890's: Life and Times of a Lost Generation.* New York: Viking, 1966, pp. 206–228.

NATHANIEL HAWTHORNE

Born: Salem, Massachusetts (July 4, 1804)
Died: Plymouth, New Hampshire (May 19, 1864)

Principal Works

NOVELS: *Fanshawe,* 1828; *The Scarlet Letter,* 1850; *The House of the Seven Gables,* 1851; *The Blithedale Romance,* 1852; *The Marble Faun,* 1860; *Septimius Felton,* 1872; *Doctor Grimshawe's Secret,* 1882.

SHORT STORIES: *Twice-Told Tales,* 1837 (2nd ed., 1842; 3rd ed., 1851); *Grandfather's Chair,* 1841; *Famous Old People,* 1841; *Mosses from an Old Manse,* 1846 (2nd ed., 1854); *The Snow Image and Other Twice-Told Tales,* 1851; *A Wonder Book for Girls and Boys,* 1851; *Tanglewood Tales,* 1853.

ESSAYS: *Our Old Home,* 1863.

JOURNALS: *The American Notebooks,* 1932; *The English Notebooks,* 1941.

Nathaniel Hawthorne, one of the greatest of all American fiction writers, was born in Salem, Massachusetts, July 4, 1804, and died in Plymouth, New Hampshire, May 19, 1864.

His first American ancestor William Hathorne (the *w* was added by Nathaniel himself while he was in college) came to Massachusetts Bay from England with John Winthrop in 1630, and as a magistrate ordered the whipping of a Quakeress in Salem; William's son John was one of the three judges who presided over the Salem witch trials in 1692. Nathaniel was sensitively aware of this inheritance. These men were important figures in the early history of the Massachusetts Bay Colony; they were also guilty of great crimes. The family fortunes had declined since those early days (Nathaniel's father was a ship captain who died in a distant port when the boy was only four years old), and Nathaniel often wondered whether the decline was a punishment for the sins of his (as he called them) "sable-cloaked, steeple-crowned progenitors."

After his graduation from Bowdoin College (where Longfellow, a lifelong friend, was a classmate) in the class of 1825, Hawthorne returned to his mother's house in Salem, where, after the publication of an immature "college novel," *Fanshawe,* in 1828, he settled down to hard application to the craft of fiction. He read much, wrote much, and destroyed much of what he wrote. The result was the appearance in the periodical press of many remarkable stories (or "tales," as he preferred to call them), published anonymously, and the collection in book form of many of these in 1837 under the title *Twice-Told Tales* (the first work to bear the author's name on the title page). Hawthorne was employed in the Boston Custom House in 1839–1840 (his publications having brought him very little money), and in 1841 he joined the socialist community at Brook Farm, where he stayed about six months. Meanwhile, he had met and fallen in love with Sophia

Peabody, and she with him, and after their marriage on July 9, 1842, they went to the "Old Manse" in Concord, Massachusetts, to live. The story of the three years there, as recorded in Hawthorne's *American Notebooks* and his essay *The Old Manse*, is one of the most charming of marital idyls.

Writing more and still more "tales," he brought out in 1846 a second collection entitled *Mosses from an Old Manse*; and, his success still consisting more of esteem than of money, he took a post in the Salem Custom House in 1846, a post which (being a good Democrat) he received from the Democratic administration of James K. Polk, and from which (being not without political enemies in his local precinct) he was ousted in 1849 by the Whig administration of Zachary Taylor. Though greatly angered at the time, Hawthorne later saw the loss of his job as a blessing in disguise; for in the gloom of this seeming misfortune, he sat down to write *The Scarlet Letter*. This novel (or "romance," as he preferred to call this and his other longer fictions) proved to be his greatest book and made him famous.

For a year and a half following the publication of *The Scarlet Letter* Hawthorne lived in the Berkshires, near Lenox, where he wrote *The House of the Seven Gables*, published in 1851, and enjoyed the stimulating friendship of Herman Melville, whose *Moby Dick*, published in the same year, was dedicated to Hawthorne. Returning to Eastern Massachusetts (he always preferred the ocean to the mountains), he wrote at West Newton *The Blithedale Romance*, based upon his Brook Farm experience and published in 1852. In 1853, he went with his wife and three children (Una, Julian, and Rose) to Liverpool, England, where he served four years as United States Consul, a comparatively lucrative post to which he had been appointed by President Franklin Pierce, whose devoted friendship went back to their college days together at Bowdoin. The Hawthornes were in Italy in 1858–1859, and in 1860, shortly after the publication of *The Marble Faun* (which was based upon Italian experiences, and appeared first in England as *Transformation*), they returned to "The Wayside," in Concord, where Hawthorne spent the remaining four years of his life. These were years of sadness, frustration, and failing health. He managed to bring out a fine collection of essays about England, *Our Old Home*, but the old skill at fiction-writing seemed to have deserted him. His death occurred while he, accompanied by the faithful Pierce, was on a recuperative journey to the White Mountains. Mrs. Hawthorne, who lived seven years longer, religiously devoted her widowhood to the publication of her husband's journals.

Hawthorne is a symbolic writer whose greatness seems to grow with the passing years. Discerning critics and readers of the mid-twentieth century and later seem tireless in discovering "layers" of meanings in his fiction. Hawthorne's work is seen more and more clearly as a criticism of life, a weighing of conflicting forces, a dramatization of the dilemmas and ambiguities which beset the human condition. His attitude toward life can be called "Puritan," but more properly it is broadly Christian in that he is concerned always with the conflict between good and evil, and the consequences to mankind which flow from "Original Sin."

In his greatest book, Arthur Dimmesdale, the Puritan minister, has committed adultery with Hester Prynne. Arthur is conscience-stricken, while Hester, a symbol of "emancipation," feels that she has not sinned. "What we did," she said, "had a consecration of its own." The tension is tautly drawn between the Puritan (or Christian) respect for law and conscience and the "Romantic" insistence upon the supremacy of the private impulse. Hester is sympathetically treated, and the Romantic position is allowed its full weight—so much so that many modern readers have believed that the Romantic position, that is, the glorification of individual desire, contains the theme of the story. But Arthur, not Hester, is the protagonist, and the resolution of the tension is brought about, not by Hester's plan of elopement, but by Arthur's confession of guilt before his assembled parishioners. The resolution (where one looks especially for "meaning") is Christian in the sense that the protagonist, after a long, agonizing conflict within himself, surrenders his own will to the Divine Will, and becomes able to say, "Father, not my will but Thine be done."

Hawthorne everywhere is concerned with moral problems which are also personality problems. The blemish on Georgiana's check in *The Birthmark* is a fascinating symbol of human imperfection. In *The House of the Seven Gables*, the author deals with the problem of heredity; in *The Blithedale Romance*, with the problem of reform; in *The Marble Faun*, with the problem of good and evil. "Is sin, then, like sorrow," Kenyon asks in the last named work, "an element of human education, through which we struggle to a higher and purer state than we could otherwise have attained? Did Adam fall, that we might ultimately rise to a loftier paradise than his?" The answers in Hawthorne to questions like these are never pat and categorical. Rather is he content to describe both sides of the human coin: the heroic and the ignoble, the unselfish and the selfish, the angelic and the diabolic. It is beside the point, critically, to apply to Hawthorne such adjectives as "morbid" or "pessimistic." He is rather a "realist" in the only worthwhile sense of that word: in the sense, that is, that he holds a true mirror to our common fallible humanity. It is for this reason, as well as his meticulous craftsmanship, that he has been attracting a growing audience of thoughtful readers in modern times.

Bibliography

The definitive edition now in progress, 1962–, is *The Centenary Edition of the Works of Nathaniel Hawthorne*, general eds., William Charvat, Roy H. Pearce, C. M. Simpson. It will supersede *The Complete Works of Nathaniel Hawthorne*, ed. by George P. Lathrop, 12 vols., 1883. Important early biographies are Julian Hawthorne, *Nathaniel Hawthorne and His Wife*, 2 vols., 1884, and George E. Woodberry, *Nathaniel Hawthorne*, 1902. A reliable factual biography is Randall Stewart, *Nathaniel Hawthorne*, 1948. See also Newton Arvin, *Nathaniel Hawthorne*, 1929; F. O. Matthiessen, *American Renaissance*, 1941; Mark Van

Doren, *Nathaniel Hawthorne*, 1949; R. H. Fogle, *Hawthorne's Fiction: The Light and the Dark*, 1952; Hyatt Waggoner, *Hawthorne: A New Evaluation*, 1955; Floyd Stovall, ed., *Eight American Authors: A Review of Research and Criticism*, 1956; Roy R. Male, *Hawthorne*, 1957; Arlin Turner, *Nathaniel Hawthorne: An Introduction and Interpretation*, 1961; and Frederick Crews, *The Sins of the Fathers: Hawthorne's Psychological Themes*, 1966. More specialized studies are found in the following: *Julian Green, Un puritan homme de lettres, Nathaniel Hawthorne*, 1928; L.-E. Chrétien, *La Pensée morale de Nathaniel Hawthorne*, 1932; Jane Lundblad, *Nathaniel Hawthorne and European Literary Tradition*, 1947; Q. D. Leavis, "Hawthorne as Poet," *Sewanee Review*, LIX (1951), 179–205, 426–458; and Randall Stewart, "Hawthorne and Faulkner," *College English*, XVII (1956), 258–262. Randall Stewart edited and annotated *The American Notebooks of Nathaniel Hawthorne*, 1932, and *The English Notebooks*, 1941.

THE BLITHEDALE ROMANCE

Type of work: Novel
Author: Nathaniel Hawthorne (1804–1864)
Type of plot: Psychological romance
Time of plot: Mid-nineteenth century
Locale: Massachusetts
First published: 1852

Although Blithedale is modeled after the Transcendentalists' utopian community of Brook Farm, the setting in the novel is incidental to plot and characterization. As in his greater works, Hawthorne probes the darker psychological side of man's nature as he explores the effects upon people of living in close proximity. The coldly inquisitive narrator Miles Coverdale; dark, queenly Zenobia; innocent and pale Priscilla; and the proud reformer Hollingsworth are typical Hawthorne characters.

Principal Characters

Miles Coverdale, a young New England poet and the narrator of the story. He is a highly sensitive young man and an eager observer of the persons he meets at Blithedale Farm, an experiment in communal living which he joins for a time. Three of his fellow experimenters particularly attract his attention: Zenobia Fauntleroy, Priscilla Moodie, and a man named Hollingsworth. As an observer of their lives, Miles is intrigued, caught by his interest in them as human souls and, as well, by his love for Priscilla Moodie, a love he never reveals to her.

Hollingsworth, a dark, powerful man who was once a blacksmith. He has fastened himself to a single project in obsessive fashion: he desires to set up a philanthropic institution for the reform of criminals and thus to reduce the amount of evil in the world. This project is Hollingsworth's ruling passion, and all else in his life must be subservient to it. He joins the experiment at Blithedale Farm because he sees in the farm a place to erect the buildings to house his reformatory and because he

sees in Zenobia, a wealthy young woman of the group, a person who can help his project with her money and influence. Unfortunately for Hollingsworth's project, he falls in love with Priscilla Moodie and thus alienates Zenobia, who is Priscilla's half sister. Zenobia's later suicide weighs heavily on Hollingsworth's conscience, for she left him with a curse. He gives up his idea of reforming other persons until he can assure himself that he is not guilty of crime. His tragedy is that of conscience, for he believes he is responsible for Zenobia's death; he believes he has driven the girl to suicide and so regards himself as her murderer. With this thought weighing upon him he can no longer consider trying to reform others guilty of crime. Though he marries Priscilla Moodie, he is a broken man.

Zenobia Fauntleroy, a wealthy young woman from another part of the United States. She is attractive both in personality and in appearance. Her vivid presence is always accentuated by her habit of wearing a flamboyant flower in her hair. She is unhappy with woman's lot in life, and her mission is to remake society so that she and her fellow women can take what she regards as their rightful places in the affairs of the world. She falls in love with Hollingsworth and offers her fortune to help him in the establishment of his reformatory, as well as her personal aid in the project. As the months pass, however, she learns that Hollingsworth loves her half sister, Priscilla Moodie. Unhappy Zenobia suffers other shocks. She loses all her wealth in a strange way, apparently to her half sister, and learns for the first time the girl's identity as a relative. These blows unnerve Zenobia, who drowns herself. Her real name is Fauntleroy, although the narrator avoids using any other than her Biblical pseudonym.

Mr. Moodie, an extremely shy and retiring man, a peddler of sorts. He reveals to Miles Coverdale that he was once wealthy and came of good family. He has given up his family name of Faunterloy, however, and assumed that of Moodie. He has been driven from home by crime and his wealth has passed to his daughter, the Zenobia of the story, inasmuch as he is supposedly dead. In New England he has remarried, and the daughter of that marriage is Priscilla Moodie, actually Zenobia's half sister. Mr. Moodie puts Priscilla under the protection of Hollingsworth and thus precipitates the tragic chain of events.

Priscilla Moodie, Zenobia's ethereal half sister, who has supported herself and her father for many years by sewing little articles for her peddler father to sell. Though she enters the story as a poor, shadowy excuse for a girl, she develops a personality through her love for Hollingsworth and his affection for her. After Zenobia's suicide Priscilla marries Hollingsworth and becomes his psychological support in his battle against feelings of guilt.

Mr. Westervelt, a fine-appearing but shallow man who is a promoter and rascal. He has a vague connection with Zenobia, as if they had known each other well at one time. Westervelt comes to dominate Zenobia and uses her in an act on the lyceum circuit, in which she figures as the Veiled Lady. He uses her, perhaps under hypnosis, to make people believe that he can forecast the future. His exploitation of the girl ends when she runs to Hollingsworth for protection during a performance.

The Story

As Miles Coverdale prepared to journey to Blithedale, where he was to join in a project in community living, he was accosted by Old Moodie, a seedy ancient who seemed reluctant to state his business. After much mysterious talk about having Coverdale do him a great favor, he changed his mind and shuffled off without telling what it was that he wanted.

It was April, but Coverdale and his companions arrived at Blithedale in a snowstorm. There they were greeted by a woman called Zenobia, a well-known magazine writer. Zenobia was a beautiful, worldly woman of wealth and position. At all times she wore a rare, exotic flower in her hair. Zenobia spent most of her energy fighting for "woman's place in the world."

On the evening of Coverdale's arrival another of the principals arrived at Blithedale. He was Hollingsworth, a philanthropist and reformer. In fact, philanthropy was to him a never-ceasing effort to reform and change mankind. With him he brought Priscilla, a simple, poorly dressed, bewildered young girl. Priscilla went at once to Zenobia and, falling at the proud woman's feet, never took her eyes from that haughty face. There was no explanation for such behavior. Hollingsworth knew only that he had been approached by Old Moodie and asked to take Priscilla to Blithedale. That was the request Old Moodie had tried to ask of Coverdale, but his courage failed him. But such was the community of Blithedale that the inhabitants made the girl welcome in spite of her strange behavior.

· It was soon evident to Coverdale that Hollingsworth's philanthropy had turned inward until that man was on the way to madness. He was convinced that the universe existed only in order for him to reform all criminals and wayward persons. The dream of his life was to construct a large edifice in which he could collect his criminal brothers and teach them to mend their ways before doom overtook them. To Coverdale he was a bore, but it was obvious that both Zenobia and Priscilla were in love with him. Priscilla blossomed as she reaped the benefits of good food and fresh air, and Zenobia viewed her as a rival with evident but unspoken alarm. Hollingsworth seemed to consider Priscilla his own special charge, and Coverdale feared the looks of thinly veiled hatred he frequently saw Zenobia cast toward the lovely girl. Priscilla, devoted to Zenobia, wanted always to be close to the beautiful woman.

When Old Moodie appeared at Blithedale to inquire of Priscilla, Coverdale tried to persuade him to reveal the reason for his interest in the girl. But the old man slipped away without telling his story.

Shortly after this incident, Professor Westervelt came to Blithedale to inquire about Zenobia and Priscilla. Coverdale saw Westervelt and Zenobia together and was sure that even though Zenobia hated him now, she once had loved and been ruined by this evil man. Coverdale knew that all of the misery which he sometimes saw in Zenobia's eyes must surely have come from this man. Coverdale felt also that there was still some bond between them.

After Westervelt's visit Zenobia was short-tempered and more vehement than usual about the poor lot of women. But she was so much in love with Hollingsworth that even the misery, or perhaps terror, caused by Westervelt did not deter her from literally worshiping at his feet. Hollingsworth, in his egotism, believed that women were placed on earth only to serve men, and so great was Zenobia's passion that she accepted his words without protest, not proclaiming her real thoughts in his presence. It was clear to Coverdale that Hollingsworth intended to use Zenobia's money to build the school for criminals of which he never ceased to talk. When Coverdale refused to join him in this project, Hollingsworth became quite cool in his dealings with Coverdale.

Tiring of the life at Blithedale, Coverdale took a vacation in town. He was greatly surprised when Zenobia, Priscilla, and Westervelt also arrived in the town shortly afterward. He called on the ladies and was disturbed by the tension that was apparent. When he chided Zenobia about Priscilla and Hollingsworth, she warned him not to interfere lest he cause serious trouble. Priscilla obviously did not know why she was there. She told Coverdale that she was like a leaf blown about by the wind. She had no will of her own, only the will of Zenobia. Then Westervelt called for the two women, and the three left Coverdale standing as if they did not know he was there.

Determined to uncover the mystery surrounding the three, Coverdale sought out Old Moodie and pried from him the story of the two girls. Once Moodie had been a wealthy and influential man until through dishonest business practices he was ruined. Then, leaving his wife and daughter Zenobia, he wandered about in poverty and disgrace. His wife died and he married again. To them Prescilla was born, as different from his first child as it was possible to be. Zenobia was beautiful and proud, Priscilla plain and shy. Neighbors thought Priscilla had supernatural powers, but her kindness and her goodness made everyone love her.

Zenobia, after Moodie's disgrace, was reared by his brother; and since Moodie was believed dead, Zenobia, as the next heir, inherited her uncle's wealth. Because she grew up a wild and willful girl, it was whispered that she had made a secret marriage with an unprincipled man. No one, however, knew anything definite. Such were her beauty and wealth that no one criticized her. Moodie called her to his home and, not telling her who he was, cautioned her to be as kind as a sister to Priscilla.

During his vacation Coverdale chanced upon a magician's show in a nearby village. There he found Hollingsworth in the audience and Westervelt on the stage. Westervelt produced a Veiled Lady, an ethereal creature whom he said he could make do his bidding. At the climax of the act Hollingsworth arose from the audience and strode to the platform. He called to the Veiled Lady to remove her veil, and as he spoke, Priscilla lifted her veil and fled into the arms of Hollingsworth with a cry of joy and of love. She looked like one who had been saved from an evil fate.

Coverdale returned to Blithedale. There he witnessed a terrifying scene between Zenobia, Priscilla, and Hollingsworth. To Zenobia, Hollingsworth admitted his love for Priscilla. Zenobia reviled him and warned her sister against the emptiness of his heart. She said she knew at last the complete ego of the man and saw that he had deceived her only to get her fortune for his great project. After the lovers left her, Zenobia sank to the ground and wept, and that night the unhappy woman drowned herself in the river flowing close by. Westervelt came to view her dead body, but his only sorrow seemed to be that he could no longer use Zenobia in his black schemes.

After Zenobia's tragedy, Coverdale left Blithedale. Priscilla and Hollingsworth lived quietly, he giving up his desire to reform other criminals because he felt himself Zenobia's murderer. In his twilight years Coverdale confessed his real interest in these ill-fated people. He had from the first been in love with Priscilla.

Critical Evaluation

Hawthorne is well known as an explorer of the darker side of human consciousness. Henry James admired his powers of psychological and moral analysis and maintained that his works gave "glimpses of a great field, of the whole deep mystery of man's soul and conscience." It is true that readers, imagining what lies behind the minister's black veil (in the story so titled) or looking into Ethan Brand's fiery kiln, encounter visions of hellish torment. In *The Blithedale Romance* there is a noticeable distancing from such visions. Evil is in the book, but largely because of calculated effects in plotting and point of view (Miles Coverdale's narration), it seems somewhat removed. The form of the work, romance, provides a filter which softens the impact of the psychological stresses the story records.

Brook Farm itself is ingenuously naïve in the earnestness with which it pursues social and moral welfare; just as the Pilgrims' isolation and religious fanaticism could not save them from the truth of the human heart—a theme Hawthorne sounded most eloquently in *The Scarlet Letter*—so this idyllically isolated settlement provides no haven from the passions animating men and women. The Hollingsworth-Zenobia-Priscilla triangle comes to a drastic head precisely because of the proximity of all the principals. Instead of a social haven, Brook Farm is finally an arena for a tragedy of love.

Miles Coverdale is perhaps the most severely judged character in the novel. His detachment and fear of accepting the consequences of his passions mark his life as wasted. He says as much about himself in the confession which ends the novel. The only thing that saves Miles Coverdale from the fate of a Roger Chillingworth is that *The Blithedale Romance* is primarily a romance and *The Scarlet Letter* categorically a tragedy.

Bibliography

Abel, Darrel. "Hawthorne's Skepticism About Social Reform with Especial Reference to *The Blithedale Romance*," in *University of Kansas City Review.* XIX (1953), pp. 181–193.

Baym, Nina. "*The Blithedale Romance*: A Radical Reading," in *Journal of English and Germanic Philology.* LXVII (October, 1968), pp. 545–569.

_____. *The Shape of Hawthorne's Career.* Ithaca, N.Y.: Cornell University Press, 1975, pp. 184–205.

Crews, Frederick C. "A New Reading of *The Blithedale Romance*," in *American Literature.* XXIX (1957), pp. 147–170.

_____. *The Sins of the Fathers: Hawthorne's Psychological Themes.* New York: Oxford University Press, 1966, pp. 194–212.

_____. "Turning the Affair into a Ballad: *The Blithedale Romance*," in

Nathaniel Hawthorne. Edited by J. Donald Crowley. New York: McGraw-Hill, 1975, pp. 87–100.

Davidson, Frank. "Toward a Re-evaluation of *The Blithedale Romance*," in *New England Quarterly*. XXV (1952), pp. 374–383.

Dryden, Edgar A. *Nathaniel Hawthorne; The Poetics of Enchantment*. Ithaca, N.Y.: Cornell University Press, 1977, pp. 72–75, 93–107.

Fogle, Richard Harter. *Hawthorne's Imagery*. Norman: University of Oklahoma Press, 1969, pp. 92–124.

Folsom, James K. *Man's Accidents and God's Purposes: Multiplicity in Hawthorne's Fiction*. New Haven, Conn.: Yale University Press, 1963, pp. 139–141, 147–151.

Gordon, Joseph T. "Nathaniel Hawthorne and Brook Farm," in *Emerson Society Quarterly*. XXXIII (1963), pp. 51–61.

Griffith, Kelley, Jr. "Form in *The Blithedale Romance*," in *American Literature*. XL (March, 1968), pp. 15–26.

Hedges, William L. "Hawthorne's *Blithedale*: The Function of the Narrator," in *Nineteenth-Century Fiction*. XIV (March, 1960), pp. 303–316.

Hoffman, Daniel G. *Form and Fable in American Fiction*. New York: Oxford University Press, 1961, pp. 202–218.

Kaul, A.N. "*The Blithedale Romance*," in *Hawthorne: A Collection of Critical Essays*. Edited by A.N. Kaul. Englewood Cliffs, N.J.: Prentice-Hall, 1966, pp. 153–163.

Lefcowitz, Allan. "Some Rents in the Veil: New Lights on Priscilla and Zenobia in *The Blithedale Romance*," in *Nineteenth-Century Fiction*. XXI (December, 1966), pp. 263–275.

Levy, Leo. "*The Blithedale Romance*: Hawthorne's 'Voyage Through Chaos,' " in *Studies in Romanticism*. VIII (Autumn, 1968), pp. 1–15.

Murray, Peter B. "Mythopoesis in *The Blithedale Romance*," in *PMLA*. LXXV (1960), pp. 591–596.

Poirier, Richard. *A World Elsewhere: The Place of Style in American Literature*. New York: Oxford University Press, 1966, pp. 93–143.

Ragan, James F. "The Irony in Hawthorne's *Blithedale*," in *New England Quarterly*. XXXV (June, 1962), pp. 239–246.

Smith, Julian. "Why Does Zenobia Kill Herself?," in *English Language Notes*. VI (September, 1968), pp. 37–39.

Stanton, Robert. "The Trial of Nature: An Analysis of *The Blithedale Romance*," in *PMLA*. LXXVI (1961), pp. 528–538.

Stewart, Randall. *Regionalism and Beyond; Essays of Randall Stewart.*

Edited by George Core. Nashville, Tenn.: Vanderbilt University Press, 1968, pp. 34–44.

Tharpe, Jac. *Nathaniel Hawthorne: Identity and Knowledge.* Carbondale: Southern Illinois University Press, 1967, pp. 40–46, 125–133.

Waggoner, Hyatt Howe. *Hawthorne: A Critical Study.* Cambridge, Mass.: Harvard University Press, 1963, pp. 175–194.

THE HOUSE OF THE SEVEN GABLES

Type of work: Novel
Author: Nathaniel Hawthorne (1804–1864)
Type of plot: Psychological romance
Time of plot: 1850
Locale: Salem, Massachusetts
First published: 1851

Woven into the ingenious plot of this novel is the theme that the sins of the fathers are passed on to the children in succeeding generations. The book reflects the author's interest in New England history and his doubts about a moribund New England that looked backward to past times.

Principal Characters

Colonel Pyncheon, a stern Massachusetts magistrate who, during the famous witchcraft trials of the seventeenth century, sent to his death a man whose property he coveted for himself. Cursed by his innocent victim, the Colonel died on the day his big new house, the House of the Seven Gables, built on his victim's land, was officially opened to guests.

Matthew Maule, Colonel Pyncheon's victim, who swore that his unjust accuser should drink blood, as Colonel Pyncheon did when he died.

Thomas Maule, the son of Matthew Maule. As the head carpenter building the House of the Seven Gables, young Maule took an opportunity to build a secret recess in which was hidden the deed by which the Pyncheons hoped to claim a vast domain in Maine.

Jaffrey Pyncheon, one of Colonel Pyncheon's nineteenth century descendants and a man like his ancestor in many ways. A judge, a member of Congress at one time, a member of many boards of directors, and an aspirant to the governorship of his state, he is a rich man who through his own efforts has multiplied the fortune he inherited from his uncle. Although he tries to present himself in a good light, Jaffrey Pyncheon is a hard man and not entirely honest. He destroys one of his uncle's wills, which names his cousin Clifford as heir, and he stands by while his cousin is wrongly sent to prison for a murder he did not commit. Convinced that his wronged cousin knows of additional family wealth hidden by their uncle, Jaffrey threatens the broken man with confinement in an insane asylum if the hiding place of the remaining wealth is not revealed. Fortunately for his cousin, Jaffrey dies of natural causes induced by emotion while making his threats.

Clifford Pyncheon, Jaffrey's unfortunate cousin, who serves a thirty-year prison term for allegedly murdering his uncle, who really died of natural causes. A handsome, carefree, beauty-loving man at one time, he emerges from prison three decades later a broken, pale, and emaciated wreck of a human being, content to hide away in the House of the Seven Gables, where he is looked after by his sister Hepzibah and their young cousin Phoebe. Clifford's mind is weakened and his spirit so broken by misfortune that he actually does strange, if harmless, acts, so that Jaffrey's threat to force Clifford into an asylum could be made good. At Jaffrey's unexpected death Clifford feels a great release after having been oppressed by his cousin for so long. Clifford, his sister, and Phoebe Pyncheon inherit Jaffrey's fortune and have the promise of a comfortable life in the future.

Hepzibah Pyncheon, Clifford's spinster sister, who lives alone for many years in shabby gentility in the House of the Seven Gables while her brother is in prison. She has few friends, for she seldom leaves the house, and she is so near-sighted that she always wears a frown, making people think she is a cross and angry woman. After the return of her brother from prison, she sets up a little shop in her house to try to provide for herself and Clifford, to whom she is devoted. Opening the shop is very difficult for her, as she dislikes meeting people and believes that entering trade is unladylike for a member of the Pyncheon family.

Phoebe Pyncheon, a young, pretty, and lively girl from the country. She comes to live with Hepzibah when her mother, a widow, remarries. Phoebe takes over the little cent-shop and makes it a profit-able venture for Hepzibah. Phoebe also brings new life to the House of the Seven Gables by cheering it with her beauty and song, as well as by tending the neglected flowers and doing other homely tasks. She is highly considerate of her elderly cousins and spends much of her time entertaining Clifford.

Mr. Holgrave, a liberal-minded young daguerreotypist who rents a portion of the House of the Seven Gables from Hepzibah. An eager, energetic young man of twenty-two, he falls in love with Phoebe Pyncheon, and they are engaged to be married. When Phoebe inherits a third of Jaffrey's large fortune, Holgrave decides to become more conservative in his thinking. It is he who reveals the secret recess hiding the now useless deed to the vast tract of land in Maine. He knows the secret because he is a descendant of Thomas Maule. In fact, his name is Maule, but he hides his true identity by assuming for a time the name of Holgrave.

Uncle Venner, an old handy man befriended by the Pyncheons. He is one of the few persons of the town to accept Hepzibah and Clifford as friends when they are in unfortunate circumstances.

The Story

The House of the Seven Gables was a colonial house built in the English style of half-timber and half-plaster. It stood on Pyncheon Street in quiet Salem. The house had been built by Colonel Pyncheon, who had wrested the desirable site from Matthew Maule, a poor man executed as a wizard. Because Colonel Pyncheon was responsible and because he was taking the doomed man's land, Maule at the moment of his execution declared that God would give the Pyncheons blood to drink. But in spite of this grim prophecy the colonel had his house, and its builder was Thomas Maule, son of the old wizard.

Colonel Pyncheon, dying in his great oak chair just after the house had been completed, choked with blood so that his shirt front was stained scarlet. Although doctors explained the cause of his death as apoplexy, the townsfolk had not forgotten old Maule's prophecy. The time of the colonel's death was inauspicious. It was said he had just completed a treaty by which he had bought huge tracts of land from the Indians, but this deed had not been confirmed by the general court and was never discovered by any of his heirs. Rumor also had it that a man was seen leaving the house about the time Colonel Pyncheon died.

More recently another startling event had occurred at the House of the Seven Gables. Jaffrey Pyncheon, a bachelor, had been found dead in the colonel's great oaken armchair, and his nephew, Clifford Pyncheon, had been sentenced to imprisonment after being found guilty of the murder of his uncle.

These events were in the unhappy past, however, and in 1850, the House of the Seven Gables was the home of Miss Hepzibah Pyncheon, an elderly, single woman, who let one wing of the old house to a young man of radical tendencies, a maker of daguerreotypes, whose name was Mr. Holgrave.

Miss Hepzibah was about to open a shop in one of the rooms of her house. Her brother Clifford was coming home from the state prison after thirty years, and she had to earn money in some way to support him. But on the first day of her venture as a storekeeper Miss Hepzibah proved to be a failure. The situation was saved, however, by the arrival of young Phoebe Pyncheon from the country. Soon she was operating the shop at a profit.

Clifford arrived from the prison a broken man of childish, querulous ways. Once he tried to throw himself from a big arched window which afforded him almost his only contact with the outside world. He was fond of Phoebe, but Miss Hepzibah irritated him with her sullen scowling. For acquaintances Clifford had Uncle Venner, a handy man who did odd jobs for the neighborhood, and the tenant of the house, Mr. Holgrave, the daguerreotypist.

The only other relative living in town was the highly-respected Judge Pyncheon, another nephew of the old Jaffrey Pyncheon, for whose murder Clifford had spent thirty years in prison. He was, in fact, the heir of the murdered man and he had been somehow involved with Clifford's arrest and imprisonment. For these reasons Clifford refused to see him when the judge offered to give Clifford and Hepzibah a home at his countryseat.

Meanwhile, Phoebe had become friendly with Mr. Holgrave. In turn, he thought that she brought light and hope into the gloomy old house, and he missed her greatly when she returned to her home in the country. Her visit was to be a brief one, however, for she had gone only to make some preparations before coming to live permanently with Miss Hepzibah and Clifford.

Before Phoebe returned from the country, Judge Pyncheon visited the House of the Seven Gables and, over Miss Hepzibah's protest, insisted on seeing Clifford, who, he said, knew a family secret which meant great wealth for the judge. When at last she went out of the room to summon her brother, Judge Pyncheon sat down in the old chair by the fireplace, over which hung the portrait of the Colonel Pyncheon who had built the house. As the judge sat in the old chair, his ticking watch in his hand, an unusually strong family likeness could be noted between the stern judge and his Puritan ancestor in the portrait. Unable to find Clifford to deliver the judge's message, Miss Hepzibah returned. As she approached the door, Clifford appeared from within, laughing and pointing to the chair where the judge sat dead of apoplexy under the portrait of the old colonel. His shirt front was stained with blood. The wizard's curse had been fulfilled once more; God had given him blood to drink.

The two helpless old people were so distressed by the sight of the dead man that they crept away from the house without notifying anyone and departed on the train. The dead body of the judge remained seated in the chair.

It was some time before the body was discovered by Holgrave. When Phoebe returned to the house, he admitted her. He had not yet summoned the police because he wished to protect the old couple as long as possible. While he and Phoebe were alone in the house, Holgrave declared his love for her. They were interrupted by the return of Miss Hepzibah and the now calm Clifford. They had decided that to run away would not solve their problem.

The police attributed the judge's death to natural causes, and Clifford, Miss Hepzibah, and Phoebe became the heirs to his great fortune. It now seemed certain that Jaffrey Pyncheon had also died of natural causes, not by Clifford's hand, and that the judge had so arranged the evidence as to make Clifford appear a murderer.

In a short time all the occupants of the House of the Seven Gables were ready to move to the judge's country estate which they had inherited. They gathered for the last time in the old room under the dingy portrait of Colonel Pyncheon. Clifford said he had a vague memory of something mysterious connected with the picture. Holgrave offered to explain the mystery and pressed a secret spring near the picture. When he did so, the portrait fell to the floor, disclosing a recess in the wall. From this niche Holgrave drew out the ancient Indian deed to the lands which the Pyncheons had claimed. Clifford then remembered he had once found the secret spring. It was this secret which Judge Pyncheon had hoped to learn from Clifford.

Phoebe asked how Holgrave happened to know these facts. The young man explained his name was not Holgrave, but Maule. He was, he said, a descendant of the wizard, Matthew Maule, and of Thomas Maule who built the House of the Seven Gables. The knowledge of the hidden Indian deed had been handed down to the descendants of Thomas Maule, who built the compartment behind the portrait and secreted the deed there after the colonel's death. Holgrave was the last of the Maules and Phoebe, the last of the Pyncheons, would bear his name. Matthew Maule's curse had been expiated.

The novel is replete with Gothic characteristics: mystery, violence, a curse, gloomy atmosphere, archaic diction, and visits from the spirit world. Yet though it is not realistic, it demonstrates what Henry James called Hawthorne's "high sense of reality," in that it reveals profound truths about how the effects of the sins of the fathers are felt by children for generations to come. The ending, however, discloses that although he recognized the deterministic effects of heredity, environment, and man's predisposition to evil, Hawthorne was essentially a hopeful man who believed that the individual does possess a residuum of will that can cope with and perhaps change "dark necessity."

Critical Evaluation

In reputation *The House of the Seven Gables* usually stands in the shadow of its predecessor, *The Scarlet Letter*. It is, however, a rich and solid achievement, a Gothic romance whose characters are among Nathaniel Hawthorne's most complex. The author himself thought it, in comparison with the earlier work, "more characteristic of my mind, and more proper and natural for me to write."

In his preface, Hawthorne explicitly states his moral: "the truth, namely that the wrong-doing of one generation lives into the successive ones, and, divesting itself of every temporary advantage, becomes a pure and uncontrollable mischief." This of course echoes the Biblical adage that "The fathers have eaten sour grapes, and the children's teeth are set on edge." Hawthorne's interest in the heritage of sin was probably whetted by the history of his own family. His first American ancestor, William Hathorne (Nathaniel himself added the *w* to the family name), was a soldier and magistrate who once had a Quaker woman publicly whipped through the streets. William's son John, having, as Nathaniel said, "inherited the persecuting spirit," was a judge at the infamous Salem witch trials, during which a defendant cursed another of the three judges with the cry, "God will give you blood to drink!" Thenceforth, as Hawthorne noted, although the family remained decent, respectable folk, their fortunes began to decline.

The fate of the Pyncheon family of the novel is considerably more dramatic. Matthew Maule's curse on Colonel Pyncheon, who has persecuted him for witchcraft and wrested from him the land on which the seven-gabled house is to be built, is precisely that which Judge John Hathorne had heard in a similar trial. It is apparently fulfilled on the day of the housewarming, when Colonel Pyncheon dies of apoplexy, the hemorrhage rising through his throat to stain his white shirt. But, Hawthorne would have us believe, such sins as Pyncheon's are not so easily paid for. The family occupies the mansion, but misfortune is their constant lot. There are repeated apoplectic deaths, sometimes heralded by an ominous gurgling in the throat; greed leads Judge Jaffrey Pyncheon, like his ancestor, to participate in a trumped-up trial, this time against his own cousin; and years of pride and isolation have thinned the family blood so that, like the scrawny chickens that peck in the Pyncheon garden, they are an unattractive, ineffectual lot. Judge Pyncheon is a monster who hides his avarice and callousness behind a façade of philanthropy and civic service. Clifford, like Hawthorne's Young Goodman Brown, is a sensitive soul who is unmanned by his confrontation with evil; after years of imprisonment he is poised on the brink of madness. Hepzibah, a spinster who has spent most of her life waiting for her brother's release, is virtually helpless either to resolve her precarious financial situation or to deal with her malevolent cousin.

Only young Phoebe possesses both goodness and energy. It is significant that she is the "country cousin" whose father married beneath his rank, and that Hepzibah observes that the girl's self-reliance must have come from her mother's blood. Thus Hawthorne casts his vote for the energizing effects of a democratic, as opposed to an aristocratic, social system; he has Holgrave, the daguerreotypist, support this view with the comment that families should continually merge into the great mass of humanity, without regard to ancestry.

The other fully vital character in the novel is Holgrave, the young daguerreotypist. He is one of Hawthorne's most charming creations: a perceptive, adventurous man who has been, it seems, almost everywhere, and done almost everything. His conversations with Phoebe reveal him as a radical who believes that the Past "lies upon the Present like a giant's dead body," preventing any generation's true fulfillment—a thesis frequently expressed by Hawthorne's contemporary, Ralph Waldo Emerson. Holgrave goes so far as to suggest that institutional buildings should "crumble to ruin once in twenty years, or thereabouts, as a hint to the people to examine into and reform the institutions which they symbolize." He is also a psychologist; his daguerreotypes, which inevitably go beyond mere pictorial likeness to expose personality, symbolize his own insight into human nature.

At the end of the novel we are led to believe that the curse is broken as Phoebe, the last of the Pyncheons, plans to marry Holgrave, who turns out to be a descendant of old Matthew Maule. The curse's effects can all be explained naturally: Holgrave observes that perhaps old Maule's prophecy was founded on knowledge that apoplectic death had been a Pyncheon trait for generations. Avarice and cruelty can certainly be passed on by example; and pride, isolation, and inbreeding can account for the "thin-bloodedness" of the once aristocratic family. Now, as Phoebe, whose blood has already been enriched by plebian stock, and Holgrave, who has escaped the stifling influence of his own declining family by traveling widely, replace a tradition of hatred with that of love, it seems plausible that the curse may indeed have run its course. Perhaps the chain of ugly events—what Chillingworth of *The Scarlet Letter* termed "dark necessity"—can be terminated by positive acts of good will.

Bibliography

Abel, Darrel. "Hawthorne's House of Tradition," in *South Atlantic Quarterly.* LII (October, 1953), pp. 561–578.

Battagua, Francis Joseph. "*The House of the Seven Gables*: New Light on Old Problems," in *PMLA.* LXXXII (December, 1967), pp. 579–590.

Baym, Nina. *The Shape of Hawthorne's Career.* Ithaca, N.Y.: Cornell University Press, 1976, pp. 153–172, 185–187.

Beebe, Maurice. "The Fall of the House of Pyncheon," in *Nineteenth-Century Fiction.* XI (1956), pp. 1–17.

Bell, Millicent. *Hawthorne's View of the Artist.* New York: State University of New York Press, 1962, pp. 159–167.

Crews, Frederick C. *The Sins of the Fathers: Hawthorne's Psychological Themes.* New York: Oxford University Press, 1966, pp. 171–194.

Dillingham, William B. "Structure and Theme in *The House of the Seven Gables,*" in *Nineteenth-Century Fiction.* XIV (1959), pp. 59–70.

Dryden, Edgar F. "Hawthorne's Castle in the Air: Form and Theme in *The House of the Seven Gables,*" in *Journal of English Literary History.* XXXVIII (1971), pp. 294–317.

————. *Nathaniel Hawthorne: The Poetics of Enchantment.* Ithaca, N.Y.: Cornell University Press, 1977, pp. 52–59, 86–89, 93–98.

Farmer, Norman, Jr. "Maule's Curse and the Rev. Nicholas Noyes: A Note on Hawthorne's Source," in *Notes and Queries.* XI (June, 1964), pp. 224–225.

Fogle, Richard Harter. *Hawthorne's Imagery.* Norman: University of Oklahoma Press, 1969, pp. 48–91.

Gerber, John C. "A Critical Exercise in the Teaching of *The House of the Seven Gables,*" in *Emerson Society Quarterly.* XXV (1961), pp. 8–11.

Havens, Elmer A. "The 'Golden Branch' as Symbol in *The House of the Seven Gables,*" in *Modern Language Notes.* LXXIV (January, 1959), pp. 20–22.

Hoffman, Daniel G. *Form and Fable in American Fiction.* New York: Oxford University Press, 1961, pp. 187–201.

Junkins, Donald. "Hawthorne's *The House of the Seven Gables*: A Prototype of the Human Mind," in *Literature and Psychology.* XVII (1967), pp. 193–209.

Levy, Alfred J. "*The House of the Seven Gables*: The Religion of Love," in *Nineteenth-Century Fiction.* XVI (December, 1961), pp. 189–203.

————. "Picturesque Style in *The House of the Seven Gables,*" in *New England Quarterly.* XXXIX (June, 1966), pp. 147–160.

Male, Roy R. *Hawthorne's Tragic Vision.* Austin: University of Texas Press, 1957, pp. 119–138.

Martin, Terence. *Nathaniel Hawthorne.* New Haven, Conn.: Yale University Press, 1965, pp. 128–144.

Orel, Harold. "The Double Symbol," in *American Literature.* XXIII (March, 1951), pp. 1–6.

Porte, Joel. "Redemption Through Art: *The House of the Seven Gables,*" in *Nathaniel Hawthorne.* Edited by J. Donald Crowley. New York: McGraw-Hill, 1975, pp. 75–86.

Rees, John O., Jr.   "Elizabeth Peabody and 'The Very A B C': A Note on *The House of the Seven Gables*," in *American Literature*. XXXVIII (January, 1967), pp. 537–540.

Sampson, Edward C.   "Sound-Imagery in *The House of the Seven Gables*," in *English Review*. XXII (1971), pp. 26–29.

Waggoner, Hyatt Howe.   *Hawthorne: A Critical Study*. Cambridge, Mass.: Harvard University Press, 1963, pp. 151–175.

Yoder, R.A.   "Transcendental Conservatism and *The House of the Seven Gables*," in *Georgia Review*. XXVIII (1974), pp. 33–51.

THE MARBLE FAUN

Type of work: Novel
Author: Nathaniel Hawthorne (1804–1864)
Type of plot: Allegorical romance
Time of plot: Mid-nineteenth century
Locale: Rome
First published: 1860

In his last completed novel, The Marble Faun, *Hawthorne transported his lifelong preoccupations with sin, alienation, and moral responsibility from Puritan New England to Rome, the center of culture, art, and Catholicism. The book is a study of the birth of the human conscience, the consequences of a crime committed by a simple, pagan spirit who, through his impulsive deed, experiences guilt, suffering, and finally, regeneration. Although the novel is too ambiguous and chaotic to rank with Hawthorne's best, the ambitiousness of its insights, complexity of its characterizations, and power of several separate scenes give a lasting impact.*

Principal Characters

Donatello, in reality the **Count of Monte Beni,** at first a naïve young man who seems to be almost dim-witted, with little formal education and almost no intellectual, moral, or emotional depth. He appears almost a creature out of the mythical past, a faun out of his time and place associating with the painters and sculptors of the artist colony in nineteenth century Rome. Feeling a kinship with nature and its inhabitants, he is truly happy only in the woods and gardens. He falls in love with Miriam Schaefer, a beautiful but mysterious young painter. One night, at her unspoken behest, Donatello murders a man. This crime brings about a change in the young Italian nobleman, who for a time retires to his ancestral home in Tuscany. He finds that he is no longer akin to nature, but in exchange for this loss he acquires new depth of soul under the torment of his crime and awakes to moral values. In the garb of a penitent he returns to Rome, where he is reunited briefly with his beloved during the carni-val season. At the end of that time he is seized by the authorities and imprisoned.

Miriam Schaefer, an exotically beautiful young woman of wealth who appears mysteriously among the people of an artist colony in Rome. She is also a painter, and her life is haunted by a man who appears to be an artist's model. He seems to have a strange hold over the girl and causes her great uneasiness. Miriam's lover, Donatello, rids her of the presence of this troublesome man by throwing him from the famous Tarpeian Rock. Because her eyes had commanded Donatello to commit the crime, Miriam feels as guilty as if the act had been her own. Also, she feels a bond with her companion-accomplice as strong as marriage ties. She, like Donatello, suffers the pangs of conscience fiercely. She and her lover, reunited after his return from a period of retirement in Tuscany, find a brief period of happiness before he is committed to prison. Miriam, who goes free, is really a member of an aristocratic

Italian family and was at one time engaged to marry the man who haunted her. Her real name is never mentioned.

Brother Antonio, a Capuchin monk, the man who haunts and hounds Miriam Schaefer until he is murdered by Donatello. Having shown himself to be of great merit, at least on the surface, he is granted unusual freedom by his order, a freedom he uses in order to dog the girl's footsteps. Once her fiancé, he had committed a crime in which Miriam, though innocent, was implicated.

Hilda, a pretty, virtuous American girl studying painting in Rome. Because she is Miriam's friend, she becomes involved in the intrigue surrounding Miriam. She witnesses the midnight murder committed by Donatello, and at Miriam's request she delivers a strange parcel which causes her to be held in a convent as a possible accessory to the crime. Hilda is much affected by the terrible deed she witnesses, even though she has no guilt. The weight of her knowledge drives the over-sensitive girl to lose all interest in her work. Though she is faithful to and proud of her Puritan heritage, she becomes so disturbed that she enters a confessional in St. Peter's Cathedral and tells her story to a priest. In the end her experiences cause her to love Kenyon, a young American in love with her.

Kenyon, a young American sculptor working in Rome. He loves Hilda and is one of the little circle of friends surrounding Miriam Schaefer. He brings Donatello and Miriam together again after they have suffered alone following the murder of Brother Antonio by Donatello. Kenyon's love for Hilda is eventually rewarded, for she comes to love him and they are married. Once after their marriage they encounter Miriam, who both blesses and repulses them silently. They do not disturb her expiation and grief.

The Story

Nothing at all was known about Miriam. In the artistic world of Rome, she lived without revealing anything about herself and without arousing the curiosity or suspicion of those living around her. With a New England girl, Hilda, and Kenyon, a sculptor, she enjoyed a friendship which even her mysterious origin did not shadow, so complete was their understanding and trust of one another.

One day the three friends, accompanied by Donatello, a young Italian, saw a statue of the faun by Praxiteles. Struck by the resemblance of the statue to Donatello, they asked jokingly to see if the Italian also had pointed ears under his golden locks. Indeed, Donatello was very much like a faun in his character. He had great agility, cheerfulness, and a sunny nature unclouded by melancholy or care. He was deeply in love with Miriam.

On another occasion, the trio went to visit the catacombs. While there, Miriam disappeared for a moment. When she came back, she returned with a strange individual whom she had met inside one of the tombs. This person followed her for months to come. No one knew anything about him. He and Miriam had conversations together, and he spoke of the hold he had on her, of their life together in a mysterious past. Miriam became more and more unhappy. She told Donatello—who was ever ready to defend her—that he must go away, for she would bring doom and destruction upon him. But Donatello stayed, as ardent as ever.

Her persecutor appeared everywhere, followed her wherever she went. One day Miriam went to Hilda and left a packet for Hilda to deliver on a certain date to the address she would find written on the outside. Shortly afterward, the friends went out one night and climbed the Tarpeian Rock, over which the old Romans used to throw their criminals. As they were getting ready to return home, Miriam's persecutor appeared. Miriam went with him, followed by Donatello. Donatello attacked the man and with the stranger secure in his grasp looked at Miriam. Her eyes gave him his answer. He threw the tormentor over a cliff to his death.

United by this crime, Miriam and Donatello also became united in love. But they did not know that Hilda had witnessed the murder, that she was suffering because of it. They had all agreed to visit the Church of the Capuchins the following afternoon in order to see a painting which supposedly bore a resemblance to Miriam's tormentor. But Hilda did not keep the appointment. The others went to find a mass for the dead in progress. The dead man was Miriam's persecutor. Later, when Miriam went to see Hilda, the American girl told Miriam that their friendship was over.

Donatello, too, had changed. He was no longer the unworried faun, but a person with a very guilty conscience. He began to avoid Miriam, even to hate her. He left Rome and went back to his ancestral home. Kenyon went there to visit his friend. Hilda stayed in Rome by herself, lonely, distraught.

At Donatello's country home, Kenyon learned the local tradition about his friend's family, a legend that Donatello was, in fact, descended from a race of fauns who had inhabited the countryside in remote times. He learned, too, of Donatello's feeling of guilt, but he, unaware of the killing, did not know the reason for Donatello's changed spirit. When Miriam followed Donatello to his home, he would not see her. Kenyon told her Donatello still loved her, however, and she agreed to meet both of them later on. When they met in the city square, Miriam stood quietly, waiting for Donatello to speak. At last he spoke her name, and she went to him. So they were united once more, but the union was haunted by their sin.

In the meantime Hilda had gone to deliver the packet Miriam had left in her keeping. The address was that of one high in the affairs of the government. Kenyon looked for Hilda everywhere, for he had seen her but briefly since his return. Realizing at last that he was in love with her, he was worried about her disappearance. During the carnival season he met Donatello and Miriam, who promised him he would soon see Hilda again. He did, on the day the carnival was at its height and the streets were filled with a merry-making throng.

Hilda told him her story. Her knowledge of the crime had weighed so heavily upon her that at last she had gone to confession in St. Peter's and had poured out the tale to a listening priest. Later she had delivered the packet, as Miriam had requested her, and afterward she had been detained in a convent until the authorities were satisfied she had taken no part in the murder on the Tarpeian Rock.

She had just been released from her strange captivity. While they stood talking, there was a commotion in the crowd nearby. The police had seized Donatello and were taking him to jail.

For his crime Donatello was sentenced to prison. Miriam was not brought to trial, for her only crime had been the look in her eyes which had told Donatello to murder her persecutor. But Miriam's history was finally revealed. Although she herself was innocent, her family had been involved in a crime which made its name infamous. She had gone to Rome and attempted to live down the past, but evil had continued to haunt her, and the past had reappeared in the form of a tormentor who had dogged her footsteps, threatening to make her identity known to the world, until Donatello had thrown him over the cliff.

Kenyon and Hilda were married. Once again they saw Miriam, kneeling in the Pantheon before the tomb of Raphael. As they passed, she stretched out her hands to them in a gesture that both blessed them and repulsed them. They left her to her expiation and her grief.

Critical Evaluation

Throughout his writing career, Nathaniel Hawthorne was preoccupied with the theme of man's fall into sin and mortality. Symbolic representations of Adam and Eden underlie much of his most exciting work, so it should be appropriate that he should turn to this theme again in his last major romance. Unfortunately, the reality of the work does not come up to its promise, and Hawthorne's use of the theme of the fall of man is far less skillful here than in some of the earlier stories. His usually subtle symbolic method turns into a somewhat heavy-handed allegory, and the rather slight and simple story is too often padded with descriptions of Rome and its art (frequently lifted with little alteration from his notebooks) which have almost no organic relation-ship to the theme of the novel. But, even though the weakest of Hawthorne's major romances, *The Marble Faun* is not without redeeming features, and its faults as well as its virtues teach us about Hawthorne's view of the world. Most accessible through its major characters, the work illustrates several of Hawthorne's most typical character types, and through their interactions dramatizes some of the themes which most preoccupied him.

The story and its theme most particularly center around Donatello, the contemporary counterpart of the Faun of Praxiteles. For Hawthorne, Dona-tello's faun-like qualities are associated with the innocence and animalistic nature of man before his fall brought him to the knowledge of sin and death. Donatello's country estate is a counterpart to Eden and suggests a pagan and pre-Christian paradise, bypassed by time, in which primordial innocence has been kept alive. But, though touching in its childlike qualities, Donatello's innocence is not one of which Hawthorne can approve. Because it lacks the knowledge of sin which is part of man's humanity, it is sub-human and cannot comprehend the real nature of the world. Even more importantly, salvation is a direct result of sin, so Donatello, existing outside the world of sin and death, is not a candidate for God's greatest gift to man. Thus, when Miriam, acting the part of an Eve figure, tempts Donatello to murder, she is the instrument bringing about his fall into humanity. The irony of Hawthorne's scheme is obvious, as the "fall" is in fact a rise from the sub-human condition. This story is a classic example of the idea of the "fortunate fall" which argues that the fall was necessary so man could achieve salvation from his sins. Thus, the price Donatello will be called upon to pay in guilt, suffering, and shame is no more than the price of his initiation into the human race with its blessing of salvation as well as its cost in pain.

The two women in *The Marble Faun* are typical of the extremes of Hawthorne's fictional women. Miriam, one of the dark ladies who frequently appear in his works, represents one moral extreme, while Hilda, whose innocence and religious faith are everywhere manifest, represents the other. Ironically, though, each of them serves as a salvation figure by becoming the instrument of humanizing the man with whom she is associated. Miriam's temptation of Donatello and her own ambiguous past with its suggestions of sin and guilt define her as an Eve figure tempting Donatello to the sin which will humanize him. Hilda, presented in terms of such innocence and virtue as to be almost unreal, is a different sort of salvation figure. In her case, she brings Kenyon from his cold isolation into the human race by awakening his ability to love. Ironically, Miriam is the more appealing of the two women for most readers because of her interesting complexities of character, but it is clearly Hilda who represents for Hawthorne the moral standard the novel is meant to affirm. But, by making her too incorruptible a symbol of Christian goodness, Hawthorne has also made her so one-dimensional as to strain our credibility.

The character in the novel closest to Hawthorne himself is the sculptor, Kenyon. Hawthorne refers to him at one point as "a man of marble," and implies that such a description fits his moral nature as well as his profession. Like the light and dark ladies, and the pre-lapsarian Adamic figure represented by Donatello, Kenyon is a recurrent type in Hawthorne's work. For Hawthorne, the artist—as well as the scientist who frequently appears in his works—by his very nature tends to isolate himself from humanity and become a cold observer who, without emotion of his own, exploits others' lives for his own ends. In his isolation, the artist suppresses what is human in himself for his art until he, in effect, loses his soul to it. Though his moral condition does not exactly parallel Donatello's, Kenyon is equally outside the human community, and he too is a candidate for salvation. It is Hilda who saves Kenyon, not through a dramatic temptation to sin, but through awakening that which is most human in his own heart—the ability to love. Though it may strain credibility to imagine Hilda as functioning within a love relationship—she seems too ethereal for so mundane a situation—Hawthorne's message of the redeeming power of love and sympathy is clear enough.

While the flaws of *The Marble Faun* are obvious faults in the total effect the novel achieves, the individual components of the work nevertheless save it from obscurity. The character types here presented are among the most important of Hawthorne's figures, while the dual themes of the "fortunate fall" and crime and punishment place the work within the great western tradition which deals with those topics, and it does bear comparison to them. Further, the setting of the novel in Rome anticipates the European novels of Henry James and the international novel which has remained a part of our literary tradition since James popularized it. Thus, though not a great novel, *The Marble Faun* is a significant work, and as such continues to hold a solid place in the American literary tradition.

Bibliography

Baym, Nina. "*The Marble Faun*: Hawthorne's Elegy for Art," in *New England Quarterly*. XLIV (1971), pp. 355–376.

————. *The Shape of Hawthorne's Career*. Ithaca, N.Y.: Cornell University Press, 1976, pp. 226–252.

Beidler, Peter G. "Theme of the Fortunate Fall in *The Marble Faun*," in *Emerson Society Quarterly*. XLVII (1967), pp. 56–62.

Bercovitch, Sacvan. "Of Wise and Foolish Virgins: Hilda Versus Miriam in Hawthorne's *Marble Faun*," in *New England Quarterly*. XLI (June, 1968), pp. 281–286.

Bicknell, John W. "*The Marble Faun* Reconsidered," in *University of Kansas City Review*. XX (Spring, 1954), pp. 193–199.

Brodtkorb, Paul, Jr. "Art Allegory in *The Marble Faun*," in *PMLA*. LXXVII (June, 1962), pp. 254–267.

Brown, Merle E. "The Structure of *The Marble Faun*," in *American Literature*. XXVIII (November, 1956), pp. 302–313.

Crews, Frederick C. *The Sins of the Fathers: Hawthorne's Psychological Themes*. New York: Oxford University Press, 1966, pp. 213–239.

Darnell, Donald G. " 'Doctrine by Ensample': The Emblem and *The Marble Faun*," in *Texas Studies in Literature and Language*. XV (1973), pp. 301–310.

Fogle, Richard Harter. "Coleridge, Hilda, and *The Marble Faun*," in *Emerson Society Quarterly*. LXXI (1973), pp. 105–111.

————. *Hawthorne's Imagery*. Norman: University of Oklahoma Press, 1969, pp. 125–172.

————. "Simplicity and Complexity in *The Marble Faun*," in *Tulane Studies in English*. II (1950), pp. 103–120.

Hart, James D. "Hawthorne's Italian Diary," in *American Literature*. XXXIV (January, 1963), pp. 562–567.

Levy, Leo B. "*The Marble Faun*: Hawthorne's Landscape of the Fall," in *American Literature*. XLII (1970), pp. 139–156.

Liebman, Sheldon W. "The Design of *The Marble Faun*," in *New England Quarterly*. XL (March, 1967), pp. 61–78.

Male, Roy R. *Hawthorne's Tragic Vision*. Austin: University of Texas Press, 1957, pp. 157–177.

Moss, Sidney P. "The Problem of Theme in *The Marble Faun*," in *Nineteenth-Century Fiction*. XVIII (March, 1964), pp. 393–399.

————. "The Symbolism of the Italian Background in *The Marble Faun*," in *Nineteenth-Century Fiction*. XXIII (December, 1968), pp. 332–336.

Pattison, Joseph C. "The Guilt of the Innocent Donatello," in *Emerson Society Quarterly*. XXXI (1963), pp. 66–68.

Pearce, Roy Harvey. "Hawthorne and the Twilight of Romance," in *Yale Review*. XXXVII (March, 1948), pp. 487–506.

Schwartz, Joseph. "Myth and Ritual in *The Marble Faun*," in *Emerson Society Quarterly*. XXV (1961), pp. 26–29.

Scrimgeour, Gary J. "*The Marble Faun*: Hawthorne's Faery Land," in *American Literature*. XXXVI (November, 1964), pp. 271–287.

Stubbs, John Caldwell. "*The Marble Faun*: Hawthorne's Romance of the Adamic Myth," in *Nathaniel Hawthorne*. Edited by J. Donald Crowley. New York: McGraw-Hill, 1975, pp. 101–114.

Waggoner, Hyatt Howe. *Hawthorne: A Critical Study*. Cambridge, Mass.: Harvard University Press, 1963, pp. 195–222.

Waples, Dorothy. "Suggestions for Interpreting *The Marble Faun*," in *American Literature*. XIII (November, 1941), pp. 224–239.

THE SCARLET LETTER

Type of work: Novel
Author: Nathaniel Hawthorne (1804–1864)
Type of plot: Psychological romance
Time of plot: Early days of the Massachusetts Colony
Locale: Boston
First published: 1850

The Scarlet Letter *is Hawthorne's masterpiece and his most profound exploration of sin, alienation, and spiritual regeneration. The novel traces the effects— social, moral, psychological, and spiritual—of Hester Prynne's adulterous relationship with the Reverend Arthur Dimmesdale on four people: the lovers themselves, their daughter, Pearl, and Roger Chillingworth, Hester's husband.*

Principal Characters

Hester Prynne, an attractive young woman living among the Puritans of Boston during the 1650's. She becomes a martyr because she, presumably a widow, bears a child out of wedlock; this sin results in her being jailed and then publicly exhibited on a pillory for three hours. When she is released from jail, she must wear for a lifetime a scarlet "A" upon her bosom. She becomes a seamstress, stitching and embroidering to earn a living for herself and for Pearl, her child. After her one act of sin, Hester behaves with such uncanny rectitude she seems an American Jeanne d'Arc, battling not against opposing armies and bigotry but against bigotry alone, the most formidable of antagonists. Hester refuses to name the child's father, who is the Reverend Arthur Dimmesdale, her minister; she does not quail when her supposedly dead husband, Roger Chillingworth, comes from out of the forest to witness her appearance on the pillory; and without complaint or self-pity she fights her way back to respectability and the rights of motherhood. Her situation is made more poignant (and heroic) by Dimmesdale's lack of sufficient moral courage to confess that he is Pearl's father. Hester seems to need no partner to share her guilt. Her life ends in tragedy (as it must) when Dimmesdale dies, but the reader feels that Hester—as strong as the oak in American clipper ships—will stoutly and resolutely make her way through life.

The Rev. Arthur Dimmesdale, a minister in Boston. Emotionally he is drawn and halved by the consequences of his sin with Hester, and he is pulled apart by responsibility. Should he confess and thus ruin his career or should he keep silent and continue the great good resulting from his sin-inspired sermons? Outwardly Dimmesdale is a living man, but inwardly he is the rubble and wreckage resulting from a Puritan conscience. One night he drags himself (along with Hester and Pearl) up to the pillory where he feels he should have stood long ago; but this confession is a sham, for only Roger Chillingworth (hidden in the darkness) observes the trio. Finally, at the end of his Election Day sermon, he takes Hester and Pearl by the hand, ascends the pillory, confesses publicly, and

---

THE SCARLET LETTER by Nathaniel Hawthorne. Published by Houghton Mifflin.

sinks down dead. When his clothing is removed, Puritans see the stigma of an "A" on the skin of his chest. Hawthorne takes no stand on Dimmesdale's weakness or strength; he says simply, "This is Dimmesdale."

Roger Chillingworth, a "physician" who might better be called "Evil." Thought to have been killed by the Indians, he reënters Hester's life when she first stands on the pillory. Pretending to minister to the physically ailing Dimmesdale, he tries only to confirm his suspicion that the minister is Pearl's father. When Arthur and Hester, in a desperate act of hope, book passage on a ship to England, Chillingworth also signs up for the voyage, and Hester knows she can never escape him. Although motivated by his wife's bearing another man's child, Chillingworth nevertheless seems inordinately twisted toward vengeance. Conniving, sly, monomaniacal, he is more a devilish force than a man.

Pearl, Hester's elfin, unpredictable daughter. She refuses to repeat the catechism for the Governor and thus risks being taken from her mother. At a meeting of Hester and Arthur in the forest she treats the minister as a rival; when he kisses her on the brow, she rushes to a stream and washes away the unwelcome kiss.

Governor Bellingham, of the Massachusetts Colony. He thinks Hester is unfit to rear Pearl but is persuaded to allow them to remain together by the plea of Dimmesdale.

The Rev. John Wilson, a stern divine. Early in the story he exhorts Dimmesdale to force Hester to reveal Pearl's father.

Mistress Higgins, the bitter-tempered sister of the Governor; she is simply and literally a witch.

The Story

On a summer morning in Boston, in the early days of the Massachusetts Colony, a throng of curious people had gathered outside the jail in Prison Lane. They were there to watch for Hester Prynne, who had been found guilty of adultery by a court of stern Puritan judges. Condemned to wear on the breast of her gown the scarlet letter, the A which stood for adulteress, she was to stand on the stocks before the meeting house, so that her shame might be a warning and a reproach to all who saw her. The crowd waited to see her ascend the scaffold with her child in her arms, and there for three hours bear her shame alone.

At last, escorted by the town beadle, the woman appeared. She moved serenely to the steps of the scaffold and stood quietly under the staring eyes that watched her public disgrace. It was whispered in the gathering that she had been spared the penalty of death or branding only through the intercession of the Reverend Arthur Dimmesdale, into whose church she had brought her scandalous sin.

While Hester stood on the scaffold, an elderly, almost deformed man appeared from the edge of the forest. When her agitation made it plain that she had recognized him, he put his finger to his lips as a sign of silence.

Hester's story was well-known in the community. She was the daughter of an ancient house of decayed fortune, and when she was young her family had married her to a husband who had great repute as a scholar. For some years they had lived in Antwerp. Two years before, the husband had sent his wife alone across the ocean to the Massachusetts Colony, intending to follow her as soon as he could put his affairs in order. There had been news of his departure, but his ship had never been heard of again. Hester, a young, attractive widow, had lived quietly in Boston until the time of her disgrace.

The scaffold of the pillory on which Hester stood was situated next to the balcony of the church where all the dignitaries of the colony sat to watch her humiliation. The ministers of the town called on her to name the man who with herself was equally guilty, and the most eloquent of those who exhorted her was the Reverend Arthur Dimmesdale, her pastor. Still Hester refused to name the father of her child, and she was led back to the prison after her period of public shame had ended.

On her return to prison Hester was found to be in a state of great nervous excitement. When at last medical aid was called, a man was found who professed knowledge of medicine. His name was Roger Chillingworth, he told the jailer, recently arrived in town after a year of residence among the Indians. Chillingworth was the stranger who had appeared so suddenly from the forest while Hester stood on the scaffold that afternoon, and she knew him as her husband, the scholar Prynne. His ship had been wrecked on the coast and he had been captive among the Indians for many months.

He also asked Hester to name the father of her child. When she refused, he stated that he would remain in Boston to practice medicine, swearing at the same time that he would devote the rest of his life to discovering the identity of the man who had dishonored him. He commanded Hester not to betray the relationship between them and she swore she would keep his secret.

When Hester's term of imprisonment was over, she found a small house on the outskirts of town, far removed from other habitation. There with her child, whom she had named Pearl, she settled down to earn a living from needlework, an outcast from society and still wearing the scarlet emblem on her breast.

Hester Prynne dressed her child in bright highly-ornamented costumes, in contrast to her sober dress. As she grew up, Pearl proved to be a capricious, wayward child, hard to discipline. One day Hester called on Governor Bellingham to deliver a pair of embroidered gloves. She also wanted to see him about the custody of Pearl, for there was a movement afoot among the strict church members to take the child away from her. In the garden of the governor's mansion, Hester found the governor, Dimmesdale, and old Roger Chillingworth. Because the perverse Pearl would not repeat the catechism, the governor was about to separate the child from her mother. Dimmesdale saved the situation, however, by a persuasive speech which resulted in the decision to let Hester keep Pearl, who seemed to be strangely attracted to the minister.

Roger Chillingworth had become intimately acquainted with Arthur Dimmesdale both as his parishioner and his doctor, for the minister had been in ill health ever since the physician had come to town. As the two men lodged in the same house, the physician came to know Dimmesdale's inmost thoughts and feelings. The minister was much perturbed by thoughts of conscience and guilt, but when he expressed these ideas in generalities to his congregation, the people thought him only the more righteous. Slowly in Chillingworth the conviction grew that Dimmesdale was Pearl's father, and he conjured up for the sick man visions of agony, terror, and remorse.

One night, unable to sleep, Dimmesdale walked to the pillory where Hester Prynne had stood in ignominy. He went up the steps and stood for a long time in the same place. A little later Hester, who had been watching at a deathbed, came by with little Pearl. The minister called them to the scaffold, saying that they had been there before when he lacked courage to stand beside them. Thus the three stood together, Dimmesdale acknowledging himself as Pearl's father and Hester's partner in sin. This striking tableau was not unobserved. Roger Chillingworth watched them from the shadows.

Hester Prynne was so shocked by Dimmesdale's feeble and unhealthy condition that she determined to see her former husband and plead with him to free the sick minister from his evil influence.

One day she met the old physician gathering herbs in the forest and begged him to be merciful to his victim. But Chillingworth was inexorable; he would not forego his revenge on the man who had wronged him. Hester then advised him that she would tell Arthur Dimmesdale their secret and warn him against his physician. A short time later, Hester and Pearl intercepted Dimmesdale in the forest as he was returning from a missionary journey to the Indians. Hester confessed her true relation with Chillingworth and warned the minister against the physician's evil influence. She and the clergyman decided to leave the colony together in secret, to take passage in a ship then in the harbor and return to the Old World. They were to leave four days later, after Dimmesdale had preached the Election Sermon.

Election Day, on which the new governor was to be installed, was a holiday in Boston, and the port was lively with the unaccustomed presence of sailors from the ship in the harbor. In the crowd was the captain of the vessel, with whom Hester had made arrangements for her own and Dimmesdale's passage. During the morning the captain informed Hester that Roger Chillingworth had also arranged for passage on the ship. Filled with despair, Hester turned away and went with Pearl to listen to Dimmesdale's sermon.

Unable to find room within the church, she stood at the foot of the scaffold where at least she could hear the sound of his voice. As the procession left the church, everyone had only words of praise for the minister's inspired address. Dimmesdale walked like a man in a dream and once he tottered and almost fell. When he saw Hester and Pearl at the foot of the scaffold, he stepped out of the procession and called them to him. Then, taking them by the hand, he climbed the steps of the pillory. Almost fainting, but with a voice terrible and majestic, the minister admitted his guilt to the watching people. With a sudden motion he tore the ministerial band from across his breast and sank dying to the platform.

When he thus exposed his breast, witnesses said that the stigma of the scarlet letter A was seen imprinted on the flesh above his heart.

Chillingworth, no longer able to wreak his vengeance on Dimmesdale, died within the year, bequeathing his considerable property to Pearl. For a time Hester disappeared from the colony, but years later she returned alone to live in her humble thatched cottage and to wear as before the scarlet emblem on her breast. But the scarlet letter, once her badge of shame, became an emblem of her tender mercy and kindness—an object of veneration and reverence to those whose sorrows she alleviated by her deeds of kindness and mercy. At her death she directed that the only inscription on her tombstone should be the letter A.

Critical Evaluation

Since it was first published in 1850, *The Scarlet Letter* has never been out of print, nor indeed out of favor with literary critics. It is inevitably included in listings of the five or ten greatest American novels. Considered the best of Nathaniel Hawthorne's writings, it may also be the most typical—the strongest statement of his recurrent themes, an excellent example of his craftsmanship.

The main thematic emphasis in *The Scarlet Letter,* as in most of Hawthorne's work, is on sin and its effects upon both the individual and society. It is frequently noted that Hawthorne's preoccupation with sin springs from the Puritan-rooted culture in which he lived, and from his awareness of two of his own ancestors who had presided over bloody persecutions during the Salem witchcraft trials. It is difficult for us, in our more permissive century, to conceive of the heavy import which seventeenth century New Englanders placed upon transgression of the moral code. As Yvor Winters has pointed out, the Puritans, believing in predestination, viewed the commission of *any* sin as evidence of the sinner's corruption and foreordained damnation. However, the harsh determinism and moralism of those early years had softened somewhat by Nathaniel Hawthorne's day; furthermore, he had worked out, perhaps during the twelve years he spent in contemplation and semi-isolation, his own notions about man's will and his nature. Thus *The Scarlet Letter* proves him closer to Paul Tillich than to Cotton Mather or Jonathan Edwards. Like Tillich, Hawthorne saw sin not as an *act* but as a *state*—that which modern existentialists refer to as alienation, and which Tillich describes as a three-fold separation from God, other men, and self. This alienation needs no fire and brimstone as consequence; it is in itself a hell.

There is a certain irony in the way in which this concept is worked out in *The Scarlet Letter*. Hester Prynne's pregnancy forces her sin to public view, and she is compelled to wear the scarlet "A" as a symbol of her adultery. Yet although she is apparently isolated from normal association with "decent" folk, Hester, having come to terms with her sin, is inwardly reconciled to God and self; and she ministers to the needy among her townspeople, reconciling herself with others until some observe that her "A" now stands for "Able." On the other hand, Arthur Dimmesdale, her secret lover, and Roger Chillingworth, her secret husband, move freely in society and even enjoy prestige, Dimmesdale as a beloved pastor, Chillingworth as a respected physician. But Dimmesdale's secret guilt gnaws so deeply inside him that he views himself with scorn as a hypocrite, and he is unable to make his peace with his God or to feel at ease with his fellow man. For his part, Chillingworth has permitted vengeance so to permeate his spirit that his alienation is absolute; he refers to himself as a "fiend," unable to impart forgiveness or change his profoundly evil path. His is the unpardonable sin—unpardonable not because God will not pardon, but because his own nature has become so depraved that he cannot repent or accept forgiveness.

Hawthorne clearly distinguishes between sins of passion and those of principle. Finally even Dimmesdale, traditional Puritan though he is, becomes aware of the difference:

> We are not, Hester, the worst sinners in the world. There is one worse than even the polluted priest! That old man's revenge has been blacker than my sin. He has violated, in cold blood, the sanctity of a human heart. Thou and I, Hester, never did so.

Always more concerned with the consequences than the cause of sin, Hawthorne anticipated Sigmund Freud's theories of the effects of guilt to a remarkable extent. Hester, whose guilt is openly known, grows through her suffering into an extraordinarily compassionate and understanding woman, a complete person who is able to come to terms with life—including sin. Dimmesdale, who yearns for the relief of confession, but hides his guilt to safeguard his role as pastor, is devoured internally. Again like Freud, Hawthorne recognized that spiritual turmoil may produce physical distress. Dimmesdale's well-being diminishes, and eventually he dies from no apparent cause other than continual emotional stress.

The Scarlet Letter reflects a number of Hawthorne's shorter works. Dimmesdale reminds one of Young Goodman Brown who, having once glimpsed the darker nature of mankind, must forevermore view humanity as corrupt and hypocritical; and of Parson Hooper in "The Minister's Black Veil," who continues to perform the duties of his calling with eloquence and compassion, but is forever separated from the company of men by the veil which he wears as a symbol of secret sin. Chillingworth is essentially like Ethan Brand, the limeburner who found the unpardonable sin in his own heart: "The sin of an intellect that triumphed over the sense of brotherhood with man and reverence for God, and sacrificed everything to its mighty claims!"

Hawthorne's craftsmanship is splendidly demonstrated in *The Scarlet Letter*. The structure is carefully unified, with three crucial scenes at the beginning, middle, and end of the action taking place on the scaffold. The scarlet "A" itself is entwined into the narrative repeatedly, as a symbol of sin or of shame, as a reminder of Hester's ability with the needle and her Ableness with people, and in Dimmesdale's case, as evidence of the searing effects of secret guilt. Several times there is forewarning or suggestion which is fulfilled later in the book: for example, notice is made that Pearl, the impish child of Hester and Dimmesdale, seems to lack complete humanity, perhaps because she has never known great sorrow; at the end of the story, when Dimmesdale dies, we are told that, "as [Pearl's] tears fell upon her father's cheek, they were the pledge that she would grow up amid human joy and sorrow, nor forever do battle with the world, but be a woman in it."

Hawthorne's skill as symbolist is fully in evidence. As one critic has noted, there is hardly a concrete object in the book that does not do double duty as a symbol: the scarlet letter; the sunlight which eludes Hester; the scaffold of public notice; the armor in which Hester's shame and Pearl's elfishness are distorted and magnified—the list could go on indefinitely. The four main characters themselves also serve as central symbols in this, the greatest allegory of a master allegorist.

Bibliography

Arden, Eugene. "Hawthorne's 'Case of Arthur D,'" in *American Imago*. XVIII (Spring, 1961), pp. 45–55.

Austin, Allen. "Satire and Theme in *The Scarlet Letter*," in *Philological Quarterly*. XLI (April, 1962), pp. 508–511.

Cowley, Malcolm. "Five Acts of *The Scarlet Letter*," in *College English*. XIX (1957), pp. 11–16.

Cox, James M. "*The Scarlet Letter*: Through the Old Manse and the Custom House," in *Virginia Quarterly Review*. LI (1975), pp. 432–447.

Crews, Frederick C. "The Ruined Wall: Unconscious Motivation in *The Scarlet Letter*," in *New England Quarterly*. XXXVIII (September, 1965), pp. 312–330.

Davidson, Edward H. "Dimmesdale's Fall," in *New England Quarterly*. XXXVI (September, 1963), pp. 358–370.

Fogle, Richard Harter. "The Poetics of Concealment: *The Scarlet Letter*," in *Nathaniel Hawthorne*. Edited by J. Donald Crowley. New York: McGraw-Hill, 1975, pp. 63–74.

Gerber, John C. "Form and Content in *The Scarlet Letter*," in *New England Quarterly*. XVII (1944), pp. 25–55.

234   *The Scarlet Letter*/HAWTHORNE

Greenwood, Douglas. "The Heraldic Device in *The Scarlet Letter*: Hawthorne's Symbolic Use of the Part," in *American Literature.* XLVI (1974), pp. 207–210.

Gross, Seymour L. " 'Solitude and Love and Anguish': The Tragic Design of *The Scarlet Letter*," in *College Language Association Journal.* III (March, 1960), pp. 154–165.

Hart, John E. "*The Scarlet Letter*: One Hundred Years After," in *New England Quarterly.* XXIII (1950), pp. 381–395.

Kaul, A.N. "Character and Motive in *The Scarlet Letter*," in *Critical Quarterly.* X (Winter, 1968), pp. 373–384.

Lasser, Michael L. "Mirror Imagery in *The Scarlet Letter*," in *English Journal.* LVI (February, 1967), pp. 274–277.

Maclean, Hugh N. "Hawthorne's *Scarlet Letter*: 'The Dark Problem of This Life,' " in *American Literature.* XXVII (1955), pp. 12–24.

McNamara, Anne Marie. "The Character of Flame: The Function of Pearl in *The Scarlet Letter*," in *American Literature.* XXVII (1956), pp. 537–553.

MacShane, Frank. "The House of the Dead: Hawthorne's Custom House and *The Scarlet Letter*," in *New England Quarterly.* XXXV (1962), pp. 93–101.

Matthiessen, F.O. *American Renaissance: Art and Expression in the Age of Emerson and Whitman.* New York: Oxford University Press, 1941, pp. 242–282.

Roper, Gordon. "The Originality of Hawthorne's *The Scarlet Letter*," in *Dalhousie Review.* XXX (1950), pp. 62–79.

Ryskamp, Charles. "The New England Sources of *The Scarlet Letter*," in *American Literature.* XXXI (1959), pp. 257–272.

Sandeen, Ernest. "*The Scarlet Letter* as a Love Story," in *PMLA.* LXXVII (September, 1962), pp. 425–435.

Scandon, Lawrence E. "The Heart of *The Scarlet Letter*," in *Texas Studies in Literature and Language.* IV (Summer, 1962), pp. 198–213.

Stubbs, John C. "Hawthorne's *The Scarlet Letter*: The Theory of the Romance and the Use of the New England Situation," in *PMLA.* LXXXIII (October, 1968), pp. 1439–1447.

Tanselle, G. Thomas. "A Note on the Structure of *The Scarlet Letter*," in *Nineteenth-Century Fiction.* XVII (1963), pp. 283–285.

Tharpe, Jac. *Nathaniel Hawthorne: Identity and Knowledge.* Carbondale: Southern Illinois University Press, 1967, pp. 110–124.

Waggoner, Hyatt Howe. *Hawthorne: A Critical Study.* Cambridge, Mass.: Harvard University Press, 1955, pp. 118–150.

LAFCADIO HEARN

Born: Leucadia, Ionian Islands (June 27, 1850)
Died: Tokyo, Japan (September 26, 1904)

Principal Works

NOVELS: *Chita: A Memory of Last Island*, 1889; *Youma*, 1890.

TALES AND SKETCHES: *Stray Leaves from Strange Literature*, 1884; *Some Chinese Ghosts*, 1887; *Kotto*, 1902; *Kwaidan*, 1904; *The Romance of the Milky Way*, 1905.

TRAVEL SKETCHES AND IMPRESSIONS: *Two Years in the French West Indies*, 1890; *Glimpses of Unfamiliar Japan*, 1894; *In Ghostly Japan*, 1899.

MISCELLANEOUS: *Gleanings in Buddha-Fields*, 1897; *Exotics and Retrospectives*, 1898; *Japan: An Attempt at Interpretation*, 1904.

Lafcadio Hearn is an excellent example of a writer who is remembered for a delicate, continuously responsive sensitivity and a carefully wrought style.

Born in the Ionian Islands on June 27, 1850, he was the son of a British army surgeon and a young Greek woman of a respected family. Her elopement with a member of the unpopular British occupational forces broke ties with her own family; thus, when she could not follow her husband to the West Indies, she and the infant Lafcadio went to Ireland to live with Surgeon Hearn's family. There, religious differences, the language barrier, and her keen sensitivity to the criticism of her in-laws and—later—of her returned husband led to a mental collapse from which she never completely recovered. She eventually returned to the Ionian Islands, married a compatriot, and died in a mental hospital on Corfu.

Hearn was left in Ireland to live an unsettled life as the ward of a very devout great-aunt, becoming prey to all sorts of fears, especially of the supernatural. He was educated at home by tutors and at a church school in Normandy before being sent to Saint Cuthbert's College near Durham, England. Here his imaginative pranks and winning nature won him many friends among the students.

Hearn left college without a degree because of three personal tragedies. Extremely myopic, he lost the sight of one of his eyes when it was accidentally struck by a classmate during a game. About this same time, his great-aunt lost her wealth through the business speculations of a relative she wished to help, and Hearn's own father, who might have contributed financially to his schooling, died on a return voyage from service in India. His father's money was left to three daughters by a second marriage.

The great-aunt, now senile, resorted to the desperate expedient of sending Hearn to Cincinnati, Ohio, where a distant relative had settled. She died soon after without ever knowing what terrible hardships her ward suffered before he received help from an English printer who gave him paternal affection and training for the superlative work he was to do for Cincinnati and New Orleans newspapers. In Cincinnati, he made his reputation locally by reporting the minute details of a sensational tan-yard murder and by writing sympathetically and perceptively about the levee life of Negro roustabouts. In New Orleans, he attacked corruption in city government, praised George Washington Cable's writing about Louisiana Creoles, reconstructed tales from Arabian and Chinese literatures, and, above all, through his translations in newspapers, introduced Zola, Maupassant, and Loti to an American reading public.

Twice he visited the West Indies, where the color and charm of native life made an immediate appeal to his senses. Exotic travel sketches and two novelettes about Creole life gained him an international audience before he departed for Japan in 1890 on an assignment from Harper and Brothers.

Hearn planned to stay in Japan for only a short time, but he was so thrilled with the veritable fairyland he discovered in Japan that he spent the rest of his life there, identifying himself with the Japanese by marrying into a Japanese family and by becoming a naturalized Japanese citizen. His penetrating studies of customs and legends and his acute interpretations of the Japanese were translated into many languages. In 1895, after teaching in several secondary schools, he was made professor of English literature in the Imperial University of Tokyo.

When he died in Tokyo on September 26, 1904, he was buried with Buddhist rites in a Buddhist cemetery. This was his wish—to die and be cremated and buried like the Japanese, though he himself was not a Buddhist. Today Hearn is nowhere so highly regarded as in Japan. Certainly, in Japan, as in so many other places, Hearn had re-created in exquisitely stylized prose whatever was wonderful and weird and beautiful.

Bibliography

The authorized biography is Elizabeth Bisland, *The Life and Letters of Lafcadio Hearn*, 2 vols., 1906. Since it glosses over certain aspects of Hearn's life and work, it should be supplemented by such later studies as Nina H. Kennard, *Lafcadio Hearn*, 1912; Edward Larocque Tinker, *Lafcadio Hearn's American Days*, 1924; Vera McWilliams, *Lafcadio Hearn*, 1946; Marcel Robert, *Lafcadio Hearn*, 3 vols., 1950–1954 (Tokyo); and O. W. Frost, *Young Hearn*, 1957 (Tokyo). Recent studies are Elizabeth Stevenson, *Lafcadio Hearn*, 1961; and Beongcheon Yu, *An Ape of Gods: The Art and Thought of Lafcadio Hearn*, 1964. Also useful are the collections of letters: *Letters from the Raven*, edited by Milton Bronner, 1907, and *The Japanese Letters of Lafcadio Hearn*, edited by Elizabeth Bisland, 1910.

For briefer studies see Percy H. Boynton, *More Contemporary Americans*, 1927; Oscar Lewis, *Hearn and His Biographers: The Record of a Literary Controversy*, 1930; Matthew Josephson, *Portrait of the Artist as American*, 1930; Elizabeth Bisland, "Some Martinique Letters of Lafcadio Hearn," *Harper's*, CXLII (1921), 516–525; Henry Tracy Kneeland, "Lafcadio Hearn's Brother," *Atlan-*

tic Monthly, CXXXI (1923), 20–27; E. C. Beck, "Letters of Lafcadio Hearn to His Brother," *American Literature*, IV (1932), 167–173; Ray M. Lawless, "A Note on Lafcadio Hearn's Brother," *ibid.*, X (1938), 80–83; and H. E. Rudkin, "Lafcadio Hearn," *Notes & Queries*, CLXXVII (1939), 419–422.

CHITA

Type of work: Novel
Author: Lafcadio Hearn (1850–1904)
Type of plot: Exotic romance
Time of plot: Nineteenth century
Locale: Louisiana coastal waters
First published: 1889

In his distinctly abrupt style, Hearn weaves in Chita *a tale that is a curious blend of narrative and poetry. The romantic story of a foundling is imbued with impressionistic, almost mystical qualities by its fusion at the climax with the progress of the hurricane.*

Principal Characters

Chita, a child rescued from the sea during a storm off the Louisiana coast. She is so young that all she can tell her rescuers on Last Island is that her real name is Lili, her Creole name is Zouzoune, and her mother and father are named Adele and Julien. Called by her new friends Chita, the little girl grows up on the island without knowing any more of her earlier existence.

Dr. Julien La Brierre, a physician from New Orleans who comes to see a patient on Last Island. He falls ill himself, and in his delirium he is reminded of his dead wife by Chita's startling resemblance to the drowned woman. He dies without realizing that the girl is really his daughter.

Feliu Viosca, a fisherman who lives on Last Island. He rescues Chita from the sea and takes her into his home.

Carmen Viosca, the fisherman's wife. She treats the foundling from the sea as though she were her own child.

Laroussel, a Creole who was Dr. La Brierre's rival for his dead wife's hand years before. At one time the doctor and Laroussel fought a duel over Adele, who became the doctor's wife. He questions Chita on Viosca's island and gives her a trinket but does not discover that she is Dr. La Brierre's child.

Captain Harris, a sea captain who checks for survivors after the storm. He decides it is best for Chita to remain with the fisherman and his wife who have given the girl a home.

Captain Abraham Smith, a sea captain who tries to rescue as many people as he can from the hurricane.

Mr. Edwards, the patient whose illness summons Dr. La Brierre to Last Island.

The Story

Southward from New Orleans one passes settlements of many nationalities and races, Western and Oriental. Beyond lies an archipelago, the islands of which are Grande Pass, Grande Terre, and Barataria. Still to the south lies Grande Isle, a modern bathing resort, the loveliest island in the Gulf of Mexico. Last Island, forty miles west of Grande Isle, is now desolate, but at an earlier time it was the most popular of the group and a fashionable resort. The hotel there was a two-story timber structure with many apartments, a dining-room, and a ballroom. One night the sea destroyed it.

On the northwest side of each island are signs of the incessant influence of the wind and sea, for the trees all bend away from the water. All along the Gulf coast, and on the island beaches, are the ruins of hurricanes, skeletons of toppled buildings and broken tree trunks. The land itself is being eaten away.

The innocent beauty of summer on these islands is impossible to express. Years ago Last Island was immersed in the azure light of a typical July. It was an unusually lovely summer and the breathless charm of the season lingered on. One afternoon the ocean began to stir and great waves started to hurl themselves over the beaches, giving warning on Last Island that a hurricane was brewing. The wind, beginning to blow, continued for a few days to stir the water. A steamer, the *Star*, due that day, was not expected to arrive.

Captain Abraham Smith, an American, knew the sea and he knew his ship. Sensing that he might be needed, he had sailed for Last Island. As he approached he saw the storm rising. He ordered the excess weight of the *Star* tossed overboard to help her ride out the storm. On the island, however, the guests at the hotel continued to dance until they noticed water at their feet and the building began to be buffeted by the waves. Captain Smith spent the night rescuing as many as he could. Buildings were ripped apart, the shores were lashed by wind and wave, lakes and rivers overflowed, and by daybreak countless corpses floated on the stormy sea.

When the hurricane subsided, scavengers came to claim whatever plunder could be salvaged from the ruins and from the bodies of the dead.

On a tiny volcanic island lived Feliu Viosca, a fisherman, and his wife Carmen. On the night of the terrible storm Carmen was awakened by the noise. Afraid, she aroused her husband, whose calmness comforted her, and he ordered her to return to sleep. In her dreams her dead child, dark-eyed Conchita, came to her.

The next day the fishermen, gathered at the shore, stood watching the wreckage and the bodies floating past. A flash of yellow caught Feliu's eye. In a moment he had stripped and was swimming out toward a child, still alive, clinging to her drowned mother. Feliu managed to rescue the baby and swim back to shore.

The half-drowned child was taken to Carmen, whose skillful hands and maternal instincts nursed the little girl into a warm, sound sleep; there was hope she would survive. Her yellow hair had saved her, for it was the flash of sun on her tresses that had caught Feliu's eye.

Captain Harris, of New Orleans, along with several other men, was sailing up and down the coast in search of missing persons, dead or still alive after the storm. Ten days after the rescue of the girl, Harris came to Viosca's wharf. Hardly able to communicate with the men, Feliu told them the story of his heroism, but cautioned them that if they wished to question the child they must proceed gently, since she was still not fully recovered from shock.

The child's Creole dialect was not comprehensible to anyone there until Laroussel, a Creole, began to question her. In her broken speech she told him that her Creole name was Zouzoune, her real one Lili. Her mother was called Adele and her father Julien. Nothing more could be determined. Realizing that the child's relatives might never be found, Harris decided to leave her with Feliu and Carmen, who promised to give her excellent care. Laroussel gave the little girl a trinket that had caught her eye. Although other searching parties stopped to see Feliu's waif, the child's identity remained a mystery. Meanwhile, near another island, a pair of bodies drifting in the sea had been identified as those of Dr. Julien La Brierre and his wife Adele. The doctor had survived, however; six months later he was in New Orleans looking at his own epitaph and that of his wife.

Dr. La Brierre had grown up in New Orleans. In maturity, to please his father, he had studied medicine in Paris. After his return to New Orleans he had fallen in love and had been wounded in a duel with a rival named Laroussel. Following the death of his father and mother, Julien had married Adele, and Zouzoune was born.

On the lonely island the small child, now called Chita, had become a member of the Viosca family. Gradually she adapted herself to the ways of her foster parents.

Years later Dr. La Brierre was practicing in New Orleans, a lonely and kindly physician. One year Edwards, an elderly patient of his, went to Viosca's Point, which Captain Harris had recommended for the sick man's recovery. While there, Edwards suffered a stroke. Hurriedly summoned, Dr. La Brierre arrived too late to help his patient.

Before the doctor could set out for home, he too became ill. Carmen nursed him. In the vague consciousness that accompanied his malady, the doctor saw Chita, whose resemblance to his dead wife greatly exicted him. In his delirium he called out to Zouzoune, to Adele, while Carmen tried to calm him.

Reliving the horror of the hurricane that had taken Adele and Zouzoune from him, the sick man died.

Critical Evaluation

Despite its graphic rendering of a devastating hurricane, *Chita* is not a naturalistic novel with a storm for its "hero." Although Hearn was attracted by Herbert Spencer's evolutionary philosophy and read Darwin avidly, his destiny was not to join the rising school of American naturalism descending from Crane and Norris to Dreiser. Hearn followed that other great trend in late nineteenth century literature—aestheticism. His kindred spirits were Keats, Walter Pater, and Oscar Wilde. He was a pursuer of beauty and a painter with words. Shortly after completing *Chita,* Hearn left for Japan and eventually became the most important literary interpreter of Japan's aesthetic culture to the English-speaking world.

Chita's sentimental plot—the lost child and her chance reunion with a dying father—is designed to arouse human emotions that will correspond in intensity to the turbulence of the storm. It is the dynamic impressionism of the storm itself that fascinates Hearn: after the deceptive calm of summer come the roaring breakers; the storm swirls houses and ships and creates an incredible magnitude of refuse in its wake. Endless wreckage and bodies are strewn everywhere—including the foundling, Chita.

The child is fished out of all this dying waste like a creature returned from the dead. Her rescue has all the aura of a miracle to the simple Vioscas, who see the child as sent "by the Virgin." At the end of the story, La Brierre's fevered imagination once more re-creates the chaotic horror of the storm, more impressionistic than ever because its setting is now an agonized brain. And once again a miracle is performed: the lost child is tossed up by the seething wreckage of La Brierre's tortured memories. She is there both in his mind and in actuality. The blurring of the two realities makes for the perfect impressionistic ending. The novel opens with the calm hues of a summery Renoir and closes with the brilliant frenzy of a Monet.

Bibliography

Kunst, Arthur E. *Lafcadio Hearn.* New York: Twayne, 1969, pp. 64–69.

Leary, L.G. "Lafcadio Hearn, 'One of Our Southern Writers': A Footnote to Southern History," in *Essays on American Literature in Honor of Jay B. Hubbell.* Edited by Clarence Gohdes. Durham, N.C.: Duke University Press, 1967, pp. 202–214.

Shuman, R. Baird. "Hearn's Gift from the Sea: *Chita,*" in *English Journal.* LVI (September, 1967), pp. 822–827.

Stokes, Edward. "Lafcadio Hearn's *Chita,*" in *Journal of the Australasian Universities Language and Literature Association.* No. 5 (1957), pp. 1–9.

Yu, Beongcheon. *An Ape of Gods: The Art of Thought of Lafcadio Hearn.* Detroit: Wayne State University Press, 1964, pp. 66–73.

E. W. HOWE

Born: Treaty, Indiana (May 3, 1853)
Died: Atchison, Kansas (October 3, 1937)

Principal Work

NOVEL: *The Story of a Country Town*, 1883.

E(dgar) W(atson) Howe, journalist and novelist, born May 3, 1853, at Treaty, Indiana, belongs to that class of prolific writers whose energy and direction come out most clearly in a book only once during a long career. His first and best novel, *The Story of a Country Town*, set in Middle Western Twin Mounds, is noteworthy in American literature for its small-town realism and its stark exposure of nastiness and loneliness. He was among the first to denigrate frontier life and portray the Midwest less in the tradition of the American Dream than in the grimness of its daily order. For these qualities he belongs in the same category as Hamlin Garland and Edgar Lee Masters, and he was noticed with appreciation by Mark Twain and William Dean Howells. The story itself, revealing conjugal betrayal in three families, is still overpowering, although in a period after Freud its undercurrent of male sexual repression reads more like a document of social psychology.

Howe published several other novels and two books of essays, but he was successful chiefly in the biting paragraphs of his journalism. He published the *Golden Globe* in Colorado and later the Atchison, Kansas, *Daily Globe*, the best-known American single sheet. He also established *E. W. Howe's Monthly* in 1911. He died at Atchison on October 3, 1937.

Bibliography

Howe told much of the story of his own life in his autobiography, *Plain Folks*, 1929. For a discussion of his novel see Carl Van Doren, Introduction to *The Story of a Country Town*, 1927; and Vernon L. Parrington, *Main Currents in American Thought*, III, 1930. See also Calder M. Pickett, *Ed Howe: Country Town Philosopher*, 1968.

THE STORY OF A COUNTRY TOWN

Type of work: Novel
Author: Edgar Watson Howe (1853–1937)
Type of plot: Social criticism
Time of plot: Mid-nineteenth century
Locale: The Middle West
First published: 1883

Historically Howe's novel is important as an early satire on the meanness of spirit, shallowness, and petty materialism of small-town America. The theme of "revolt from the village" was to become a major subject of social criticism in American literature during the 1920's.

Principal Characters

Abram Nedrow (Ned) Westlock, a Middle Border boy (and man), the narrator of the story. He is a farm helper for his father, later an apprentice in journalism, and he becomes a successful editor of the paper his father leaves him. For years in love with Agnes, he marries her after his mother's death. A close observer of people, he is also a moralist on such matters as temperance and personal industry. As a critic of small-town temperament and mores, he anticipates Sinclair Lewis's Carol Kennicott.

The Reverend John Westlock, his father, a Methodist minister, a strong, capable, independent, thrifty man; a domestic tyrant, a hard worker, strongly opinionated. Suffering from a gnawing discontent, he leaves the ministry, becomes the editor of a newspaper, and later deserts his family, informing Ned of a seven-year liaison with Mrs. Tremaine, who accompanies him in his flight.

Mrs. Westlock, the minister's weak, timid, submissive wife. She dies just before her repentant husband returns.

Jo Erring, her younger brother, in early youth a member of the Westlock household and throughout his life a close friend of Ned. Stout, energetic, and ambitious, but rather crude and uneducated, he works hard to prove himself worthy of Mateel. Having learned milling under Damon Barker, he builds a mill of his own and marries Mateel. Doomed from the beginning, the marriage is never happy, and it finally disintegrates. After Mateel divorces him and marries Bragg, Jo murders him and later poisons himself in prison.

Mateel Shepherd, Jo Erring's sweetheart. Though in love with Bragg, she marries Jo, whom she later divorces to marry Bragg. Driven insane by Bragg's murder, she dies shortly afterward.

Clinton Bragg, Jo's rival for Mateel. He is boastful, sullen, insolent, lazy, an ostentatious drinker, educated and scornful of others' ignorance. He is murdered by Jo.

Damon Barker (in reality **Captain Deming**), a former ship captain now a miller, a friend of Ned and Jo. After his wife's death he reveals his identity to his daughter Agnes, who goes to live with him.

Agnes Deming, his daughter, a young and pretty schoolteacher. Popular in Fairview, she is a kindly friend and adviser to everyone. Though older than Ned, she accepts his love. They grow closer when she cares for his ailing mother, and at the end of the story she and Ned have been happily married for several years.

The Reverend Goode Shepherd, the father of Mateel and successor to Mr. Westlock at the Fairview church.

Mrs. Tremaine, the widowed half sister of Damon Barker, for whom she keeps house. She elopes with Mr. Westlock but leaves him when she learns he has left Ned his money and property.

Dad Erring, Jo's father, a shingle-maker,

non-religious, eccentric, and reticent, a man who attends to his own business and ignores that of others.

Mr. Lytle (Little) Biggs, Agnes' uncle, the father of eight children. A free-spoken little man, he is critical of others' follies and faults as well as his own, such as his penchant for lying.

Big Adam, Mr. Biggs' hired man, a fat, bull-voiced country lout with a habit of drawing imaginary corks and pouring imaginary drinks. He becomes Barker's helper and later the mill operator.

The Story

The Westlocks had gone west to grow up with the country. They lived first on a farm near a church where the father acted as the volunteer preacher. It was a life of toil and privation on the bleak prairie. Days began early and ended soon after supper, when fatigue drove the Westlocks to bed. There were four of them, John Westlock and his wife, their son Ned, and Mrs. Westlock's younger brother, Jo Erring. The only real amusement Ned had was visiting a nearby miller with his young uncle. The miller, Mr. Barker, had been a sailor in early life and he regaled the boys with stories of his travels.

When Ned was eleven years old a minister was sent from the East to take charge of the country church where Mr. Westlock had been acting as preacher. Erring immediately fell in love with Mateel Shepherd, the daughter of the new preacher, but he found no favor in her eyes because he was uneducated and crude. With the miller's help he began to improve himself. The miller became so fond of Erring that he took him on as an apprentice who would some day take over the mill. This was a great opportunity for the seventeen-year-old boy. The only flaw in his happiness then was that Mateel Shepherd was being courted by a young lawyer named Clinton Bragg.

Shortly after Erring left the farm, Mr. Westlock sold his farm and bought the almost defunct paper in the town of Twin Mounds. When the Westlocks moved into town, Ned went to the office every day to learn the printing trade and to help his father in the newspaper office.

Twin Mounds was an unprepossessing village with a post-office, several stores, a jail, and about six hundred people. The only pleasures in which the people seemed to indulge, so far as Ned could see, were drinking, gossiping, and fighting. Although the Westlocks lived in a large stone house, the father had Ned stay at the newspaper office in the company of one of the printers, under whom he was learning the trade.

Erring, apprenticed to the miller, made such excellent progress that after a year or so the community subscribed to a fund so that he could build a mill of his own, the growing population justifying a second mill in the district. He was also successful in his suit with Mateel Shepherd, who had promised to marry him when his mill was completed and in operation.

One day the quiet life of the Westlock family was rudely shattered. Mr. Westlock left the deeds to all his property in the custody of Ned and his mother and ran away with another woman. Ned took over the newspaper, which became more profitable under his management than it had been under his father, for the people in the community had not liked Mr. Westlock. He had been too solitary and strange to suit their natures.

The family gradually began to grow out of the feeling of disgrace which had fastened itself upon them when the father disappeared. Their friends did what they could for them and rallied in support of Mrs. Westlock and her son. At times it seemed as if the disappearance of Mr. Westlock were of more benefit than harm. Ned was left with some valuable property and a chance to make a name for himself at a very early age.

The following Christmas Eve Erring married Mateel Shepherd. Just before the marriage he and Ned had a long talk, in which he told Ned that in some way he was not as anxious for the marriage as he had been when he first met Mateel. What Erring did not realize was that he had been so zealous in getting an education that he had not only reached Mateel's level but he had already passed her. It was not a happy wedding. Only a handful of guests came to the wedding supper, and those who stayed away did not bother to send their regrets. The Shepherds were not popular in the community.

After the marriage of Mateel and Erring, life in the community of Twin Mounds settled into a quiet routine for everyone. Ned was more disappointed than ever in the town. Its people seldom thought out anything for themselves, and every opinion they had was made for them, often by Ned's own editorials. Their shallowness and smugness irked him.

One cold winter night Erring appeared at the door of the Westlock home. Nervous and disheveled, he had come because he felt the need to talk to someone whom he could trust. He had found a letter which his wife had written to his rival before her marriage, a letter disclosing Mateel's belief that she could never love any man but Bragg. This idea rankled in Erring's mind. He had been thoughtful and tender with his wife, but she had always been distant and cool to him, in keeping with the vow she had made in her letter to Bragg.

Ned listened to his uncle's story and then took him back to the mill and Mateel. After Erring had confronted his wife with what he had discovered, he and Ned sat up all night, unable to sleep. Clinton Bragg disappeared from Twin Mounds within a few days, apparently afraid of Mateel's husband.

That same winter Ned's father returned to Twin Mounds and accidentally met his son on the street at a late hour. He told Ned that he had been faced with misfortune ever since he had left his wife and son. The woman with whom he had run away had not really loved him and had deserted him soon after she learned that he had left his money and property in Ned's hands. John Westlock was a pathetic and broken figure, unwilling to face the wife he had deserted. Ned gave him the little money he happened to have in his pocket, and the older man then turned away into the snowy night and was soon lost to sight. Ned knew that he had seen his father for the last time.

Meanwhile matters between Erring and his wife had gone from bad to worse. He had taken a vow never to speak to his wife or touch her again, and Mateel began to fade quickly under his harsh treatment. At last she asked Erring to let her return to her father's home. He agreed. A day later Bragg drove up in a buggy to take the girl back to her father and mother. It was a bitter experience for Erring to see another man carry his wife away from his house. Ned was with his uncle and left only when the older man had fallen asleep, exhausted.

When Ned arrived home he discovered that his mother had died in his absence. Always quiet and subdued, she had died as she had lived, asking nothing from anyone.

In the spring Ned braved a heavy rainstorm to visit his uncle. He arrived to find the mill deserted. Suddenly the door opened and Erring walked in, carrying Mateel, who was unconscious. In a calm voice he told Ned how he had lain in wait along the road until Bragg and Mateel had come along in a buggy. He had dragged his rival from the vehicle and killed him with his bare hands while Mateel looked on. Then he had carried Mateel back to the mill. Unable to face the fact that Mateel had divorced him and married Bragg, he felt it was better to murder and then to die himself than to live with Mateel married to another.

Erring surrendered quietly to the authorities and was taken to jail. He was never tried, however, because one night he took poison. The jailer discovered him with a letter for Ned clutched in his hand.

After Erring's burial, Ned stopped at the Shepherd home to ask about Mateel. The poor girl was demented. While he was in the house she came into the room and mistook Ned for Erring. She drew a dagger from her dress and told Ned she had gone by the mill that day to have one last look at the place where she had been happy. Now she intended to kill herself. Her mother led her away. That same night she died, shortly after telling her father and mother she hoped to see Jo Erring soon.

Critical Evaluation

Howells and Twain praised Edgar W. Howe's novel, and one early reviewer believed that at last someone had created the "great American novel." For the modern reader, however, its interest is historical rather than literary. Howe's style is often cumbersome with frequent errors of spelling, word usage, and construction.

Many reviewers have noted the novel's Dickensian tones. The most obvious influence is in the characters' names—Jo Erring, Ned's tragic, misunderstood uncle; the Reverend Goode Shepherd; the worthless but wordy philosopher, Lytle Biggs; and the boastful villain, Clinton Bragg. There is also the sense of melancholy Dickens gives to his child heroes. Ned resembles Pip and David Copperfield in the dismal circumstances of his early life. Dominated by work, death, religion, and rejection, Ned comes to a fatalistic acceptance that life is a wretched experience.

Unfortunately, the adult Ned is less interesting. His story is submerged as the book sinks into trite melodrama, and Ned remains important only as narrator of the misfortunes of Jo and Mateel. Another departure from Dickens is that there is no humor to relieve the book's starkness. The gray, wooden church with its graveyard dominates Fairview, and the Indian graves of Twin Mounds oversee the meanness of small-town culture.

Howe implies that country living makes men cruel. Trying desperately to wring an existence from the dry soil, the characters find the work ethic to be all-encompassing. Their only relief is religion, which is grimly Calvinistic. Ned begins his narrative by observing that his father's religion would have been incomplete without a hell, for Mr. Westlock hoped that everyone who did not share his piety would be punished. It is ironic that through the church Mr. Westlock meets Mrs. Tremaine, a temperance fanatic, with whom he elopes. When last seen, he is a broken, guilt-ridden old man who returns to Twin Mounds on the snowy eve of his wife's funeral.

The melodrama and sketchy characterization weaken the novel, but the book is of definite value when seen as a precursor to *Winesburg, Ohio*; *Main Street*; and *Spoon River Anthology*.

WILLIAM DEAN HOWELLS

Born: Martins Ferry, Ohio (March 1, 1837)
Died: New York, N.Y. (May 11, 1920)

Principal Works

NOVELS: *Their Wedding Journey,* 1872; *A Chance Acquaintance,* 1873; *A Foregone Conclusion,* 1875; *The Lady of the Aroostook,* 1879; *The Undiscovered Country,* 1880; *A Modern Instance,* 1882; *A Woman's Reason,* 1883; *The Rise of Silas Lapham,* 1885; *Indian Summer,* 1886; *The Minister's Charge,* 1887; *April Hopes,* 1888; *Annie Kilburn,* 1889; *A Hazard of New Fortunes,* 1890; *The Quality of Mercy,* 1892; *An Imperative Duty,* 1892, *The World of Chance,* 1893; *The Coast of Bohemia,* 1893; *A Traveler from Alturia,* 1894; *The Day of Their Wedding,* 1896; *A Parting and a Meeting,* 1896; *An Open-Eyed Conspiracy,* 1897; *The Landlord at Lion's Head,* 1897; *Their Silver Wedding Journey,* 1899; *Ragged Lady,* 1899; *The Kentons,* 1902; *The Son of Royal Langbrith,* 1904; *Through the Eye of the Needle,* 1907; *New Leaf Mills,* 1913; *The Leatherwood God,* 1916.

SHORT STORIES: *A Fearful Responsibility and Other Stories,* 1881; *Christmas Every Day,* 1893.

PLAYS: *The Parlor Car,* 1876; *Out of the Question,* 1877; *A Counterfeit Presentment,* 1877; *The Register,* 1884; *A Sea-Change,* 1888; *The Albany Depot,* 1892; *A Letter of Introduction,* 1892; *The Unexpected Guests,* 1893; *A Previous Engagement,* 1897; *Room Forty-five,* 1900; *The Smoking Car,* 1900; *An Indian Giver,* 1900; *Parting Friends,* 1911.

TRAVEL SKETCHES: *Venetian Life,* 1866; *Italian Journeys,* 1867; *Tuscan Cities,* 1886; *London Films,* 1905; *Certain Delightful English Towns,* 1906; *Roman Holidays,* 1908; *Seven English Cities,* 1909; *Familiar Spanish Travels,* 1913.

AUTOBIOGRAPHY AND REMINISCENCE: *A Boy's Town,* 1890; *My Year in a Log Cabin,* 1893; *Impressions and Experiences,* 1896; *Stories of Ohio,* 1897; *Letters Home,* 1903; *My Mark Twain,* 1910; *Years of My Youth,* 1916; *Eighty Years and After,* 1921; *The Life in Letters of William Dean Howells,* 1928.

ESSAYS AND CRITICISM: *Criticism and Fiction,* 1891; *My Literary Passions,* 1895; *Literary Friends and Acquaintances,* 1900; *Heroines of Fiction,* 1901; *Literature and Life,* 1902; *Imaginary Interviews,* 1910.

Concerning the literary greatness of William Dean Howells, some dissent is now being heard on the grounds that he is too quiet and unhurried for our own frenetic generation, but it is hard to exaggerate the influence which he once exerted upon American writing. A prolific and versatile author of novels, plays, essays, poems, reviews, travel pieces—the author of too much, it must be said— he achieved a remarkable degree of success in consistently expressing himself with ease, exactness, and felicity. Furthermore, his long connection with the *Atlantic Monthly* and other important publications enabled him to encourage some potentially able writers to whom an editor's approval could make a great difference. The list of struggling authors thus benefited would be a long one; and it would show such notables-to-be as Mark Twain and Henry James, both of whom received Howells' endorsement at times when it was needed most.

Howells was born March 1, 1837, at Martins Ferry, Ohio. His father, William Cooper Howells, was of Welsh descent, a former Quaker who had drifted into the "New Church" of Emanuel Swedenborg; his mother, Mary Dean Howells, was of Irish and Pennsylvania Dutch stock. The elder Howells was a man of ability and character whose craftsman's skill as a printer was offset by a distressing lack of business acumen. With, eventually, ten mouths to feed, he led a wandering and straitened life as editor and printer in various sections of Ohio; and his second son, William Dean, got much of his education in a printing office. Fortunately, there have been worse places, as Bret Harte and Mark Twain could have joined Howells in testifying. The latter's formal schooling occupied as little as sixteen or eighteen months; and these were in random doses, mainly at Hamilton, Ohio. Nevertheless, the boy's keen appetite for learning was soon discernible to and encouraged by his understanding father. William eagerly read and wrote; he developed a passion for languages, at one period studying five simultaneously, and he acquired such a devotion to Heinrich Heine that Lowell was later to write: "You must sweat the Heine out of you as men do mercury."

At fourteen Howells became a compositor on the *Ohio State Journal* at Columbus. Other newspaper jobs followed, but the young man found time to write and send off poetry to the *Atlantic Monthly*, some of it finding acceptance. Energy and ambition began to pay off, though all was not clear sailing. One of his biggest handicaps was a sort of psychic malaise, featuring a fear of hydrophobia, which haunted his childhood and adolescence, once driving him into a complete breakdown. Nevertheless, Howells' will was indomitable. At twenty-one he was dining with the governor of the state; at twenty-four—largely as the result of a campaign life of Lincoln—he was appointed American Consul at Venice.

His four years in Venice were the equivalent of a university education for Howells; they gave him not only an acquaintance with the riches of Europe but enough time to read, write, and improve his knowledge of languages. During his consulship, in 1862, he married Elinor Meade of Brattleboro, Vermont, whom he had previously met in Columbus. Their stay abroad inspired the writing of *Venetian Life* and *Italian Journeys*, which were published in 1866 and 1867.

Returning to America in 1865, Howells intensified his pursuit of a literary career. After a few months of free-lancing in New York, a break came when he was offered the post of editorial assistant on *The Nation*. Even this, however, was merely the prelude to one of the most important steps of his life. Early in 1866 he attracted the attention of James T. Fields, editor of the *Atlantic Monthly*; and a few weeks later, on his twenty-ninth birthday, he became assistant editor of that influential literary organ. For fifteen years Howells' fate and fortunes were to be connected with those of the *Atlantic Monthly*; in 1872 he became chief editor, remaining in that capacity until 1881, when he resigned to devote himself more exclusively to writing. During his years with the *Atlantic Monthly* he exercised a wide and wholesome influence, mediating busily between the old and the new, compromising differences between East and West, and sponsoring such new and diverse talents as those of Mark Twain and Henry James. Not even these activities, however, could shut off the flow of his own writing; and his contributions to the magazine began to display, more and more strongly, the type of realistic writing which stamps his major pieces of fiction.

The quality of Howells' realism finds effective illustration in what are generally considered his best novels: *A Modern Instance, The Rise of Silas Lapham*, and *A Hazard of New Fortunes*. In these, he largely concerns himself with everyday people and the realistic translation of their experiences. However, his picture of humanity omitted the rougher aspects of life, and his standards of good taste did not permit the revelations of sex and violence which punctuate the writing of the twentieth century. Because of these omissions, the characters of his novels have been accused of being commonplace, but it is certain that modern realism owes a debt to Howells' pioneering which it has not always been very prompt to acknowledge.

After leaving the *Atlantic Monthly* in 1881, Howells moved to New York, which had become the publishing center of the nation. There he wrote novels for the *Century Magazine* and became literary adviser to Harper and Brothers; in 1900 he took over editorship of The Easy Chair, that notable department of *Harper's Monthly*. Novels and shorter fiction continued to pour from his pen, with side excursions into poetry and drama. In literary criticism, also, he achieved what some literary historians consider his finest work, reaching its peak with *Criticism and Fiction* in 1891.

Howells' later years were rich in honors. His last two decades brought satisfying recognition to a man who, despite varying estimates of his literary significance, had always refused to compromise on matters involving principle. Harvard, Yale, and Columbia conferred degrees upon him; Oxford bestowed a doctorate of literature in 1904; leading institutions sought his services as lecturer and teacher. For many years he was president of the American Academy of Arts and Letters. Before his wife's death in 1909 he frequently traveled abroad with her; afterwards his companion became his daughter Mildred. Howells died May 11, 1920, at his home in New York.

Bibliography

The definitive biography is E. H. Cady, *The Road to Realism: The Early Years, 1837–1885*, 1956; and *The Realist at War: The Mature Years, 1885–1920*, 1958. Also to be consulted is Mildred Howells, ed., *The Life in Letters of William Dean Howells*, 2 vols., 1928. The best critical studies are Delmar G. Cooke,

William Dean Howells: A Critical Study, 1922; Oscar W. Firkins, *William Dean Howells: A Study*, 1924; Everett Carter, *Howells and the Age of Realism*, 1954; and Edward Wagenknecht, *William Dean Howells: The Friendly Eye*, 1969. See also Clara and Rudolph Kirk, *Introduction to William Dean Howells: Representative Selections*, American Writers Series, 1950; Arthur H. Quinn, *American Fiction*, 1936; Alexander Cowie, *The Rise of the American Novel*, 1948; and Gordon S. Haight, "Realism Defined: William Dean Howells," in *Literary History of the United State*, Vol. II, edited by Robert E. Spiller, Willard Thorp, Thomas H. Johnson, and Henry S. Canby, 1948.

A HAZARD OF NEW FORTUNES

Type of work: Novel
Author: William Dean Howells (1837–1920)
Type of plot: Novel of manners
Time of plot: The 1880's
Locale: New York City
First published: 1890

A complex novel containing some of Howells' most deft characterizations, A Hazard of New Fortunes *reflects both the author's own life and his dissatisfaction with America. It also reveals his interest in social improvement. The novel is considered one of the finest of Howells' fictional works.*

Principal Characters

Basil March, an unsuccessful Boston insurance man who accepts the editorship of a literary magazine in New York. His adventures with the magazine's promoters, financial backers, and staff members constitute the story. Though March has little self-confidence, the magazine thrives. Eventually he has a chance to buy the publication, in partnership with the promoter, a happy circumstance which will make him not only financially successful but also spiritually fulfilled.

Mr. Dryfoos, a rustic who had made a fortune from his natural gas holdings. It is he who finances the magazine March edits. He lives a harassed existence: his womenfolk are socially ambitious, he cannot approve his daughter's choice in suitors, his son, determined to be a minister, makes a bad businessman, and a socialist on the magazine's staff plagues him on political issues. Dryfoos finally solves his problems by selling the magazine to March and the promoter, Fulkerson, and taking his family on an extended trip to Europe.

Henry Lindau, March's tutor, a German socialist who becomes the magazine's foreign editor and reviewer. His clash with Dryfoos results in Lindau's dismissal from "Every Other Week," Dry-

foos' periodical. While demonstrating with the workers in a streetcar strike, Lindau is set upon by the police and beaten so severely that he eventually dies. He receives a proper funeral by a contrite Dryfoos.

Conrad Dryfoos, Dryfoos' son and the ostensible publisher of "Every Other Week." While defending the one-armed Lindau from the police who are beating him, he is struck by a stray bullet and killed.

Mr. Fulkerson, the promoter who invites March to accept the editorship of the magazine. He is happy when he and March buy the magazine because in this act he sees a secure future for himself and the girl he wants to marry, a Southern belle whose Virginia colonel father loves to extol the merits of slavery.

Christine Dryfoos, Dryfoos' daughter, who is bent on entering society and who finally has her way. First, however, she loves a young man to whom her father objects, but whom she rejects when her father later approves of him. In Europe her fondest dreams come true when she becomes engaged to a penniless French nobleman.

Mrs. March, March's wife, who, though

reluctant to leave Boston, persuades her husband to take the editorship in New York.

Angus Beaton, the art director of "Every Other Week," who loves Christine and is paid for his trouble when, despite her love for him, she scratches his face and forcibly ejects him from her father's house.

The Story

In his youth Basil March had wished for a literary career. Family responsibilities turned him, however, to the insurance business, a field in which he proved to himself and his employers that he was but mediocre. After eighteen years with his firm, his employers decided to replace him and put him into a somewhat meaningless position. Rather than be so embarrassed, March resigned. Fortunately for him and his family's future, Mr. Fulkerson, a promoter of syndicated newspaper material, who had met the Marches years before, proposed that March take over the editorship of a new literary magazine that he was promoting. March at first demurred at Fulkerson's proposal, but the promoter, certain that March had the necessary taste and tact to be sucessful, finally persuaded him to take the position.

Mrs. March and their children had always lived in Boston, and so when the prospect of moving to New York City appeared, even though it meant a career for the husband and father, they needed considerable persuasion. At last Mrs. March was convinced that the removal to the larger city was imperative. She and her husband went to New York to find a flat in which they could make themselves comfortable. After many days of searching, Mrs. March returned to Boston, leaving her husband to make a decision about the editorship. He did so a short time later.

March's problems in connection with a staff did not prove as difficult as he had imagined. Fulkerson, the promoter, had engaged an artist, Angus Beaton, to serve as art director, procured a cover sketch for the first issue, and made all the financial arrangements with the magazine's backer, Mr. Dryfoos, who had recently made a fortune for himself through the control of natural gas holdings. Mr. Dryfoos, who was trying to win his son away from a career as a minister, had undertaken to finance the magazine in order to give his son Conrad a chance to enter business as the ostensible publisher of the periodical. Foreign articles and reviews were to be handled by an old German socialist, Henry Lindau, who had been March's tutor and whom the younger man had met accidentally in New York.

Despite March's fear and lack of confidence, the new magazine, *Every Other Week*, was a success from the very first issue; both the illustrations and the material caught the public fancy. On the periphery of the activities concerning the magazine, however, there were many complications. The Dryfoos family, who had been simple farm folk, wanted to be taken into society; at least the two daughters wanted to enter society. In addition, Christine, the older daughter, fell in love with the art editor, who was not in love with her. Fulkerson, the promoter, had also fallen in love. He was busy paying court to a southern girl who boarded at the same house he did, and the girl's father, a Virginia colonel, was after Fulkerson to have the magazine print at least a portion of his great work extolling the merits of slavery.

Because the magazine had been a success, Fulkerson suggested that for publicity purposes they should give a dinner party for members of the staff and the press. Mr. Dryfoos, who was asked to pay the bill for the proposed affair, vetoed the idea, but he agreed to have a small dinner party at his home for several of the men connected with the magazine. Among the guests was Henry Lindau, who had struck the millionaire's fancy because he had lost a hand fighting in the Civil War. Dryfoos did not realize that Mr. Lindau, who was doing the foreign language work for the magazine, was a socialist. At the dinner party the personalities and the principles of the men clashed openly. The next day the millionaire told Basil March bluntly that the old man was to be fired. March wished to stick by the old German socialist, but Mr. Lindau forced the issue by refusing to do any more work for the capitalistic owner of the magazine.

Another crisis occurred a short time later when Mr. Dryfoos and his son, who hated being a businessman rather than a minister, had an open clash of wills. The situation became so acute that the father, calling one day when his son was alone in the office, struck the young man in the face. Outside the office, the father also had trouble with his daughter, Christine, for he had forbidden his house to the art editor of the magazine, with whom she was in love.

At that time there was a streetcar strike in New York City. Young Conrad Dryfoos was very much in sympathy with the strikers, many of whom he knew as a result of his church work among the poor and sick of the city. At the instigation of a young woman whom he loved, he went out upon the streets to try to bring peace among the rioting strikers and the police. He saw Mr. Lindau, the aged, one-armed socialist, being beaten by a policeman; when he ran to interfere, he was struck by a stray bullet and was killed.

Mr. Dryfoos was heartbroken at the loss of his son, particularly because he felt that he had mistreated the young man. When he learned that his son had died trying to save Mr. Lindau from the policeman's club, he decided to accept the old man as a friend and to take care of him for the rest of his life. The decision came too late, however, for the old man died as a result of the beating he had received. In a last effort to show his change of heart, Mr. Dryfoos had Mr. Lindau's funeral conducted in his own home.

Still wishing to try to make his family happy, Mr. Dryfoos then swallowed his pride and went to see Angus Beaton, the artist. Confessing that he was sorry to have caused the young people unhappiness, he invited Beaton to resume his calls on Christine. The young man eventually pocketed his pride and called, but in spite of her love for him Christine rejected his suit forcibly and scratched his face.

A few days later, Mr. Dryfoos resolved to take his wife and daughters to Europe. Before he left, he went to the offices of the magazine, where everyone had been wondering what the fate of the publication would be and whether Conrad Dryfoos' death had destroyed his father's interest in the periodical. Mr. Dryfoos magnanimously consented to sell the periodical to Fulkerson and March at a low figure and with very low interest on the money they needed in order to purchase it. Both March and Fulkerson were extremely happy about the turn of events. March saw his future secure at last, and he also saw that he would have a free hand in shaping the editorial policy. Fulkerson was happy because he too foresaw a prosperous future. As the result of his expectations, he was able to marry and settle down.

Some months afterward they learned that the Dryfoos family had been taken up promptly by at least a portion of Parisian society. Christine Dryfoos had even become engaged to a penniless but proud French nobleman.

The Story

The plot of *A Hazard of New Fortunes* is strikingly autobiographical; the various events reflect Howells' hazarding of his own fortunes in leaving his literary domain in Boston for New York City and the editor's chair at *Harper's Magazine*. It was an astute move, for the literary center of America seemed to follow him.

The protagonists of this novel are also autobiographical. Featured in Howells' first novel, *Their Wedding Journey* (1872), which parallels the Howells' own honeymoon, Basil and Isabel March are also central to several of Howells' works of the 1890's. In *A Hazard of New Fortunes* they mature noticeably and develop a sense of the complicity of all men in one another's affairs. But learning this lesson took Howells himself beyond the comfortable surface of American life and exposed him to social and economic problems that aroused his concern but with which he was temperamentally unable to deal. Mr. Dryfoos' attempt to make amends after the death of his son reads like the end of *A Christmas Carol*. However, the labor unrest that indirectly caused Conrad's death calls for more than the redemption of a Scrooge. Naturalists such as Dreiser and Norris were to provide the fiction that would bring such social forces into focus.

Howells after *A Hazard of New Fortunes* is, therefore, a changed man. While he struggled with a new range of experience, the school of literary realism he had developed and propounded as editor and novelist proved inadequate for dealing with the more grim aspects of real life in America. Howells' succeeding novels reveal a new pensiveness, tentativeness, and diminished self-assurance. While no abrupt transition can be noted, experimentation with new literary forms in the utopian Altrurian romances, psychological symbolism in *The Shadow of a Dream,* manipulation of point of view in *The Landlord at Lion's Head,* all point to a diminishing confidence in the capacity of literary realism, and in Howells himself, to render into fiction the increasingly complex reality of American life.

Bibliography

Arms, George W. "Howells' *A Hazard of New Fortunes*," in *Explicator*. I (November, 1942), item 14.

————. "Howells' New York Novel: Comedy and Belief," in *Critics on William Dean Howells: Readings in Literary Criticism*. Edited by Paul A. Eschholz. Coral Gables, Fla.: University of Miami Press, 1975, pp. 102–111.

————. "Introduction," in *A Hazard of New Fortunes*. By William Dean Howells. New York: Dutton, 1952, pp. vii–xviii.

Behrens, Ralph. "Howells' *A Hazard of New Fortunes*," in *Explicator*. XVIII (June, 1960), item 52.

Bennett, George N. *The Realism of William Dean Howells, 1889–1920*. Nashville, Tenn.: Vanderbilt University Press, 1973, pp. 35–44.

————. *William Dean Howells: The Development of a Novelist*. Norman: University of Oklahoma Press, 1959, pp. 185–199.

Cady, Edwin H. *The Realist at War: The Mature Years, 1885–1920, of William Dean Howells*. Syracuse, N.Y.: Syracuse University Press, 1958, pp. 93–96, 100–113.

Carrington, George C., Jr. *The Immense Complex Drama: The World and Art of Howells' Novels*. Columbus: Ohio State University Press, 1966, pp. 82–100, 206–211.

Carter, Everett. *Howells and the Age of Realism*. Philadelphia: Lippincott, 1954, pp. 201–224.

Cooke, Delmar Gross. *William Dean Howells: A Critical Study*. New York: Dutton, 1922, pp. 226–230.

Eschholz, Paul A. "William Dean Howells' Recurrent Character Types: The Realism of *A Hazard of New Fortunes*," in *English Record*. XXIII (1973), pp. 40–47.

Evanoff, Alexander. "William Dean Howells' Economic Chance-World in *A Hazard of New Fortunes*: An American Classic Reviewed," in *Discourse*. VI (Winter, 1962–1963), pp. 382–388.

Firkins, Oscar W. *William Dean Howells: A Study*. New York: Russell and Russell, 1963, pp. 164–168.

Frazier, David L. "Howells' Symbolic Houses: The Plutocrats and Palaces," in *American Literary Realism 1870–1910*. XI (Summer, 1977), pp. 267–279.

Gibson, William M. *William Dean Howells*. Minneapolis: University of Minnesota Press, 1967, pp. 34–36.

Kraus, W. Keith. "The Convenience of Fatalism: Thematic Unity in William Dean Howells' *A Hazard of New Fortunes*," in *English Record*. XVIII (1967), pp. 33–36.

McMurray, William. *The Literary Realism of William Dean Howells*. Carbondale: Southern Illinois University Press, 1967, pp. 67–75.

Martin, Jay. *Harvests of Change: American Literature 1865–1914*. Englewood Cliffs, N.J.: Prentice-Hall, 1967, pp. 42–45.

Morgan, H. Wayne. *American Writers in Rebellion*. New York: Hill and Wang, 1965, pp. 64–67.

Tanner, Tony. "Introduction," in *A Hazard of New Fortunes*. By William Dean Howells. London: Oxford University Press, 1967, pp. vii–xxxv.

Trilling, Lionel. "W.D. Howells and the Roots of Modern Taste," in *Partisan Review*. XVIII (September–October, 1951), pp. 516–536.

Vanderbilt, Kermit. *The Achievement of William Dean Howells: A Reinterpretation*. Princeton, N.J.: Princeton University Press, 1968, pp. 144–191.

Walsh, Harry. "Tolstoy and the Economic Novels of William Dean Howells," in *Comparative Literature Studies*. XIV (June, 1977), pp. 143–165.

INDIAN SUMMER

Type of work: Novel
Author: William Dean Howells (1837–1920)
Type of plot: Domestic realism
Time of plot: Shortly after the American Civil War
Locale: Florence, Italy
First published: 1886

A masterpiece of the realism of the commonplace, this book details life in the American colony in Florence shortly after the American Civil War. Howells wrote with sympathy and affection of his aging, cultured characters. Some critics consider this work his best novel.

Principal Characters

Theodore Colville, a middle-aged American architect who leaves Italy for the United States when a young woman rejects his suit. In America he runs a newspaper for a time and then enters Indiana politics. Defeated at the polls, he returns to Italy to resume his study of architecture. He learns to love two American women, one a middle-aged widow, the other a girl half his age. He almost marries the girl but complications and misunderstandings prevent him from doing so. Finally, he marries the widow.

Imogene Graham, a young girl who falls in love with Colville, though he is old enough to be her father. She finally understands, chiefly through the influence of her mother and the appearance of a young minister, that her love is actually infatuation. She returns to America from Italy and marries the minister, who is now established in a prosperous church near Buffalo.

Lina Bowen, a widow who has known Colville for some time. She acts as Imogene's chaperone while Imogene and Colville see each other. She tries to act properly toward the Colville-Imogene affair by not allowing her personal bias to enter her discussions with Imogene about the problems that her marriage with Colville may produce. When Imogene at last rejects Colville, Mrs. Bowen accepts Colville's suit.

Effie Bowen, Mrs. Bowen's thirteen-year-old daughter, who is very fond of Colville. It is largely through Effie's efforts that Colville and Mrs. Bowen finally decide to marry.

Mr. Morton, a young minister who loves Imogene and comes to Italy to court her. Both return to the United States and the Colvilles suspect that they will marry.

Mrs. Graham, Imogene's mother, who comes to Italy when she learns that her daughter is thinking seriously of marrying Colville. Her influence on her daughter is instrumental in causing the girl to see that her love for Colville is only infatuation.

The Story

Theodore Colville studied architecture as a young man and in order to continue his professional education he spent some months in Italy. While there he went about with two young women and fell in love with one of them. The girl rejected his suit. Soon afterward he went back to the United States at the request of his older brother, who had recently purchased a newspaper. Returning to America, Colville became the editor of his brother's paper and finally purchased it. He entered politics in his fortieth year. After his defeat he left his home in Indiana and went at once again to Italy.

In Italy he tried to resume the study of architecture, but his interest was soon diverted by his meeting with Mrs. Bowen, who had been one of his companions in Italy years before, the one with whom he had not fallen in love. Mrs. Bowen, now a widow, invited Colville to visit at her home. When he went there, Colville met Mrs. Bowen's thirteen-year-old daughter Effie, who quickly became fond of him, and Imogene Graham, a twenty-year-old American woman whom Mrs. Bowen was chaperoning.

In company with Mrs. Bowen, Imogene Graham, and Effie Bowen, Mr. Colville spent a number of pleasant days and evenings. At first Imogene regarded him as an old man, since he was twice her age, but she soon realized that she enjoyed his company much more than that of many men her own age. In an effort to be companionable with her, Colville danced and went about socially as he had not done for many years. Mrs. Bowen also enjoyed Colville's company; the result was that they were together a great deal.

Mrs. Bowen chose carefully the places where she and her charges went. During the carnival season she permitted Colville to take them all to a masked ball. At the ball little Effie became ill and had to be taken home unexpectedly. As a result, Imogene and Colville were together unchaperoned during much of the evening. At that time they began to realize their affection for each other.

Mrs. Bowen quickly realized that a love affair was developing. She also realized that no one, least of all herself, had expected it. She tactfully pointed out to Imogene the differences between the girl and a man so much older. When she said, rather less tactfully, that she thought Colville had been trying only to be amusing, the girl reported the conversation to Colville. Hurt, he went to Mrs. Bowen and talked with her, finally agreeing to her suggestion that for propriety's sake he leave Florence. Unfortunately, it was a weekend, and Colville having insufficient funds to leave the city after settling his hotel bills, was forced to wait until the following Monday. By that time Imogene had decided that it was unfair to make him leave the city because of her. She requested that he stay. He decided to do so.

A few days later Colville and Imogene met accidentally in a public park. Quickly coming to an agreement that they loved one another, they went back to Mrs. Bowen's residence and told her that they had decided to be married. Mrs. Bowen, as Imogene's chaperone, told them she would be forced to write immediately to the girl's parents to inform them of this recent development. The lovers, agreeing to her plan, also promised to say nothing about an official engagement until they heard from America. Imogene warned her chaperone, however, that she would marry Colville, even without her parents' consent.

While they were awaiting word from America, a young minister named Morton, also in love with Imogene, returned to Florence to pay her court. Both Colville and Mrs. Bowen wished to let the young man know the state of affairs, but the girl refused to permit them to tell Mr. Morton of her engagement. To make the situation appear normal, the four—Mrs. Bowen, Mr. Morton, Imogene, and Colville—went about together. Finally word came from Imogene's parents. Her mother had decided to sail for Europe, to see Colville for herself before giving her decision.

During the intervening days before Mrs. Graham's arrival, the four people went on an excursion to Fiesole to see the Etruscan ruins there. At one interval Colville and the young minister walked a short distance beside the carriage. While they were doing so, a peasant driving a band of sheep came over the brow of a hill. The horses, frightened at the sight of the sheep, began to back the carriage dangerously close to a precipitous drop at the side of the road. The two men rescued the women from the carriage. While Mr. Morton was taking Imogene from the vehicle, Colville ran to the horses' heads in an attempt to hold them. Unable to do so, and with his hand caught in the curb strap, he was dragged with the team when the carriage plunged over the edge of the road.

For two weeks Colville lay very ill. When he was finally able to have visitors, Imogene's mother came to see him. She told him that she was taking her daughter to America immediately, even though she felt that Colville had acted as a gentleman in the entire affair. She then gave her reason for preventing the marriage. Her daughter, she said, was not really in love with Colville, although she thought too much of him to break the engagement. The shock was a great one to Colville, but he immediately saw that the girl's departure was the only answer to the problems that the situation had developed. After her mother left, Imogene herself came into the sickroom and bade Colville a hasty goodbye.

Some time later Mrs. Bowen and Colville talked over the affair. During the conversation they both admitted their love for each other. Mrs. Bowen refused to marry Colville, however, because of the embarrassing position in which she had been placed during his affair with Imogene. She had hated herself the whole time she tried to prevent the affair because, although she hoped she could see the situation objectively, she had always feared that her actions and thinking had been colored by her feeling for Colville.

Little Effie Bowen, having formed a very strong attachment for Colville, refused to hear of his departure. Within a few months, under the influence of their mutual love and Effie's attitude toward her mother's suitor, Mrs. Bowen was reconciled to a marriage. They were married quietly and then moved to Rome, where no one who knew them could spread gossip about the affair with Imogene.

Not long after their marriage they heard that Mr. Morton, who had been deeply in love with Imogene, had been appointed to a church in a community near Buffalo, where the Grahams lived. Both Mr. and Mrs. Colville hoped that he and Imogene Graham would make a match of their own.

Critical Evaluation

Indian Summer represents Howells at his best; psychological acuteness, facile development, and deft delineation of character all typify Howells at the top of his form. A European love story in the American mode, the delicate handling of manners, marriage, and travel made *Indian Summer* an immensely popular work.

Howells was well equipped for this particular task. Set in Italy, the novel capitalizes on Howells' experience as consul to Venice during the Civil War. He revisited Italy a few years before writing *Indian Summer,* and worked on that novel concurrently with *Tuscan Cities,* thus keeping the intricacies of the place of Americans in Italian society fresh in his mind. Howells was, in 1886, in the ripe Indian summer of his own career, and the Old World setting and subtle, intricate relationships of the characters provided a most appropriate vehicle for the delicate touch he had perfected in *A Modern Instance* and *The Rise of Silas Lapham.*

Furthermore, while Howells' later fictions were to strain his social consciousness and force him to question the ability of literary realism to deal with real life, *Indian Summer* is a precise embodiment of his own critical theory. It is the commonplace, rather than the fantastic, elaborate, or unusual that provides the material for the novel. The focus of the story is not on plot but rather on the development of character. The story is deliberately antiromantic; real life is shown to be more good than evil, and democracy comes off better than decaying European aristocracy.

Recent criticism, moreover, has uncovered symbolic and even allegorical levels of meaning beneath the quaint and quiet surface of *Indian Summer.* The novel is to be appreciated as vintage Howells, most of all because he was perhaps never to write as well again.

Bibliography

Bennett, George N.   *William Dean Howells: The Development of a Novelist.* Norman: University of Oklahoma Press, 1959, pp. 146–149.

Cady, Edwin H.   *The Road to Realism: The Early Years, 1837–1855, of William Dean Howells.* Syracuse, N.Y.: Syracuse University Press, 1956, pp. 224–229.

Carter, Everett.   *Howells and the Age of Realism.* Philadelphia: Lippincott 1954, pp. 66–67.

Cooke, Delmar Gross.   *William Dean Howells: A Critical Study.* New York: Dutton, 1922, pp. 203–206.

Cumpiano, Marion W.   "Howells' Bridge: A Study of the Artistry of *Indian Summer*," in *Modern Fiction Studies.* XVI (1970), pp. 363–382.

Firkins, Oscar W.   *William Dean Howells: A Study.* New York: Russell and Russell, 1963, pp. 123–131.

Frazier, David L.   "Time and the Theme of *Indian Summer*," in *Arizona Quarterly.* XVI (Autumn, 1960), pp. 260–267.

Gibson, William M.   "Introduction," in *Indian Summer.* By William Dean Howells. New York: Dutton, 1951, pp. vii–xix.

————.   *William Dean Howells.* Minneapolis: University of Minnesota Press, 1967, pp. 21–25.

Kirk, Clara Marburg.   *W.D. Howells and Art in His Time.* New Brunswick, N.J.: Rutgers University Press, 1965, pp. 87–96.

Lynn, Kenneth S.   *William Dean Howells: An American Life.* New York: Harcourt Brace Jovanovich, 1971, pp. 166–167.

Woodress, James L., Jr.   *Howells & Italy.* Durham, N.C.: Duke University Press, 1952, pp. 184–185.

A MODERN INSTANCE

Type of work: Novel
Author: William Dean Howells (1837–1920)
Type of plot: Domestic realism
Time of plot: Nineteenth century
Locale: New England
First published: 1882

The "modern instance" is that of divorce, a subject seldom treated in nineteenth century American fiction. Although the divorce never actually occurs, the issue permeates the book and serves as a moral catalyst. While Howells' treatment of the subject may seem archaic, even quaint, to the modern reader, his willingness to deal with it forthrightly was a step in the direction of a more candid treatment of intimate relations between the sexes.

Principal Characters

Bartley Hubbard, a newspaperman of the eighties of the last century who ranges from Equity, a small town in New England, to Whited Sepulchre, Arizona. His moral weakness manifests itself in his affairs with women, his shoddy business ethics, his indifferent attitude toward money, and his love of liquor. He spends most of his time running from debts and family obligations. He dies, shot down by an irate citizen, while he is editor of a small western newspaper.

Marcia Gaylord, an innocent New England girl whose impetuous marriage to Hubbard brings her unhappiness. Hubbard takes her to Boston, where their child, Flavia, is born. When pressed by financial problems, Hubbard deserts his wife and child and goes West. He attempts to divorce Marcia and is foiled only by the intervention of her father. Hubbard's death makes it possible for Marcia to marry a good man and have a decent home.

Squire Gaylord, Marcia's father and Hubbard's first employer on a New England newspaper, the "Free Press."

The Squire recognizes Hubbard's talent, but he opposes Hubbard's suit for Marcia's hand. He looks after his daughter's affairs throughout her unfortunate marriage to the errant newspaperman. He dies of a stroke suffered during the trial for divorce Hubbard initiates against Marcia.

Ben Halleck, a member of one of Boston's older families who is a man of means and a college classmate of Hubbard. Halleck does not like Hubbard, but he feels sorry for Marcia, and befriends her. He helps Hubbard by lending him money—which is never returned—and helps Marcia by standing by her during her divorce trial. After Hubbard's death, Halleck tries to decide whether it would be morally right to ask Marcia to marry him.

Atherton, a conservative Boston lawyer who is a friend to Halleck and the Hubbards.

Kinney, a tramp philosopher who provides Hubbard with many stories Hubbard sells to magazines and newspapers without asking Kinney's permission.

Hannah Morrison, the daughter of the town drunk, who works with her mother in the newspaper office in Equity. Hannah has had few advantages in her life and claims, when Marcia meets her drunk on the streets of Boston, that Hubbard is responsible for her destitution.

Witherby, an unscrupulous publisher of a Boston newspaper who hires Hubbard as managing editor. Witherby sells some stock in the paper to Hubbard, who borrows from Halleck the money to buy it. When Hubbard's work appears in a rival newspaper, Witherby fires him.

Henry Bird, a shop foreman on the "Free Press" with whom Hubbard has a fight over Hannah. The resulting scandal causes Hubbard to leave his job on the paper.

Willett, the owner of the New England logging camp to which Hubbard flees when scandal drives him out of Equity.

Mrs. Macallister, a fashionable woman who, at the logging camp, flirts with Hubbard. To impress her, Hubbard pokes fun at his quaint friend Kinney, who takes offense at such treatment and the two men part angrily.

The Story

In the little town of Equity, in northern New England, Bartley Hubbard was an up-and-coming young man. An orphan whose life had so far been one of great promise, he had a free and easy way about him and a ready tongue that made him a general favorite. Squire Gaylord was well pleased with his work as editor of the village paper, the *Free Press*, but not so well pleased when Bartley became engaged to Marcia Gaylord, the squire's only daughter.

One afternoon Bartley and Marcia went for a sleigh ride. In a swamp they met another cutter which overturned in deep snow while trying to pass them on the narrow trail. The women in the overturned vehicle were Mrs. Morrison and her daughter Hannah, who worked in the office of the *Free Press*. Bartley jumped out to help them. Mrs. Morrison got into the cutter by herself. Because Bartley lifted Hannah Morrison to her place, Marcia was angry enough to precipitate their first quarrel.

Hannah was the daughter of the town drunkard. Young Bartley encouraged her greatly, thinking to improve the quality of her work, but she interpreted his interest as love. Her father called on Bartley one morning, drunk as usual, and asked Bartley's intentions toward his daughter. The young editor was so vexed and infuriated that he ejected Hannah's father bodily. His foreman, Henry Bird, in his turn accused Bartley of stealing Hannah's affections. When he hit Bartley in the face, the latter retaliated with an open-handed slap. Henry fell, suffering a concussion when his head hit the floor.

The scandal was immense. Squire Gaylord took a legal view of the possibility that Bird might die. Marcia took the fight as proof of an affair between Bartley and Hannah and broke their engagement. Bartley resigned his job, even though Bird soon recovered. Bartley went to stay with Kinney, a crackerbox philosopher who cooked in a nearby logging camp.

At the camp Willett, the owner, came to visit with a fashionable party. Mrs. Macallister, one of the guests, flirted with Bartley, and he tried to curry favor by poking fun at the quaint Kinney. That same night Bartley and Kinney parted in anger, and the young man walked back to town.

After selling his horse and cutter, Bartley went to the station to catch the Boston train. Marcia caught up with him at the depot. Asking his forgiveness, she begged him to take her back. They were married that same day and left for Boston together.

In the city Bartley went to work. He turned his visit to the logging camp into a feature article which he sold for twenty-five dollars. That was the start of his fairly comfortable, although uncertain, income as a free-lance writer. Marcia and he could afford only one room, but they were happy together. Marcia's father, Squire Gaylord, came to see her once, to make cerain she was married. He refused to meet her husband again.

About the time Marcia learned that she was pregnant, Bartley was offered a job as managing editor of *Events*, whose publisher was a shrewd, unprincipled man named Witherby. With a regular salary at last, Bartley moved his wife into a private house.

In college Bartley had known Ben Halleck, a member of one of Boston's older families. Marcia knew no one at all, and she often wondered why Bartley did not resume his acquaintance with the Hallecks. Now that Bartley had a better job, he did call on the Hallecks, and they at once befriended the Hubbards. Through them the young couple also got acquainted with Mr. Atherton, a conservative lawyer. Halleck cared no more for Bartley than he ever had, but he was sorry for trusting Marcia, saddled with a shallow husband. After the birth of her child Flavia, Marcia saw less and less of Bartley, who spent many of his evenings away from home.

Witherby offered to sell some stock in the newspaper. For this deal Bartley borrowed fifteen hundred dollars from Halleck. Before long he had assumed a prosperous air, and his drinking added greatly to his girth. After a quarrel with Marcia, one night, he stayed out late and became quite drunk. Halleck saw him on the street and rescued him from a policeman. When Halleck took the drunken man back to Marcia, his pity for the poor wife increased.

Kinney, visiting the Hubbards, entertained Bartley and another newspaperman with stories of his picturesque life. After he left, Bartley wrote up the tales and sold them to another paper without Kinney's permission. Witherby was upset at seeing Bartley's work in a rival newspaper, and when he learned that his managing editor had written the article in violation of ethical considerations he dismissed Bartley.

Bartley returned to free-lancing. Halleck was absent from the city; hence Bartley could not repay the fifteen hundred dollars. He intended to do so, but he gambled with the money and before long lost several hundred dollars. Atherton and Halleck were confirmed in their suspicions of Bartley's moral weakness.

Marcia, returning from the Halleck house one evening, saw a drunken woman on the street. To her surprise she recognized Hannah Morrison. When she tried to talk with Hannah, the latter insisted that Bartley was to blame for her present status in life. Suspecting and believing the worst of Bartley, Marcia rushed home and accused him of having seduced Hannah. During the ensuing quarrel they separated, and Bartley took a train for Cleveland.

On the train Bartley's wallet was stolen; in consequence he was unable to send money back to Halleck. In Boston, Marcia regretted her hasty conclusions and stayed on at their house awaiting her husband's return. When creditors began to hound her, she enlisted Atherton's sympathetic aid. He and Halleck continued to look after the deserted wife. In time she thought of Bartley as dead, and Halleck wondered when he would be free to speak to her of his love.

By chance a western newspaper came into Halleck's hands, a paper in which Bartley had given notice of suit for divorce. Marcia, her small daughter, Squire Gaylord, and Halleck took a train to Indiana to contest the suit. They arrived in time to have the divorce set aside, but during the trial Marcia's father had a stroke from which he never recovered. After the trial Bartley drifted farther west and became the editor of a weekly paper in Whited Sepulchre, Arizona. He was shot there by a citizen of the town. When Bartley's death was reported, Halleck wondered whether morally he was free to ask Marcia to marry him.

Critical Evaluation

A reader of American novels who cut his teeth on Steinbeck and Hemingway and was perhaps adventurous enough to move on to Thomas Wolfe, Norman Mailer, and perhaps even Hunter Thompson would be baffled to find that William Dean Howells was once considered to be a modern writer. In fact, Howells is a prime example of the post-Civil War "realist" school. At first glance there would be little that would make him seem modern to today's readers.

One of the most glaringly antiquated aspects of *A Modern Instance* is the attitude it shows towards divorce. Divorce was cause for grave alarm. If it became accepted in society or easy to obtain, civilization, held together by strong family bonds, would crumble disastrously, Howells seems to tell the reader. If Halleck were to ask Marcia to marry him, even after Bartley's death, the moral depravity of this act would doom Western culture to the fate of Nineveh and Tyre, because Halleck had fallen in love with Marcia before she was abandoned by Bartley. Thus, to marry her would put a retroactive seal of approval upon his love of a married woman. This is too close to divorce for comfort, even though Howells leaves the matter unresolved at the end of the book.

What could be modern about this attitude towards divorce? The answer is simply that Howells must be taken in terms of his own time. The period of American history between the Civil War and Spanish-American War was one that corresponded to the high point of the Victorian Age in England. The attitude towards divorce described above and shown in *A Modern Instance* was not an odd one for that time. It is in this fact that the justification for Howells' claim to realism and modernism lies.

Divorce was one of those things that happened in America in the 1880's but was never recognized. The fact that Howells treated that theme was itself innovative and startling to many. Even though Howells' realism was part of a larger literary movement, this novel was a marvelously modern publication. America at that time was also a nation very proud of itself and of its new postwar vigor. Howells' Social Darwinism shows us the vitality of the American belief in pragmatism and rationality, and the desire to see things as they actually were without moral or stylistic frills. This movement was not unique to America, of course, but Howells' novels show to what extent it affected American literature of the period. In effect, *A Modern Instance* claims that it is a true picture of an aspect of life—divorce—and the way people act when confronted with it.

To what extent did Howells reach his goal? He was modern for his time, but was he realistic? The two questions cannot be separated fairly because realism, meaning here accurate description of persons and places together with credible characterization and dialogue, would have been considered innovative. A consideration of the points of crisis in the novel would contribute to an answer.

One such point is Marcia and Bartley's elopement. A nonrealistic treatment of this would be romantic in the extreme. The central motif might be a romantic haze through which the reader would glimpse two hearts beating at last as one, secure and happy in their conquest of all obstacles. Instead, Howells treats the reader to a scene in which the first consideration is the sale of the horse and sled.

The period of marriage is also treated realistically. The problem of finding decent housing at an affordable price, the struggle to secure a living, and the routine of domestic life are all presented matter-of-factly. One episode from this part of the book seems particularly to have been drawn from life, and given a life of its own by Howells' skill. This is the scene in which Bartley begins his career as a journalist by drinking with a group of newspapermen at their club. In a spirit of slightly drunken camaraderie he is nominated and chosen a member. Then he pays his dues. This inclusion, in passing, of the matter of an entrance fee into the club is one of those gem-like little touches by which Howells is able to freeze an instant in the mind of the reader and to show realistically more than was thought to be there. This episode is one of several such gems.

The divorce crisis is handled without false sentiment or melodramatic histrionics. After a quarrel Marcia flees the house. Bartley packs a bag and waits for her to return. He finally gives up his waiting and leaves, as he had wanted to do. Marcia returns a half hour later and refuses to believe he has abandoned her. Far longer than one might think possible she keeps up the pretense that he is merely away on a trip. She eventually knows that she is fooling only herself, but not even this recognition, hinted at by Howells, forces her to drop the game. Such naïveté could strain a reader's credulity except that Howells has drawn by this point in the novel such a deft portrait of her that she is clearly recognizable as a woman who is essentially still a sheltered girl.

As for characterization, one of the elements of Howells' realism, the characters are exceptionally well drawn until the last quarter of the book, at which point the novel seems to fall apart. It rushes to an inconclusive ending. It is true, however, that the novel was written when Howells was exhausted, ill, and under pressure of a deadline. (The work was originally published as a serial in *Scribner's Magazine* under the title of "The New Medea.") Even though the characterizations and the structure of *A Modern Instance* falter towards the end of the book, the first parts offer well-delineated characterizations that seem to have been taken from life. Perhaps no higher compliment can be paid an author with pretensions to realism.

The major exception to this rule is the characterization of Kinney. He is of such a stock line, the philosophical backwoodsman, that it is possible that Howells intended him as comic relief. If this is the case, then it is a tribute to Howells' craftsmanship that he can skillfully use this buffoon to further the exposition of Bartley's character. Kinney does not seem so much to be drawn from life as he seems a fugitive from *Roughing It* or from one of the better works of Petroleum V. Nasby.

A Modern Instance is one of those few books which even after a century can reach us and awaken a sense of what life must have been like in a time that is farther off and further removed from us than most people today realize. It is a novel that deserves to be better known.

Bibliography

Bennett, George N. *William Dean Howells: The Development of a Novelist.* Norman: University of Oklahoma Press, 1959, pp. 113–123.

Brockway, Wallace. "Afterword," in *A Modern Instance.* By William Dean Howells. New York: New American Library, 1964, pp. 422–430.

Cady, Edwin H. *The Road to Realism: The Early Years, 1837–1885, of William Dean Howells.* Syracuse, N.Y.: Syracuse University Press, 1956, pp. 206–216.

Carrington, George C., Jr. *The Immense Complex Drama: The World of Art of the Howells Novel.* Columbus: Ohio State University Press, 1966, pp. 69–77.

Cooke, Delmar Gross. *William Dean Howells: A Critical Study.* New York: Dutton, 1922, pp. 240–243.

Eschholz, Paul A. "Howells' *A Modern Instance*: A Realist's Moralistic Vision of America," in *Critics on William Dean Howells: Readings in Literary Criticism*. Edited by Paul A. Eschholz. Coral Gables, Fla.: University of Miami Press, 1975, pp. 71–79.

Falk, Robert P. *The Victorian Mode in American Fiction 1865–1885*. East Lansing: Michigan State University Press, 1975, pp. 43–53.

Fertig, Walter L. "Maurice Thompson and *A Modern Instance*," in *American Literature*. XXXVIII (March, 1966), pp. 103–111.

Firkins, Oscar W. *William Dean Howells: A Study*. New York: Russell and Russell, 1963, pp. 100–107.

Gargano, James W. "*A Modern Instance*: The Twin Evils of Society," in *Texas Studies in Literature and Language*. IV (Autumn, 1962), pp. 399–407.

Gibson, Walker. *Tough, Sweet and Stuffy: An Essay on Modern American Prose Styles*. Bloomington: Indiana University Press, 1966, pp. 29–37.

Gibson, William M. "Introduction," in *A Modern Instance*. By William Dean Howells. Boston: Houghton Mifflin, 1957, pp. v–xviii.

————. *William Dean Howells*. Minneapolis: University of Minnesota Press, 1967, pp. 26–28.

Girgus, Sam B. "Bartley Hubbard: The Rebel in Howells' *A Modern Instance*," in *Research Studies*. XXXIX (1971), pp. 315–321.

Gross, Seymour and Rosalie Murphy. "Commonplace Reality and the Romantic Phantoms: Howells' *A Modern Instance* and *The Rise of Silas Lapham*," in *Studies in American Fiction*. IV (1976), pp. 1–14.

Lynn, Kenneth S. *William Dean Howells: An American Life*. New York: Harcourt Brace Jovanovich, 1971, pp. 252–267.

Perkins, George. "*A Modern Instance*: Howells' Transition to Artistic Maturity," in *New England Quarterly*. XLVII (1974), pp. 427–439.

See, Fred G. "The Demystification of Style: Metaphoric and Metonymic Language in *A Modern Instance*," in *Nineteenth-Century Fiction*. XXVIII (1974), pp. 379–403.

Sirluck, Ernest. "Howells' *A Modern Instance*," in *Manitoba Arts Review*. X (Winter, 1956), pp. 66–72.

Spangler, George M. "Moral Anxiety in *A Modern Instance*," in *New England Quarterly*. XLVI (1973), pp. 236–249.

Stronks, James. "*A Modern Instance*," in *American Literary Realism*. I (Fall, 1968), pp. 87–89.

Sweeney, Gerard M. "The Medea Howells Saw," in *American Literature*. XLII (March, 1970), pp. 83–89.

Tavernier-Courbin, Jacqueline. "Towards the City: Howells' Characterization in *A Modern Instance*," in *Modern Fiction Studies*. XXIV (Spring, 1978), pp. 111–128.

Vanderbilt, Kermit. *The Achievement of William Dean Howells: A Reinterpretation*. Princeton, N.J.: Princeton University Press, 1968, pp. 49–95.

Wright, Nathalia. "The Significance of the Legal Profession in *A Modern Instance*," in *From Irving to Steinbeck: Studies of American Literature in Honor of Harry R. Warfel*. Edited by Motley Deakin and Peter Lisca. Gainesville: University of Florida Press, 1972, pp. 57–70.

THE RISE OF SILAS LAPHAM

Type of work: Novel
Author: William Dean Howells (1837–1920)
Type of plot: Domestic realism
Time of plot: Nineteenth century
Locale: New England
First published: 1885

In outline The Rise of Silas Lapham *reads like a typical naturalistic novel: a poor man struggles to success only to have it dissipate and collapse, leaving him broken and destitute. In actuality, however, the novel is inspired by Howells' moral vision of the universe. Lapham's failure is not due to impersonal forces, but to his own false values, and his financial ruin is no catastrophe, only a prelude to his moral regeneration.*

Principal Characters

Silas Lapham, a millionaire paint manufacturer in Boston. He is respected in business circles, but his family is not accepted socially. Garrulous, bourgeois, burly, brusque, he reflects traits of the self-made man who loves his maker; yet he is compassionate with outsiders and loving to his family. Babbitt-like, he emulates men he has admired for their savoir-faire. Bankrupt after a series of business reverses, he gladly leaves the material comforts of Boston, to return with his family to the modest living of their earlier days. Lapham is called "Colonel," his rank when he was injured at Gettysburg during the Civil War.

Persis Lapham, his wife. Like her husband, she has kept the ways of the country. More aware of present social conduct than is her husband, she is no more capable of observing the proprieties. Interested in marriage for her daughters, prudent and self-effacing in social matters, she restrains herself in advising them. An influence in his affairs, she goads Lapham into business dealings, to her involving morality, only to regret later the action taken. When

uninformed of his activities, she becomes suspicious; she is remorseful and self-reproaching when she senses her unfounded jealousies. To Persis, returning to the country is escape from the rigors of Boston's social life and her inability to cope with status.

Irene, the Laphams' younger daughter. Quiet, reserved, beautiful, and domestic, she infers that Tom Corey is interested in her, only to learn that he is in love with her sister. She escapes the sympathy and questioning of her family and the trials of the family's financial reverses through a month-long visit with relatives in the Middle West. Returning to Boston, to let the family know that her cousin's evident interest in her is another misleading affair, she becomes a virtual recluse other than for visits to the Middle West.

Penelope, the Laphams' older daughter. She is satirical, humorous, droll. Inferring that Tom Corey is in love with Irene, but secretly in love with him herself, Penelope is guilt-stricken when Corey reveals his affection for her. She refuses Corey's attentions, thinking her father's financial adversity would imply the wrong motivations for her accepting Corey. Ultimately, they are married and go to Mexico and Central America, where Cory will be in business.

Tom Corey, the son of a proper Bostonian family. Shaking off the effects of hereditary stratification, he displays considerable business acumen. In his attentions to Irene he is hoping to attract Penelope to him. This indirection misleads the Laphams and the Coreys. However, his stability, self-reliance, and graciousness in personal affairs, as well as removal from their families, assure marital happiness for him and Penelope.

Milton K. Rogers, Lapham's former business partner. His recurrent appearances for assistance create situations to point up Lapham's character and the attitudes and rapport between the Laphams. Unsuccessful in appeals to Lapham, Rogers turns to Persis, who intercedes with her husband.

Anna Corey, Tom's mother. In her seeming innocuous role of an aristocrat whose chief occupation is the comfort of her husband and children, she is likable. In protecting her son from questionable associations, as with the Laphams, she is protective in a genteel way.

Bromfield Corey, Tom's father. A rich young painter in Rome at the time of his marriage, he has never changed his pace. Sedentary, he remains unassuming in social matters. Nothing surprises him; nothing shocks him; nothing upsets him. In his self-imposed isolation, he views life as an amusing process and expresses his ready opinions on happenings accordingly.

Zerilla Dewey, a typist in Lapham's office, the butt of Mrs. Lapham's jealousy.

Mrs. James Millon (Moll), Zerilla's mother. Moll Millon is the ne'er-do-well widow of the man who was killed by a bullet intended for Lapham in an early labor dispute.

**Lily and
Nanny,** Tom Corey's young sisters. Their behavior toward the Laphams and Tom's marriage reflects their mother's influence.

Walker, a bookkeeper in Lapham's office. His garrulousness in office matters helps to define Corey's discretion and business attitudes.

Bartley Hubbard, a journalist who writes Lapham's biography.

Mr. Sewell, a minister, the adviser to the Laphams in their dilemma after Tom's indirection with Irene and Penelope.

James Bellingham, Mrs. Corey's brother and a business adviser to Lapham at the time of Lapham's financial losses.

The Story

Silas Lapham was being interviewed for a Boston paper. The journalist was secretly mocking Lapham's way of life, but Lapham, content with his success, paid little attention to his interviewer as he proudly exhibited a photograph of his two daughters and his wife. He told how he had been brought up in a large family, how he had gone West with his brothers, how he had returned, bought a stage route, married the village schoolteacher and finally hit upon making paint from a mineral his father had discovered on his farm.

The story of his success was a story of determination and hard work. During the Civil War his wife had kept the paint works going and after the war he had taken a man named Rogers as a partner for a short time.

After the interview Lapham and his wife drove out to see the site of a house they were building in a more fashionable part of Boston. Although both looked with pride upon the place soon to be their residence, they pretended not really to want the house at all. They merely suggested the new home would be a greater advantage for Penelope and Irene when their friends came to call.

But neither Penelope nor Irene anticipated with any great joy their coming change of living. They said they felt the present house was more convenient to the horsecars. Secretly, both realized that their parents were awkward in social life. At the same time they themselves had never been brought up to feel comfortable in the presence of people whose families had been accustomed to wealth for generations.

One day, as Mr. and Mrs. Lapham were dismounting from their carriage, Lapham's former partner appeared unexpectedly. Rogers had furnished money to help Lapham get started, but later Lapham had crowded Rogers out. Lapham insisted that what he had done had merely been good business. But Mrs. Lapham maintained that she never felt quite right about what had happened to Rogers, and seeing him again took all the happiness out of her plans for the new house.

The next time the family ventured out to visit the partly-completed house, Irene was surprised by the arrival of Tom Corey, a young man who had shown some interest in her. Immediately Mr. Lapham took over the occasion, and by his bragging greatly embarrassed his daughters.

That evening young Corey talked to his father about the Laphams. Bromfield Corey did not agree with his son's easy acceptance of the Laphams, but he did not object when his son announced his intention to apply for a position in Lapham's firm.

Young Corey visited Lapham in his office in order to ask for a job. Lapham was so pleased that he invited Corey to go with him to Nantasket where Mrs. Lapham and the girls were expecting Lapham for the weekend. At the Nantasket cottage the girls and their mother could not understand what had brought young Corey for the weekend visit. They had thought Lapham's bragging would have kept him away forever.

That evening Lapham discussed Corey with his wife. Mrs. Lapham contended that Corey was interested not in the paint but in Irene. Her husband commented that unless the young man were interested in the paint he would never get a chance to be interested in Irene. When Lapham said he intended to give the young man a chance, Mrs. Lapham warned him that he was playing with a situation which was bound to bring trouble.

Tom Corey's mother was concerned when she heard what her son had done. She admitted she would not object if he made a fortune from the paint business, but she did not want him to fall in love with either of the Lapham girls.

After Corey entered Lapham's employ, he was invited frequently to the Lapham home, for Irene was beginning to fall in love with him. Bromfield Corey grew more and more curious about the Laphams. He decided that he would encourage his wife to give a dinner for them in the autumn.

The cost of the new house worried Mrs. Lapham, and she asked her husband to stop his lavish spending. She learned he had given a substantial loan to Rogers, his former partner.

When Mrs. Corey returned from Bar Harbor, she debated a long time about giving a dinner party for the Laphams. In the first place, the Laphams were newcomers. On the other hand, she wanted to give public recognition of the new connection between her son and the Lapham family. She finally decided to give a formal dinner early in the season, before her more prominent friends returned to the city.

On the night of the dinner the Laphams tried to appear at ease. Penelope had refused to attend, thus causing her mother considerable embarrassment. Lapham watched the other men carefully, feeling sure he had not made too many social blunders. The next day, however, he was not so sure, for he had taken too much wine at dinner.

At the office Lapham sought out Corey and mentioned with embarrassment his behavior of the night before. He offered Corey his liberty to seek another job, a position among gentlemen, but Corey refused to go, saying that Lapham's tipsy talk had been only an unfortunate accident. When they parted, Corey insisted that Lapham's conduct had been proper and entertaining.

That night, feeling that he had actually patronized Lapham, Corey resolved to go to his employer and apologize. Lapham was out, but Penelope received Corey. At the end of a long talk he stammeringly confessed his love for her. In great confusion he left without waiting to speak to Lapham.

The next day Mrs. Lapham informed her husband that Corey had been coming to see Penelope all the time. She could only imagine what the shock would do to Irene. They felt, however, that Penelope would never permit Corey to become her suitor, for Penelope was convinced he belonged to Irene.

Irene was informed of the situation by her mother that evening. Immediately she carried to her sister's room every memento of Corey's attentions she possessed. After a few days Lapham took her to his boyhood village in Vermont.

Corey called on the Laphams to present his explanation, saying that he had cared more for Penelope all the time. Penelope refused to give him any satisfaction. She said she owed more to her sister's hurt feelings.

At the same time Lapham's finances were troubling him greatly. People who owed him money were unable to pay; his own creditors were pressing him. Lapham determined to take a trip west to inspect some mills held as security for his loan to Rogers. When he returned he was even more concerned. Rogers had drawn him into a trap with his securities, for a railroad controlled the value of the property. Lapham decided it would be necessary to sell the new house unfinished. Learning of Lapham's difficulties, Corey offered to lend his employer thirty thousand dollars, but Lapham rejected the offer.

Lapham's affairs took a turn for the worse. An added blow was the destruction of the unfinished Back Bay house. Wandering through the house one night he decided to test one of the chimneys and made a fire from blocks and shavings the workmen had left scattered about. He thought the fire had burned out before he left. That night the house burned to the ground. The insurance policy had expired a week before.

Determined to raise money by selling everything he could, Lapham visited his competitors who were working on a new mineral paint. They were willing to merge with him if he could raise money to help develop their plant. While he was trying to secure a loan, he learned from Rogers that some English gentlemen were interested in buying the property which Rogers had put up as security and which Lapham had thought valueless. Lapham refused to sell the mills however, because he believed a sale would be unethical as long as the railroad controlled their value.

He asked for time to think over the proposition. Shortly afterward the railroad forced him to sell the mills at a ruinous figure. Lapham felt that his honesty, which had kept him from selling the property to the Englishmen, had been unjustly abused. Rogers claimed Lapham had made it impossible for him to recover his losses. Lapham was now ruined, for he could not raise capital to merge with the rival paint firm.

Tom Corey was determined to marry Penelope in spite of her father's impending ruin. He did marry her after Lapham went into bankruptcy, and his family accepted her for their own sake as well as for his. Irene, who had returned as soon as she heard of her father's troubles, was pleased with her sister's happiness.

Lapham managed to save a part of his fortune, but more important to him was the belief that he had acted honestly in all his business dealings.

Critical Evaluation

The reputation of William Dean Howells has suffered much from the charge of many modern critics that his scope was too limited to satisfy the requirements of complexity demanded by the sophisticated twentieth century reader. It is argued that his insights into man's social existence, for example, were based on tenets from a past age that are no longer viable in the face of present realities; the absence of certain intense passions and obsessions in the novels, as well as Howells' failure to explore in depth such areas as human sexuality and man's capacity for violence, are cited as evidence. Similarly, *The Rise of Silas Lapham*—the author's most popular work and in many ways his masterpiece—has been adversely judged by some on the grounds that its plot is too slender to support the weight of its own implications. To support such charges, however, is either to misunderstand the nature of Howells' moral vision of life, or to overlook its depth and breadth, its universality, its applicability to all times and places.

Howells believed in the interdependence of people upon one another; he viewed each person's life as inextricably caught up with the lives of others, thus creating the web of interrelationships which forms societies. Such a belief

meant that for Howells, man's personal moral life and his life as a social
being were fused; there was no such thing as a purely individual moral act,
whether good or evil, since each personal act had its inevitable consequences
in the interpersonal or social realm. This in turn led to the morally pragmatic
stance that the proper course of action can often be chosen on the basis of
which course will result in "the most good for the greatest number" of people.
This utilitarian viewpoint is reflected in such concepts as "the economy of
pain" principle, propounded by Howells through the character of David
Sewell in the scene from *The Rise of Silas Lapham* in which Silas and his
wife seek the minister's advice concerning the triangular love complication
between their two daughters and Tom Corey. He tells them that in such a
situation, for which no one is to blame, the best solution is the one that will
cause suffering to the fewest number of people. In this case, therefore, Penelope
would be wrong to sacrifice Tom to Irene, which would make all three persons
suffer miserably; she should marry him herself, which would result in the
great happiness of two people and the temporary hurt of only one.

Underlying this moral outlook were three basic assumptions: that all aspects
of human life, including the social, are infused with moral purpose, thus
making society an extremely precious commodity; that the preservation of
society depended upon man's overcoming destructive passions with reason;
and that the function of art is to reveal the superiority of the civilized and
reasoning side of man's nature over the primitive and ignorant side. Howells'
first assumption was shared by most people in his age, but it was his fervent
espousal of the last proposition that placed him at the philosophical head of
a group of writers whose aim it was to reveal the morality of life through the
use of realism in their fiction. Yet Howells abhorred sermonizing, and attacked
the didactic element in writing wherever he encountered it.

This seeming paradox is cleared up, however, when one examines more
closely Howells' theory of literature. What he objected to was not the presence
of moral purpose in a work, but rather any attempt by an author to force
artificially his set of beliefs into a fictional structure without regard to the
organic dictates of the work itself. When Howells was finally asked to sum-
marize explicitly his theory of the moral purpose of literature, he began by
identifying the three progressively worse stages of "immorality" often practiced in fiction. The first involves the obscuring of the reader's judgment
through indulgence of his "gross appetite for the marvelous"; the second, the
elevation of passion over principles; and the third (and most pernicious), the
presentation of characters who commit serious sins, but are left unpunished by
the penalties which follow such sins in the real world. The true function of the
writer, Howells argued, is first to reject any absolute standard of morality,
and then to portray lives of characters in honest and careful detail; as the
characters meet each new situation in their everyday lives, as they are faced
with decisions over what is right and what is wrong, they will respond as

people do in life. Sometimes they will act in morally responsible ways, and will be rewarded, if not with worldly success, with inner peace; at other times they will commit wrong, and will suffer the inevitable consequences. Thus, Howells believed, all the author need do is describe reality truthfully, and the morality of life will come through the narrative naturally, as it does in life.

Howells carried out his theory to near-perfection in *The Rise of Silas Lapham*. This novel tells the story of a man who has been led astray from the true values in life by the corrupting influence of wealth. The action centers around Silas Lapham's fall into financial ruin, which turns out to be his salvation, his rise (hence the title) back into a morally healthy state. The plot is organic, reflecting the theme of the novel, and growing out of the main character's growth. The beginning and end are linked masterfully, while the midway point in the story—the dinner party given by the Coreys—serves to converge all the threads spun out so far, suspend them momentarily for our contemplation, and then direct them toward their climax and natural conclusion. In his interview with Bartley Hubbard at the opening of the novel, we see Silas in all the glory of his material success: he is proud of his rise from humble beginnings, of his newly-acquired social position, and of the new house he is just starting to build. The house becomes a symbol of Silas' fortunes; destined to be a magnificent mansion, it rises quickly until its construction is slowed down because of lack of funds. In the end it is burned to the ground. The destruction of the house represents Silas' rebirth, however, since his moral regeneration can only occur after he has been stripped of the false trappings of materialism. In his talk with David Sewell at the end, Silas' transformation is set in dramatic contrast to his initial appearance in the Bartley interview: he has grown humble and honest; bragging has been replaced by sincerity.

Lapham has been able to reach this new stage of awareness by progressing through a series of moral "tests," culminating in the legal, but morally dishonest deal urged upon him by Milton Rogers and the Englishmen; when he refuses to participate, both his financial ruin and his personal salvation are secured. He has painfully but steadily moved from the easiest stages of redemption—acts of unselfishness and generosity on a personal, one-to-one basis—through a wider area of commitment to people in large groups, and has finally reached the highest, most difficult to attain level of good action. This level involves an individual's commitment to the social body as a whole, to the welfare not of a personally known individual or group, but to all men as they comprise society.

Although Howells' efforts to uncover the underlying morality of all human action by focusing on the commonplace and familiar in his fiction reached a pinnacle in *The Rise of Silas Lapham,* he was not fully conscious of the nature of his achievement until a year after the novel's publication. It was in that year—1886—that he began reading Tolstoy. His exposure to the

Russian novelist was like a religious experience for him; of its effects he wrote, "What I had instinctively known before, I now knew rationally." Following this illumination of his own motives and absorbing concerns as an artist, Howells was able to sum up the vision which inspired not only *The Rise of Silas Lapham,* but all his work: "Morality penetrates all things, it is the soul of all things."

Bibliography

Arms, George W. "Introduction," in *The Rise of Silas Lapham.* By William Dean Howells. New York: Rinehart, 1949, pp. v–xvi.

Arms, George W. and William M. Gibson. "Silas Lapham, Daisy Miller, and the Jews," in *New England Quarterly.* XVI (March, 1943), pp. 118–122.

Berces, Francis A. "Mimesis, Morality and *The Rise of Silas Lapham,*" in *American Quarterly.* XXII (Summer, 1970), pp. 190–202.

Cady, Edwin H. "Introduction," in *The Rise of Silas Lapham.* By William Dean Howells. Boston: Houghton Mifflin, 1957, pp. v–xviii.

————. *The Road to Realism: The Early Years, 1837–1885, of William Dean Howells.* Syracuse, N.Y.: Syracuse University Press, 1956, pp. 230–240.

Carter, Everett. "Introduction," in *The Rise of Silas Lapham.* By William Dean Howells. New York: Harper, 1958, pp. v–xiv.

Clark, Harry H. "Introduction," in *The Rise of Silas Lapham.* By William Dean Howells. New York: Modern Library, 1951, pp. v–xix.

Edwards, Herbert. "The Dramatization of *The Rise of Silas Lapham,*" in *New England Quarterly.* XXX (June, 1957), pp. 235–243.

Firkins, Oscar W. *William Dean Howells: A Study.* New York: Russell and Russell, 1963, pp. 111–119.

Fiske, Horace S. *Provincial Types in American Literature.* Chatauqua, N.Y.: Chatauqua Press, 1907, pp. 11–42.

Gibson, William M. *William Dean Howells.* Minneapolis: University of Minnesota Press, 1967, pp. 28–31.

Hart, John E. "The Commonplace as Heroic in *The Rise of Silas Lapham,*" in *Modern Fiction Studies.* VIII (Winter, 1962–1963), pp. 375–383.

Hough, Robert L. "William Dean Howells and *The Rise of Silas Lapham,*" in *The American Novel from James Fenimore Cooper to William Faulkner.* Edited by Wallace Stegner. New York: Basic Books, 1965, pp. 73–85.

Kirk, Rudolf and Clara Kirk. "Introduction," in *The Rise of Silas Lapham.* By William Dean Howells. New York: Collier Books, 1962, pp. 5–11.

McMurray, William. *The Literary Realism of William Dean Howells.* Carbondale: Southern Illinois University Press, 1967, pp. 13–54.

Manierre, William R.   "*The Rise of Silas Lapham*: Retrospective Discussion as Dramatic Technique," in *College English*. XXIII (February, 1962), pp. 357–361.

Mead, C. David.   "Introduction," in *The Rise of Silas Lapham*. By William Dean Howells. New York: Dodd, Mead, 1964, pp. v–x.

Pizer, Donald.   "The Ethical Unity of *The Rise of Silas Lapham*," in *American Literature*. XXXII (November, 1960), pp. 322–327.

Solomon, Eric.   "Howells, Houses, and Realism," in *American Literary Realism*. IV (Fall, 1968), pp. 89–93.

Steinmetz, Marion L.   "Problems in Connection with *The Rise of Silas Lapham*," in *Exercise Exchange*. III (February, 1956), pp. 6–10.

Stronks, James.   "The Boston Seasons of Silas Lapham," in *Studies in the Novel*. I (1969), pp. 60–66.

Tanselle, G. Thomas.   "The Architecture of *The Rise of Silas Lapham*," in *American Literature*. XXXVII (January, 1966), pp. 430–457.

Vanderbilt, Kermit.   *The Achievement of William Dean Howells: A Reinterpretation*. Princeton, N.J.: Princeton University Press, 1968, pp. 96–143.

————.   "Howells Among the Brahmins: Why 'the bottom dropped out' during *The Rise of Silas Lapham*," in *New England Quarterly*. XXXV (September, 1962), pp. 291–317.

Van Nostrand, Albert D.   "Fiction's Flagging Man of Commerce," in *English Journal*. XLVIII (January, 1959), pp. 1–11.

HENRY JAMES

Born: New York, N.Y. (April 15, 1843)
Died: London, England (February 28, 1916)

Principal Works

NOVELS: *Roderick Hudson,* 1876; *The American,* 1877; *The Europeans,* 1878; *Daisy Miller,* 1879; *An International Episode,* 1879; *Confidence,* 1880; *Washington Square,* 1881; *The Portrait of a Lady,* 1881; *The Bostonians,* 1886; *The Princess Casamassima,* 1886; *The Reverberator,* 1888; *The Tragic Muse,* 1890; *The Other House,* 1896; *The Spoils of Poynton,* 1897; *What Maisie Knew,* 1897; *In the Cage,* 1898; *The Awkward Age,* 1899; *The Sacred Fount,* 1901; *The Wings of the Dove,* 1902; *The Ambassadors,* 1903; *The Golden Bowl,* 1904; *Julia Bride,* 1909; *The Outcry,* 1911; *The Ivory Tower,* 1917; *The Sense of the Past,* 1917.

SHORT STORIES: *A Passionate Pilgrim,* 1875; *The Madonna of the Future,* 1879; *The Siege of London,* 1883; *Tales of Three Cities,* 1884; *The Author of Beltraffio,* 1885; *The Aspern Papers,* 1888; *The Lesson of the Master,* 1892; *The Real Thing,* 1898; *Terminations,* 1895; *Embarrassments,* 1896; *The Two Magics: The Turn of the Screw* and *Covering End,* 1898; *The Soft Side* 1900; *The Better Sort,* 1903; *The Finer Grain,* 1910; *A Landscape Painter,* 1919; *Traveling Companions,* 1919; *Master Eustace,* 1920.

AUTOBIOGRAPHY: *A Small Boy and Others,* 1913; *Notes of a Son and Brother,* 1914; *The Middle Years,* 1917.

PLAYS: *Theatricals: Tenants and Disengaged,* 1894; *Theatricals, Second Series: The Album* and *The Reprobate,* 1895; *The Complete Plays of Henry James,* 1949.

TRAVEL SKETCHES AND IMPRESSIONS: *Transatlantic Sketches,* 1875; *Portraits of Places,* 1883; *A Little Tour in France,* 1884; *English Hours,* 1905; *The American Scene,* 1907; *Italian Hours,* 1909.

CRITICISM: *French Poets and Novelists,* 1878; *Hawthorne,* 1879; *Partial Portraits,* 1888; *Essays in London,* 1893; *Views and Reviews,* 1908; *Notes on Novelists,* 1914; *Within the Rim,* 1918.

The world of Henry James's novels, with its international outlook, its very intimate human relationships, and its ideal abundance of money, distinction, intelligence, and good will, was derived in part from the circumstances of his own childhood and youth. He was born in New York City on April 15, 1843, the second son of Henry James and Mary Walsh James, both of whom belonged to wealthy New York State families of Irish Protestant descent. Henry James, Senior, was a dissident religious philosopher, a man of many ideas, an affectionate father, and a charming if highly independent social figure. His personal vitality and speculative mind descended to the eldest son, William James, the future scientist and philosopher, and in some degree to the younger brothers, Wilkinson and Robertson, and the younger sister, Alice. The Jameses were a gifted and vivacious circle; and their frequent changes of residence in the United States (Albany, New York, Newport, Cambridge); the lengthy stay they made in Europe during Henry's boyhood; the perpetual experiments in schooling to which the young Jameses were subjected—all this promoted the self-sufficiency of the family as a whole and the close interdependence of its members on one another. Henry and William were, and remained, especially intimate.

Illness and mental tension also haunted the James family. Passive and withdrawn in childhood, Henry suffered a back injury in his nineteenth year which made him a semi-invalid throughout his youth. He never married. His experience was notably inward and his mind highly contemplative from the start. He felt unsure of his talents and of his place in the family, the United States, and the world. But these uncertainties determined him in his search for a vocation and a mind of his own. From his early love of paintings and stage plays arose a passion for artistic form and for the representation of life in what he called "images." In the Europe, especially the Paris, of his boyhood he found the image of a high culture and a complex social history as distinguished from the more meager culture and history of his own country at the time. He profited by the James family culture in the degree that he gently dissociated himself from some of its ideals, retaining the family faith in self-culture and moral disinterestedness but pursuing these aims from a point of view which was more international, aristocratic and conservative. Despite his family's wealth and his own preference for good society, he largely supported himself by his writings and was a tireless critic of the manners and morals of good society.

These and other considerations made him finally take up residence in Europe. Meanwhile he had served his literary apprenticeship in the United States. At Cambridge, where he was briefly enrolled in the Harvard Law School in 1862, he applied himself seriously to writing and formed enduring literary friendships with William Dean Howells, Charles Eliot Norton and others. His first publication seems to have been an unsigned tale, "A Tragedy of Error," which appeared in the *Continental Monthly* in February, 1864. He was soon a steady contributor of stories, critical articles, and travel essays to American periodicals. Between 1868 and 1874 he made two long stays in Europe; and in 1872, after a prolonged debate with himself and others, he decided to settle in Europe. Paris, where he first resided and where he came to know Turgenev, Flaubert, and other writers, proved uncongenial for his purposes, and in 1876 he removed to England. London was for many years his home; but in 1898 he acquired a small estate in Rye, Sussex, which was his main residence for the rest of his life. He continued to travel in Europe and paid three lengthy visits to America. He had a genius for friendship and its amenities, including letter writing. For many years his social life in Europe was very active; he frequented fashionable society as well as that of other writers and artists, English, American, and French. Essentially he remained a rather solitary bachelor, preoccupied with his own art and point of view as a kindly but austere moralist. His literary reputation, which was high in his early London years, declined during the later 1880's; and in the next decade he turned to writing for the theater in the hope of recouping his losses. The experiment failed; and gradually he ceased to expect a wide popularity. His novels became increasingly intricate and original in language and form; and while they antagonized the large public, they attracted readers of advanced taste. His remarkable powers of conversation were also widely appreciated. He felt, said one listener, "a deep impression of majesty, beauty and greatness." Beginning in 1907, there appeared the New York Edition of *The Novels and Tales of Henry James*, for which he selected, revised, and prefaced his writings. In 1911, following the death of William James, he issued two autobiographical volumes, *A Small Boy and Others* and *Notes of a Son and Brother*; the fragment of a third, *The Middle Years*, was published posthumously. With the outbreak of the war of 1914, he devoted himself to England's cause and in 1915 he made the sympathetic gesture of becoming a British subject. But his health was failing, and following a heart attack he died in London on February 28, 1916, aged 72.

James's work is massive and complex and, in its themes and techniques, extremely various. The twenty-six volumes of the New York Edition include only about two-thirds of his published fiction, which ranges in scope and subject from great international panoramas like *The Wings of the Dove* to unpretentious comedies of manners, fables of the artist life, ghost stories, and anecdotal tales. He was most famous in his lifetime for novels and stories showing the impact of Europeans and Americans on one another. His best early writings (e.g. *Daisy Miller*, *The American*, *The Europeans*, and *The Portrait of a Lady*) deal with this subject; and he returned to it in the three long novels of his later maturity (*The Ambassadors*, *The Wings of the Dove*, and *The Golden Bowl*). In the later 1880's and the 1890's, he wrote much on the subject of English life proper or American life proper (e.g. *The Bostonians*, *The Princess Casamassima*, *The Spoils of Poynton*, *What Maisie Knew*, *The Awkward Age*). These books, which had little success in their day, have since been recognized as among his greatest. Besides his fiction, he also wrote biographies (of Hawthorne and William Wetmore Story), literary essays, and cultural studies (*The American Scene*), and was one of the major Anglo-American critics between the age of Matthew Arnold and that of T. S. Eliot.

His fiction and his criticism rest on the same general interests and assumptions. Like Matthew Arnold he was greatly concerned with the state of culture, and he believed that culture included art, ideas, and manners, but consisted essentially in "the perfection of the self." In all his major novels, his men and women seek self-knowledge of the world and pleasure in the world's appearances. He was, Joseph Conrad said, "the historian of fine consciences." Men and women become true heroes for James in the degree that they reach a state of consciousness concerning their own natures and aims, cast off their illusions and their emotional dependency on other persons, act decisively on the data of consciousness, and are willing to renounce some immediate material advantage in the expectation of some ultimate and higher good. This is success in life for Henry James; while failure and evil, which also abound in his fictional world, consist in the substitution of material aims and of personal power for the practice of intelligence, good will, and love. His high evaluation of human consciousness gives rise to the peculiar methods of the James novel. The events of the story are transmitted to us through the minds of the chief protagonists. The minds of his observers frequently develop in clarity and power of sympathy as the story progresses, though sometimes they remain closed to reality and record experience falsely. From these methods arises the profound irony of many of James's performances; and some few of his tales (*The Sacred Fount*, *The Turn of the Screw*) seem to be deliberate exercises in ambiguity. Other similar tales ("The Aspern Papers," "The Beast in Jungle"), in which the observer is denied real vision altogether or until the last moment, may be James's most original and perfect writings. In recent years, some English critics claim him for the great tradition of novel writing in that country, while some American critics describe him as among the greatest of our own writers, the disciple of Hawthorne and the forerunner of T. S. Eliot. Both claims are justified by the range of his sympathy, knowledge, and art.

Bibliography

The standard but incomplete edition is the New York Edition of *The Novels and Tales of Henry James*, 26 vols., 1907–1917, containing the author's final revisions and valuable prefaces. A London edition, *The Novels and Stories of Henry James*, 36 vols., was published 1921–1923. Percy Lubbock edited *The Letters of Henry James*, 2 vols., 1920. Varied selections include *The Art of Henry James: Critical Prefaces*, edited by R. P. Blackmur, 1934; *The Great Short Novels of Henry James*, edited by Philip Rahv, 1944; *Stories of Writers and Artists*, edited by F. O. Matthiessen, 1944; *The Short Stories of Henry James*, edited by Clifton Fadiman, 1945; *The American Novels and Stories of Henry James*, edited by F. O. Matthiessen, 1947; *The Notebooks of Henry James*, edited by F. O. Matthiessen and K. B. Murdock, 1947; *The Ghostly Tales of Henry James*, edited by Leon Edel, 1948; *The Portable Henry James*, edited by Morton Dauwen Zabel, 1951; *Henry James: Autobiography*, edited by F. W. Dupee, 1956; and *The Complete Tales of Henry James*, edited by Leon Edel, 12 vols., 1962–1965.

The definitive biography is now Leon Edel, *Henry James: The Untried Years, 1843–1870*, 1953; *The Conquest of London, 1870–1881*, 1962; *The Middle Years, 1882–1895*, 1962; and *The Treacherous Years, 1895–1901*, 1969; and *The Master, 1901–1916*, 1972. An early comprehensive study is Pelham Edgar, *Henry James: Man and Author*, 1927. A recent valuable study is F. W. Dupee, *Henry James*, in the American Men of Letters Series, 1951 (rev. ed., 1956). See also E. L. Cary, *The Novels of Henry James: A Study*, 1905; Joseph Warren Beach, *The*

Method of Henry James, 1918; Theodora Bosanquet, *Henry James at Work*, 1924; Van Wyck Brooks, *The Pilgrimage of Henry James*, 1925; Cornelia P. Kelly, *The Early Development of Henry James, University of Illinois Studies in Language and Literature*, XV (1930), Nos. 1–2; Stephen Spender, *The Destructive Element*, 1935; F. O. Matthiessen, *Henry James: The Major Phase*, 1944; *idem, The James Family*, 1947; F. W. Dupee, ed., *The Question of Henry James*, 1945; Elizabeth Stevenson, *The Crooked Corridor*, 1949; Henry S. Canby, *Turn West, Turn East: Mark Twain and Henry James*, 1951; Roger Gard, ed., *Henry James: The Critical Heritage*, 1968; Walter Isle, *Experiments in Form: Henry James's Novels 1896–1901*, 1968; and Lyall H. Powers, *Guide to Henry James*, 1969.

The Henry James Special Number of *Modern Fiction Studies*, III (1957) contains an extensive and valuable selected checklist of James criticism with an index to studies of separate works, 73–96.

THE AMBASSADORS

Type of work: Novel
Author: Henry James (1843–1916)
Type of plot: Psychological realism
Time of plot: About 1900
Locale: Paris, France
First published: 1903

The Ambassadors *marks a turning point in James's attitude toward his American characters. This novel contains none of the embarrassment found in many of the earlier works, which portray the author's fellow Americans as slightly barbaric in their inability to appreciate the fineness and subtlety of European culture.*

Principal Characters

Lambert Strether, the chief ambassador of Mrs. Newsome, his betrothed, sent to summon her son Chad back from Paris to the family business in Wollett, Massachusetts. A fifty-five-year-old editor of a review, Lambert Strether has all the tact and diplomacy necessary to accomplish his task, but his sensitivity will not allow him either to complete it or to take advantage of Chad's situation to gain his own ends. He sees Chad as immeasurably better off in Paris, himself as somehow changed and strengthened by his sojourn abroad, though he will not allow himself to stay in Europe after having failed his benefactress. His heady experiences renew his earlier impressions, and he forms friendships, visits cathedrals, and lives easily for the first time since his wife died while bearing their son, also dead. His delicacy—in approaching young Newsome and his mistress, Mme. de Vionnet; in handling Chadwick's sister, brother-in-law, and childhood sweetheart, and in breaking off from Maria Gostrey, who loves him—is the more remarkable when one considers that his own hopes of a rich marriage and great influence have been shattered by his actions.

Chadwick Newsome, called **Chad,** the handsome, twenty-eight-year-old successor to a family business on the one hand and the heir to a modest income from another source. Candid and openhearted, the graying young man has been so improved by his years in Europe, largely under the tutelage of Mme. de Vionnet, that no thought of his return can really be habored by anyone who has seen him. Although he himself is willing to return for a visit and to consider taking over the advertising and sales promotion of the business he is well equipped to run, his proposed marriage to Mamie Pocock is unthinkable. His greatest triumph comes as the result of his mannerly presentation of his sister's group of ambassadors to his Parisian friends, while his saddest duty is to allow his good friend Lambert Strether to return to face the consequences of a diplomatic failure.

Maria Gostrey, a self-styled introducer and tour director and a chance acquaintance of Lambert Strether. A sensitive, genial, and understanding woman, she proves to be the agent through whom the ambassador discovers the irony of Chad Newsome's situation. Her generosity and devotion to her new friend first touch him and then move him deeply when he sees her loyalty and love unencumbered by desire for personal gain.

Mme. Marie de Vionnet (mä·rē′ də vē·ôn·nä′), the beautiful Comtesse whose religion and social position will not allow her to divorce an unloved and faithless husband. Gravely lovely and charming, she has educated young Chad Newsome in the social graces and has won his heart and soul. Called a virtuous connection by intimate friends, the arrangement seems shabby to Mr. Waymarsh and Mrs. Pocock, typically closed-minded Americans. Through the efforts of good friends, especially those of Lambert Strether, Mme. de Vionnet is allowed to retain her younger lover in spite of the fact that they have no future beyond their immediate happiness. Her daughter, who was believed by some to be in love with Chad Newsome, settles on a marriage more reasonable and agreeable to all.

John Little Bilham, called **Little Bilham,** an American expatriate artist and Chad Newsome's close friend. A perceptive, bright young man, little Bilham becomes the confidant of the ambassadors and, along with a friend, Miss Barrace, their interpreters of social and artistic life in Paris.

Miss Barrace, a shrewd, witty, understanding woman living in Paris. She asks Lambert Strether not to force the issue of Chad Newsome's return home.

Mr. Waymarsh, an American lawyer residing in England, Lambert Strether's friend. He accompanies Strether to Paris and directly involves himself in Chad Newsome's affairs when he writes a letter informing Mrs. Newsome that her ambassador is not fulfilling his mission.

Sarah Newsome Pocock, Chad Newsome's older sister. She, her husband, and her sister-in-law are also dispatched as Mrs. Newsome's ambassadors to make certain that Chad returns to America. She and Mr. Waymarsh join forces to separate Chad and Mme. de Vionnet.

James Pocock, Sarah's husband, who during Chad Newsome's absence is in control of the Newsome mills. He enjoys his trip to Paris, sympathizes with Chad, and becomes Lambert Strether's tacit ally.

Mamie Pocock, James Pocock's younger sister, the girl Mrs. Newsome has selected as a suitable wife for her son. Although she accompanies her brother and his wife on their mission to persuade Chad Newsome to return, she loses her personal interest in the young man after meeting John Little Bilham. Little Bilham's announced intention of marrying Mamie helps Chad solve his own problems of loyalty and love in his affair with Mme. de Vionnet.

Jeanne de Vionnet, Mme. de Vionnet's daughter. For a time society assumed that Chad Newsome might be in love with the daughter. Jeanne becomes engaged to M. de Montbron.

M. Gloriani, a sculptor, Mme. de Vionnet's friend, famous in the artistic and fashionable circles of Parisian society.

Mme. Gloriani, his lovely wife.

The Story

Lambert Strether was engaged to marry Mrs. Newsome, a widow. Mrs. Newsome had a son Chadwick, whom she wanted to return home from Paris and take over the family business in Woollett, Massachusetts. She was especially concerned for his future after she had heard that he was seriously involved with a Frenchwoman. In her anxiety she asked Strether to go to Paris and persuade her son to return to the respectable life she had planned for him.

Strether did not look forward to his task, for the young man had ignored all his mother's written requests to return home. Nor did Strether know what hold Chadwick's mistress might have over him or what sort of woman she might be. He strongly suspected that she was a young girl of unsavory reputation. Strether realized, however, that his hopes of marrying Mrs. Newsome depended upon his success in bringing Chad back to America, where his mother could see him married to Mamie Pocock.

Leaving his ship at Liverpool, Strether journeyed across England to London. On the way he met Miss Gostrey, a young woman who was acquainted with some of Strether's American friends, and she promised to aid Strether in getting acquainted with Europe before he left for home again. Strether met another old friend, Mr. Waymarsh, an American lawyer living in England, whom he asked to go with him to Paris.

A few days after arriving in Paris, Strether went to Chad's house. The young man was not in Paris, and he had temporarily given the house over to a friend, Mr. Bilham. Through Bilham, Strether got in touch with Chad at Cannes. Strether was surprised to learn of his whereabouts, for he knew that Chad would not have dared to take an ordinary mistress to such a fashionable resort.

About a week later Strether, Miss Gostrey, and Waymarsh went to the theater. Between the acts of the play, the door of their box was opened and Chad entered. He was much changed from the adolescent college boy Strether remembered. He was slightly gray, although only twenty-eight.

Both Strether and Chad Newsome pleased each other on sight. Over coffee after the theater, the older man told Chad why he had come to Europe. Chad answered that all he asked was an opportunity to be convinced that he should return.

A few days later Chad took Strether and his friends to a tea where they met Mme. and Mlle. de Vionnet. The former, who had married a French count, turned out to be an old school friend of Miss Gostrey. Strether was at a loss to understand whether Chad was in love with the comtesse or with her daughter Jeanne. Since the older woman was only a few years the senior of the young man and as beautiful as her daughter, either was possibly the object of his affections.

As the days slipped by it became apparent to Strether that he himself wanted to stay in Paris. The French city and its life were much calmer and more beautiful than the provincial existence he had known in Woollett, and he began to understand why Chad was unwilling to go back to his mother and the Newsome mills.

Strether learned that Chad was in love with Mme. de Vionnet, rather than with her daughter. The comtesse had been separated from her husband for many years, but their position and religion made divorce impossible. Strether, who was often in the company of the Frenchwoman, soon fell under her charm. Miss Gostrey, who had known Mme. de Vionnet for many years, had only praise for her and questioned Strether as to the advisability of removing Chad from the woman's continued influence.

One morning Chad announced to Strether that he was ready to return immediately to America. The young man was puzzled when Strether replied that he was not sure it was wise for either of them to return, that it would be wiser for them both to reconsider whether they would not be better off in Paris than in New England.

When Mrs. Newsome, back in America, received word of that decision on the part of her ambassador, she immediately sent the Pococks, her daughter and son-in-law, to Paris along with Mamie Pocock, the girl she hoped her son would marry. They were to bring back both Strether and her son.

Mrs. Newsome's daughter and her relatives did not come to Paris with an obvious ill-will. Their attitude seemed to be that Chad and Strether had somehow drifted astray, and it was their duty to set them right. At least that was the attitude of Mrs. Pocock. Her husband, however, was not at all interested in having Chad return, for in the young man's absence Mr. Pocock controlled the Newsome mills. Mr. Pocock further saw that his visit was probably the last opportunity he would have for a gay time in the European city, and so he was quite willing to spend his holiday going to theaters and cafés. His younger sister, Mamie, seemed to take little interest in the recall of her supposed fiancé, for she had become interested in Chad's friend, Mr. Bilham.

The more Strether saw of Mme. de Vionnet after the arrival of the Pococks, the more he was convinced that the Frenchwoman was both noble and sincere in her attempts to make friends with her lover's family. Mrs. Pocock found it difficult to reconcile Mme. de Vionnet's aristocratic background with the fact that she was Chad's mistress.

After several weeks of hints and genteel pleading, the Pococks and Mamie went to Switzerland, leaving Chad to make a decision whether to return to America. As for Mr. Strether, Mrs. Newsome had advised that he be left alone to make his own decision, for the widow wanted to avoid the appearance of having lost her dignity or her sense of propriety.

While the Pococks were gone, Strether and Chad discussed the course they should follow. Chad was uncertain of his attitude toward Mamie Pocock. Strether assured him that the girl was already happy with her new love, Mr. Bilham, who had told Strether that he intended to marry the American girl. His advice, contrary to what he had thought when he had sailed from America, was that Chadwick Newsome should remain in France with the comtesse, despite the fact that the young man could not marry her and would, by remaining in Europe, lose the opportunity to make himself an extremely rich man. Chad decided to take his older friend's counsel.

Waymarsh, who had promised his help in persuading Chad to return to America, was outraged at Strether's changed attitude. Miss Gostrey, however, remained loyal, for she had fallen deeply in love with Strether during their time together in Paris. But Strether, realizing her feelings, told her that he had to go back to America alone. His object in Europe had been to return Chad Newsome to his mother. Because he had failed in that mission and would never marry Mrs. Newsome, he could not justify himself by marrying another woman whom he had met on a journey financed by the woman he had at one time intended to marry. Only Mme. Vionnet, he felt, could truly appreciate the irony of his position.

Critical Evaluation

In Henry James's *The Ambassadors* plot is minimal; the storyline consists simply in Mrs. Newsome sending Lambert Strether to Europe to bring home her son, Chad. The important action is psychological rather than physical; the crucial activities are thought and conversation. The pace of the novel is slow. Events unfold as they do in life: in their own good time.

Because of these qualities, James's work demands certain responses from the reader. He must not expect boisterous action, shocking or violent occurrences, sensational coincidences, quickly mounting suspense, or breathtaking climaxes: these devices have no place in a Henry James novel. Rather, the reader must bring to the work a sensitivity to problems of conscience, an appreciation of the meaning beneath manners, and an awareness of the intricacies of human relationships. Finally, and of the utmost importance, the reader must be patient; the power of a novel like *The Ambassadors* is only revealed quietly and without haste. This is why, perhaps more than any other modern author, James requires rereading—not merely because of the complexity of his style, but because the richly layered texture of his prose contains a multiplicity of meanings, a wealth of subtle shadings.

In *The Ambassadors,* which James considered his masterpiece, this subtlety and complexity is due partially to his perfection of his technique for handling point of view. Departing from traditional eighteenth and nineteenth century use of the omniscient narrator, James experimented extensively with the limited point of view, exploring the device to discover what advantages it might have over the older method. He found that what was lost in panoramic scope and comprehensiveness, the limited viewpoint more than compensated for in focus, concentration, and intensity. It was the technique perfectly suited to an author whose primary concern was with presenting the thoughts, emotions, and motivations of an intelligent character, with understanding the psychological makeup of a sensitive mind and charting its growth.

The sensitive and intelligent character through whose mind all events in the novel are filtered is Lambert Strether. The reader sees and hears only what Strether sees and hears; all experiences, preceptions, and judgments are his.

Strictly adhered to, this device proved too restricted for James's purpose; therefore, he utilized other characters—called confidants—who enabled him to expand the scope of his narrative without sacrificing advantages inherent in the limited point of view. The basic function of these "listening characters" is to expand and enrich Strether's experience. Miss Gostrey, Little Bilham, Waymarsh, and Miss Barrace—all share with him attitudes and insights arising from their widely diverse backgrounds; they provide him with a wider range of knowledge than he could ever gain from firsthand experience. Maria Gostrey, who is Strether's primary confidante, illustrates the fact that James's listening characters are deep and memorable personalities in their own right. Miss Gostrey not only listens to Strether but she also becomes an important figure in the plot, and as she gradually falls in love with Strether, engages the reader's sympathy as well.

Lambert Strether interacts with and learns from the environment of Paris as well as from the people he meets there; thus, the setting is far more than a mere backdrop against which events in the plot occur. To understand the significance of Paris as the setting, the reader must appreciate the meaning which the author, throughout his fiction, attached to certain places. James was fascinated by what he saw as the underlying differences in the cultures of America and Europe, and in particular in the opposing values of a booming American factory town like Woollett and an ancient European capital such as Paris. In these two places, very different qualities are held in esteem. In Woollett, Mrs. Newsome admires practicality, individuality, and enterprise, while in Paris, her son appreciates good food and expensive wine, conversation with a close circle of friends, and leisure time quietly spent. Woollett pursues commercialism, higher social status, and rigid moral codes with untiring vigor; Paris values the beauty of nature, the pleasure of companionship, and an appreciation of the arts with studied simplicity. Thus, the implications of a native of Woollett, like Lambert Strether, going to Paris at the end of his life are manifold; and it is through his journey that the theme of the novel is played out.

The theme consists of a question of conscience: Should Strether, in his capacity as Mrs. Newsome's ambassador, be faithful to his mission of bringing Chad home, once he no longer believes in that mission? That he ceases to believe is the result of his conversion during his stay in Paris. He is exposed to a side of life that he had not known previously; furthermore, he finds it to be good. As a man of noble nature and sensitive conscience, he cannot ignore or deny, as Sarah Newsome later does, that life in Paris has vastly improved Chad. Ultimately, therefore, he must oppose rather than promote the young man's return. The honesty of this action not only destroys his chance for financial security in marriage to Chad's mother, but also prevents him from returning the love of Maria Gostrey. Although Strether's discovery of a different set of values comes too late in life for his own benefit, he at least can save Chad. The lesson he learns is the one he passionately seeks to impart to Little Bilham: "Live all you can; it's a mistake not to. It doesn't so much matter what you do in particular, so long as you have your life. . . . Don't, at any rate, miss things out of stupidity. . . . Live!"

If in reading *The Ambassadors* the reader's expectations are for keenness of observation, insight into motivations, comprehension of mental processes, and powerful characterizations, he will not be disappointed. If Henry James demands the effort, concentration, and commitment of his reader, he also— with his depth and breadth of vision and the sheer beauty of his craftsmanship —repays him a hundredfold.

Bibliography

Anderson, Quentin. *The American Henry James.* New Brunswick, N.J.: Rutgers University Press, 1957, pp. 207–231.

Beach, Joseph Warren. *The Method of Henry James.* New Haven: Yale University Press, 1918, pp. 255–270. Reprinted in *Twentieth Century Interpretations of* The Ambassadors: *A Collection of Critical Essays.* Edited by Albert E. Stone, Jr. Englewood Cliffs, N.J.: Prentice-Hall, 1969, pp. 37–42.

Bennett, Joan. "The Art of Henry James: *The Ambassadors,*" in *Chicago Review.* IX (Winter, 1956), pp. 16–26. Reprinted in *Twentieth Century Interpretations of* The Ambassadors: *A Collection of Critical Essays.* Edited by Albert E. Stone, Jr. Englewood Cliffs, N.J.: Prentice-Hall, 1969, pp. 57–65.

Cargill, Oscar. *The Novels of Henry James.* New York: Macmillan, 1961, pp. 303–337.

Chase, Richard. "James' *Ambassadors,*" in *Twelve Original Essays on Great American Novels.* Edited by Charles Shapiro. Detroit: Wayne State University Press, 1958, pp. 124–147.

Crews, Frederick C. *The Tragedy of Manner: Moral Drama in the Later Novels of Henry James.* New Haven, Conn.: Yale University Press, 1957, pp. 30–56.

Dupee, F.W. *Henry James: His Life and Writings.* Garden City, N.Y.: Doubleday, 1956, pp. 207–216. Reprinted in *Twentieth Century Interpretations of* The Ambassadors: *A Collection of Critical Essays.* Edited by Albert E. Stone, Jr. Englewood Cliffs, N.J.: Prentice-Hall, 1969, pp. 33–34.

Edel, Leon. "Henry James: *The Ambassadors,*" in *Landmarks of American Writing.* Edited by Hennig Cohen. New York: Basic Books, 1969, pp. 182–193.

Edgar, Pelham. *Henry James: Man and Author.* Boston: Houghton Mifflin, 1927, pp. 310–324.

Forster, E.M. "*The Ambassadors,*" in *Aspects of the Novel.* New York: Harcourt, 1927, pp. 218–234. Reprinted in *The Ambassadors.* Edited by S.P.

Rosenbaum. New York: Norton, 1964, pp. 421–427.

Geismar, Maxwell. *Henry James and the Jacobites.* Boston: Houghton Mifflin, 1963, pp. 271–290. Reprinted in *Twentieth Century Interpretations of* The Ambassadors*: A Collection of Critical Essays.* Edited by Albert E. Stone., Jr. Englewood Cliffs, N.J.: Prentice-Hall, 1969, pp. 96–105.

Hardy, Barbara. *Tellers and Listeners: The Narrative Imagination.* Atlantic Highlands, N.J.: Humanities, 1975, pp. 56–101.

Holland, Laurence Bedwell. *The Expense of Vision: Essays on the Craft of Henry James.* Princeton, N.J.: Princeton University Press, 1964, pp. 229–282.

Lubbock, Percy. "The Point of View: *The Ambassadors*," in *The Craft of Fiction: Picture, Drama and Point of View.* London: Jonathan Cape, 1921, pp. 156–171. Reprinted in *Henry James: A Collection of Critical Essays.* Edited by Leon Edel. Englewood Cliffs, N.J.: Prentice-Hall, 1963, pp. 37–46.

McElderry, Bruce R., Jr. *Henry James.* New York: Twayne, 1965, pp. 129–135.

Marks, Robert. *James's Later Novels: An Interpretation.* New York: William-Frederick, 1960, pp. 57–110.

Matthiessen, F.O. *Henry James: The Major Phase.* New York: Oxford University Press, 1944, pp. 19–41. Reprinted in *Twentieth Century Interpretations of* The Ambassadors*: A Collection of Critical Essays.* Edited by Albert E. Stone, Jr. Englewood Cliffs, N.J.: Prentice-Hall, 1969, pp. 43–48. Also reprinted in *The Ambassadors.* Edited by S.P. Rosenbaum. New York: Norton, 1964, pp. 427–438.

Mizener, Arthur. "*The Ambassadors*," in *Twelve Great American Novels.* New York: New American Library, 1967, pp. 49–67.

Putt, S. Gorley. *Henry James: A Reader's Guide.* Ithaca, N.Y.: Cornell University Press, 1966, pp. 343–359.

Sears, Sallie. *The Negative Imagination: Form and Perspective in the Novels of Henry James.* Ithaca, N.Y.: Cornell University Press, 1968, pp. 101–151.

Sharp, Sister M. Corona. *The Confidante in Henry James: Evolution and Moral Value of a Fictive Character.* Notre Dame, Ind.: University of Notre Dame, 1963, pp. 150–180.

Tomlinson, Thomas B. *The English Middleclass Novel.* New York: Barnes & Noble, 1976, pp. 148–165.

Ward, J.A. *The Imagination of Disaster: Evil in the Fiction of Henry James.* Lincoln: University of Nebraska Press, 1961, pp. 110–126.

Wegelin, Christof. *The Image of Europe in Henry James.* Dallas: Southern Methodist University Press, 1958, pp. 86–105. Reprinted in *The Ambassadors.* Edited by S.P. Rosenbaum. New York: Norton, 1964, pp. 442–458.

THE AMERICAN

Type of work: Novel
Author: Henry James (1843–1916)
Type of plot: Psychological realism
Time of plot: Mid-nineteenth century
Locale: Paris, France
First published: 1877

In this novel James juxtaposes the pragmatic and materialistic values of American democratic society, as exhibited in Christopher Newman, with the traditional complex aristocratic French culture in which he becomes involved.

Principal Characters

Christopher Newman, a young American millionaire who is looking for more in life than a business career. He goes to Paris to experience European culture, and he hopes to find a wife who can aid in developing his natural abilities. Both modest and astute, he has a depth of integrity that is recognized by both men and women. He is also generous in his response to the qualities of others. When he meets Claire de Cintré though his friend, Mrs. Tristram, he is drawn to her noble character and touched by her adverse situation. In his relationship with the Bellegarde family, Newman's innate decency stirs some of them to admiration and others to a desire to exploit Newman's naïveté. Newman is refused Claire, who retires to a convent; he is tempted to bargain for her because he has evidence showing that her father was put to death by his wife. But the family knows their man: his innate decency leads him to destroy the incriminating evidence. This action, as his friend Mrs. Tristram points out, was a part of the Bellegarde calculations.

Claire de Cintré, nee **Bellegarde,** a young French woman locked in the rigid confines of her mother's domination. When she was forced into marriage with a worldly old man, her invalid father could not save her; but a few years later her husband's death released her. This is the woman Newman meets and loves. Seeing in Newman a sensitive and reliable man, she responds to his goodness. She is just beginning to feel strength and freedom when the Bellegardes withdraw their permission for her marriage to Newman. She is further distressed when her amiable younger brother dies in a duel. She knows intuitively of her mother's crime of murder, but there seems no way out of her dilemma. She chooses the only path open to her—the convent—where she can at least escape her family. One senses that sorrow has taught her only to endure; she does not know the enormity of her sacrifice in giving up Newman.

Mr. Tristram, Newman's somewhat boisterous American friend.

Mrs. Tristram, a woman much more perceptive than her husband. Her warmth is a kind of sisterly affection for Newman to fall back upon.

Madame de Bellegarde (bĕl·gȧrd'), a French aristocrat by title but in actuality a hard woman with neither morality nor integrity.

The Marquis de Bellegarde (Urbain), the elder son in the family; he is like his mother in character.

Valentin de Bellegarde, the younger son He is a man of wit and kindliness. He loves his sister and dies in Switzerland as the result of a duel motivated by his affair with Mlle. Nioche.

Mrs. Bread, the Bellegarde servant who is taken over by Newman after Valentin's dying words instruct her to reveal Madame de Bellegarde's secret.

M. Nioche, an elderly French shopkeeper whose age and experience permit him some philosophical observations.

Mlle. Nioche, his daughter. An indifferent artist, she is able to support herself by her physical charms. She is last seen in London escorted by Valentin's distant cousin, Lord Deepmere.

The Story

In 1868 Christopher Newman, a young American millionaire, withdrew from business and sailed for Paris. He wanted to loaf, to develop his aesthetic sense, and to find a wife for himself. One day, as he wandered in the Louvre, he made the acquaintance of Mlle. Nioche, a young copyist. She introduced him to her father, an unsuccessful shopkeeper. Newman bought a picture from Mlle. Nioche and contracted to take French lessons from her father.

Later, through the French wife of an American friend named Tristram, he met Claire de Cintré, a young widow, daughter of an English mother and a French father. As a young girl, Claire had been married to Monsieur de Cintré, an evil old man. He had soon died, leaving Claire with a distaste for marriage. In spite of her attitude, Newman saw in her the woman he wished for his wife. But an American businessman was not the person to associate with French aristocracy. On his first call, Newman was kept from entering Claire's house by her elder brother, the Marquis de Bellegarde.

True to his promise, M. Nioche appeared one morning to give Newman his first lesson in French. Newman enjoyed talking to the old man. He learned that Mlle. Nioche dominated her father and that he lived in fear that she would leave him and become the mistress of some rich man. M. Nioche assured Newman that he would shoot her if she did. Newman took pity on the old man and promised him enough money for Mlle. Nioche's dowry if she would paint some more copies for him.

Newman left Paris and traveled through Europe during the summer. When he returned to Paris in the autumn he learned that the Tristrams had been helpful; the Bellegardes were willing to receive him. One evening Claire's younger brother, Valentin, called on Newman and the two men found their opposite points of view a basis for friendship. Valentin envied Newman's liberty to do as he pleased; Newman wished himself acceptable to the society in which the Bellegardes moved. After they had become good friends, Newman told Valentin that he wished to marry his sister and asked Valentin to plead his cause. Warning Newman that his social position was against him, Valentin promised to help the American as much as he could.

Newman confessed his wish to Claire, and asked Madame de Bellegarde,

Claire's mother, and the marquis for permission to be her suitor. The permission was given, grudgingly. The Bellegardes needed money in the family.

Newman went to the Louvre to see how Mlle. Nioche was progressing with her copying. There he met Valentin and introduced him to the young lady.

Mrs. Bread, an old English servant of the Bellegardes, assured Newman that he was making progress with his suit. He asked Claire to marry him and she accepted. Meanwhile, Valentin had challenged another man to a duel in a quarrel over Mlle. Nioche. Valentin left for Switzerland with his seconds. The next morning Newman went to see Claire. Mrs. Bread met him at the door and said that Claire was leaving town. Newman demanded an explanation. He was told that the Bellegardes could not allow a commercial person in the family. When he arrived home, he found a telegram from Valentin stating that he had been badly wounded and asking Newman to come at once to Switzerland.

With this double burden of sorrow, Newman arrived in Switzerland and found Valentin near death. Valentin guessed what his family had done and told Newman that Mrs. Bread knew a family secret. If he could get the secret from her, he could make them return Claire to him. Valentin died the next morning.

Newman attended the funeral. Three days later he again called on Claire, who told him that she intended to enter a convent. Newman begged her not to take this step. Desperate, he called on the Bellegardes again and told them that he would uncover their secret. Newman arranged to see Mrs. Bread that night. She told him that Madame de Bellegarde had killed her invalid husband because he had opposed Claire's marriage to M. de Cintré. The death had been judged natural, but Mrs. Bread had in her possession a document which proved that Madame de Bellegarde had murdered her husband. She gave this paper to Newman.

Mrs. Bread left the employ of the Bellegardes and came to keep house for Newman. She told him that Claire had gone to the convent and refused to see anyone, even her own family. The next Sunday Newman went to mass at the convent. After the service he met the Bellegardes walking in the park and showed them a copy of the paper Mrs. Bread had given him.

The next day the marquis called on Newman and offered to pay for the document. Newman refused to sell. He offered, however, to accept Claire in exchange for it. The marquis refused.

Newman found he could not bring himself to reveal the Bellegardes' secret. On the advice of the Tristrams he traveled through the English countryside and in a melancholy mood went to some of the places he had planned to visit on his honeymoon. Then he went to America. Restless, he returned to Paris and learned from Mrs. Tristram that Claire had become a nun.

The next time he went to see Mrs. Tristram, he dropped the secret document on the glowing logs in her fireplace and told her that to expose the Bellegardes now seemed a useless and empty gesture. He intended to leave Paris forever. Mrs. Tristram told him that he probably had not frightened the Bellegardes with his threat, because they knew that they could count on his good nature never to reveal their secret. Newman instinctively looked toward the fireplace. The paper had burned to ashes.

Critical Evaluation

Christopher Newman of *The American* represents new world culture in conflict with the rigid traditions of the European aristocracy. Newman, a natural aristocrat in his own right, epitomizes the democratic spirit and pragmatic values of a culture in which accomplishment is alone the measure of individual worth. Though Newman suffers from a naïveté which blinds him to the complications of the complex society he encounters in France, he is an essentially moral person whose values ultimately prove superior to those of his detractors.

True to his materialistic background, Newman comes to Paris determined to acquire the best that European culture has to offer. He quickly reveals that he has little instinct for the best in art, and his judgment of people will prove equally inept. His choice of Claire de Cintré is based equally upon his vision of her as his ideal woman and as the ultimate possession to crown his success. His failure to achieve her depends upon his failure to recognize her subordination to the family will and the Bellegarde family's determination not to surrender the aristocratic tradition which is all that remains of their nobility.

Expecting that the Bellegardes will finally sacrifice family tradition to their material interests, Newman enters into a game with rules he never fully understands. His own democratic spirit makes it impossible that he should ever comprehend the almost religious idolatry of family which characterizes the Bellegardes. As the Bellegardes show their true colors, including criminal responsibility for the death of Claire's father, their "nobility" is shown to be based entirely upon tradition—it has no moral and human equivalent. Newman, on the other hand, rises in our estimation as a natural aristocrat whose moral superiority makes him the real measure of the best in the human condition.

Bibliography

Beach, Joseph Warren. *The Method of Henry James.* New Haven, Conn.: Yale University Press, 1918, pp. 199–205. Reprinted in *The Merrill Studies in* The American. Edited by William T. Stafford. Columbus, Oh.: Merrill, 1971, pp. 33–37.

Bowden, Edwin T. *The Themes of Henry James.* New Haven, Conn.: Yale University Press, 1956, pp. 28–36.

Brooks, Cleanth. "The American 'Innocence,' " in *Shenandoah*. XVI (Autumn, 1964), pp. 21–37. Reprinted in *A Shaping Joy: Studies in the Writer's Craft*. New York: Harcourt Brace Jovanovich, 1972, pp. 181–197.

Butterfield, R.W. *"The American,"* in *The Air of Reality: New Essays on Henry James*. Edited by John Goode. London: Methuen, 1972, pp. 5–35.

Canby, Henry Seidel. *Turn West, Turn East: Mark Twain and Henry James*. Boston: Houghton Mifflin, 1951, pp. 117–121.

Cargill, Oscar. *The Novels of Henry James*. New York: Macmillan, 1961, pp. 41–61. Reprinted in *The Merrill Studies in* The American. Edited by William T. Stafford. Columbus, Oh.: Merrill, 1971, pp. 45–62.

Cary, Elizabeth L. *The Novels of Henry James: A Study*. New York: Putnam's, 1905, pp. 59–74.

Clair, John A. *"The American*: A Reinterpretation," in *PMLA*. LXXIV (December, 1959), pp. 613–618. Reprinted in *The Merrill Studies in* The American. Edited by William T. Stafford. Columbus, Oh.: Merrill, 1971, pp. 80–91.

Dupee, F.W. *Henry James*. Garden City, N.Y.: Doubleday Anchor, 1956, pp. 82–85.

Edel, Leon. *Henry James: The Conquest of London, 1870–1881*. Philadelphia: Lippincott, 1962, pp. 246–260.

Edgar, Pelham. *Henry James: Man and Author*. Boston: Houghton Mifflin, 1927, pp. 237–245.

Geismar, Maxwell. *Henry James and the Jacobites*. Boston: Houghton Mifflin, 1963, pp. 22–26.

Kelley, Cornelia Pulsifer. *The Early Development of Henry James*. Urbana: University of Illinois Press, 1930, pp. 234–244.

Knox, George. "Romance and Fable in James's *The American*," in *Anglia*. LXXXIII (1965), pp. 308–323. Reprinted in *The Merrill Studies in* The American. Edited by William T. Stafford. Columbus, Oh.: Merrill, 1971, pp. 65–79.

Krutch, Joseph Wood. *The Modern Temper: A Study and a Confession*. New York: Harcourt, 1929, pp. 105–108.

McElderry, Bruce R., Jr. *Henry James*. New York: Twayne, 1965, pp. 44–47.

Maseychik, William J. "Points of Departure from *The American*," in *Henry James: Modern Judgments*. Edited by Tony Tanner. London: Macmillan, 1968, pp. 116–127.

Nettels, Elsa. *James and Conrad*. Athens: University of Georgia Press, 1977, pp. 88–93.

Pearce, Roy Harvey. "Henry James and His *American*," in *Historicism Once More: Problems and Occasions for the American Scholar*. Princeton, N.J.: Princeton University Press, 1969, pp. 240–260.

Poirier, Richard. *The Comic Sense of Henry James: A Study of the Early Novels*. New York: Oxford University Press, 1960, pp. 44–94.

Putt, S. Gorley. *Henry James: A Reader's Guide*. Ithaca, N.Y.: Cornell University Press, 1966, pp. 110–115.

Rourke, Constance. *American Humor: A Study of the National Character*. New York: Harcourt, 1931, pp. 235–265. Reprinted in *The Question of Henry James: A Collection of Critical Essays*. Edited by F.W. Dupee. New York: Holt, 1945, pp. 138–159.

Spengemann, William C. *The Adventurous Muse: The Poetics of American Fiction, 1789–1900*. New Haven, Conn.: Yale University Press, 1977, pp. 241–263.

Traschen, Isadore. An American in Paris," in *American Literature*. XXVI (March, 1954), pp. 67–77.

West, Ray B., Jr. *The Writer in the Room: Selected Essays*. East Lansing: Michigan State University Press, 1968, pp. 60–73.

THE AWKWARD AGE

Type of work: Novel
Author: Henry James (1843–1916)
Time: The 1890's, presumably
Locale: London, and outlying estates
First published: 1899

Essay-Review

The *Awkward Age* stems from that intensely experimental period at the turn of the century in which Henry James laid the groundwork for the major accomplishments of *The Ambassadors*, *The Wings of the Dove*, and *The Golden Bowl*. Coming as it does between *What Maisie Knew*, in which the point of view is that of a narrator for whom the actions of the other characters are the subject of endless but unconfirmable speculation, *The Awkward Age* is more technically dazzling, and possibly more enigmatic, than either in that James restricts himself almost entirely to dialogue and eschews, except for two or three very brief passages, his customary practice of "going behind," that is, of entering the minds of any of his characters. The effect is rather that of a lengthy closet drama (James admits in the preface that his model has been the *roman dialogué* of the French authoress Gyp), but a drama surpassing in subtlety, intricacy, and elusiveness anything heretofore written in that genre. With the help only of those few occasions when James renders Nanda's and Vanderbank's thoughts, and of a hypothetical spectator to whom James attributes hypothetical interpretations of tones of voice and facial expressions, the reader is left to infer, as the characters themselves do, the motivational and situational realities behind the labyrinth of the novel's conversation, or at least to register how the characters' own inferences bring about the events in which they participate.

The central characters of the novel are members of Mrs. Brookenham's "group," a select circle of sophisticated conversationalists for whom innuendo and the immediately perceived hinted nuance have become a style of life. Beyond mere talk—their lives reside so largely in their talk—is the prospect of what will happen to the group's tone, what restraints will be imposed, upon the admission into the drawing room of Mrs. Brook's marriageable but unmarried daughter, Nanda. Into this distinctly "modern" society comes Mr. Longdon, and the novel opens on a lengthy conversation between him and Vanderbank following the occasion of their having spent the evening—Mr. Longdon's first—at Mrs. Brook's. Vanderbank, who presents, it emerges, a remarkably handsome and imposing appearance, but whose means are hardly commensurate with the impression he creates, is taken with the older man who so charmingly contrasts with the tone he is accustomed to, and Mr. Longdon, despite misgivings about that tone—which finds its quintessence in Mrs. Brook—is similarly pleased. Mr. Longdon confides to Van that he has been a suitor to both Van's mother and Mrs. Brook's mother, Lady Julia, and that he has never forgotten his feeling for the latter, from whom her own daughter differs so radically. Upon seeing a picture of Nanda, Mr. Longdon exclaims on her similarity to Lady Julia. The conversation ends on Mr. Longdon's revealing that the conversational tone of the evening has indeed shocked him.

The next "act," so to speak (there are ten), presents us immediately with Mrs. Brook in colloquy with her son Harold, whom she catches in the act of stealing a five-pound note. Mrs. Brook is operating in her family mode, a studied and languorous melancholy quite at odds with her public performances, and her conversation turns on the problem of getting Harold invited to house parties (her son has obviously taken lessons in manipulation from her) and the family's financial straits. With Harold's exit and the entrance of the Duchess, the talk turns to Nanda, who is visiting her married friend Tishy Grendon. The Duchess chides Mrs. Brook for allowing her daughter to mingle with such questionable associates, whereas she, in the European manner, has carefully sheltered her niece, Little Aggie, from any such possible contaminations, has preserved her a perfect little *tabula rasa* until the time of her marriage. She then urges Mrs. Brook to snare Mitchy as a husband for Nanda; she adds that his ugliness and his being the son of a shoemaker render him totally unsatisfactory as a potential mate for Aggie, though she will shortly thereafter instigate a maneuver designed to land him for Aggie. After a brief conversation between Mrs. Brook and her husband, Mitchy and Petherton enter, and it is shown that Petherton is probably the Duchess' lover. Mrs. Brook attributes to Mitchy, despite his outrageous talk, a gentleness and "niceness" lacking in the rest of them, and her comment, sincere or not, will be borne out in the development of the novel. The Duchess re-enters, this time with Aggie, and when Carrie Donner's arrival is shortly followed by that of Lady Fanny, the talk turns to the erotic entanglements of the Grendon-Donner-Cashmore set, the Duchess informing Mitchy that it is Nanda who is her mother's source on the degree of intimacy between Mrs. Donner and Mr. Cashmore.

In the following scene Mr. Longdon, and the reader, are confronted for the first time with Nanda, whose resemblance to Lady Julia overwhelms Mr. Longdon. He and Nanda develop an immediate rapport.

Mrs. Brook sounds Van on the subject of Mr. Longdon's fortune and what he may do for Nanda, and in the same dialogue indicates that she is possibly in love with Van.

At a weekend party given by Mitchy, Mr. Longdon urges Nanda to marry, but she rejects Mitchy as impossible and confides to him that she will probably never marry. The Duchess tries to persuade Mr. Longdon to settle on Van a sum which will allow him to marry Nanda (thus leaving Mitchy, upon whom Mrs. Brook has designs for Nanda, free for Aggie), who is "as sick as a little cat—with her passion" for him. Mr. Longdon makes his offer to the uncertain Van, who requests time to consider the proposition and refuses to allow his prospective benefactor to name a sum.

In the ensuing conversation, Van reveals to Mrs. Brook Mr. Longdon's generous offer, which that lady—whether merely prophetically or in an attempt to determine his hand—enigmatically hints he will refuse. Mrs. Brook then, against Van's articulated wishes, imparts to Mitchy the information she has just gained and suggests that Van will pass up the chance to propose to Nanda rather than appear to accept a bride. She has, she says, made her revelation simply in accordance with that principle of openness and honesty which is so much the note of their society, and the scene concludes with the mutual bestowal of lavish accolade, somewhat undercut by Van's ironic awareness of the prevalent duplicity and the possible mixture of motive for Mrs. Brook's behavior. Nanda enters shortly after the departure of her mother's guests, and Mrs. Brook questions her about her relation with Mr. Longdon and broaches the possibility and advisability of his adopting the girl.

At Mr. Longdon's, Nanda approaches Mitchy, whom she knows to be in love with her, and urges him, for his own sake and that of Aggie, to marry the Duchess' niece, thus effectually eliminating him as a candidate for her own hand. Mitchy, to gratify Nanda and to enjoy the only proximity of relation with her now open to him, that of simply being thoroughly together with her on the matter of Aggie, acquiesces to her promptings and reveals his intentions to Van, indicating that the way is now completely open to the latter. Van, however, remains uncommitted and indecisive. The conversation ends rather darkly on the question of what Mr. Longdon will do for Nanda should Van fail to propose.

The climactic scene of the novel occurs several months later at Tishy Grendon's, where all the principal characters are gathered. At this time Nanda has been Mr. Longdon's guest for several months; Harold has ably distracted Lady Fanny from her design to run off with another gentleman; and Little Aggie, after her marriage, has been divested with a vengeance of her innocence and has taken up with her aunt's lover, Petherton. Mrs. Brook, in a tremendous scene, demands Nanda's return from Mr. Longdon and forces the public exposure of the group, climaxing her performance with the revelation that Nanda has read a scabrous French novel lent to her by Vanderbank, and has even pronounced it unfit for the presumably far more experienced Tishy to read. The effect is to reveal to Vanderbank the depths of knowledge already open to Nanda, depths in the unveiling of which he has been instrumental but which, with cruel irony, render her an impossible choice for his wife. Mrs. Brook, who knows her Van all too well, has eliminated the possibility of losing him to her daughter.

The scene at Tishy Grendon's however, has served to destroy the solidarity of the group, and it is only after months that Van returns to Mrs. Brook's, supposedly to see Nanda but ultimately avoiding the chance to do so, an avoidance which Mrs. Brook interprets as his finally having given Nanda up. This information she enjoins Mitchy to give Mr. Longdon, for, as she has explained to her remarkably obtuse husband, her purpose in creating the horrid scene at Tishy's had been simply to confirm Mr. Longdon's belief that she and her world were impossible for Nanda and to insure his taking care of the girl.

The final "act" occurs two weeks later, with the overwrought and embarrassed Van making what is presumably his final visit to Nanda. Nanda, however, lets the now awkward young man off easily by assuming the role of herself being in the false position, and she generously entreats him not to desert her mother, a plea she repeats to Mitchy in her next interview. Finally there is only Mr. Longdon, and before him she breaks down in the fullness of her suffering. It is Little Aggie whom Vanderbank ought to have married, they agree. Only that innocence could have met his measure, though an innocence capable of becoming its own obverse at the first taste of experience. Even under such a circumstance, however, Mitchy would still have been totally out of the question for her; it has been his fate, as it has been Nanda's, to love only that person for whom he is an impossibility. Around the suffering Mitchy Nanda's thoughts revolve as she prepares to be taken away the following day by Mr. Longdon.

Turning as it seems to on the question of a girl's reading a questionable book, *The Awkward Age* may appear to the superficial glance as a period piece, elaborate and elegant, but without the reverberating significance of James's three final masterpieces. To see the novel in this light, however, is to neglect its hard and lucid inquiry into the coexistence of moral vision and the knowledge of a world seemingly its antithesis. Little Aggie is innocent of such knowledge, but her innocence is the merest ignorance of that which she will become. Paradoxically, Nanda's knowledge, the superficial taint as opposed to the inward blight, of the world in which she is so thoroughly implicated, a knowledge which is perhaps instrumental in creating Nanda's moral dimension, renders her unacceptable to Vanderbank. And yet if Nanda's magnanimous vision can exist only in her retreat with Mr. Longdon from the world, there is a sense in which she too, by her pressuring Mitchy into marrying Aggie, has been implicated in the network of selfishness, guilt, and suffering which is perhaps the inevitable result of the brush of human contact.

Finally there is the pragmatism of the magnificent Mrs. Brook, the ability to make do in a world where one is unlikely to get what one wants. What Mrs. Brook wants is unquestionably Van. The book leaves the question moot whether they have ever been lovers, though most of evidence points to the fact that they have not. Her scene at Tishy Grendon's appears from one angle a wanton destruction of her daughter's hopes; yet, given her knowledge of Van's nature, a nature it must be said, which contact with her has in no small measure formed, her seemingly brutal actions may just as well be motivated, as she explains to Edward, by a desire to provide, no matter how deviously, for a daughter who has no other chance, to ensure for her the opening of an escape from a world which has already left its mark. To acknowledge that the selfish desire to retain Van for herself enters Mrs. Brook's design is only to admit the necessary multiplicity of motive inherent in taking any course of human action. Mrs. Brook's motives are decidedly mixed—and her awareness of the fact is part of her limited triumph. She provides the only alternative, if a partially cruel one, to the very different satisfactions offered by renunciation.

Bibliography

Bass, Eben, "Dramatic Scene and *The Awkward Age*," in *PMLA*. LXXIX (March, 1964), pp. 148–157.

Cargill, Oscar. *The Novels of Henry James*. New York: Macmillan, 1961, pp. 263–279.

Dupee, F.W. *Henry James*. Garden City, N.Y.: Doubleday Anchor, 1956, pp. 170–176.

Edgar, Pelham. *Henry James: Man and Author*. Boston: Houghton Mifflin, 1927, pp. 131–144.

Firebaugh, Joseph. "The Pragmatism of Henry James," in *Virginia Quarterly Review*. XXVII (Summer, 1951), pp. 419–435.

Gargano, James W. "The Theme of 'Salvation' in *The Awkward Age*," in *Texas Studies in Language and Literature*. IX (Summer, 1967), pp. 273–287.

Gregor, Ian and Brian Nicholas. "The Novel of Moral Consciousness: *The Awkward Age*," in *The Moral and the Story*. London: Faber and Faber, 1962, pp. 151–184.

Hall, William F. "James's Conception of Society in *The Awkward Age*," in *Nineteenth Century Fiction*. XXIII (June, 1968), pp. 28–48.

Hartsock, Mildred. "The Exposed Mind: A View of *The Awkward Age*," in *Critical Quarterly*. IX (Spring, 1967), pp. 49–59.

Isle, Walter. "*The Awkward Age*," in *Experiments in Form: Henry James's Novels, 1896–1901*. Cambridge, Mass.: Harvard University Press, 1968, pp. 165–204.

Jefferson, D.W. *Henry James and the Modern Reader*. New York: St. Martin's, 1964, pp. 164–176.

Krook, Dorothea. *The Ordeal of Consciousness in Henry James*. New York: Cambridge University Press, 1962, pp. 135–166.

Leavis, F.R. *The Great Tradition: George Eliot, Henry James, Joseph Conrad*. New York: George Stewart, 1949, pp. 169–171.

Leyburn, Ellen Douglass. *The Strange Alloy: The Relation of Comedy to Tragedy in the Fiction of Henry James*. Chapel Hill: University of North Carolina Press, 1968, pp. 110–121.

Lubbock, Percy. *The Craft of Fiction.* New York: Scribner's, 1921, pp. 189–202.

McElderry, Bruce R., Jr. *Henry James.* New York: Twayne, 1965, pp. 113–114.

Marks, Robert. *James's Later Novels: An Interpretation.* New York: William-Frederick, 1960, pp. 15–43.

Nelson, Carl. "James' Social Criticism: The Voice of the Ringmaster in *The Awkward Age*," in *Arizona Quarterly.* XXIX (Summer, 1973), pp. 151–168.

Owen, Elizabeth. "*The Awkward Age* and the Contemporary English Scene," in *Victorian Studies.* XI (September, 1967), pp. 63–82.

Putt, S. Gorley. *Henry James: A Reader's Guide.* Ithaca, N.Y.: Cornell University Press, 1966, pp. 253–258.

Tanner, Tony. *The Reign of Wonder: Naivety and Reality in American Literature.* New York: Cambridge University Press, 1965, pp. 298–308.

Tomlinson, Thomas B. *The English Middleclass Novel.* New York: Barnes & Noble, 1976, pp. 114–130.

Walters, Margaret. "Keeping the Place Tidy for the Young Female Mind: *The Awkward Age*," in *The Air of Reality.* Edited by John Goode. London: Methuen, 1972, pp. 190–218.

Ward, J.A. *The Imagination of Disaster: Evil in the Fiction of Henry James.* Lincoln: University of Nebraska Press, 1961, pp. 90–101.

Wiesenfarth, Joseph. *Henry James and the Dramatic Analogy: A Study of the Major Novels of the Middle Period.* New York: Fordham University Press, 1963, pp. 76–95.

DAISY MILLER

Type of work: Novelette
Author: Henry James (1843–1916)
Type of plot: Psychological realism
Time of plot: Mid-nineteenth century
Locale: Vevey, Switzerland, and Rome
First published: 1878

This almost plotless James novelette concerns itself with a conflict between European and American customs and ideals. Daisy Miller, an unsophisticated, "strikingly, admirably pretty" girl, clashes with the conventions of Europeanized, expatriate Americans who enforce society's regulations with severity and thoughtlessness. The diversity in characterization makes Daisy Miller *an ironic study of contrasts.*

Principal Characters

Daisy Miller, the charming and unconforming American tourist whose inattention to decorum (she walks unchaperoned with an Italian suitor in the daytime) results in her ostracism by the Europeanized Americans in Rome. In defiance, she visits the Colosseum at night with the same young man and later dies of a fever contracted there.

Frederick Winterbourne, an American expatriate from whose point of view the story is told. At first puzzled by Daisy, he soon becomes convinced that she is immoral. However, after her death, he realizes that her manners indicated only a native American freedom, and that he loved her.

Giovanelli, the young Italian whose companionship causes the scandal involving Daisy. An adventurer interested primarily in Daisy's money, he admits to Winterbourne after her death that she never would have consented to marry him.

Mrs. Walker, an American expatriate. Because Daisy rejects Mrs. Walker's efforts to preserve her from scandal, Mrs. Walker cuts her at a party, thus beginning Daisy's complete ostracism.

Randolph Miller, Daisy's young and spoiled brother. His impudence also shocks the American expatriates.

Mrs. Costello, Winterbourne's aunt. She refuses to meet Daisy because she is convinced that the Millers are common.

Eugenio, the Millers' courier and servant. That the Millers treat him almost as a member of the family also causes talk among the American expatriates.

The Story

Winterbourne was a young American who had lived in Europe for quite a while. He spent a great deal of time at Vevey, which was a favorite spot of his aunt, Mrs. Costello. One day, while he was loitering outside the hotel, he was attracted by a young woman who appeared to be related to Randolph Miller, a

young American boy with whom he had been talking. After a while the young
woman exchanged a few words with him. Her name was Daisy Miller. The boy
was her brother, and they were in Vevey with their mother. They came from Sche-
nectady, Winterbourne learned, and they intended to go next to Italy. Randolph
insisted that he wanted to go back home. Winterbourne learned that Daisy hoped
to visit the Castle of Chillon. He promised to take her there, for he was quite
familiar with the old castle.

Winterbourne asked his aunt, Mrs. Costello, to meet Daisy. Mrs. Costello, however, would not agree because she thought the Millers were common. That evening Daisy and Winterbourne planned to go out on the lake, much to the horror
of Eugenio, the Millers' traveling companion, who was more like a member of the
family than a courier. At the last moment Daisy changed her mind about the
night excursion. A few days later Winterbourne and Daisy visited the Castle of
Chillon. The outing confirmed Mrs. Costello's opinion that Daisy was uncultured
and unsophisticated.

Winterbourne made plans to go to Italy. When he arrived, he went directly to
the home of Mrs. Walker, an American whom he had met in Geneva. There he
met Daisy and Randolph. Daisy reproved him for not having called to see her.
Winterbourne replied that she was unkind, as he had just arrived on the train.
Daisy asked Mrs. Walker's permission to bring an Italian friend, Mr. Giovanelli,
to a party Mrs. Walker was about to give. Mrs. Walker agreed. Then Daisy said
that she and the Italian were going for a walk. Mrs. Walker was shocked, as
young unmarried women did not walk the streets of Rome with Italians. Daisy
suggested that there would be no objection if Winterbourne would go with her to
the spot where she was to meet the Italian and then walk with them.

Winterbourne and Daisy set out and eventually found Giovanelli. They walked
together for a while. Then Mrs. Walker's carriage drew alongside the strollers.
She beckoned to Winterbourne and implored him to persuade Daisy to enter her
carriage. She told him that Daisy had been ruining her reputation by such behavior; she had become familiar with Italians and was quite heedless of the scandal
she was causing. Mrs. Walker said she would never speak to Winterbourne again
if he did not ask Daisy to get into the carriage at once. But Daisy, refusing the
requests of Mrs. Walker and Winterbourne, continued her walk with the Italian.

Mrs. Walker determined to snub Daisy at the party. When Winterbourne arrived, Daisy had not made her appearance. Mrs. Miller arrived more than an
hour before Daisy appeared with Giovanelli. Mrs. Walker had a moment of weakness and greeted them politely. But as Daisy came to say goodnight, Mrs. Walker
turned her back upon her. From that time on Daisy and Giovanelli found all doors
shut to them. Winterbourne saw her occasionally, but she was always with the
Italian. Everyone thought they were carrying on an intrigue. When Winterbourne
asked her if she were engaged, Daisy said that she was not.

One night, despite the danger from malarial fever, Giovanelli took Daisy to the
Colosseum. Winterbourne, encountering them in the ancient arena, reproached

the Italian for his thoughtlessness. Giovanelli said that Daisy had insisted upon viewing the ruins by moonlight. Within a few days Daisy was dangerously ill. During her illness she sent word to Winterbourne that she had never been engaged to Giovanelli. A week later she was dead.

As they stood beside Daisy's grave in the Protestant cemetery in Rome, Giovanelli told Winterbourne that Daisy would never have married her Italian suitor, even if she had lived. Then Winterbourne realized that he himself had loved Daisy without knowing his own feelings, that he could have married her had he acted differently. He reasoned, too late, that he had lived in Europe too long, that he had forgotten the freedom of American manners and the complexity of the American character.

Critical Evaluation

In *Daisy Miller*, James represents the conflicts between American innocence and independence and the rigid social conventions characteristic of the American colony in Rome. While Daisy deliberately flaunts convention by her unorthodox behavior, Mrs. Costello and Mrs. Walker make appearance their only basis for moral judgment. Winterbourne, troubled by the ambiguity in Daisy's character, seeks some objective basis for making a judgment.

Daisy realizes that the other Americans have no interest in her as an individual. Living in a world of moral judgments based entirely upon social conventions, they are only concerned to preserve the appearance of morality through "proper" behavior. Determined to be accepted on more meaningful grounds than these, Daisy asserts those freedoms she would be allowed in America, but which are clearly out of place in Rome. Confident in her own innocence, she refuses to conform to the restrictions her compatriots would place upon her.

Innocence and crudity are the terms characterizing Daisy, and these conflicting qualities are the source of Winterbourne's confusion about her. He, like his aunt and Mrs. Walker, has a tendency to make judgments on the basis of superficial appearances. Daisy, however, seems innocent to him in spite of her unconventional behavior, so he cannot fit her into a neat category as he would like. But discovering Daisy in a seemingly compromising position with Giovanelli in the Colosseum gives Winterbourne the evidence he needs, and with some relief he declares Daisy morally corrupt. In so doing, he places himself solidly among the other Americans who, like himself, have lived too long abroad to appreciate the real innocence which underlies Daisy's seeming moral laxity. Too late Winterbourne realizes at the graveside that his formulation of Daisy has been unjust.

Bibliography

Booth, Wayne C. *The Rhetoric of Fiction.* Chicago: University of Chicago Press, 1961, pp. 282–284. Reprinted in *James's* Daisy Miller: *The Story, the Play, the Critics.* Edited by William T. Stafford. New York: Scribner's, 1963, pp. 157–158.

Coffin, Tristram P. *"Daisy Miller,* Western Hero," in *Western Folklore.* XVII (October, 1958), pp. 273–275. Reprinted in *James's* Daisy Miller: *The Story, the Play, the Critics.* Edited by William T. Stafford. New York: Scribner's, 1963, pp. 136–137.

Dupee, F.W. *Henry James.* Garden City, N.Y.: Doubleday Anchor, 1956, pp. 92–96. Reprinted in *James's* Daisy Miller: *The Story, the Play, the Critics.* Edited by William T. Stafford. New York: Scribner's, 1963, pp. 147–149.

Edel, Leon. *Henry James: The Conquest of London, 1870–1881.* Philadelphia: Lippincott, 1962, pp. 302–312.

Edgar, Pelham. *Henry James: Man and Author.* Boston: Houghton Mifflin, 1927, pp. 25–27.

Fiedler, Leslie A. *Love and Death in the American Novel.* New York: Criterion Books, 1960, pp. 298–300. Reprinted in *James's* Daisy Miller: *The Story, the Play, the Critics.* Edited by William T. Stafford. New York: Scribner's, 1963, pp. 140–141.

Fryer, Judith. *The Faces of Eve: Women in the Nineteenth Century American Novel.* New York: Oxford University Press, 1976, pp. 97–101.

Gargano, James W. *"Daisy Miller:* An Abortive Quest for Innocence," in *South Atlantic Quarterly.* LIX (Winter, 1960), pp. 114–120. Reprinted in *James's* Daisy Miller: *The Story, the Play, the Critics.* Edited by William T. Stafford. New York: Scribner's, 1963, pp. 150–153.

Geist, Stanley. "Fictitious Americans—Portraits from a Family Album: *Daisy Miller,*" in *Hudson Review.* V (Summer, 1952), pp. 203–206. Reprinted in *James's* Daisy Miller: *The Story, the Play, the Critics.* Edited by William T. Stafford. New York: Scribner's, 1963, pp. 131–133.

Graham, Kenneth. *Henry James: The Drama of Fulfillment, An Approach to the Novels.* Oxford: Clarendon Press, 1975, pp. 15–28.

Hagopian, John V. *Insight I: Analyses of American Literature.* Frankfurt, Germany: Hirschgraben-Verlag, 1964, pp. 132–139.

Hoffmann, Charles G. *The Short Novels of Henry James.* New York: Bookman, 1957, pp. 19–25. Reprinted in *James's* Daisy Miller: *The Story, the Play, the Critics.* New York: Scribner's, 1963, pp. 155–156.

Kelley, Cornelia P. "Debut of the American Girl," in *The Early Development of Henry James*. Urbana: University of Illinois Press, 1930, pp. 266–269. Reprinted in *James's* Daisy Miller: *The Story, the Play, the Critics*. Edited by William T. Stafford. New York: Scribner's, 1963, pp. 144–145.

Kennedy, Ian. "Frederick Winterbourne: The Good Bad Boy in *Daisy Miller*," in *Arizona Quarterly*. XXIX (Summer, 1973), pp. 139–150.

McElderry, Bruce R., Jr. "The 'Shy, Incongruous Charm' of *Daisy Miller*," in *Nineteenth Century Fiction*. X (September, 1955), pp. 162–165.

Monteiro, George. " 'Girlhood on the American Plan': A Contemporary Defense of *Daisy Miller*," in *Books at Brown*. XIX (May, 1963), pp. 89–93.

Ohmann, Carol. "*Daisy Miller*: A Study of Changing Intentions," in *American Literature*. XXXVI (March, 1964), pp. 1–11.

Putt, S. Gorley. *Henry James: A Reader's Guide*. Ithaca, N.Y.: Cornell University Press, 1966, pp. 122–123.

Randall, John H., III. "The Genteel Reader and *Daisy Miller*," in *American Quarterly*. XVII (Fall, 1965), pp. 568–581.

Sharp, Sister M. Corona. *The Confidante in Henry James: Evolution and Moral Value of a Fictive Character*. Notre Dame, Ind.: University of Notre Dame Press, 1963, pp. 9–14.

Stone, Edward. *The Battle and the Books: Some Aspects of Henry James*. Athens: Ohio University Press, 1964, pp. 88–93, 120–122.

Wasserstrom, William. *Heiress of all the Ages: Sex and Sentiment in the Genteel Tradition*. Minneapolis: University of Minnesota Press, 1959, pp. 61–64. Reprinted in *James's* Daisy Miller: *The Story, the Play, the Critics*. Edited by William T. Stafford. New York: Scribner's, 1963, pp. 138–139.

Wegelin, Christof. *The Image of Europe in Henry James*. Dallas: Southern Methodist University Press, 1958, pp. 61–64. Reprinted in *James's* Daisy Miller: *The Story, the Play, the Critics*. Edited by William T. Stafford. New York: Scribner's, 1963, pp. 134–135.

West, Rebecca. *Henry James*. New York: Holt, 1916, pp. 44–47. Reprinted in *James's* Daisy Miller: *The Story, the Play, the Critics*. Edited by William T. Stafford. New York: Scribner's, 1963, pp. 142–143.

THE GOLDEN BOWL

Type of work: Novel
Author: Henry James (1843–1916)
Type of plot: Psychological realism
Time of plot: c. 1900
Locale: England and the Continent
First published: 1904

The Golden Bowl *is a meticulous, involved, and incredibly detailed exploration of the subtleties of thought and nuances of emotion of a small circle of wealthy, cultured Americans living in Europe. James's collection of psychological shades and discriminations are at times almost overwhelming to the reader. A forerunner of psychological expressionism, the novel describes characters who live in a world shut off from homely realities, a world that will not tolerate crudities.*

Principal Characters

Maggie Verver, the motherless daughter of an American millionaire. For a number of years the Ververs have spent much of their time abroad, where Mr. Verver has devoted himself to acquiring a magnificent art collection for the museum he plans to build in American City. Sharing her father's quiet tastes and aesthetic interests, Maggie has become his faithful companion, and they have created for themselves a separate, enclosed world of ease, grace, and discriminating appreciation, a connoisseurship of life as well as of art. Even Maggie's marriage to Prince Amerigo, an Italian of ancient family, does not change greatly the pattern of their lives, a pattern that she believes complete when Mr. Verver marries her best friend, Charlotte Stant. What Maggie does not know is the fact that before her marriage the Prince and Charlotte, both moneyless and therefore unable to marry, had been lovers. Several years later the Prince, bored by his position as another item in the Verver collection, and Charlotte, restless because she takes second place beside her elderly husband's interest in art, resume their former intimacy. Maggie finds her happiness threatened when her purchase of a flawed gold-and-crystal bowl leads indirectly to her discovery of the true situation. Her problem is whether to disclose or conceal her knowledge. Deeply in love with her husband and devoted to her father, she decides to remain silent. Her passivity becomes an act of drama because it involves a sense of ethical responsibility and a moral decision; her predicament is the familiar Jamesian spectacle of the innocent American confronting the evil of European morality, in this case complicated by Maggie's realization that she and her father are not without guilt, that they have lived too much for themselves. In the end her generosity, tact, and love resolve all difficulties. Mr. Verver and his wife leave for America and Maggie regains her husband's love, now unselfishly offered.

Prince Amerigo, a young Italian noble-

---

man, handsome, gallant, sensual, living in England with his American wife. A man of politely easy manners, he is able to mask his real feelings under an appearance of courteous reserve. Though he has loved many women, he has little capacity for lies or deception in his dealings with them; he objects when Charlotte Stant, his former mistress, wishes to purchase a flawed golden bowl as a wedding gift to his wife, for he wants nothing but perfection in his marriage. He and Charlotte are often thrown together after she marries his father-in-law, and they become lovers once more. When his wife learns, through purchase of the same flawed bowl, the secret of his infidelity, he tries to be loyal to all parties concerned, and he so beautifully preserves the delicate harmony of family relationships that no outsiders except their mutual friends, the Assinghams, know of the situation. Maggie, his wife, is able to save her marriage because his delicacy in the matter of purchased and purchasable partners makes tense situations easier. After Mr. Verver and his wife return to America, the Prince shows relief as unselfish as it is sincere; their departure allows him to be a husband and a father in his own right.

Charlotte Stant, the beautiful but impecunious American girl who needs a wealthy husband to provide the fine clothes and beautiful things she believes necessary for her happiness. Because Prince Amerigo is poor, she becomes his mistress but never considers marrying him. After his marriage to Maggie Verver, her best friend, Mr. Verver proposes to Charlotte. She accepts him and, though Mr. Verver cannot understand her claim of unworthiness, declares herself prepared to be as devoted as possible, both as a wife and as a stepmother to the Prince's good friend. Often left in the Prince's company while Maggie and her father pursue their interest in art, she resumes her affair with her former lover. When the truth is finally revealed, Charlotte, determined to prove her loyalties to all concerned, persuades Mr. Verver to re-

turn with her to America. Her poised and gracious farewell to Maggie and the Prince is more than a demonstration of her ability to keep up appearances; it shows the code of responsibility she has assumed toward her lover, her friend, and her husband.

Adam Verver, a rich American who has given over the pursuit of money in order to achieve the good life for himself and his daughter Maggie. In his innocence he believes that this end may be attained by seeing and collecting the beautiful art objects of Europe. A perfect father, he cannot realize that there is anything selfish in the close tie that exists between himself and his daughter, and he tries to stand in the same relationship with his son-in-law, Prince Amerigo, and Charlotte Stant, his daughter's friend, whom he marries. All he really lives for is to provide for Maggie and his grandson the life of happiness and plenty he envisions for them. When he finally realizes that the pattern of his life has been a form of make-believe, he sacrifices his own peace of mind and agrees to return with his wife to make the United States his permanent home.

Fanny Assingham, the friend of Maggie and Adam Verver, Prince Amerigo, and Charlotte Stant, and the guardian angel of their secret lives. As one who senses the rightness of things, she helps to bring about both marriages with a sensitive understanding of the needs of all, a delicacy she will not allow to be disrupted by Maggie's discovery of her husband's infidelity. Her belief is that even wickedness is more to be condoned than wrongness of heart. She helps to resolve the situation between Maggie and Prince Amerigo when she hurls the golden bowl, symbol of Maggie's flawed marriage and the Prince's guilt, to the floor and smashes it.

Colonel Robert Assingham, called **Bob,** a retired army officer who understands his wife's motives in the interest she takes in the Verver family but who manages to keep himself detached from her complicated dealings with the lives of others.

The Principino, the small son of Prince Amerigo and his wife Maggie.

The Story

Maggie Verver was the daughter of a wealthy American widower who had devoted all his life to his daughter. The Ververs lived a lazy life. Their time was spent in collecting items to decorate their own existence and to fill a museum which Mr. Verver was giving to his native city back in the United States. They had few friends. Maggie's only confidante was Mrs. Assingham, the American-born wife of a retired British army officer.

It was Mrs. Assingham who introduced the Ververs to Prince Amerigo, a handsome, quiet young Italian nobleman who struck Maggie's fancy. When she informed her father that she would like to marry the Prince, Mr. Verver provided a handsome dowry so that the wedding might take place.

A few days before the wedding a painful scene occurred in Mrs. Assingham's home, where the Prince and Charlotte Stant, deeply in love with each other, met to say goodbye. Each was penniless and a marriage had been out of the question. Since both were friends of Maggie, the present situation was painful for them. As a farewell lark they spent the last afternoon searching for a wedding present for Charlotte to present to Maggie. In a tiny shop they discovered a golden bowl which Charlotte wished to purchase as a remembrance for the Prince from her. He refused it because of superstitious fears that a crack in the golden bowl might bring bad luck.

After the wedding of the Prince and Maggie, the lives of the pair coincided with the life that the Ververs had been living for years. Maggie and her father spent much of their time together. The Prince, although he did not complain, was really only a convenience that they had purchased because Maggie had reached the age when she needed to have a husband.

After a year and a half a baby was born to the Prince and Maggie, but the child made no apparent difference in the relationships between the girl and her father or the girl and her husband. Maggie decided that her father also needed a wife. She went to Mrs. Assingham and told her friend that she planned to have Charlotte Stant marry her father. Charlotte was a quiet person aware of the love between the girl and her father, and she was the sort of person who would be so thankful to marry a wealthy man that she would cause little trouble. Neither Maggie nor Mrs. Assingham put this aspect into words, but it was tacitly understood.

Mr. Verver, anxious to please his daughter in this as in everything else, married Charlotte a short time later. This second marriage created a strange situation. Maggie and her father both took houses in London where they could be together a great deal of the time. The association of father and daughter left the Prince and Charlotte much together. Maggie encouraged them to go out, to represent her and her father at balls and dinners. But Maggie did not know that her husband and her stepmother had been intimate before her own marriage to the Prince.

Several years went by in this manner, but slowly the fact that there was something strange in the relationships dawned upon Maggie's sensitive feelings. She eventually went to Mrs. Assignham and poured out her suspicions to her. Mrs. Assignham, in full knowledge of the circumstances, decided to keep silence.

Maggie resolved to say nothing of her suspicions to anyone else. But her attitude of indifference, her insistence in throwing the Prince and Charlotte together, aroused their suspicions that she knew they had been sweethearts, that she suspected them of being lovers after marriage.

Each one of the four speculated at length as to what the other three knew or suspected. Yet their mutual confidence and love prevented each one of them from ever asking anything of the others.

One day Maggie went shopping for some unusual art object to present to her father on his birthday. She accidentally happened into the same shop where the Prince and Charlotte had gone several years before, and she purchased the golden bowl which they had passed over because of its flaw. The following day the shopkeeper visited her. The name and address had told him that she was the wife of the Prince who had passed up the bowl years before. He knew that the existence of the crack would quickly come to the attention of the Prince, and so he had hastened to inform Maggie of the flaw and to return part of the purchase price. He also told her of the Prince's first visit to the shop and of the young woman who had been with him. Maggie then knew that the Prince and Charlotte had known each other before her marriage and that they had spent an afternoon together the day before she was married. She was upset. Again she confided in Mrs. Assignham.

Having learned that there was no serious relationship between the Prince and Charlotte, Mrs. Assignham informed Maggie that she was making a great ado over nothing at all. To point up her remark, she raised the bowl above her head and smashed it to the floor, where it broke into several pieces. As she did so, the Prince entered the room and saw the fragments of the bowl. After Mrs. Assignham's departure he tried to learn how much Maggie knew. Maggie and her husband agreed to say nothing to either Maggie's father or to Charlotte.

Charlotte, too, began to sense that something had disturbed Maggie, and she shrewdly guessed what it was. Then Maggie tried to realign the relationships of the four by proposing that she and Charlotte stay together for awhile and that the Prince and her father go to the Continent to buy art objects. This proposal was gently put forward and as gently rebuffed by the other three.

Maggie and her father began to realize that their selfishness in trying to keep up the father-daughter relationship which they had had before her marriage was wrong. Shortly after that selfishness had been brought into the open and discussed by Maggie and Mr. Verver, Charlotte told Maggie that she wished to return to America and to take her husband with her. She bluntly informed Maggie she was afraid that if Mr. Verver continued to live so close to his daughter he would lose interest in his wife. Mr. Verver agreed to accompany Charlotte back to the United States. It was a difficult decision for him to make. He realized that once he was away, Charlotte would never agree to his coming back to Europe to live.

On an autumn afternoon Mr. Verver and Charlotte went to have tea with Maggie and the Prince before leaving England. It was almost heartbreaking to Maggie to see her father's carriage take him out of sight and to know that her old way of life was really ended. The only thing which kept her from breaking down completely was the look on the Prince's face as he turned her face away from the direction her father's carriage had taken. At that moment, seeing his eyes, Maggie knew she had won her husband for herself and not for her money.

Critical Evaluation

The Golden Bowl, along with *The Ambassadors* and *The Wings of the Dove,* is one of the novels of the triad of works upon which the high reputation of James's "major phase" rests. In these novels, James's already complex style reaches new levels of sophistication as, increasingly, the writing becomes more and more intricate and convoluted as it tends toward ever-increasingly subtle levels of analysis of character and event. Gradually the "center of consciousness" in the mind of a character, which had been essential to James's earlier works, gives way to an omniscient narrative point of view, and a narrative voice which is James's own. Though it hardly appears so to the eye, James's style of this period is essentially oral—he had developed the habit of dictating his material to a secretary—and reflects his characteristically ponderous manner of speech. Seeming to move endlessly to circle or enfold a subject or an idea without ever touching it directly, James's language and technique in these late novels has been admired highly by critics who place a premium on style, while frequently being disparaged by those who stress content and clarity of thought. For James himself, the art of the novel was everything in writing, and there is little doubt that in *The Golden Bowl* his artistry reached a peak.

With this novel, James continues the subject matter of the "international theme" which had characterized his work from its beginning by dealing with a group of Americans in Europe. Adam Verver, in particular, can be seen as an avatar of the American Adam who recurs in James's fiction, often, as here, in search of European culture which he will take back to his culturally barren homeland. Prince Amerigo is linked by his name to the historic connection between America and Europe, and, by his marriage to Maggie, might be seen as dramatizing a new dependence of the Old World upon the New. Yet, *The Golden Bowl* ultimately is less an international novel than such works as *The*

American, Daisy Miller, or *The Ambassadors* because its concerns are finally more with individuals than with cultures. Though the Ververs begin in America and Adam returns there at the novel's end, neither his experience nor that of Maggie or Charlotte is essentially contingent upon the sort of conflict of cultural values which is at the heart of James's international novels and stories. Rather, the problems of love and marriage at the heart of *The Golden Bowl* are truly universal, neither their nature nor their solution dependent upon an American perspective.

Like many of James's works, *The Golden Bowl* began in his notebooks with the recording of an anecdote he had heard concerning a young woman and her widower father, each of whom had taken spouses, who learned their partners were engaged in an affair. From this scant beginning, James crafted his longest and most elaborate novel not by greatly complicating the essential material of this simple plot, but by scrupulous elaboration of the conflicts and resolutions resulting from the complex relations among his four central characters. By making his characters members of the wealthy leisure class, James frees them from the mundane worries of the world so he can focus his, and their, entire attention on the one particular problem without regard to external complications. Ultimately, the novel seeks to pose moral and philosophical questions which transcend either the psychological or social levels of the work to confront the basic question of Maggie's adjustment to a less-than-perfect world.

The golden bowl is James's metaphor for the marriage between Amerigo and Maggie, and perhaps, in its larger implications, for life itself. The bowl, not really "golden" at all, but crystal gilded with gold leaf, has the superficial appearance of perfection, but is, in fact, cracked. As a symbol of Maggie's "perfect" marriage, the bowl very clearly illustrates the flaw at the heart of the relationship—a flaw which no doubt existed even before the Prince and Charlotte resume their old love affair, and which represents a potential threat to the marriage. Both Maggie and her father are guilty of treating the Prince as nothing more than one of the valuable objects they have come to Europe to purchase—they have bought the perfect marriage for Maggie. Unlike art, however, human relationships are not subject to purchase, nor can they, as in the case of Adam's marriage to Charlotte, be arranged for convenience without regard to the human factors concerned. In fact, both Maggie and her father tend to live in a small, supremely selfish world. Insulated by their money from the actuality of life, they isolate themselves from the real complexities of daily existence. Their world is, in effect, itself more "art" than "life."

The resolution of the novel turns around Maggie's positive act, but in the earlier parts of the novel she is more passive than active. The marriage itself, for example, seems more of an arrangement between the Prince and Adam Verver than a particular choice of Maggie's—Adam wants the perfect marriage for his daughter, and Prince Amerigo wants access to the Verver millions, so they come to an agreement between themselves. Maggie apparently has little to say about it, and even, judging from her relationship to the Prince throughout most of the novel, no very great interest in the marriage. Her real desire seems to be to continue life with her father pretty much as always, rather than to begin an independent life with her husband. Only when confronted with the Prince's infidelity does Maggie recognize that she must confront this reality for all their sakes. In choosing to separate from her father in order to begin making the best of her imperfect marriage, Maggie discovers a latent ability to confront the world as it really is, and to rise above the romantic idealism which had characterized her life with Adam Verver.

Bibliography

Anderson, Quentin. *The American Henry James.* New Brunswick, N.J.: Rutgers University Press, 1957, pp. 281–346.

Bayley, John. "Love and Knowledge: *The Golden Bowl*," in *The Characters of Love: A Study in the Literature of Personality.* New York: Basic, 1961, pp. 203–262.

Bersani, Leo. *A Future for Astyanax: Character and Desire in Literature.* Boston: Little, Brown, 1976, pp. 128–155.

Bowden, Edwin T. *The Themes of Henry James.* New Haven, Conn.: Yale University Press, 1956, pp. 102–113.

Cargill, Oscar. *The Novels of Henry James.* New York: Macmillan, 1961, pp. 383–440.

Crews, Frederick C. *The Tragedy of Manners: Moral Drama in the Later Novels of Henry James.* New Haven, Conn.: Yale University Press, 1957, pp. 81–114.

Dupee, F.W. *Henry James.* Garden City, N.Y.: Doubleday Anchor, 1956, pp. 224–324.

Edel, Leon. *Henry James, the Master, 1901–1916.* Philadelphia: Lippincott, 1972, pp. 208–223.

Edgar, Pelham. *Henry James: Man and Author.* Boston: Houghton Mifflin, 1927, pp. 324–343.

Fryer, Judith. *The Faces of Eve: Women in the Nineteenth Century American Novel.* New York: Oxford University Press, 1976, pp. 112–126.

Geismar, Maxwell. *Henry James and the Jacobites.* Boston: Houghton Mifflin, 1963, pp. 297–338.

Holland, Laurence B. *The Expense of Vision: Essays on the Craft of Henry James.* Princeton, N.J.: Princeton University Press, 1964, pp. 331–407.

Jefferson, D.W. *Henry James and the Modern Reader.* New York: St. Martin's, 1964, pp. 216–225.

Krook, Dorothea. *The Ordeal of Consciousness in Henry James.* New York: Cambridge University Press, 1962, pp. 232–324.

Lebowitz, Naomi. *The Imagination of Loving: Henry James's Legacy to the Novel.* Detroit: Wayne State University Press, 1965, pp. 71–85, 99–103, 121–127, 130–142.

Marks, Robert. *James's Later Novels: An Interpretation.* New York: William-Frederick, 1960, pp. 111–130.

Matthiessen, F.O. *Henry James: The Major Phase.* New York: Oxford University Press, 1944, pp. 81–104. Reprinted in *Critics on Henry James: Readings in Literary Criticism.* Edited by J. Don Vann. Coral Gables, Fla.: University of Miami Press, 1973, pp. 57–69.

Nuhn, Ferner. "The Enchanted Kingdom of Henry James—*The Golden Bowl,*" in *The Wind Blew from the East: A Study in the Orientation of American Culture.* New York: Harper and Row, 1940, pp. 116–158.

Pearson, Gabriel. "The Novel to End All Novels: *The Golden Bowl,*" in *The Air of Reality.* Edited by John Goode. London: Methuen, 1972, pp. 301–362.

Putt, S. Gorley. *Henry James: A Reader's Guide.* Ithaca, N.Y.: Cornell University Press, 1966, pp. 363–386.

Sears, Sallie. *The Negative Imagination: Form and Perspective in the Novels of Henry James.* Ithaca, N.Y.: Cornell University Press, 1968, pp. 155–222.

Sharp, Sister M. Corona. *The Confidante in Henry James: Evolution and Moral Value of a Fictive Character.* Notre Dame, Ind.: University of Notre Dame Press, 1963, pp. 214–246.

Todasco, Ruth T. "Theme and Imagery in *The Golden Bowl,*" in *Texas Studies in Language and Literature.* IV (Summer, 1962), pp. 228–240.

Ward, J.A. *The Imagination of Disaster: Evil in the Fiction of Henry James.* Lincoln: University of Nebraska Press, 1961, pp. 139–156.

Wright, Walter F. *The Madness of Art: A Study of Henry James.* Lincoln: University of Nebraska Press, 1962, pp. 242–254.

THE PORTRAIT OF A LADY

Type of work: Novel
Author: Henry James (1843–1916)
Type of plot: Psychological realism
Time of plot: About 1875
Locale: England, France, Italy
First published: 1881

In this novel crowded with brilliantly subtle and penetrating character studies, James explores the ramifications of a naïve, young, high-minded American girl's first exposure and gradual acclimatization to the traditions and decadence of an older European culture. The reader follows step by step the mental processes of Isabel Archer as she gravitates away from the staunch and stuffy American, Caspar Goodwood, and her frail, intelligent, and devoted cousin Ralph Touchett, into a marriage with Gilbert Osmond, a worthless, tyrannical dilettante. The Portrait of a Lady *is an excellent example of the Jamesian technique of refracting life through the mind and temperament of an individual.*

Principal Characters

Isabel Archer, the heroine of the novel. Orphaned at an early age and an heiress, she uses her freedom to go to Europe to be educated in the arts of life lacking in her own country. She draws the interest and adoration of many people, all of whom feel that they can make a contribution to her growth, or at least can use her. Isabel is somewhat unworldly at the time of her marriage to Gilbert Osmond. After three years of resisting the social mold imposed on her by Osmond and his Roman ménage, Isabel faces a dilemma in which her intelligence and honesty vie with her sense of obligation. Sensitive to her own needs as well as to those of others, she is aware of the complicated future she faces.

Gilbert Osmond, an American expatriate. He finds in Rome an environment suited to his artistic taste and devotes his time and tastes solely to pleasing himself.

Madame Merle, Isabel's friend. Madame Merle was formerly Osmond's mistress and is the mother of his daughter Pansy.

A clever, vigorous woman of considerable perspicacity, she promotes Isabel's marriage to Osmond.

Ralph Touchett, Isabel's ailing cousin. He appreciates the fine qualities of Isabel's nature. Distressed by what he considers her disastrous marriage, he sees to it that his own and his father's estates come to Isabel.

Caspar Goodwood, Isabel's faithful American suitor. He has the simplicity and directness of American insight that Isabel is trying to supplement by her European "education." He does not understand why he fails with Isabel.

Lord Warburton, a friend of Ralph Touchett. Like all the other unsuccessful men in Isabel's life, he deeply admires the young American woman and is distressed by her marriage to Gilbert Osmond.

Henrietta Stackpole, an American journalist and a girlhood friend of Isabel.

Henrietta is, in her own right, an amusing picture of the sensation-seeking uncritical American intelligence ranging over the length and breadth of Europe. She is eager to "save" Isabel.

Pansy Osmond, the illegitimate daughter of Osmond and Madame Merle. Pansy is unaware of her situation, and she welcomes Isabel as her stepmother; she feels that in Isabel she has an ally, as indeed she has. Determined to endure gracefully what she must, she feels increasingly the strictures of her father's dictates.

Edward Rosier, a suitor for Pansy's hand. This kindly, pleasant man lacks means sufficient to meet Osmond's demands.

Countess Gemini, Osmond's sister. She is a woman who has been spoiled and corrupted by her European experience, and she finds Isabel's behavior almost boring in its simplicity. Several motives prompt her to tell Isabel about Osmond's first wife and his liaison with Madame Merle. She does not spare Isabel a clear picture of Osmond's lack of humanity.

Mrs. Touchett, Isabel's vigorous and sympathetic aunt. Mrs. Touchett is the one responsible for the invitation that brings Isabel to Europe and the world.

The Story

Isabel Archer, upon the death of her father, had been visited by her aunt, Mrs. Touchett. She proved so attractive to the older woman that Mrs. Touchett decided to give her the advantage of more cosmopolitan experience, and Isabel was quickly carried off to Europe so she might see something of the world of culture and fashion.

On the day the women arrived at the Touchett home in England, Isabel's sickly young cousin, Ralph Touchett, and his father were taking tea in the garden with their friend, Lord Warburton. When Isabel appeared, Warburton had been confessing to the two men his boredom and his distaste for his routine existence. The young nobleman was much taken with the American girl's grace and lively manner.

Isabel had barely settled at Gardencourt, her aunt's home, before she received a letter from an American friend, Henrietta Stackpole, a newspaper woman who was writing a series of articles on the sights of Europe. At Ralph's invitation, Henrietta went to Gardencourt to spend some time with Isabel and to obtain material for her writing.

Soon after Henrietta's arrival, Isabel heard from another American friend. Caspar Goodwood, a would-be suitor, had followed her abroad. Learning her whereabouts from Henrietta, he wrote to ask if he might see her. Isabel was much irked by his aggressiveness, and she decided not to answer his letter.

On the day she received the letter from Goodwood, Lord Warburton proposed to her. Not wishing to seem indifferent to the honor of his proposal, she asked for time to consider it. At last she decided she could not marry the young Englishman, for she wished to see considerably more of the world before she married. She was afraid that marriage to Warburton, although he was a model of kindness and thoughtfulness, would prove stifling.

Because Isabel had not seen London on her journey with Mrs. Touchett and since it was on Henrietta Stackpole's itinerary, the two young women, accompanied by Ralph Touchett, went to the capital. Henrietta quickly made the acquaintance of a Mr. Bantling, who undertook to squire her around. When Caspar Goodwood visited Isabel at her hotel, she again refused him, though his persistence made her agree that if he still wished to ask for her hand he might visit her again after two years had passed.

While the party was in London a telegram came from Gardencourt. Old Mr. Touchett was seriously ill of the gout, and his wife was much alarmed. Isabel and Ralph left on the afternoon train. Henrietta remained under the escort of her new friend.

During the time Mr. Touchett lay dying and his family was preoccupied, Isabel was forced to amuse herself with a new companion. Madame Merle, an old friend of Mrs. Touchett, had come to Gardencourt to spend a few days. She and Isabel, thrown together a great deal, exchanged many confidences. Isabel admired the older woman for her ability to amuse herself, for her skill at needlework, at painting, at the piano, and for her ability to accommodate herself to any social situation. On the other hand, Madame Merle spoke enviously of Isabel's youth and intelligence, lamenting the life which had left her, at middle age, a widow with no children and no visible success in life.

When her uncle died, he left Isabel, at her cousin's instigation, one-half of his fortune. Ralph, greatly impressed with his young kinswoman's brilliance, had persuaded his father that she should be given an opportunity to fly as far and as high as she might. For himself, he knew he could not live long because of his pulmonary illness, and his legacy was enough to let him live in comfort.

As quickly as she could, Mrs. Touchett sold her London house and took Isabel to Paris with her. Ralph went south for the winter to preserve what was left of his health. In Paris the new heiress was introduced to many of her aunt's friends among American expatriates, but she was not impressed. She thought their indolent lives worthy only of contempt. Meanwhile Henrietta and Mr. Bantling had arrived in Paris, and Isabel spent much time with them and Edward Rosier. She had known Rosier when both were children and she was traveling abroad with her father. Rosier was another dilettante, living on the income from his inheritance. He explained to Isabel that he could not return to his own country because there was no occupation there worthy of a gentleman.

In February Mrs. Touchett and her niece went to the Palazzo Crescentini, the Touchett house in Florence. They stopped on the way to see Ralph, who was staying in San Remo. In Florence they were joined once more by Madame Merle.

Unknown to Isabel or her aunt, Madame Merle also visted her friend, Gilbert Osmond, another American who lived in voluntary exile outside Florence with his art collection and his young, convent-bred daughter, Pansy. Madame Merle told Osmond of Isabel's arrival in Florence saying that as the heir to a fortune, Isabel would be a valuable addition to Osmond's collection.

The heiress who had rejected two worthy suitors did not refuse the third. She was quickly captivated by the charm of the sheltered life Gilbert Osmond had created for himself. Her friends were against the match. Henrietta Stackpole, who was inclined to favor Caspar Goodwood, was convinced that Osmond was interested only in Isabel's money, as was Isabel's aunt. Mrs. Touchett had requested Madame Merle, the good friend of both parties, to discover the state of their affections; she was convinced that Madame Merle could have prevented the match. Ralph Touchett was disappointed that his cousin should have fallen to the ground from her flight so quickly. Caspar Goodwood, learning of Isabel's intended marriage when he revisited her after the passage of the two years agreed upon, could not persuade her to reconsider her step. Isabel was indignant when he commented on the fact that she did not even know her intended husband's antecedents.

After her marriage to Gilbert Osmond, Isabel and her husband established their home in Rome, in a setting completely expressive of Osmond's tastes. Before three years had passed, Isabel began to realize that her friends had not been completely wrong in their objections to her marriage. Osmond's exquisite taste had made their home one of the most popular in Rome, but his ceaseless effort to press his wife into a mold, to make her a reflection of his own ideas, had not made their marriage one of the happiest.

He had succeeded in destroying a romance between Pansy and Edward Rosier, who had visited the girl's stepmother and found the daughter attractive. He had not succeeded, however, in contracting the match he desired between Pansy and Lord Warburton. Warburton had found Pansy as pleasing as Isabel had once been, but he had dropped his suit when he saw that the girl's affections lay with Rosier.

Ralph Touchett, his health growing steadily worse, gave up his wanderings on the continent and returned to Gardencourt to die. When Isabel received a telegram from his mother telling her that Ralph would like to see her before his death, she felt it her duty to go to Gardencourt at once. Osmond reacted to her wish as if it were a personal insult. He expected that, as his wife, Isabel would want to remain at his side, and that she would not disobey any wish of his. He also made it plain that he disliked Ralph.

In a state of turmoil after her conversation with her husband, Isabel met the Countess Gemini, Osmond's sister. The countess, visiting the Osmonds, had seen how matters lay between her brother and Isabel. An honest soul, she had felt more sympathy for her sister-in-law than for her brother. To comfort Isabel, she told her the story of Gilbert's past. After his first wife had died, he and Madame Merle had an affair that lasted six or seven years. During that time Madame Merle, a widow, had borne him a child, Pansy. Changing his residence, Osmond had been able to pretend to his new circle of friends that the original Mrs. Osmond had died in giving birth to the child.

With this news fresh in her mind, and still determined to go to England, Isabel stopped to say goodbye to Pansy, who was staying in a convent where her father had sent her to recuperate from her affair with Rosier. There, too, she met Madame Merle. Madame Merle, with her keen perception, had no difficulty realizing that Isabel knew her secret. When she remarked that Isabel would never need to see her again, that she would go to America, Isabel was certain Madame Merle would also find in America much to her own advantage.

Isabel was in time to see her cousin before his death. She stayed on briefly at Gardencourt after the funeral, long enough to bid goodbye to Lord Warburton, who had come to offer condolences to her aunt, and to reject a third offer from Caspar Goodwood, who knew of her husband's treatment. When she left to start her journey back to Italy, Isabel knew what she must do. Her first duty was not to herself, but to put her house in order.

Critical Evaluation

The Portrait of a Lady first appeared serially in England and America (*Macmillan's Magazine,* Oct., 1880-Nov., 1881; *Atlantic,* Nov., 1880-Dec., 1881); it was published as a book in 1881. Usually regarded as the major achievement of James's early period of fiction writing, *The Portrait of a Lady* is one of the great novels of modern literature. In it James demonstrates that he has learned well from two European masters of the novel. Turgenev had taught him how to use a single character who shapes the work and is seen throughout in relationship to various other characters. From George Eliot he had learned the importance of tightening the structure of the novel and giving the story an architectural or organic form which develops logically from the given materials. He advances in *The Portrait of a Lady* beyond George Eliot in minimizing his own authorial comments and analysis and permitting his heroine to be seen through her own tardily awakening self-realization and also through the consciousness of the men and women who are closest to her. Thus his "portrait" of a lady is one which slowly grows stroke by stroke as touches are added which bring out both highlights and shadows, until Isabel Archer stands before us at the end a woman whose experiences have brought her excitement, joy, pain, and knowledge and have given her an enduring beauty and dignity.

Isabel is one of James's finest creations and one of the most memorable women in the history of the novel. A number of sources have been suggested for her. She may have been partly drawn from James's cousin Mary ("Minny") Temple, whom he was later to immortalize as Milly Theale in *The Wings of the Dove.* She has been compared to two of George Eliot's heroines, Dorothea Brooke in *Middlemarch* and Gwendolen Harleth in *Daniel Deronda;* to Diana Belfield in an early romantic tale by James entitled "Longstaff's Marriage"; to Bathsheba Everdene in Thomas Hardy's *Far from the Madding Crowd;* and even to Henry James himself, some of whose early experiences closely parallel those of Isabel. Yet, though James may have drawn from both real and fictional people in portraying Isabel Archer, she possesses her own identity; she grew from James's original "conception of a certain young woman affronting her destiny," as he later wrote in his Preface to the novel. He visualized her as "an intelligent but presumptuous girl" who would yet be "complex" and who would be offered a series of opportunities for free choice in the affronting of that destiny. Because of her presumption that she knew more than she did about herself and the world, Isabel was to make mistakes, including the tragic error of misjudging the nature of Gilbert Osmond. But her intelligence, though it was not sufficient to save her from suffering, would enable her to achieve a moral triumph in the end.

Of the four men in Isabel's life, three love her and one uses her innocence to gain for himself what he would not otherwise have had. She refuses marriage to Lord Warburton because, though he offers her a great fortune, a title, an entry into English society, and an agreeable and entertaining personality, she believes she can do better. She turns down Caspar Goodwood, who also offers wealth, because she finds him stiff and she is frightened by his aggressiveness. Her cousin, Ralph Touchett, does not propose because he does not wish her to be tied to a man who daily faces death. She does not even suspect the extent of his love and adoration until she is almost overwhelmed by learning it just as death takes him from her. She accepts Gilbert Osmond because she is deceived by his calculated charm and because she believes that he deserves what she can offer him: first, a fortune that will make it possible for him to live in idleness but surrounded by the objects of the "culture" she believes he represents; and second, a mother's love and care for his supposedly motherless daughter. Half of the novel is given over to Isabel's living with, adjusting to, and, finally, triumphing over the disastrous choice she has made.

In his Preface, James uses an architectural figure to describe *The Portrait of a Lady*. He says the "large building" of the novel "came to be a square and spacious house." Much of what occurs in the novel does so in or near a series of houses each of which relates significantly to Isabel or to other characters. The action begins at Gardencourt, the Tudor English country house of Daniel Touchett which Isabel finds more beautiful than anything she has ever seen. The charm of the house is enhanced by its age and its natural setting beside the Thames above London. It contrasts greatly with the "old house at Albany, a large, square, double house" belonging to her grandmother which Isabel in her childhood had found romantic and in which she had indulged in dreams stimulated by her reading. Mrs. Touchett's taking Isabel from the Albany house to Gardencourt is a first step in her plan to "introduce her to the world." When Isabel visits Lockleigh, Lord Warburton's home, she sees it from the gardens as resembling "a castle in a legend," though inside it has been modernized. She does not view it as a home for herself, or its titled owner as her husband, despite the many advantages he offers.

The front of Gilbert Osmond's house in Florence is "imposing" but of "a somewhat uncommunicative character," a "mask." It symbolizes Osmond whose mask Isabel does not see through until she has married him. The last of the houses in *The Portrait of a Lady* is the Palazzo Roccanera, the Roman home of the Osmonds, which James first describes as "a kind of domestic fortress . . . which smelt of historic deeds, of crime and craft and violence." When Isabel later broods over it during her night-long meditation in Chapter 42, it is "the house of darkness, the house of dumbness, the house of suffocation."

We first see Isabel at Gardencourt on her visit with Mrs. Touchett, and it is here that she turns down the first of three proposals of marriage. It is fitting that also we should last see her here and by turns with each of the three men who have loved her. Asserting the independence on which she has so long prided herself, she has defied her imperious husband by going to England to see the dying Ralph, whose last words tell her that if she has been hated by Osmond she has been adored by her cousin. In a brief conversation with Lord Warburton after Ralph's death, Isabel turns down an invitation to visit him and his sisters at Lockleigh. Shortly afterward a scene six years earlier is reversed. Then she had sat on a rustic bench at Gardencourt and looked up from reading Caspar Goodwood's letter implying that he would come to England and propose to her—only to see and hear Warburton preparing to offer his own proposal. Now Caspar surprises her by appearing just after she has dismissed Warburton. There follows the one sexually passionate scene in the novel. In it Isabel has "an immense desire to appear to resist" the force of Caspar's argument that she should leave Osmond and turn to him. She pleads with streaming tears, "As you love me, as you pity me, leave me alone!" Defying her plea, Caspar kisses her:

> His kiss was like white lightning, a flash that spread, and spread again, and stayed; and it was extraordinarily as if, while she took it, she felt each thing in his hard manhood that had least pleased her, each aggressive fact of his face, his figure, his presence, justified of its intense identity and made one with this act of possession.

Caspar has possessed her for a moment only. "But when darkness returned she was free" and she flees into the house—and thence to Rome, as Caspar learns in the brief scene in London with Henrietta Stackpole which closes the novel.

James leaves the reader to conclude that Isabel's love for Pansy Osmond has principally determined her decision to continue enduring a marriage that she had freely—though so ignorantly and foolishly—chosen.

Bibliography

Anderson, Quentin. *The American Henry James.* New Brunswick, N.J.: Rutgers University Press, 1957, pp. 183–198. Reprinted in *The Merrill Studies in* The Portrait of a Lady. Edited by Lyall H. Powers. Columbus, Oh.: Merrill, 1970, pp. 67–79.

Cargill, Oscar. *The Novels of Henry James.* New York: Macmillan, 1961, pp. 78–119. Reprinted in *Perspectives on James's* Portrait of a Lady: *A Collection of Critical Essays.* Edited by William T. Stafford. New York: New York University Press, 1967, pp. 256–286.

Chase, Richard. *The American Novel and Its Tradition.* New York: Doubleday, 1957, pp. 117–137. Reprinted in *Critics on Henry James: Readings in Literary Criticism.* Edited by J. Don Vann. Coral Gables: University of Miami Press, 1972, pp. 89–94. Also reprinted in *Perspectives on James's* The Portrait of a Lady: *A Collection of Critical Essays.* Edited by William T. Stafford. New York: New York University Press, 1967, pp. 148–165.

Drew, Elizabeth. *The Novel: A Modern Guide to Fifteen English Masterpieces.* New York: Norton, 1963, pp. 224–244.

Eakin, Paul J. *The New England Girl: Cultural Ideals in Hawthorne, Stowe, Howells, and James.* Athens: University of Georgia Press, 1977, pp. 168–194.

Edel, Leon. *Henry James: The Conquest of London, 1870–1881.* Philadelphia: Lippincott, 1962, pp. 417–436. Reprinted in *The Merrill Studies in* The Portrait of a Lady. Edited by Lyall H. Powers. Columbus, Oh.: Merrill, 1970, pp. 94–105.

Edgar, Pelham. *Henry James: Man and Author.* Boston: Houghton Mifflin, 1956, pp. 245–255. Reprinted in *Twentieth Century Interpretations of* The Portrait of a Lady. Edited by Peter Buitenhuis. Englewood Cliffs, N.J.: Prentice-Hall, 1968, pp. 112–113.

Fryer, Judith. *The Faces of Eve: Women in the Nineteenth Century American Novel.* New York: Oxford University Press, 1976, pp. 126–142.

Galloway, David D. *Henry James:* The Portrait of a Lady. London: Edward Arnold, 1967.

Holland, Laurence B. *The Expense of Vision: Essays on the Craft of Henry James.* Princeton, N.J.: Princeton University Press, 1964, pp. 3–54. Reprinted in *The Portrait of a Lady.* Edited by Robert D. Bamberg. New York: Norton, 1975, pp. 730–741.

Kelley, Cornelia Pulsifer. *The Early Development of Henry James.* Urbana: University of Illinois Press, 1930, pp. 284–300. Reprinted in *Perspectives on James's* The Portrait of a Lady: *A Collection of Critical Essays.* Edited by William T. Stafford. New York: New York University Press, 1967, pp. 51–62.

Kettle, Arnold. "Henry James: *The Portrait of a Lady,*" in *An Introduction* *to the English Novel*, Volume II. London: Hutchinson's, 1953, pp. 13–34. Reprinted in *Perspectives on James's* The Portrait of a Lady: *A Collection of Critical Essays*. Edited by William T. Stafford. New York: New York University Press, 1967, pp. 91–112.

Krook, Dorothea. *The Ordeal of Consciousness in Henry James*. New York: Cambridge University Press, 1962, pp. 26–61, 357–369. Reprinted in *The Portrait of a Lady*. Edited by Robert D. Bamberg. New York: Norton, 1975, pp. 713–729.

Leavis, F.R. *The Great Tradition: George Eliot, Henry James, Joseph Conrad*. Garden City, N.Y.: Doubleday, 1954, pp. 155–187.

Matthiessen, F.O. *Henry James: The Major Phase*. New York: Oxford University Press, 1944, pp. 152–186.

Poirier, Richard. *The Comic Sense of Henry James*. London: Chatto and Windus, 1960, pp. 237–246. Reprinted in *The American Novel from James Fenimore Cooper to William Faulkner*. Edited by Wallace Stegner. New York: Basic Books, 1965, pp. 47–60.

Powers, Lyall H. "*The Portrait of a Lady*: The Eternal Mystery of Things," in *Nineteenth Century Fiction*. XIV (September, 1959), pp. 143–155.

Putt, S. Gorley. *Henry James: A Reader's Guide*. Ithaca, N.Y.: Cornell University Press, 1966, pp. 137–160.

Rahv, Philip. "The Heiress of all the Ages," in *Image and Idea: Fourteen Essays on Literary Themes*. New York: New Directions, 1957, pp. 51–76. Reprinted in *Perspectives on James's* The Portrait of a Lady: *A Collection of Critical Essays*. Edited by William T. Stafford. New York: New York University Press, 1967, pp. 139–147. Also reprinted in *The Merrill Studies in* The Portrait of a Lady. Edited by Lyall H. Powers. Columbus, Oh.: Merrill, 1970, pp. 19–27.

Roberts, James L. The Portrait of a Lady: *A Critical Study*. Lincoln: University of Nebraska Press, 1965.

Sharp, Sister M. Corona. *The Confidante in Henry James: Evolution and Moral Value of a Fictive Character*. Notre Dame, Ind.: University of Notre Dame Press, 1963, pp. 67–96.

Tanner, Tony. "The Fearful Self: Henry James's *The Portrait of a Lady*," in *Critical Quarterly*. VII (Autumn, 1965), pp. 205–219. Reprinted in *The Merrill Studies in* The Portrait of a Lady. Edited by Lyall H. Powers. Columbus, Oh.: Merrill, 1970, pp. 106–122. Also reprinted in *Henry James: Modern Judgments*. Edited by Tony Tanner. London: Macmillan, 1968, pp. 143–159. Also reprinted in *Twentieth Century Interpretations of* The Portrait of a Lady: *A Collection of Critical Essays*. Edited by Peter Buitenhuis. Englewood Cliffs, N.J.: Prentice-Hall, 1968, pp. 67–82.

Van Ghent, Dorothy. *"The Portrait of a Lady,"* in *The English Novel: Form and Function.* New York: Holt, Rinehart and Winston, 1953, pp. 211–228. Reprinted in *Critics on Henry James: Readings in Literary Criticism.* Edited by J. Don Vann. Coral Gables: University of Miami Press, 1972, pp. 83–85. Also reprinted in *Perspectives on James's* The Portrait of a Lady: *A Collection of Critical Essays.* Edited by William T. Stafford. New York: New York University Press, 1967, pp. 113–131.

Ward, J.A. *The Imagination of Disaster: Evil in the Fiction of Henry James.* Lincoln: University of Nebraska Press, 1961, pp. 44–55.

Wegelin, Christof. *The Image of Europe in the Fiction of Henry James.* Dallas: Southern Methodist University Press, 1958, pp. 63–78.

THE PRINCESS CASAMASSIMA

Type of work: Novel
Author: Henry James (1843–1916)
Type of plot: Social criticism
Time of plot: Late nineteenth century
Locale: London
First published: 1886

This novel takes up the later career of a character from an earlier work, Roderick Hudson, *which saw beautiful Christina Light married to the powerful Italian Prince Casamassima. The Princess, some ten years later, is now separated, and in* The Princess Casamassima *we follow her new life of social involvement with proletarian revolutionaries. James examines not only the motives of upper-class "reformers," but also the interaction between the world of princes and dukes and the world of bookbinders, dressmakers, and chemists.*

The Story

Florentine Vivier, a French dressmaker, gave birth to an illegitimate son and accused an Englishman, Lord Frederick Purvis, of being the boy's father. Because Lord Frederick and his family refused to recognize the baby, Florentine Vivier stabbed Lord Frederick to death, a crime for which she received the maximum prison sentence. Her son, called Hyacinth Robinson, she entrusted to another poor dressmaker, Miss Amanda Pynsent, who brought him up without telling him the unfortunate circumstances surrounding his birth.

Years later Mrs. Bowerbank, a prison matron, visited Miss Pynsent to tell her that Florentine Vivier was dying in the prison hospital and had asked to see her son, now ten years of age. Miss Pynsent consulted Mr. Vetch, a violinist in a Bloomsbury theater, who was her closest friend. On his advice she took Hyacinth to the prison. He did not know that the woman was his mother. The grim prison frightened him, and at first his mother spoke only in French, saying that she feared he was ashamed of her. She embraced him pitifully before the matron bustled the visitors away.

Years again passed. In the interval the rowdy family of Millicent Henning, the childhood friend of Hyacinth, had been ejected from their quarters next to Miss Pynsent's shop in Lomax Place. Mr. Vetch had a copy of Lord Bacon's *Essays* bound as a gift for Hyacinth and thus had met the master bookbinder Eustache Poupin, exiled from France after the Commune of 1871. Mr. Vetch learned that he and Poupin had a common bond of hate for the existing social and political fabric. Poupin secured for Hyacinth an apprenticeship with Crookenden's bookbindery and taught him French and socialism.

Millicent Henning, grown to a bold, handsome young woman, unexpectedly appeared once more in Lomax Place to renew her friendship with Hyacinth. Poupin introduced Paul Muniment to Hyacinth. Paul took him to visit his crippled sister, Rose Muniment, and there they met Lady Aurora Langrish, who devoted her time to caring for the poor and who admired Paul a great deal. She was a spinster much neglected by her large and wealthy family. Paul led Hyacinth more deeply into revolutionary activity. In the meantime Hyacinth had looked up the newspaper reports of his mother's trial, and he considered himself the aggrieved son of Lord Frederick Purvis.

Mr. Vetch got for Hyacinth tickets to take Millicent to see the play, *The Pearl of Paraguay*. Captain Godfrey Sholto, whom Hyacinth had met at a revolutionists' discussion group at "The Sun and Moon" public house, came from his box at the theater to invite Hyacinth to meet his companions, the Princess Casamassima and her old companion, Madame Grandoni.

Prince Casamassima tried to see the princess to beg her to return to living with him, but she refused to see him. As the prince was leaving her house, he saw Hyacinth ushered in, at the princess' invitation, to tea. Later, Hyacinth bound a copy of Tennyson as a gift for the princess, but when he tried to deliver his gift he learned that she had left London for a series of visits in the country. Hyacinth also encountered Captain Sholto in a bar and, as Sholto hurried him strangely along, they encountered Millicent. Hyacinth suspected that Millicent had arranged to meet Sholto.

Paul Muniment announced at a meeting at "The Sun and Moon" that the revolutionary organizer, Hoffendahl, who had spent twelve years in Prussian prisons, was in London. After Hyacinth declared his readiness to give his life for the cause, Paul took him to see Hoffendahl. There he swore an oath to perform an act of violence whenever Hoffendahl should send the order. Meanwhile, the princess had invited Hyacinth to stay at her country house, Medley. The princess was extremely pleasant and Hyacinth stayed on in the country. One day Captain Sholto rode up to Hyacinth as he was walking on the estate and asked Hyacinth to obtain an invitation to dinner for him. Clearly, Hyacinth had replaced Sholto as the princess' favorite.

He returned from Medley to find Miss Pynsent dying. In her will she left a small sum of money to him. Mr. Vetch added to this sum and advised Hyacinth to travel on the Continent. On his return, he heard that the princess had sold all her beautiful furnishings, moved to a tawdry, lower-middle-class house in Madeira Crescent, and become friendly with Paul Muniment, who was now deeply involved in revolutionary activities. In the meantime Hyacinth's own contact with wealth and leisure had made life seem more valuable and the society which produces and appreciates art more tolerable.

The prince followed the princess and observed her going out with Paul Muniment. He demanded that Madame Grandoni tell him what she was doing. As the prince left with Madame Grandoni, he met Hyacinth. While they were walking away from the house they saw Paul and the princess return and enter together. Madame Grandoni abandoned the princess. The prince wrote to Paul saying that he would send no more money to his wife.

At Poupin's Hyacinth found the German worker Schinkel with sealed orders for him. He was to go to a grand party and there assassinate a duke. Mr. Vetch tried to keep Hyacinth from doing some desperate action. Hyacinth went to the store where Millicent worked, only to find her talking to Captain Sholto. The princess, going to Hyacinth's room, found Schinkel waiting. She demanded that he break in. Inside, they find that Hyacinth had shot himself in the heart.

Critical Evaluation

The Princess Casamassima is James's most concerted effort to catch the revolutionary atmosphere of the London during the 1870's and 1880's. In his Preface to the novel he speaks of his awareness of political forces brewing beneath the vast surface of society. He did not know these forces in any intimate detail, however, and the novel shows it. His portraits of lower-class characters are solid enough (Hyacinth Robinson, Miss Pynsent, Mr. Vetch) and even brilliant (Millicent Henning).

The trouble lies in the portrayal of the revolutionaries. Paul Muniment, who introduces Hyacinth into revolutionary work is vague at the center. The famous revolutionary leader Hoffendahl does not even appear on stage; his "potency" is merely a felt presence. Nevertheless, James's political fable has its finenesses. The drama of Hyacinth's gradual awareness of what revolutionary behavior amounts to is superbly done. The little bookbinder finds that he has been used by Muniment and the Princess, and at the same time he discovers that he has become deeply attached to those objects of art possessed by the class he has been working to overturn. In his youthful idealism, he has been working against all he now respects and wishes to preserve. The irony here is compounded by the case of the Princess herself. Under the influence of Muniment and her own idealism she comes to repudiate her wealth and position at the very time Hyacinth aspires to the finer things to which she has introduced him. In the Princess, James gives us a vivid picture of the upper-class revolutionary—a person in full-fledged rebellion from her class. In contrast to Lady Aurora Langrish whose enthusiasm for the revolution fades when she discovers she cannot catch Paul Muniment, the Princess' revolutionary sympathies are not so easily dissipated. There is something about her seriousness which is cold and inhuman. She is a good portrait of a revolutionary fanatic and reactionary. Needless to say, for James revolutionary politics was not a pleasing spectacle.

Bibliography

Bogan, Louise. *Selected Criticism: Prose, Poetry.* New York: Noonday, 1955, pp. 112–121.

Cargill, Oscar. *The Novels of Henry James.* New York: Macmillan, 1961, pp. 146–173.

Cox, James M. "Henry James: The Politics of Internationalism," in *Southern Review.* VIII (July, 1972), pp. 493–506.

Dolan, Paul J. *Of War and War's Alarms: Fiction and Politics in the Modern World.* New York: Free Press, 1976, pp. 70–95.

Dubler, Walter. "*The Princess Casamassima*: Its Place in the James Canon," in *Modern Fiction Studies.* XII (Spring, 1966), pp. 44–60.

Dupee, F.W. *Henry James.* Garden City, N.Y.: Doubleday Anchor, 1956, pp. 132–140.

Edel, Leon. *Henry James: The Middle Years, 1882–1895.* Philadelphia: Lippincott, 1962, pp. 179–192.

Edgar, Pelham. *Henry James: Man and Author.* Boston: Houghton Mifflin, 1927, pp. 269–283.

Geismar, Maxwell. *Henry James and the Jacobites.* Boston: Houghton Mifflin, 1963, pp. 66–76.

Halliburton, D.G. "Self and Secularization in *The Princess Casamassima*," in *Modern Fiction Studies.* XI (Summer, 1965), pp. 116–128.

Hartsock, Mildred E. "*The Princess Casamassima*: The Politics of Power," in *Studies in the Novel.* I (Fall, 1969), pp. 297–309.

Harvey, William J. *Character and the Novel.* Ithaca, N.Y.: Cornell University Press, 1965, pp. 81–89.

Howe, Irving. "Henry James: The Political Vocation," in *Politics and the Novel.* New York: Horizon, 1957, pp. 139–156. Reprinted in *Henry James: A Collection of Critical Essays.* Edited by Leon Edel. Englewood Cliffs, N.J.: Prentice-Hall, 1963, pp. 156–171.

Kimmey, John L. "*The Princess Casamassima* and the Quality of Bewilderment," in *Nineteenth Century Fiction.* XXII (June, 1967), pp. 47–62.

Leyburn, Ellen Douglass. *The Strange Alloy: The Relation of Comedy to Tragedy in the Fiction of Henry James.* Chapel Hill: University of North Carolina Press, 1968, pp. 96–103, 121–130.

Lucas, William J. "Conservatism and Revolution in the 1880's," in *Literature and Politics in the Nineteenth Century.* London: Methuen, 1971, pp. 173–219.

McElderry, Bruce R., Jr. *Henry James.* New York: Twayne, 1965, pp. 68–72.

Monteiro, George. "The Campaign of Henry James's Disinherited Princess," in *English Studies.* XLV (December, 1964), pp. 442–454.

Oliver, Clinton F. "Henry James as a Social Critic," in *Antioch Review.* VII (June, 1947), pp. 243–258.

Putt, S. Gorley. *Henry James: A Reader's Guide.* Ithaca, N.Y.: Cornell University Press, 1966, pp. 163–178.

Swan, Michael. *Henry James.* London: Barker, 1952, pp. 66–74.

Tilley, W.H. *The Background of* The Princess Casamassima. Gainesville: University of Florida Press, 1960.

Trilling, Lionel. "*The Princess Casamassima,*" in *The Liberal Imagination.* New York: Viking, 1950, pp. 58–92. Reprinted in *Critics on Henry James: Readings in Literary Criticism.* Edited by J. Don Vann. Coral Gables: University of Miami Press, 1972, pp. 70–74. Also reprinted in *The Modern Critical Spectrum.* Edited by Gerald Jay Goldberg. Englewood Cliffs, N.J.: Prentice-Hall, 1962, pp. 134–155.

Ward, J.A. *The Search for Form: Studies in the Structure of James's Fiction.* Chapel Hill: University of North Carolina Press, 1967, pp. 114–140.

Woodcock, George. "Henry James and the Conspirators," in *Sewanee Review.* LX (Spring, 1952), pp. 219–229.

RODERICK HUDSON

Type of work: Novel
Author: Henry James (1843–1916)
Type of plot: Psychological realism
Time of plot: The 1870's
Locale: Chiefly Rome, also Florence and Switzerland
First published: 1876

In this early novel, Henry James presents themes and character types that were to be central to all his works. Most notable is the "international theme": the clash between the innocent, energetic, even vulgar American and the beautiful, complex, sometimes decadent European milieu. Also in Roderick Hudson, *James develops the character of the artist whose talents and passions carry the possibilities of both brilliant creativity and tragic self-destruction.*

The Story

Rowland Mallet, expecting to sail for Europe in September, visited his cousin Cecilia in Northampton, Massachusetts. He was an idle bachelor, having inherited money, and he felt that he was leading a useless life. Having a passion for art, he was interested to learn of a young sculptor who lived in the town. On meeting the intense, impetuous Roderick Hudson and seeing proof of his talent, he offered to subsidize the young artist for a period of study in Rome. Rowland gained the assent of Hudson's widowed mother. At a farewell picnic Rowland had a last talk with Mary Garland, distant cousin of Mrs. Hudson, who had been visiting in Northampton. Rowland realized that he would not see her for perhaps three years. In their brief acquaintance she had come to mean a great deal to him. But on the Atlantic voyage Roderick Hudson told Rowland that he was engaged to Mary.

In Rome that autumn, as Rowland had expected, Roderick responded to the stimulus provided by the art treasures of the city. He assimilated experience readily and became eager to create masterpieces of his own. Rowland was pleased with his role as patron and nourisher of talent.

One day, while Roderick sat sketching in the Villa Ludovisi, the two companions observed a trio of passers-by—a shabbily-appearing man, a middle-aged woman, and a young girl with blue eyes, dusky hair, and perfect features. Roderick was enraptured and yearned to model her. But they did not stop.

Rowland began to introduce Roderick into society. The young and handsome sculptor, attractively impertinent and strident, became a favorite. He spent the days hard at work and the nights in Roman drawing rooms. His first work, a life-sized Adam, drew admirers to his studio. Among them were another sculptor, Gloriani, and a young American painter, Sam Singleton. Gloriani was skeptical of Roderick's staying power, while Singleton was an uncritical worshiper. Roderick frequently grew lyrical about his own brilliant future.

But the onset of summer brought Roderick to an impasse. His exuberance and inspiration departed. Rowland Mallet prescribed a change of scenery, and the two left Rome to ramble northward. Roderick desired to spend most of the summer alone.

In England, after a month with no word from Roderick, Rowland dispatched a letter. The reply was unsettling; Roderick had been gambling and was heavily in debt. When the two friends met in Geneva, Roderick admitted debauchery but felt no remorse. He had learned his susceptibility to the beauty and mystery of women.

Back in Rome, Roderick was discontented and worked only by fits and starts. Then one day into his studio burst the man and woman and the beautiful young girl whom he had observed in the Ludovisi gardens. Madame Light, her daughter Christina, and the Cavaliere Giacosa, had come to see the rising young sculptor and his works. Roderick insisted he must do a bust of Christina.

Mrs. Light was a vain, silly widow. She had picked up the old Cavaliere in her European ramblings and now lived solely to marry Christina to a fortune. Christina's beauty was supplemented by wit, will, and education.

During the winter Roderick worked on his bust of Christina and became enamored of her. Rowland feared her influence on him. She seemed selfish and vicious, a complex person who demanded worship. Meanwhile Christina's mother was becoming established in Roman society. Roderick took a commission from an American snob to create in marble the idea of Intellectual Refinement.

The old Cavaliere became Rowland's confidant. Roderick would find his love unrequited, he said. Mrs. Light was determined that Christina should marry a man of wealth and position. Though Rowland and Christina disliked each other, they achieved a certain understanding. Christina confessed that she despised her own egotism and longed for someone to free her from herself. Roderick's adoration continued.

In an effort to cool the relationship, Rowland informed Christina of Roderick's engagement. Roderick's subsequent anger revealed something to Rowland: his friend lacked a feeling heart; he did not mind hurting Mary. Rowland's faith in Roderick's potential had been foolish. The artistic temperament was amoral.

Winter brought a new personage on the scene. Prince Casamassima was seen with the Light entourage. He was Mrs. Light's choice for Christina.

Rowland encountered Christina at various places in Rome, and their exchange of frank confidences continued. Rowland requested her to leave Roderick alone. She seemed to desire Rowland's respect, but when she left Rome briefly, Roderick followed.

Despite Roderick's interlude of riotous living in Naples, Rowland's fondness for him was undiminished. Even when he stopped work on Intellectual Refinement, Rowland tried to understand.

Christina's engagement to Prince Cassmassima was announced, but Roderick continued his pursuit. Rowland admitted himself disgusted with people. His good deed had turned sour; Mrs. Hudson and Mary Garland would be hurt to learn the truth about Roderick. His thoughts kept going back to Mary.

Hoping to save the situation he cabled for Mrs. Hudson and Mary. Roderick greeted Mary in a state of drunkenness. To Rowland she was more attractive than before.

Although Christina's wedding date was set for June, Roderick's infatuation continued. Rowland was astonished to learn from Madame Grandoni that his own love for Mary Garland was perfectly evident. Then Christina broke off with the prince. Roderick isolated himself in his quarters for a week to contemplate this good fortune. Mrs. Light summoned Rowland to talk sense to Christina. Mrs. Hudson and Mary, still unaware of the complex situation, suffered in silence.

Rowland unwillingly conversed with Christina. Although Prince Casamassima's money did not excite her, she refused to accept Roderick's proposal of marriage. Three days later Christina and the prince were suddenly and privately married. Simultaneously a secret came to light: Christina's father had been Mrs. Light's lover, the Cavaliere. Christina had married quickly, before such a scandal could cause the prince to break with her.

Roderick, angry, disappointed, miserable, was ready to leave Rome. He placed himself entirely in Rowland's hands. Rowland agreed when Roderick confessed to his mother and Mary that he was a failure. Mrs. Hudson was appalled to learn that the uncompleted Intellectual Refinement was a $5,000 commission.

They all went to Florence for the summer. Rowland vaguely hoped that Roderick could still pull himself together. Rowland admired Mary more and more. After an idle, dreary summer they moved on to Switzerland. Roderick's perceptions of beauty were as acute as ever, but he was unable to do anything constructive.

Rowland pressed the point about Roderick's engagement. Mary did not interest him, but he did not break off. Roderick saw no point in Rowland's desire to keep secret his admiration for Mary.

In one of their daily rambles, Roderick and Rowland encountered the Prince and Princess Casamassima. Christina detested her husband. Hitherto petulant and unforgiving of her, Roderick turned to pursuit again. The next day he asked Rowland for one thousand francs to meet her at Interlaken. He got some money from Mary when Rowland, at the end of patience, refused the request. He chided Rowland for moralizing, but Rowland admitted his love for Mary.

Roderick then disappeared. A spectacular mountain thunderstorm arose in the afternoon. He had not returned by dawn the next day. Sam Singleton, who had been diligently sketching all the while Roderick had idled, had stopped for a visit. He and Rowland went to look for Roderick. His body lay beneath a high cliff three hours' walk from the inn. He had fallen, apparently, on his way to Interlaken.

Mrs. Hudson and Mary Garland went back to Northampton. Rowland, with his inexhaustible patience, frequently came to call on Mary.

Critical Evaluation

This novel opened one of the richest and most complicated careers in American literature. Themes and devices which James was to employ over and over again are used in *Roderick Hudson* for the first time.

Roderick Hudson may, of course, be viewed as a signal achievement of American literary independence, as a reflection of the clash between the old world and the new, or as a story of the corruption of innocence by decadence. It is also important to note that *Roderick Hudson* has an artist as its central character. The novel asks what it takes for an American artist to survive as a creative talent. For James, always self-conscious in his role as an artist, and especially an American artist, this was a pressing question. So James's first novel, then, may be considered in many ways as a catalogue of temptations, temptations which must be resisted if an artist is to survive and succeed.

It is Roderick's egoism and self-absorption that are ultimately fatal. In order to develop his talent he must be exposed to the cultural experiences of the civilizations of Europe. At the same time, his selfishness makes him vulnerable to the temptation of Christina Light, and especially to the temptation of possessing her. Plunging into relationships in Europe separates Roderick from the healthy, stabilizing American influence of Mary Garland.

James argues that unless an American artist is able to preserve a certain simplicity and honesty, qualities associated with American civilization, he will be distracted and finally destroyed as a talent by European decadence. At the same time it is clear from Rowland Mallet's experience, and the experiences of others like him in later works by James, that creative accomplishment also requires a sense of daring and risk. The unwillingness or inability to take those risks also dooms talent.

In *Roderick Hudson,* then, it is balance and poise which are crucial for artistic survival. One may also conclude that *Roderick Hudson* is not merely a prescription for survival in general, but expresses James's strategy and hope for himself and reveals those temptations he felt were dangerous for his own development.

Bibliography

Beach, Joseph Warren. *The Method of Henry James.* Philadelphia: Albert Saifer, 1954, pp. 191–199.

Bewley, Marius. "Henry James and 'Life,' " in *Hudson Review.* XI (Summer, 1958), pp. 167–185.

Bowden, Edwin T. *The Themes of Henry James.* New Haven, Conn.: Yale University Press, 1956, pp. 24–28.

Cargill, Oscar. *The Novels of Henry James.* New York: Macmillan, 1961, pp. 19–40.

Conn, Peter J. "Roderick Hudson: The Role of the Observer," in *Nineteenth Century Fiction.* XXVI (1971–72), pp. 65–82.

Daiches, David. "Sensibility and Technique (Preface to a Critique)," in *Kenyon Review.* V (Autumn, 1943), pp. 569–579.

Dunbar, Viola R. "The Problem of *Roderick Hudson*," in *Modern Language Notes.* LXVII (February, 1952), pp. 109–113.

Edel, Leon. *The Unknown Distance: From Consciousness to Conscience, Goethe to Camus.* Cambridge, Mass.: Harvard University Press, 1972, pp. 154–172.

Edgar, Pelham. *Henry James: Man and Author.* Boston: Houghton Mifflin, 1927, pp. 232–237.

Geismar, Maxwell. *Henry James and the Jacobites.* Boston: Houghton Mifflin, 1963, pp. 19–22.

Graham, Kenneth. "*Roderick Hudson*: Tragedy of the Will," in *Henry James: The Drama of Fulfillment, an Approach to the Novels.* Oxford: Clarendon Press, 1975, pp. 29–57.

Hoffman, Frederick J. *The Mortal No: Death and the Modern Imagination.* Princeton, N.J.: Princeton University Press, 1964, pp. 41–50.

Jefferson, D.W. *Henry James.* Edinburgh: Oliver and Boyd, 1960, pp. 22–26.

Kelley, Cornelia Pulsifer. *The Early Development of Henry James.* Urbana: University of Illinois Press, 1930, pp. 182–194.

Leavis, F.R. "Henry James's First Novel," in *Scrutiny.* XIV (September, 1947), pp. 235–301.

Leyburn, Ellen Douglass. *The Strange Alloy: The Relation of Comedy to Tragedy in the Fiction of Henry James.* Chapel Hill: University of North Carolina Press, 1968, pp. 11–20.

McElderry, Bruce R., Jr. *Henry James.* New York: Twayne, 1965, pp. 41–44.

Nettels, Elsa. "Action and Point of View in *Roderick Hudson*," in *English Studies.* LIII (June, 1972), pp. 238–247.

Poirier, Richard. *The Comic Sense of Henry James: A Study of the Early Novels.* New York: Oxford University Press, 1960, pp. 11–43.

Putt, S. Gorley. *Henry James: A Reader's Guide.* Ithaca, N.Y.: Cornell University Press, 1966, pp. 94–100.

Scherting, John. "*Roderick Hudson*: A Re-evaluation," in *Arizona Quarterly.* XXV (Summer, 1969), pp. 101–119.

Speck, Paul. "A Structural Analysis of James's *Roderick Hudson*," in *Studies in the Novel.* II (Autumn, 1970), pp. 292–305.

Spender, Stephen. *The Destructive Element.* London: Jonathan Cape, 1935, pp. 26–32.

Taylor, Gordon O.   *The Passages of Thought: Psychological Representation in the American Novel, 1870–1900.* New York: Oxford University Press, 1969, pp. 42–84.

Weinstein, Philip M.   "The Romantic and the Real: Beliefs and Roles in *Roderick Hudson,*" in *Henry James and the Requirements of the Imagination.* Cambridge, Mass.: Harvard University Press, 1971, pp. 8–30.

THE SACRED FOUNT

Type of work: Novel
Author: Henry James (1843–1916)
Time: The 1890's
Locale: Newmarch, a British country estate, and the train from Paddington Station to Newmarch
First published: 1901

Essay-Review

To the mystification engendered by the late novels of Henry James possibly no work has contributed more spectacularly than *The Sacred Fount*, that relatively slight book which falls between the weightier *The Awkward Age* and *The Ambassadors.* The elaborate account of a weekend guest's attempt to fathom the relations existing among his fellow guests, the novel baffles in no small part because it is as short on facts—that Mrs. Server has "none too much money" and has lost three children, and that Ford Obert is a painter are virtually the only ones to which the reader is treated—as it is long on speculation, so much so that the very concept of "fact" comes under question. James has in this, more than in any other of his novels, ruthlessly stripped away those historical and environmental encrustations which we ordinarily read for clues to character, in order to concentrate on those relationships which for the book's narrator are alone telling, if ultimately untold. That the narrator's speculations are finally refutable or, worse, uncorroborable is perhaps the ultimate mystification, one compounded even further by James's feat in casting the ironic spotlight on this his sole novelistic first person narrator (and hence our only source of information, other than reproduced dialogue) in order to call both his motivation and his interpretation into question. Yet this extraordinarily modern opacity of the novel anticipates Robbe-Grillet, even, if antithetically and is hardly attributable, as has often been said, to a failure of James's imagination. For the book is itself about the failure of the imagination. It is the fullest, wittiest, and darkest development of that breakdown of consciousness which hovers behind all the major James works and its opacity is only the lucid rendering of such a subject.

The Sacred Fount begins as the nameless narrator, said by many critics to be a novelist—although the only evidence for his being so is the curiosity of the typical Jamesian observer—encounters two former acquaintances, Gilbert Long and Grace Brissenden, both of whom are also going to the party at Newmarch, and both of whom appear to him considerably changed. Long, who has previously struck him as a handsome clod, seems suddenly to have become clever, and Mrs. Brissenden, who is supposedly at least forty, seems to have grown younger, or at least not to have aged. In conversation with Mrs. Briss, as she is called, the narrator receives the *donnée* for what is to become his theory, that Gilbert Long's intellectual improvement is the result of his having entered into relation with a clever woman, identified by Mrs. Briss as Lady John, another guest at Newmarch, who is coming on a later train with Guy Brissenden, her screen, as that gentleman's wife intimates, for her affair with Long.

Arriving at the party, the narrator fails, just as he has initially failed in the case of the wife, to recognize Guy Brissenden, who, though only in his late twenties, looks older now than his wife—appears, in fact, "quite sixty." This discovery completes his theory that as one party to a relationship gains, either physically or intellectually, the other loses, is drained by the "sacrificer" until quite depleted, a theory which he communicates to Ford Obert, who has assumed Mrs. Briss to be considerably younger than her husband.

The remainder of the novel details the narrator's attempts to corroborate his theory. His discovery that Lady John is as witty, and superficial, as ever leads him to reject her, in a conversation with Mrs. Briss, as Long's "victim," for the partner to such a relationship would of necessity lack her former attributes. At this juncture the two conspirators discover in colloquy two figures who prove to be Briss and May Server, and the latter presumably using Briss as a screen, just as Lady John was formerly said to have done. Mrs. Briss happily lights upon her as the very woman for whom they have been looking to serve as the replacement for the now unacceptable Lady John. Mrs. Server is "all over the place," flitting from man to man in an attempt to mask the loss of her faculties, Mrs. Briss confides to the narrator in their next interview (which is their last, save for the extraordinary showdown between the two which occupies the book's last three chapters), and her description tallies remarkably with that given the narrator by Ford Obert, who sees Mrs. Server greatly changed from the self-possessed woman she was when she sat for him to have her portrait painted. By this time the narrator, on the grounds of both Mrs. Briss's and Obert's testimony and of an encounter with Mrs. Server herself, has come around to accepting Mrs. Briss's account, but his tender feeling for Mrs. Server, his sense that he and his collaborator are poking into a matter which is none of their business, and perhaps also his pique that Mrs. Briss is beating him at his own game, prevent him from acknowledging to her fully the degree of conviction to which she has brought him around.

The amount of data with which the narrator is confronted becomes prodigious, but the theory expands to accommodate all of it: Lady John makes up to Briss to conceal the fact that she is in love with Long; Mrs. Server's single appearance with Long (the point is actually made by Mrs. Briss) is the exception which proves the rule; Mrs. Server's avoidance of the narrator, out of all the men at the party, indicates her awareness that he is on to her predicament (it never strikes him that she may find his patent inquisitiveness obnoxious); and Mrs. Server's frequent juxtaposition with Briss is less Mrs. Briss's postulated screen than the mutual tacit commiseration of the two victims, each conscious of the other's depletion (it has been the narrator's hypothesis that the two victims know while the two victimizers do not). A conversation with Briss, who tells the narrator that

Mrs. Server has nothing to say and confesses a certain terror of, and yet fascination with, her, confirms his view of their condition and mutual relation—even
though Briss's confusion might as easily be sincere, and Mrs. Server's evidently
morbid state attributable to the loss of her three children. Briss, however, may be
covering an actual affair which he is having with Mrs. Server and which prompts
him to send Briss off in pursuit of her. In the next scene the narrator himself
engages in talk with Mrs. Server, hinting in a veiled manner at her relation with
Briss and gleaning that she takes comfort in his awareness of her plight and his
tolerant sympathy. Mrs. Server's participation in the dialogue is, however, so
vague and so slight (most of the chapter is simply given up to the narrator's
ruminations on the scene's meaning) that the reader can take it as evidence of
everything or nothing.

In the ensuing scene Lady John confronts the narrator with the fact that his
supersubtlety and passion for reading meanings into everything have the rest of
the company in mortal terror, and she chastises him for sending Briss off to Mrs.
Server when it is perfectly obvious to everyone with what loathing she inspires
him. The narrator, in an elaborate subterfuge, attempts to convince Lady John
that as Long is in love with her and he himself with Mrs. Server, she ought to
relinquish Briss so that the narrator might at least have the pleasure of seeing the
woman he loves, Mrs. Server, get the man she loves, Briss. Their conversation is
halted when they see Mrs. Briss and Long deep in talk, a fact which leads the
narrator to speculate that Lady John benightedly and jealously conceives a liaison between the two, whereas he, by dint of his "superior wisdom," knows them
now to have come to a knowledge, and by the very agency of his inquiries, of their
"bloated" or victimizing conditions, and to be joining together for mutual protection. As their talk ends, Mrs. Briss approaches him and briefly informs him that
she wishes to speak to him later in the evening, after the other guests have
retired.

From here on the narrator's theory begins to crumble into myriad shards. First
Ford Obert appears to inform him that Mrs. Server is no longer in her drained
condition and that the man, whoever he may be, is out of the question since she
has given him up. To top this blow, Mrs. Briss arrives to demolish what is left of
the narrator's theory. There is nothing in what he says, she informs him, and she
has speculated along his lines only under his spell. Mrs. Server is not the woman
because there is no woman. Gilbert Long, as her conversation with him has amply
testified, is as stupid as he ever had been. As a matter of fact, he and Lady John
are lovers, a fact which squares perfectly with his theory because she is not
drained (there being very little to drain) nor he improved. Moreover, she has it
from Briss that Lady John and Long are intimate. What the narrator has thought
he has seen is simply his insanity. Finally, to clinch her argument, to explain, in
fact, her wriggling and self-contradiction throughout the course of the interview,
Mrs. Server has not been using Briss as a screen; she has—and this from Briss's
own lips—been making love to him. Also, Mrs. Server is sharply perceptive. At

the narrator's amazed gasp, Mrs. Briss asks if that was not the very thing he had maintained. She then tells him he is crazy and bids him goodnight! And on this the narrator can only wanly observe that she has had the last word.

The facts toward which the narrator works, then, are finally unknowable. Whether Mrs. Briss is at the end telling the truth, lying in collusion with Long to protect their status in the sacred fount relationships to which they are parties, or attempting to shield the fact that she is actually carrying on an affair with Long, cannot be resolved. Pointing toward the last interpretation are the "facts" that Mrs. Briss and Long happened to be on the same train for Newmarch, that Briss had been placed in bachelor quarters, the latter a circumstance peculiarly at odds with the narrator's belief that his wife's draining him is sexual in origin.

Such evidence is, like the rest in the book, more suggestive than conclusive. It is interesting to note that both Mrs. Briss and Long broach to the narrator the improvement in the other and that his theory thus receives its impetus and codification in terms which they provide but which she will, later, take great pains to deny. Even more interesting, perhaps, is the fact that the narrator's sense of Long's improvement stems from Long's cordially recognizing him instead of, as is his habit, snubbing him. Here is an indication of the tenuous and egotistical base upon which the entire theory possibly rests, especially as, outside of Mrs. Briss's initial testimony, there is no external evidence whatsoever of Long's presumed metamorphosis. Add to these a propensity and necessity to lie, surely almost as great on the part of the other characters as on the narrator's, and any theory as to the relations at Newmarch collapses because it is incapable of accommodating all the possibilities invoked.

What remains, then, is the discrimination between the narrator's method and Mrs. Briss's tone, his method itself the very preclusion of his sharing her tone, which is that of involvement in his theory. Not only is the possibility of participation in life as coincident with artistic creation called into question, but also art's validity in its own terms, for the novel's end relegates art and the creative imagination to the realm of delusion and madness, containing within themselves the principle of their own destruction.

The narrator is an example of the Jamesian creative imagination, reduced in this case to absurdity, and his theory a type of the work of art, the inclusive imaginative construct. Before his interview with Mrs. Server, the would-be ultimate test of his theory, he pictures himself at the center of the imaginative vision, where possibility looms in every direction and symmetry is achieved. His passion for symmetry even leads him to postulate that should Gilbert Long change back to his old condition Mrs. Briss would, in exemplification of the same law, change back too. But the inclusive theory must rest on exclusive facts, and the narrator, working inductively from presumed effect to presumptive cause which exemplifies a general law, must depend upon particulars which exclude other possibilities and alternative hypotheses. To be inclusive in application, the theory must be exclusive in exemplification. The antinomy is present in most of James's fiction and in the Prefaces, but in *The Sacred Fount* it receives its most desperate turn, for not only is the imaginative construct necessarily subject to limitation, but its relevance to actuality is unknowable, perhaps a phantasm.

If, however, the limitations of artistic creation can be construed as analogous to those of actively living, the narrator's theory may be viewed as in some way figuring his own state. Early in the novel Grace Brissenden tells him that he has affected her quite as Mrs. Server has affected Mr. Long, and at the end he feels totally drained by her. This ironic application of the book's central image may be variously interpreted: perhaps Mrs. Briss is draining him by leading him totally astray; more likely, however, the efforts of the creative imagination drain him of vitality, rendering him incapable of life, and, conversely, his imaginative strength is sapped in the presence of Mrs. Briss, life's indelicate child. Life is the sacred fount for art, but art is divergent from life. At one point the narrator confesses that it would have been as embarrassing to reveal how little he knew of experience as it would have been to tell how much he had lived in fancy. He might well be summing up his entire condition, the condition of being thoroughly out of things, for which he tries to compensate in his hypothetical feeling for Mrs. Server.

In a much discussed scene early in the novel, the narrator and Mrs. Server pronounce antithetical views of a portrait of a young man holding what is presumably a mask. The scene is a nicely comic version—comic because, though his intent is to draw from Long a brilliant commentary which will corroborate his theory, the narrator proves himself so garrulous that Long is unable to get a word in—of the doubloon chapter of *Moby Dick* in that the external object, in this case an aesthetic object, is merely the receptacle for a solipsistic projection of individual consciousness. The narrator sees the mask, the work of art, as creating life, giving it meaning, but the book's final view is already latent here, that of the impossibility of ultimate knowledge or absolute meaning. Meaning is relational to the individual consciousness, and the creative consciousness collapses at the end a method without meaning, a form without content. The "palace of thought" crumbles a "house of cards," not necessarily under pressure from the truth but of internal necessity. For his is the "imagination of atrocity" of which Lady John has accused him, atrocity which of its own nature it necessarily wreaks upon itself. If there is a Sacred Fount, it is inaccessible to the narrator, and his vision perishes of its own aridity and impossibility.

Bibliography

Beebe, Maurice. *Ivory Towers and Sacred Founts: The Artist as Hero in Fiction from Goethe to Joyce.* New York: New York University Press, 1964, pp. 197–231.

Blackall, Jean F. *Jamesian Ambiguity and* The Sacred Fount. Ithaca, N.Y.: Cornell University Press, 1965.

Blackmur, R.P. *"The Sacred Fount,"* in *Kenyon Review.* IV (Autumn, 1942), pp. 328–352.

Brooks, Van Wyck. *The Pilgrimage of Henry James.* New York: Octagon, 1972, pp. 88–105.

Cargill, Oscar. *The Novels of Henry James.* New York: Macmillan, 1961, pp. 280–299.

Edel, Leon. *Henry James: The Treacherous Years, 1895–1901.* Philadelphia: Lippincott, 1969, pp. 338–350.

Edgar, Pelham. *Henry James: Man and Author.* Boston: Houghton Mifflin, 1927, pp. 144–148.

Finkelstein, Sidney. "The 'Mystery' of Henry James's *The Sacred Fount,*" in *Massachusetts Review.* III (Summer, 1962), pp. 753–776.

Folsom, James K. "Archimago's Well: An Interpretation of *The Sacred Fount,*" in *Modern Fiction Studies.* VII (Summer, 1961), pp. 136–145.

Geismar, Maxwell. *Henry James and the Jacobites.* Boston: Houghton Mifflin, 1963, pp. 197–218.

Holland, Laurence B. *The Expense of Vision: Essays on the Craft of Henry James.* Princeton, N.J.: Princeton University Press, 1964, pp. 183–226.

Isle, Walter. *Experiments in Form: Henry James's Novels, 1896–1901.* Cambridge, Mass.: Harvard University Press, 1968, pp. 205–233.

Jefferson, D.W. *Henry James and the Modern Reader.* New York: St. Martin's, 1964, pp. 176–187.

Krook, Dorothea. *The Ordeal of Consciousness in Henry James.* New York: Cambridge University Press, 1962, pp. 167–194.

Lebowitz, Naomi. *The Imagination of Loving: Henry James's Legacy to the Novel.* Detroit: Wayne State University Press, 1965, pp. 119–129.

Levy, Leo B. "What Does *The Sacred Fount* Mean?" in *College English.* XXIII (February, 1962), pp. 381–384.

Macnaughton, W.R. "The Narrator in Henry James's *The Sacred Fount,*" in *Literature and Ideas in America: Essays in Memory of Harry Hayden Clark.* Edited by Robert Falk. Athens: Ohio University Press, 1975, pp. 155–181.

Ozick, Cynthia. "The Jamesian Parable: *The Sacred Fount,*" in *Bucknell Review.* XI (May, 1963), pp. 55–70.

Putt, S. Gorley. *Henry James: A Reader's Guide.* Ithaca, N.Y.: Cornell University Press, 1966, pp. 258–262.

Samuels, Charles Thomas. *The Ambiguity of Henry James.* Urbana: University of Illinois Press, 1971, pp. 25–39.

Stein, William Bysshe. "*The Sacred Fount*: The Poetics of Nothing," in *Criticism*. XIV (Fall, 1972), pp. 373–389.

Tanner, Tony. *The Reign of Wonder: Naivety and Reality in American Literature*. New York: Cambridge University Press, 1965, pp. 319–331.

Weinstein, Philip M. "The Exploitative and Protective Imagination: Aspects of the Artist in *The Sacred Fount*," in *Henry James and the Requirements of the Imagination*. Cambridge, Mass.: Harvard University Press, 1971, pp. 97–120.

————. "The Exploitative and Protective Imagination: Unreliable Narration in *The Sacred Fount*," in *The Interpretation of Narrative: Theory and Practice*. Edited by Morton W. Bloomfield. Cambridge, Mass.: Harvard University Press, 1970, pp. 189–209.

Wiesenfarth, Joseph. "*The Sacred Fount* and the Perspective Achievement," in *Henry James and the Dramatic Analogy: A Study of the Major Novels of the Middle Period*. New York: Fordham University Press, 1963, pp. 96–111.

THE SPOILS OF POYNTON

Type of work: Novel
Author: Henry James (1843–1916)
Type of plot: Social morality
Time of plot: Late nineteenth century
Locale: England
First published: 1897

A finely perceived psychological novel written during the middle period of James's career, The Spoils of Poynton *turns upon the theme of conflicting values— material as opposed to moral—as they affect the acquisition both of property and love rights.*

Principal Characters

Mrs. Gereth, the mistress of Poynton. During her husband's lifetime, she and Mr. Gereth had filled Poynton with carefully chosen, exquisite furnishings that had made her beloved house a place of beauty and charm. Apprehensive over the fate of her cherished objects in the hands of Poynton's heir, her insensitive son Owen, she attempts to manipulate his relationships to guarantee the preservation of the estate and its contents as they are, only to see the house and furnishings finally consumed by fire.

Owen Gereth, Mrs. Gereth's son and the heir to Poynton. Insensitive to the real beauty of Poynton but loving it as his home, he is torn, abetted by his mother's manipulations, between Mona Brigstock, who desires the house for the value of its contents, and Fleda Vetch, who loves it for its beauty. He marries Mona and loses Poynton in a fire.

Mona Brigstock, Owen Gereth's fiancée and later his wife. Although she fails to appreciate Poynton's beauty, she is fully aware of the value of its contents. Finally, triumphant over the manipulations of Mrs. Gereth, she marries Owen shortly before Poynton and its contents are lost in a fire.

Fleda Vetch, Mrs. Gereth's companion. Loving Poynton for the beauty of the place, she is chosen by Mrs. Gereth as a suitable wife for her son Owen, the heir to Poynton. Fleda falls in love with Owen but loses him to Mona Brigstock.

The Story

While visiting one weekend at Waterbath, the country house of the Brigstock family, Mrs. Gereth met and was immediately drawn to a young woman named Fleda Vetch. The basis of the attraction was a mutual sensitiveness to beautiful things; each guessed that the other possessed such a feeling when they met one morning while obviously trying to escape the house and the rest of the party. Their aversion was caused not by the fact that Waterbath was exceptionally ugly, but rather because it was so very ordinary while pretending to be lovely. The house and the garden might have been quite attractive, and should have been so, but the Brigstocks, people without even a hint of feeling or taste, had had everything done over to fit the very latest fashion. It was this air of fashionable conformity that Fleda and Mrs. Gereth objected to. They recognized what the estate would have been naturally, and they could only be repulsed by what it had become.

Mrs. Gereth's horror of Waterbath was particularly acute because of the comparison she inevitably made between it and her own home at Poynton. Everything at Poynton was exquisite. She and her late husband had gradually furnished it after years of scraping and saving so that they might have the best. Every article in the house had been carefully chosen during their travels in various parts of the world, and she rightly considered it the most beautiful place in England. Unfortunately, the estate had been left to her son Owen, and she knew that she would have to give it up, along with her beloved treasures, when he married. Her secret dread was that he would marry a woman with as little a sense of the beautiful as he himself had. She therefore spent much of her time at Waterbath trying to turn his attention from Mona Brigstock, who personified everything she dreaded, to Fleda Vetch, the one person of her acquaintance who would appreciate and preserve Poynton as it was.

When Mrs. Gereth, with somewhat ulterior motives, invited Fleda to come to Poynton as a friend and permanent companion, Fleda, who had no real home of her own, readily accepted. To the chagrin of both women, Owen soon wrote that he was planning to marry Mona and that he was bringing her down within a week to see the estate. Mona, of course, approved. Although she failed to appreciate its beauty and immediately began planning certain changes, she did realize that every article in the house had some value, and she insisted that Mrs. Gereth leave all but her personal belongings as they were. Mrs. Gereth was to be given the smaller, but still charming, estate called Ricks.

At first Mrs. Gereth refused to be moved, but she finally agreed to make the change when it was decided that she could take a few of her prized objects with her. Owen, who was very much disturbed at being pushed by Mona to the point of having a serious conflict with his mother, had solicited Fleda's aid in getting his mother to make the move quickly. This request only complicated matters, however, for Fleda soon fell in love with Owen and could not really be effective as an agent for both parties in the controversy. She encouraged Mrs. Gereth to move quickly and quietly, leaving Poynton essentially as it was; but, because of her feelings toward both her friend and the estate, she also encouraged Owen to give his mother more time.

During these negotiations it became necessary for Fleda to go to London to see her father. While she was gone Mrs. Gereth left Poynton. Her moving was quick and quiet. When Fleda rejoined her at Ricks, she found that the woman had moved virtually all of the furnishings from Poynton. Needless to say, Owen and Mona were less than pleased. In fact, Mona postponed the wedding; she refused to marry Owen until Poynton again held its rightful belongings. Again Mrs. Gereth was stubborn, and more negotiations ensued, with both sides once more depending on Fleda for aid.

This time it was Owen's turn to fall in love. His strained relations with Mona, which caused a rather close relationship with Fleda, left him emotionally unstable. He had also lately come to realize how much Poynton, as he had always known it, meant to him and to appreciate anyone who understood its beauty and value as Fleda did. He knew that his life would have been much more satisfactory at this time if he were about to marry Fleda instead of Mona. Mrs. Gereth, who had always been willing to give up Poynton to anyone who could love it as she did, would gladly send back everything for Fleda. A realization of this fact finally caused Owen to declare his love for Fleda and to ask her to marry him.

Fleda, although she acknowledged her own feelings, would make no move until Owen had completely broken with Mona Brigstock, and it was to this end that she sent him away. When Mrs. Gereth heard of these developments she thought that the situation had finally worked out to her liking, and she immediately sent everything back to Poynton. This act proved a mistake, however, for as soon as Mona heard that the furnishings had been returned she immediately became her former charming self and again captivated Owen. Unfortunately, because of his honor as a gentleman, Owen could not break the engagement unless the lady demonstrated that she wished to do so; Mona Brigstock now made it clear that she did not wish to end the engagement. She quickly married him and moved at once to Poynton in order to acknowledge and secure her possession of the house and its contents. Soon the couple began an extended tour of the Continent.

Fleda and Mrs. Gereth again took up residence at Ricks and succeeded in making quite a charming place out of it, in spite of having little to work with and of having to do it with broken hearts. Sometime later Fleda received a letter from Owen asking her to go to Poynton and take whatever object she most prized, and because of her love both for Owen and the estate, she resolved to do so. When she arrived at the station, still more than a mile from Poynton, she saw great billows of smoke rising from that direction. It was a porter who told her that everything was lost. In a fire which was probably caused by a faulty lamp and aided tremendously by a strong wind, Poynton and all its beautiful furnishings were destroyed.

Critical Evaluation

According to Henry James in his "Preface" to *The Spoils of Poynton,* he perceived the "germ" of the short novel in a friend's casual mention of an acrimonious conflict between a mother and her son over the disposition of the family furniture following the death of the father. "There had been but ten words, yet I recognized in them, as in a flash, all the possibilities of the little drama of my 'Spoils.'" "On the face of it," he went on to say, "the 'things' themselves would form the very center of such a crisis; these grouped objects, all conscious of their eminence and their price, would enjoy, in any picture of a conflict, the heroic importance."

But the "things" alone must not have been enough to provoke James to immediate creation, since he left the idea unused for almost two years. In 1895, however, needing a story to fulfill an obligation to the *Atlantic,* James returned to the "spoils" idea and added the necessary missing ingredient, the central character. "For something like Fleda Vetch had surely been latent in one's first appreciation of the theme."

Thus James found the two lines of action that give the story its final shape: the conflict between Mrs. Gereth and her son, goaded on by Mona Brigstock, over the furnishings of Poynton and the romance between Owen Gereth and Fleda Vetch. The problem of who is to get the "spoils" dominates the first third of the book, but by chapter eight the center of interest has shifted to the question of who will marry Owen. The two issues are, of course, completely intertwined since Owen is actually one of the "spoils" himself and his marital decision also determines the disposition of the "things."

The dispute over the "spoils" is really a trial between two strong-willed, determined women, Mona Brigstock and Mrs. Gereth, who direct their strategies through Owen Gereth and Fleda Vetch. The contest becomes ambiguous and the outcome doubtful because the "agents" prove unreliable: Owen's emotional involvement with Fleda upsets Mona's calculations, and Fleda's ambivalent reactions threaten Mrs. Gereth's design.

It is unlikely that Mona cares much for the "things" of Poynton for themselves. After she finally wins Owen and Poynton, she flaunts her indifference to the house by not even living there. Her tenacity in seeking the "spoils" is a matter of willful pride: "Mona," wrote James, "is *all* will." She insists on the furniture because it "goes with the house"—and the house goes with Owen. In addition, it is probable that Mona sees the dispute as a "test" of Owen; or, rather, of her ability to control him. If she can force him to act against his mother's deepest wishes, then she can be confident of dominance in their marriage.

Even though Mrs. Gereth is no less strong-willed and ruthless in her passion to keep control of the artifacts of Poynton, she is a considerably more sympathetic figure. If her attitude toward Poynton reveals her to be a thorough materialist, she is at least a materialist with taste; Poynton, the fruit of her labors, is a fine art product and her devotion to it is passionate and complete. If she is a snob, judging people solely in terms of their taste and "cleverness," she seems accurate in her judgments: Mona is vulgar, Owen is stupid, and Fleda is superior. If Mrs. Gereth's actions are arrogant and extreme, they are mitigated by her situation; the English law that grants all inheritance rights directly to the son, regardless of the widow's needs, is an unjust one. And, if she "collected" Fleda to use as part of a scheme to regain Poynton, she does, in the end, show genuine feeling and concern toward the girl as a person, not just a "piece of furniture."

However, the most sympathetic and interesting person in the story is Fleda Vetch. In his "Preface" James identifies her as the only real "character" in the story; that is, the one figure of feeling and intelligence who is capable of development and change. It is through her perception and sensibility that the reader experiences the story and, in James's words, "the progress and march of my tale became and remained that of her understanding."

Not surprisingly, Fleda is the most complex and puzzling character in the book. Although her intelligence and moral superiority are evident throughout, her behavior frequently seems contradictory and self-defeating. Critics have disputed the motivations behind many of her actions and especially those during the crucial scenes that determine the outcome of her romance with Owen. The primary question is this: at the point where Owen says he loves her and wants to marry her, why does she send him straight back to Mona with "conditions" that virtually guarantee losing him? Or, to put it more generally, why does she throw away her one chance for happiness at the very time she seems to have it within her grasp?

In attempting to answer that question, three variables must be kept in mind: Fleda's relationship with Mrs. Gereth, her relationship with Owen, and her own aesthetic and moral values.

From the beginning Fleda is flattered and awed by Mrs. Gereth's attentions and compliments. The older woman sees in Fleda the perfect protégée, a girl gifted with intelligence and intuitive good taste, but with little background experience, who can be influenced, even molded, by an astute mentor. Thus, Mrs. Gereth grooms a "replacement" for herself who can not only keep Poynton out of Mona's grasp, but can even minister to its treasures long after she, Mrs. Gereth, is gone. In matters of artistic taste Mrs. Gereth probably has her way with Fleda, but after Owen becomes a factor her control over the girl becomes doubtful. In addition, as the book progresses Fleda becomes increasingly aware of being manipulated by Mrs. Gereth and, while she may not personally object to being a "piece of furniture," she does feel quite guilty about being used as bait in a trap for Owen.

Fleda's relations with Owen are equally problematical. At first she rejects him on the grounds that he is "too stupid," but even from the beginning his amiable personality and physical desirability make a strong impression on her. As their relationship grows, Fleda's view of him becomes more and more clouded by self-deception. Her first impressions of him as "stupid" and "weak" are accurate, but, as she falls in love with him, she suppresses these obvious insights or rationalizes them into strengths. She insists that he act with "independence" and "maturity," yet, like Mona, she fully expects to dominate him after marriage ("It's because he's so weak that he needs me").

352 The Spoils of Poynton/JAMES

Fleda feels strongly attracted and obligated to both people, so she gives each of them the impression that she favors their cause. From these contending loyalties come such self-defeating acts as her persistent claim to Owen that she is winning his mother over and her lies to Mrs. Gereth regarding her emotions and, more importantly, Owen's feelings for her.

Thus, conflicting impulses probably determine her final self-defeating act. Because of her innate morality and her Victorian upbringing, Fleda is unable to accept the idea of winning a previously committed man away from his intended; she cannot act the part of the "designing woman"—especially in someone else's design. Given her tendency to self-deception, she probably convinces herself that Owen can, in fact, meet the conditions she imposes; unfortunately "her Owen" is largely imaginary and the real Owen cannot resist a fully aroused Mona Brigstock. And emotionally Fleda seems to lack the capacity, as Mrs. Gereth put it, to "let go."

But these speculations do not answer the central question about Fleda. Does her final act represent a failure of nerve, a running away from life and experience? Or does it represent the moral victory of a woman too proud to jeopardize her ethics in return for a chance at happiness? Both views, and most positions in between, have been argued by the critics with little consensus. Each reader must make up his or her own mind on the point.

However, if Fleda's actions cost her a life with Owen, her reaction to that loss demonstrates her strength of character and her mature appreciation of life. It is she who senses the "meaning" of Ricks and brings a measure of solace to the defeated Mrs. Gereth. It is here that we come really to understand Fleda's aesthetic sensibility; to her, objects have moral qualities and their beauty is a product of the human experience they reflect. If she can succeed in impressing that view on her companion, a mellowed Mrs. Gereth may find a measure of happiness at Ricks—even after that accidental fire which resolves forever the fate of the "spoils" of Poynton.

Bibliography

Baym, Nina. "Fleda Vetch and the Plot of *The Spoils of Poynton*," in *PMLA*. LXXXIV (January, 1969), pp. 102–111.

Bowden, Edwin T. *The Themes of Henry James*. New Haven, Conn.: Yale University Press, 1956, pp. 72–77.

Broderick, John C. "Nature, Art, and Imagination in *The Spoils of Poynton*," in *Nineteenth-Century Fiction*. XIII (March, 1959), pp. 295–312.

Cargill, Oscar. *The Novels of Henry James*. New York: Macmillan, 1961, pp. 218–243.

Clair, John A. *The Ironic Dimension in the Fiction of Henry James*. Pittsburgh: Duquesne University Press, 1965, pp. 59–78.

Edelstein, Arnold. " 'The Tangle of Life': Levels of Meaning in *The Spoils of Poynton*," in *Hartford Studies in Literature*. II (1970), pp. 133–150.

Edgar, Pelham. *Henry James: Man and Author.* Boston: Houghton Mifflin, 1927, pp. 105–118.

Ford, Ford Madox. *Henry James: A Critical Study.* New York: Dodd, Mead, 1916, pp. 28–38.

Gargano, James W. "*The Spoils of Poynton*: Action and Responsibility," in *Sewanee Review.* LXIX (October–December, 1961), pp. 650–660.

Geismar, Maxwell. *Henry James and the Jacobites.* Boston: Houghton Mifflin, 1963, pp. 141–146.

Graham, Kenneth. "The Passion of Fleda Vetch," in *Henry James: The Drama of Fulfillment, An Approach to the Novels.* Oxford: Clarendon Press, 1975, pp. 127–159.

Greene, Philip L. "Point of View in *The Spoils of Poynton*," in *Nineteenth-Century Fiction.* XXI (March, 1967), pp. 359–368.

Hoffmann, Charles G. *The Short Novels of Henry James.* New York: Bookman, 1957, pp. 55–70.

Holland, Laurence B. *The Expense of Vision: Essays on the Craft of Henry James.* Princeton, N.J.: Princeton University Press, 1964, pp. 57–113.

Isle, Walter. *Experiments in Form: Henry James's Novels, 1896–1901.* Cambridge, Mass.: Harvard University Press, 1968, pp. 77–119.

Lewis, R.W.B. *Trials of the Word: Essays in American Literature and the Humanistic Tradition.* New Haven, Conn.: Yale University Press, 1965, pp. 77–96, 116–120.

Leyburn, Ellen Douglass. *The Strange Alloy: The Relation of Comedy to Tragedy in the Fiction of Henry James.* Chapel Hill: University of North Carolina Press, 1968, pp. 75–81.

McElderry, Bruce R., Jr. *Henry James.* New York: Twayne, 1965, pp. 105–107.

McLean, Robert C. "The Subjective Adventure of Fleda Vetch," in *American Literature.* XXXVI (March, 1964), pp. 12–30. Reprinted in *Henry James: Modern Judgments.* Edited by Tony Tanner. London: Macmillan, 1968, pp. 204–221.

Putt, S. Gorley. *Henry James: A Reader's Guide.* Ithaca, N.Y.: Cornell University Press, 1966, pp. 241–247.

Samuels, Charles Thomas. *The Ambiguity of Henry James.* Urbana: University of Illinois Press, 1971, pp. 61–88.

Sharp, Sister M. Corona. *The Confidante in Henry James: Evolution and Moral Value of a Fictive Character.* Notre Dame, Ind.: University of Notre Dame Press, 1963, pp. 97–126.

354

Stein, William Bysshe. "The Method at the Heart of Madness: *The Spoils of Poynton*," in *Modern Fiction Studies*. XIV (Summer, 1968), pp. 187–202.

Ward, J.R. *The Imagination of Disaster: Evil in the Fiction of Henry James*. Lincoln: University of Nebraska Press, 1961, pp. 57–63.

Wiesenfarth, Joseph. *Henry James and the Dramatic Analogy: A Study of the Major Novels of the Middle Period*. New York: Fordham University Press, 1963, pp. 44–56.

THE TURN OF THE SCREW

Type of work: Novelette
Author: Henry James (1843–1916)
Type of plot: Moral allegory
Time of plot: Mid-nineteenth century
Locale: England
First published: 1898

More than a horrific ghost story, The Turn of the Screw *is an enigmatic and disturbing psychological novel that probes the sources of terror in neurosis and moral degradation.*

Principal Characters

The Governess, from whose point of view the story is told. Employed to look after his orphaned niece and nephew by a man who makes it clear that he does not wish to be bothered about them, she finds herself engaged in a struggle against evil apparitions for the souls of the children. There has been a good deal of the "Is-Hamlet-mad?" sort of inconclusive speculation as to whether "The Turn of the Screw" is a real ghost story or a study of a neurotic and frustrated woman. Probably both interpretations are true: the apparitions are real; the children are indeed possessed by evil; and the governess is probably neurotic.

Miles, a little boy, one of the governess' charges. At first he seems to be a remarkably good child, but gradually she learns that he has been mysteriously corrupted by his former governess and his uncle's former valet, whose ghosts now appear to maintain their evil control. Miles dies in the governess' arms during her final struggle to save him from some mysterious evil.

Flora, Miles' sister and feminine counterpart. The governess finally sends her away to her uncle.

Miss Jessel, the former governess, now dead. She appears frequently to the governess and to the children, who refuse to admit the appearances.

Peter Quint, the uncle's former valet, now dead. Drunken and vicious, he was also Miss Jessel's lover. The governess sees his apparition repeatedly.

Mrs. Grose, the housekeeper of the country estate where the story is set. Goodhearted and talkative, she is the source of what little concrete information the governess and the reader get as to the identities and past histories of the evil apparitions. Allied with the governess against the influence of Peter Quint and Miss Jessel, she takes charge of Flora when the child is sent to her uncle.

The Story

It was a pleasant afternoon in June when the governess first arrived at the country estate at Bly where she was to take charge of Miles, aged ten, and Flora, eight. She faced her new position with some trepidation because of the unusual circumstances of her situation. The two children were to be under her complete care, and the uncle who had engaged her had been explicit in the fact that he did not wish to be bothered with his orphaned niece and nephew. Her uneasiness disappeared, however, when she saw her charges, for Flora and Miles seemed incapable of giving the slightest trouble.

The weeks of June passed uneventfully. Then, one evening, while she was walking in the garden at twilight, the governess was startled to see a strange young man at a distance. The man looked at her challengingly and disappeared. The incident angered and distressed the young woman, but she decided the man was a trespasser.

On the following Sunday evening the young woman was startled to see the same stranger looking in at her through a window. Once again he stared piercingly at her for a few seconds and then disappeared. This time the governess realized that the man was looking for someone in particular and that perhaps he boded evil for the children in her care. A few minutes later the governess told the housekeeper, Mrs. Grose, of the incident and described the appearance of the man. Mrs. Grose told her that it was a perfect description of Peter Quint, the valet to the governess' employer, but that Mr. Quint was dead.

One afternoon shortly afterward, a second apparition appeared. This time the ghost of Miss Jessel, the former governess, appeared in the garden to both the governess and the little girl, Flora. The strange part of the situation was that the little girl refused to let the governess know that she had seen the figure and knew who it was, though it was obvious that she had understood the appearance fully.

From the housekeeper the governess learned that the two apparitions had been lovers while alive, though the girl had been of a very fine family and the man had been guilty of drunkenness and worse vices. For what evil purpose these two spirits wished to influence the seemingly innocent children, neither the housekeeper nor the governess could guess. The secrecy of the children about seeing the ghosts was maddening to the two women.

They both felt that the boy was continuing to see the two ghosts in private and concealed that fact, just as he had known of the illicit affair between the valet and the former governess in life and had helped them to conceal it. Yet, when in the presence of the children, the governess sometimes felt that it would be impossible for the two children to be influenced into evil.

The third time the ghost of Quint appeared to the governess inside the house. Unable to sleep, she had sat reading late at night. Hearing someone on the stairs, she went to investigate and saw the ghost, which disappeared when faced by her unflinching gaze. Each night after that she inspected the stairs, but she never again saw the ghost of the man. Once she glimpsed the apparition of Miss Jessel as it sat dejectedly on the lowest stair. Worse than the appearance of the ghosts was the discovery that the children had left their beds at night to wander on the lawn in communication with the spirits who were leading them to unknown evil. It became apparent to the governess that the children were not good within themselves. In their imaginations they were living in a world populated by the evil dead restored.

In such an atmosphere the summer wore away into autumn. In all that time the children had given no sign of awareness of the apparitions. Knowing that her influence with the children was as tenuous as a thread which would break at the least provocation, the governess did not allude to the ghosts. She herself had seen no more manifestations, but she had often felt by the children's attitude that the apparitions were close at hand. What was worse for the distressed woman was the thought that what Miles and Flora saw were things still more terrible than she imagined, visions that sprang from their association with the evil figures in the past.

One day Miles went to her and announced his desire to go away to school. The governess realized it was only proper that he be sent to school, but she feared the results of ghostly influences once he was beyond her care. Later, opening the door of the schoolroom, she again saw the ghost of her predecessor, Miss Jessel. As the apparition faded the governess realized that her duty was to stay with the children and combat the spirits and their deadly influence. She decided to write immediately to the children's uncle, contradictory to his injunction against being bothered in their behalf. That night before she wrote she went into Miles' room and asked the boy to let her help him in his secret troubles. Suddenly a rush of cold air filled the room, as if the window had been blown open. When the governess relighted the candle blown out by the draft, the window was still closed and the drawn curtain had not been disturbed.

The following day Flora disappeared. Mrs. Grose and the governess found her beside the garden pond. The governess, knowing she had gone there to see the ghost, asked her where Miss Jessel was. The child replied that she only wanted to be left alone. The governess could see the apparition of Miss Jessel standing on the opposite side of the pond.

The governess, afraid that the evil influence had already dominated the little girl, asked the housekeeper to take the child to London, and to request the uncle's aid. In place of the lovable angelic Flora there had suddenly appeared a little child with a filthy mind and filthy speech, which she used in denouncing the governess to the housekeeper. The same afternoon Mrs. Grose left with the child as the governess had requested.

That evening, immediately after dinner, the governess asked Miles to tell her what was on his mind before he left the dining-room. When he refused, she asked him if he had stolen the letter she had written to his uncle. As she asked the question she realized that standing outside the window, staring into the room, was the ghost of Peter Quint. She pulled the boy close to her, shielding him from any view of the ghost at the window, while he told her that he had taken the letter. He also informed her that he had already been expelled from one school because of his lewd speech and actions. Noting how close the governess was holding him, he suddenly asked if Miss Jessel were near. The governess, angry and distraught, shrieked at him that it was the ghost of Peter Quint, just outside the window. When Miles turned around, the apparition was gone. With a scream he fell into the governess' arms. At first, she did not realize that she had lost him forever—that Miles was dead.

Critical Evaluation

One of Henry James's best known, most written about stories, *The Turn of the Screw*, was published serially in Collier's Weekly (January 27–April 16, 1898) and in book form with another story later that year. That the work is considered a novel by many thoughtful readers and a short story by others should be noted; however, the more discordant apparitionist/nonapparitionist dichotomy has overshadowed the short story/novel question.

For an intelligent appreciation of the tale's literary merits, no resolution to either issue is necessary. To whatever genre one assigns the story, its action remains dynamic, its events extraordinary. Any reader who so chooses may observe complex symbolic patterns and the rich suggestiveness of their texture. The governess remains, in either case, a young woman who, with limited experience and education but high moral principles, attempts to protect seemingly innocent children from the corrupting influence of ghosts but ends up killing one of them. Her culpability remains unchanged in either instance; for, even if the ghosts are real, can the death of the boy be preferable to that other course, however unthinkable it might be?

A quarter of a century passed after publication of the work before anyone questioned in print the reality of the ghosts. Another decade passed before the matter intensified with Edmund Wilson's "The Ambiguity of Henry James," in which he argued that the narrator suffered a neurosis stemming from repressed sexuality and that the ghosts were her resultant hallucinations. James's own words about the story are inconclusive; his actions, however, are much clearer. For one thing, he chose to place the piece in the New York edition of his works not among his other ghost tales but between "The Aspern Papers," a tale of prying destruction, and "The Liar." The revisions made for that edition are also instructive: in addition to the already numerous uses of *felt*, *sense*, *appear*, and *fancy* in the 1898 version, he amended such words as *perceived* and *saw* to *felt* and *knew* so that the sense of "felt" trouble pervaded the text from the first chapter of the governess's manuscript to the last.

The balancing of "felt" trouble at the beginning and end and its recurrence throughout the text contribute to the sense of doubling characters and pairs of characters: for example, the dead governess, Miss Jessel, and the living one; the Peter Quint/Miss Jessel pair doubled with Miles and Flora; the relation of Quint and Miles and that of Miss Jessel and Flora; the suggestion of duality in the man/woman nature of Peter Quint's name; the equal division of the visitations between Quint and Miss Jessel; the reflection of faces in polished surfaces; and so on. All of these examples remind us of the frequency with which James employed the doubling device and the frequency with which he used it to develop the duality theme in his fiction.

The same sort of duality is present in the description of the lake at Bly, which had impressed the governess with its extent and agitation. We must pay attention when a writer as careful as James does something unusual in his work. In this instance, he gives through his mouthpiece, the governess, a thorough description of the lake and topography of the estate at the expense of interrupting a rather breathless scene. The prolonged passage contributes significantly to the theme and symbolism: the expanse of the lake becomes, at the usual point of embarkation, unexpectedly oblong in shape and so narrow when measured against its length that it might have been taken for a scant river. This shifting, highly suggestive imagery complements the symbolism of Quint's appearance on the tower (at a time when the governess has been longing for her handsome employer to arrive and approve her care of the children) and his subsequent appearances at windows, which stand as opposites in a binary relation with the tower. Miss Jessel's appearance by the lake reinforces the theme as she watches Flora, also watched absorbedly by the governess, play her suggestive little game:

> She had picked up a small flat piece of wood, which happened to have in it a little hole that had evidently suggested to her the idea of sticking in another fragment that might figure as a mast and make the thing a boat. This second morsel . . . she was very markedly and intently attempting to tighten in its place.

All of this imagery and these occurrences have a way of building in our minds until the overall pattern, James's figure in the carpet, begins to form before our eyes after first being "felt" as trouble, then being recognized as the very horror that we somehow share and for which we feel responsible. At this point, readers will certainly wish to keep James's instructions to himself in mind: "Only make the reader's general vision of evil intense enough . . . and his own experience, his own imagination, his own sympathy (with the children) and horror (of their false friends) will supply him quite sufficiently with all particulars." Wondering just whom exactly he meant by *false friends* (the ghosts or the governess?), one begins to subordinate the matter of ghosts to the matter of the particular horror that we begin to suspect either in reality (if the ghosts are real) or in the governess's mind (if they are not real). The matter had to be handled with the greatest delicacy in Victorian times; indeed, the matter would still have to be handled with the greatest delicacy today to prevent rejection as the writing of a very dirty and sick old man.

That is exactly what James did; he wrote the story with brilliant delicacy, injecting so much ambiguity that the horror still remains checked by modern readers who are unwilling to accept the reality of what they suspect but repress. This was the reaction James intended: that propensity within us to doubt our worst fears and suspicions—the psychological monster that lurks deep within all of us, the righteous and the wicked.

Bibliography

Booth, Wayne. " 'The Turn of the Screw' as Puzzle," in *The Rhetoric of Fiction*. Chicago: University of Chicago Press, 1961, pp. 311–323.

Briggs, Julia. *Night Visitors: The Rise and Fall of the English Ghost Story*. Salem, N.H.: Faber, 1977, pp. 142–164.

Cargill, Oscar. "Henry James as Freudian Pioneer," in *Chicago Review*. X (Summer, 1956), pp. 13–29. Revised and reprinted in *Toward A Pluralistic Criticism*. Carbondale: Southern Illinois University Press, 1965, pp. 95–117.

Clair, John A. *The Ironic Dimension in the Fiction of Henry James*. Pittsburgh: Duquesne University Press, 1965, pp. 37–58.

Cranfill, Thomas M. and Robert L. Clark, Jr. *An Anatomy of "The Turn of the Screw."* Austin: University of Texas Press, 1965.

Enck, John J. " 'The Turn of the Screw' and the Turn of the Century," in *The Turn of the Screw*. Edited by Robert Kimbrough. New York: Norton, 1966, pp. 259–269.

Evans, Oliver. "James's Air of Evil: 'The Turn of the Screw,' " in *Partisan Review*. XVI (February, 1949), pp. 175–187. Reprinted in *A Casebook on Henry James's "The Turn of the Screw."* Edited by Gerald Willen. New York: Crowell, 1960, pp. 201–211.

Firebaugh, Joseph J. "Inadequacy in Eden: Knowledge and 'The Turn of the Screw,' " in *Modern Fiction Studies*. III (Spring, 1957), pp. 57–63. Reprinted in *A Casebook on "The Turn of the Screw."* Edited by Gerald Willen. New York: Crowell, 1960, pp. 291–297.

Geismar, Maxwell. *Henry James and the Jacobites*. Boston: Houghton Mifflin, 1963, pp. 156–167.

Goddard, Harold C. "A Pre-Freudian Reading of 'The Turn of the Screw,' " in *Nineteenth-Century Fiction*. XII (June, 1957), pp. 1–36. Reprinted in *A Casebook on Henry James's "The Turn of the Screw."* Edited by Gerald Willen. New York: Crowell, 1960, pp. 244–272. Also reprinted in *Twentieth Century Interpretations of "The Turn of the Screw": A Collection of Critical Essays*. Edited by Jane Tompkins. Englewood Cliffs, N.J.: Prentice-Hall, 1970, pp. 60–87.

Heilman, Robert B. " 'The Turn of the Screw' as Poem," in *University of Kansas City Review*. XIV (Summer, 1948), pp. 277–289. Reprinted in *Five Approaches to Literary Criticism*. Edited by Wilbur Stewart Scott. New York: Macmillan, 1962, pp. 283–301. Also reprinted in *A Casebook on "The Turn of the Screw."* Edited by Gerald Willen. New York: Crowell, 1960, pp. 174–188. Also reprinted in *Forms of Modern Fiction*. Edited by William Van O'Connor. Minneapolis: University of Minnesota Press, 1948, pp. 211–228.

Hoffmann, Charles G. "Innocence and Evil in James' 'The Turn of the Screw,'" in *University of Kansas City Review.* XX (Winter, 1953), pp. 97–105. Reprinted in *A Casebook on "The Turn of the Screw."* Edited by Gerald Willen, New York: Crowell, 1960, pp. 212–222.

Krook, Dorothea. *The Ordeal of Consciousness in Henry James.* New York: Cambridge University Press, 1962, pp. 106–134. Partly reprinted in *The Theory of the Novel: New Essays.* Edited by John Halperin. New York: Oxford University Press, 1974, pp. 353–372.

Lydenberg, John. "The Governess Turns the Screws," in *Nineteenth-Century Fiction.* XII (June, 1957), pp. 37–58. Reprinted in *A Casebook on "The Turn of the Screw."* Edited by Gerald Willen. New York: Crowell, 1960, pp. 273–290.

McElderry, Bruce R., Jr. *Henry James.* New York: Twayne, 1965, pp. 117–120.

Putt, S. Gorley. *Henry James: A Reader's Guide.* Ithaca, N.Y.: Cornell University Press, 1966, pp. 396–399.

Rubin, Louis D., Jr. "One More Turn of the Screw," in *Modern Fiction Studies.* IX (Winter, 1963–1964), pp. 314–328. Reprinted in *The Curious Death of the Novel.* Baton Rouge: Louisiana State University Press, 1967, pp. 67–87.

Samuels, Charles Thomas. *The Ambiguity of Henry James.* Urbana: University of Illinois Press, 1971, pp. 11–22.

Siegel, Eli. *James and the Children: A Consideration of Henry James's "The Turn of the Screw."* New York: Definition, 1963.

Solomon, Eric. "'The Return of the Screw,'" in *University Review.* XXX (1964), pp. 205–211. Reprinted in *The Turn of the Screw.* Edited by Robert Kimbrough. New York: Norton, 1966, pp. 237–245.

Thomson, A.W. "'The Turn of the Screw': Some Points on the Hallucination Theory," in *Review of English Literature.* VI (October, 1965), pp. 26–36.

West, Muriel. "The Death of Miles in 'The Turn of the Screw,'" in *PMLA.* LXXIX (June, 1964), pp. 283–288. Reprinted in *A Casebook on "The Turn of the Screw."* Edited by Gerald Willen. New York: Crowell, 1960, pp. 338–349.

——————. *A Stormy Night with "The Turn of the Screw."* Phoenix, Ariz.: Frye and Smith, 1964.

Wilson, Edmund. "The Ambiguity of James," in *Hound and Horn.* VII (April–June, 1934), pp. 385–406. Revised and reprinted in *The Question of Henry James.* Edited by F.W. Dupee. New York: Holt, 1954, pp. 160–190.

Wright, Walter F. *The Madness of Art: A Study of Henry James.* Lincoln: University of Nebraska Press, 1962, pp. 176–185.

WASHINGTON SQUARE

Type of work: Novel
Author: Henry James (1843–1916)
Type of plot: Psychological realism
Time of plot: About 1850
Locale: New York City
First published: 1881

The publication of Washington Square *a psychological novella of great poignancy, marks the end of the first period of Henry James's work. Set in New York City about the middle of the nineteenth century, this lucid book explores the theme of a father's harshly authoritarian control of his daughter.*

Principal Characters

Catherine Sloper, an heiress who remains steadfast to her ideal of loyalty. Irreparably harmed by the harshness of her father and the coldness of a calculating suitor, Catherine reëstablishes her life to fill the void of love removed. True to her vision, she neither mopes nor is vindictive; she merely compensates by filling her time with charitable and sociable acts, blending her life into her fashionable but anachronistic Washington Square home. Never one to complain, she does one time cry out against her father's heartlessness, her lover's lack of heart, and her meddling aunt's perverse though romantic indiscretions. She forever after forgives but never really forgets, something of tenderness and devotion having gone out of her who was, in the beginning, richly endowed with these virtues.

Austin Sloper, her socialite physician father whose unfortunate loss of a beautiful wife and son leaves him with no comfort in his plain, simple-hearted daughter. Brilliant and incisive as he is, Dr. Sloper is unable to ridicule Catherine's love out of existence or to supplant love with surface intellectuality. Although he sees clearly the suitor's contrivance, he can never act unselfishly or with unattached love to the humble daughter who both dotes on him and fears him. He lives on and by irony, himself finally the victim of a deeper sarcasm. Though his perspicacity makes him aware of events and their consequences, he never understands their meanings. He dies believing that he has thwarted a lovers' plot to gain his fortune, without knowing he has helped kill that love.

Morris Townsend, the suitor who gives up a small fortune offered with love and devotion for a larger fortune which he cannot manage to earn or contrive. As Catherine thinks, he is a man with charming manners and unrealized intellectual abilities; but he is also a shallow, egoistic, altogether selfish aging young man who has squandered his own small inheritance, sponged off his poor and widowed sister, and set his cap for a plain heiress whose love he rejects when the larger fortune is withheld by her father. Aging as a caricature of his youthful self, he unsuccessfully offers himself to the heiress as one worth waiting for. Soft-spoken Catherine has forgiven him, feels friendly toward him, and never wishes to see again this man whom she only accuses of "having treated me badly."

Lavinia Penniman, the widowed sister of Dr. Sloper and the unremitting confidante of the mercenary suitor. Wife of a deceased clergyman, Mrs. Penniman is a hopeless romantic who has taken upon herself the playing of Catherine's love and small inheritance against the handsome Townsend's expectation of the doctor's wealth. Badly frightened by the miscarriage of her conspiracy and aware of the possibility of losing her parasitic position in the household, she becomes circumspect, cautious against her brother's wrath and her niece's mute accusations. Gay and indestructible after her brother's death, she once again attempts the part of duenna for the middle-aged Catherine and Townsend, with results her narrowness of vision can never comprehend.

Marian Almond, Catherine Sloper's sensible and observant aunt. Mrs. Almond, aware of her responsibility in the matter, since her niece met Morris Townsend at a party given in the Almond house, dislikes the match but hates the meddling of both her brother and sister. She thinks more highly of Catherine and her simple virtues than do the others; she wishes Morris were as sympathetic and kind as the proud but humble sister whom the selfish man lives on. Her own deep sympathies make for ease with Catherine and antagonism toward Lavinia, the weak-minded matchmaker. Even she is not able to win the jilted girl's confidence, though she manages to relieve the pain of Dr. Sloper's satiric inquiries and Lavinia's fatuous comments.

Mrs. Montgomery, Morris Townsend's widowed sister. A call on Mrs. Montgomery confirms Dr. Sloper's belief that Townsend is a fortune hunter.

The Story

Peace, especially of the domestic variety, was becoming increasingly important to Dr. Sloper as he entered his fifties. Intelligent, poised, distinguished in his profession, he was accustomed to meeting life on his own terms. Not entirely unscarred by fate, he had suffered the loss of his wife and a young son many years before; but the passage of time had helped to soften even this blow. Now he dwelt quietly and comfortably in his mansion on Washington Square with his only remaining child, his daughter Catherine, and his widowed sister, Mrs. Penniman.

Neither of these companions, oddly enough, inspired the doctor with any great fondness. His sister had just the sort of nature, incurably romantic and deviously feminine, to set his teeth on edge; he saw her presence in his establishment as merely an inconvenience to be overlooked in the interest of providing female supervision of his growing daughter. Nor, regarding the daughter herself, was Dr. Sloper any less candid in his private appraisal. Catherine was a good girl, he thought, but incurably dull. Entering her twenties, she had never had a romantic interest or a prospect of any. She was shyly fond of her father and very much afraid of him, especially when an ironical tone crept into his voice. However, he was generally kind and courteous to her, even if more self-contained than an adoring daughter might always wish.

Catherine's taste for ornate dress was one of the characteristics which her father found especially trying. She had long cherished this taste without venturing to express it, but when she reached the age of twenty she bought a red satin gown trimmed with gold fringe. It made her look like a woman of thirty, and her father inwardly grimaced at the thought that a child of his should be both ugly and overdressed.

Catherine was wearing her red gown on the evening when she first met Morris Townsend. The occasion was a party, given by her aunt, Mrs. Almond. Catherine became quickly convinced that she had never met a young man so handsome, clever, and attentive. When his absorption with Catherine began to attract notice, Townsend quickly shifted his attentions to Mrs. Penniman, whose romantic sensibilities were soon aflutter with delight and anticipation. Before the evening ended, she had managed to intimate to this agreeable young man that he would be welcome to call in Washington Square.

The visit soon occurred, to be quickly followed by another; and presently young Townsend was in regular attendance upon Catherine. This development was far from unobserved by the other two members of the household, though their reactions were entirely different. Mrs. Penniman, undertaking the role of a middle-aged Cupid, pressed Townsend's claims and assisted his cause as ardently as she dared. Dr. Sloper, on the other hand, became first skeptical and then concerned. An interview with the young man strengthened his conviction that Townsend's charming manner was only a mask for irresponsibility and selfishness. He suspected that Townsend was living off the meager resources of the latter's sister, a widow with five children, and the doctor determined to investigate the matter. Before he could do so, however, Catherine brought him word that Morris Townsend had proposed to her and that she was anxious to accept him.

His suspicions confirmed by a talk with Mrs. Montgomery, Townsend's sister, the doctor came away from his call more convinced than ever that Catherine's young man was a fortune hunter. For once, however, his objections failed to sway the infatuated girl. As a last resort Dr. Sloper declared that if Catherine married Townsend he would disinherit her. This measure would not leave her penniless by any means, since an inheritance from her mother would still supply her with a comfortable income. Nevertheless it would reduce, by two-thirds, the amount Catherine could eventually expect; and the doctor's announcement gave both Townsend and Mrs. Penniman, also the object of her brother's displeasure, something to think about.

Mrs. Penniman, alarmed, counseled delay, and Townsend agreed to part with Catherine while she accompanied her father to Europe. Both Townsend and Mrs. Penniman hoped that the passage of time would soften the doctor's obdurate opposition to the match. Catherine, while agreeing to make the trip, cherished no such illusions. After several months the travelers returned, but the situation remained unchanged. Catherine was determined to go ahead with the marriage; Townsend kept putting her off. Suddenly he vanished from New York altogether.

Years passed before she saw him again. In the meantime Dr. Sloper had died and, fearful to the end that Townsend might re-enter Catherine's life, had left his own fortune to charity. One night while Catherine was sitting quietly at home, there was a ring at the door. Morris Townsend had come back, secretly encouraged by the unwearying Mrs. Penniman. Bearded, heavier, and forty-five years of age, he was still fluent and personable; his whole manner made it clear that he expected to be made welcome in Washington Square. The lapse of twenty years might have taken much from him, including the European wife of whom Catherine had vaguely heard, but he had not lost the bright assurance with which he now waited for his words to work their old-time magic on Catherine's heart.

He stood, hat in hand, murmuring his warm phrases, but Catherine did not ask him to sit down. She looked at him as if he were a stranger, repelling all advances and brushing off all explanations with a cool imperturbability which would have been worthy of the old doctor himself. With Catherine there was no longer any question of yielding to his charm: she had suffered too much. This time it would be she who sent him away; and she gave him his dismissal with a finality which he had no choice but to accept and understand.

Critical Evaluation

Though one of Henry James's least complex and ambiguous novels, *Washington Square* is scarcely below the more complicated works in artistic quality. With characteristic skill, James explores the complex relationship between Dr. Sloper, disappointed because his plain and somewhat dull daughter cannot replace either his deceased wife or his lost son, and Catherine Sloper, whose essential goodness makes her one of James's most appealing heroines. Catherine, surviving and growing through the callous treatment by her father and her great disappointment in Morris Townsend, gradually develops a stoic strength and dignity which give her a tragic quality.

When we first encounter Catherine, she is torn between the extremes of her aunt's foolish romanticism and her father's hardheaded realism. In the course of the novel, she will move from one extreme to the other, but James does not present her growth as necessarily a victory of knowledge over naïveté. From the start, Dr. Sloper recognizes Morris' motives, but his handling of the situation borders on the sadistic. He neither tries to understand Catherine nor to consider her feelings or happiness. Rather, he devotes his attention to causing Morris finally to reveal his mercenary plans, thus making marriage impossible for his daughter. One wonders if marriage to Morris could have been worse than the lonely spinsterhood to which Catherine finally comes.

Catherine reveals her strength and pride in defying her father's demand that she renounce Townsend. Though, purged of her girlish romanticism, she undoubtedly knows already that she will never marry Morris, she nevertheless retains her autonomy by refusing on principle to submit to Dr. Sloper's demands. Unfortunately, however, neither the loss of romantic dreams of happiness nor the development of real inner strength has offered Catherine a fuller or richer life. At the end of the novel, we find her alone, facing an empty future.

Bibliography

Beach, Joseph Warren. *The Method of Henry James.* New Haven, Conn.: Yale University Press, 1918, pp. 228–232. Reprinted in *Washington Square.* Edited by Gerald Willen. New York: Crowell, 1970, pp. 177–181.

Bell, Millicent. "Style as Subject: *Washington Square*," in *Sewanee Review.* LXXXIII (1975), pp. 19–38.

Bowden, Edwin T. *The Themes of Henry James.* New Haven, Conn.: Yale University Press, 1956, pp. 40–44. Reprinted in *Washington Square.* Edited by Gerald Willen. New York: Crowell, 1970, pp. 190–198.

Cambon, Glauco. "The Negative Gesture in Henry James," in *Nineteenth Century Fiction.* XV (1961), pp. 335–340. Reprinted in *Washington Square.* Edited by Gerald Willen. New York: Crowell, 1970, pp. 221–230.

Canby, Henry Seidel. *Turn West, Turn East: Mark Twain and Henry James.* Boston: Houghton Mifflin, 1951, pp. 152–153. Reprinted in *Washington Square.* Edited by Gerald Willen. New York: Crowell, 1970, pp. 187–188.

Dupee, F.W. *Henry James.* Garden City, N.Y.: Doubleday Anchor, 1956, pp. 54–56. Reprinted in *Washington Square.* Edited by Gerald Willen. New York: Crowell, 1970, pp. 188–190.

Edel, Leon. *Henry James: The Conquest of London, 1870–1881.* Philadelphia: Lippincott, 1962, pp. 387–400. Reprinted in *Washington Square.* Edited by Gerald Willen. New York: Crowell, 1970, pp. 215–218.

Geismar, Maxwell. *Henry James and the Jacobites.* Boston: Houghton Mifflin, 1963, pp. 36–40. Reprinted in *Washington Square.* Edited by Gerald Willen. New York: Crowell, 1970, pp. 218–221.

Gordon, David J. "*Washington Square*: A Psychological Perspective," in *Washington Square.* Edited by Gerald Willen. New York: Crowell, 1970, pp. 263–271.

Gurko, Leo. "The Dehumanizing Mind in *Washington Square*," in *Washington Square.* Edited by Gerald Willen. New York: Crowell, 1970, pp. 230–243.

Hoffmann, Charles G. *The Short Novels of Henry James.* New York: Bookman, 1957, pp. 25–37.

Johannsen, Robert R. "Two Sides of *Washington Square*," in *South Carolina Review.* VI (April, 1974), pp. 60–65.

Kelley, Cornelia P.   *The Early Development of Henry James.* Urbana: University of Illinois Press, 1930, pp. 278–283. Reprinted in *Washington Square.* Edited by Gerald Willen. New York: Crowell, 1970, pp. 181–187.

Kronenberger, Louis.   "*Washington Square,*" in *The Polished Surface: Essays in the Literature of Worldliness.* New York: Knopf, 1969, pp. 233–245.

Lucas, John.   "*Washington Square,*" in *The Air of Reality: New Essays on Henry James.* Edited by John Goode. London: Methuen, 1972, pp. 36–59.

McElderry, Bruce R., Jr.   *Henry James.* New York: Twayne, 1965, pp. 51–53.

Matthiessen, F.O.   *The American Novels and Stories of Henry James.* New York: Knopf, 1947, pp. x–xi. Reprinted in *Washington Square.* Edited by Gerald Willen. New York: Crowell, 1970, pp. 175–177.

Pendo, Mina.   "Reason Under the Ailanthus," in *Washington Square.* Edited by Gerald Willen. New York: Crowell, 1970, pp. 243–252.

Poirier, Richard.   " 'Confidence' and *Washington Square,*" in *The Comic Sense of Henry James: A Study of the Early Novels.* New York: Oxford University Press, 1960, pp. 165–182. Reprinted in *Washington Square.* Edited by Gerald Willen. New York: Crowell, 1970, pp. 196–215.

Putt, S. Gorley.   *A Reader's Guide to Henry James.* Ithaca, N.Y.: Cornell University Press, 1966, pp. 46–51.

Roddman, Philip.   "The Critical Sublime: A View of *Washington Square,*" in *Washington Square.* Edited by Gerald Willen. New York: Crowell, 1970, pp. 253–263.

Samuels, Charles T.   *The Ambiguity of Henry James.* Urbana: University of Illinois Press, 1971, pp. 141–149.

Schecter, Harold.   "The Unpardonable Sin in *Washington Square,*" in *Studies in Short Fiction.* X (1973), pp. 137–141.

Stone, Donald D.   *Novelists in a Changing World: Meredith, James, and the Transformation of English Fiction in the 1880's.* Cambridge, Mass.: Harvard University Press, 1972, pp. 201–204.

Veeder, William.   *Henry James: The Lesson of the Master.* Chicago: University of Chicago Press, 1975, pp. 184–206.

WHAT MAISIE KNEW

Type of work: Novel
Author: Henry James (1843–1916)
Type of plot: Social morality
Time of plot: 1890's
Locale: London, Folkestone, Boulogne
First published: 1897

This novel, one of the greatest of James's middle period, is the story of the growing moral and intellectual perception of the neglected daughter of divorced and irresponsible parents. The moral core of What Maisie Knew *is the child's incorruptible innocence.*

Principal Characters

Maisie Farange, the neglected daughter of divorced and irresponsible parents. Shuttled back and forth between her father and mother, Maisie at first lacks moral perception, although she herself is incorruptibly innocent. Then, under the tutelege of Mrs. Wix, she grows in moral and intellectual sense, rejects the immorality of her stepparents, and chooses to live with Mrs. Wix.

Mrs. Wix, a governess. Employed to replace Miss Overmore, Mrs. Wix alone seems concerned for Maisie's welfare. Refusing to condone the immorality around her, she is the moral influence in the young girl's environment.

Sir Claude, Ida Farange's second husband. Genuinely interested in Maisie, Sir Claude most nearly approaches the fatherly role. However, he is unable to

end his affair with Mrs. Farange (Miss Overmore) and Maisie refuses to live with them.

Miss Overmore, Maisie's governess, later the second Mrs. Beale Farange. After she tires of her husband, she begins an affair with Sir Claude, who is captivated by her beauty. She does not love Maisie, but she feels that she can hold Sir Claude through his devotion to the girl.

Ida Farange, Maisie's mother. Divorced from Beale Farange, Ida marries Sir Claude but soon loses interest in her daughter and husband. She turns Maisie over to him and goes out of their lives.

Beale Farange, Maisie's father. After his divorce, Beale marries Miss Overmore, but they soon tire of each other. Beale goes to America and out of the story.

The Story

Beale and Ida Farange were divorced with much publicity. At first each fought to possess their daughter Maisie, but at last it was arranged that the girl should spend six months with each in turn. The first period was to be spent with her father.

Maisie was confused by the divorce. At first she truthfully reported to her parents what they said about each other, but finding that her candor provoked furious outbursts and that she was being used as an innocent messenger, she soon became silent on the subject of the absent parent and appeared to absorb no knowledge during her visits.

Ida engaged Miss Overmore, a pretty governess, for Maisie, and Maisie was unhappy to leave her when she returned to her father. Soon, however, Miss Overmore went to Beale Farange's house where she was, to Ida's fury, also engaged as Maisie's governess. Upon her subsequent return to Ida, Maisie was placed in the care of Mrs. Wix. She learned no lessons from Mrs. Wix, but adored her conversation and felt comfortable and secure with her.

During Maisie's next stay with Beale he went for a few days to Brighton with Miss Overmore. When the governess returned, she found Mrs. Wix waiting for her. Mrs. Wix alone was preoccupied with Maisie's welfare, and was outraged by the child's environment. She announced to Miss Overmore that Ida was about to remarry and she gave Maisie a photograph of Sir Claude, her future stepfather. Miss Overmore outdid her, as it were, by announcing that she had just married Beale Farange.

Some time after his marriage Sir Claude called and was received by the new Mrs. Beale Farange. Maisie was delighted by their apparent understanding and declared that she had brought them together. Sir Claude won Maisie's love by his gentleness toward her and by his declared intent to make her his responsibility. In spite of the pain of leaving the new Mrs. Farange, the girl was pleased to go home with him. But Ida's love for her new husband soon waned and she had several lovers. When she accused Sir Claude of basely stealing Maisie's affections, and threatened to drive Mrs. Wix out of the house for supporting him, Maisie felt that she belonged nowhere. In this disturbed situation Mrs. Wix was determined to meet her responsibility for Maisie, and she desired to "save" Sir Claude from Mrs. Beale Farange, whom he frequently visited. Also, fearing the loss of her livelihood, she wished that Sir Claude would take a house for himself where she and Maisie would also live.

On one outing Sir Claude took Maisie to her father's new house, which she was afraid to enter for fear of losing him if she remained there. Once in the house, however, she was again enthralled by Mrs. Farange's beauty and was interested to learn that Beale mattered no more to his wife than Sir Claude did to Ida. Maisie remained happily with her stepmother after Sir Claude had assured her that he would provide for Mrs. Wix and visit her frequently.

After a long absence Sir Claude visited Maisie again. While they were walking in the park they met Ida with an unknown, military-appearing man. Ida and Sir Claude were immensely angry at their meeting, and Maisie was sent to talk with Ida's escort, whom her mother had called the Captain, while they finished their argument. Maisie, who was by that time thoroughly aware that neither parent loved her, wept when the Captain praised her mother highly and was eager to agree that she was "good." After this episode Sir Claude, unable to learn from Maisie what the Captain had said to her, sent her home alone in a cab.

Mrs. Farange told Maisie that she met Sir Claude away from her home, but that he was reluctant to visit them and thus compromise Maisie. The three hoped to meet at a London exhibition; instead, they unexpectedly encountered Beale Farange. After a subdued but violent quarrel, Maisie was whisked away by her father to the house of his mistress. There he offered, in such a way that Maisie could only refuse, to take her to America with him.

Sir Claude, encouraged by Mrs. Wix, took Maisie to Folkestone as the first step toward making a home for them in France. There Ida arrived suddenly and surrendered Maisie to Sir Claude's guardianship. The following day they crossed to France, where Mrs. Wix joined them. Sir Claude was to return to England and to Mrs. Beale Farange, when Maisie's father had finally left. Sir Claude confessed that he feared Mrs. Farange as he had formerly feared Ida. Mrs. Wix, still strongly opposed to Mrs. Farange, asked to be sent to England to sever their relationship. This request was refused by Sir Claude, who went off to England alone.

While he was away Mrs. Wix explained to a bewildered Maisie that she refused to condone the immorality of Mrs. Farange and Sir Claude in living together with them. Also, she declared that she would never again leave Maisie. After several walks and much thought the full implications of what this situation might mean became apparent to Maisie. She realized, too, that she had no moral "sense," and having rapidly absorbed the idea of such a sense from vague but emphatic conversations with Mrs. Wix, she decided to show in her future responses that she did indeed possess it.

When they returned to their hotel after a morning walk, Maisie was unexpectedly greeted by her stepmother. Mrs. Wix's own "moral sense" was nearly destroyed by Mrs. Farange's charm and her determination to have the governess-companion as an ally. According to Mrs. Farange, now that the girl's father had left, Maisie was her own daughter. In this way she intended to hold Sir Claude, through his devotion to the girl. Mrs. Wix wavered, but Maisie declared that she would stay with Sir Claude only if he were alone.

The next morning Mrs. Wix awakened Maisie with the news that Sir Claude had arrived. When Maisie breakfasted alone with him, he asked her if she would leave Mrs. Wix and live with him and Mrs. Farange. She asked to see Mrs. Wix before deciding. Later, while walking with Sir Claude, she said she would give up Mrs. Wix only if he would give us Mrs. Farange. Maisie made her decision when the four people confronted one another in a final struggle at the hotel. After she had failed in her appeal to have Mrs. Farange give up Sir Claude, Maisie decided to stay with Mrs. Wix.

Critical Evaluation

Henry James is credited with freeing fiction from a "moral" purpose. His influential theories on point of view and scenic power educated succeeding generations of writers to the formal capacities of the novel. However, the ultimate purpose of his dismissal of a simple-minded didacticism from fiction was not the eradication of moral vision as such. On the contrary, as his "technique" grew more subtle, the result was an increasingly profound exploration of human values and motives. He was reluctant to judge, which was probably the outstanding naturalist trait in his fiction, but he nevertheless served an ethical muse by demonstrating and revealing the moral realities of life.

What Maisie Knew has often been singled out as a neglected masterpiece; neither "early" nor "late" James, it is credited with combining the "storytelling virtues" of the earlier novels with the "psychological complexity" of the later. The truth is that its central position in James's canon invests it with almost more weight than it can bear. As the psychological intensity grows, the plot is contorted to keep up. Maisie's parents divorce, remarry, and *their* new spouses become lovers and finally surrogate parents to Maisie. It is diabolically neat, but almost farcical. And farce is not what James wants as a background for his moral and psychological development of Maisie.

The point is that Maisie herself is not always a convincing protagonist, especially as a vehicle for the novel's intricate, and often tortured, shifts in point of view: " . . . if he (Sir Claude) had an idea at the back of his head she had also one in a recess as deep, and for a time, while they sat together, there was an extraordinary mute passage between her vision of this vision of his, his vision of her vision, and her vision of his vision of her vision." Unlike Mrs. Wix, who never loses her "wonder" over what Maisie knew, the reader sometimes doubts that James was sure what she knew. He could, of course, experiment very freely with her capacity to know: she is only a child and therefore has an openended mind. But her child's identity is never adequately established. It is revealing that we never have a clear idea of her exact age. Lewis Carroll's Alice is a real child in an imaginary world; James's Maisie is an imaginary child in a moral jungle.

Bibliography

Bewly, Marius. *The Complex Fate: Hawthorne, Henry James, and Some Other American Writers.* London: Chatto and Windus, 1952, pp. 96–113, 132–143.

Brebner, Adele. "How to Know Maisie," in *College English.* XVII (February, 1956), pp. 283–285.

Cargill, Oscar. *The Novels of Henry James.* New York: Macmillan, 1961, pp. 244–262.

Dupee, F.W. *Henry James.* Garden City, N.Y.: Doubleday Anchor, 1956, pp. 166–170.

Dyson, A.E. "On Knowing What Maisie Knew Perhaps," in *On the Novel: A*

Present for Walter Allen on His 60th Birthday from His Friends and Colleagues. Edited by B.S. Beneditz. London: Dent, 1971, pp. 128–139.

Edgar, Pelham. *Henry James: Man and Author.* Boston: Houghton Mifflin, 1927, pp. 118–127.

Fahey, Paul. *"What Maisie Knew*: Learning Not to Mind," in *Critical Quarterly.* XIV (1971), pp. 96–108.

Gargano, James W. *"What Maisie Knew*: The Evolution of a 'Moral Sense,' " in *Nineteenth-Century Fiction.* XVI (June, 1961), pp. 33–46. Reprinted in *Henry James: Modern Judgments.* Edited by Tony Tanner. London: Macmillan, 1968, pp. 222–235.

Geismar, Maxwell. *Henry James and the Jacobites.* Boston: Houghton Mifflin, 1963, pp. 146–155.

Hamblen, Abigail A. "Henry James and the Power of Eros: *What Maisie Knew,*" in *Midwest Quarterly.* IX (July, 1968), pp. 391–399.

Isle, Walter. *"What Maisie Knew,*" in *Experiments in Form: Henry James's Novels, 1896–1911.* Cambridge, Mass.: Harvard University Press, 1968, pp. 120–164.

Leavis, F.R. *"What Maisie Knew,*" in *Anna Karenina and Other Essays.* New York: Random House, 1933, pp. 75–91.

McCloskey, John C. "What Maisie Knows: A Study of Childhood and Adolescence," in *American Literature.* XXXVI (January, 1965), pp. 485–513.

McElderry, Bruce R., Jr. *Henry James.* New York: Twayne, 1965, pp. 107–109.

Mitchell, Juliet. *"What Maisie Knew*: Portrait of the Artist as a Young Girl," in *The Air of Reality.* Edited by John Goode. London: Methuen, 1972, pp. 168–189.

Putt, S. Gorley. *A Reader's Guide to Henry James.* Ithaca, N.Y.: Cornell University Press, 1969, pp. 247–252.

Samuels, Charles Thomas. *The Ambiguity of Henry James.* Urbana: University of Illinois Press, 1971, pp. 178–209.

Sears, Sallie. *The Negative Imagination: Form and Perspective in the Novels of Henry James.* Ithaca, N.Y.: Cornell University Press, 1968, pp. 20–34.

Sharp, Sister M. Corona. *The Confidante in Henry James: Evolution and Moral Value of a Fictive Character.* Notre Dame, Ind.: University of Notre Dame Press, 1963, pp. 127–149.

Tanner, Tony. *The Reign of Wonder: Naivety and Reality in American Literature.* New York: Cambridge University Press, 1965, pp. 278–308.

Wasiolek, Edward. "Maisie: Pure or Corrupt?," in *College English.* XXII (December, 1960), pp. 167–172.

Weinstein, Philip M. "Resisting the Assault of Experience: *What Maisie Knew*," in *Henry James and the Requirements of the Imagination.* Cambridge, Mass.: Harvard University Press, 1971, pp. 72–96.

Wiesenfarth, Joseph. *Henry James and the Dramatic Analogy: A Study of the Major Novels of the Middle Period.* New York: Fordham University Press, 1963, pp. 57–75.

Wilson, Harris W. "What *Did* Maisie Know?," in *College English.* XVII (February, 1956), pp. 279–282.

Wright, Walter F. *The Madness of Art: A Study of Henry James.* Lincoln: University of Nebraska Press, 1962, pp. 162–168.

THE WINGS OF THE DOVE

Type of work: Novel
Author: Henry James (1843–1916)
Type of plot: Psychological realism
Time of plot: c. 1900
Locale: London and Venice
First published: 1902

One of the major psychological novels of James's final period, The Wings of the Dove *concerns a young, fine-spirited woman afflicted by an incurable malady who attempts to live a lifetime in a few precious months. The admirable character of "the dove," Milly Theale, was modeled avowedly on the author's own cousin, Mary Temple.*

Principal Characters

Mildred Theale (Milly), "the dove" who comes to Europe to learn to live and to die there of an incurable disease. A handsome young woman of great means, inherited through the deaths of her entire family of six, this New Yorker with her Bostonian writer friend and a companion her own age tries to extend her experiences so as to encompass a lifetime in a few short months. Although Milly seems never to suffer, she is the first to know that her sickness will be fatal, and she needs only the strength and subtlety of an eminent physician to confirm this fact. Her fine manners and sensitivity to others' needs make her a delightful companion to all, even when the truth of her condition would otherwise make others pity her. Bright, vivacious, and charming in all ways, she finally wins a heart and ironically loses both hers and his to the tragic situation. Her generosity in remembering her two closest friends (whom she forgives for plotting a scheme of marriage) is unacceptable finally. The wings meant for sheltering then become symbols of religious purity.

Kate Croy, the young woman who befriends Milly Theale in England and seeks through her a solution to her own problems. A victim of her father's bad reputation and her uncompromising aunt's machinations, Kate is a beautiful, stylish, and acute observer of the society in which her aunt, Mrs. Lowder, has placed her. Her hopeless love for a young newspaper reporter only makes her decisions more poignant, for she decides he must marry the rich and doomed Milly in order for their own marriage finally to be realized. Sparkling and perceptive as she is, Kate fails to live the lie so calmly planned and must live out her existence in her aunt's entourage.

Merton Densher, Kate Croy's unacceptable lover and Milly Theale's beloved. Densher, just returned from a journalistic assignment in America to a secret engagement with Kate, finds that his charms, good looks, and good manners are the pawns to two separate schemes.

He is rejected as her niece's fiancé by Mrs. Lowder but encouraged as a suitor of Milly Theale, whom he had met briefly in America. His fine perceptions and sensitivities are so keenly balanced that he can neither propose nor reject, have or hold. He binds Kate as his lover to an agreement, only to find at last that he loves Milly; but he cannot break off his engagement to Kate. Both he and Kate suffer.

Lord Mark, a nobleman encouraged by Mrs. Lowder as a suitor for her niece. He is attentive to both Kate and Milly, and both reject him. He then gains an unconscious revenge by informing the dying girl of the relationship between Kate and Densher. Neither young nor old-appearing, Lord Mark is supercilious to the point of caricature. Without intending malice, he nonetheless manages to do harm more efficiently than if he had. He is considered a good catch by older matchmakers and abhorred by the objects of his attentions.

Mrs. Lowder, a managing woman who succeeds in convincing everyone that her own will is the strongest and that her judgments are infallible. Though Mrs. Lowder intimidates more than she inspires, her nature is not altogether cold. She simply sees the world as it is and tries to fit those nearest her into the mold.

Mrs. Stringham, a schoolmate and long-time friend of Mrs. Lowder and the companion to Milly Theale. Her warm nature and compassionate responses offset the calculating forces of the highborn English. As a writer, she observes and comments wisely on human character and manners the more so because she observes the tragedy unfold.

Sir Luke Strett, the distinguished physician who involves himself more than professionally in order to make of Milly Theale's living death an experience in vivid life. Although there is nothing he can do for her, he extends his great humanity to the young and lovely American so desirous of life and so tragically doomed.

The Story

Kate Croy was dependent upon her aunt, Mrs. Lowder, because Kate's own father was a ne'er-do-well. Mrs. Lowder had great plans for her niece, and she encouraged Lord Mark as a suitor for Kate's hand. Kate's own mind was set on a young reporter, Merton Densher, who worked on one of the London papers. While Mrs. Lowder liked Densher, and even invited him to her home, she did not want him to marry her niece, for he had no apparent prospects of money or a place in society. Mrs. Lowder breathed easier when she learned that the young man was being sent by his newspaper to America, to write a series of articles on life in the United States.

While he was in New York, Densher made the acquaintance of a pretty young American, Milly Theale, who had recently inherited a large fortune through the death of her parents.

A few weeks later Milly Theale asked a Boston friend, Mrs. Susan Stringham, widow and a writer, to go with her to Europe. Within a matter of days they had taken passage on a liner and soon arrived in Italy. They traveled up the Italian peninsula and into Switzerland. Restless, Milly soon decided that she would like to go to London.

When they had arrived in England, Mrs. Stringham sent word of her arrival to Mrs. Lowder, the one real acquaintance she had in that country from her school-days many years before. Mrs. Stringham and Milly Theale immediately became familiar callers at Mrs. Lowder's home. Because of her beauty, money, and attractive personality, Milly was a great success. Lord Mark became infatuated with her. Milly and Kate Croy became fast friends.

Aware that she was ill, Milly went to see Sir Luke Strett, an eminent surgeon who informed her that there was nothing surgery or medicine could do to save her, and he advised her to make the best of the time she had left. Although Kate Croy, Mrs. Lowder, and Mrs. Stringham knew that she had only a few months to live, Milly requested them to keep silent in the matter. Her intention was to enjoy herself as much as possible.

Great friends as Kate Croy and Milly Theale were, they never mentioned their mutual acquaintance, Merton Densher. One day, while walking in the National Art Galleries, Milly saw him and her friend Kate together. Kate and Densher enlisted the aid of Mrs. Stringham and Milly to further their courtship. Milly, herself a little in love with Densher, was only too glad to help him be near Kate.

Soon Kate hit upon a way to bring her affair with Densher to a happy conclusion. She told the young man to marry Milly, thus making her happy for the few remaining months of her life. Kate had seen clearly that Milly was falling in love with Densher. Kate realized that Milly's fortune would be left after her death to Densher, who would then be free to marry Kate and would have sufficient money to allay any objections Mrs. Lowder might have to the match. Kate was sure that Mrs. Lowder or Mrs. Stringham would not try to prevent a marriage between Milly and Merton Densher, for she knew that the two older women loved Milly enough to go to any lengths to make her final days happy.

The four women, accompanied by Densher, went to Venice for the winter months, Milly on the advice of Sir Luke Strett. Densher made little headway with his plan to marry Milly until Mrs. Lowder and Kate returned to England for a few weeks. Before they left, Kate made Densher promise that he would do as she had planned. Densher's conscience rebelled at the duplicity of the scheme, and he was not sure that when the plan was worked out to its finish Kate would still want him. As a sign that there was mutual trust between them, he asked Kate to go to his rooms with him. She did so the day before she left Venice, leaving her lover honor-bound to try to marry another woman.

One day, as Densher approached the house Milly had taken for the winter, he saw Lord Mark leaving. He soon found out from Mrs. Stringham that Lord Mark had proposed to Milly and had been rejected because the girl had detected unwanted sympathy in his proposal and had suspected that he was after her money rather than her love. Densher believed, rightly, that Lord Mark's rejection gave him some reason to be hopeful. He informed Milly that she was the only reason he was neglecting his work. She was highly pleased and hoped that he would propose.

Lord Mark disappeared from Venice for almost a month. Then Densher discovered him in a café, shortly after Densher had been refused admittance to Milly's house. Immediately Densher knew what had happened. Lord Mark had, in some way, discovered the engagement between Densher and Kate and had informed Milly. Densher attempted to hit upon some plan to right the situation. Three days later Mrs. Stringham came to him and told him what had happened. It was as he had guessed. What he had not guessed, however, was that Milly had ceased to take any interest in living and was refusing to eat or talk to anyone. Mrs. Stringham, desperate, had sent for Sir Luke Strett.

Densher returned to London but did not, at first, go to see Kate. He could not face her after the turn which their plans had taken, and he could not bear the idea of having hurt Milly as he had done. Finally, on Christmas Day, he had a premonition. He hurried to Sir Luke Strett's residence. There he found Mrs. Lowder, who told him that the previous day she had received a telegram telling of Milly's death. A few days later a letter arrived from Venice. Without opening it, Densher knew what the message was, for it was addressed in Milly's handwriting. He went immediately to see Kate, who also guessed that it was a letter informing Densher that she had left him part of her fortune so that he and Kate might marry. Neither of them dared to open the letter because they were ashamed of their conduct toward Milly. They burned the letter in the fireplace.

Within ten days another letter came from a New York law firm. Densher did not open it, but sent it with a short note to Kate. She came to his rooms with it. She wanted to know why he had sent it on to her. He replied that it was up to her to answer whether he should take the money that was offered by it, for he could never marry her with the money Milly had left him.

Kate refused to answer him or to open the letter, lest the large amount of the fortune tempt either of them into accepting it. Finally Densher said he wanted to marry her, but only as they had been before the arrival of Milly Theale. Kate left, after reminding him that they could never be the same, that such was impossible, for the events pertaining to Milly Theale had imbedded themselves into their souls.

Critical Evaluation

Henry James came of a family whose members considered themselves viewers of, rather than participators in, society. Their wealth enabled them to remove themselves from the common rout, and Henry and his father both suffered from physical disabilities which to some degree enforced this detachment, which was emotional as well as physical. The family traveled continually during the author's youth; as an adult he lived chiefly in Europe, though maintaining nonetheless close relations with his parents and siblings. The ties of blood, for him, took the place of national feeling. He considered himself a citizen of the world, and took of the life of his countrymen the same objective, albeit curious and sympathetic, view as of society in general.

Coming as he did of parents whose chief business in life was the cultivation of their own and their children's sensibilities, and sharing the family's strong if eccentric religious bent, he took it as his artistic mission to examine the condition of human society at large as that condition manifested itself in the most subdued and civilized of human milieus.

The specifics of the plot of *The Wings of the Dove* were suggested to the author by the premature death of his cousin Mary Temple, called Minny. The girl had charm, beauty, money, and love. She had, as it is said, everything to live for, and grimly resisted her fate to the end. After her death of tuberculosis in 1870, James was, as he later wrote, "haunted" by the tragedy of her situation. Two of his most appealing heroines take their essential lines from her: Isabel Archer of *The Portrait of a Lady,* and Milly Theale.

James wrote three of his best novels in quick succession shortly after 1900. As the new century began, he produced *The Ambassadors* (1902), *The Wings of the Dove* (1903), and *The Golden Bowl* (1904). These three novels represent the highest expression of those ideas of art and life gleaned over nearly six decades of observation and analysis of European and American mores. The three themes that impel these novels, as well as most of his previous works, are: "the contrast of American sincerity and crudity with European deceit and culture, the conflicting realities of life and art, and the substitution of psychological for ethical measurements of good and evil " (Robert E. Spiller, *The Cycle of American Literature*). *The Wings of the Dove* treats all three.

The first is most neatly illustrated by the counterpoise of Mrs. Maud Lowder and Mrs. Stringham. Aunt Maud's wardship of Kate has a monetary quality made explicit in her remark to Merton Densher: " 'I've been saving (Kate's presence) up and letting it, as you say of investments, appreciate, and you may judge whether, now it has begun to pay so, I'm likely to consent to treat for it with any but a high bidder.' " Mrs. Stringham's attachment to Milly, on the other hand, takes for her the shape of a holy mission to shepherd through the hazards of the world a being so exalted that the heroines of literature pale beside her. Her view of Milly is essentially romantic; she calls her "an angel," "a princess in a palace," and ironically "the real thing"; ironically, because *real* is exactly what Milly is not for her companion, any more than Kate is at bottom anything more than a marketable commodity to Mrs. Lowder. The difference in the characters of Kate and Milly enlarges on this theme; Kate accepts that definition of herself, using it to her own purpose, but succumbs at the last to its corrupting influence in using Densher as just such another counter, thus losing both love and honor. Milly, resisting the dehumanizing effects of both hero worship and pity, works her own salvation as well as Densher's.

The life that Milly makes for herself, knowing her days are numbered and knowing, almost, their number, comprehends abysses both sublime and terrible. For she recognizes from the first the effects of her money on the company into which she is betrayed by her shepherd, so graphically if unintentionally particularized for her by kind, corrupt Lord Mark, who brings her before the Bronzino portrait; so like her but, most poignantly to Milly's sense, "dead, dead, dead." She has, even before she hears her sentence pronounced by Sir Luke Strett, a trick of deferring judgment, of not permitting the baseness of others to circumscribe or debase her experience. Afterward, this tendency flowers into a kind of divine duplicity, a double reverse which consists of her keeping from everyone but Mrs. Stringham the fact that she is dying. We are to keep in mind that after a certain point in the story she must inevitably see everyone else as acting in the light of this knowledge of her limited future. Yet she makes no move to defend herself; she simply, profoundly, trusts. In short, she offers herself as a dove for sacrifice, a gesture that parallels the willingness of others to sacrifice her to their own designs. All her putative friends deceive themselves in regard to her, acting for their own good but in the name of her happiness. But Milly does not deceive herself. Her surrender is deliberate. In this she is a supreme artist; she makes of her life an instrument for Mrs. Stringham's gratification, for Kate's enlightenment, and for Densher's redemption, a creative act of the highest kind.

And all this great work, as well as diverse strokes of wickedness, is done in a few murmured words, a nod or a look, an invitation accepted or declined, gestures always within the bounds of propriety. Such an exposition of the instincts of the jungle expressed in the manners of the salon generates, in the end, more force than many a less subdued narrative. For we are treated not only to the powerful spectacle of Kate Croy prowling her situation with the disciplined rage of a caged tigress, but also to the glorious vision of Milly Theale, triumphant over betrayal and death, fulfilling her extraordinary nature to its highest potential.

Bibliography

Anderson, Quentin. *The American Henry James.* New Brunswick, N.J.: Rutgers University Press, 1957, pp. 233–280.

Bersani, Leo. *A Future for Astyanax: Character and Desire in Literature.* Boston: Little, Brown, 1976, pp. 128–155.

Bowden, Edwin T. *The Themes of Henry James.* New Haven, Conn.: Yale University Press, 1956, pp. 88–96.

Cargill, Oscar. *The Novels of Henry James.* New York: Macmillan, 1961, pp. 338–382.

Dupee, F.W. *Henry James.* Garden City, N.Y.: Doubleday Anchor, 1956, pp. 215–223.

Edel, Leon.   *Henry James, the Master, 1901–1916.* Philadelphia: Lippincott, 1972, pp. 108–122.

Edgar, Pelham.   *Henry James: Man and Author.* Boston: Houghton Mifflin, 1927, pp. 298–310.

Fryer, Judith.   *The Faces of Eve: Women in the Nineteenth Century American Novel.* New York: Oxford University Press, 1976, pp. 101–112.

Geismar, Maxwell.   *Henry James and the Jacobites.* Boston: Houghton Mifflin, 1963, pp. 226–243.

Graham, Kenneth.   "The Sense of Life in *The Wings of the Dove,*" in *Henry James: The Drama of Fulfillment, An Approach to the Novels.* Oxford: Clarendon Press, 1975, pp. 160–232.

Holland, Laurence B.   *The Expense of Vision: Essays on the Craft of Henry James.* Princeton, N.J.: Princeton University Press, 1964, pp. 285–327.

Jefferson, D.W.   *Henry James and the Modern Reader.* New York: St. Martin's, 1964, pp. 201–216.

Krook, Dorothea.   *The Ordeal of Consciousness in Henry James.* New York: Cambridge University Press, 1962, pp. 195–231.

Lewis, R.W.B.   *Trials of the Word.* New Haven, Conn.: Yale University Press, 1965, pp. 120–128.

McElderry, Bruce R., Jr.   *Henry James.* New York: Twayne, 1965, pp. 135–139.

Marks, Robert.   *James's Later Novels: An Interpretation.* New York: William-Frederick, 1960, pp. 44–56.

Matthiessen, F.O.   *Henry James: The Major Phase.* New York: Oxford University Press, 1944, pp. 42–80.

Putt, S. Gorley.   *A Reader's Guide to Henry James.* Ithaca, N.Y.: Cornell University Press, 1966, pp. 307–339.

Samuels, Charles Thomas.   *The Ambiguity of Henry James.* Urbana: University of Illinois Press, 1971, pp. 61–88.

Sears, Sallie.   *The Negative Imagination: Form and Perspective in the Novels of Henry James.* Ithaca, N.Y.: Cornell University Press, 1968, pp. 61–98.

Sharp, Sister M. Corona.   *The Confidante in Henry James: Evolution and Moral Value of a Fictive Character.* Notre Dame, Ind.: University of Notre Dame Press, 1963, pp. 181–213.

Ward. J.A.   *The Imagination of Disaster: Evil in the Fiction of Henry James.* Lincoln: University of Nebraska Press, 1961, pp. 127–139.

————.   *The Search for Form: Studies in the Structure of James's Fiction.* Chapel Hill: University of North Carolina Press, 1967, pp. 164–198.

Wegelin, Christof. *The Image of Europe in Henry James.* Dallas: Southern Methodist University Press, 1958, pp. 106–121. Reprinted in *Discussions of Henry James.* Edited by Naomi Lebowitz. Boston: Heath, 1962, pp. 71–79.

Wright, Walter F. *The Madness of Art: A Study of Henry James.* Lincoln: University of Nebraska Press, 1962, pp. 219–232.

SARAH ORNE JEWETT

Born: South Berwick, Maine (September 3, 1849)
Died: South Berwick (June 24, 1909)

Principal Works

SHORT STORIES: *Deephaven*, 1877; *Old Friends and New*, 1879; *A White Heron and Other Stories*, 1886; *The King of Folly Island*, 1888; *Strangers and Wayfarers*, 1890; *A Native of Winby*, 1893; *The Life of Nancy*, 1895; *The Country of the Pointed Firs*, 1896; *The Queen's Twin*, 1899.

NOVELS: *A Country Doctor*, 1884; *A Marsh Island*, 1885; *The Country of the Pointed Firs*, 1896; *The Tory Lover*, 1901.

Born in South Berwick, Maine, on September 3, 1849, Sarah Orne Jewett lived a quiet and happy childhood distinguished only by the fact that she developed a keen interest in people and an insight into culture through traveling about the countryside with her father, who was a country doctor. Her interest in the people of Maine never diminished, even though she later traveled widely in Europe. She seems to have been much more interested in the people of the coastal villges and upland farms of Maine than she was in such friends as William Dean Howells, Annie Fields, and Thomas Bailey Aldrich, famous literary personages of the time. Jewett's private life was always undistinguished; she never married, nor did she go to college, although Bowdoin College awarded her an honorary Litt.D. degree in 1901, making her the first woman to receive such a degree from that institution.

What education Jewett had she acquired by herself or at the local academy in Berwick. As a young woman she began to serve a writer's apprenticeship by writing for children's magazines. Her first published attempt at adult fiction appeared in the *Atlantic Monthly* for December, 1869, when she was but twenty years old. By 1877 she had published many stories in periodicals and collected thirteen of them into a volume published as *Deephaven* in 1877. During the following two decades Jewett continued to write many stories for magazines and collected them at intervals in volumes. Of the several collections, two are outstanding: *Tales of New England* (1890), selected from earlier volumes, and *The Country of the Pointed Firs*, published in 1896. Critics, scholars, and fellow authors have termed the latter volume one of the great examples of American regional fiction during the period 1865–1900. Willa Cather, famous American woman writer, enthusiastically compared *The Country of the Pointed Firs* in greatness to Mark Twain's *Huckleberry Finn* and Hawthorne's *The Scarlet Letter*.

The Country of the Pointed Firs, as well as other volumes by Jewett, is generally considered a novel. The book is divided into chapters, each "chapter" a separate local color character sketch, with the series held together by the device of having a summer visitor to the fictional town of Dunnet Landing, Maine, narrate the fiction through her impressions. The device is a common one in Jewett's writings, and she used it as early as her first collection, *Deephaven*, in 1877.

All of Jewett's important writings deal with the country she knew so well, the coastal towns and upland farms of Maine. Her method of approach to her material is realistic, and her brand of realism is very similar to the realism of the commonplace familiar to readers of William Dean Howells. Some readers have been dismayed because the subject matter—background, characters, and action—is often so simple and commonplace as to seem to border on the trivial. Twentieth century readers, reared on a lustier diet of fiction—like that of Hemingway and Faulkner—may find Jewett's work boring, despite a poetic air which pervades it. Perhaps Jewett's fiction, like that of other women authors of the nineteenth century, is to become fare for the passionate few, rather than for a wide but less enthusiastic group of readers.

Technically, the fiction written by Jewett is outstanding, despite the shortcomings some readers may find in it. She studied the craft of writing more seriously than most writers, becoming an avid student of fiction-writing and especially the work of Zola, Tolstoy, Flaubert, and Henry James. She appreciated their work because they, like her, gave weight in their writings to the commonplace, even the trivial, lending an importance to elements in everyday life which ordinarily are not seen thoroughly enough to be regarded as important. Like Henry James, Jewett sought to see beneath the surface of existence. The result is that her stories attain artistry, although they may seem brittle. Certainly she has given American literature a better picture of New England than such writers as Harriet Beecher Stowe and Rose Terry Cooke.

Jewett saw everything and wrote about everything from the standpoint of a woman. Her female characters are splendidly portrayed, as is their life, but she seems to have regarded the world of men as of little consequence for her art.

Rather than whole volumes, present-day readers tend to read individual stories from her work. Some which seem particularly attractive for readers now are "A White Heron," "Marsh Rosemary," "A Lost Lover," "Miss Tempy's Watchers," and "The Courting of Sister Wisby."

In addition to her stories and some juvenile fiction, Miss Jewett made excursions into other areas of writing. She wrote a non-fictional *Story of the Normans* (1887) and three novels in addition to *The Country of the Pointed Firs*. Her first novel, *A Country Doctor*, described in fiction the character and life of her father. In *The Tory Lover* she attempted a historical novel dealing with John Paul Jones and a company of men he recruited from her native Berwick, Maine. She died in the town of her birth on June 24, 1909.

Bibliography

The best study is F. O. Matthiessen, *Sarah Orne Jewett*, 1929. See also Jean

Sougnac, *Sarah Orne Jewett*, 1937; Willa Cather, Introduction to *The Best Stories of Sarah Orne Jewett*, 2 vols., 1925; Arthur H. Quinn, *American Fiction*, 1936; Richard Cary, *Sarah Orne Jewett*, 1962; C. M. Thompson, "The Art of Miss Jewett," *Atlantic Monthly*, XCIV (1904), 485–497; E. M. Chapman, "The New England of Sarah Orne Jewett," *Yale Review*, III (1913), 157–172; Martha H. Shackleford, "Sarah Orne Jewett," *Sewanee Review*, XXX (1922), 20–26; Edward Garnett, *Friday Nights*, 1922; Anon, "The New England Spirit," *London Times Literary Supplement*, XLVI (1947), p. 602, and the Jewett issue, *Colby Library Quarterly*, Ser. VI, No. X (June, 1964).

See also Carl J. Weber, *A Bibliography of the Published Writings of Sarah Orne Jewett*, 1949, and *Letters of Sarah Orne Jewett Now in the Colby College Library*, 1948; also "New England Through French Eyes Fifty Years Ago," *New England Quarterly*, XX (1947), 385–396.

A COUNTRY DOCTOR

Type of work: Novel
Author: Sarah Orne Jewett (1849–1909)
Type of plot: Regional romance
Time of plot: Mid-nineteenth century
Locale: Oldfields, Maine
First published: 1884

In this successful local color novel, Jewett describes an intelligent girl's maturing process in the midst of people who consider her independence and her desire to remain single and pursue a career strange and unladylike. The customs and habits of the Oldfields community are painted with warmth and sympathy.

Principal Characters

Nan Prince, a young girl who, in the nineteenth century, wants to become a medical doctor. As a child she is mischievous, but likes to care for animals. She assists the local doctor, who rears her after her mother's and grandmother's deaths. The girl attends medical school, despite pressure from her relatives and her suitor. Upon receiving her medical education she returns to the town to assist the doctor and eventually to take over his practice.

Adeline Thacher Prince, Nan's mother. She returns home to Oldfields to die, bringing her infant daughter. She is a wild, rebellious woman who reputedly is addicted to drink. She resents her husband's family because they opposed her marriage.

Mrs. Thacher, Nan's maternal grandmother, who cares for the child until her own death.

Dr. Leslie, the doctor in Oldfields. He looks after Nan and rears her in his own home after her grandmother's death. He encourages her study of medicine.

Miss Nancy Prince, a wealthy spinster, Nan's aunt. She is shocked at Nan's seemingly unladylike ambition to be a doctor and tries to dissuade the girl from studying medicine. She also tries to interest Nan in a young man, George Gerry, in hopes that Nan will marry and abandon her ambition to practice medicine.

George Gerry, a young friend of Miss Nancy Prince. He and Nan fall in love, as Nan's aunt hopes, but George cannot persuade Nan to marry him and abandon medicine.

The Story

One cold winter night while Mrs. Thacher and two of her neighbors were sitting around the stove and gossiping about neighborhood activities, they were interrupted by a noise at the door. Adeline Thacher Prince had fallen on the doorstep. In her arms she held her infant daughter, Nan. Dr. Leslie was sent for at once but by the next day Adeline was dead. According to her wishes, Dr. Leslie became the little child's guardian, though she lived with her maternal grandmother.

Nan's mother had left home to go to work in a textile mill in Lowell. There she had fallen in love with a young man from Dunport, Maine, and after a short courtship she had married him. The marriage had been far from happy. Adeline had inherited a wild, rebellious tendency, and it was whispered in Dunport that she had eventually taken to drink. She resented, furthermore, the opposition of her husband's family to the marriage, especially the views of her husband's sister, Miss Nancy Prince. After Adeline's husband died, she tried for a time to support herself and the child. When she could do so no longer, she trudged back to Oldfields to die in her mother's home.

Little Nan seemed to exhibit some of her mother's characteristics, for she was mischievous and inclined to pleasure. Her grandmother often thought her a trial, but to Dr. Leslie she was something quite different. One day Nan retrieved a fallen bird with a fractured leg and applied a splint, as she had seen Dr. Leslie do to his patients. The doctor began to wonder if Nan had not inherited some tendency toward medicine which her father had had. He did not insist that she go to school. He thought that the training she received in the woods and the fields was far more beneficial than any she would obtain in the schoolroom.

When Mrs. Thacher died, Nan went to live with Dr. Leslie. Between the two there was a great feeling of affection. Nan, who continued to go out on calls with the doctor, exhibited much interest in his work. The time came at last for her to be sent to boarding school. At first she was shy and rather backward in her studies, but after a while she made admirable progress. She would have been completely satisfied with her life if she had not wondered, from time to time, about the mysterious aunt of whom she had heard only rumors. Mrs. Thacher had never explained anything of the girl's family background to her, and Nan had conjured up the figure of a wealthy aristocratic relative who would one day send for her. Miss Prince, who had inherited a large estate, regularly sent money to Dr. Leslie to provide for Nan's upkeep. The doctor never touched a penny of it. When Adeline had died, Miss Prince had asked for the custody of the child, but Mrs. Thacher and Dr. Leslie had refused her request.

When Nan grew older, she told Dr. Leslie of her desire to study medicine. Although the doctor was aware of the difficulties she would face, he approved heartily of her interest. But the town of Oldfields did not, and many were shocked at the idea of a woman doctor. Nan continued her studies in the doctor's books, however, and acted as his nurse. That training she was to continue at a medical school in a nearby city.

When the time came for her to leave Oldfields, Nan wrote a brief note to her aunt, Miss Prince, and asked if she might visit her father's sister. Miss Prince, although she feared that Nan might be like her mother, consented to receive her niece. On Nan's arrival in Dunport, Miss Prince, genuinely pleased with her, helped Nan to make friends and openly acknowledged her young relative. But when Nan expressed her wish to study medicine, everyone was shocked, even

Miss Prince, who in a large measure blamed Dr. Leslie for Nan's unladylike desire for a professional career. Nan, although made unhappy by her aunt's objections, remained adamant.

Her aunt and her friends, however, sought to lead her astray from her work. Miss Prince had a favorite friend, young George Gerry, to whom she intended leaving her money. When Nan grew fond of George, everyone hoped that they would marry. One day, during an outing, Nan and George stopped at a farmhouse, and Nan treated a farmer who had thrown his arm out of joint. Sometime later, George asked Nan to marry him. She refused, both because she wanted to become a doctor and because she was afraid that her inherited characteristics might cause her to be a bad wife.

At last she told her aunt that she would have to return to Oldfields. On her arrival, the doctor, who had been apprehensive that Nan might have been influenced by Miss Prince and her money, was pleasantly surprised. She was the same Nan she had been before, and all the more ambitious for a successful medical career.

Nan went away to study. When she returned, Dr. Leslie was older and needed more help in his practice. Nan settled down in Oldfields and slowly the community accepted her. Before many years passed she had succeeded Dr. Leslie in the affections of the men and women of the village.

Critical Evaluation

A Country Doctor is a novel of development rather than plot. With sensitivity and insight, Sarah Orne Jewett traces the growth and awakening of an intelligent young girl. Nan Prince has more imagination and energy than the village people are accustomed to seeing in a young girl. They like her, but don't quite approve of her; they wonder what will become of such a fanciful, harum-scarum female who doesn't act as a girl ought to act and do what is expected of her. "I don't mean to be discontented," she says, but it is clear that she has a will of her own. Nan is taught that she owes something to the world besides following her own selfish plans; duty to society is early instilled into her by the doctor, who feels that Nan is not the kind of girl who is likely to marry: she is too independent and self-reliant.

The difficulties Nan encounters because she wants to be a doctor are explored in detail. People tell Nan that a woman's place is in the home, but she insists that since any man who aspires to be a doctor is helped, so should she be. God wouldn't have given her talents equal to those of a man if she were not meant to use them, she tells her aunt. Her family tries to marry her off, but she resists, and dedicates herself entirely to her career.

Another theme mentioned in this book and elaborated in nearly all of Sarah Orne Jewett's books is that of the old people taking with them when they die their lifetime's store of local social history and tradition. Jewett saw that this valuable source should be tapped, and somehow saved for posterity. Perhaps, she suggests, the country doctors could record the memories of their old patients, rather than let them perish.

No American writer had a better ear than Jewett for the speech patterns of her people, for their selection of words and phrases, the rhythms and cadences of their conversation, and their humor. Jewett never satirizes her characters, but presents them with both affection and objectivity. She recognizes the flaws in these unsophisticated, work-hardened people, but she forgives them, and in *A Country Doctor,* she shows how a strong and intelligent person such as Nan can rise from among these people, and shine with all of the stubborn virtues of the native American tradition.

Bibliography

Auchincloss, Louis. *Pioneers and Caretakers: A Study of American Women Novelists.* Minneapolis: University of Minnesota Press, 1965, pp. 6–19.

Bentzon, Th. "Le Roman de la Femme-Medecin," in *Revue des Deux Mondes.* LXVII (February 1, 1885), pp. 598–632. Translated and reprinted in *Appreciation of Sarah Orne Jewett: 29 Interpretive Essays.* Edited by Richard Cary. Waterville, Me.: Colby College Press, 1973, pp. 3–15.

Cone, Helen Gray. "Woman in American Literature," in *Century.* XL (October, 1890), pp. 926–927.

Eakin, Paul John. "Sarah Orne Jewett and the Meaning of Country Life," in *American Literature.* XXXVIII (1967), pp. 508–531. Reprinted in *Appreciation of Sarah Orne Jewett: 29 Interpretive Essays.* Edited by Richard Cary. Waterville, Me.: Colby College Press, 1973, pp. 203–222.

Forbes, Esther. "Sarah Orne Jewett, The Apostle of New England," in *Boston Evening Transcript.* (May 16, 1925), Section VI, p. 1. Reprinted in *Appreciation of Sarah Orne Jewett: 29 Interpretive Essays.* Edited by Richard Cary. Waterville, Me.: Colby College Press, 1973, pp. 70–80.

Forrey, Carolyn. "The New Woman Revisited," in *Women's Studies.* II (1974), pp. 42–44.

Matthieseen, F.O. "Sarah Orne Jewett," in *Responsibilities of the Critic: Essays and Reviews.* New York: Oxford University Press, 1952, pp. 64–66.

More, Paul Elmer. "A Writer of New England," in *Nation.* XCI (October 27, 1910), pp. 386–387. Reprinted in *Appreciation of Sarah Orne Jewett: 29 Interpretive Essays.* Edited by Richard Cary. Waterville, Me.: Colby College Press, 1973, pp. 49–51.

Pool, Eugene Hillhouse. "The Child in Sarah Orne Jewett," in *Colby Library Quarterly.* VII (September, 1967), pp. 503–509. Reprinted in *Appreciation of Sarah Orne Jewett: 29 Interpretive Essays.* Edited by Richard Cary.

Waterville, Me.: Colby College Press, 1973, pp. 223–228.

Shackford, Martha Hale. "Sarah Orne Jewett," in *Sewanee Review.* XXX (1922), pp. 20–26. Reprinted in *The World of Dunnet Landing: A Sarah Orne Jewett Collection.* Edited by David Bonnell Green. Lincoln: University of Nebraska Press, 1962, pp. 353–364. Also reprinted in *Appreciation of Sarah Orne Jewett: 29 Interpretive Essays.* Edited by Richard Cary. Waterville, Me.: Colby College Press, 1973, pp. 64–69.

Thorp, Margaret F. *Sarah Orne Jewett.* Minneapolis: University of Minnesota Press, 1966, pp. 30–32.

Wilbanks, Evelyn. "The Doctor as Romantic Hero: A Study of Idealization," in *Journal of the American Medical Association.* CCXX (1972), pp. 54–57.

THE COUNTRY OF THE POINTED FIRS

Type of work: Novel
Author: Sarah Orne Jewett (1849–1909)
Type of plot: Regional romance
Time of plot: Late nineteenth century
Locale: Maine seacoast
First published: 1896

Told from the point of view of a summer visitor to Dunnet Landing, Maine, this work is very slender in plot; it consists mainly of character sketches, nature descriptions, and short tales told to Mrs. Todd's boarder by local residents of the seacoast town. The book is a masterpiece of local-color writing, and is considered by most readers to be Jewett's finest work.

Principal Characters

The Boarder, a woman writer who comes to Dunnet Landing, Maine, to work in seclusion. Here she meets many people and finds friendly, interesting characters.

Mrs. Almira Todd, a friendly widow who accepts the writer as a boarder. She is also an herb doctor, growing herbs in her garden and searching out others in the fields.

Captain Littlepage, an elderly, retired sea captain who tells the writer a yarn about his own shipwreck and a town of ghosts near the North Pole, where souls await their passage to the next world.

Mrs. Blackett, Mrs. Todd's aged mother. She lives on an island with her son William and does her own housework.

William Blackett, Mrs. Todd's brother, a bashful man. He loves Esther Hight and finally is able to marry her when he is in his fifties.

Mrs. Fosdick, a friend of Mrs. Todd. She comes often to visit with her friend and to tell stories about the local folk.

Mr. Tilley, an old fisherman. He is reserved with strangers, but he accepts the writer as a friend and shows her the house he has kept for eight years the same as it was when his wife died.

Esther Hight, a woman loved by William Blackett. She supports herself and her elderly mother by tending sheep. After her mother's death she is free to marry William.

The Story

A woman writer came one summer to Dunnet Landing, a Maine seacoast town, to find seclusion for her work. She boarded with Mrs. Almira Todd, a friendly widow and the local herb doctor. Besides having a garden full of herbs, Mrs. Todd often roamed far afield for rarer specimens. The boarder sometimes took care of

Mrs. Todd's sales of herbs and birch beer when Mrs. Todd was away.

At last the boarder realized that she must get to work on her book and give up the society of Mrs. Todd in the daytime. The boarder found the village schoolhouse a quiet place for her writing, and she spent most of her days there. One morning she was surprised to have a visit from old Captain Littlepage, a retired seaman who seldom left his house. For a time he spoke seriously of the great English poets. When he saw that the boarder did not laugh at him, he launched upon a long narrative. It seemed that he had been shipwrecked upon a small island and had met there another sailor who had been to the North Pole. He told Captain Littlepage of a town of ghosts he had discovered. It was Captain Littlepage's theory that in this town souls awaited their passage into the next world. The old man's narrative stopped suddenly as his mind returned to the present. The boarder helped him home and told no one about his strange story.

On another day Mrs. Todd took her boarder out to Green Island, where Mrs. Todd's mother lived. Mrs. Blackett was over eighty, her daughter past sixty. Mrs. Blackett still did her own work and kept house for her son William, who was past fifty. William was a bashful man, but he found a friend to his liking in the boarder. Mrs. Todd and the boarder gathered some herbs before they left the island, and Mrs. Todd showed her the spot offshore where her husband had gone down in his boat.

Mrs. Fosdick came to visit Mrs. Todd. The two old ladies and the boarder often spent their evenings together. One night Mrs. Todd told of her husband's Cousin Joanna, who had lived on Shell-heap Island. Disappointed in love, Joanna went to live alone on the tiny island. Passing fishermen often left presents on the shore for her, but no one ever visited her. Finally Mrs. Todd and the minister went to see her, for the minister was worried about the state of Joanna's soul. They found Joanna living comfortably but simply. Satisfied with her lonely life, she could not be induced to return to the mainland. Joanna lived out her life on the island and was buried there.

Late in August Mrs. Todd took her boarder and Mrs. Blackett to the Bowden family reunion. They hired a carriage and drove far inland to the family seat. All the Bowdens for miles around came to the reunion, and Mrs. Blackett was one of the privileged guests because of her age. For once Mrs. Todd forgot her herbs and spent the entire day in the enjoyment of the society of her friends. William had not come to the gathering because of his bashfulness. Mrs. Blackett treasured every moment of the day, for she knew it was one of the last reunions she would attend.

One day the boarder stood on the shore below Dunnet Landing. There she met Mr. Tilley, one of the oldest fishermen in the village. Mr. Tilley was reserved toward strangers, but he had at last accepted the boarder as a friend and he invited her to visit him that afternoon. When the boarder arrived, he was knitting some socks. The two friends sat in the kitchen while Mr. Tilley told the boarder about his wife. She had died eight years before, but her husband had never got over his sorrow. He kept the house just as she had left it. Proudly he showed the boarder the seldom-used parlor and Mrs. Tilley's set of china. She left the cottage feeling the loneliness that surrounded the old fisherman.

When the clear, cool autumn came, it was time for the boarder to leave. Mrs. Todd helped her pack and get her belongings down on the wharf for the steamer. Mrs. Todd took her leave of the boarder before she left the house. From the deck of the steamer the boarder watched Dunnet Landing fade into the distance. She recalled a day of the past summer when William had come to the mainland. He was going trout fishing in an inland stream. Self-consciously he asked the boarder to go with him. They caught no fish, but William took her afterward to see Mrs. Hight and her daughter Esther. The boarder stayed to talk to Mrs. Hight, while William went out to speak to Esther, who supported her aged and crippled mother by tending sheep. As William and the boarder left, she realized that William and Esther were lovers.

When the boarder returned to Dunnet Landing in the spring, Mrs. Todd told her that Mrs. Hight had recently died and that Esther and William were to be married immediately. He was to come to the mainland the next day if the weather proved good.

Early in the morning Mrs. Todd was up to watch for a sail from Green Island. Finally she saw it approaching. Then neighbors began to drop in to inquire why William was coming to the mainland. After the ceremony William and Esther stopped for a moment at Mrs. Todd's house before returning to the island. Mrs. Todd and the boarder accompanied the pair to the landing to see them off. The older woman expressed no emotion at the leavetaking; but as she and the boarder returned to the house, they walked holding hands all the way.

Critical Evaluation

Willa Cather, when asked to name three American novels "deserving of a long, long life," selected *The Country of the Pointed Firs* to share this honor with *The Scarlet Letter* and *Huckleberry Finn*. One of Sarah Orne Jewett's last works, and probably her highest achievement, the novel is a moving and wise chronicle, unquestionably a genuine and great work of art. The gentle, thoughtful narrative flows with a precision of description worthy of Flaubert or Turgenev. The apparently effortless and ever graceful prose is the work of a master craftsman and a refined and gifted sensibility. The work is rich in symbols that arise naturally from the world about which the author is writing. Perhaps the dominant symbol is that of the great army of pointed firs, darkly cloaked and "standing as if they wait to embark."

The theme of balance is fundamental to the book, as much a part of it as the carefully structured narrative and perfectly poised sentences. Why, for example, does the major character, Mrs. Todd, choose to live in this tiny community? To keep the world balance true, suggests the author, to offset some other, unknown, existence. There is always a reason, if one but knows it. Hand in hand with the theme of balance moves that of solitude. Paths are trodden to the shrines of solitude the world over, writes the narrator, whether it be the island of Miss Joanna or the island of Mrs. Todd's mother, or the caves of the saints of the past. The old sea captain's story of the "Waiting Place," the strange, twilight land hovering by the North Pole, again suggests this theme. Perhaps solitude serves humanity as a kind of purgatory, a way station of the soul on its way to paradise. It can be fearful, this uncharted, inner space, but it must be encountered to achieve our full humanity. The ship that carried Captain Littlepage to this land was not accidentally named "Minerva."

The characterizations in *The Country of the Pointed Firs* are among the finest in American literature. Mrs. Todd is perhaps the glory of the book, a creation worthy of Dickens. She might belong to any age, as the narrator says, "like an idyl of Theocritus"; but with her potions and herbs, her Puritan ancestors probably would have burned her as a witch. She is an unlikely classic heroine, yet the narrator cannot resist some flattering comparisons. Mrs. Todd is likened to a grand and architectural caryatid and compared to Antigone standing alone on the Theban plain. But it is her language, her way with the Old Maine way of speaking, that breathes life into her bulky figure. One can *taste* the salty old expressions as they roll off her tongue.

The past of the whalers, so recently behind the characters, is ever present in the book. Indeed, the past is important on many levels to the characters in the novel. Mrs. Fosdick remarks: "Conversations got to have some root in the past, or else you've got to explain every remark you make. . . ." The rule might be said to apply to all civilized social intercourse. People with no respect for the past are left isolated and hopeless. In the world of Sarah Orne Jewett the present and past mutually enrich each other, and mortals wise enough to accept this are the benefactors.

The Country of the Pointed Firs is a treasure of wisdom and a lesson in the writing of pure, unaffected prose as the highest art. The individuals who stalk through its pages are loners, but they are not unhappy or unloving. Sara Orne Jewett has realized that "in the life of each of us . . . there is a place remote and islanded, and given to endless regret and secret happiness; we are each the uncompanioned hermit and recluse of an hour or a day. . . ." When she writes about her isolated New Englanders on their saltwashed islands, she is writing about all of us, about all of humanity.

Bibliography

Auchincloss, Louis. *Pioneers and Caretakers: A Study of American Women Novelists.* Minneapolis: University of Minnesota Press, 1965, pp. 6–19.

Bender, Bert. "To Calm and Uplift 'Against the Dark': Sarah Orne Jewett's Lyric Narratives," in *Colby Library Quarterly*. XI (1975), pp. 219–229.

Berthoff, Warner. "The Art of Jewett's *Pointed Firs*," in *New England Quarterly*. XXXII (1959), pp. 31–53. Reprinted in *Fictions and Events: Essays in Criticism and Literary History*. New York: Dutton, 1971, pp. 243–263. Also reprinted in *The World of Dunnet Landing: A Sarah Orne Jewett Collection*. Edited by David Bonnell Green. Lincoln: University of Nebraska Press, 1962, pp. 385–411. Also reprinted in *Appreciation of Sarah Orne Jewett: 29 Interpretive Essays*. Edited by Richard Cary. Waterville, Me.: Colby College Press, 1973, pp. 144–161.

Cather, Willa. *Not Under Forty*. New York: Knopf, 1936, pp. 76–95.

Chapman, Edward M. "The New England of Sarah Orne Jewett," in *Yale Review*. III (1913), pp. 157–172. Reprinted in *Appreciation of Sarah Orne Jewett: 29 Interpretive Essays*. Edited by Richard Cary. Waterville, Me.: Colby College Press, 1973, pp. 52–63.

Chase, Mary Ellen. "Sarah Orne Jewett as a Social Historian," in *The World of Dunnet Landing: A Sarah Orne Jewett Collection*. Edited by David Bonnell Green. Lincoln: University of Nebraska Press, 1962, pp. 365–372. Reprinted in *Appreciation of Sarah Orne Jewett: 29 Interpretive Essays*. Edited by Richard Cary. Waterville, Me.: Colby College Press, 1973, pp. 181–186.

Eakin, Paul John. "Sarah Orne Jewett and the Meaning of Country Life," in *American Literature*. XXXVIII (1967), pp. 508–531. Reprinted in *Appreciation of Sarah Orne Jewett: 29 Interpretive Essays*. Edited by Richard Cary. Waterville, Me.: Colby College Press, 1973, pp. 203–222.

Fike, Francis. "An Interpretation of *Pointed Firs*," in *New England Quarterly*. XXXIV (1961), pp. 478–491. Reprinted in *Appreciation of Sarah Orne Jewett: 29 Interpretive Essays*. Edited by Richard Cary. Waterville, Me.: Colby College Press, 1973, pp. 170–180.

Green, David Bonnell. "The World of Dunnet Landing," in *New England Quarterly*. XXXIV (1961), pp. 514–517. Reprinted in *The World of Dunnet Landing: A Sarah Orne Jewett Collection*. Edited by David Bonnell Green. Lincoln: University of Nebraska Press, 1962, pp. 412–417.

Hicks, Granville. *The Great Tradition: An Interpretation of American Literature Since the Civil War*. New York: Macmillan, 1933, pp. 101–105.

Howe, Irving. "*The Country of the Pointed Firs*," in *The Critic as Artist: Essays on Books, 1920–1970*. Edited by Gilbert A. Harrison. New York: Liveright, 1972, pp. 162–166.

Magowan, Robin. "The Outer Island Sequence in *Pointed Firs*," in *Colby Library Quarterly*. VI (1964), pp. 418–424.

————. "Pastoral and the Art of Landscape in *The Country of the Pointed Firs,*" in *New England Quarterly.* XXXVI (1963), pp. 229–240. Reprinted in *Appreciation of Sarah Orne Jewett: 29 Interpretive Essays.* Edited by Richard Cary. Waterville, Me.: Colby College Press, 1973, pp. 187–195.

Martin, Jay. *Harvests of Change: American Literature 1865–1914.* Englewood Cliffs, N.J.: Prentice-Hall, 1967, pp. 142–148.

Matthiessen, F.O. *Sarah Orne Jewett.* Boston: Houghton Mifflin, 1929, pp. 100–110.

Quinn, Arthur Hobson. *American Fiction: An Historical and Critical Survey.* New York: Appleton, 1936, pp. 324–330.

Shackford, Martha Hale. "Sarah Orne Jewett," in *Sewanee Review.* XXX (1922), pp. 20–26. Reprinted in *The World of Dunnet Landing: A Sarah Orne Jewett Collection.* Edited by David Bonnell Green. Lincoln: University of Nebraska Press, 1962, pp. 353–364. Also reprinted in *Appreciation of Sarah Orne Jewett: 29 Interpretive Essays.* Edited by Richard Cary. Waterville, Me.: Colby College Press, 1973, pp. 64–69.

Short, Clarice. "Studies in Gentleness," in *Western Humanities Review.* II (1957), pp. 387–393. Reprinted in *Appreciation of Sarah Orne Jewett: 29 Interpretive Essays.* Edited by Richard Cary. Waterville, Me.: Colby College Press, 1973, pp. 128–134.

Stouck, David. "*The Country of the Pointed Firs*: A Pastoral of Innocence," in *Colby Library Quarterly.* IX (December, 1970), pp. 213–220. Reprinted in *Appreciation of Sarah Orne Jewett: 29 Interpretive Essays.* Edited by Richard Cary. Waterville, Me.: Colby College Press, 1973, pp. 249–254.

Thorp, Margaret F. *Sarah Orne Jewett.* Minneapolis: University of Minnesota Press, 1966, pp. 41–44.

Toth, Susan A. "The Value of Age in The Fiction of Sarah Orne Jewett," in *Studies in Short Fiction.* VIII (1971), pp. 433–441. Reprinted in *Appreciation of Sarah Orne Jewett: 29 Interpretive Essays.* Edited by Richard Cary. Waterville, Me.: Colby College Press, 1973, pp. 255–263.

Vella, Michael W. "Sarah Orne Jewett: A Reading of *The Country of the Pointed Firs,*" in *Emerson Society Quarterly.* LXXIII (1973), pp. 275–282.

Voelker, Paul D. "*The Country of the Pointed Firs*: A Novel by Sarah Orne Jewett," in *Colby Library Quarterly.* IX (December, 1970), pp. 201–213. Reprinted in *Appreciation of Sarah Orne Jewett: 29 Interpretive Essays.* Edited by Richard Cary. Waterville, Me.: Colby College Press, 1973, pp. 238–248.

Waggoner, Hyatt H. "The Unity of *The Country of the Pointed Firs,*" in *Twentieth Century Literature.* V (1959), pp. 67–73. Reprinted in *The World of Dunnet Landing: A Sarah Orne Jewett Collection.* Edited by David Bonnell Green. Lincoln: University of Nebraska Press, 1962, pp. 373–384. Also reprinted in *Appreciation of Sarah Orne Jewett: 29 Interpretive Essays.* Edited by Richard Cary. Waterville, Me.: Colby College Press, 1973, pp. 162–169.

Wood, Ann Douglas. "The Literature of Impoverishment: The Women Local Colorists in America, 1865–1914," in *Women's Studies.* I (1972), pp. 3–45.

Ziff, Larzer. *The American 1890's: Life and Times of a Lost Generation.* New York: Viking, 1966, 286–291.

JACK LONDON

Born: San Francisco, California (January 12, 1876)
Died: Santa Rosa, California (November 22, 1916)

Principal Works

NOVELS: *A Daughter of the Snows*, 1902; *The Call of the Wild*, 1903; *The Sea Wolf*, 1904; *The Game*, 1905; *White Fang*, 1906; *Before Adam*, 1906; *The Iron Heel*, 1907; *Martin Eden*, 1909; *Burning Daylight*, 1910; *Adventure*, 1911; *Smoke Bellew*, 1912; *John Barleycorn*, 1913; *The Valley of the Moon*, 1913; *The Mutiny of the Elsinore*, 1914; *The Star Rover*, 1915; *The Scarlet Plague*, 1915; *Jerry of the Islands*, 1917; *Michael, Brother of Jerry*, 1917; *Hearts of Three*, 1920.

SHORT STORIES: *The Son of the Wolf*, 1900; *The God of His Fathers*, 1901; *The Faith of Men*, 1904; *Tales of the Fish Patrol*, 1905; *Moon-Face*, 1906; *Love of Life*, 1906; *When God Laughs*, 1911; *The House of Pride*, 1912; *The Strength of the Strong*, 1914; *Dutch Courage*, 1922.

PLAY: *Theft*, 1910.

ESSAYS: *Revolution and Other Essays*, 1910.

Jack (John Griffith) London, the ardent Socialist whose individualistic tales of adventure have long made him the idol of American boys, was born in the squalor of a San Francisco slum on January 12, 1876. His mother was a girl called Flora Wellman, his father an Irish adventurer and roving astrologer, W. H. Chaney. A few months after the child's birth Flora married John London, whose name was to be adopted and made famous by a child not his own.

Increasing poverty forced London to leave school after the eighth grade; thenceforth his literary education was dependent upon the books he borrowed from the Oakland Public Library. The fictional productions of his maturity reflect the influence of his early favorites, Rudyard Kipling, Karl Marx, and, later, Herbert Spencer and Friedrich Nietzsche. Not that young London had much leisure for reading; during the five years after he left school he was an oyster pirate, a seaman, an unsuccessful Yukon prospector, and a tramp throughout the entire North American continent. In 1893, shortly after he had won a newspaper prize for his account of a typhoon off Japan, he spent a month in a Niagra Falls jail as a vagrant. Upon his release he returned to Oakland and, intending to mend his ways, entered high school there. After only a year he passed the entrance examinations of the University of California with high honors. After only one semester he left college for financial reasons, to devote himself to the writing which was to be his principal occupation for the rest of his life.

In 1898 the *Overland Monthly* published London's tale of the Yukon, *To The Man on the Trail*, the first of a steady stream of stories which were to pour from

his prolific pen. By 1903 he had published more than one hundred pieces in periodicals as well as eight full-length volumes. During that year *The Call of the
Wild* appeared, the story of the magnificent lone dog Buck, king of the Alaskan
wilderness, which has become something of an American classic. But London's
socialistic class-consciousness was already warring with his love of adventurous
individualism; during the same year the American public was shocked to read his
first-hand account, in *The People of the Abyss*, of life among the derelicts of
London, who grubbed for garbage in the mud as food.

During the next ten years London's novels followed upon each other with
amazing rapidity. Whether dealing with high adventure and the thrills of the
individual torn loose from the encumbrances of civilization, battling nature as in
The Sea Wolf, or with the growing consciousness of the downtrodden masses
under a powerful leader, as in *The Iron Heel*, his books are alike in their exalta-
tion of violence and essential solitude. This love of violence is reflected in the very
titles of some of the later books, as in *The Strength of the Strong or The Abysmal
Brute*. Only two of the novels, *Martin Eden* and *John Barleycorn*, are frankly
autobiographical, but most of them reflect some aspects of the author's own character and ideals. The fortune his writing quickly brought him London spent with
reckless abandon, seeking to "show the world" and satisfy his own ego with his
enormous ranch, his fantastic yacht, his many loves. But neither writing nor his
pursuit of pleasure could ward off the despair which came increasingly to supplant the glorious illusions in his mind. On November 22, 1916, at the age of
forty, Jack London took his own life at Santa Rose, California.

At its best, Jack London's style is characterized by color, vigor, and brutal
directness rather than by literary refinement or excellence; at its worst it is that of
any cheap, pot-boiling hack. But it is for the tales of violence conceived by his
fertile imagination, not for beauty of prose style, that London is remembered.
Socialist though he may have been by intellectual choice, he was at heart an
unadulterated individualist and romantic, and his personal dream was not the
Socialist paradise of mass security but the primordial wilderness, untouched by
civilization, where every man and beast is king in his own domain. Egotism and
vitality were the keys to London's personality, just as they are the central qualities
of all his books. It was as "king of the adventure story" that Jack London was
hailed in his own era and is read and remembered today.

Bibliography

The basic story of London's life is Charmian London, *The Book of Jack
London*, 2 vols., 1921; but this has been supplanted by Richard O'Connor, *Jack
London: A Biography*, 1964. See also Irving Stone, *Sailor on Horseback*, 1938;
and Joan London, *Jack London and His Times: An Unconventional Biography*,
1939. Reminiscences of London and related background studies will also be
found in Stephen Graham, *The Death of Yesterday*, 1930; Georgia L. Bamford,
The Mystery of Jack London, 1931; and Joseph Noel, *Footloose in Arcadia*,
1940.

For criticism see Thomas K. Whipple, *Study Out the Land*, 1943; H. L. Mencken, *Prejudices, First Series*, 1919; King Hendricks, *Jack London: Master Craftsman of the Short Story*, 1966; Lewis Mumford, "Jack London," *New Republic*, XXX (1922), 145–147; Stephen Graham, "Jack London," *English Review*, XXXVIII (1924), 732–737; C. Hartley Grattan, "Jack London," *Bookman*, LXVIII (1929), 667–671; and Charles C. Walcutt, "Naturalism and the Superman in the Novels of Jack London," *Papers of the Michigan Academy of Science, Arts and Letters*, XXIV (1938), 89–107.

THE CALL OF THE WILD

Type of work: Novel
Author: Jack London (1876–1916)
Type of plot: Adventure romance
Time of plot: 1897
Locale: Alaska
First published: 1903

London's most popular novel, The Call of the Wild *tells the story of Buck, who is stolen and taken to Alaska to be trained as a sled dog. In his new environment he must learn the elements of survival, from cunning and ruthlessness to courage and loyalty.*

Principal Characters

Buck, a cross between a St. Bernard and an intelligent Scotch shepherd. He is the leader of all the dogs on Judge Miller's estate in California until stolen and carted off to the Alaska gold rush. Passed from one owner to another, he finally breaks away to run with a wolf pack.

A Spitz, the bloodthirsty enemy of Buck and lead dog on the sled, until killed by Buck.

John Thornton, a prospector who protects Buck from stupid gold seekers. After John is killed by Indians, his body is left at the river, to which once a year Buck returns and utters the call of the wild, the howl of a savage beast for his human friend.

The Story

Buck was the undisputed leader of all the dogs on Judge Miller's estate in California. A crossbreed of St. Bernard and Scottish shepherd, he had inherited the size of the first and the intelligence of the other. Buck could not know that the lust for gold had hit the human beings of the country and that dogs of his breed were much in demand as sled dogs in the frozen North. Consequently he was not suspicious when one of the workmen on the estate took him for a walk one night. The man took Buck to the railroad station, where the dog heard the exchange of money. Then a rope was placed around his neck. When he struggled to get loose, the rope was drawn so tight that it shut off his breath and he lost consciousness.

He recovered in a baggage car. When the train reached Seattle, Buck tried to break out of his cage while he was being unloaded. A man in a red shirt hit him with a club until he was senseless. After that, Buck knew that he could never win a fight against a club. He retained that knowledge for future use.

Buck was put in a pen with other dogs of his type. Each day some of the dogs went away with strange men who came with money. One day Buck was sold. Two French-Canadians bought him and some other dogs and took them on board a ship sailing for Alaska. The men were fair, though harsh, masters, and Buck respected them. Life on the ship was not particularly enjoyable, but it was a paradise compared to that which awaited Buck when the ship reached Alaska. There he found men and dogs to be little more than savages, with no law but the law of force. The dogs fought like wolves, and when one was downed the pack moved in for the kill. Buck watched one of his shipmates being torn to pieces after he lost a fight, and he never forgot the way one dog in particular, a Spitz, watched sly-eyed as the loser was slashed to ribbons. The Spitz was Buck's enemy from that time on.

Buck and the other dogs were harnessed to sleds on which the two French-Canadians carried mail to prospectors in remote regions. It was a new kind of life to Buck, but not an unpleasant one. The men treated the dogs well, and Buck was intelligent enough to learn quickly those things which made him a good sled dog. He learned to dig under the snow for a warm place to sleep and to keep the traces clear and thus make pulling easier. When he was hungry, he stole food. The instincts of his ancestors came to life in him as the sled went farther and farther north. In some vague manner he sensed the great cunning of the wolves who had been his ancestors in the wilderness.

Buck's muscles grew firm and taut, his strength greater than ever. But his feet became sore and he had to have moccasins. Occasionally one of the dogs died or was killed in a fight, and one female went mad. The dogs no longer worked as a team, and the two men had to be on guard constantly to prevent fights. One day Buck saw his chance. He attacked the Spitz, the lead dog on the sled, and killed him. After that Buck refused to be harnessed until he was given the lead position. He proved his worth by whipping the rebellious dogs into shape, and he became the best lead dog the men had ever seen. The sled made record runs, and Buck was soon famous.

When they reached Skaguay, the two French-Canadians had official orders to turn the team over to a Scottish half-breed. The sled was heavier and the weather bad on the long haul back to Dawson. At night Buck lay by the fire and dreamed of his wild ancestors. He seemed to hear a faraway call which was like a wolf's cry.

After two days' rest in Dawson, the team started back over the long trail to Skaguay. The dogs were almost exhausted. Some died and had to be replaced. When the team arrived again in Skaguay, the dogs expected to rest, but three days later they were sold to two men and a woman who knew nothing about dogs or sledding conditions in the northern wilderness. Buck and the other dogs started out again, so weary that it was an effort to move. Again and again the gallant dogs stumbled and fell and lay still until the sting of a whip brought them to their feet for a few miles. At last even Buck gave up. The sled had stopped at the cabin of John Thornton, and when the men and the woman were ready to leave Buck refused to get up. One of the men beat Buck with a club and would have killed him had not Thornton intervened, knocking the man down and ordering him and his companions to leave. They left Buck with Thornton.

As Thornton nursed Buck back to health, a feeling of love and respect grew between them. When Thornton's partners returned to the cabin, they understood this affection and did not attempt to use Buck for any of their heavy work.

Twice Buck saved Thornton's life and was glad that he could repay his friend. In Dawson Buck won more than a thousand dollars for Thornton on a wager, when the dog broke loose from the ice a sled carrying a thousand-pound load. With the money won on the wager, Thornton and his partners went on a gold-hunting expedition. They traveled far into eastern Alaska, where they found a stream yellow with gold.

In his primitive mind Buck began to see a hairy man who hunted with a club. He heard the howling of the wolves. Sometimes he wandered off for three or four days at a time, but he always went back to Thornton. At one time he made friends with a wolf that seemed like a brother to Buck.

Once Buck chased and killed a great bull moose. On his way back to the camp, he sensed that something was wrong. He found several dogs lying dead along the trail. When he reached the camp, he saw Indians dancing around the bodies of the dogs and Thornton's two partners. He followed Thornton's trail to the river, where he found the body of his friend full of arrows. Buck was filled with such a rage that he attacked the band of Indians, killing some and scattering the others.

His last tie with man broken, he joined his brothers in the wild wolf packs. The Indians thought him a ghost dog, for they seldom saw more than his shadow, so quickly did he move. But had the Indians watched carefully, they could have seen him closely. Once each year Buck returned to the river that held Thornton's body. There the dog stood on the bank and howled, one long, piercing cry that was the tribute of a savage beast to his human friend.

Critical Evaluation

On its simplest, most superficial and insensitive level, *The Call of the Wild* is just another of Jack London's "dog stories," which also include *White Fang* (1906) and *Jerry of the Islands* (1917). But so cavalier a dismissal of *The Call of the Wild*—usually accompanied by contemptuous allegations that the novel is nothing more than a potboiler—is quite unwarranted. Buck's story has far broader implications than the first, hasty reading may reveal. Admittedly, the book's popular success stems largely from its romantic-adventure qualities, yet there is much more to the novel than mere entertainment.

Jack London led a checkered life and had a checkered career; his experiences and knowledge are reflected in his novels and short stories, particularly his sociopolitical and economic views. At best, London's position could be described as eclectic; at worst, vacillating. He admired Herbert Spencer, Charles Darwin, Karl Marx, and Friedrich Nietzsche simultaneously and without much recognition of the contradictions among them. He embraced socialist causes while espousing Nietzschean "superman" theories. It is thus that Buck—under the presumably civilizing influence of John Thornton—becomes a good socialist; that is, Buck works for the common good rather than for his individual advancement. But, bereft of Thornton's guidance when his mentor dies, Buck reverts to the Darwinian survival of the fittest and the Nietzschean superman principles for his own protection.

To be sure, the novel has been faulted for Buck's so-called reversion to the wild. Even the most venerable of critics have praised *White Fang* and *Jerry of the Islands* for depicting savagery under civilized control, while disparaging *The Call of the Wild* as a clarion call to brute force. Yet, however such critics deplore the Darwinian-Nietzschean point of view, they seem to ignore the realities of the Marxian position: peasants and poor people—like Buck—can work with their kind for mutual benefit; but without a spirit of cooperation and without leadership or guidance, they must fend for themselves, or they will not endure. The cruelties of life are severe for both man and dog. And here the dog Buck is virtually an allegory for Everyman, in the pristine medieval sense, symbolizing the plight of the oppressed and the downtrodden everywhere in their struggle to maintain life. Whatever his intentions or his convictions, and no matter how skewed, London has portrayed, in *The Call of the Wild,* a vivid picture of the dilemma of the disadvantaged, even though he did so by using a dog as his protagonist.

Bibliography

Benoit, Raymond. "Jack London's *The Call of the Wild*," in *Arizona Quarterly.* XX (Summer, 1968), pp. 246–248.

Clayton, Lawrence. "The Ghost Dog, A Motif in *The Call of the Wild*," in *Jack London Newsletter.* V (September–December, 1972), p. 158.

Flink, Andrew. "*The Call of the Wild*: Parental Metaphor," in *Jack London Newsletter.* VII (May–August, 1974), pp. 58–61.

Geismar, Maxwell. *Rebels and Ancestors: The American Novel, 1890–1915.* Boston: Houghton Mifflin, 1953, pp. 149–152.

Labor, Earle G. *Jack London.* New York: Twayne, 1974, pp. 69–81.

————. "Jack London's 'Monde Cane': *The Call of the Wild* and *White Fang*," in *Jack London Newsletter.* I (July–December, 1967), pp. 2–13.

Markham, Edwin. *Songs and Stories.* Los Angeles: Powell, 1931, pp. 16–17.

Mitchell, Theodore C. "Introduction," in *The Call of the Wild.* By Jack London. New York: Macmillan, 1917, pp. vii–xxxi.

Roden, Donald.   *London's* The Call of the Wild *also:* White Fang. New York: Monarch Press, 1965.

Rothberg, Abraham.   The Call of the Wild *and* White Fang. New York: Bantam, 1963, pp. 1–17.

Spinner, Jonathan H.   "A Syllabus for the 20th Century: Jack London's *The Call of the Wild*," in *Jack London Newsletter*. VII (May–August, 1974), pp. 73–78.

Starrett, Vincent.   "*The Call of the Wild*," in *Best Loved Books of the Twentieth Century*. New York: Bantam, 1965, pp. 91–101.

Taylor, Walter.   *A History of American Letters*. New York: American Book Company, 1937, pp. 315–318.

Walcutt, Charles Child.   *American Literary Naturalism: A Divided Stream*. Minneapolis: University of Minnesota Press, 1956, pp. 96–97, 103–107.

————.   *Seven Novelists in the American Naturalist Tradition*. Minneapolis: University of Minnesota Press, 1974, pp. 144–149.

Wilcox, Earl J.   "Jack London's Naturalism: The Example of *The Call of the Wild*," in *Jack London Newsletter*. II (May–August, 1969), pp. 91–101.

THE SEA WOLF

Type of work: Novel
Author: Jack London (1876–1916)
Type of plot: Adventure romance
Time of plot: 1904
Locale: Pacific Ocean, Bering Sea
First published: 1904

The plot of The Sea Wolf *becomes progressively unbelievable, but this defect is overcome by the visceral description of shipboard life and the energetically written action scenes. The conflict between the erratic, dangerous, animalistic captain, Wolf Larsen, and the delicate, civilized, sympathetic Maud Brewster assumes an almost allegorical quality.*

Principal Characters

Humphrey Van Weyden, called **Hump,** picked up by the sealer "Ghost" after a shipwreck. He has a perilous existence until the crew kill off one another. He and Miss Brewster navigate the crippled ship back to the United States.

Wolf Larsen, called **The Sea Wolf,** brutal Captain of the "Ghost." He is buried at sea.

Maud Brewster, the survivor of a wreck, rescued by Wolf and protected from him by Hump.

Death Larsen, Captain of the "Macedonia." He is Wolf's brother and enemy. He steals his brother's skins.

Johansen, the cruel mate of the "Ghost," drowned during a mutiny.

Johnson, a seaman beaten by the officers. He tries to desert with Leach but is drowned.

Leach, the former cabin boy, who tries to kill the cook and the Captain.

Mugridge, the ship's cook, to whom Hump is assigned. The cook abuses and robs him until the "cabin boy" turns on him.

Louis, the only crew member friendly to Hump.

The Story

When the ship in which he was a passenger sank in a collision off the coast of California, Humphrey Van Weyden was picked up by the crew of Wolf Larsen's ship, the *Ghost,* a sailing vessel headed for seal hunting ranges in the Bering Sea. Wolf Larsen was a brute. Van Weyden witnessed the inhuman treatment of a sick mate who died shortly afterward. He saw a cabin boy badly beaten. In his own interview with the captain, he fared little better. Instead of promising to help him return to San Francisco, Wolf demanded that Van Weyden sign as cabin boy and stay with his ship.

The crew set to work taking in the topsails and jibs. From that moment Hump, as the crew called Van Weyden, learned life the hard way. He had to get his sea legs and he had to learn the stoical indifference to pain and suffering which the sailors seemed to have mastered already. As cabin boy, he peeled potatoes and washed greasy pots and pans. Mugridge, the cook, abused him and robbed him of his money.

Only one man, Louis, seemed to share Hump's feelings about the captain and his ship. Louis predicted many deaths would result from this voyage. He said that Wolf Larsen was a violent, dangerous man, that the crew and seal hunters were vicious outcasts. Wolf did seem mad. He varied from moods of wild exultation to spells of extreme depression. In his cabin were classic books of literature, and when he spoke he chose either to use excellent English or the lingo of the sailors. Sometimes he amused himself by arguing with Hump. He claimed that life was without meaning.

During a southeaster Hump badly dislocated his knee, and Wolf unexpectedly allowed Hump to rest for three days while he talked to him about philosophy and literature. When Hump returned to the galley, the cook was whetting his knife. In return, Hump obtained a knife and began whetting it also. His actions so frightened the cowardly cook that Hump was no longer the victim of his abuse.

Louis talked of the coming season with the seals. Moreover, he hinted that trouble would come if the *Macedonia*, a sealing steamer, came near. Captained by Death Larsen, the brother and enemy of Wolf, the *Macedonia* was a certain menace. As a prelude to things to come, an outbreak of fury took place aboard the *Ghost*. First, Wolf Larsen and the mate beat a seaman named Johnson to a pulp because he complained of ill treatment; then Leach, the former cabin boy, beat the cook. Later two hunters exchanged shots, severely wounding each other, and Wolf beat them because they had crippled themselves before the hunting season began. Afterward Wolf suffered from one of his periodic headaches. To Hump, life on shipboard was a tremendous experience in human cruelty and viciousness.

A few days later the men tried to mutiny. In the row which followed, Johansen, the mate, was drowned and Wolf was nearly killed. While Hump dressed Wolf's wounds, Wolf promoted him to mate in Johansen's place. Both Leach and Johnson would have killed Wolf in a second, but he remained too wary for them.

At the seal hunting grounds a terrific storm cost them the lives of four men. The ship itself was beaten, its sails torn to shreds and portions of the deck swept into the sea.

When Leach and Johnson deserted in a small skiff, Wolf started out in pursuit. On the morning of the third day an open boat was sighted. The boat contained a young woman and four men, survivors from a sinking steamer. Wolf took them aboard, planning to make sailors of the men as he had of Hump. Shortly afterward the *Ghost* overtook Johnson and Leach. Refusing to pick them up, Wolf let them struggle to get aboard until their small craft capsized. He watched them drown without comment and then ordered the ship's course set for a return to the seal hunting grounds.

The woman survivor was Maud Brewster, a rich woman and a poet, as weak physically for a woman as Hump had been for a man. Wolf resented the intimacy which sprang up at once between Maud Brewster and Hump, but he took out his resentment by deciding to give the cook the first bath the cook had ever been known to take.

At his orders Mugridge was thrown into the water with a tow rope slung about his middle. First, however, the cook fled madly about the ship, causing one man to break a leg and another to be injured in a fall. Before Wolf was ready to bring Mugridge back aboard ship, a shark bit off the cook's right foot at the ankle. Dragged aboard, Mugridge in his fury tried to bite Wolf's leg, and the captain almost strangled him. Then Hump bandaged the wounded man's leg. Maud Brewster looked on, nearly fainting.

The *Macedonia* appeared one day and robbed Wolf's hunters of their day's catch of seals by cutting off the line of approach to the *Ghost*. In revenge, Wolf set his men to work capturing hunters from the *Macedonia*. When the *Macedonia* gave chase, Wolf sailed his ship into a fog bank.

That night Wolf tried to seize Maud, but Hump, awakening, ran his knife into Wolf's shoulder. At the same time, Wolf was overcome by one of his headaches, this seizure accompanied by blindness. Hump helped him to his bunk and under cover of darkness he and Maud made their escape in an open boat. After days of tossing they came to a small island. Using supplies they had taken from the *Ghost*, they set about making themselves houses and gathering food for the coming winter.

One morning Hump saw the wreck of the *Ghost* lying offshore. Going aboard, he discovered Wolf alone, his crew having deserted him to go aboard Death Larsen's ship. Wolf seemed nearly insane and had only a sick man's desire to sleep. Hump stole some pistols and food which he took to the island.

Hump, planning to repair the masts of the *Ghost*, began work on the crippled ship. That night Wolf undid all Hump's work, and cast the masts off the vessel.

Hump and Maud began anew to refit the ship. One day Wolf attempted to murder Hump, but during the struggle he had one of his spasms and fainted. While he was still unconscious, they handcuffed him and shut him in the hold.

Then they moved aboard the *Ghost* and the work of refitting the vessel went forward. Wolf became more than a prisoner. He had a stroke which paralyzed the right side of his body.

Hump continued to repair the vessel. At last it was able to sail. Wolf Larsen finally lost the use of his muscles and lay in a coma. When he died, Hump and Maud buried him at sea. By that time they were deeply in love. When a United States revenue cutter discovered them one day, they felt that their dangerous odyssey was at an end. But they were about to begin another, less perilous journey, together.

Critical Evaluation

The Sea Wolf, published in 1904, is still an exciting yarn; it can also be read as an allegory of the deepest hopes and fears of an age. The hopes were that mankind was becoming more spiritual, that his moral fiber was becoming stronger, his institutions enlightened, and his tastes elevated. The fears were that man's animal nature might frustrate his aspirations and that he might slip backward into a bestial state where his violence, greed, and lust would make a shambles of civilization. Such hopes and fears were a culmination of people's preoccupation with the theories of Charles Darwin (referred to by Wolf and Humphrey), who had shown man to be a product of evolution and a creature of nature.

Jack London was well prepared to write about this tension between man's upward and downward possibilities. Raised in a knockabout way in the San Francisco Bay area, he was on his own at fifteen, a drinking man and oyster pirate by sixteen, and a crewman on a sealing ship at seventeen. He knew the seamy side of life. He was also an avid reader, a man capable of strong romantic attachments, and a worker for social and economic justice. He aspired to a finer life.

In the novel Wolf Larsen represents the primitive and feral in man and Maud Brewster the spiritual. They stand, as Humphrey observes, at opposite ends of the ladder of evolution; both tug at him. Humphrey rejects Wolf's philosophy that life is a meaningless and brutal struggle, but he is toughened in body and mind by Wolf's harsh regimen. Maud's beauty and idealism fill Humphrey with love, tenderness, and chivalric courage. We may conclude that London was hopeful about man's future. Amoral Wolf's fierce vitality slowly ebbs. Ethereal Maud, brought at last to safety by Humphrey, unites with him in a chaste embrace. In this symbolic union Humphrey as modern man rejects the cruel and brutish and dedicates himself to what is saving and civilized.

Bibliography

Bruccoli, Matthew J. "Introduction," in *The Sea Wolf.* By Jack London. Boston: Houghton Mifflin, 1964, pp. v–xv, 1–2.

Bukoski, Anthony. "Jack London's Wolf Larsen: Nietzschean Superman at All?," in *Jack London Newsletter.* VII (September–December, 1974), pp. 109–110.

Clayton, Lawrence. "*The Sea Wolf*: London's 'Commedia,' " in *Jack London Newsletter.* VIII (May–August, 1975), pp. 50–54.

Ellis, James. "A New Reading of *The Sea Wolf*," in *Western American Literature.* II (Summer, 1967), pp. 127–134.

Forrey, Robert. "Male and Female in London's *The Sea Wolf*," in *Literature and Psychology.* XXIV (1974), pp. 135–143.

Gurian, Jay. "The Romantic Necessity in Literary Naturalism: Jack London," in *American Literature.* XXXVIII (March, 1966), pp. 112–114.

Hartwick, Harry. *The Foreground of American Fiction.* New York: Century, 1934, pp. 67–84.

Hindman, Kathleen B. "Jack London's *The Sea Wolf*: Naturalism with a Spiritual Bent," in *Jack London Newsletter.* VI (September–December, 1973), pp. 99–110.

Labor, Earle G. *Jack London.* New York: Twayne, 1974, pp. 94–100.

Lynn, Kenneth. *The Dream of Success.* Boston: Little, Brown, 1955, pp. 92–97.

Parkay, Forrest Winston. "The Influence of Nietzsche's *Thus Spake Zarathustra* on London's *The Sea Wolf*," in *Jack London Newsletter.* IV (January–April, 1971), pp. 16–24.

Pearsall, Robert Brainard. "Elizabeth Barrett Meets Wolf Larsen," in *Western American Literature.* IV (Spring, 1969), pp. 3–13.

Walcutt, Charles Child. *American Literary Naturalism: A Divided Stream.* Minneapolis: University of Minnesota Press, 1956, pp. 107–113.

————. *Jack London.* Minneapolis: University of Minnesota Press, 1966, pp. 24–27.

————. *Seven Novelists in the American Naturalist Tradition.* Minneapolis: University of Minnesota Press, 1974, pp. 149–151.

Watson, Charles N., Jr. "Sexual Conflict in *The Sea Wolf*: Further Notes on London's Reading of Kipling and Norris," in *Western American Literature.* XI (1976), pp. 239–248.

Woodward, Robert H. "Jack London's Code of Primitivism," in *Folio.* XVIII (May, 1936), pp. 39–44.

HERMAN MELVILLE

Born: New York, N.Y. (August 1, 1819)
Died: New York (September 28, 1891)

Principal Works

NOVELS: *Typee*, 1846; *Omoo*, 1847; *Mardi*, 1849; *Redburn*, 1849; *White-Jacket*, 1850; *Moby Dick*, 1851; *Pierre*, 1852; *Israel Potter*, 1855; *The Confidence Man*, 1857; *Billy Budd, Foretopman*, 1924.

SHORT STORES: *Piazza Tales*, 1856.

POEMS: *Battle Pieces and Aspects of the War*, 1866; *Clarel*, 1876; *John Marr and Other Sailors*, 1888; *Timoleon*, 1891.

MISCELLANEOUS: *Journal Up the Straits*, 1935; *Journal of a Visit to London and the Continent*, 1948.

Herman Melville's first five books were based in part on the varied experiences of his youth. It is therefore necessary to have the main facts of the author's early life before us.

Melville was born in New York City on August 1, 1819. His family was of English, Scotch, and Dutch ancestry and had some claims to eminence on both sides. Both the Presbyterianism of his father and the Dutch Reformed views of his mother gave Melville that partly Calvinistic concern with good and evil which we find in his writings, most notably *Moby Dick*. Melville's father, a prosperous merchant until 1826, failed financially in that year of depression and died in 1832, leaving the family close to poverty.

After a number of years in Albany as a student and a clerk, Melville embarked in 1837 on his first voyage, as a cabin boy on a merchant ship bound for Liverpool. In 1841 he sailed from New Bedford on the whaleship *Acushnet*, beginning a series of adventures in the Pacific which lasted until 1844. Returning to New York, he began to write of his experiences.

His first book, *Typee*, was a popular success, and this exciting narrative, part memoir, part romance, which described the hero's sojourn among the cannibals of the Marquesas Islands, remained for many decades the author's most widely known work. *Omoo*, a sequel to *Typee*, was followed by *Mardi*. This book, which readers found baffling, begins as a travel narrative but quickly becomes a fanciful mixture of allegory, satire, and extravaganza somewhat in the tradition of the imaginary voyage, such as *Gulliver's Travels*. A new note of stark and somber realism is struck in *Redburn*, based on Melville's voyage to Liverpool. The note of realism is maintained in *White-Jacket*, a book which benefits from Melville's memories of his days as a common sailor aboard the U.S.S. *United States*, on which he had returned from the Pacific in 1844. The best of these early books is *Typee*, although parts of *Redburn* are moving and authentic and certain scenes in

White-Jacket rival Smollett's in their vivid impression of sea-going life.

But *Typee* turned out to be something of an evil fate for its author, since it had conditioned Melville's available audience to pleasurable travel romance. Unwilling and unable to continue in the *Typee* vein, Melville lost his audience and suffered more and more, as he grew older, from his increasing sense of alienation from the conventional life of his time. Even *Moby Dick*, which seems to us now one of the great books of world literature, had no more than a scattered reputation until about 1920. And only in recent years has Melville been generally accepted as one of the greatest of American writers.

Moby Dick was written mostly in Pittsfield, Massachusetts, where Melville, now married and beginning to raise a family, had settled in 1850. Like the early novels, *Moby Dick* mirrors actual experience, being an account of the author's voyage on the *Acushnet*. The accepted view of *Moby Dick* is that as Melville first conceived it, it was to be merely a realistic narrative. As he wrote, however, the pursuit of the whale, which was to constitute the main plot, took on ever new meanings. This imaginative proliferation was the result of the natural unfolding of Melville's genius, but also of his reading, at the time, of Shakespeare and Hawthorne. Besides being a magnificent account of the whaling enterprise, the book became, as Melville reconceived it, an epic romance.

Moby Dick has manifold meaning, but its complexity is often exaggerated. Much confusion can be avoided by noting that the white whale is not allegorical, and therefore cannot be explained as "standing for" this or that. The whale is a poetic symbol deliberately intended to reflect the ambiguity of nature, at once terrible and beautiful, threatening and beneficent. It is a part of Captain Ahab's madness that he understands the whale allegorically, thinking of it (and thus thinking of nature itself) as representing Evil. In Ahab we see a man alienated from mankind by a fanatical will and intellect which have distorted all the genial emotions into a vindictive hatred of life itself. All the rich poetry of life, so memorably expressed by Melville, is unavailable to him. Whether or not Ahab is intended in a sinister way as the representative American individualist, it is certain that, in the manner of epics, *Moby Dick* copiously reflects the folkways of the culture that gave it birth.

The later writings of Melville may be dealt with briefly, although he wrote several interesting works at Pittsfield and later in New York, where he was a District Inspector of Customs from 1866 until 1885. *Pierre* is a powerful but incoherent melodrama of incest and struggling genius, murkily reflecting Melville's own inner struggles. *The Confidence Man* is a dark comedy or masque, having for its central figure an elusive character representing the huckstering tendencies of American life as Melville saw them—from ordinary salesmanship to Emersonian transcendentalism. Sometimes extremely effective, the book never quite finds a way of clearly expressing the author's intense satire. Certain prose pieces of the 1850's, like *Bartleby the Scrivener*, *Benito Cereno*, and *The Encantadas*, are next to perfect in their way, and *Israel Potter* is, though not a great, a neglected piece of picaresque narrative. After the Civil War Melville wrote poetry. But his poems, with certain notable exceptions, such as "The Portent," "Shiloh," and "The Maldive Shark," are the work of a thoughtful amateur rather than a skillful poet.

There remains *Billy Budd*, the product of Melville's last years. In its concern with the inhumanity of martial law, it reminds us of *White-Jacket*. But in the hanging of the innocent Billy by Captain Vere, a good and honorable man, Melville found one of his most effective symbols for the inscrutable ambiguity of the universe and of the moral ideas man derives from the universe. As befits the author's last work, the tone is one of elegy and recompense. *Billy Budd* stands near the top of Melville's achievement, a fitting last word of the all but unknown author who died on September 28, 1891, and was obscurely buried in a New York cemetery.

Bibliography

What will probably be the definitive edition is that being edited by Harrison Hayford, 1968— (Vol. V by 1971). The *Letters* were edited by Merrill R. Davis and William H. Gilman, 1960. The present collected edition is *The Works of Herman Melville*, 16 vols., London, 1922–1924. For biographical and critical studies see the following: Raymond Weaver, *Herman Melville: Mariner and Mystic*, 1921; John Freeman, *Herman Melville*, 1926; Lewis Mumford, *Herman Melville*, 1929; Charles R. Anderson, *Melville in the South Seas*, 1939; William Braswell, *Melville's Religious Thought*, 1943; W. E. Sedgwick, *Herman Melville: The Tragedy of Mind*, 1944; Howard P. Vincent, *The Trying Out of Moby Dick*, 1949; Richard Chase, *Herman Melville: A Critical Study*, 1949; Geoffrey Stone, *Melville*, 1949; Newton Arvin, *Herman Melville*, 1950; Leon Howard, *Herman Melville: A Biography*, 1951; Jay Leyda, *The Melville Log: A Documentary Life of Herman Melville*, 1951; Eleanor Melville Metcalf, *Herman Melville: Cycle and Epicycle*, 1953; E. H. Rosenberry, *Melville and the Comic Spirit*, 1955; Hershel Parker, ed., *The Recognition of Herman Melville: Selected Criticism since 1846*, 1967; Edgar A. Dryden, *Melville's Thematics of Form: The Great Art of Telling the Truth*, 1968; and Howard P. Vincent, *Studies in Moby Dick*, 1969.

See also Willard Thorp, Introduction to *Melville* in the American Writers series, 1931, and Introduction to *Moby Dick*, Oxford University Press, 1947; R. P. Blackmur, *The Expense of Greatness*, 1940; F. O. Matthiessen, *American Renaissance*, 1941; and W. H. Auden, *The Enchafèd Flood, 1950*.

BILLY BUDD, FORETOPMAN

Type of work: Novel
Author: Herman Melville (1819–1891)
Type of plot: Symbolic tragedy
Time of plot: 1797
Locale: Aboard a British man-of-war
First published: 1924

In this last of Melville's works, published posthumously, the author dramatized the clash between natural goodness and innocence as personified by Billy Budd, and unprovoked evil as embodied in Claggart. Captain Vere, as his name suggests, is the upholder of truth and right in the story. When Billy inadvertently kills his antagonizer in a fight, Vere is caught between his love for Billy and his duty to uphold the law and maintain order; he opts for justice over mercy, and decides that he must hang the boy.

Principal Characters

Billy Budd, a youthful member of the crew of the merchantman *Rights-of-Man,* who is impressed into service aboard H.M.S. *Bellipotent* during the last decade of the eighteenth century. Billy is twenty-one, "welkin-eyed," and possessed of great masculine beauty; he has no idea who his father and mother were, having been left a foundling in a basket on the doorstep of a "good man" in Bristol, England. Billy was a cheerful, stabilizing influence on the rough crew of the merchantman; when he is taken aboard the *Bellipotent,* he is popular with all the officers and crew except John Claggart, the master-at-arms, who is envious of Billy's almost perfect physique and personality. Claggart falsely accuses Billy of fomenting a mutiny aboard the ship. When he repeats the charges in the Captain's quarters while Billy is present, the young man (who stutters under stress and sometimes suffers a total speech block) can say nothing in his own defense and hits Claggart on the forehead with his fist. Claggart falls and dies. In the subsequent trial at which the Captain is the sole wit-

ness, there can be no leniency because of the recent Great Mutiny in the fleet. Billy is sentenced to hang. At the execution his last words are, "God bless Captain Vere!"

Captain the Honourable Edward Fairfax Vere, of the *Bellipotent.* He is known in the fleet as "Starry" Vere to distinguish him from a kinsman and officer of like rank in the navy. The nickname is a misnomer, however, for Captain Vere, a bachelor of about forty, is a quiet, brooding intellectual who reads a great deal. He is also a fine commander, but he lacks the flamboyance of the more famous Nelson. He seems trapped by regulations (tightened during the Great Mutiny) which state that striking an officer is a capital offense. When Claggart comes to Captain Vere with his foggy, unsubstantiated charges that Billy is mutinuous, the Captain summons Billy to his quarters only to prove that Claggart is a false witness.

John Claggart, the master-at-arms of the ship. Since guns have replaced the many small arms used in naval fight-

BILLY BUDD, FORETOPMAN by Herman Melville. By permission of Mrs. Eleanor Melville Metcalf. From SHORTER NOVELS OF HERMAN MELVILLE. Copyright, 1928, by Horace

ing, his duties are mainly to oversee the crew and its work. When Claggart observes Billy Budd, he quickly becomes envious of the personal beauty of the young man. In this respect he is like Iago in "Othello"; Iago hates Cassio partly because he is an open, honest, handsome man. So with the Claggart-Budd relationship. The only basis for the charges Claggart makes against Billy is that an afterguardsman, a troublemaker, tries to be friendly and confidential with the foretopman. Because he joined the navy for no apparent reason and because he never makes any reference to his previous life ashore, Claggart is a man of mystery about whom many rumors are circulated on the ship.

The Dansker, an old veteran who serves as mainmast-man in his watch. He likes Billy from the start and is the one who nicknames him "Baby." When Billy comes to him for counsel and to ask why his petty mistakes are getting him into trouble, the Dansker astutely remarks that "Jimmy Legs" (meaning the master-at-arms) is down on him.

The Story

In 1797 the British merchant ship *Rights-of-Man*, named after Thomas Paine's famous reply to Edmund Burke's criticism of the French Revolution, was close to home after a long voyage. As it neared England, the merchant vessel was stopped by a man-of-war, H. M. S. *Bellipotent*, and an officer from the warship went aboard the *Rights-of-Man* to impress sailors for military service. This practice was necessary at the time to provide men to work the large number of ships which Britain had at sea for protection against the French.

The captain of the *Rights-of-Man* was relieved to have only one sailor taken from his ship, but he was unhappy because the man was his best sailor, Billy Budd. Billy was what his captain called a peacemaker; because of his strength and good looks he was a natural leader among the other sailors, and he used his influence to keep them contented and hard at work. Billy Budd seemed utterly without guile, a man who tried to promote the welfare of the merchant ship because he liked peace and was willing to work hard to please his superiors. When informed that he was not to return to England, but was to head for duty with the fleet in the Mediterranean Sea he did not appear disturbed; he liked the sea and he had no family ties. He was an orphan who had been left in a basket as a tiny baby on the doorstep of a family in Bristol.

As the boat from the warship took him away from the merchant ship, Billy called farewell to the *Rights-of-Man* by name, a deed which greatly embarrassed the naval officer who had impressed him. The remark was unwittingly satirical of the treatment to which Billy was being subjected by the navy.

Once aboard the *Bellipotent*, Billy quickly made himself at home with the ship and the men with whom he served in the foretop. Because of his good personality and his willingness to work, he soon made a place for himself with his messmates and also won the regard of the officers under whom he served.

At first the master-at-arms, a petty officer named Claggart, seemed particularly friendly to Billy, a fortunate circumstance, Billy thought, for the master-at-arms was the equivalent of the chief of police aboard the warship. The young sailor was rather surprised, therefore, when he received reprimands for slight breaches of conduct which were normally overlooked. The reprimands came from the ship's corporals who were Claggart's underlings. Since the reprimands indicated that something was wrong, Billy grew perturbed; he had a deadly fear of being the recipient of a flogging in public. He thought he could never stand such treatment.

Anxious to discover what was wrong, Billy consulted an old sailor, who told him that Claggart was filled with animosity for the young man. The reason for the animosity was not known, and because the old man could give him no reason Billy refused to believe that the master-at-arms was his enemy. Claggart had taken a deep dislike to Billy Budd on sight, however, and for no reason except a personal antipathy that the young man's appearance had generated. Sly as he was, Claggart kept, or tried to keep, his feelings to himself. He operated through underlings against Billy.

Not long after he had been warned by the old sailor, Billy spilled a bowl of soup in the path of Claggart as he was inspecting the mess. Even then, Claggart smiled and pretended to treat the incident as a joke, for Billy had done the deed accidentally. But a few nights later someone awakened Billy and told him to go to a secluded spot in the ship. Billy went and met a sailor who tried to tempt him into joining a mutiny. The incident bothered Billy, who could not understand why anyone had approached him as a possible conspirator. Such activity was not a part of his personality, and he was disgusted to find it in other men.

A few days later the master-at-arms approached the captain of the ship and reported that he and his men had discovered that a mutiny was being fomented by Billy Budd. Captain Vere reminded Claggart of the seriousness of the charge and warned the master-at-arms that bearing false witness in such a case called for the death penalty. Because Claggart persisted in his accusations, Captain Vere ended the interview on deck, which place he thought too public, and ordered the master-at-arms and Billy Budd to his cabin. There Captain Vere commanded Claggart to repeat his accusations. When he did, Billy became emotionally so upset that he was tongue-tied. In utter frustration at being unable to reply to the infamous charges, Billy hit the master-at-arms. The petty officer was killed when he fell heavily to the floor.

Captain Vere was filled with consternation, for he, like everyone except the master-at-arms, liked Billy Budd. After the surgeon had pronounced the petty officer dead, the captain immediately convened a court-martial to try Billy for assaulting and murdering a superior officer. Because England was at war, and because two mutinies had already occurred in the British navy that year, Captain Vere believed that corrective action had to be taken immediately. Though Vere believed Billy innocent of the charges brought against him by Claggart; and though Vere knew Billy did not contemplate murder but was, rather, trying to let his fists say what his lips could not, nevertheless, the Captain insisted that a court martial be immediately set into motion. In addition, Vere put on the court officers he knew he could manipulate, and though declaring he would have no part in the proceedings, the Captain argued with the court until they agreed that they must act under regulations, find Billy guilty, and sentence him to be hanged from a yardarm the following morning.

All the ship's company were dismayed when informed of the sentence. But Billy bore no animosity for the captain or for the officers who had sentenced him to die. When he was placed beneath the yardarm the following morning, he called out a blessing on Captain Vere, who, he believed, had no other choice in the matter but to hang him. It was quite strange, too, that Billy Budd's calm seemed even to control his corpse. Unlike most hanged men, he never twitched when hauled aloft by the neck. The surgeon's mate, when queried by his messmates, had no answer for the unique behavior of the corpse.

Some months later Captain Vere was wounded in action. In the last hours before his death he was heard to murmur Billy Budd's name over and over again. Nor did the common sailors forget the hanged man. For many years the yardarm from which he had been hanged was kept track of by sailors, who regarded it almost as reverently as Christians might revere the Cross.

Critical Evaluation

According to Harrison Hayford and Merton M. Sealts, the editors of *Billy Budd, Sailor,* Melville began the novel in 1886, developed and revised it through several stages, and then left if unpublished when he died in 1891. The Hayford-Sealts text, published in 1962, differs considerably from earlier ones published in 1924 and 1948. Among the noteworthy differences is the change of name for the ship on which the action occurs from *Indomitable* to *Bellipotent*. The symbolism of the latter name relates it to the emphasis which Melville places in the novel on war, man's involvement in it, and the effects of war on the individual.

That Melville did not wish his readers to mistake the nature or the general intent of his novel is clear in his early warning that Billy "is not presented as a conventional hero" and "that the story in which he is the main figure is no romance." The story itself is extremely simple. A young sailor on a British merchant ship is impressed for service on a British warship. He offers no resistance but accepts his new assignment with good will and attempts to be an ideal sailor. The ship's master-at-arms takes an immediate and unwarranted dislike to the sailor, plots to cause him trouble, and then accuses him to the captain of having plotted mutiny. The captain summons the sailor, asks him to defend himself, and sees him strike and accidentally kill his accuser. The captain imprisons him, convenes a court-martial, condemns him to death, and has him hanged. This plot is the vehicle for Melvill's extended use of moral symbolism throughout the novel.

Billy Budd, Claggart, and Captain Vere are all clearly symbolic characters, and Melville brings out the symbolism through information supplied about their backgrounds, language used to describe them, and authorial comment of moral, theological, and philosophical import.

Melville employs a double symbolism for Billy; he is both a Christ figure and a representation of innocent or Adamic man. Before Billy is removed from the merchant ship, the captain explains to the lieutenant from the warship that Billy has been most useful in quieting the "rat-pit of quarrels" that formerly infested his forecastle. "Not that he preached to them or said or did anything in particular, but a vitrue went out of him, sugaring the sour ones." The captain's words echo Luke, 6:19: "And the whole multitude sought to touch him: for there went virtue out of him, and healed them all." When the lieutenant is adamant about Billy's impressment, the captain's last words to him are: " . . . you are going to take away my peacemaker." Again, there is no mistaking the reference to the Prince of Peace. In describing Billy as he appears to the men and officers on the warship, Melville mentions "something in the mobile expression, and every chance attitude and movement, something suggestive of a mother eminently favored by Love and the Graces." An officer asks, "Who was your father?" and Billy answers, "God knows, sir." Though Billy explains that he was a foundling, the hint has already been given of a divine paternity. Melville drops the Christ symbolism of Billy until the confrontation with Claggart when Billy, unable to reply to Captain Vere's request that he defend himself, shows in his face "an expression which was a crucifixion to behold." At the hanging, Billy's last words are, "God bless Captain Vere!" and the reader recalls Chirst's words on the Cross, "Father, forgive them; for they know not what they do." The symbolism continues with the hanging itself. Captain Vere gives a silent signal and "At the same moment it chanced that the vapory fleece hanging low in the East was shot through with a soft glory as of the fleece of the Lamb of God seen in mystical vision, and simultaneously therewith, watched by the wedged mass of upturned faces, Billy ascended; and, ascending, took the full rose of dawn." In the final chapter, Melville adds that "The spar from which the foretopman was suspended was for some few years kept trace of by the bluejackets. . . . To them a chip from it was as a piece of the Cross. . . . They recalled a fresh young image of the Handsome Sailor, that face never deformed by a sneer or subtler vile freak of the heart within. This impression of him was doubtless deepened by the fact that he was gone, and in a measure mysteriously gone." Even in the verses which close the novel, with Billy's words, "They'll give me a nibble—bit o' biscuit ere I go. Sure a messmate will reach me the last parting cup," one cannot miss the Last Supper reference.

Yet, though Billy is Christlike, he belongs to the race of man, and Melville repeatedly employs him as an archetype. His complete innocence is first suggested in Mellville's comment that " . . . Billy in many respects was little more than a sort of upright barbarian, much such perhaps as Adam presumably might have been ere the urbane Serpent wriggled himself into his company." Later, Captain Vere thinks of the handsome sailor as one "who in the nude might have posed for a statue of young Adam before the Fall." But innocence will not protect Billy. As Adam's human imperfection led to his fall, so an imperfection in Billy leads to his destruction. In times of stress Billy stutters or is even speechless and, says Melville, "In this particular Billy was a striking instance that the arch interferer, the envious marplot of Eden, still has more or less to do with every human consignment to this planet of Earth."

The innocence that is his "blinder" causes Billy (or "Baby" as he is called) to fail to see and be on guard against the evil in Claggart, and his "vocal defect" deprives him of speech when he faces his false accuser. He strikes out as instinctively as a cornered animal, and his enemy dies. Billy did not intend to commit murder but, as Captain Vere tells his officers, "The prisoner's deed—with that alone we have to do." Billy does not live in an animal's instinctive world of nature. His life is bound by social law and particularly by naval law in a time of war. As Captain Vere explains, innocent Billy will be acquitted by God at "the last Assizes," but "We proceed under the law of the Mutiny Act." The act demands death for Billy's deed, and he dies in order that discipline may be maintained in the great navy which must protect Britain against her enemies.

As Billy symbolizes innocent man, Claggart represents the spirit of evil, the foe of innocence. There is a mystery in Claggart's enmity toward harmless Billy. For, says Melville, "what can more partake of the mysterious than an antipathy spontaneous and profound such as is evoked in certain exceptional mortals by the mere aspect of some other mortal, however harmless he may be, if not called forth by this very harmlessness itself?" Claggart's evil nature was not acquired, "not engendered by vicious training or corrupting books or licentious living, but born with him and innate. . . ." He can recognize the good but is "powerless to be it." His energies are self-destructive; his nature is doomed to "act out to the end the part allotted to it." Though he destroys an innocent man, he must himself be destroyed as well.

As Billy at one extreme is Christlike and childishly innocent and Claggart at the other is Satanic, Captain Vere represents the kind of officer needed to preserve such an institution as the navy he serves. He is a man of balance, "mindful of the welfare of his men, but never tolerating an infraction of discipline; thoroughly versed in the science of his profession, and intrepid to the verge of temerity, though never injudiciously so." His reading tastes incline toward "books treating of actual men and events . . . history, biography, and unconventional writers like Montaigne, who, free from cant and convention, honestly and in the spirit of common sense philosophize upon realities." More intellectual than his fellow officers, he seems somewhat "pedantic" to them, and Melville hints that, in reporting Vere's long speech to his junior officers of the drumhead court, he has simplified the phrasing of the argument. Yet elsewhere Captain Vere's speech is simple, brief, and direct.

The action in *Billy Budd* together with the symbolism attached to characters, setting, and conflict, suggests that in his last novel Melville was working not only with questions of morality having to do with social structures and morés but also with archetypal patterns seeming to govern human behavior. Though high-principled, Captain Vere is a dedicated representative of the state, and especially in a time of war believes he must protect the state even if it involves the sacrifice of an individual.

On one level, then, Melville seems to conclude that imperfect man living in an imperfect world has no guarantee against suffering an unjust fate. But to accept this conclusion is no reason to believe that Melville has reconciled to it; indeed the substructure of symbols in *Billy Budd* creates ambiguities not easily disposed of. The symbolism suggests that Vere, playing the role of God the Father, Claggart, playing the role of Lucifer, a fallen angel still desirous of merging with a better half, and Billy, playing the role of Christ/Adam are involved in a drama necessary to be carried out, a fated action which nothing can stop, but which must continue until all the parts are acted out. Indeed, Melville's replication of the crucifixion suggests a human need for a continual reenactment of a necessary rite. And the allusions to Billy as an arisen Christ are undercut by the novel's end where the sailor's sing not of a ordered world under the supervision and attention of a benevolent god whose actions imply harmony and grace, but rather of a drowned Billy twisted over with oozy weeds.

A rich novel, *Billy Budd* resists facile interpretations and stands as a last testament to one of our greatest novelists.

Bibliography

Anderson, Charles R. "The Genesis of *Billy Budd*," in *American Literature*. XII (1940), pp. 328–346.

Arvin, Newton. *Herman Melville: A Critical Biography*. New York: William Sloane, 1950, pp. 292–299.

————. "A Note on the Background of *Billy Budd*," in *American Literature*. XX (1948), pp. 51–55.

Berthoff, Warner. "Certain Phenomenal Men: The Example of *Billy Budd*," in *English Literary History*. XXVII (1960), pp. 334–351.

Braswell, William. "Melville's *Billy Budd* as 'An Inside Narrative,'" in *American Literature*. XXIX (1957), pp. 133–146.

Bredahl, A. Carl. *Melville's Angles of Vision*. Gainesville: University of Florida Press, 1972, pp. 63–73.

Chase, Richard. *Herman Melville: A Critical Study*. New York: Macmillan, 1949, pp. 258–277.

Fogle, Richard H. "*Billy Budd*—Acceptance or Irony," in *Tulane Studies in English*. VIII (1958), pp. 107–113.

Franklin, H. Bruce. *The Wake of the Gods: Melville's Mythology*. Stanford, Calif.: Stanford University Press, 1963, pp. 188–202.

Glick, Wendell. "Expediency and Absolute Morality in *Billy Budd*," in *PMLA*. LXVIII (1953), pp. 103–110.

Hillway, Tyrus. "*Billy Budd*: Melville's Human Sacrifice," in *Pacific Spectator*. VI (1952), pp. 342–347.

Howard, Leon. *Herman Melville: A Biography.* Berkeley: University of California Press, 1951, pp. 324–328.

Lemon, Lee T. "*Billy Budd*: The Plot Against the Story," in *Studies in Short Fiction.* II (1964), pp. 32–43.

Lewis, R.W.B. *The American Adam: Innocence, Tragedy, and Tradition in the Nineteenth Century.* Chicago: University of Chicago Press, 1955, pp. 147–152.

McCarthy, Paul. "Character and Structure in *Billy Budd*," in *Discourse.* IX (1966), pp. 201–217.

Mason, Ronald. *The Spirit Above the Dust: A Study of Herman Melville.* London: John Lehmann, 1951, pp. 245–260.

Matthiessen, F.O. *American Renaissance.* New York: Oxford University Press, 1941, pp. 500–514.

Merrill, Robert. "The Narrative Voice of *Billy Budd*," in *Modern Language Quarterly.* XXXIV (1973), pp. 283–291.

Miller, James E. "Billy Budd: The Catastrophe of Innocence," in *Modern Language Notes.* LXXIII (1958), pp. 168–176.

Rathbun, John W. "*Billy Budd* and the Limits of Perception," in *Nineteenth-Century Fiction.* XX (1965), pp. 19–34.

Reich, Charles A. "The Tragedy of Justice in *Billy Budd*," in *Yale Review.* LVI (1967), pp. 368–389.

Rosenberry, Edward H. "The Problem of *Billy Budd*," in *PMLA.* LXXX (1965), pp. 489–498.

Schroth, Evelyn. "Melville's Judgment on Captain Vere," in *Midwest Quarterly.* X (1969), pp. 189–200.

Sten, Christopher W. "Vere's Use of Forms: Means and Ends in *Billy Budd*," in *American Literature.* XLVII (1975), pp. 37–51.

Stern, Milton R. *The Fine Hammered Steel of Herman Melville.* Urbana: University of Illinois Press, 1957, pp. 206–239.

Thompson, Lawrance. *Melville's Quarrel with God.* Princeton, N.J.: Princeton University Press, 1952, pp. 355–414.

Tindall, William Y. "The Ceremony of Innocence," in *Great Moral Dilemmas in Literature, Past and Present.* Edited by R.M. MacIvor. New York: Harper, 1956, pp. 73–81.

Watson, E.L. Grant. "Melville's Testament of Acceptance," in *New England Quarterly.* VI (1933), pp. 319–327.

Zink, Karl E. "Herman Melville and the Forms—Irony and Social Criticism in *Billy Budd*," in *Accent.* XII (1952), pp. 131–139.

THE CONFIDENCE MAN

Type of work: Novel
Author: Herman Melville (1819–1891)
Type of plot: Social satire
Time of plot: Nineteenth century
Locale: The Mississippi River
First published: 1857

Episodic in structure, this symbolic story of a con man is a quietly bitter castigation of human nature. With a pessimism to rival Mark Twain's in his darker moods, Melville relentlessly depicts man's loss of faith in his fellows and shows the facility with which most men can be duped.

Principal Characters

The Confidence Man, masquerading, in turn, as a deaf-mute beggar; as a crippled Negro beggar named Black Guinea; as John Ringman; as a solicitor of funds for the Seminole Widow and Orphan Society; as Mr. Truman, president of the Black Rapids Coal Company; as an herb doctor; as a representative of the Philosophical Intelligence Office; and as Francis Goodman, world traveler. By means of his glib tongue and show of sympathetic camaraderie, he succeeds in duping the passengers on board the "Fidele" even as a placard offering a reward for the impostor is posted on the steamship's deck.

Mr. Roberts, a kindly, gullible merchant swindled by the confidence man.

An Episcopal Clergyman, an officious demander of references who is blandly gulled out of alms for "Black Guinea" as well as a contribution to the Seminole Widow and Orphan Society.

Pitch, a misanthropic frontiersman inspired by the confidence man's glib tongue to hire a boy through the impostor's "employment agency."

Charles Noble, a garrulous passenger who succeeds in evading the confidence man's appeals for a loan.

Mark Winsome, a mystic philosopher who accuses Charles Noble of being the confidence man.

Egbert, a disciple of Mark Winsome. He disgusts the confidence man by relating a long story concerning the folly of making loans between friends.

The Story

Aboard the steamboat *Fidele*, in dock at St. Louis, a group of passengers stood reading a placard which offered a reward for the capture of an impostor from the East—a confidence man. A deaf-mute beggar joined the group and began displaying a slate on which he wrote several mottoes praising the virtue of charity. Jeered at by the crowd, the deaf-mute lay down and slept on the forecastle as the steamboat pulled out for New Orleans.

A short time later Black Guinea, a crippled Negro, appeared on deck to beg for pennies, which he skillfully caught in his mouth. A man with a wooden leg broke up this cruel game by loudly accusing the Negro of fraud, but Black Guinea protested his innocence and, in reply to an Episcopal clergyman's request for references, described several persons on the boat, all of whom, along with Black Guinea himself and the deaf-mute as well, were one and the same man— the confidence man. After the clergyman left to find one of these references, only a kindly country merchant gave Black Guinea alms, an act which had unfortunate consequences, since he dropped one of his business cards while he was fishing in his pocket for a coin.

To this merchant, Mr. Roberts by name, the impostor introduced himself as John Ringman. Pretending that he had met Mr. Roberts six years earlier, on a business matter, Ringman won his confidence and talked him out of a sum of money. To repay Mr. Roberts, Ringman gave him a tip on some valuable stock which could be bought aboard ship from the president of the Black Rapids Coal Company.

Next, Ringman accosted a college student who was reading Tacitus. Before Ringman could make a pitch for money, the student left in embarrassment at a lecture Ringman was delivering on the decadence of Tacitus.

The confidence man appeared next as a solictor of funds for the Seminole Widow and Orphan Society. In this disguise he was recognized as one of Black Guinea's references by the Episcopal clergyman. The clergyman gave his alms for Black Guinea and was prevailed upon to contribute to the Seminole Fund also. In the same disguise the impostor gulled a widow and a gentleman into donating to the fund. Somewhat reluctantly, the gentleman also contributed to a plan for the worldwide consolidation of all charities.

Disguised as Mr. Truman, the president of the Black Rapids Coal Company, the impostor met the student again. Ironically, since he prided himself on his cynicism and circumspection, the student insisted on buying some stock, despite the impostor's feigned reluctance to sell. The good merchant, Mr. Roberts, was also pleased to purchase some of the shares which his friend Ringman had recommended. During the conversation which followed this transaction, Mr. Roberts happened to mention the presence of a sickly old miser aboard ship and thus informed the confidence man of another victim.

The confidence man succeeded in gulling the miser twice: once by selling him some of the bogus stock and once, posing as an herb doctor, by selling him a supply of Omni-Balsamic Reinvigorator, guaranteed, if taken with confidence, to cure a consumptive cough.

A Missouri frontiersman's scorn for herbs and natural healing transformed the herb doctor into a representative of an employment agency, the Philosophical Intelligence Office. This Missourian, named Pitch, had resolved to purchase machinery to work his farm rather than rely on another boy, having had thirty-five unpleasant experiences with as many boys. Through brilliantly specious rhetoric the impostor persuaded him to hire still another boy.

The impostor appeared to Pitch once more, this time disguised as Francis Goodman, a friendly world traveler and cosmopolitan. But Pitch, brooding over his own gullibility, was in no mood for fellowship. After trying unsuccessfully to dispel Pitch's misanthropic melancholia, the cosmopolitan moved on in search of more susceptible prey.

He was accosted by one Charles Noble, a garrulous passenger who, having overheard the colloquy with Pitch, was reminded of another bitter frontiersman: Colonel John Moredock, a notorious Indian hater. Goodman being agreeable, Noble proceeded to narrate a long tale of Moredock's vendetta against Indians and to expound the philosophy of Indian-hating.

Needless to say, the confidence man was appalled by such a misanthropic tale. Finding that Noble shared his feeling, Goodman agreed to split a bottle of port with him. Over their port, the two found that they shared a high regard for wine, but their incipient friendship was strained by Goodman's suspicion that Noble was trying to get him drunk. Cordiality and noble sentiments prevailed, however, until Goodman asked Noble to prove his professed confidence in mankind by lending him fifty dollars. This startling request produced such a violent reaction that the friendship would have ended then and there had not Goodman pretended that he had been joking. Confidence restored, Goodman told the story of Charlemont, an aristocrat of singularly peculiar behavior, as a prelude to another request for a loan. Before Goodman could make his appeal, Noble abruptly retired.

A passenger who had been watching the two men warned Goodman to beware of Noble's companionship. Goodman had difficulty in extracting a comprehensible reason for this warning because the passenger turned out to be Mark Winsome, a mystic philosopher of no plain, ordinary tongue. Finally, Winsome stated clearly that Noble was a confidence man. Of course the real confidence man expressed incredulity, whereupon Winsome withdrew, leaving behind a disciple, a young man named Egbert, to explain the Winsome mystic philosophy, which was, in effect, quite practical.

To explore the philosophy on a practical level, Goodman suggested that Egbert use it to answer a hypothetical request for a loan. Steadfastly and consistently Egbert rejected the plea and finally told a long story to illustrate the folly, the tragedy, of loans between friends. Disgusted by such complete cynicism, the confidence man retreated.

Still in the guise of the cosmopolitan, he visited the ship's barber shop. There he succeeded in cheating the barber out of the price of a shave but failed, ultimately, in persuading the barber to extend credit to his customers.

Later that night, in the gentleman's sleeping cabin, the confidence man found only one person still awake, an old man reading the Bible. Though he mouthed pious sentiments attesting his faith in mankind and God, the old man eagerly bought a traveler's lock and a money belt from a child peddler and accepted a counterfeit detector as a premium. Commenting that the two of them put equal trust in man and God, the confidence man led the old gentleman, who was now carrying a life preserver, off to bed.

Critical Evaluation

The white-clad mute and Black Guinea symbolize the cosmic forces Melville dramatizes in *The Confidence Man*. While it is uncertain whether one or both these figures are manifestations of the Confidence Man, they clearly represent the Christian appeal to love and charity at one extreme, and the power of the diabolic that preys upon human weakness and gullibility at the other. Melville generalizes the *Fidele's* passengers to represent "that multiform pilgrim species, man," so the Mississippi River setting has universal as well as particularly American implications. Finally, the barber's "No Trust" sign ironically suggests the prevailing attitude of the world in which the action takes place.

In the confrontations between the Confidence Man and his victims, the inappropriateness of the Christian values of faith, hope, and charity are explored. The Con Man, in his various guises, is actually able to elicit far more trust than the barber's sign would suggest is possible, but he does so only to victimize those with whom he succeeds. At the opposite extreme from those who trust are the misanthropes who, though immune from the devil's wiles, are in their mistrust and isolation as far from the Christian ideal as those who are gulled. The most ironic examples of the extremes of attitude are Winsome and his disciple Egbert, who make a fine theoretical case for brotherly love but offer an equally compelling pragmatic argument against helping a fellow man.

The encounter with the Bible-reading old man at the end of the novel seems to represent Melville's final commentary on the practical impossibility of a world based on Christian principles. In spite of his ostentatious display of religion, the old man is hopelessly insecure and an easy victim. As the world is plunged into darkness, we sense the final triumph of evil.

Bibliography

Cawelti, John G. "Some Notes on the Structure of *The Confidence Man*," in *American Literature*. XXIX (November, 1957), pp. 278–288.

Chase, Richard. "Melville's Confidence Man," in *Kenyon Review*. XI (Winter, 1944), pp. 122–140.

Drew, Philip. "Appearance and Reality in Melville's *The Confidence Man*," in *ELH*. XXXI (1965), pp. 418–442.

Dubler, Walter. "Theme and Structure in Melville's *The Confidence Man*," in *American Literature*. XXXIII (November, 1961), pp. 308–319.

Foster, Elizabeth. "Introduction," of *The Confidence Man* in the *Complete Works of Herman Melville*. Edited by Howard P. Vincent. New York: Hendricks House, 1954.

Hayford, Harrison. "Poe in *The Confidence Man*," in *Nineteenth-Century Fiction*. XIV (December, 1959), pp. 207–218.

Hoffman, Daniel G. "Melville's Story of China Aster," in *American Literature*. XXII (May, 1950), pp. 137–149.

Mason, Ronald. *The Spirit Above the Dust: A Study of Herman Melville*. London: John Lehmann, 1951, pp. 198–207.

Miller, James E., Jr. "The Confidence Man: His Guises," in *PMLA*. LXXIV (March, 1959), pp. 102–111.

Mumford, Lewis. *Herman Melville*. New York: Harcourt, Brace, 1924, pp. 247–255.

Oliver, Egbert S. "Melville's Goneril and Fanny Kemble," in *New England Quarterly*. XVIII (December, 1945), pp. 489–506.

————. "Melville's Picture of Emerson and Thoreau in *The Confidence Man*," in *College English*. VIII (November, 1946), pp. 61–72.

Pearce, Roy Harvey. "Melville's Indian Hater: A Note on the Meaning of *The Confidence Man*," in *PMLA*. LXVII (December, 1952), pp. 942–948.

Rosenberry, Edward H. *Melville and the Comic Spirit*. Cambridge, Mass.: Harvard University Press, 1955, pp. 146–178.

Sedgwick, William Ellery. *Herman Melville: The Tragedy of Mind*. Cambridge, Mass.: Harvard University Press, 1944, pp. 186–193.

Shroeder, John W. "Sources and Symbols for Melville's Confidence Man," in *PMLA*. LXVI (June, 1951), pp. 363–380.

Stone, Geoffrey. *Melville*. New York: Sheed and Ward, 1949, pp. 228–234.

Thompson, Lawrance. *Melville's Quarrel with God*. Princeton, N.J.: Princeton University Press, 1952, pp. 297–328.

Tuveson, Ernest. "The Creed of the Confidence Man," in *ELH*. XXXIII (1966), pp. 247–270.

Weissbuch, T.N. "A Note on the Confidence Man's Counterfeit Detector," in *Emerson Society Quarterly*. XIX (1960), pp. 16–18.

ISRAEL POTTER

Type of work: Novel
Author: Herman Melville (1819–1891)
Type of plot: Social satire
Time of plot: 1774–1826
Locale: Vermont, Massachusetts, England, France, the Atlantic Ocean
First published: 1855

A mock picaresque novel, Israel Potter *satirizes a great many ideas and institutions, from the pious morality of Benjamin Franklin to the brutality of wars and the idiocy of jingoistic patriotism. The hero,* Israel Potter, *wanders about America and Europe for more than fifty years, forever innocent and often stumbling into difficult situations.*

Principal Characters

Israel Potter, a wanderer. Brought up in the rugged New England hills and immersed in their austere virtues, he quarrels with his father and leaves home. He wanders about, the innocent American, for fifty years, and in the course of his many adventures, he becomes the spokesman through whom the author satirizes various ideas and institutions, among them war, patriotism, and so-called civilized behavior.

King George III, whom Israel Potter meets in London. The mad King, realizing that Israel is an American, is ineffectually kind to him after the many snubs Israel has received because of his nationality.

Squire Woodcock, a secret friend of America who befriends Israel Potter and sends him on a mission to Benjamin Franklin.

Benjamin Franklin, who gives Israel Potter lessons in proper behavior based on maxims from "Poor Richard's Almanack." The lessons, carefully learned, are quickly forgotten.

John Paul Jones, with whom Israel Potter engages in piracy and in the sea fight between the "Bon Homme Richard" and the "Serapis."

The Earl of Selkirk, whose home is plundered by the pirate companions of Israel Potter and John Paul Jones. After receiving a large sum of money from another exploit, the two Captains buy back and return the Earl's possessions.

Ethan Allen, whom Israel Potter tries unsuccessfully to help escape from England.

The Story

Born among the rugged stones of the New England hills, in the Housatonic Valley, Israel Potter grew up with all the virtues of the hard, principled, new land. After an argument with his father over a girl whom his stern parent did not think a suitable match, Israel decided to run away from home while his family was attending church. He wandered about the countryside, hunting deer, farming land, becoming a trapper, dealing in furs. During his wanderings he learned that most men were unscrupulous. He also hunted whales from Nantucket to the coast of Africa.

In 1775, Israel joined the American forces and took part in the Battle of Bunker Hill. He fought bravely, but the battle, as he saw it, was simply disorganized carnage. Wounded, Israel enlisted aboard an American ship after his recovery. Once at sea, the ship was captured by the British. Israel was taken prisoner and conveyed to England on the British ship, but on his arrival in London he managed to make his escape.

Wandering about London, Israel met various Englishmen who mocked his American accent. Some of the English were kind and helpful to him; others cuffed him about and berated the scurrilous Yankee rebels. He found various odd jobs, including one as a gardener working for a cruel employer. He escaped from this job and found one as a gardener on the king's staff at Kew Gardens. One day Israel met King George III. The king, completely mad, realized that Israel was an American and was ineffectually kind to him. Eventually, in a slack season, Israel was discharged. He then worked for a farmer, but when neighboring farmers discovered that he was an American, he was forced to run away.

Israel met Squire Woodcock, a wealthy and secret friend of America, who sent him on a secret mission to Benjamin Franklin in Paris. Israel carried a message in the false heel of his new boots. On his arrival in Paris, while he was looking for Benjamin Franklin, a poor man tried to shine his boots on the Pont Neuf. Israel, in fright, kicked the man and ran off. At last he found Benjamin Franklin, who took the message and then insisted that Israel return and pay damages to the bootblack.

In this fashion Israel, under the tutelage of Franklin, learned his first lesson in European politeness and consideration. From this incident Franklin proceeded to instruct Israel in the ways of proper behavior, deriving many of his lessons from the simple maxims in *Poor Richard's Almanack.* Israel, still innocent, absorbed the teaching carefully, although none of it ever applied to his later experiences. Franklin promised that Israel would be sent back to America, if he would first return to England with a message. While still in Paris, Israel met the stormy and ferocious Captain John Paul Jones, who also visited Franklin. John Paul Jones found Israel a bright and likely young man.

Israel made his way back across the Channel and went to Squire Woodcock. The squire urged him to hide in the dungeon cell for three days, since their plot was in danger of discovery. When Israel emerged from the cell, he recognized that the good squire must have been killed for his activities in the American cause.

Having appropriated some of the squire's clothes, Israel masqueraded as Squire Woodcock's ghost and escaped from a house filled with his enemies. He then traded clothes with a farmer, wandered to Portsmouth, and signed on as a foretopman on a British ship bound for the East Indies. In the Channel, his ship met another ship whose captain had authority to impress some of the men; Israel was among those taken. That same night the ship was captured by an American ship under the command of John Paul Jones. Having revealed himself to his old friend, Israel soon became the quartermaster of the *Ranger*. With John Paul Jones, Israel engaged in piracy, capturing and looting ships.

In Scotland they called on the Earl of Selkirk in order to rob him, but the nobleman was not at home. Israel impressed the earl's wife with his Parisian manners, drank tea with her, and assured her that he and John Paul Jones did not intend to do the lady any harm. The crew, however, insisted that plunder was a part of piracy, and so Israel and John Paul Jones were forced to allow the men to take the family silver and other valuables. Israel promised to restore all articles of value, and when he received a large sum of money from another exploit, he and John Paul Jones bought back all the earl's articles from the men and returned them to the Selkirk family.

Other adventures did not end so cheerfully. The sea fight between the *Bon Homme Richard* and the *Serapis* was a violent and bloody battle, fought along national lines and devoid of all the amenities of piracy. Both ships were lost, and Israel and John Paul Jones, still hoping to get to America, sailed on the *Ariel*. The *Ariel* was captured by the British and Israel was again impressed into the British Navy. By feigning madness to hide his Yankee origins, he got back to England safely.

In England, Israel met Ethan Allen, a strong, heroic, Samson-like figure, held prisoner by the English. Israel tried to help Allen escape but was unsuccessful. Disguised as a beggar, he went to London, where he remained for over forty years. During that time he worked as a brick-maker and laborer, always hoping to save enough money to return to America but never finding the economic situation in London stable enough to permit saving. A wanderer in an alien land, he became part of the grime and poverty of London. During those years he married a shopgirl who bore him a son. Finally, in 1826, he secured some credit and, with the help of the American consul, sailed for America with his son.

Israel arrived in Boston on July 4, during a public celebration of the Battle of Bunker Hill. No one recognized him or acknowledged his right to be there. Instead, people laughed at him and thought he was mad. He returned to his father's farm, but the homestead had long since disappeared. Old Israel, his wanderings ended, found no peace, comfort, or friendship in his old age. Although heroes of the Revolution were publicly venerated, the aged man could not even get a small pension.

Critical Evaluation

"Is civilization a thing distinct, or is it an advanced state of barbarism?" Melville asks the question after describing in vivid detail, but with cynical detachment, the canine ferocity of the fight to the death between John Paul

Jones's *Bon Homme Richard* and the British man of war *Serapis*. Joined by their smashed and burning rigging, the two vessels are a fitting symbol of the fratricidal struggle between Britain and the young United States. What bemuses Melville is the insanity of a fight in which both parties literally destroy themselves in pursuit of victory over the other; when the *Serapis* finally strikes her colors, it is almost impossible to determine the true victor because both ships were disemboweled wrecks with half their crews killed or wounded. Ironically, Jones and his men board the *Serapis* the morning after battle because they are unable to put out the flames on the *Richard*.

In *Moby Dick* and *Pierre,* written a few years before *Israel Potter,* Melville had traced the consequences of erratic and self-destructive behavior in titanic and tormented individuals: satanic Ahab and maddeningly idealistic Pierre. In *Israel Potter* Melville broadens his focus to include the world at large; instead of cosmic tragedy, we have cosmic laughter, a kind of grim snicker at the absurdity and contemptuous pettiness of the real world. There is no doubt that this minor work is an important bridge between *Moby Dick* and *The Confidence Man,* that dark social satire which Lewis Leary has called "the inevitable sequel" to *Israel Potter.*

The famous portraits in the novel of actual historical figures (Franklin, John Paul Jones, and Ethan Allen) are artful exercises in debunking and anticipate by more than sixty years the biographical intentions of Lytton Strachey. Great men are mirrors to the corruption and vanities of their time. Israel Potter, the common man, despite the adventurous promise of his youth fails to realize the American imperative of independence and self-realization. Although brave and gifted with the shrewdness necessary for survival, he lives out his days in mediocrity and helpless exile. When he finally does return to America, he is unrecognized and denied his pension—a hero of Bunker Hill.

Bibliography

Chase, Richard. *Herman Melville: A Critical Study.* New York: Macmillan, 1949, pp. 176–184.

Farnsworth, R.M. "*Israel Potter*: Pathetic Comedy," in *Bulletin of the New York Public Library.* LXV (February, 1961), pp. 125–132.

Frederick, John T. "Symbol and Theme in Melville's *Israel Potter,*" in *Modern Fiction Studies.* VIII (Autumn, 1962), pp. 265–275.

Hull, Raymond. "London and Melville's *Israel Potter,*" in *Emerson Society Quarterly.* XLVII (1967), pp. 78–81.

Jackson, Kenny. "*Israel Potter*: Melville's Fourth of July Story," in *College Language Association Journal.* VI (March, 1963), pp. 194–204.

Keyssar, Alexander. *Melville's* Israel Potter, *Reflections on the American Dream.* Cambridge, Mass.: Harvard University Press, 1969.

McCutcheon, Roger P. "The Technique of Melville's *Israel Potter*," in *South Atlantic Quarterly.* XXVII (April, 1928), pp. 161–174.

Rampersad, Arnold. *Melville's* Israel Potter: *A Pilgrimage and Progress.* Bowling Green, Oh.: Bowling Green University Popular Press, 1969.

Watson, Charles N., Jr. "Melville's Israel Potter: Fathers and Sons," in *Studies in the Novel.* VII (1975), pp. 563–568.

————. "Premature Burial in *Arthur Gordon Pym* and *Israel Potter*," in *American Literature.* XLVII, pp. 105–107.

Weaver, Raymond M. "Introduction in *Israel Potter* by Herman Melville. New York: A & C. Boni, 1924, p. xvii.

Yates, Norris. "An Instance of Parallel Imagery in Hawthorne, Melville, and Frost," in *Philological Quarterly.* XXXVI (April, 1957), pp. 276–280.

MARDI

Type of work: Novel
Author: Herman Melville (1819–1891)
Type of plot: Symbolic allegory
Time of plot: Mid-nineteenth century
Locale: Chiefly Mardi, a group of islands located somewhere in the Western Pacific
First published: 1849

Mardi *represented a double turning point in Herman Melville's career. On the one hand, it was his first attempt to deal with serious social, philosophical, and moral issues in a quasi-symbolic narrative form, and, as such, it prefigures* Moby Dick. *On the other, it was this book that lost him the audience he had entertained with his earlier sea adventures,* Typee *and* Omoo. *From this point on Melville's popularity rapidly declined as the profundity of his work increased.*

Principal Characters

The Narrator, a young American sailor in the South Seas who, with a companion, jumps ship and leaves in a small boat for hospitable islands. He meets, at sea, a blond native girl named Yillah. The party is welcomed to an island, where the Narrator assumes the identity of Taji, a god. The Narrator falls in love with Yillah and when she mysteriously disappears he wanders the seas, visiting many islands, looking for her.

Yillah, the Narrator's sweetheart, the symbol for psychic wholeness in the novel. After her disappearance the Narrator's search for her is the symbolic quest to understand the mystical identity of the divine and human consciousness.

Hautia, a dark native queen who is Yillah's rival for the Narrator's love. She and her heralds pursue the Narrator.

Jarl, a sailor who, with the Narrator,

leaves the whaling vessel and travels among the islands of the South Seas.

Samoa, a native whom Jarl and the Narrator find hiding in a derelict ship. The sailors befriend him, and he accompanies them on their travels.

Media, a native king who accepts the Narrator as the god Taji and offers him the hospitality of the island.

Babbalanja, a wise man in Media's court who tells the Narrator that having lost Yillah, he will never again find her.

King Donjalolo, monarch of the island of Juam, who moves from place to place on his island home in order to escape reality.

Yoomy, the minstrel-poet of King Media's court.

Mohi, a historian at King Media's court.

The Story

The Narrator of the novel, a young American sailor, was picked up by a whaling vessel at Ravavai, a Pacific Island, but a combination of circumstances made him want to leave the ship. He and Jarl, an old sailor, provisioned a whaleboat and made their escape. After sailing for some time, they came upon a drifting ship. Boarding it, they noted that it appeared to be the scene of some tragedy. Samoa and Annatoo, a native couple, were discovered on the ship the following morning. Samoa told the Narrator and Jarl that the ship's captain and crew had been murdered by some islanders who had been hired to dive for pearls. Only he and his wife had escaped. With the Narrator acting as captain, the four continued to sail in a westerly direction. The Narrator, however, soon became annoyed with Annatoo. Although he admitted that she had some admirable qualities, he also stated that she was sly, possessive, and domineering. He and Jarl were almost out of patience with her when she was killed accidentally during a storm.

Because the ship had been damaged beyond repair during the storm, the Narrator, Jarl, and Samoa abandoned it for the whaleboat. After traveling for a number of days, they spied a sail in the distance. Approaching it, they saw a double canoe with a tentlike shelter. More than two dozen young men and one old, authoritative looking man were seen on board. Samoa surmised that the old man was a priest who was carrying out a sacred mission. Curious to know more, the Narrator succeeded in learning that a beautiful young woman was being taken by them to an island to be sacrificed in a whirlpool. Although the young woman was neither seen nor heard by the Narrator, he decided to rescue her. In the exchange which followed, the Narrator killed the old priest. Samoa and Jarl held the young men at bay while the Narrator entered the tentlike structure. He found a lovely blonde woman inside the tent. She was wearing a rose-colored pearl. She told him that her name was Yillah and revealed that she believed herself to be a goddess. The old priest had told her that she was on her way home to paradise.

The Narrator convinced Yillah to go with him by telling her that he, too, was a divine being from paradise. He also told her that the old priest had entrusted her to his care. Once on board the whaleboat, they were pursued by the young men who, as sons of the old priest, were determined to avenge his death, but the Narrator and his companions eluded them. The time spent on the whaleboat with Yillah, the Narrator claimed, was a time of happiness, for he and Yillah fell in love. Sometimes, however, Yillah was downcast because she was convinced that she was destined to descend into the enchanted whirlpool. The Narrator concentrated on leading Yillah to give up her belief in their divinity. He was pleased with the knowledge that she was becoming dependent on him.

Eventually they landed on an island which was part of a group that was known as Mardi. As they were making contact with the natives, Samoa advised the Narrator to claim that he was Taji, one of the islander's gods. Media, a king of one of the islands of Mardi and a divinity in his own right, accepted the Narrator as Taji and took the Narrator and his companions to his kingdom. On Odo, Media's island, the Narrator discovered that the king had a double personality. Although Media was a gracious host, he was a repressive monarch. Soon another personality made a strong impression on the Narrator. One day the Narrator became aware of a heavily draped figure whom he thought was watching Yillah with an air of hostility. Much later he learned that this figure was Hautia, a mysterious queen of one of the islands of Mardi. After his first encounter with the shrouded figure, three young women ritualistically presented him with a symbolic message in the form of flowers. They told him that they were the heralds of Queen Hautia.

One morning the Narrator woke to find that Yillah was gone. Hautia's heralds approached him, but he spurned them and their flower message. When the Narrator announced that he must leave Media's island to search for Yillah, the king surprised Taji by suggesting that he and three of his companions—Babbalanja, a philosopher, Mohi, a historian, and Yoomy, a poet—accompany the Narrator, Jarl, and Samoa. Together they set out in three of Media's royal canoes.

During the months that followed, the group visited extensively throughout the islands of Mardi and circumnavigated the world. All the islands that they visited were plagued with social unrest or were inhabited by different kinds of fools. All the travelers, to greater or lesser extents, were concerned with the great religious and philosophic questions of life. As the Narrator described their conversations, Media instigated and directed much of the talk, but Babbalanja contributed to it more than the others. The Narrator as Taji did not participate in their discussions. Instead, he began to speak occasionally in an omniscient, oracular voice. But the Narrator was not the only one with double or multiple personalities. Babbalanja attributed many of his ideas and theories to a devil personality whom he claimed inhabited him. Throughout the journey, Taji continued to be accosted by three of the old priest's sons, the avengers, who succeeded in killing Jarl and Samoa about midway in the journey. Hautia's heralds, too, continued to appear with flower messages for the Narrator, which he spurned.

As the Narrator and his party were coming to an end of their journey, Babbalanja, Media, Yoomy, and Mohi found a people whose religious philosophy and way of life impressed them. Babbalanja, relinquishing the devil aspect of his personality, had a mystical vision and decided to remain on the Isle of Serenia. Media relinquished his claim to divinity and vowed to return to his kingdom to put the Serenia philosophy into practice. Nevertheless, the Narrator was determined to continue his search for Yillah.

Leaving Babbalanja on Serenia, the Narrator and the others continued to visit more islands and were again approached by the avengers as well as by Hautia's heralds. The last time that Hautia's heralds approached them, the Narrator agreed to meet Hautia, for her heralds' message seemed to promise that Hautia could tell him of Yillah's fate. Although Yoomy, Media, and Mohi accompanied the Narrator to Hautia's island, they left him after they had met Hautia to return to Media's kingdom. On Hautia's island, Taji drank a magic potion which made him desire Hautia, but when he reached for her, she eluded him. When she reappeared, she led him to a lake in a cavern to dive for pearls, but he did not secure any. After several other experiences, the Narrator threatened to kill Hautia unless she told him what she knew about Yillah. Then, on her head, he saw the rose-colored pearl which Yillah had worn. After he grasped it, Hautia implied that Yillah may have drowned or was drowning in another hidden lake. He ran to it but arrived only in time to see a form which he thought might be Yillah circling about in dark water and floating seaward through a low arch.

That night, as he wandered on the beach, Yoomy and Mohi appeared. As they forced him into their boat, the Narrator told them that Taji was dead. Mohi reported that when he, Yoomy, and Media had reached Media's kingdom, they found an insurrection in progress which was led by the old priest's sons. Media had instructed them to get Taji and proceed to Serenia. The Narrator suddenly announced that he would not go with them: he was going to steer the boat out into the open sea. Believing that Taji was crazed and that their lives were in danger, Yoomy and Mohi jumped out of the boat and began to swim for the shore. As the boat shot through a narrow channel and into the open sea, the Narrator saw the old priest's sons, weapons poised, intently pursuing him.

Critical Evaluation

In the prefaces to his first two novels, Herman Melville told his readers that for the most part the events which he related in *Typee* and *Omoo* did take place. Moreover, he emphasized that he tried to be as objective as possible in regard to his observations about the impact of Westerners on the pagan cultures of the South Sea Islands. Some of his readers, however, felt that Melville had attacked Christendom. As a way of undermining his authority, they criticized his truthfulness.

Melville was angered and insulted by the reaction of these readers, and he was determined to continue to combat unreflective, dogmatic thinking. Thus, in the preface to *Mardi: And a Voyage Thither*, his third novel, he drew attention to the satire in *Mardi*. Tongue in cheek, he wrote that since some of the readers of his first two books seemed bent on taking fact for fiction, he intended in *Mardi*, a romance, to see if they would take fiction for fact.

But *Mardi* is much more than a novel of social satire. Complex and daring, *Mardi* reveals that Melville was capable of creating fiction with mythological and metaphysical dimensions.

Mardi met with a hostile response from its first reviewers, and it has continued to receive negative criticism in the twentieth century. The recent trend among *Mardi*'s critics, however, constitutes a reversal of these negative views and suggests that the novel may be one of the most extraordinary achievements in American literature.

Conceptually and stylistically, *Mardi* is a challenging novel. It is an intellectualized yet mystical allegory of the way in which the divine operates as it creatively explores its own infinite potentialities. As a novel which describes reality as a process of "becoming," it poses the tendency toward the static and fixed against the tendency toward the dynamic and anarchistic. Neither of these tendencies, however, is seen as wholly good or evil.

The complexity of the allegory centers on a paradox that on the esoteric level the divine and the human are one in essence. As a symbolic character, the narrator of *Mardi* represents this paradox, for he is both subject and agent, the creator and the created, the divine and the human consciousness in the novel. At the time at which he experienced the events which form *Mardi*'s plot, however, he was unenlightened in regard to the mystical identity of the human and the divine. Thus, on one level, *Mardi* is a novel of initiation.

As the young American sailor who is immature, the narrator undergoes an initiation experience. His test is to come to a profound understanding of the nature of reality and thus to become aware of the mystical identity of the divine and human consciousness. Yillah and her rose-colored pearl are symbols of attaining psychic wholeness. As the human consciousness, the American sailor, the narrator who is only pretending that he is a god loses Yillah, who is his psychic opposite, because he is not able to overcome the linear, dualistic mode of thinking which divides reality into such absolute categories as good and evil, light and dark, and the divine and human. That he does overcome the linear, dualistic mode of thinking—after the events which he relates have taken place—is indicated by the fact that he does acquire Yillah's rose-colored pearl, a symbol of non-duality, shortly before the end of the narrative and by the fact that the narrator lapses occasionally into an omniscient, oracular method of narration.

One of the basic metaphors in *Mardi* which posits the identity of the human and divine is the metaphor of the hunter and the hunted. In terms of the ordinary consciousness, the hunter and the hunted are categorical opposites, but in terms of the mystical consciousness, they are both manifestations of the same divine energy and are thus one in essence. The narrator of *Mardi* symbolizes this metaphor, for he is both the hunter and the hunted. While pursuing Yillah, he himself is pursued by Hautia's heralds and the sons of the old priest whom he murdered. Esoterically considered, they are all aspects of his own consciousness, and his own consciousness is an aspect of the divine. From the point of view of the mystical consciousness, therefore, the emnity between the hunter and the hunted is a farcical game, a ritual of life and death which insures the transformation of energy. That the title of the novel is derived from Mardi Gras, the day of carnival which precedes Lent, suggests that Melville was striving in *Mardi* to synthesize the sacred and the profane. Certainly *Mardi* is replete with the imagery of digestion, games, masks, and costumes.

Bibliography

Arvin, Newton. "Melville's *Mardi*," in *American Quarterly*. II (Spring, 1950), pp. 71–81.

Bernard, Kenneth. "Melville's *Mardi* and the Second Loss of Paradise," in *Lock Haven Review.* VII (1965), pp. 23–30.

Blansett, B.N. "From Dark to Dark; *Mardi*, A Foreshadowing of *Pierre*," in *Southern Quarterly.* I (April, 1963), pp. 213–227.

Braswell, William. *Melville's Religious Thought: An Essay in Interpretation.* Durham, N.C.: Duke University Press, 1943, pp. 86–106.

Davis, Merrell R. "The Flower Symbolism in *Mardi*," in *Modern Language Quarterly.* II (December, 1941), pp. 625–638.

————. *Melville's* Mardi: *A Charter Voyage.* New Haven, Conn.: Yale University Press, 1952.

Freeman, John. *Herman Melville.* New York: Macmillan, 1926, pp. 95–108.

Graham, Philip. "The Riddle of Melville's *Mardi*: A Reinterpretation," in *Texas Studies in English.* XXXVI (1957), pp. 93–99.

Hillway, Tyrus. "Toji's Abdication in Herman Melville's *Mardi*," in *American Literature.* XVI (November, 1944), pp. 204–207.

————. "Toji's Quest for Certainty," in *American Literature.* XVIII (March, 1946), pp. 27–34.

Jaffe, David. "Some Sources of Melville's *Mardi*," in *American Literature.* IX (March, 1937), pp. 56–69.

Larrabee, Stephen A. "Melville Against the World," in *South Atlantic Quarterly.* XXXIV (October, 1935), pp. 410–418.

Mason, Ronald. *The Spirit Above the Dust: A Study of Herman Melville.* London: John Lehmann, 1951, pp. 38–65.

Miller, James E., Jr. "The Many Masks of *Mardi*," in *Journal of English and Germanic Philology.* LVIII (July, 1959), pp. 400–413.

Mills, Gordon. "The Significance of Arcturus in *Mardi*," in *American Literature.* XIV (May, 1942), pp. 158–161.

Mumford, Lewis. *Herman Melville.* New York: Harcourt, Brace, 1929, pp. 93–107.

Rosenberry, Edward H. *Melville and the Comic Spirit.* Cambridge, Mass.: Harvard University Press, 1955, pp. 57–89.

Sedgwick, William Ellery. *Herman Melville: The Tragedy of Mind.* Cambridge, Mass.: Harvard University Press, 1944, pp. 37–61.

Stern, Milton R. *The Fine Hammered Steel of Herman Melville.* Urbana: University of Illinois Press, 1957, pp. 66–149.

Stone, Geoffrey. *Melville.* New York: Sheed and Ward, 1949, pp. 86–108.

Thompson, Lawrance. *Melville's Quarrel with God.* Princeton, N.J.: Princeton University Press, 1952, pp. 59–69.

Wright, Nathalia. "The Head and the Heart in Melville's *Mardi*," in *PMLA*. LXVI (June, 1951), pp. 351–362.

MOBY DICK

Type of work: Novel
Author: Herman Melville (1819–1891)
Type of plot: Symbolic allegory
Time of plot: Early nineteenth century
Locale: The high seas
First published: 1851

Herman Melville brought many disparate elements together in Moby Dick: *a realistic picture of the whaling industry, an adventure-romance of the sea, an epic quest, a Faustian bargain, and metaphysical speculation. Although it is unlikely that any one interpretation of Ahab's obsessive pursuit of the white whale will ever be generally accepted, the depth, sweep, and power of the author's vision guarantees the novel's stature as one of the world's proven masterpieces.*

Principal Characters

Ishmael, a philosophical young schoolmaster and sometime sailor who seeks the sea when he becomes restless, gloomy, and soured on the world. With a newfound friend Queequeg, a harpooner from the South Seas, he signs aboard the whaler "Pequod" as a seaman. Queequeg is the only person on the ship to whom he is emotionally and spiritually close, and this closeness is, after the initial establishment of their friendship, implied rather than detailed. Otherwise Ishmael does a seaman's work, observes and listens to his shipmates, and keeps his own counsel. Having been reared a Presbyterian (as was Melville), he reflects in much of his thinking the Calvinism out of which Presbyterianism grew; but his thought is also influenced by his knowledge of literature and philosophy. He is a student of cetology. Regarding Ahab's pursuit of Moby Dick, the legendary white whale, and the parts played by himself and others involved, Ishmael dwells on such subjects as free will, predestination, necessity, and damnation. After the destruction of the "Pequod" by Moby Dick, Ishmael, the lone survivor, clings to Queenqueg's floating coffin for almost a day and a

night before being rescued by the crew of another whaling vessel, the "Rachel."

Queequeg, Starbuck's veteran harpooner, a tattooed cannibal from Kokovoko, an uncharted South Seas island. Formerly zealous of learning about Christianity, he has become disillusioned after living among so-called Christians and, having reverted to paganism, he worships a little black idol, Yojo, that he keeps with him. Although he appears at ease among his Christian shipmates, he keeps himself at the same time apart from them, his only close friend being Ishmael. In pursuit of whales he is skilled and fearless. When he nearly dies of a fever he has the ship's carpenter build him a canoe-shaped coffin which he tries out for size and comfort; then, recovering, he saves it for future use. Ironically it is this coffin on which Ishmael floats after the sinking of the "Pequod" and the drowning of Queequeg.

Captain Ahab, the proud, defiant, megalomaniacal captain of the "Pequod." He is a grim, bitter, brooding, vengeful madman who has only one goal in life: the killing of the white whale that had deprived him of a leg in an earlier encounter. His most prominent physical peculiarity is a livid scar that begins under the hair of his head and, according to one crewman, extends the entire length of his body. The scar symbolizes the spiritual flaw in the man himself. His missing leg has been replaced by one of whalebone for which a small hole has been bored in the deck. When he stands erect looking out to sea, his face shows the unsurrenderable willfulness of his spirit and to Ishmael a crucifixion also, a "regal overbearing dignity of some mighty woe." Ahab is in complete, strict command of his ship, though he permits Starbuck occasionally to disagree with him. Ahab dies caught, like Fedallah, the Parsee, in a fouled harpoon line that loops about his neck and pulls him from a whaleboat.

Starbuck, the first mate, tall, thin, weathered, staid, steadfast, conscientious, and superstitious, a symbol of "mere unaided virtue or right-mindedness." He dares to criticize Ahab's desire for vengeance, but he is as ineffectual as a seaman trying to halt a storm. Ahab once takes his advice about repairing some leaking oil casks; but when Starbuck, during a typhoon off Japan, suggests turning home, Ahab scorns him. Starbuck even thinks of killing or imprisoning Ahab while the Captain is asleep, but he cannot. Having failed to dissuade Ahab from the pursuit of Moby Dick, Starbuck submits on the third day to Ahab's will, though feeling that in obeying Ahab he is disobeying God. When he makes one final effort to stop the doomed Ahab, the captain shouts to his boatmen, "Lower away!"

Stubb, the second mate, happy-go-lucky, indifferent to danger, good-humored, easy; he is a constant pipe-smoker and a fatalist.

Flask (King-Post), the young third mate, short, stout, ruddy. He relishes whaling and kills the monsters for the fun of it

or as one might get rid of giant rats. In his shipboard actions Flask is sometimes playful out of Ahab's sight but always abjectly respectful in his presence.

Fedallah, Ahab's tall, diabolical, white-turbaned Parsee servant. He is like a shadow of Ahab or the two are like opposite sides of a single character and Ahab seems finally to become Fedallah, though retaining his own appearance. The Parsee prophesies that Ahab will have neither hearse nor coffin when he dies. Fedallah dies caught in a fouled harpoon line which is wrapped around Moby Dick.

Moby Dick, a giant albino sperm whale that has become a legend among whalers. He has often been attacked and he has crippled or destroyed many men and boats. He is both a real whale and a symbol with many possible meanings. He may represent the universal spirit of evil, God the indestructible, or indifferent Nature; or perhaps he may encompass an ambiguity of meaning adaptable to the individual reader. Whatever his meaning, he is one of the most memorable non-human characters in all fiction.

Pip, the bright, jolly, genial little Negro cabin boy who, after falling from a boat during a whale chase, is abandoned in midocean by Stubb, who supposes that a following boat will pick him up. When finally taken aboard the "Pequod," he has become demented from fright.

Tashtego, an American Indian, Stubb's harpooner. As the "Pequod" sinks, he nails the flag still higher on the mast and drags a giant seabird, caught between the hammer and the mast, to a watery grave.

Daggoo, a giant African Negro, Flask's harpooner.

Father Mapple, a former whaler, now the minister at the Whaleman's Chapel in New Bedford. He preaches a Calvinistic sermon, on Job, filled with seafaring terms.

Captain Peleg and
Captain Bildad, fighting, materialistic
Quakers who are the principal owners
of the "Pequod."

Elijah, a madman who warns Ishmael
and Queequeg against shipping with
Captain Ahab.

Dough-Boy, the pale, bread-faced, dull-
witted steward who, deathly afraid of
Queenqueg, Tashtego, and Daggoo, does
his best to satisfy their enormous appe-
tites.

Fleece, the old Negro ship's cook. At
Stubb's request he preaches a sermon to
the voracious sharks and ends with a

hope that their greed will kill them. He
is disgusted also by Stubb's craving for
whale meat.

Bulkington, the powerfully built, deeply
tanned, sober-minded helmsman of the
"Pequod."

Perth, the ship's elderly blacksmith, who
took up whaling after losing his home
and family. He makes for Ahab the
harpoon intended to be Moby Dick's
death dart, which the captain baptizes
in the devil's name.

Captain Gardiner, the skipper of "Rachel" for whose lost son Captain Ahab
refuses to search.

The Story

Ishmael was a schoolmaster who often felt that he must leave his quiet existence and go to sea. Much of his life had been spent as a sailor, and his voyages
were a means for ridding himself of the restlessness which frequently seized him.
One day he decided that he would sign on a whaling ship, and packing his carpet-
bag he left Manhattan and set out, bound for Cape Horn and the Pacific.

On his arrival in New Bedford he went to the Spouter Inn near the waterfront
to spend the night. There he found he could have a bed only if he consented to
share it with a harpooner. His strange bedfellow frightened him when he entered
the room, for Ishmael was certain that he was a savage cannibal. After a few
moments, however, it became evident that the native, whose name was Queequeg,
was a friendly person, for he presented Ishmael with an embalmed head and
offered to share his fortune of thirty dollars. The two men quickly became
friends, and decided to sign on the same ship.

Eventually they signed on the *Pequod*, a whaler out of Nantucket, Ishmael as a
seaman, Queequeg as a harpooner. Although several people seemed dubious
about the success of a voyage on a vessel such as the *Pequod* was reported to be
under so strange a man as Captain Ahab, neither Ishmael nor Queequeg had any
intention of giving up their plans. They were, however, curious to see Captain
Ahab.

For several days after the vessel had sailed there was no sign of the captain, as
he remained hidden in his cabin. The running of the ship was left to Starbuck and
Stubb, two of the mates, and although Ishmael became friendly with them, he
learned very little more about Ahab. One day, as the ship was sailing southward,
the captain strode out on deck. Ishmael was struck by his stern, relentless expression. In particular, he noticed that the captain had lost a leg and that instead
of a wooden leg he now wore one cut from the bone of the jaw of a whale. A livid

white scar ran down one side of his face and was lost beneath his collar, so that it seemed as though he were scarred from head to foot.

For several days the ship continued south looking for the whaling schools. The sailors began to take turns on masthead watches to give the sign when a whale was sighted. Ahab appeared on deck and summoned all his men around him. He pulled out an ounce gold piece, nailed it to the mast, and declared that the first man to sight the great white whale, known to the sailors as Moby Dick, would have the gold. Everyone expressed enthusiasm for the quest except Starbuck and Stubb, Starbuck especially deploring the madness with which Ahab had directed all his energies to this one end. He told the captain that he was like a man possessed, for the white whale was a menace to those who would attempt to kill him. Ahab had lost his leg in his last encounter with Moby Dick; he might lose his life in the next meeting. But the captain would not listen to the mate's warning. Liquor was brought out, and at the captain's orders the crew drank to the destruction of Moby Dick.

Ahab, from what he knew of the last reported whereabouts of the whale, plotted a course for the ship which would bring it into the area where Moby Dick was most likely to be. Near the Cape of Good Hope the ship came across a school of sperm whales, and the men busied themselves harpooning, stripping, melting, and storing as many as they were able to catch.

When they encountered another whaling vessel at sea, Captain Ahab asked for news about the white whale. The captain of the ship warned him not to attempt to chase Moby Dick, but it was clear by now that nothing could deflect Ahab from the course he had chosen.

Another vessel stopped them, and the captain of the ship boarded the *Pequod* to buy some oil for his vessel. Captain Ahab again demanded news of the whale, but the captain knew nothing of the monster. As the captain was returning to his ship, he and his men spotted a school of six whales and started after them in their rowboats. While Starbuck and Stubb rallied their men into the *Pequod*'s boats, their rivals were already far ahead of them. But the two mates urged their crew until they outstripped their rivals in the race and Queequeg harpooned the largest whale.

Killing the whale was only the beginning of a long and arduous job. After the carcass was dragged to the side of the boat and lashed to it by ropes, the men descended the side and slashed off the blubber. Much of the body was usually demolished by sharks, who streamed around it snapping at the flesh of the whale and at each other. The head of the whale was removed and suspended several feet in the air, above the deck of the ship. After the blubber was cleaned, it was melted in tremendous try-pots, and then stored in vats below deck.

The men were kept busy, but their excitement increased as their ship neared the Indian Ocean and the probable sporting grounds of the white whale. Before long they crossed the path of an English whaling vessel, and Captain Ahab again demanded news of Moby Dick. In answer, the captain of the English ship held out his arm, which from the elbow down consisted of sperm whalebone. Ahab demanded that his boat be lowered at once, and he quickly boarded the deck of the other ship. The captain told him of his encounter, and warned Captain Ahab that it was foolhardy to try to pursue Moby Dick. When he told Ahab where he had seen the white whale last, the captain of the *Pequod* waited for no civilities, but returned to his own ship to order the course changed to carry him to Moby Dick's new feeding ground.

Starbuck tried to reason with the mad captain, to persuade him to give up this insane pursuit, but Ahab seized a rifle and in his fury ordered the mate out of his cabin.

Meanwhile, Queequeg had fallen ill with a fever. When it seemed almost certain he would die, he requested that the carpenter make him a coffin in the shape of a canoe, according to the custom of his tribe. The coffin was then placed in the cabin with the sick man, but as yet there was no real need for it. Queequeg recovered from his illness and rejoined his shipmates. He used his coffin as a sea chest and carved many strange designs upon it.

The sailors had been puzzled by the appearance early in the voyage of the Parsee, Fedallah. His relationship to the captain could not be determined, but that he was highly regarded was evident. Fedallah had prophesied that the captain would die only after he had seen two strange hearses for carrying the dead upon the sea, one not constructed by mortal hands, and the other made of wood grown in America. But he said that the captain himself would have neither hearse nor coffin for his burial.

A terrible storm arose one night. Lightning struck the masts so that all three flamed against the blackness of the night, and the men were frightened by this omen. It seemed to them the hand of God was motioning them to turn from the course to which they had set themselves and return to their homes. Only Captain Ahab was undaunted by the sight. He planted himself at the foot of the mast and challenged the god of evil which the fire symbolized for him. He vowed once again his determination to find and kill the white whale.

A few days later a cry rang through the ship. Moby Dick had been spotted. The voice was Captain Ahab's, for none of the sailors, alert as they had been, had been able to sight him before their captain. Then boats were lowered and the chase began, with Captain Ahab's boat in the lead. As he was about to dash his harpoon into the side of the mountain of white, the whale suddenly turned on the boat, dived under it, and split it into pieces. The men were thrown into the sea, and for some time the churning of the whale prevented rescue. At length Ahab ordered the rescuers to ride into the whale and frighten him away, so he and his men might be picked up. The rest of that day was spent chasing the whale, but to no avail.

The second day the men started out again. They caught up with the whale and buried three harpoons in his white flanks. But he so turned and churned that the lines became twisted, and the boats were pulled every way, with no control over their direction. Two of them were splintered, and the men hauled out of the sea, but Ahab's boat had not as yet been touched. Suddenly it was lifted from the water and thrown high into the air. The captain and the men were quickly picked up, but Fedallah was nowhere to be found.

When the third day of the chase began, Moby Dick seemed tired, and the *Pequod*'s boats soon overtook him. Bound to the whale's back by the coils of rope from the harpoon poles they saw the body of Fedallah. The first part of his prophecy had been fulfilled. Moby Dick, enraged by his pain, turned on the boats and splintered them. On the *Pequod* Starbuck watched and turned the ship toward the whale in the hope of saving the captain and some of the crew. The infuriated monster swam directly into the *Pequod*, shattering the ship's timbers. Ahab, seeing the ship founder, cried out that the *Pequod*—made of wood grown in America—was the second hearse of Fedallah's prophecy. The third prophecy, Ahab's death by hemp, was fulfilled when rope from Ahab's harpoon coiled around his neck and snatched him from his boat. All except Ishmael perished. He was rescued by a passing ship after clinging for hours to Queequeg's canoe-coffin, which had bobbed to the surface as the *Pequod* sank.

Critical Evaluation

Although his early adventure novels—*Typee* (1846), *Omoo* (1847), *Redburn* (1849), and *White Jacket* (1850)—brought Melville a notable amount of popularity and financial success during his lifetime, it was not until nearly fifty years after his death—in the 1920's and 1930's—that he received universal critical recognition as one of the greatest American authors of the nineteenth century. Melville took part in the first great period of American literature—the period that included Poe, Emerson, Hawthorne, Whitman, and Thoreau. For complexity, originality, psychological penetration, breadth, and symbolic richness, Melville achieved his greatest artistic expression with the book he wrote when he was thirty, *Moby Dick*. Between the time of his birth in New York City and his return there to research and write his masterpiece, Melville had circled the globe of experience—working as a bank messenger, salesman, farmhand, schoolteacher (like his narrator, Ishmael), engineer and surveyor, bowling alley attendant, cabin boy, and whaleman in the Pacific on the *Acushnet*. His involvement in the mutinous Pacific voyage, combined with J. N. Reynold's accounts of a notorious whale called "Mocha Dick" (in *The Knickerbocker Magazine,* 1839) that wrought havoc in the 1840's and 1850's, certainly influenced the creation of *Moby Dick*.

The intertangled themes of this mighty novel express the artistic genius of a mind that, according to Hawthorne, "could neither believe nor be comfortable in unbelief." Many of those themes are characteristic of American romanticism: the "isolated self" and the pain of self-discovery, the insufficiency of conventional practical knowledge in the face of the "power of blackness," the demonic center to the world, the confrontation of evil and innocence, the fundamental imperfection of man, Faustian heroism, search for the ultimate truth, the inadequacy of human perception. The conflict between faith and doubt was one of the major issues of the century and *Moby Dick,* as Eric Mottram points out, is part of "a huge exploration of the historical and psychological origins and development of self, society and the desire to create and destroy gods and heroes."

Moby Dick is, moreover, a unique literary form, combining elements of the psychological and picaresque novel; sea story and allegory; the epic of "literal and metaphorical quest"; the satire of social and religious events; the emotional intensity of the lyric genre, both in diction and metaphor; Cervantian romance; Dantesque mysticism; Rabelaisian humor; Shakespearean drama (both tragedy and comedy), complete with stage directions; journalistic travel book; and scientific treatise on cetology. Melville was inspired by Hawthorne's example to give his story the unifying quality of a moral parable, although his own particular genius refused to allow that parable an unequivocal, single rendering. Both in style and theme, Melville was also influenced by Spenser, Shakespeare, Dante, Cervantes, Robert Burton, Sir Thomas Carlyle, Thomas Browne, and vastly miscellaneous reading in the New York Public Library (as witnessed by the two "Etymologies" and the marvelous "Extracts" that precede the text itself, items from the writer's notes and files that he could not bear to discard). It was because they did not know how to respond to its complexities of form and style that the book was "broiled in hell fire" by contemporary readers and critics. Even today the rich mixture of its verbal texture—an almost euphuistic flamboyance balanced by dry, analytical expository prose—requires a correspondingly unique sensitivity on the part of the reader. The most remarkable thing about the plot is that Moby Dick does not appear physically until after five hundred pages; and is not even mentioned by name until nearly two hundred pages have passed.

Whether it be the knowledge of reality, an embodiment of the primitive forces of nature, the deep subconscious energies of mankind, fate or destiny inevitably victorious over illusory free will, or simply the unknown in experience, it is what Moby Dick stands for that occupies the narrator's emphasis and the reader's attention through the greater part of the novel. In many ways, the great white whale may be compared to Spenser's "blatant beast" (who, in *The Faerie Queene,* also represents the indeterminable elusive quarry, and also escapes at the end to continue haunting the world). Nor is it surprising that *Moby Dick* is often considered to be "the American epic." The novel is replete with the elements characteristic of that genre: the piling up of classical, Biblical, historical allusions to provide innumerable parallels and tangents that have the effect of universalizing the scope of action; the narrator's strong sense of the fatefulness of the events he recounts, and his corresponding awareness of his own singular importance as the narrator of momentous, otherwise unrecorded, events; Queequeg as Ishmael's "heroic companion"; the "folk" flavor provided by countless proverbial statements; the leisurely pace of the narrative, with its frequent digressions and parentheses; the epic confrontation of life and death on a suitably grand stage (the sea), with its consequences for the human City (the *Pequod*); the employment of microcosms to explicate the whole (for example, the painting in the Spouter Inn, the Nantucket pulpit, the crow's nest); epithetical characterization; a cyclic notion of time and events; an epic race of heroes, the Nantucket whalers with their Biblical and exotic names; the mystical power of objects like Ahab's chair, the doubloon, or the *Pequod* itself; the alienated, sulking hero (Ahab); the use of lists to enhance the impression of an all-inclusive compass. Finally, *Moby Dick* shares the usually didactic purpose of folk epic; on one level, its purpose is to teach the reader about whales; on another level, it is to inspire the reader to become, himself, a heroic whaleman.

All this richness of purpose and presentation is somehow made enticing by Melville's masterly invention of his narrator. Ishmael immediately establishes a comfortable rapport with the reader in the unforgettable opening lines of the novel. He is both the objective observer and a participant in the events observed and recounted, both spectator and narrator. But he is much more than the conventional wanderer-witness. As a schoolmaster and sometime voyager, he combines his book learning with firsthand experience to make him an informed observer and a convincing, moving reporter. Simply by surviving he transcends the Byronic heroism of Ahab, as the wholesome overcoming the sinister.

Bibliography

Anderson, Charles Robert. *Melville in the South Seas.* New York: Columbia University Press, 1939, pp. 11–65.

Arvin, Newton. *Herman Melville.* New York: William Sloane, 1950, pp. 143–193.

Austin, Allen. "The Three-Stranded Allegory of *Moby Dick*," in *College English.* XXVI (February, 1965), pp. 344–349.

Bernstein, John. *Pacifism and Rebellion in the Writings of Herman Melville.* The Hague: Newton, 1964, pp. 82–125.

Berthoff, Warner. *The Example of Melville.* Princeton, N.J.: Princeton University Press, 1962, pp. 78–98, 159–170, 175–182.

Boath, T.Y. "*Moby Dick*: Standing Up to God," in *Nineteenth-Century Fiction.* XVII (June, 1962), pp. 33–43.

Bowden, Edwin T. *The Dungeon of the Heart: Human Isolation and the*

American Novel. New York: Macmillan, 1961, pp. 156–172.

Bowen, Merlin. *The Long Encounter: Self and Experience in the Writings of Herman Melville*. Chicago: University of Chicago Press, 1960, pp. 143–157, 240–252.

Braswell, William. "The Main Theme of *Moby Dick*," in *Emerson Society Quarterly*. XXVIII (October, 1962), pp. 15–17.

Chase, Richard. *Herman Melville: A Critical Study*. New York: Macmillan, 1949, pp. 43–102.

Cowan, S.A. "In Praise of Self-Reliance; The Role of Bulkington in *Moby Dick*," in *American Literature*. XXXVIII (January, 1967), pp. 547–556.

Dillingham, William B. "The Narrator of *Moby Dick*," in *English Studies*. XLIX (February, 1968), pp. 20–29.

Dryden, Edgar E. *Melville's Thematics of Form: The Great Art of Telling the Truth*. Baltimore: Johns Hopkins University Press, 1968, pp. 81–113.

Eldridge, H.G. "Careful Disorder: The Structure of *Moby Dick*," in *American Literature*. XXXIX (May, 1967), pp. 145–162.

Ellen, Sister Mary, I.H.M. "Duplicate Imagery in *Moby Dick*," in *Modern Fiction Studies*. VIII (Autumn, 1962), pp. 252–275.

Fiedler, Leslie A. *Love and Death in the American Novel*. New York: Criterion Books, 1960, pp. 520–552.

Finkelstein, Dorothee. *Melville's Orienda*. New Haven, Conn.: Yale University Press, 1961, pp. 223–234.

Franklin, H. Bruce. *The Wake of the Gods: Melville's Mythology*. Stanford, Calif.: Stanford University Press, pp. 53–98.

Frederix, Pierre. *Herman Melville*. Paris: Gallimard, 1950, pp. 185–203.

Freeman, John. *Herman Melville*. New York: Macmillan, 1926, pp. 114–131.

Friedrich, Gerhard. *In Pursuit of* Moby Dick. Wallingford, Pa.: Pendle Hill, 1958.

Gleim, William S. *The Meaning of* Moby Dick. New York: Edmond Byrne Hackett, 1938.

————. "The Meaning of *Moby Dick*," in *New England Quarterly*. II (July, 1929), pp. 402–419.

Green, Martin. *Re-Appraisals: Some Commonsense Readings in American Literature*. New York: Norton, 1963, pp. 87–108.

Hayford, Harrison and Hershel Parker, Editors. Moby Dick: *An Authoritative Text: Reviews and Letters by Melville; Analogues and Sources; Criticism*. New York: Norton, 1967.

Hillway, Tyrus. *Herman Melville*. New York: Twayne, 1963, pp. 83–106.

————. *Melville and the Whale*. Stonington, Conn.: Stonington, 1950.

Horsford, Howard C. "The Design of the Argument in *Moby Dick*," in *Modern Fiction Studies*. VIII (Autumn, 1962), pp. 233–251.

Humphreys, A.R. *Melville*. London: Oliver and Boyd, 1962, pp. 41–82.

Mason, Ronald. *The Spirit Above the Dust: A Study of Herman Melville*. London: John Lehmann, 1951, pp. 111–157.

Matthiessen, F.O. *American Renaissance: Art and Expression in the Age of Emerson and Whitman*. New York: Oxford University Press, 1949, pp. 282–291, 409–466.

Maxwell, D.E.S. *Herman Melville*. New York: Humanities Press, 1968, pp. 32–53.

Mengeling, Marvin E. "*Moby Dick*: The Fundamental Principles," in *Emerson Society Quarterly*. XXXVIII (1965), pp. 74–87.

Miller, James E., Jr. *Quests Surd and Absurd: Essays in American Literature*. Chicago: University of Chicago Press, 1967, pp. 196–198, 206–207, 227–238.

Mumford, Lewis. *Herman Melville*. New York: Harcourt, Brace, 1929, pp. 158–195.

————. "The Writing of *Moby Dick*," in *American Mercury*. XV (December, 1928), pp. 482–490.

Murray, Henry A. "In Nomine Diaboli," in *New England Quarterly*. XXIV (December, 1951), pp. 435–452.

Myers, Henry Alonzo. "Captain Ahab's Discovery: The Tragic Meaning of *Moby Dick*," in *New England Quarterly*. XV (March, 1942), pp. 15–34.

Olson, Charles. *Call Me Ishmael*. New York: Reynad & Hitchcock, 1947.

Parke, John. "Seven Moby Dicks," in *New England Quarterly*. XXVIII (September, 1955), pp. 319–338.

Parker, Hershel and Harrison Hayford, Editors. *Essays and Extracts:* Moby Dick *as Doubloon, 1851–1970*. New York: Norton, 1970.

Percival, M.O. *A Reading of* Moby Dick. Chicago: University of Chicago Press, 1950.

Rosenberry, Edward H. *Melville and the Comic Spirit*. Cambridge, Mass.: Harvard University Press, 1955, pp. 93–138.

Sedgwick, William Ellery. *Herman Melville: The Tragedy of Mind*. Cambridge, Mass.: Harvard University Press, 1944, pp. 82–136.

Sewall, Richard B. "*Moby Dick* as Tragedy," in Moby Dick: *An Authoritative Text; Reviews and Letters by Melville; Analogues and Sources; Criticism*. Edited by Harrison Hayford and Hershel Parker. New York: Norton, 1967, pp. 692–702.

Short, R.W. "Melville as Symbolist," in *University of Kansas City Review*. XV (Autumn, 1948), pp. 38–46.

Shulman, Robert. "The Serious Functions of Melville's Phallic Jokes," in *American Literature.* XXXIII (May, 1961), pp. 179–194.

Stern, Milton R., Editor. *Discussions of* Moby Dick. Boston: Heath, 1960.

————. "Melville's Tragic Imagination: The Hero Without a Home," in *Patterns of Commitment in American Literature.* Edited by Marston La France. Toronto: University of Toronto Press, 1967, pp. 42–50.

Stewart, George R. "The Two *Moby Dicks,*" in *American Literature.* XXV (January, 1954), pp. 417–448.

Stone, Edward. *Voices of Despair.* Athens: Ohio University Press, 1966, pp. 93–102.

Stone, Geoffrey. *Melville.* New York: Sheed and Ward, 1944, pp. 160–186.

Thompson, Lawrance. *Melville's Quarrel with God.* Princeton, N.J.: Princeton University Press, 1952, pp. 127–243.

Vincent, Howard P. *The Trying-Out of Moby Dick.* Boston: Houghton Mifflin, 1949.

Vogel, Dan. "The Dramatic Chapters in *Moby Dick,*" in *Nineteenth-Century Fiction.* XIII (December, 1958), pp. 239–247.

Walcutt, Charles Child. "The Fire Symbolism in *Moby Dick,*" in *Modern Language Notes.* LIX (May, 1944), pp. 304–310.

————. *Man's Changing Mask: Modes and Methods of Characterization in Fiction.* Minneapolis: University of Minnesota Press, 1966, pp. 104–123.

Ward, J.A. "The Function of the Cetological Chapters in *Moby Dick,*" in *American Literature.* XXVIII (May, 1956), pp. 164–183.

Watters, R.E. "The Meanings of the White Whale," in *University of Toronto Quarterly.* XX (January, 1951), pp. 155–168.

Woodson, Thomas. "Ahab's Greatness: Prometheus as Narcissus," in *ELH.* (September, 1966), pp. 351–369.

Young, James Dean. "The Nine Gams of the Pequod," in *American Literature.* XXV (January, 1954), pp. 449–463.

Yu, Beongcheon. "Ishmael's Equal Eye: The Source of Balance in *Moby Dick,*" in *ELH.* XXXII (March, 1965), pp. 110–125.

OMOO

Type of work: Novel
Author: Herman Melville (1819–1891)
Type of plot: Adventure romance
Time of plot: Early 1840's
Locale: Tahiti and the South Seas
First published: 1847

This sequel to Typee *takes its title from a word in the native dialect of the Marquesas Islands which signifies a wanderer among islands. The wanderer in the novel is Melville himself, whose twofold purpose in the novel is to relate his adventures in the Society Islands, and to expose the ill effects of the missionaries' presence in Polynesia. The novel contrasts the hypocrisy of pseudo-Christians to the sincerity and naïveté of the pagan islanders.*

Principal Characters

The Narrator, a young American sailor who acquires the name Tommo in *Typee.* He is rescued from a cannibal island by the crew of a British whaler, the *Julia,* and he signs on the ship as a deck hand. He is soon relieved of duty because of lameness in his leg. Conditions on the ship are bad, so Tommo and the rest of the crew put ashore at Papeetee, on the island of Tahiti, and are imprisoned when they refuse to return in their ship. After the ship sails away with a new crew, Tommo and the other sailors are freed by their Tahitian jailer. Later Tommo and his friend, Doctor Long Ghost, have several adventures in the islands together. Tommo finally ships on a whaler which will take him to Japan and eventually home. In the course of his island-hopping, he becomes convinced that the natives have been corrupted by their contact with the white missionaries and were better off as primitive pagans.

Doctor Long Ghost, the ship's doctor on the British whaler which rescues Tommo. The doctor becomes his close friend and companion in his adventures. The doctor tries to sign on the same ship with Tommo when he decides to leave the islands; but the captain refused to allow the doctor to sign on, either as a deck hand or as a ship's doctor, and he is left behind.

Captain Bob, the Tahitian jailer of Tommo and the rest of the crew. He is jolly and easy-going, and after the whaler sails away the old man frees his prisoners.

John Jermin, first officer of the British whaler.

The Story

After Tommo escaped from the island of Nukuheva where he had been held captive by the Typee tribesmen, he joined the crew of the *Julia,* a British whaler. He agreed to stay on board as a deckhand until it reached the next port, where he was to be placed ashore. But the *Julia* was not a well-managed vessel, and soon after Melville joined it several of the men made an attempt to desert. These unfortunates were recovered quickly, however, by the timely aid of the islanders and the crew of a French man-of-war.

In the weeks of cruising that followed, Tommo, relieved from duty because of a lameness in his leg, spent his time reading the books of the ship's doctor, Doctor Long Ghost, and playing chess with him. Those were not weeks of pleasure. In that time two of the man in the forecastle died and the entire crew lived under the most abominable conditions, in the rat-infested, rotten old ship which should have been condemned years before. Finally, when the captain himself fell ill, the ship changed its course to Tahiti, the nearest island.

Having convinced themselves that when the captain left the ship they would no longer be bound by the agreements they had signed, the crew intended to leave the ship when she arrived in the harbor at Papeetee. The captain attempted to prevent their desertion by keeping the ship under way just outside the harbor while he went ashore in a small boat. Tommo and Doctor Long Ghost's influence among the rebellious crew members prevented these men from disregarding orders and taking the vessel into harbor to anchor her. Tommo sympathized with the unhappy crew members because he felt that the ship's captain was endangering their lives by making them stay on the *Julia* when it was not seaworthy, but he and Doctor Long Ghost did not want to risk the punishment for mutiny and did not like violence. To provide the rebels with an outlet for their anger as well as to seek a solution peaceably, Tommo suggested that they protest their treatment in a letter. After they signed the letter, it was conveyed to the British consul by the ship's Negro cook. Unfortunately, the acting consul in Papeetee and the captain of the *Julia* were old acquaintances, and the official's only action was to inform the men they would have to stay with the ship and cruise for three months under the command of the first mate. The captain himself would remain in Tahiti. But after a Mauri harpooner attempted to wreck the ship, the drunken mate decided to take the whaler into the harbor, regardless of consequences.

In Papeetee, the acting consul had the disgruntled crew members, including Tommo and Doctor Long Ghost, imprisoned on a French frigate. After five days aboard the French ship, they were removed and were once more given an opportunity to return to their ship. When they refused, the mutineers were taken into custody by a Tahitian native called Captain Bob, who took them to an oval-shaped thatched house which was to be their jail.

There they were confined in stocks, two timbers about twenty feet long serving to secure all the prisoners. Each morning the jailer came to free the men and supervise their baths in a neighboring stream. The natives, in return for hard ship's biscuit from the *Julia*, fed the men baked breadfruit and Indian turnips. Sometimes the kindly jailer led the men to his orange grove, where they gathered fruit for their meals. This fruit diet was precisely what they needed to regain the health they had lost while eating sea rations of salt pork and biscuit.

The prisoners in the thatched hut were in sight of Broom Road, the island's chief thoroughfare. Since they were easily accessible, the idle, inquisitive Tahitians were constantly visiting, and they did not lack for company.

Within a few days, their jailer freed the sailors from the stocks during the daytime, except when white men were in the vicinity. Once this leniency was granted, the men roamed the neighborhood to take advantage of the natives' hospitality. Doctor Long Ghost always carried salt with him, in case he found some food to flavor.

When the consul sent a doctor to look at the prisoners, all the sailors pretended to be sick. Shortly after the doctor had made his examinations and departed, a native boy appeared with a basket of medicines. The sailors discarded the powders and pills, but eagerly drank the contents of all the bottles which smelled the least bit alcoholic.

British missionaries on the island took no notice of the sailors from the *Julia* other than sending them a handful of tracts. Three French priests, however, came to see the men. The natives, it seemed, looked upon the priests as magicians, and so they had been able to make only a few converts among the islanders. The priests were popular with the sailors because they gave freshly baked wheat bread and liquor to the prisoners.

Three weeks after arriving in the port of Papeetee, the captain of the *Julia* sailed away with a new crew recruited from beachcombers idling about the island. After his departure the mutineers were no longer confined to their jail, but continued to live there because the building was as convenient as any other thatched dwelling in the neighborhood. They existed by foraging the surrounding country and smuggling provisions from visiting ships with the aid of the sailors aboard.

Tommo found this life not unpleasant at first, but after a time he grew bored. He even went to a native church to hear the missionary preach. The theme of the sermon was that all white men except the British were bad and so were the natives, unless they began to contribute more baskets of food to the missionary's larder. Tommo did not go to the missionary church again.

Several weeks after the *Julia* had sailed, Tommo met two white men who informed him that a plantation on a neighboring island was in need of laborers. Tommo and Doctor Long Ghost, introduced to the planters as Peter and Paul, were immediately hired. One moonlight night the pair boarded the boat belonging to their employer. They left their former shipmates without ceremony, lest the authorities prevent their departure.

The planters lived by themselves in an inland valley on the mosquito-infested island of Imeeo. The prospect of plying a hoe in the heat of the day and amid swarms of insects did not appeal to the two sailors, and so at noon of the first day in the fields Doctor Long Ghost pretended illness. He and Tommo agreed to do as little work as possible. After a few days they gave up farming for good and went afoot to Tamai, an inland village unspoiled by missionaries or other white men. There they saw a dance by native girls, a rite which had been banned as pagan by the missionaries on the island. Doctor Long Ghost behaved in a lecherous way during the performance. A day or two later, while the two white men were considering settling permanently at Tamai, the natives forced them to flee, perhaps because of Doctor Long Ghost's behavior at the natives' dance and afterwards, for the morning following the secret rite, Doctor Long Ghost had accosted several of the women of Tamai.

The next adventure they comtemplated was an audience with the deposed queen of Tahiti who was living in seclusion in Partoowye. Hearing that the queen was considering going to war against the French, they were prepared to offer their service to her cause. Traveling by easy stages from one village to the next, they made their way to the queen's village. There they met a runaway ship's carpenter who had settled there and who kept busy building boxes and cabinets for the natives. From him they learned that a whaler was in the local harbor. But when they talked to the crew of the vessel, they were told that it was not a good ship on which to sail, and they gave up all thought of shipping away from the islands aboard the whaler.

After five weeks in the village, Doctor Long Ghost and Tommo finally obtained admittance to the queen through the good offices of a Marquesan attendant at her court. When Tommo saw the queen, he noticed that although she conducted herself regally, she seemed careworn and depressed. They were told to leave the court, however, before they could speak with her because Doctor Long Ghost behaved unceremoniously. After Doctor Long Ghost's blunder, they had no opportunity to meet with the queen again, for she had given orders that no strangers were to be admitted to the palace. The two travelers again decided to go to sea. They made friends with the third mate of the whaler, which was still in the harbor. The mate reassured them concerning conditions aboard the ship. The other sailors, knowing the ship could not sail away from the pleasant islands without more men in the crew, had deliberately lied.

Having confidence in the mate, Doctor Long Ghost and Tommo then approached the captain and asked to sign on as members of the crew. The captain, however, would not accept Doctor Long Ghost as a deckhand or as the ship's doctor. Reluctantly Tommo shipped alone on the voyage which would take him to the coast of Japan and, he hoped, eventually home.

Critical Evaluation

The title of this book, a sequel to Melville's earlier *Typee*, was borrowed from the native dialect of the Marquesas Islands. The word signifies a person who wanders, like the narrator of the book, from one island to another. Melville's object in writing *Omoo* was twofold. He wished to relate his own adventures in the Society Islands and to make people realize the effects promiscuous social intercourse with white men, generally, and missionaries, particularly, had had upon the Polynesians. Contact between Western and Polynesian cultures, Melville felt, could be beneficial to both, but only if Westerners admitted that the Polynesian way of life had some good qualities and a special character which were worth preserving. He hoped that some kind of synthesis which combined the best features of each culture could be achieved.

Following his pattern in *Typee*, Melville in *Omoo* combines his own experiences and observations during his brief stay on several islands with material gathered from several books. The reader is led to believe that this account contains the narrator's true adventures supplemented by stories and other information given him by various friends or acquaintances. Early British reviewers of *Omoo* questioned whether a book which appeared to have been written by a cultured gentleman could really be the work of an ordinary American sailor. Twentieth century scholars have shown the considerable extent of Melville's borrowings, yet they grant that he added much style and insight to what he borrowed from others. In fact, the episodic picaresque tale contains a kind of unity through the revealed personality and turn of mind of the narrator.

Omoo, like *Typee*, is an adventure romance set on an island semi-paradise. In both, the tone is largely comic and satiric. The Tahitians and other islanders are presented with less verisimilitude than were the Typees. The narrator Tommo and his friend Doctor Long Ghost (in reality a dissolute ship's steward named John Troy), however, are finely drawn characters. Although throughout much of the book the narrator appears to be lazy and irresponsible, he is actually reflecting closely on the people and social life that he finds himself among.

Omoo continues an attack, begun in *Typee*, against missionaries, rebuking them for their venality and their foolish attempts to change the lives and ways of the South Sea natives. The people of Tahiti and the other islands visited by the two rovers had experienced far more contact with Western vistors than had the Typees, and Melville was appalled by many of the harmful effects he observed. For the modern reader, *Omoo* is both a serious narrative of social commentary and angry condemnation and a rollicking adventure tale of faraway places.

Bibliography

Anderson, Charles Roberts. "Contemporary American Opinions of *Typee* and *Omoo*," in *American Literature*. IX (March, 1937), pp. 1–25.

————. "Melville's English Debut," in *American Literature*. XI (March, 1939), pp. 23–38.

————. *Melville in the South Seas*. New York: Columbia University Press, 1939, pp. 199–345.

Bernstein, John. *Pacifism and Rebellion in the Writings of Herman Melville*. The Hague: Mouton, 1964, pp. 126–145.

Canaday, Nicholas. "The Theme of Authority in Melville's *Typee* and *Omoo*," in *Forum*. IV (Fall, 1963), pp. 38–41.

Dryden, Edgar A. *Melville's Thematics of Form: The Great Art of Telling the Truth*. Baltimore: Johns Hopkins University Press, 1968.

Eigner, Edwin M. "The Romantic Unity of Melville's *Omoo*," in *Philological Quarterly*. XLVI (January, 1967), pp. 95–108.

Forsythe, Robert S. "Herman Melville in the Marquesas," in *Philological Quarterly*. XV (January, 1936), pp. 1–15.

————. "Herman Melville in Tahiti," in *Philological Quarterly*. XVI (October, 1937), pp. 344–357.

————. "Herman Melville's Father Murphy," in *Notes and Queries*. CLXXII (April 10, 1937), pp. 254–258.

————. "More upon Herman Melville in Tahiti," in *Philological Quarterly*. XVII (January, 1938), pp. 1–17.

Frederix, Pierre. *Herman Melville*. Paris: Gallimard, 1950, pp. 132–147.

Kaplan, Sidney. "Herman Melville and the Whaling Enderbys," in *American Literature*. XXIV (May, 1952), pp. 224–230.

Lawrence, D.H. *Studies in Classic American Literature*. New York: Doubleday, 1955, pp. 142–156.

Levin, Harry. *The Power of Blackness: Hawthorne, Poe, Melville*. New York: Knopf, 1960.

Mason, Ronald. *The Spirit Above the Dust: A Study of Herman Melville*. London: John Lehmann, 1951, pp. 31–37.

Miller, James E., Jr. *A Reader's Guide to Herman Melville*. New York: Noonday, 1962, pp. 18–37.

Rosenberry, Edward. *Melville and the Comic Spirit*. Cambridge, Mass.: Harvard University Press, 1955.

PIERRE

Type of work: Novel
Author: Herman Melville (1819–1891)
Type of plot: Philosophical tragedy
Time of plot: Early nineteenth century
Locale: New York
First published: 1852

This novel is the story of Pierre Glendinning, whose defense of his illegitimate half-sister Isabel leads to incestuous desires which finally provoke Pierre's suicide and bring misery and ruin to his entire family. Probably the least read of Melville's works because of its obscure and sometimes confused symbolism, this novel is considered by scholars as an experiment on the author's part and an attempt to break away from the mold set by his previous novels of the sea and the Pacific islands.

Principal Characters

Pierre Glendinning, a wealthy young easterner of the early nineteenth century. When he claims his half sister as his wife in order to shield her from the world, his decision causes him to lose his inheritance, his fiancée and eventually his life. Having shot and killed a male cousin, he is sent to prison. During a visit from his fiancée and his half sister he swallows poison and dies.

Isabel, Pierre's half sister, the illegitimate daughter of an alliance Pierre's father had with a young French woman. Her love for Pierre is not the typical love of a sister for a brother. She is jealous of the attention he pays another woman, and finally, after Pierre has taken his life by poison, she kills herself by drinking from the vial he had used.

Lucy Tartan, Pierre's fiancée. Though she has wealth and many friends, she follows Pierre and Isabel to New York to live with them and earn her living by painting portraits. When Pierre tells her, during the prison scene, that Isabel is his half sister and not his wife, Lucy dies of shock.

Mrs. Glendinning, Pierre's mother, a proud woman who is jealous of her influence over her son. Because Pierre claims Isabel as his wife, she drives him from home and, at her death, cuts him off without a cent.

Glen Stanly, Pierre's cousin, the relative to whom Mrs. Glendinning leaves the family fortune. Stanly is in love with Lucy. In concert with Lucy's brother, he provokes Pierre, with whom Lucy is now living. Pierre shoots and kills him during a fight.

Delly Ulver, an illegitimate farm girl befriended by Isabel and Pierre. She becomes their servant.

The Story

Pierre Glendinning was a young man who lived amid luxury and ease, the heir to vast estates that formed the larger portion of two counties in New York State. His time was taken up with outdoor recreation, reading, and the courting of beautiful and well-to-do Lucy Tartan, a girl of whom Pierre's mother approved completely. Mrs. Glendinning, who was jealous of her influence over her son, saw nothing to fear in quiet, unaggressive Lucy Tartan.

One evening, however, a strange incident occurred when Mrs. Glendinning and Pierre visited a sewing bee in a nearby home. One of the girls who was there shrieked and fainted when she saw Pierre. The incident bothered the young man, but he was totally unprepared for a note which he received from the girl a short time later. In the note she requested that Pierre visit her in the evening at the farm where she was employed. Pierre, disturbed by the mystery involved, went to the farm and discovered that the girl, Isabel, was his half-sister, the illegitimate child of his father and a young Frenchwoman. Pierre resolved immediately to acknowledge Isabel as his sister, but the question of how to accomplish the acknowledgment was a weighty one.

At first Pierre intended to tell his mother of his discovery, but his mother's attitude toward Delly Ulver, a farm girl who had been born an illegitimate child, warned Pierre that he could expect no sympathetic understanding from Mrs. Glendinning. He next thought of approaching his minister for help with his problem, but the discovery that the minister followed his mother's opinion caused Pierre to fall back on his own thinking. He realized also that his mother could not bear to have it proved that her husband had been an adulterer, nor could he bring himself to dishonor his father's name. The only road which seemed open to Pierre was to acknowledge Isabel as his wife rather than his sister.

When Pierre told his mother that he had been married secretly, she ordered him to leave the house immediately. Disowned and cast forth from his mother's affections, he also told Lucy Tartan that he had married another girl. His story threw Lucy into an almost fatal illness.

Having been disowned by his family, Pierre took Isabel from her home at the farm and went to New York City. They were accompanied by Delly Ulver, whom Pierre had decided to help. Although he had announced that he and Isabel had been married, Pierre and his half-sister had entered into no such union; the announcement was only a means to permit them to live together. In New York City they found life barren and difficult, for Pierre had only a small supply of money. He had hoped to find a haven for himself and the two girls with his wealthy cousin, Glen Stanly, but the cousin refused to recognize Pierre and had him thrown out of his home.

Forced to rely upon his own resources, Pierre resolved to become an author. He had, he thought, acquired quite a reputation by publishing some short poems and some essays in various periodicals. He also thought he had great talent, sufficient, at least, to enable him to write a philosophical work. After much difficulty he managed to find a publisher who agreed to take his unwritten novel and to advance him enough money to live. For months Pierre, struggling to write his great work, lived in three miserable, unheated rooms in a vast tenement, along with Isabel and Delly Ulver, who acted in the capacity of servant to them both.

One day word came to Pierre that his mother had died just a few weeks after he had left for New York City; her heir was Pierre's cousin, Glen Stanly. The news made Pierre very bitter, particularly when he discovered that his cousin was a suitor for the hand of Lucy Tartan, whom Pierre still loved dearly. Despite the feeling of utter helplessness which the news created in his mind, Pierre kept at work upon his book. Because he was unable to keep Isabel from realizing that she was not alone in his affections, the girl became jealous and disliked the fact that another woman could claim his attentions and love. Her attachment for Pierre went much deeper than ordinary love for a brother by a sister.

Some time later Pierrre received a letter from Lucy. She had rebuffed Glen Stanly's suit, and she wrote to tell Pierre that he alone had her affections. She told Pierre that, even though he was married, she wished to travel to New York City to live near him. Pierre could not prevent her from joining his household, although he lied to Isabel and told her that Lucy was his cousin. Lucy arrived the next day. As she entered the tenement where Pierre lived, her brother and Glen Stanly tried to take her away by force. Pierre interfered on her behalf, and the two men had to leave without the girl.

Lucy, listening only to the promptings of her heart, refused to leave Pierre, even though he told her that Isabel was his wife. Having brought along her painting materials, she intended to support herself as a painter of portraits. Isabel disliked the idea of a third woman in the home, but she was powerless to turn Lucy out. The two women lived in a state of distrustful and watchful truce.

Glen Stanly and Lucy's brother, not wishing to see Lucy remain near Pierre, sent him a letter of premeditated insults in hopes of provoking him. Angered by their message, Pierre found two pistols in the apartment of a friend and set out to find Stanly and Lucy's brother. He encountered them on a crowded street. When they met, Stanly lashed at Pierre with a whip, whereupon Pierre drew his pistols and killed his cousin. The police immediately seized Pierre and took him to prison.

In prison, Pierre had no hope of life. Nor did he care to live, for he felt that fate had been too cruel to him. One evening Isabel and Lucy were allowed to visit him for a few hours. When Isabel revealed that she was Pierre's sister, the shock of her announcement killed Lucy immediately. Pierre, driven mad by her death, seized a vial of poison which he knew Isabel carried in her bosom. He drank a portion of the poison, and Isabel emptied the vial of the remainder.

A short time later Lucy's brother came looking for her, still hoping to rescue her from Pierre's influence. When the turnkey opened the cell door, Pierre was already dead, lying close to Lucy. Isabel still had sufficient life to say that no one had known the real Pierre. Then she too died, completing the tragedy of their ambiguous relationships.

Critical Evaluation

Pierre is a Hamlet in reverse; he acts too soon, in everything that he does, and brings about catastrophes greater than anything brought on by Hamlet's delay. That ironic observation, made by F. O. Matthiessen in his classic study, *American Renaissance* (1941), is the key to understanding what Melville meant by his novel's subtitle, *The Ambiguities*. Pierre finds it impossible to hedge, to be anything but purely realistic in all his actions. The result is that despite his pure intentions, his conduct results in great suffering for all those around him.

If Pierre had mastered the gist of "Chronometricals and Horologicals," the pamphlet he read on his way to New York, he would have understood that the only way "God's truth and man's truth correspond is through their contradictions." But such ambiguity is unacceptable to his idealism, and he literally immolates himself to a totally unrealistic ethics. In order to save his half-sister's honor, he lives with her in what looks to the world like marital respectability; instead of providing for her security, the arrangement ultimately destroys both of them. Pierre can do no right, because he tries to live as if he could avoid doing any wrong at all.

These are strong suggestions that Pierre is driven by subconscious desires that actually force him into his self-destructive behavior. Perhaps the greatest ambiguity—and irony—of all is that his supposed idealism is merely a sublimation of his darkest instincts, that the incestuous attraction to "dark" Isabel is actually stronger than the claims of Lucy's innocent "whiteness." The Oedipal relationship to his mother is certainly an indication of psychological pressures. Again, the similarities to Hamlet are striking.

There are finally too many "ambiguities" for us to trust Melville's control of his own theme. *Pierre* seems an incoherent nightmare in comparison to *Moby Dick*, but the spiritual courage of its agonizing questions reminds us of the exploratory vision of his masterpiece.

Bibliography

Bernstein, John. *Pacifism and Rebellion in the Writings of Herman Melville.* The Hague: Mouton, 1964, pp. 126–145.

Berthoff, Warner. *The Example of Melville.* Princeton, N.J.: Princeton University Press, 1962, pp. 47–54.

Braswell, William. "Melville's Opinion of *Pierre*," in *American Literature.* XXIII (May, 1951), pp. 246–250.

————. *Melville's Religious Thought: An Essay in Interpretation.* Durham, N.C.: Duke University Press, 1943, pp. 75–106.

————. "The Satirical Temper of Melville's *Pierre*," in *American Literature.* VII (January, 1936), pp. 424–438.

Chase, Richard. *Herman Melville: A Critical Study.* New York: Macmillan, 1949, pp. 103–141.

Dryden, Edgar E. *Melville's Thematics of Form: The Great Art of Telling the Truth.* Baltimore: Johns Hopkins University Press, 1968, pp. 115–148.

Fiedler, Leslie A. *Love and Death in the American Novel.* New York: Criterion Books, 1960, pp. 403–408.

Franklin, H. Bruce. *The Wake of the Gods: Melville's Mythology.* Stanford, Calif.: Stanford University Press, 1963, pp. 99–125.

Frederix, Pierre. *Herman Melville.* Paris: Gallimard, 1950, pp. 204–213.

Freeman, John. *Herman Melville.* New York: Macmillan, 1926, pp. 108–113.

Fussell, Edwin. "Herman Melville," in *Frontier: American Literature and the American West.* Princeton, N.J.: Princeton University Press, 1965.

Gupta, R.K. "Melville's Use of Non-Novelistic Conventions in *Pierre*," in *Emerson Society Quarterly.* XLVIII (1967), pp. 141–145.

Hillway, Tyrus. *Herman Melville.* New York: Twayne, 1963.

————. "Pierre, the Fool of Virtue," in *American Literature.* XXI (May, 1949), pp. 201–211.

Howard, Leon. "Herman Melville," in *Six American Novelists of the Nineteenth Century: An Introduction.* Edited by Richard Foster. Minneapolis: University of Minnesota Press, 1968, pp. 101–105.

Humphreys, A.R. *Melville.* London: Oliver and Boyd, 1962, pp. 83–92.

Kissane, James. "Imagery, Myth, and Melville's *Pierre*," in *American Literature.* XXVI (January, 1955), pp. 564–572.

Mason, Ronald. *The Spirit Above the Dust: A Study of Herman Melville.* London: John Lehmann, 1951, pp. 158–178.

Mayoux, Jean-Jacques. *Melville.* London: Evergreen Books, 1960, pp. 100–111.

Miller, James E., Jr. *A Reader's Guide to Herman Melville.* New York: Noonday, 1962, pp. 118–139.

Mogan, Joseph J., Jr. "Pierre and Manfred: Melville's Study of the Byronic Hero," in *Papers on English Language and Literature.* I (Summer, 1965), pp. 230–240.

Moorman, Charles. "Melville's Pierre in the City," in *American Literature.* XXVII (January, 1956), pp. 571–577.

————. "Melville's Pierre and the Fortunate Fall," in *American Literature.* XXV (March, 1953), pp. 13–30.

Mumford, Lewis. *Herman Melville.* New York: Harcourt, Brace, 1929, pp. 203–222.

Sedgwick, William Ellery. *Herman Melville: The Tragedy of Mind.* Cambridge, Mass.: Harvard University Press, 1944, pp. 137–172.

Stern, Milton R. *The Fine Hammered Steel of Herman Melville.* Urbana: University of Illinois Press, 1957, pp. 150–205.

Stone, Geoffrey. *Melville.* New York: Sheed and Ward, 1949, pp. 187–210.

Thompson, Lawrance. *Melville's Quarrel with God.* Princeton, N.J.: Princeton University Press, 1952, pp. 247–294.

Watson, E.L. Grant. "Melville's *Pierre*," in *New England Quarterly.* III (April, 1930), pp. 195–234.

Wright, Nathalia. "*Pierre*: Herman Melville's Inferno," in *American Literature.* XXXII (May, 1960), pp. 167–181.

Yaggy, Elinor. "Shakespeare and Melville's *Pierre*," in *Boston Public Library Quarterly.* VI (January, 1954), pp. 43–51.

REDBURN

Type of work: Novel
Author: Herman Melville (1819–1891)
Type of plot: Adventure romance
Time of plot: Mid-nineteenth century
Locale: New York, the Atlantic Ocean, and England
First published: 1849

In this authentic treatment of sailors and life on the sea, Melville presents events from the perspective of a common sailor who learned his trade the hard way. As a teenager, the author made a similar trip to that described in Redburn, *aboard a merchant vessel bound for Liverpool. The novel is also interesting in its fore-shadowing of those philosophical concerns which were to lead to the writing of Melville's masterpiece,* Moby Dick.

Principal Characters

Wellingborough Redburn, a young American who leaves his widowed mother and his brothers at home on the Hudson River in New York to go to sea. He learns, during a voyage from New York to Liverpool and return, that a sailor's life is a good but rugged one, that each generation makes its own world, and that true joy and sorrow are components of the human condition.

Harry Bolton, a young English prodigal son of good family who becomes Redburn's friend during the voyage from Liverpool to New York. Bolton is a misfit aboard ship, thus belying the stories he tells of his voyages as a crew member on other vessels. His pride is so injured when the Captain pays him a dollar and a half as wages at the voyage's end that he throws the money back on the Captain's desk.

Captain Riga, the tough, shrewd master of the "Highlander," Redburn's first ship. He pays Redburn three dollars a month for his work on the voyage, but when the ship returns to New York he dismisses Redburn without a penny because he says Redburn had left the ship for a day at Liverpool and, furthermore, had lost tools overboard.

The Story

Wellingborough Redburn's father had died, leaving the mother and children poorly provided for, even though the father had been a highly successful merchant and at one time a wealthy man. When Redburn was in his middle teens, he decided to take some of the burden off his mother by going to sea. Given an old gun and a hunting jacket by an older brother, young Redburn left his home along the Hudson River and went to New York to seek a berth on a ship.

A college friend of his older brother aided Redburn in finding a berth on a ship bound for Liverpool. Unfortunately the friend had emphasized the fact that Redburn came from a good family and had wealthy relatives; consequently, Captain

Riga, master of the *Highlander*, was able to hire the young lad for three dollars a month. Having spent all his money, and unable to get an advance on his wages, Redburn had to pawn his gun for a shirt and cap to wear aboard ship.

During his first few days out of port Redburn thought that he had made a dreadful mistake in going to sea. His fellow sailors jeered at him as a greenhorn; he made many silly mistakes; he became violently seasick; and he discovered that he did not even have a spoon with which to take his portion of the food from the pots and pans in which it was sent to the forecastle. Most horrifying of all was the suicide of a sailor who dived over the side of the ship in a fit of delirium tremens.

As the thirty-day cruise to Liverpool from New York wore on, Redburn learned how to make himself useful and comfortable aboard the ship. When he went aloft alone to release the topmost sails, he earned a little respect from his fellow seamen, although they never did, throughout the voyage, let him forget that he was still a green hand and had signed on as a "boy." Redburn found the sea fascinating in many ways; he also found it terrifying, as when the *Highlander* passed a derelict schooner on which three corpses were still bound to the railing.

For Redburn one of the liveliest incidents of the voyage was the discovery of a little stowaway on board the *Highlander*. The small boy had been on board the vessel some months before, when the father had been a sailor signed on for a trip from Liverpool to New York. The father had since died, and the boy had stowed himself away in an effort to return to England. Everyone on the ship, including the usually irascible Captain Riga, took a liking to the homesick stowaway and made much of him.

Redburn had little in common with his fellow crew members, most of whom were rough fellows many years older than he. Through them, however, he received an education quite different from that which he had learned in school. At first he tried to talk about church and good books to them, but he soon discovered that such conversation only irritated them into more than their usual profanity and obscenity. Redburn thought they were not really very bad men; they had never had the chance to be good men. Most of all, he disliked them because they looked upon anyone who could not follow the seaman's trade as a fool.

A long, low skyline in the distance was Redburn's first glimpse of Ireland. He met his first true European when an Irish fisherman hailed the *Highlander* and asked for a line. When he had hauled fifteen or so fathoms of the line into his boat, the Irishman cut the line, laughed, and sailed away. Even though the rope was not Redburn's, he, boylike, felt that he man had played a scurvy trick.

When the *Highlander* arrived at Liverpool, Redburn decided that the English city was not a great deal different from New York. Sailors and ships, he found, were the same in one place as in another, with a few notable exceptions. His trips into the city, away from the waterfront, and excursions into the Lancashire countryside convinced him that he, as an alien, was not welcome. People distrusted him because of his ragged clothing, and he had no money to purchase a new outfit, even though Captain Riga had advanced him three dollars, one month's pay, upon the ship's arrival in port.

Redburn's greatest disappointment came when he tried to use for his excursions an old guidebook he had brought from his father's library. The guidebook, almost half a century old, was no longer reliable, for streets and structures it mentioned were no longer in existence. Redburn felt that the whole world must have changed since his father's time; he saw in the unreliable guidebook a hint that as the years passed the habits and ideals of youth had to be charted anew. Each generation, he learned, had to make its own guidebook through the world.

While in Liverpool, Redburn met Harry Bolton, a young Englishman of good family but a prodigal son. Bolton said that he had shipped on two voyages to the East Indies; now he wanted to emigrate to America. With Redburn's help Harry Bolton was enrolled as a "boy" on the *Highlander* for its return trip to New York. The two boys, traveling on Bolton's money, made a quick excursion to London before the ship sailed, but they were back in Liverpool within forty-eight hours. Redburn saw little of England beyond the port where he had arrived.

On the return trip to America the ship carried a load of Irish emigrants. Redburn quickly felt sorry for them but at the same time superior to the miserable wretches crowded between decks. The steerage passengers suffered a great deal during the voyage. Their quarters were cramped at best, and during heavy weather they could not remain on deck. For cooking they had a stove placed on one of the hatches, one stove for five hundred people. Worst of all, an epidemic of fever broke out, killing many of the emigrants and one of the sailors.

Bolton had a miserable trip, and Redburn was sorry for him, too. The English boy had lied in saying he had been at sea before. Because he could not bear to go aloft in the rigging, he, in place of Redburn, became the butt of all the jokes and horseplay that the crew devised.

After the ship reached America, however, the voyage seemed to both Redburn and Bolton to have been a good one. They discovered that they really hated to leave the vessel which had been home to them for several weeks. But their nostalgia for the vessel was soon dissipated by Captain Riga. The captain dismissed Redburn without any pay because the lad had left his duties for one day while the ship was at Liverpool. The captain even told Redburn that he owed the ship money for tools he had dropped into the sea. Bolton was given a dollar and a half for his work; the pittance made him so angry he threw it back on the captain's desk. The two boys then left the ship, glad to be back on land once more.

Critical Evaluation

The best way to read *Redburn* is as a prologue to *Moby Dick*. The story of the white whale is anticipated by the tragic themes of the earlier novel: its relentless depiction of misery and cruelty on board Captain Riga's ship, as well as in Liverpool port, develops a universal consciousness of human suffering, of the crushing effect of experience on innocence. F. O. Matthiessen called *Redburn* "the most moving of its author's books before *Moby Dick*." Redburn is abused by the other sailors for openly showing his fright when a man with delerium tremens throws himself over the side; the isolation makes him dread lest he become "a sort of Ishmael." He does, of course, become just that (and seems strengthened by the transformation) in *Moby Dick*, which was published two years after *Redburn* appeared.

Not only is Redburn similar to Melville's narrator in *Moby Dick*, but the whole novel is strewn with anticipations of the great novel's themes and characterizations. The mad sailor Jackson foreshadows Ahab: "He was a Cain afloat; branded on his yellow brow with some inscrutable curse; and going about corrupting and searing every heart that beat near him." The friendship between Harry Bolton and Redburn is curiously similar to that between the cannibal Queequeg and Ishmael: Harry is the prodigal son of a genteel family and Queequeg a royal personage; Harry introduces Redburn to London, Queequeg introduces Ishmael to the *Pequod*; Harry is finally killed when he is crushed between a ship and a whale, while Queequeg dives into the heart of a whale to rescue Tashtego.

All these similarities indicate the direction of Melville's art. He was moving from a fiction of initiation and adventure to one of philosophical depth. The symbolic action of Redburn is a cruder version of the same superstructure that supports Melville's masterpiece.

Bibliography

Bell, Michael D. "Melville's Redburn: Initiation and Authority," in *New England Quarterly*. XLVI (1973), pp. 558–572.

Bercovitch, Sacvan. "Melville's Search for National Identity: Son and Father in *Redburn, Pierre* and *Billy Budd*," in *College Language Association Journal*. X (March, 1967), pp. 217–228.

Bernstein, Warner. *Pacifism and Rebellion in the Writings of Herman Melville*. The Hague: Mouton, 1964, pp. 57–67.

Berthoff, Warner. *The Example of Melville*. Princeton, N.J.: Princeton University Press, 1962, pp. 30–36.

Davison, R.A. "Redburn, Pierre, and Robin: Melville's Debt to Hawthorne?," in *Emerson Society Quarterly*. XLVII (1967), pp. 32–34.

Dryden, Edgar A. *Melville's Thematics of Form: The Great Art of Telling the Truth*. Baltimore: Johns Hopkins University Press, 1968, pp. 58–67.

Fiess, Edward. "Byron's Dark Blue Ocean and Melville's Rolling Sea," in *English Language Notes*. III (June, 1966), pp. 274–278.

Franklin, H. Bruce. "Redburn's Wicked End," in *Nineteenth-Century Fiction*. XX (September, 1965), pp. 140–194.

Freeman, John. *Herman Melville.* New York: Macmillan, 1926, pp. 84–88.

Gilman, William H. *Melville's Early Life and* Redburn. New York: New York University Press, 1951.

————. "Melville's Liverpool Trip," in *Modern Language Notes.* LXI (December, 1946), pp. 543–547.

Gozzi, Raymond D. "Melville's *Redburn*: Civilization and Its Discontents," in *Literature and Psychology.* XIII (Fall, 1963), p. 104.

Gross, John J. "The Rehearsal of Ishmael: Melville's *Redburn*," in *Virginia Quarterly Review.* XXVII (Summer, 1951), pp. 581–600.

Humphreys, A.R. *Melville.* London: Oliver and Boyd, 1962, pp. 28–40.

Huntress, Keith. "A Note on Melville's *Redburn*," in *New England Quarterly.* XVIII (June, 1945), pp. 259–260.

Kosak, Heinz. "Redburn's Image of Childhood," in *Emerson Society Quarterly.* XXXIX (1965), pp. 40–42.

Lisk, T.G. "Melville's Redburn: A Study in Dualism," in *English Language Notes.* V (December, 1967), pp. 113–120.

Mason, Ronald. *The Spirit Above the Dust: A Study of Herman Melville.* London: John Lehmann, 1951, pp. 67–79.

Miller, James E. "Redburn and White Jacket: Initiation and Baptism," in *Nineteenth-Century Fiction.* XIII (March, 1959), pp. 273–293.

Schweter, James. "Redburn and the Failure of Mythic Criticism," in *American Literature.* XXXIX (November, 1967), pp. 274–297.

Sedgwick, William Ellery. *Herman Melville: The Tragedy of Mind.* Cambridge, Mass.: Harvard University Press, 1944, pp. 62–81.

Thompson, Lawrance. *Melville's Quarrel with God.* Princeton, N.J.: Princeton University Press, 1952, pp. 73–89.

Thorp, Willard. "Redburn's Prosy Old Guidebook," in *PMLA.* LIII (1938), pp. 1146–1156.

TYPEE

Type of work: Novel
Author: Herman Melville (1819–1891)
Type of plot: Adventure romance
Time of plot: Mid-nineteenth century
Locale: Marquesas Islands
First published: 1846

The first significant romance of the South Seas, Typee *is a fictionalized narrative of the actual adventures of young Herman Melville. More than a fascinating travel book, the novel foreshadows the development of many qualities later to appear in the writer's major productions.*

Principal Characters

Tom called Tommo by the natives, an American sailor on the whaler "Dolly" who, with his friend Toby, jumps ship at Nukuheva, and immediately contracts a disease which makes his leg swell and become very painful. When their food runs out, they give themselves up to the Typee tribe of natives on the island. They are treated kindly and Tom is given a native servant to take care of him. Toby leaves to seek medical aid and never returns, leaving Tom alone with the natives, who, the friends had discovered, are cannibals. Tom is allowed a fair amount of freedom but is always attended by Kory-Kory, his servant, and Fayaway, a beautiful native girl. Tom is finally allowed to go down to the beach to see a boat from an Australian vessel. Though watched carefully by the natives, he manages to break away from his guards and is taken on board by the Australians.

Toby, Tom's friend, who leaves the whaler with him and shares his adventures on the island until he goes to find medical help for Tom and is tricked into boarding a vessel which leaves the island the next day. Years later he meets Tom and is happy to learn that his friend escaped and is well.

Kory-Kory, Tom's faithful native servant, who is always by his side. Tom very much regrets having to leave him behind when he escapes.

Fayaway, the native girl who is Tom's constant companion while he is among the Typees.

Marnoo, a native taboo man who is free to move among all the tribes on the island without danger. Tom asks Marnoo to help him escape, but Marnoo cannot do so without arousing the natives' anger. He does, however, tell the captain of the Australian vessel of Tom's situation.

Mehevi, the Typees' chief, who is typical of the relaxed Polynesian.

The Story

The whaler *Dolly* had been long at sea, and the men were discontented and restless when the captain finally gave orders to put in at Nukuheva, one of the Marquesas Islands. This was the chance Tom and Toby, two young sailors, had been waiting for. Even though the natives of the island were known to be can-nibals, Tom and Toby deserted the ship and fled inland, planning to hide until the *Dolly* sailed. Then they hoped to sign aboard another ship where they would get better treatment.

Tom and Toby began their flight with only a few biscuits for food. On the first night away from the ship Tom contracted some disease which caused his leg to swell, and he was in much pain. Nevertheless, he and Toby went on. At last, when their food was all gone, they realized that they could stay alive only by giving themselves up to one of the savage tribes that inhabited the island.

They discovered too late that the natives to whom they surrendered themselves were the Typee tribe, the most ferocious cannibals on Nukuheva. Tom and Toby were treated with respect, however, and were given food and comfortable quar-ters. All the natives came to see the strangers. Mehevi, the king of the Typees, appointed Kory-Kory as personal servant to Tom. The captives went to live in the home of Tinor, Kory-Kory's mother. Mehevi had a medicine man examine Tom's swollen leg, but the native remedies had no effect on the disease.

Tom, unable to walk, spent most of his time reclining in the house while Kory-Kory attended to his needs. A beautiful young maiden, Fayaway, was also his constant companion. She, among all the Typees, seemed to understand the pain-ful situation of the two captives.

Toby convinced the Typees that he should be allowed to return to the main harbor on the island to seek medical aid for Tom. On the trail he was attacked by hostile warriors from a neighboring tribe, and he returned to the Typees with an ugly head wound.

A few days later Toby discovered a boat offshore. He was allowed to go down by the beach, but Tom was detained in his house. Toby promised to bring medical aid to Tom within three days. But the three days passed without the return of Toby. Tom could learn nothing from the natives; he realized that now he was the single captive of the Typees. Somewhat recovered, he was allowed to roam almost at will within the country of the Typees. But he was always accompanied by Kory-Kory; there was no chance for escape.

As Tom's leg improved, he began to indulge in the pleasures allowed him and to observe the native life with interest. The Typees seemed to exist in a perpetual state of happiness, interrupted only by skirmishes with neighboring tribes.

One of Tom's greatest pleasures was to paddle a canoe about a small lake in company with Fayaway. For the privilege of taking Fayaway with him he had to ask special permission, since entering a canoe was ordinarily taboo for a woman.

One day a handsome stranger appeared among the Typees bearing news from other parts of the island. He was Marnoo, a taboo man, who was free to go among all the tribes without harm. When Tom learned that Marnoo knew English, he asked the native to help him escape. This Marnoo could not do for fear of arous-ing the anger of the Typees.

The daily life of the natives was extremely regular. Each morning they bathed and ate breakfast. After the meal they smoked their pipes. The rest of the morning they spent sleeping, conversing, or doing odd jobs about their houses. The men often spent the afternoon in the large meeting house of Mehevi; there they relaxed and joked in a sort of bachelors' club. Before the evening meal they bathed again. After the meal the young girls entertained the rest with dancing. Everyone retired at an early hour.

Tom was present at the Feast of the Calabashes. It seemed to have some religious significance, but most of the time was spent in eating and drinking. During the two days of the festival Tom decided the natives did not take their religion seriously. They possessed many idols not treated with any high degree of respect. The most universal religious observance was that of tattooing; everyone was tattooed upon the face, even the women. The bodies of some of the men were completely covered with intricate designs.

Since the men outnumbered the women in the tribe, the women often had two or three husbands. But the men never had more than one wife. All in the tribe seemed happy with the various aspects of their social organization. Private property was limited to household goods, food was common property. All understood and followed the laws and customs of the tribe; there were never disputes among the Typees.

One day a battle was fought between the Typees and a neighboring tribe. Afterward the bodies of the dead enemies were taken to the ceremonial feasting place. For the next day or two Tom was not allowed to leave the vicinity of his house. He suspected that the Typees were making a meal of their dead enemies. Later he discovered the remains of the meal and found that he was correct, though the Typees denied they were cannibals.

A few days later Marnoo again appeared among the Typees. This time he told Tom to try to escape by means of the same path by which he left. Tom was unable to leave the village, however, for Kory-Kory kept close watch on him day and night.

Not many days after Marnoo had left, the Typees excitedly announced the approach of a boat. Tom argued with the natives and finally persuaded them to let him go to the beach. He had some difficulty in getting there, since his leg had begun to swell again.

At the beach Tom found a boat from an Australian ship standing just outside the surf. Marnoo had told the Australian captain of Tom's trouble, and he had sent a boat loaded with presents to obtain Tom's release. The Typees, however, had no wish to release their captive. In desperation, Tom broke away from the guard which had been placed around him and plunged into the surf. He managed to reach the boat, and the sailors pulled away from shore.

Thus ended Tom's captivity among the Typees. His only regret was in leaving the faithful Kory-Kory and the beautiful Fayaway.

Many years later Tom again met Toby and learned from him that he had intended to return to the aid of his injured friend, but he had been tricked into boarding a vessel which sailed from Nukuheva the following day. It was only long after Toby had given Tom up for lost that the two friends learned of each other's fate after their separation.

Critical Evaluation

Melville's assertion in *Moby Dick* that a whale ship was his Yale and Harvard reminds us of how central to his development the sea adventures of his youth were, and how strongly they would shape his writing. It was from the whaler *Acushnet* that Melville jumped ship in the Marquesas to spend a few weeks among the Nukuheva natives. The episode ended, sooner and less dramatically than in *Typee*, when he departed the island on another whaler, eventually to join the American warship, *United States*, for a voyage back to Boston. But, though the adventure had ended in actuality, it only began imaginatively for Melville when he sought to discover its meaning in a fictionalized account of his sojourn among the cannibals which he called *Typee*. Though actually a novel based upon experience, *Typee* was regarded generally as simply a travel narrative when it appeared, and the work's reputation since has had to fight against that classification. In fact, *Typee* contains more of the basic elements of Melville's later fiction than its detractors have realized, and it deserves a primary place among such other early works as *Redburn* and *White-Jacket* which give meaning to the idea of Melville's education on board the ships he sailed as a young man.

The essential facts of *Typee*, except for the time which Melville considerably exaggerates, are true: he did jump ship in company of a friend named Toby Greene and spend a few weeks among the natives of the Typee valley where he enjoyed a somewhat ambiguous status as a prisoner-guest; Melville did injure his leg escaping the *Acushnet* and allowed Toby to go for medical supplies; Toby failed to return, having been shanghaied by another whaler; and, after a few weeks, Melville was taken off the island by a whaler in search of crewmen. The novel, however, is considerably more than the sum of these few facts, and it cannot be done justice by a reading which regards it as no more than a slightly fictionalized autobiographical narrative. Far from simply recounting his adventures, Melville explores in *Typee* the fundamental ambiguities in man and nature which would characterize his best work as the basis for the unanswerable questions his novels propose.

From its very beginning, the boys' journey into Typee valley promises to be more than it seems. Running not only from the ship and its cruelly authoritarian master, but from the world of the coast natives which has been hopelessly corrupted by sailors, administrators, and missionaries, these adventurers make their way down a precipitous route which carries them metaphorically backward in time as it takes them beyond the reach of civilization. Eventually reaching the valley floor, the boys initially encounter Typee (which they still believe to be Happar) as a new paradise. Not only the fecundity and lushness of the rich valley but also the young lovers who are the first inhabitants encountered, point to the discovery of a South Sea Eden. This vision of innocence and beauty in the South

Sea islands was, to some extent, typical of nineteenth century Romanticism with its recurrent theme of the Noble Savage, but Melville, even this early in his career, was no typical Romantic writer.

From the time Tom (now renamed Tommo) settles, albeit unwillingly, into life with the Typees, Melville begins to develop around him a series of symbols which point to the fundamental ambiguity which lies at the heart of the island "paradise." On the one hand, the simplicity, loyalty, and unselfconscious devotion offered by Kory-Kory, and, more particularly, the innocent love and natural sexuality of Fayaway, keep alive the vision of an Edenic garden. On the other hand, Tommo's discovery that he is in the land of the dread Typees rather than among the peaceful Happars leads to his fear of cannibalism, the most dread of all man's aberrations. Tommo's injured leg, which mysteriously grows worse as his suspicions of cannibalism near confirmation, becomes an objective correlative for his sick spirit which, cut off from the civilization it sought to escape, languishes. Tatooing also develops a symbolic value, since it would complete the initiation into the Typean world begun with the ritual name-change. Once tatooed, Tommo would never again be able to return to his own world.

The essential ambiguity in *Typee* centers around the prospect of a paradise corrupted at its heart by the horror of cannibalism. In later years, Melville would assert that he could look upon a horror and be familiar with it, but this is not so of Tommo, who cannot reconcile himself to this discovery. More generally, the implications of the innate evil of *Typee* seriously challenges the view of optimistic philosophers of Melville's period who argued that the universe, and man, were essentially good, evil being only an appearance rather than a reality. Tommo might like to think that he, as a civilized human being, somehow transcends the essentially savage nature of man, but Melville will not have it so. In the escape scene, Tommo repays the hospitality of his hosts by driving the boat hook into the throat of one of his recent friends. Even as Tommo feels the horror of his violent act, we feel the horror of Melville's world in which the savage impulse dwells even in the most civilized breast.

Though perhaps less orderly than this reading suggests, Melville's symbols are clearly present, and they serve to put his vision in a direct line of descent from that of his Calvinist forebearers who endorsed the doctrine of the essential depravity of man. It is only because the symbols are tentative and nascent, rather than fully developed into Melville's mature symbolism, that *Typee* must be seen more as an anticipation of later Melville than as a fully realized work of art in itself. *Typee* does reveal, however, how early Melville began to develop the symbolic mode which would become the hallmark of his greatest romances, and how soon he began to discover those unsolvable questions of the nature of good and evil which would preoccupy him throughout his career.

Bibliography

Anderson, Charles Roberts. "Contemporary American Opinions of *Typee* and *Omoo*," in *American Literature*. IX (March, 1937), pp. 1–25.

————. "Melville's English Debut," in *American Literature*. XI (March, 1939), pp. 23–38.

————. *Melville in the South Seas*. New York: Columbia University Press, 1939, pp. 69–195.

Bernstein, John. *Pacificism and Rebellion in the Writings of Herman Melville*. The Hague: Mouton, 1964.

Birss, John H. "The Story of Toby, A Sequel to *Typee*," in *Harvard Library Bulletin*. I (Winter, 1947), pp. 118–119.

Canaday, Nicholas. "The Theme of Authority in Melville's *Typee* and *Omoo*," in *Forum*. IV (Fall, 1963), pp. 38–41.

Dryden, Edgar A. *Melville's Thematics of Form: The Great Art of Telling the Truth*. Baltimore: Johns Hopkins University Press, 1968, pp. 37–46.

Firebaugh, J.J. "Humanist as Rebel: The Melville of *Typee*," in *Nineteenth-Century Fiction*. IX (September, 1954), pp. 108–120.

Forsythe, Robert S. "Herman Melville in the Marquesas," in *Philological Quarterly*. XV (January, 1936), pp. 1–15.

Frederix, Pierre. *Herman Melville*. Paris: Gallimard, 1950, pp. 132–147.

Freeman, John. *Herman Melville*. New York: Macmillan, 1926, pp. 74–80.

Gobdes, Clarence. "Gossip About Melville in the South Seas," in *New England Quarterly*. X (September, 1937), pp. 526–531.

————. "Melville's Friend Toby," in *Modern Language Notes*. LIX (January, 1944), pp. 52–55.

Houghton, D.E. "The Incredible Ending of Melville's *Typee*," in *Emerson Society Quarterly*. XXII (1961), pp. 28–31.

Ishoy, Saada. *The American Novel: Two Studies*. Emporia: Kansas State Teachers College, 1965, pp. 7–13.

Jones, B.C. "American Frontier Humor in Melville's *Typee*," in *New York Folklore Quarterly*. XV (Winter, 1950), pp. 283–288.

Lawrence, D.H. *Studies in Classic American Literature*. New York: Doubleday, 1955, pp. 142–156.

Mason, Ronald. *The Spirit Above the Dust: A Study of Herman Melville*. London: John Lehmann, 1951, pp. 21–30.

Mayoux, Jean-Jacques. *Melville*. London: Evergreen Books, 1960, pp. 36–42.

Miller, James E., Jr. *A Reader's Guide to Herman Melville*. New York: Noonday, 1962, pp. 18–37.

Petrullo, H.B.   "The Neurotic Hero of *Typee*," in *American Imago*. XII (Winter, 1955), pp. 317–323.

Ruland, Richard.   "Melville and the Fortunate Fall: Typee as Eden," in *Nineteenth-Century Fiction*. XXIII (December, 1968), pp. 312–323.

Sedgwick, William Ellery.   *Herman Melville: The Tragedy of Mind*. Cambridge, Mass.: Harvard University Press, 1944, pp. 19–35.

Stern, Milton R.   *The Fine Hammered Steel of Herman Melville*. Urbana: University of Illinois Press, 1957, pp. 29–65.

Thomas, Russell.   "Yarn for Melville's *Typee*," in *Philological Quarterly*. XV (January, 1936), pp. 16–29.

Thompson, Lawrance.   *Melville's Quarrel with God*. Princeton, N.J.: Princeton University Press, 1952, pp. 45–55.

Weathers, Winston.   "Melville and the Comedy of Communications," in *ETC*. XX (December, 1963), pp. 411–420.

WHITE-JACKET

Type of work: Novel
Author: Herman Melville (1819–1891)
Type of plot: Adventure romance
Time of plot: The 1840's
Locale: A vessel of the U.S. Navy
First published: 1850

Based in part upon the author's experiences on board the U.S. frigate United States *in 1843–1844,* White-Jacket *is a loosely knit narrative that exposes a number of vicious practices of the day: flogging, the tyranny of commanders, issuance of liquor to sailors, and poor messing facilities of the naval vessels.*

Principal Characters

White-Jacket, a common seaman aboard the United States frigate "Neversink" on a voyage from the Pacific around Cape Horn to the eastern seaboard. White-Jacket gets his name aboard the ship when he sews for himself a canvas jacket for protection against the cold of the Cape. He is a sensitive young man and is greatly disturbed by practices common aboard United States naval vessels of the last century; floggings, tyrannical officers, issuance of liquor to crewmen, all draw his fire. White-Jacket's story ends when he falls overboard off the Virginia capes and throws off the canvas coat to be better able to swim for his life. White-Jacket's account was instrumental in abolishing flogging as punishment in

the United States Navy.

Jack Chase, a Britisher in United States service aboard the U.S.S. "Neversink." He is the educated, civil, petty officer under whom White-Jacket serves. His good work in getting privileges for the crew earns him the respect of the coarse seamen with whom he sails.

Captain Claret, a typical commander of naval vessels of the last century. He, along with his officers, feels that naval officers should drive men, not lead them. The Captain is stern, usually fair, but sometimes peevish and unpredictable. He never feels that common seamen deserve even a modicum of the respect ordinarily paid human beings.

The Story

White-Jacket, as he was later nicknamed, was a common sailor, a member of the crew of the United States frigate *Neversink* on a cruise of the Pacific Ocean during the 1840's. After the ship left Callao, Peru, the sailor tried to purchase a heavy jacket, needed protection when the *Neversink* passed into the colder climate off Cape Horn. Because a heavy jacket was not available from the ship's purser, the vessel having been at sea for over three years, the sailor had to make a canvas jacket for himself.

The jacket was full of pockets and quilted with odds and ends of rags and clothing for warmth. When the maker requested some paint to make it waterproof and darken its color, he was told that no paint was available for the purpose.

As the ship moved southward toward the Antarctic, the sailor gradually came to be called White-Jacket by the crew because of the strange garment he wore. Some of the sailors, superstitious as old wives, disliked him because of the jacket; they said that White-Jacket was too much like a ghost as he went about his duties high in the rigging of the frigate.

The offensiveness of White-Jacket's strange apparel was revealed only a few days after the ship's anchor had been weighed at Callao. White-Jacket was forced to leave the mess group to which he had been assigned, for the sailors told him openly that anyone who wore such a weird garment was unwelcome. That White-Jacket had proved himself a very poor cook during his tour of duty for the group had not helped his cause.

Forced from his original messmates' company, White-Jacket was taken into the mess to which belonged the petty officer of the maintop under whom White-Jacket served. The petty officer was Jack Chase, a gentlemanly Britisher who shared White-Jacket's love of literature. Chase, who had returned to the *Neversink* after an absence of months, during which he had served as an officer on a Peruvian insurrectionist vessel, was looked up to by the rough sailors and respected by all the officers aboard the ship.

As the *Neversink* sailed southward along the western coast of South America the general ship's duties continued. White-Jacket and his fellows set sails and took them in, washed down the decks, stood their watches, and prepared for colder weather. To relieve the tedium of the long voyage, Captain Claret gave out word that the men would be permitted to stage a theatrical entertainment. The captain had permitted such entertainments in the earlier stages of the cruise, but he had discontinued them because one of the actors had behaved in an objectionable manner. White-Jacket noted that before the play the captain perused and censored the script. Neither the captain nor the commodore who was aboard the *Neversink* dignified the men's entertainment by being present.

During the coastal voyage a man fell overboard and was drowned. The incident demonstrated to White-Jacket how risky life aboard a ship was and how quickly a lost man was forgotten.

The *Neversink* was becalmed in the waters off Cape Horn. After three days of cold and calm the captain gave the unusual order for the crew to "skylark." The men gave themselves over to all kinds of activity and games of a rougher sort, all in an attempt to keep warm and to prevent frozen hands and feet. Shortly thereafter a wind came up. The ship rounded the Cape and began to cruise steadily northward.

One day the lookout sighted a number of casks floating on the ocean. Word was given that they should be picked up, and when they were hauled aboard it was discovered that they contained very fine port wine. The discovery caused great joy among the crew. In the 1840's the navy still clung to the custom of serving spirits to the men twice a day, but the *Neversink's* steward, for some unaccountable reason, had neglected to replenish the ship's supply of rum during the stop at Callao.

The most significant happenings during the run from Cape Horn northward to Rio de Janeiro, so far as White-Jacket was concerned, were a series of floggings. At that time the American navy still made flogging a punishment for offenses at sea. White-Jacket hated the cruel whippings, which all crew members and officers were forced to watch. White-Jacket reflected that even in Rome no citizen could be flogged as punishment and that the great naval officers of the nineteenth century were opposed to a practice so brutal and unnecessary.

The *Neversink* finally reached Rio de Janeiro. During many days in port the men were not to be permitted ashore. At last the petty officers appointed Jack Chase, the captain of the maintop, to request shore leave for the men. At first the captain was unwilling to grant leave, but the commodore interceded and gave his approval to sending the men ashore. Once again Chase was the hero of the men aboard the vessel.

One day the Emperor of Brazil was expected to visit the vessel. White-Jacket, amazed at preparations made by men and officers for the royal visit, wondered how men from a democratic nation could so easily fawn upon royalty. He decided the men would have made fewer preparations to receive the President of the United States.

On the voyage northward along the eastern coast of South America one of White-Jacket's shipmates fell ill and died. White-Jacket watched the preparations for burial, including the traditional final stitch of the shroud through the nose, then stood by during the service. That event was as moving to him as an amputation demonstrated by the ship's doctor while the *Neversink* lay in the harbor at Rio de Janeiro. The operation was performed, White-Jacket believed, because the surgeon wished to show off to colleagues from other vessels anchored there at the same time. Convinced that the operation was unnecessary, White-Jacket was very bitter when the injured man died of shock.

White-Jacket himself had a close escape from death when the ship was off the Virginia capes. Sent aloft to reeve a line through some blocks, he lost his balance and fell from the rigging a hundred feet into the sea. He had to cut away his white jacket in order to keep afloat. He was barely out of his garment when a sailor, mistaking the jacket for a white shark, threw a harpoon into it. White-Jacket, rescued from the sea, was sent aloft ten minutes later to complete his task. White-Jacket was content to close his story of the voyage with the loss of his unlucky garment.

Critical Evaluation

Though ostensibly an autobiographical exposé of the abuses against crewmen aboard American naval vessels in the 1840's, *White-Jacket* nevertheless contains essential elements of a novel of initiation into a complex world of good and evil. White-Jacket's bizarre garment develops into a symbol of the naïve innocence of its wearer, who, through his adventures on the *Neversink*, comes to a knowledge of the real world as represented by the man-of-war. The boy's final plunge into the sea as a result of having become entangled in his white coat represents his baptism into the world of adult knowledge and the shedding of his childhood innocence.

Though not clearly developed in novelistic form, a number of themes in *White-Jacket* tie this novel to Melville's more mature works. The evil resulting from insecure authority and arbitrary laws underlies much of the abuse of power aboard ship, for example. In fact, Melville seems to suggest a distinction along class lines of the problems resulting from an abuse of power by the officers, and the "sins" of the sailors, both seen as resulting from the inhumane conditions aboard ship. But while these forms of physical abuse account for one type of evil aboard ship, and the behavior of the sailors at their worst represents another, a typically Melvillian suggestion of innate evil can be seen in certain characters. The inhumanity of Cadwallader Cuticle, M.D., who murders a sailor in the name of science, and the master-at-arms, Bland, said to be "without a soul," are manfestations of such innate evil.

Melville's world, however, is always ambiguous. Thus, in *White-Jacket* the evil represented by Bland and the doctor is balanced by Jack Chase, who epitomizes all that is best in man.

Bibliography

Allen, Priscilla. *"White-Jacket* and the Man-of-War Microcosm," in *American Quarterly*. XXV (1973), pp. 32–47.

Anderson, Charles Roberts. *Melville in the South Seas.* New York: Columbia University Press, 1939, pp. 349–434.

————. "A Reply to Herman Melville's *White-Jacket* by Rear-Admiral Thomas O. Selfridge, Sr.," in *American Literature*. VII (May, 1935), pp. 123–144.

Bernstein, John. *Pacifism and Rebellion in the Writings of Herman Melville.* The Hague: Mouton, 1964, pp. 68–81.

Dryden, Edgar A. *Melville's Thematics of Form: The Great Art of Telling the Truth.* Baltimore: Johns Hopkins University Press, 1968, pp. 67–79.

Freeman, John. *Herman Melville.* New York: Macmillan, 1926.

Hayford, Harrison. "The Sailor Poet of *White-Jacket*," in *Boston Public Library Quarterly*. III (July, 1951), pp. 221–228.

Humphreys, A.R. *Melville.* London: Oliver and Boyd, 1962, pp. 28–40.

Huntress, Keith. "Melville's Use of a Source for *White-Jacket*," in *American Literature*. XVII (March, 1945), pp. 66–74.

McCarthy, Paul. "Symbolic Elements in *White-Jacket*," in *Midwest Quarterly*. VII (Summer, 1966), pp. 309–329.

Mason, Ronald. *The Spirit Above the Dust: A Study of Herman Melville.* London: John Lehmann, 1951, pp. 80–95.

Miller, James E. "*Redburn* and *White-Jacket*: Initiation and Baptism," in *Nineteenth-Century Fiction.* XIII (March, 1959), pp. 273–293.

Mordell, Albert. "Melville and *White-Jacket*," in *Saturday Review of Literature.* VII (July 4, 1931), p. 946.

Nichol, John W. "Melville's Soiled Fish of the Sea," in *American Literature.* XXI (November, 1949), pp. 338–339.

Philbrick, Thomas L. "Another Source for *White-Jacket*," in *American Literature.* XXIX (January, 1958), pp. 431–439.

————. "Melville's Best Authorities," in *Nineteenth-Century Fiction.* XV (September, 1960), pp. 171–179.

Procter, Page S. "A Source for the Flogging Incident in *White-Jacket*," in *American Literature.* XXII (May, 1958), pp. 176–182.

Regan, Charles L. "Melville's Horned Woman," in *English Language Notes.* V (September, 1967), pp. 34–39.

Sedgwick, William Ellery. *Herman Melville: The Tragedy of Mind.* Cambridge, Mass.: Harvard University Press, 1944.

Seelye, John D. " 'Spontaneous Impress of Truth': Melville's Jack Chase: A Source, an Analogue, a Conjecture," in *Nineteenth-Century Fiction.* XX (March, 1966), pp. 367–376.

Stone, Geoffrey. *Melville.* New York: Sheed and Ward, 1949, pp. 125–135.

Thompson, Lawrance. *Melville's Quarrel with God.* Princeton, N.J.: Princeton University Press, 1952, pp. 93–124.

Vincent, Howard P. "*White-Jacket*: An Essay in Interpretation," in *New England Quarterly.* XXII (September, 1949), pp. 304–315.

Walker, Warren S. "A Note on Nathaniel Ames," in *American Literature.* XXVI (May, 1954), pp. 239–241.

Zirker, Priscilla. "Evidence of the Slavery Dilemma in *White-Jacket*," in *American Quarterly.* XVIII (Fall, 1966), pp. 477–492.

EDGAR ALLAN POE

Born: Boston, Massachusetts (January 19, 1809)
Died: Baltimore, Maryland (October 7, 1849)

Principal Works

POEMS: *Tamerlane and Other Poems,* 1827; *Al Aaraaf, Tamerlane and Minor Poems,* 1829; *Poems,* 1831; *The Raven and Other Poems,* 1845; *Eureka: A Prose Poem,* 1848

SHORT STORIES: *Tales of the Grotesque and Arabesque,* 1840 (2 vols.); *Tales,* 1845.

NOVELLA: *The Narrative of Arthur Gordon Pym,* 1838.

CRITICISM: *The Literati,* 1850.

The parents of Edgar Allan Poe were David Poe and Elizabeth Arnold Poe. They had three children: William Henry Leonard, Edgar, and Rosalie. Edgar was born on January 19, 1809, in Boston. His mother died in Richmond, Virginia, on December 8, 1811, and the circumstances of David Poe's death are unknown. It is believed that he died not long before or after the death of his wife. The pretty little boy, Edgar, though not legally adopted, became a member of the childless family of John Allan, a Scottish tobacco merchant of the Richmond firm of Ellis and Allan. He was given the name of Edgar Allan and treated as the son of the family. When Mr. Allan sailed for England to establish a branch of the firm, Edgar went with him and his wife. He was kept in an English school most of the time until the Allans returned home in 1820. After further school days in Richmond, Poe was taken to Charlottesville where on February 14, 1826, he was entered as a student in the University of Virginia. He continued as a student for the more than ten months' session until it closed in December. He excelled in his classes, but he accumulated some debts over which he and Mr. Allan quarreled; and as a result Poe left Richmond a penniless youth.

Why Poe chose to go to Boston is unknown but he arranged there for the publication of a little volume of poems, *Tamerlane and Other Poems,* and on May 26, 1827, he enlisted under the name of Edgar A. Perry in the United States Army. In 1829 he secured a discharge from the army and entered West Point in 1830 as a cadet. After the death of his first wife, John Allan married again. Soon afterward there was a final break with Poe, and Poe himself was dismissed from the Academy. He had published *Al Aaraaf, Tamerlane and Minor Poems* in 1829 and upon leaving West Point he published *Poems, Second Edition,* 1831. There followed an obscure period in Baltimore before he went to Richmond in 1835 to work on the *Southern Literary Messenger* until the end of 1836. He had married his cousin, Virginia Clemm, in 1836, and he now took her and his aunt, Mrs. Clemm, to New York, but soon he removed to Philadelphia where he became first an associate editor of *Burton's Gentleman's Magazine* and later editor of its successor, *Graham's Magazine*. In April, 1844, he returned to New York and in 1846 rented the little cottage in Fordham, just out of the city, where Virginia died on January 30, 1847, and where Poe and Mrs. Clemm continued to live until Poe's death. He had published stories and articles in various magazines and had worked on the New York *Mirror* and edited the *Broadway Journal*.

Of his books, *The Narrative of Arthur Gordon Pym* was published in 1838, *Tales of the Grotesque and Arabesque*, in two volumes, in 1840, *Tales* and *The Raven and Other Poems* in 1845, and *Eureka* in 1848. The publication of his prize-winning story, "The Gold Bug" in the Philadelphia *Dollar Newspaper* in 1843 brought him some recognition, but he became famous in 1845 with the printing of "The Raven" in the *Evening Mirror* and the *Whig Review*. In 1849, the year in which appeared "Annabel Lee," "The Bells," and others of his best-known poems, Poe visited Norfolk and Richmond on a lecture tour. He had broken his engagement to marry the poetess, Mrs. Helen Whitman, and in Richmond he had become engaged to his former sweetheart, Sarah Elmira Royster, now the widow Shelton. From the time of his leaving Richmond his movements are unknown until he was found in an unconscious condition in Baltimore. He died in a hospital on October 7, 1849. In the churchyard of the Westminster Prebyterian Church he was interred the next day. His wife, Viriginia, was later removed from the vault of the Valentines, owners of the Fordham cottage, to a place beside his grave.

Edgar Allan Poe is as important for his influence upon the literature of the world as he is for the works in themselves. He is known as poet, critic, short story writer, and mystic theorist. The quality of about twenty of his poems is unique. He was an innovator in the field of pure poetry and of symbolism. Of lesser importance was his mastery of certain technical devices, such as assonance, rhythm and rhyme, as evidenced in his "The Raven," "The Bells," and "Ulalume." His influence was especially great in France through Baudelaire, Mallarmé, and the Symbolists. Certainly, "To Helen," "Annabel Lee," "The Haunted Palace," "The Raven," "Israfel," "The City in the Sea," and "Ulalume" are among the most universally admired short poems in the language.

Poe, at the time of his death, was best known in America as a critic. He defined the short story and developed the theory of what has come to be known as "pure poetry."

His prose tales were unique for his day. He invented the detective story, as illustrated by such tales as "The Murders in the Rue Morgue" and "The Purloined Letter." His most characteristic tales were stories of impressionistic effect, often containing a psychological theme or built on a study of conscience, as seen in "Ligeia" or "William Wilson"; or tales of terror, such as "The Black Cat," "The Tell-Tale Heart," or "The Cask of Amontillado."

The magic of Poe, his power to arouse our terror, and to make us partake of the sensations that he evokes by his stories as though we had lived them, are the effects of his conscious art. His poems are remarkable for their beauty and melody, his tales for the intensity with which the artist brings us under his spell. He is associated especially with his dark and terror-filled stories with which all readers are familiar and he is, perhaps, the world's master of the macabre. He was the product of the Gothic influence infused with the curiosity as to all things psychological that came from Germany. When all the stories that he wrote, however, are considered, he is seen to have a wider range as a prose writer than is generally recognized.

Bibliography

The standard editions are *The Complete Works of Edgar Allan Poe*, edited by James A. Harrison, 17 vols., 1902, now out of print, and the less complete but reliable *Works of Edgar Allan Poe*, edited by George E. Woodberry and Edmund C. Stedman, 10 vols., 1894–1895 (reprinted 1914); but a new edition is needed to incorporate the letters and other findings of recent scholarship. One such contribution is John W. Ostrom, *The Letters of Edgar Allan Poe*, 2 vols., 1948. The best editions of the short stories are James Southall Wilson, *Tales of Edgar Allan Poe*, 1927; and Killis Campbell, *Poe's Short Stories*, 1927. The latter also edited *The Poems of Edgar Allan Poe*, 1917. An edition in 3 vols. of the *Collected Works*, edited by Thomas Oliver Mabbott, is in progress, Vol. I, *Poems*, 1970.

The standard biography is Arthur H. Quinn, *Edgar Allan Poe: A Critical Biography*, 1941. See also J. H. Ingram, *Edgar Allan Poe: His Life, Letters, and Opinions*, 2 vols., 1880; George E. Woodberry, *The Life of Edgar Allan Poe, Personal and Literary*, 2 vols., 1885 (rev. ed., 1909); Hervey Allen, *Israfel: The Life and Times of Edgar Allan Poe*, 2 vols., 1926; N. B. Fagin, *The Histrionic Mr. Poe*, 1949; and Edward Wagenknecht, *Poe: The Man behind the Legend*, 1963.

See also Margaret Alterton, *Origins of Poe's Critical Theory*, 1925; Norman Foerster, *American Criticism*, 1928; S. F. Damon, *Thomas Holley Chivers, Friend of Poe*, 1930; Killis Campbell, *The Mind of Poe and Other Studies*, 1933; Gay Wilson Allen, *American Prosody*, 1935; Van Wyck Brooks, *The World of Washington Irving*, 1944; and "Edgar Allan Poe," in *The Literary History of the United States*, Vol. II, edited by Robert E. Spiller, Willard Thorp, Thomas H. Johnston, and Henry S. Canby, 1948.

For briefer criticism and special studies consult the extensive bibliography in *The Literary History of the United States*, Vol. III, 689–696.

THE NARRATIVE OF ARTHUR GORDON PYM

Type of work: Novella
Author: Edgar Allan Poe (1809-1849)
Type of plot: Adventure romance
Time of plot: Early nineteenth century
Locale: High seas
First published: 1838

This extended tale, Poe's longest narrative fiction, has been given many labels—horror story, gothic parody, sea-adventure-romance, literary hoax, even a Western of a kind—but it continues to defy categorization. Whatever its type, however, it is one of the most startling revelations of Poe's bleak vision of the cosmos and man's precarious place in it.

Principal Characters

Arthur Gordon Pym, the narrator, young son of a Nantucket trader in ship stores. Desirous of adventure, he stows away on a whaling ship, the "Grampus"; helps to overpower and kill the mutineers who seize the ship; becomes briefly a cannibal before he and Dirk Peters are rescued by the "Jane Guy"; survives with Peters after the slaughter of the captain and all of the crew of the "Jane Guy" by natives on an uncharted Antarctic island; and dies of an unexplained accident after most of his story had been prepared for publication. How he managed to travel from the Antarctic to the United States is not revealed, as the last part of his story was lost at his death.

Augustus Barnard, his friend who aids Pym in hiding aboard the "Grampus" and who shares his experiences and his dangers until he dies from gangrene resulting from an arm wound received in the capture of the ship from the mutineers.

Captain Barnard, Augustus' father, skipper of the "Grampus." With four loyal sailors he is set adrift in a rowboat after his ship is seized by the mutineers.

Dirk Peters, a mutineer sailor on the "Grampus." He is the son of an Indian woman and a white trader. Ferocious-looking, grotesquely misshapen like a dwarf, with huge hands and bowed arms and legs, an immense head, and a ludicrously demonic countenance, he at first joins the mutineers but later turns upon them. He helps Pym and Augustus seize the "Grampus" and becomes a good friend and companion to Pym in all of his later adventures.

Seymour, a Negro cook, leader of one party of the "Grampus" mutineers.

Hartman Rogers, a mutineer who dies in convulsions after being poisoned by the mate, who leads the other party of mutineers.

Richard Parker, a mutineer who joins Pym, Barnard, and Peters. He is the first to suggest cannibalism for survival, and ironically he draws the short straw and is killed by Peters.

Captain Guy, skipper of the "Jane Guy," a schooner which rescues Pym and Peters from the battered hulk of the "Grampus."

Too-Wit, chief of a black-skinned tribe

of savages on Tsalal Island in the Antarctic Ocean. Through treachery, the chief and his men entomb by a landslide Captain Guy and all of the "Jane Guy's" crew except six men left on board, and Pym and Peters, who survive both the landslide and a later attack by the savages.

Nu-Nu, a Tsalal native captured and used as a guide by Pym and Peters in their escape from the island. He dies shortly afterward.

The Story

Arthur Gordon Pym was born the son of a respectable trader at Nantucket. While still young he attended an academy and there met Augustus Barnard, the son of a sea captain, and the two became close friends. One night after a party Augustus awoke Pym from his sleep and together they set off for the harbor. There, Augustus took charge of a small boat and they headed out to sea.

Before long, Pym, seeing that his companion was unconscious, realized the sad truth of the escapade. Augustus had been drunk, and now in the cold weather was lapsing into insensibility. As a result their boat was run down by a whaler and the two narrowly escaped with their lives. They were taken aboard the ship which had run them down and returned to port at Nantucket.

The two friends became ever more intimate after this escapade. Captain Barnard was at that time preparing to fit out the *Grampus,* an old sailing hulk, for a voyage on which Augustus was to accompany him. Against his father's wishes, Pym planned to sail with his friend. Since Captain Barnard would not willingly allow Pym to sail without his father's permission, the two boys decided to smuggle Pym aboard and hide him in the hold until the ship should be so far at sea the captain would not turn back.

At first everything went according to schedule. Pym was hidden below in a large box with a store of water and food to last him approximately four days. Great was his consternation to discover, at the end of the fourth day, that his way to the main deck was barred. His friend Augustus did not appear to rescue him. In that terrible state he remained for several days, coming each day closer to starvation or death from thirst.

At last his dog, which had followed Pym aboard the ship, found his way to his master. Tied to the dog's body was a paper containing a strange message concerning blood and a warning to Pym to keep silent if he valued his life.

Pym was sick from hunger and fever when Augustus at last appeared. The story he had to tell was a terrible one. Shortly after the ship had put to sea the crew had mutinied, and Captain Barnard had been set adrift in a small boat. Some of the crew had been killed, and Augustus himself was a prisoner of the mutineers. Pym and Augustus located a place of comparative safety where it was agreed Pym should hide.

Pym now began to give his attention to the cargo, which seemed not to have been stowed in accordance with the rules for safety. Dirk Peters, a drunken mutineer, helped both Pym and Augustus and provided them with food.

When the ship ran into a storm, some of the mutineers were washed overboard. Augustus was once more given free run of the ship. Augustus, Pym, and Peters planned to overcome the other mutineers and take possession of the ship. To frighten the mutineers during a drunken brawl, Pym disguised himself to resemble a sailor recently killed. The three killed all of the mutineers except a sailor named Parker. Meanwhile a gale had come up, and in a few hours the vessel was reduced to a hulk by the heavy seas. Because the ship's cargo was made up of empty oil casks, there was no possibility of its sinking from the violence of the heavy seas. When the storm abated, the four survivors found themselves weak and without food or the hope of securing stores from the flooded hold. One day a vessel was sighted, but as it drew near those aboard the *Grampus* saw that it was adrift and all of its passengers were dead.

Pym tried to go below by diving, but he brought up nothing of worth. His companions were beginning to go mad from strain and hunger. Pym revived them by immersing each of them in the water for awhile. As their agony increased, a ship came near, but it verred away without coming to their rescue.

In desperation the men considered the possibility of eating one of their number. When they drew lots, Parker was chosen to be eaten. For four days the other three lived upon his flesh.

At last they made their way into the stores and secured food. Rain fell, and the supply of fresh water, together with the food, restored their hope. Augustus, who had suffered an arm injury, died. He was devoured by sharks as soon as his body was cast overboard.

A violent lurch of the ship threw Pym overboard, but he regained the ship with Peters' help just in time to be saved from sharks. The floating hulk having overturned at last, the two survivors fed upon barnacles. Finally, when they were nearly dead of thirst, a British ship came to their rescue. It was the *Jane Guy* of Liverpool, bound on a sealing and trading voyage to the South Seas and Pacific.

Peters and Pym began to recover. Within two weeks they were able to look back upon their horrible experiences with almost the same feeling with which one recollects terrible dreams.

The vessel stopped at Christmas Harbor, where some seals and sea elephants were killed for their hides. The captain was anxious to sail his vessel into Antarctica on a voyage of exploration. The weather turned cold. There was an adventure with a huge bear which Peters killed in time to save his companions. Scurvy afflicted the crew. Once the captain decided to turn northward, but later he foolishly took the advice of Pym to continue on. They sailed until they sighted land and encountered some savages whom they took aboard.

The animals on the island were strange, and the water was of some peculiar composition which Pym could not readily understand. The natives on that strange coast lived in a state of complete savagery. Bartering began. Before the landing party could depart, however, the sailors were trapped in what seemed to be an earthquake, which shut off their passage back to the shore. Only Pym and Peters escaped, to learn that the natives had caused the tremendous earth slide by pulling great boulders from the top of a towering cliff. The only white men left on the island, they were faced by the problem of evading the natives, who were now preparing to attack the ship. Unable to warn their comrades, Pym and Peters could only watch helplessly while the savages boarded the *Jane Guy* and overcame the six white men who had remained aboard. The ship was almost demolished. The savages brought about their own destruction, however, for in exploring the ship they set off the ammunition and the resulting explosion killed about a thousand of them.

In making their escape from the island Pym and Peters discovered ruins similar in form to those marking the site of Babylon. When they came upon two unguarded canoes, they took possession of one and pushed out to sea. Savages chased them but eventually gave up the pursuit. They began to grow listless and sleepy when their canoe entered a warm sea. Ashy material fell continually around and upon them. At last the boat rushed rapidly into a cataract, and a human figure, much larger than any man and as white as snow, arose in the pathway of the doomed boat. So ended the journal of Arthur Gordon Pym.

Critical Evaluation

Though incomplete and uneven, *The Narrative of Arthur Gordon Pym* is nevertheless one of Poe's most important evocations of the irrational power which ultimately dominates his universe. In this novella, the appearance of reason and order always deceives—the apparently benign is nothing more than a mask over horrors almost too frightening to contemplate. Poe repeatedly demonstrates this as, in the course of the story, an idyllic moonlight cruise leads to near-disaster, Pym's adventurous dream of stowing away becomes the nightmare of being buried alive, faithful Tiger changes into a raging beast. Men are subject to the same forces. Pym, first horrified by Peters' proposal, joins his companions in cannibalizing Parker's body. The "friendly" natives of Tslal prove treacherous savages. Finally, Nature itself, as exemplified by the strangely ambiguous white sea (which some critics have seen as suggestive of life-giving milk) flows into the ultimate horror of the metaphysical void.

Arthur Gordon Pym is the archetypal voyager or quester after knowledge whose initiation into the secrets of the universe is the substance of the work. Beginning as the adventurous boy of the opening chapter, he becomes, by the end of the story, the tragic pilgrim who dies a "sudden and distressing death" before he can relate the full extent of his discoveries. Like many of Poe's narrators, Pym represents himself as the epitome of the reasonable man, and throughout his adventures he seeks assurances that the universe reflects similar principles. Self-deceived on both counts, Pym seems unaware that his description of the Tslalians as "the most wicked, hypocritical, vindictive, bloodthirsty, and altogether fiendish race of men upon the face of the globe" is equally applicable to himself. Perhaps it is this knowledge that Pym comes to by his look upon the void, and with which he is unable to live.

Bibliography

Bezanson, Walter E.   "The Troubled Sleep of Arthur Gordon Pym," in *Essays in Literary History*. Edited by Rudolf Kirk and C.F. Main. New York: Russell and Russell, 1965, pp. 149–177.

Campbell, Josie P.   "Deceit and Violence: Motifs in *The Narrative of Arthur Gordon Pym*," in *English Journal*. LIV (February, 1970), pp. 206–212.

Candelaire, Cordelia.   "On the Whiteness at Tsalal: A Note on *Arthur Gordon Pym*," in *Poe Studies*. VI (June, 1973), p. 26.

Carringer, Kenneth Walter.   "Circumscription of Space and the Form of Poe's *Arthur Gordon Pym*," in *PMLA*. LXXXIX (1974), pp. 506–516.

Cecil, L. Moffitt.   "Poe's Tsalal and the Virginia Springs," in *Nineteenth-Century Fiction*. XIX (March, 1965), pp. 398–402.

_____.   "Two Narratives of Arthur Gordon Pym," in *Texas Studies in Literature and Language*. V (Summer, 1963), pp. 232–241.

Covici, Pascal.   "Toward a Reading of Poe's *The Narrative of Arthur Gordon Pym*," in *Mississippi Quarterly*. XXI (Spring, 1968), pp. 111–118.

Fiedler, Leslie A.   "The Blackness of Darkness: The Negro and the Development of American Gothic," in *Images of the Negro in American Literature*. Edited by Seymour L. Gross and John Edward Hardy. Chicago: University of Chicago Press, 1966, pp. 84–89.

_____.   *Love and Death in the American Novel*. New York: Criterion Books, 1960, pp. 370–382.

Fussell, Edwin.   *Frontier: American Literature and the American West*. Princeton, N.J.: Princeton University Press, 1965, pp. 149–155.

Harp, Richard L.   "A Note on the Harmony of Style and Theme in Poe's *Narrative of Arthur Gordon Pym*," in *CEA Critic*. XXXVI (1974), pp. 8–11.

Hinz, Evelyn J.   "Tekeli-li: *The Narrative of Arthur Gordon Pym* as Satire," in *Genre*. III (1970), pp. 379–397.

Hussey, John P.   " 'Mr. Pym' and 'Mr. Poe': The Two Narrators of *Arthur Gordon Pym*," in *South Atlantic Bulletin*. XXXIX (1974), pp. 22–32.

Kaplan, Sidney.   "Introduction to *Pym*," in *The Narrative of Arthur Gordon Pym*. By Edgar Allan Poe. New York: Hill and Wang, 1960. Reprinted in *Poe: A Collection of Critical Essays*. Edited by Robert Regan. Englewood Cliffs, N.J.: Prentice-Hall, 1967, pp. 145–163.

La Guardia, David. "Poe, Pym, and Initiation," in *Emerson Society Quarterly.* LX (Fall, 1970), pp. 82–85.

Lee, Grace F. "The Quest of Arthur Gordon Pym," in *Southern Literary Journal.* IV (Spring, 1972), pp. 22–33.

Lee, Helen. "Possibilities of *Pym*," in *English Journal.* LV (December, 1966), pp. 1149–1154.

Maxwell, D.E.S. *American Fiction: The Intellectual Background.* New York: Columbia University Press, 1963, pp. 84–94.

Moldenhauer, J.J. "Imagination and Perversity in *The Narrative of Arthur Gordon Pym*," in *Texas Studies in Literature and Language.* XIII (Summer, 1971), pp. 267–280.

Moss, Sidney P. "*Arthur Gordon Pym*, or the Fallacy of Thematic Interpretation," in *University Review.* XXXIII (Summer, 1967), pp. 298–306.

O'Donnell, Charles. "From Earth to Ether: Poe's Flight into Space," in *PMLA.* LXXVII (March, 1962), pp. 85–89.

Porte, Joel. *The Romance in America: Studies in Cooper, Poe, Hawthorne, Melville and James.* Middletown, Conn.: Wesleyan University Press, 1969, pp. 53–94.

Quinn, Patrick F. "Poe's Imaginary Voyage," in *Hudson Review.* IV (Winter, 1952), pp. 562–585.

Ridgely, J.V. and Iola S. Haverstick. "Chartless Voyage: The Many Narratives of Arthur Gordon Pym," in *Texas Studies in Literature and Language.* VII (Spring, 1966), pp. 63–80.

Stroupe, John H. "Poe's Imaginary Voyage: Pym as Hero," in *Studies in Short Fiction.* IV (Summer, 1967), pp. 315–322.

SUSANNA ROWSON

Born: Portsmouth, England (1762)
Died: Boston, Massachusetts (November 2, 1824)

Principal Works

NOVELS: *Victoria,* 1786; *The Inquisition,* 1788; *Charlotte Temple,* 1791; *Mentoria,* 1791; *Rebecca,* 1794; *Reuben and Rachel,* 1798; *Sarah,* 1813; *Lucy Temple,* 1828.
PLAYS: *Slaves in Algiers,* 1794; *Americans in England,* 1796.
POETRY: *A Trip to Parnassus,* 1788; *Miscellaneous Poems.*

Born Susanna Haswell in Portsmouth, England, 1762, the author of America's first best-selling novel led an extremely active and varied life, especially so for a woman at that time. Her mother, Susanna Musgrove Haswell, died at her daughter's birth, and her father shortly thereafter came to America as the royal customs collector. Five years later he returned to England, picked up Susanna and brought her back to his home and new wife in Nantasket, Massachusetts. There with three younger half brothers she lived pleasantly enough until her father, distrusted for his service to the crown, lost his property and was interned in virtual poverty during the Revolutionary War. When Haswell was returned to England in 1778, Susanna became a governess to the Duchess of Devonshire, secured a pension for her father, and began her career as a writer.

Shortly after she published her first novel *Victoria,* in 1786, she married William Rowson. Within six years his hardware business failed, and although Mrs. Rowson had continued to publish, *Charlotte: A Tale of Truth* (1791), the *Inquisition or the Invisible Rambler* (1792), and *Rebecca, or the Fille de Chambre* (1794), the Rowson family, including William's sister, Charlotte, turned to acting. Finding little success in England, they joined Thomas Wignell and came to America on tour in 1793.

For Wignell's company Mrs. Rowson acted but wrote more—both drama and music. Her topical comedies, especially *Americans in England* (1796), and musical numbers had some success, but in 1797, after having moved from Philadelphia to Boston, Mrs. Rowson left the stage and opened a Young Ladies' Academy. The school began humbly, but soon attracted more students than she could accept. Although she relocated the school several times, Mrs. Rowson ran it for twenty-five years, retiring finally in ill-health two years before her death. She not only administered the school, but taught, wrote textbooks on several subjects, created poetic dialogues for the student's moral instruction, and frequently led the dancing. Meanwhile, she continued to write novels, poetry, essays, plays, and between 1802 and 1807 edited the *Boston Weekly Magazine.* Mrs. Rowson died in 1824, but her last novel *Lucy Temple, or the Three Orphans: A Sequel to Charlotte Temple* was published in 1828.

The highlight of Susanna Rowson's writing career was *Charlotte Temple*, perhaps the most frequently reprinted American novel ever (over two hundred editions), but she also wrote seven more novels, two collections of fictional sketches; seven works for the theater, two poetry collections, six textbooks, numerous occasional works, and many song lyrics. Her novels reflect some attempts to employ the American scene: for example, the autobiographical *Rebecca, or the Fille de Chambre* which recounts her own adventures on both sides of the Atlantic, *Charlotte Temple* which is set partly in New York, and *Reuben and Rachel; or Tales of Old Times* (1799) which traces the ancestors of Columbus to contemporary Americans. However, with their concern with seduction, heavy didacticism, and plots and characters derived from Samuel Richardson's novels, these works are well within the European tradition of sentimental romance. The popularity of *Charlotte Temple* in America, therefore, testifies as much to its uniqueness as to its familiarity, and, of course, draws as well on the mixture of sensationalism and moral instruction that were part of such romances. Moreover, that mixture, in slightly different terms, seems to lie at the center of Susanna Rowson's career, for she was both teacher and entertainer, quite effective at giving her lessons zest.

Bibliography

Dorothy Weil's *In Defense of Women*, 1976, is a recent full length study of Susanna Rowson's life and work. The introductions to Francis W. Halsey, ed., *Charlotte Temple*, 1905, William S. Kable, ed., *Three Early American Novels*, 1970, and Clara M. and Rudolf Kirk, eds., *Charlotte Temple*, 1964 also have useful biographical and critical information. See also, Herbert Brown, the *Sentimental Novel in America 1789–1860*, 1940; Alexander Cowie, *the Rise of the American Novel*, 1948; Leslie Fiedler, *Love and Death in the American Novel*, 1960; Henri Petter, *The Early American Novel*, 1971; and Constance Rourke, *The Roots of American Culture*, 1942. Bibliographical information can be found in Weil and in Robert W. G. Vail, "Susanna Haswell Rowson, the author of *Charlotte Temple*: A Bibliographical Study, " *Proceedings of the American Antiquarian Society* 42 (1932), 47–160.

CHARLOTTE TEMPLE
A Tale of Truth

Type of work: Novel
Author: Susanna (Haswell) Rowson (1762–1824)
Type of plot: Didactic sentimental romance
Time of plot: Late eighteenth century
Locale: England and America
First published: 1791

The first American best-seller, Charlotte Temple *employs an ornate style and rapid pace to illustrate Rowson's moral in this domestic Richardsonian sentimental romance of a young woman's seduction.*

Principal Characters

Charlotte Temple, the only child of Henry and Lucy Temple. She is seduced by a British officer, John Montraville, and taken to America. Ultimately abandoned there, she bears Montraville's child and then, within a few days, dies. Rowson characterized Charlotte not as lascivious, but weak, innocent, and easily misled both by Montraville and by her teacher, Mlle. La Rue. Charlotte's fate is designed to warn others, but by the example of Mrs. Beauchamp's and her own family's forgiveness, the reader is also made to pity her.

Lieutenant John Montraville, a British officer, Charlotte's seducer, and father of her child. When his father bought him a military commission, he sternly warned against marriage unless to a wealthy woman or until he had risen enough in rank to avoid the battlefield. When he learns that Charlotte has only modest means, he therefore knows he will not marry her and his continued wooing is clearly ignoble. But, Montraville is less vicious than thoughtless and, like Charlotte, easily influenced to wrong by his friends. Until deceived by Belcourt to think Charlotte unfaithful, Montraville is troubled by his treatment of Charlotte, and

even after marrying Julia Franklin, when he learns of Charlotte's death, he partially atones by killing Belcourt. He lives the rest of his life melancholy and conscience striken.

Mademoiselle La Rue, Charlotte's teacher and companion, who misguides her pupil into error and then, having married to wealth and surface respectability, denies her in the hour of need. She is clever, attractive, polished, but extremely selfish, deceitful, and adventurous. Her high and licentious living as Colonel Crayton's wife eventually leads to her ruin—abandonment, poverty, sickness, and death—thus proving that crime does not pay.

Belcourt, Montraville's fellow officer and friend. Unlike Montraville he is thoroughly corrupt. He begins to lust for Charlotte in mid-Atlantic, attracted by her beauty and vulnerability, and continues to alienate Montraville from her after they are in New York. His worst crime is to abandon her entirely, once he has driven away Montraville, pocketed the money left for her support, and discovered a more attractive and reciprocating object for his affection in a nearby farmer's daughter.

494

Charlotte Temple/ROWSON

Henry Temple, Charlotte's father. Disinherited youngest son of the Earl of D___, he was attracted by Lucy Eldridge, because of her beauty and devotion to her father. He never condemns Charlotte for her fall and is present at her deathbed to offer forgiveness and assume custody of her granddaughter.

Lucy (Eldridge) Temple, Charlotte's mother. When a friend of her brother living at their home made advances to her, she told her parents and thereby illustrates what Charlotte should have done. In fact, this and her continued devotion to her father while he was in prison make her the very soul of filial duty.

Captain Eldridge, Lucy's father, Charlotte's grandfather. He was imprisoned for debt when he came between his daughter and his son's friend to whom he owed money.

Mrs. Beauchamp, Colonel Crayton's daughter. She risks public censure to aid Charlotte.

Colonel Crayton, a wealthy officer. Generous and foolish, he is easily deceived by Mlle. La Rue into marrying her.

Earl of D___, Temple's father. When his plan goes awry to have his son marry a wealthy landowner's daughter, he marries her himself.

Madame Du Pont, the proprietor of the boarding school where Charlotte is sent. She is highly respectable, but hires unwisely in the case of Mlle. La Rue.

Julia Franklin, a beautiful, wealthy, fashionable young woman, the kind of girl Montraville's father advised him to marry.

Miss Weatherby, a gorgeous, wealthy, but empty headed counterpoint to Lucy Eldridge. She is offered to Temple, but he refuses her.

John, a servant to Colonel Crayton. He gives aid to Charlotte when Mrs. Crayton denies her.

Mr. Lewis, a friend of Eldridge's son. He loans Eldridge money, and when rebuffed in his attempted seduction of Lucy, he ruins her father.

Corydon, the favorite of Mrs. Crayton. He silently pities Charlotte, when she appears at the Crayton house.

The Story

Until Charlotte Temple was fifteen her life centered on her family. Her father, the son of an English nobleman, had given up his claim to the family title and inheritance when he fell in love with Lucy Eldridge. He met her while she was attending to her father who had been imprisoned for debt. Temple had been so taken by the father's sad tale and Lucy's stalwart devotion, that he had paid off Eldridge's debts and married Lucy, thereby thwarting his father's plans to have him marry the beautiful, and wealthy (but deplorably shallow) Miss Weatherby. Instead, Temple had settled Lucy and her father in a small rural cottage and, especially when Charlotte arrived, pursued a life of domestic bliss.

Affectionate and loyal, Charlotte was everything parents devoted to religion, home, and duty could wish. To finish her education, the Temples sent her to a highly respectable boarding school in Chichester, where she came under the influence of one of her teachers, an unscrupulous and lascivious but amiable and superficially proper Frenchwoman, Mademoiselle La Rue. Mlle. La Rue had been clandestinely meeting a young man at night in the garden adjoining the boarding school, and on one of these forays, since the young man wanted to bring a friend, she persuaded her favorite pupil, Charlotte, to accompany her. Charlotte went innocently enough, unaware of the danger to her honor and reputation, thinking instead of the delight in an outdoor picnic and in meeting a young man of fashion whom Mlle. La Rue called her cousin.

However, before this rendezvous another young man accosted them in the garden. He was Lieutenant John Montraville, a British officer awaiting orders that would send him overseas to war against the American rebels. He had seen Charlotte a few days before walking home from church with a group of girls from Madame Du Pont's boarding school and had recognized her as a girl he had seen at a ball in Portsmouth two years before. Her newly matured beauty but still preserved innocence had aroused his interest in her, but all his efforts to meet her had been thwarted until he found her walking with her companion in the garden.

Montraville seized the opportunity of the chance meeting to win the support of Mlle. La Rue (a bribe helped) and to press a love note into Charlotte's hand. When Charlotte returned to her room, she realized that the young lieutenant had been much too forward and that she should report their meeting and give his note, unread, to Madame Du Pont. But Mlle. La Rue played on Charlotte's sympathies by pointing out that Madame Du Pont would discharge her if she learned of their nightime journey and that would be an unkind return for all the special favors she had given her favorite pupil.

Charlotte was moved by Mlle. La Rue's guile and also by her own attraction to the handsome officer. She kept their meeting a secret and, in fact, agreed to a number of others. Each meeting she resolved would be her last, and she only convinced herself to go on the basis that it would be an occasion for her to convince Montraville that they should meet no more. Montraville, however, also played on Charlotte's sympathies, reminding her that he was scheduled for battle and might very well be killed, even suggesting that he would rush to battle, like a Roman to his own sword, if he thought Charlotte were rejecting him. Montraville was aided in his wooing, not only by Mlle. La Rue, but also by a fellow officer, and more thoroughgoing roué, Belcourt, who kept Mlle. La Rue entertained and discreetly out of the way. The example of Belcourt's and La Rue's relationship, in fact, was instrumental in finally persuading Charlotte to elope with Montraville first to Portsmouth and then to America.

The day they were to elope also happened to be the day Charlotte's parents had planned a surprise birthday party for her, in part as a reward for her being such a dutiful daughter. When Charlotte learned of the party, she repented of her earlier decision, but once again agreed to keep her appointment only to reject Montraville in person. However, the confrontation with Montraville turned out to be more than Charlotte could handle. In a moment of giddy confusion over the conflict of love and duty, she fainted and was literally carried away. Before they were at sea, Charlotte tried once to write her parents and ask for their under-standing and forgiveness, but the letter was intercepted by Montraville, and thus Charlotte was left entirely at the mercy of her lover.

On the journey to America Montraville remained attentive to Charlotte and this, with the added thought that she would eventually hear from her family and friends, kept Charlotte generally cheerful, despite her troubled conscience and seasickness. Mlle. La Rue, however, soon realized that Belcourt intended neither to marry or otherwise to support her, so she interested herself in another pas-senger, Colonel Crayton. Wealthy, widowed, and much traveled, Crayton fancied all things foreign, was generally open and trusting in manner, and, therefore, be-came an easy mark for the clever Mlle. La Rue. She saw in him a chance to secure both the means and the necessary cloak of propriety for a life of pleasure. Their engagement shocked Charlotte into realizing the precariousness of her own situation, since in so short a time she had seen Belcourt's "promise" forgotten. Belcourt, in fact, had begun to plot taking Montraville's place with Charlotte when the opportunity should arise.

At their arrival in New York, then, Charlotte's and Mlle. La Rue's statuses had somewhat reversed. Mlle. La Rue soon became Mrs. Crayton, while Charlotte was set up as a mistress in a modest, rented house just outside New York. With a few servants to care for her, Charlotte was reasonably comfortable, but not at all content. The facts of her situation weighed on her conscience and also began to frighten her. Military duties and flagging interest kept Montraville away much of the time, and this combined with not hearing from her family made her feel lonely and abandoned. About this time Montraville met and fell in love with fashionable and wealthy Julia Franklin. Troubled by his relationship with Char-lotte he thought himself unworthy of Julia, but continued to see more of her and less of Charlotte anyway. Belcourt now recognized the opportunity to wedge Charlotte away from Montraville and began to spend more time with her while Montraville was absent.

Charlotte, meanwhile, had aroused the sympathies of Crayton's daughter, Mrs. Beauchamp, who had seen and pitied Charlotte when she had met her on the dock in New York and heard about her situation with Montraville. Discovering that they were also neighbors, Mrs. Beauchamp risked possible censure and de-vised a way to befriend Charlotte. On Mrs. Beauchamp's advice Charlotte wrote to her parents asking their forgiveness and revealing not only her whereabout but that she was now pregnant.

This letter was the only message to get through, for Belcourt had become much more aggressive in his pursuit of Charlotte and had bribed one of the ser-vants into intercepting all her mail for him. He also helped Montraville ease his conscience about Charlotte by telling him that she had been unfaithful, entertain-ing various men, including himself, while Montraville had been away. The tie was finally severed when Montraville visited Charlotte unannounced and discovered Belcourt lying beside Charlotte in bed. In fact, Belcourt had known of

Montraville's visit and had sneaked in beside Charlotte, while she was sleeping, but Montraville was all too ready to believe what he saw and now felt relieved of his moral obligation to Charlotte. He married Julia Franklin, suffering in conscience only so far as to try to provide continued support for Charlotte and the soon to be born child, whoever its father might have been.

With Montraville's withdrawal, Charlotte's doom was sealed. The money for her support was entrusted to Belcourt, who kept it for himself. Soon Charlotte's health failed and with it her looks, so that Belcourt was easily diverted by a nearby farmer's daughter and forgot about Charlotte altogether. Even Mrs. Beauchamp was away so that when the landlady came and demanded Charlotte either pay or leave, Charlotte had no one to turn to for help and was forced to quit the house on a stormy, wintry night. She headed for New York hoping to find at least temporary sanctuary with Mrs. Crayton, but her former companion refused even to acknowledge their acquaintance. Mrs. Crayton has made good on her plans to live extravagantly and licentiously under the cloak of marriage. She had deceived her husband about her past and so viewed Charlotte's sudden appearance as a threat to the advantage she now enjoyed. One of her servants, however, pitied Charlotte and took her to his home where she soon gave birth to a daughter and died after a few days.

In the last days and hours before Charlotte's death, Mrs. Beauchamp found her and provided some comfort. Having received the one letter, Charlotte's father was also at her death bed to assure her of her family's forgiveness and to take custody of her child. Montraville happened upon the funeral and ultimately salvaged some honor, first by finding and killing Belcourt for his perfidy, and then by the evidences of his sorrow in yearly visits to her grave site. Finally, years later, Mrs. Crayton showed up, abandoned, impoverished, sick and dying on Temple's doorstep. She admitted her role in both Charlotte's seduction and her death, but Temple helped her, nevertheless, until, within a week, she too died. The Temple's were left only with the happiness of raising their granddaughter and the hope that she would fare better than her unfortunate mother.

Critical Evaluation

A novel such as Susanna Rowson's *Charlotte Temple*, clumsily written, no longer much read, inevitably invites discussion of its place in history. Despite the novel's present obscurity, that place has several interesting aspects. The novel's immense popularity (more than two hundred editions to date) argues that it was a significant book. As a publishing phenomenon, this popularity registers the American reader's appetite for novels—and a rather sensational one at that—despite the vociferous objection of those, Puritan or otherwise, who held that novel reading was immoral. In that regard also, the novel may have served as evidence that a fiction writing career was possible in America if the right balance of titillation and piety were struck.

Yet, despite all that popularity, neither *Charlotte Temple*, nor Susanna Rowson have had any discernible impact on the ideas or art of America's more significant writers. The novel's place in literary history is more as a curiosity of the transitional early national period, when American literature was not yet fully "American," but not entirely European either. *Charlotte Temple*, like William Hill Brown's, *The Power of Sympathy*, Hannah Foster's, *The Coquette*, and a few others, is a partially Americanized *Clarissa*, representing from the English standpoint the end and decline of a tradition, but from the American standpoint a beginning. Thus, this very English, Richardsonian novel (first published in London, 1791, and then in Philadelphia, 1794) had its vogue only in America. Mrs. Rowson similarly lived and wrote novels in both England and America.

Charlotte Temple reflects this bi-polar world in its own setting, beginning as it does in England, climaxing in New York during the Revolution, and then anticlimaxing back across the Atlantic. The use of native materials by an American author in the 1790's is, of course, a significant development, but those materials are rather sparse, little more than place names. Montraville and Belcourt are British officers, fighting the American rebels, but there are no battle scenes, no descriptions of the effects of war, no discussions of the issues of the war. It may be that some concrete images were evoked for American readers in the eighteenth or early nineteenth centuries, aware of the real lives (Charlotte Stanley, granddaughter of the Earl of Derby and John Montrésor, a noted soldier and engineer) and of the grave site in Trinity Churchyard, New York, bearing Charlotte Temple's name. But, within the text, there is quite simply little sense of time or place, whether it be England or America, the Temple's cottage, Madame Du Pont's boarding school, on board the ship, in Charlotte's rented love nest, or the servant's quarters where she dies.

Some other features of the novel, therefore, better explain its native quality, its appeal to American readers, and its place in literary history. For one, the novel depicts a daughter of the English aristocracy falling prey to a British officer. This gives the novel's didactic purpose of saving "the young and thoughtless of the fair sex" from the "errors which ruined poor Charlotte" a patriotic tinge. The preaching for the virtues of domesticity, religion, and duty is presented in a context where the guilty, including Charlotte, are all Europeans, and the seducers in particular are the recently defeated enemy.

Looked at in this way, however, the meanings associated with the New World within the novel's moral frame become interestingly complex, prefiguring themes that will recur throughout American literature. America is first mentioned as a place of danger and Montraville repeatedly uses the threat of death there to arouse Charlotte's sympathies. Even more it is the place of escape, of freedom from restraint, of separation from home, of alienation and isolation. Put baldly, to go to America (or as Huck Finn would later say to "light out for the territories") is to revolt, and indeed, however meekly and unconsciously, Charlotte revolts from the authority of her parents, Mlle. La Rue revolts from the entrapment in

Madame Du Pont's boarding school, and Montraville and Belcourt revolt from the morality necessary to hold society together. Even Henry Temple, it should be noted, has revolted from his father and against the meretricious values of a decadent aristocracy, choosing a lifestyle that, while still in England, is clearly pastoral. Also, that revolt is for a time, at least, devilishly attractive. Of course, Rowson in no way justifies sensuality; her ideal virtue, "lovely Virgin," is attended by the "handmaids . . . *Humility, Filial Piety, Conjugal Affection, Industry,* and *Benevolence*" and "her name is *Content.*" But, the chief villainy of the work is less sensuality than social sins: deceit of friends, false education, and failure of charity.

In short, *Charlotte Temple* reflects ambivalences Americans have long and early felt about themselves and their experiences, their separation from England, the promise as well as the dangers of freedom and renewal. In Rowson's novel these issues are largely implicit, beneath the surface morality of virtue rewarded and vice punished. Her only obviously mixed feelings are whether or not to feel sorry for Charlotte and thereby seem to condone her actions. Nevertheless, the presence of these issues helps explain what is American about the novel and perhaps a little more why it has been so popular.

Bibliography

Fiedler, Leslie A. *Love and Death in the American Novel.* New York: Stein and Day, 1966, pp. 93–98.

Parker, P.L. "*Charlotte Temple*: America's First Best Seller," in *Studies in Short Fiction.* XIII (Fall, 1976), pp. 518–520.

Sargent, M.E. "Susanna Rowson," in *Medford Historical Review.* (April, 1904), n.p.

Spiller, Robert. *Literary History of the United States.* New York: Macmillan, 1963, pp. 177–178.

Vail, R.W.G. "Foreword: Susanna Haswell Rowson, Author of *Charlotte Temple*: Bibliographical Study," in *American Antiquarian Society Proceedings.* XLII (1932), pp. 62–68.

Van Doren, Carl. *American Novel.* New York: Macmillan, 1922, pp. 7–8.

Wagenknecht, Edward C. *Cavalcade of the American Novel.* New York: Holt, 1952, pp. 4–5.

Whittier, John Greenleaf. "Susanna Rowson," in *Whittier on Writers and Writing.* Syracuse, N.Y.: Syracuse University Press, 1950, pp. 15–18.

WILLIAM GILMORE SIMMS

Born: Charleston, South Carolina (April 17, 1806)
Died: Charleston (June 11, 1870)

Principal Works

NOVELS: *Guy Rivers*, 1834; *The Partisan*, 1835; *The Yemassee*, 1835; *Mellichampe*, 1836; *Pelayo*, 1838; *Richard Hurdis*, 1838; *The Damsel of Darien*, 1839; *The Border Beagles*, 1840; *The Kinsmen*, 1841 (*The Scout*, 1854); *Beauchampe*, 1842; *Helen Halsey*, 1845; *Count Julian*, 1845; *Katherine Walton*, 1851; *The Golden Christmas*, 1852; *As Good as A Comedy*, 1852; *Vasconselors*, 1853; *The Sword and Distaff*, 1853 (*Woodcraft*, 1854); *The Forayers*, 1855; *Eutaw*, 1856; *Charlemont*, 1856; *The Cassique of Kiawah*, 1859.

SHORT STORIES: *The Wigwam and the Cabin*, 1845–1846.

HISTORY: *A History of South Carolina*, 1840; *South Carolina in the Revolution*, 1854.

POEM: *Atalantis*, 1832.

William Gilmore Simms, born in Charleston, South Carolina, on April 17, 1806, was known in his lifetime as a novelist, short story writer, poet, historian, and journalist; but his reputation rests today on his novels.

Simms's childhood was an unusual one. His mother died while he was still an infant, and his father left the baby in the care of its maternal grandmother. Under her care he seems to have had but casual schooling, but he read widely and listened intently to his grandmother's stories of the Revolutionary War as it had occurred in the South. In 1816, when the boy was ten years old, his father, a frontiersman who had gone westward toward the Mississippi River, paid a visit to Charleston, and eight years later the boy went to visit his father on his plantation in what is now Mississippi. Upon his return to Charleston after that visit Simms published some poems, most of them with a Byronic flavor. In 1828 he entered upon the editorship of a short-lived magazine entitled *The Tablet*. After its failure he became editor of the Charleston *City Guzette*, which opposed the election of John C. Calhoun. Because of the political animosity he incurred as a result, plus the deaths of his wife, grandmother, and father, Simms left for the North, where he found friends and a future.

Some early work was published shortly after he left Charleston, but his first important success came with the publication of *Guy Rivers* in 1834. A story of gold-mining in northern Georgia, the novel, packed with action, is a romantic piece of writing, but one with a realistic, native theme. His next work was *The Partisan*, which was probably inspired by his grandmother's accounts of the Revolutionary War. In the same year appeared *The Yemassee*, destined to remain his most popular book. It is an exciting tale of early days in South Carolina, especially important because of the realistic portrayal of the Indians. Indeed Simms's portrayal of the Indians has been adjudged by scholars to be essentially better than the more popular, idealized pictures given by James Fenimore Cooper in his novels. Simms's realism was a little too much for his own day. Two of his novels, *Beauchampe* and *Charlemont*, both about a celebrated Kentucky murder case, were considered in his lifetime too realistic for what was then called good taste, although they seem tame enough for today.

Following his second marriage in 1836, Simms's life began to change. Filling the position of a wealthy planter on his wife's plantation and rearing a family of fifteen children made him an outstanding spokesman for the Southern notion of Greek democracy in America, a concept which implied a defense of slavery. Simms's theories on slavery were found in his *History of South Carolina.* His viewpoint and his reputation as an author made him a great man in the South, but they caused unpopularity in the North. While his works were in vogue before the Civil War, they were neglected afterward. All Simms's important writing came before that war, for while the war ruined his reputation in the North, it also destroyed his home and way of life in the South.

Simms's reputation has been slow in returning. For a half century his books were out of print, except for *The Yemassee.* A frequent comparison of Simms to Cooper as a novelist generally is without critical foundation and really unfair to Simms. His novels are vigorous, and the materials he used and the realism he employed were his own. He wrote about South Carolina during the eighteenth century and about the pre-Civil War frontier, then east of the Mississippi River. He celebrated little-known elements of American history and culture. In three kinds of fiction he excelled: the border romance, of which *Guy Rivers* is his best; the novel of Indian warfare, of which *the Yemassee* is a classic; and the romance about the American Revolution, of which *The Partisan* is a good example. In addition to fiction, poetry and history, Simms also wrote biographies of Francis Marion, Captain John Smith, and Nathaniel Greene.

Simms died in Charleston, June 11, 1870.

Bibliography

The Works of William Gilmore Simms, 20 vols., 1853–1866 is not complete. *The Letters of William Gilmore Simms* have been edited by Mary C. Simms Oliphant, Alfred T. Odell, and T. C. D. Eaves, 5 vols., 1952–1956. The standard biography is William P. Trent, *William Gilmore Simms*, 1892. Alexander Cowie's 1937 edition of *The Yemassee* includes an introduction and an excellent bibliography. Outstanding studies of Simms appear in Vernon L. Parrington, *Main Currents in American Thought*, Vol. II, 1927; Van Wyck Brooks, *The World of Washington Irving*, 1944; and Jay B. Hubbell, *The South in American Literature, 1607–1900*, 1954, the latter the leading work on the subject of Southern literature. See further E. W. Parks, *William Gilmore Simms as Literary Critic*, 1961; and J. V. Ridgely, *William Gilmore Simms*, 1962.

THE YEMASSEE

Type of work: Novel
Author: William Gilmore Simms (1806–1870)
Type of plot: Historical romance
Time of plot: Early eighteenth century
Locale: South Carolina
First published: 1835

The Yemassee *tells a fast-moving story of adventure and love during the days of Indian warfare in Colonial South Carolina. Simms is most effective in his characterization of the Indians, who are neither idealized nor despised, but shown as human beings fated by race to suffer defeat at the hands of the whites.*

Principal Characters

Gabriel Harrison (Governor Charles Craven), a young man of commanding presence and gay, worldly manner. A stranger looked on with suspicion by some of the South Carolina frontiersmen, he wins them over by his valiant leadership in defending the colony against the Yemassee uprising. He then reveals that he is the new Governor of the province in disguise.

Parson Matthews, who dislikes Harrison until won over by his heroism. Matthews' insistence on the friendliness of the Indians, in spite of Harrison's warnings, results in his and his daughter's capture and in their subsequent rescue by Harrison.

Bess Matthews, the parson's daughter, in love with and loved by Harrison. The parson finally gives permission for their marriage.

Hector, Harrison's devoted Negro slave and constant companion. After undergoing various ordeals on behalf of or with his master, he refuses Harrison's offer to give him his freedom.

Sanutee, the last great Yemassee chief. Proud, and suspicious of the increasing encroachments of the colonists upon

Yemassee territory, he rouses his people to cast out the land-selling chiefs and to make war on the settlers. At last he is killed in battle.

Occonestoga, Sanutee's son. A drunkard, he is friendly with the whites, an alliance which forces him to flee his tribe. He saves Bess Matthews' life and is consequently befriended by Harrison. Returning to the Indian stronghold to spy for Harrison, he is discovered by his father.

Matiwan, Sanutee's wife, torn between loyalty to her husband and devotion to her son. Finally, to prevent the carrying out of Sanutee's order that Occonestoga have the tribal mark cut from his skin and be executed, she herself kills her son.

Hugh Grayson, a rival of Harrison for the affections of Bess Matthews. He, too, is finally won to friendship by Harrison's bravery. After revealing himself as the Governor, Harrison makes Hugh Grayson commander of the garrison forces.

Walter Grayson, Hugh's brother, an honorable young farmer.

Dick Chorley, a sailor whom Harrison discovers to be a Spanish agent come to arm the Indians against the English settlers.

Ishiagaska, another Yemassee chief.

Enoree Mattee, an Indian prophet who aids Sanutee in rousing his people against the settlers.

Granger, a trader.

Mrs. Granger, his brave and quick-witted wife.

Dugdale, Harrison's strong and faithful dog.

The Story

The English settlers, who at first had to accept aid from the Yemassee Indians when the white men landed on the South Carolina shores, had become quite powerful by 1715. No longer did they have to be careful not to offend the Indians; instead, they continually set up farms on the wrong side of the boundary lines between white and Indian territory. Sanutee, one of the Yemassee chiefs, had become suspicious of the colonists; he was afraid that they would soon take over all the Yemassee land. In order to keep them from occupying Indian territory, he had made treaties with other tribes and with the Spanish, who were willing to help the Indians defeat the English. Sanutee's life was made unhappy by his son, Occonestoga, who had been tempted by liquor to become a close friend of the whites. Sanutee was too proud of his ancestry and his position to call a drunkard his son, and it was only by constant pleas that his wife, Matiwan, was able to keep him from completely disowning Occonestoga.

One of the recent settlers was Gabriel Harrison, a strange young man whose commanding presence and jolly manner made him both admired and disliked. Among those who liked him was Bess Matthews, the daughter of the old parson, and Walter Grayson, an honorable young farmer. Parson Matthews disliked Harrison because he was too gay and worldly in his manner, and Walter's brother, Hugh, disliked Harrison because he was also an admirer of Bess. Harrison had brought with him a fine Negro slave named Hector, who was his constant companion, and a strong and faithful dog named Dugdale. With these two companions Harrison wandered about the district.

One day in the forest Harrison came upon Sanutee fighting with a stranger over the carcass of a deer. He arrived in time to save Sanutee's life, but the proud Indian expressed no gratitude. Harrison learned that Sanutee's opponent was a sailor named Dick Chorley, who had recently arrived on the coast. Although Chorley said that he had come to trade, Harrison rightly suspected that he was really a Spanish agent who had come to arm the Indians against the English. Harrison sent Hector to spy on Chorley and Sanutee, who had been joined by Ishiagaska, another Yemassee chief.

Hector, hiding in the brush, overheard Chorley's declaration that he had come to South Carolina to arm the Indians. Displaying the wampum belt of an Indian treaty, he asked the Yemassee tribe to join the tribes who were willing to fight the English. Before Hector could return to tell Harrison what he had learned, the slave was captured and taken aboard Chorley's ship.

Harrison guessed what had become of Hector. He found Chorley in the parson's cabin and by threats forced the seaman to sign an order freeing Hector. His action angered the parson, who refused to suspect Chorley of treason. He denied Harrison the right to wed his daughter Bess.

In the meanwhile the Yemassee chiefs were called to a council and asked to sell more land to the English. Most of the chiefs were willing to sell, but Sanutee, who arrived late at the meeting, made a stirring speech against the sale. Interrupted by his drunken son, the old Yemassee almost killed Occonestoga. When he heard that the chiefs intended to sell the land over his protests, Sanutee left the meeting and went to arouse the people against their chiefs. With the aid of an Indian prophet named Enoree Mattee, he so infuriated the crowd that they repudiated the other chiefs and punished them by having the tribal mark cut from their skins, so that they became outcasts from the tribe. Only Occonestoga escaped this punishment.

Occonestoga hid in the woods. One day he saved Bess Matthews' life by killing a rattlesnake that was about to strike her. For his deed Harrison rewarded the young Yemassee with his friendship. Soon afterward he sent Occonestoga back to the Indian stronghold to learn what the Indians were planning. Occonestoga secretly made his way to his mother, Matiwan, who hid him in her tent. By chance Sanutee discovered the boy and ordered that he be killed after having the tribal mark cut from his skin. In desperation, Matiwan killed her son before the sentence could be carried out, for the tribal mark could not be cut from a dead man.

Harrison, realizing that Sanutee was about to lead the Indians against the whites, did his best to get all the settlers to go to the blockhouse for protection. Parson Matthews insisted that the Indians had never been more friendly, and he refused to leave his cabin. Harrison, while scouting in the woods, was captured by Indians. With the aid of Matiwan, who had heard of his kindness to her dead son, he escaped. In his attempt to save Bess before the Indians could seize her, he was almost recaptured. Hector and his dog Dugdale arrived just in time to save him.

Meanwhile Chorley had led a party of Indians and sailors to the parson's cabin and had captured both Bess and her father. Harrison was able to rescue them and lead them to the blockhouse before the Indian attack began. A furious struggle took place, with even the women aiding in the fight to hold off the Indians. Both the Grayson brothers became friendly with Harrison because of the bravery he had shown in saving their families, and together they fought valiantly to save the community. At last the Indians were forced to withdraw.

Harrison made plans to send many of the settlers to Charleston, where they would be safe until troops could be mustered to defeat the Indians permanently. After winning the parson's permission to marry Bess, consent freely given after his heroic defense of the colony, Harrison astonished the group by announcing that he was in reality Charles Craven, the new governor of the province. He had come to the region in disguise so that he could see for himself the true state of affairs on the frontier. He made Hugh Grayson commander of the garrison forces. When he offered Hector his freedom, the old slave refused to be parted from his kind master.

In Charleston, Craven raised a considerable fighting force and returned to battle with the Yemassee Indians on the banks of the Salkehatchie River. When the Indians attacked the camp of the white men, the governor's troops, firing from ambush, shot them down. Sanutee fell, mortally wounded, and Craven saw Matiwan run upon the field and fall weeping by her husband's body. The last of the Yemassee braves was dead.

Critical Evaluation

In early American frontier novels the Indian was inevitably characterized in one of two ways, either as a "noble savage," a natural primitive untainted by civilization's corrupting influences, or, more commonly, a savage barbarian who took pleasure in cruelty and violence toward innocent white settlers. Even America's most famous author of historical romances, James Fenimore Cooper, divided his Indians into absolutely "good" and "bad" types and developed his novels accordingly. Perhaps only William Gilmore Simms in *The Yemassee* succeeded in creating believable, human Indians with mixed qualities, natures, and potentials; and that is the primary reason why *The Yemassee,* in spite of severe artistic flaws, must be acknowledged as one of the best nineteenth century frontier novels.

Through the first third of the book, the action is seen primarily from the Indian viewpoint. Simms carefully describes the Yemassee tribe as they plan and attempt to execute an uprising against the white settlers. Their motives, however, spring not from innate hostility or cruelty, but from a realization that the powers and needs of the white man make the conflict—and their own ultimate defeat—inevitable. Thus, Simms imports to the Yemassee a kind of doomed, almost tragic grandeur.

But it is in his presentation of the intimate life of the Indian that Simms is most impressive. Unlike Cooper, Simms describes the natives in their own environment and shows their daily routines, tribal mores, rituals, and politics in minute, careful detail. This Indian culture is presented with respect and individual tribe members are presented as fallible, but admirable human beings.

The most vivid portraits are those of Chief Sanutee, his wife, and their son. Sanutee is a proud, intelligent, brave, but flawed leader, who understands and accepts the unavoidable dissolution of his tribe, but who, nevertheless, inspires his men to heroic resistance. His wife, Matiwan, shares her husband's courage and insight, but her compassion elevates her above racial identity to become a kind of "Earth Mother" figure. Their son, Occonestoga, contaminated by contact with the white man's whiskey and promises, finally finds his courage and nobility in a time of crisis, although too late to salvage his tribal status. Few scenes in nineteenth century fiction are as powerful as the one in which, during the ritual that is to strip Occonestoga of his tribal identity, Matiwan kills her own son before the assembled Indians to save his honor and dignity.

Had Simms been able to sustain the insights and intensity of the first third of the book, *The Yemassee* might have been a great novel. But, unfortunately, once the focus of the novel shifts to the white man's world, the characters, both Indians and whites, become stock characters, and the novel degenerates into a clichéd chase-capture-escape romance.

Simms's sympathetic treatment of the Indians, however, does not mean that he considered them the white man's equal. Even Sanutee "well knew that the superior must necessarily be the ruin of the race which is inferior." As a staunch upholder of the Southern position in the pre-Civil War South, Simms firmly believed in racial superiority and what he and others called an "organic society." In Simms's view the Indian was doomed because he was an inferior race and culture and, unlike the black, could not be fit into a useful place in the white man's world. However tragic and seemingly unjust the displacement or destruction of the red man might be, it was, to Simms, the necessary price that had to be paid in order to establish the superior society.

Bibliography

Cecil, L.M.   "Symbolic Pattern in *The Yemassee*," in *American Literature*. XXXV (January, 1964), pp. 510–514.

Erskine, John.   "William Gilmore Simms," in *Leading American Novelists*. New York: Holt, 1910, pp. 142–149.

Gendron, D.   "Source for Simms' *Yemassee*," in *American Literature*. XLVIII (November, 1976), pp. 368–370.

Holman, C.H.   "Hiawatha Meter in *Yemassee*," in *Modern Language Notes*. LXVII (June, 1952), pp. 418–419.

Parks, Edd Winfield.   *William Gilmore Simms as Literary Critic*. Athens: University of Georgia Press, 1961, pp. 11–12.

Shelton, A.J.   "African Realistic Commentary on Culture Hierarchy and Racistic Sentimentalism in *The Yemassee*," in *Phylon*. XXV (Spring, 1964), pp. 72–78.

Trent, William P.   *William Gilmore Simms*. New York: Haskell House, 1968, pp. 89–94.

Van Doren, Carl.   *The American Novel*. New York: Macmillan, 1922, pp. 60–66.

Wagenknecht, Edward.   *Cavalcade of the American Novel.* New York: Holt, 1952, pp. 33–37.

Wakelyn, Jon L.   *The Politics of a Literary Man: William Gilmore Simms.* Westport, Conn.: Greenwood Press, 1973, pp. 58–60.

HARRIET BEECHER STOWE

Born: Litchfield, Connecticut (June 14, 1811)
Died: Hartford, Connecticut (July 1, 1896)

Principal Works

NOVELS: *Uncle Tom's Cabin, or Life Among the Lowly*, 1852; *Dred: A Tale of the Great Dismal Swamp*, 1856; *The Minister's Wooing*, 1859; *The Pearl of Orr's Island*, 1862; *Agnes of Sorrento*, 1862; *Oldtown Folks*, 1869; *Pink and White Tyranny*, 1871; *My Wife and I*, 1871; *We and Our Neighbors*, 1875; *Poganuc People*, 1878.

SHORT STORIES AND SKETCHES: *Sam Lawson's Oldtown Fireside Stories*, 1872.

TRAVEL SKETCHES: *Sunny Memories of Foreign Lands*, 1854.

Harriet (Elizabeth) Beecher Stowe presented two regional backgrounds in her fiction: the South before the Civil War and the rural area of New England (Maine). Her novels of the antebellum South, were less authentic as well as more melodramatic in style. They were more popular, however, because of the timeliness of their theme and the antislavery feeling they created.

Born in Litchfield, Connecticut, on June 14, 1811, Harriet Elizabeth Beecher was the daughter of a famous minister, the Reverend Lyman Beecher, and sister of Henry Ward Beecher. She was educated in the school of her older sister Catherine, who encouraged her inclination to write. The family moved to Cincinnati when Harriet was eighteen. There she married Calvin Ellis Stowe, a professor in the Lane Theological Seminary, and spent eighteen years across the river from a slave state.

Uncle Tom's Cabin, written after the Stowes had moved to Maine, brought its author immediate worldwide fame. The literature of the period generally was influenced by a humanitarian impulse, and Mrs. Stowe had a ready audience for her romantic, even melodramatic history of the relations of a group of southern white families and their slaves. Of her material, she said, "Two nations, the types of two exactly opposite styles of existence, are here struggling; and from the intermingling of these two a third race has arisen, and the three are interlocked in wild and singular relations, that evolve every possible combination of romance." She added, "It is the moral bearings of the subject involved which have had the chief influence in its selection."

The success of her first novel encouraged Stowe to write a second on the same theme. The Dred Scott decision, stating that the Negro is not a human being, served as the catalyst for *Dred*, a novel in which her purpose of showing the general corruption of Christian principles brought on by slavery remained the same. Attacked by the critics, like the first novel, for artistic faults, mainly those of artificiality of language, contrived plotting, and sentimental characterizations, the book was less popular than its predecessor.

Turning next to her New England background, Stowe wrote four novels in a manner that did not increase her fame but did raise her position on the ground of literary merit. These novels were *The Minister's Wooing, The Pearl of Orr's Island, Oldtown Folks*, and *Poganuc People*. She also wrote society novels and in *Agnes of Sorrento* produced a didactic historical romance. Stowe was the first writer to use New England dialect for the sake of realism, becoming a pioneer in the tradition of Mary E. Wilkins Freeman and Sarah Orne Jewett. But her constant interpolation of Christian aphorisms and her use of routine plots kept these novels on the level of conventional nineteenth century romance and local color fiction. A daughter of the transcendental period, she was the most famous sentimental novelist of her time. She died at Hartford, Connecticut, July 1, 1896.

Bibliography

The collected edition is *The Writings of Harriet Beecher Stowe*, 16 vols., 1896. There are several authorized biographies: Annie A. Fields, *Life and Letters of Harriet Beecher Stowe*, 1897; Charles E. Stowe, *Life of Harriet Beecher Stowe: Compiled from her Journals and Letters*, 1899; and Charles E. Stowe and Lyman Beecher Stowe, *Harriet Beecher Stowe: The Story of her Life*, 1911. There are two recent biographies: Catherine Gilbertson, *Harriet Beecher Stowe*, 1937; and Forrest Wilson, *Crusader in Crinoline: The Life of Harriet Beecher Stowe*, 1941— the most valuable single work. A useful critical study is Charles H. Foster, *The Rungless Ladder: Harriet Beecher Stowe and New England Puritanism*, 1954. See also Constance Rourke, *Trumpets of Jubilee*, 1927; Jay B. Hubbell, *The South in American Literature*, 1954; John R. Adams, *Harriet Beecher Stowe*, 1963; and Alice C. Crozier, *The Novels of Harriet Beecher Stowe*, 1969.

OLDTOWN FOLKS

Type of work: Novel
Author: Harriet Beecher Stowe (1811–1896)
Type of plot: Social chronicle
Time of plot: Late eighteenth century
Locale: Massachusetts
First published: 1869

Drawing upon her husband's recollections of his Massachusetts village of Natick for her picture of Oldtown and its citizens, Stowe presents quiet reminiscences through her narrator Horace Holyoke. Rather than having a definite plot, the novel consists of vivid pictures of New England life shortly after the Revolutionary War with particular emphasis on changing social patterns and new religious movements which replaced the collapsed Puritan theocracy.

Principal Characters

Horace Holyoke, the narrator of this social chronicle of post-Revolutionary War New England. Born to poverty, he is ten when his schoolteacher father dies. Thanks to his abilities and his industry, and to the benefaction of friends, he attends Harvard and at last becomes a successful lawyer.

Harry Percival, Horace's closest friend. Harry's mother, brought to America after an elopement and secret marriage, is deserted by her English officer husband and dies, leaving Harry and his sister. They are brought up with Horace, and the boys attend Harvard together. Harry's legitimacy is established, and on the death of his father he goes to England as Sir Harry.

Eglantine (Tina) Percival, Harry's sister, who is loved by Horace. She marries another man, but after ten years of unhappy marriage he dies; two years later she and Horace are married.

Ellery Davenport, handsome and clever and a grandson of Jonathan Edwards. He holds a succession of diplomatic posts abroad, and so is able to aid Harry with

information about his father. Upon the death of his mad wife, he marries Tina; almost immediately a girl he had seduced appears with their child, whom Tina generously takes. Unprincipled and ambitious, Ellery is close to madness when he is killed in a political duel.

Esther Avery, the daughter of a minister, and a close friend of Tina, Harry, and Horace. She marries Harry and goes to England with him.

Mr. Lothrop, the minister and leading citizen of Oldtown. An Arminian in his views, he is sedate and sensible.

Mrs. Lothrop, his wife and Ellery's cousin. She is called "Lady Lothrop" by the people of Oldtown in a not disrespectful allusion to her aristocratic Boston background and her lingering adherence to the Church of England. She promises to provide for Harry's clothing and education.

Deacon Badger, Harry's grandfather, a leading farmer and miller of Oldtown, in whose home Horace lives after his father's death. An Arminian like Mr. Lothrop, he is also serene and affable.

Mrs. Badger, Horace's grandmother, who is a strict Puritan Calvinist. The Badgers take in Harry and Tina when they are found in a deserted house in which they took refuge. Harry stays on with them.

Susy Badger Holyoke, their daughter and Horace's mother. Her beauty faded because of hardship and poverty, she returns to her parents with her children after her husband's death.

Miss Mehitable Rossiter, the daughter of a former minister of Oldtown. Her life has been saddened by the disappearance some years before of her half sister. She adopts Tina.

Emily Rossiter, Mehitable's half sister, who appears with her child by Ellery shortly after his marriage to Tina. Tina uses her newly inherited fortune to establish the sisters in a house near Boston.

Sir Harry Percival, the worthless and dissipated father of Harry and Tina. Deserting his wife and children, he takes the wedding certificate and leaves a letter denying the legality of the marriage. Only a "younger son" at the time of the elopement, he succeeds to the family title and property.

Caleb (Old Crab) Smith, a miser, in whose house Harry's mother dies. He decides to keep the boy as a field hand.

Miss Asphyxia Smith, Caleb's sister. She takes in Tina, but the children are so harshly treated that they run away.

Bill Holyoke, Horace's older brother. He gives little promise as a scholar and so goes to work on the farm with his uncle Jacob.

Jacob Badger, the son of Mr. and Mrs. Badger, and Horace's uncle.

Sam Lawson, the village handyman and do-nothing. Called shiftless by some, he is Horace's chief comfort in the days after his father's death. Sam is never too busy to tell stories to the small boys or to take them hunting and fishing.

Keziah Badger, one of Mr. and Mrs. Badger's unmarried daughters. Romantic-minded, she has a reputation for homeliness in the village.

Lois Badger, Keziah's sister, who also is a spinster. She is sharp-tongued but warm-hearted.

Jonathan Rossiter, Miss Mehitable's half brother and master of the academy in Cloudland. Horace and Harry study there and live with him.

Mr. Avery, the minister at Cloudland and Esther's father. Tina boards with him.

Madame Kittery, Mrs. Lothrop's mother. The children are taken to visit her in Boston as a special Easter treat. She takes an interest in Horace and provides money to send him to Harvard.

Major Broad and
Squire Jones, friends who meet in the spacious Badger kitchen to discuss politics, religion, and philosophy.

The Story

Years later Horace Holyoke could remember Oldtown as he had known it when he was a boy, a quiet little village beside a tranquil river in Massachusetts. Surrounded by farmhouses deep in green hollows or high on windy hilltops, Oldtown consisted of one rustic street where stood the chief landmarks of the community. Among these were the meeting house with its classic white spire, the schoolhouse, the academy, a tavern, and the general store which was also the post-office.

As was common in those days, when New England was changing from a Puritan theocracy of little villages to a group of states under a federal government, the minister was still the leading citizen of the town. Mr. Lothrop, descended from generations of ministers, was an Arminian in his views, a sedate, sensible man whose sermons were examples of elegant Addisonian English. His wife, the daughter of an aristocratic family of Boston, had never forsaken the Church of England, and each Easter, Whitsunday, and Christmas she traveled in her coach to Boston to attend services in Christ Church. The people of Oldtown called her, without disrespect, Lady Lothrop.

To Oldtown the famous John Eliot had come as an apostle to the Indians. Three generations later Horace Holyoke's father had arrived in the town to teach in the local academy. There he fell in love with Susy Badger, one of the prettiest of his pupils, and married her. With marriage came responsibilities that dimmed forever his hopes of completing his education at Harvard College. When Horace was a little boy, his father's household was a place of penny-pinching hardships. The mother's beauty faded and the father's health, weakened by his attempts to provide for his family and to continue his studies, broke slowly. Horace was ten and his brother Bill a few years older when their father died of consumption.

Horace grieved as only a small boy can over his father's death. His chief comfort in those dark days came from Sam Lawson, the village handyman and do-nothing. Many people called Sam shiftless. A few pitied him because his wife was a scold. A man of good humor and garrulous tongue, he was never too busy to take small boys on fishing or hunting trips and to tell them stories.

After the funeral Mrs. Holyoke and her sons went to live with her father, Deacon Badger, a leading farmer and miller of Oldtown. He, like Mr. Lothrop, was an Arminian, and a serene, affable man. His wife, on the other hand, was a strict Puritan Calvinist, as fond of theological dispute as she was of cleanliness. Many were the arguments Horace overheard between the two, with scriptural texts flying thick and fast in proof of their contentions. Their unmarried daughters were named Keziah and Lois. Keziah was a romantic-minded woman with a reputation for homeliness throughout the township. Lois was like a chestnut bur, prickly and rough on the outside but soft and smooth within, as her tart tongue and warm-hearted nature proved.

Just as the life of the village revolved around the meeting house, so the center of the Badger household was the spacious, white-sanded kitchen. There the friends of the family gathered—Miss Mehitable Rossiter, daughter of a former minister of the town, Major Broad, Squire Jones, Sam Lawson, and others. There Horace listened to discussions on politics, religion, philosophy, and varied local lore that were to influence him throughout his lifetime. There, too, it was decided that his brother Bill, who gave little promise as a scholar, was to work on the farm with Jacob Badger, his mother's brother, while Horace would be allowed to continue his studies in the village school.

Horace grew into a dreamy, imaginative boy. Sometimes he felt that auras suggestive of good or evil surrounded people whom he met. Often he dreamed of a silent, lonely lad of about his own age. The boy began to fade from Horace's visions, however, after he found a friend in young Harry Percival.

Harry's father was an English officer, the younger son of a landed family, who had brought his wife to America near the end of the Revolutionary War. The wife was a curate's daughter whom the officer had married secretly after their elopement. The husband proved worthless and dissipated, and at last he deserted his wife and two children when his regiment returned to England. With him he took his wife's wedding certificate and left behind a letter denying the legality of their marriage. Friendless and without funds, the wife set out to walk to Boston with Harry and his sister Eglantine. On the way the mother fell sick and died in the house of miserly Caleb Smith, called by his neighbors Old Crab Smith. The farmer decided to keep the boy as a field hand. Eglantine, or Tina, as her brother called her, was taken in by Caleb's sister, Miss Asphyxia. The children were treated so harshly, however, that at last they decided to run away. After a night spent with an old Indian woman in the woods they found a refuge in the abandoned Dench mansion, reported to be haunted, on the outskirts of Oldtown. There Sam Lawson and some neighbors found the children after smoke had been seen coming from the chimney of the old house.

Harry and Tina were befriended by Deacon Badger and his wife. Within a few days it had been decided that Harry was to remain with the Badgers, an arrangement made even more satisfactory by Mrs. Lothrop's promise to provide for the boy's clothing and education. Miss Mehitable Rossiter, whose life had been saddened some years before by the mysterious disappearance of her young half-sister Emily, adopted Tina. From that time on Horace's, Harry's, and Tina's lives were to be closely intertwined.

As a special Easter treat, Mrs. Lothrop arranged to take the children to Boston with her. There they were entertained by Madame Kittery, Mrs. Lothrop's mother, and during their stay they met Ellery Davenport. Ellery, Mrs. Lothrop's cousin, had served in the Continental army and had held several diplomatic posts abroad. He was handsome and clever. A grandson of the great Jonathan Edwards, he had turned away from the church; his preceptors were the French philosophers of the day. Horace heard that his wife was mad.

Madame Kittery, a kindly old woman, took a great interest in Horace and listened sympathetically while he told of his father's death and of his own desire to attend college. Shortly after the party returned to Oldtown he was told that money would be provided so that he and Harry could go to Harvard together. Madame Kittery had become his benefactress.

Over Thanksgiving, Ellery Davenport and Mrs. Lothrop's sister Deborah came to Oldtown for a visit. At a harvest dance at the Badger homestead Ellery paid marked attentions to young Tina. He also promised Miss Mehitable that on his return to France he would look for her lost sister, who was believed to have fled to that country.

Tina became more beautiful as she grew older. When the schoolmaster fell in love with her, and Miss Mehitable's cousin Mordecai, hired as her tutor, also succumbed to her charms, it was finally decided that she, with Horace and Harry, would go to Cloudland, where Jonathan Rossiter, Miss Mehitable's half-brother, was master of the academy. The boys lived with Mr. Rossiter. Tina boarded with the minister, Mr. Avery, whose danghter Esther became the friend and companion of the three newcomcrs. Esthcr and Harry soon fell in love. Under Mr. Avery's influence Harry decided to study for the ministry. Horace dreamed of a career that would insure his future with Tina, whom he had loved since childhood.

When Ellery Davenport returned from England, he had important news for Harry. The boy's father was now Sir Harry Percival. Ellery had also secured possession of the stolen marriage certificate, which he gave to Mr. Lothrop for safekeeping.

Horace and Harry entered Harvard as sophomores. Tina, visiting with the Kitterys in Boston or staying with Miss Mehitable in Oldtown, wrote them letters that were playful, almost mocking in tone. Horace began to worry about Ellery Davenport's influence on the girl. A short time later he heard that Ellery's insane wife had died. Then word came that Harry's father had died in England. Harry was now Sir Harry Percival. The two friends returned to Oldtown for the spring vacation, to learn on their arrival that Tina was engaged to marry Ellery. Horace, reflecting wryly on the contrast between his own humble position and the high estate to which his friends had been lifted, concealed with stubborn pride the deep hurt he felt.

Because Ellery was soon to return to the embassy in London, preparations for the wedding were hurried. After the ceremony Ellery and his bride planned to spend a short time, before sailing, in the reconditioned Dench mansion. When they arrived, they found a woman dressed in black waiting for them in the parlor of the old house. The caller was Emily Rossiter, whom Ellery had seduced and taken away from her family years before. Emily, spurning the settlement he had provided for her, had followed him to America. To her horror, Tina learned also that he was the father of the unfortunate woman's child.

The course Tina took was both noble and tragic. In spite of the wrong Ellery had done, both to Emily and to his bride, Tina refused to desert him. Instead, she used the fortune she had inherited from her father to establish Miss Mehitable and her sister in a house near Boston. The child she took with her to England when she went there with Ellery.

After his graduation Harry married Esther Avery and left for England with his bride. At first he planned to return shortly to America, but as time passed it became apparent that his interests lay abroad and that he intended to make his home there. Horace felt that he had been left alone in the world.

Eight years went by before Ellery and Tina returned to make their home near Boston. By that time Tina had grown faded and worn. Horace, a successful lawyer, saw her and her husband frequently; as a sympathetic spectator he watched the course of Ellery's reckless and unprincipled career, which, fed by his ambition, was to bring him close to madness. Ten years after his marriage Ellery was killed in a political duel.

Two more years passed before Horace and Tina were married. Their wedding journey took them to England to see Harry and Esther. Later, as the years came and went softly, Horace and his wife often visited Oldtown and there renewed the familiar associations of earlier days.

Critical Evaluation

Harriet Beecher Stowe's popular reputation rests on *Uncle Tom's Cabin* but her other novels, especially *Oldtown Folks,* also deserve attention for their literary qualities as distinct from the propagandistic aspects of her abolitionist novel. Indeed, *Oldtown Folks* is a fine example of realistic literature with a regional flavor, in its way a herald of such later works as Edgar Lee Masters' *Spoon River Anthology* and the regional novels of Sarah Orne Jewett.

In *Oldtown Folks,* Stowe recreates the ambience of delicately balanced life in a small New England town through her narrator Horace Holyoke. Three quite distinct religious persuasions, for example, coexisted in Oldtown, if not always amicably at least civilly. Yet the differences between strict, predestination Calvinists and potential-salvation-for-all Arminians could hardly be more vivid, while the Church of England (later Episcopalian) affiliation of "Lady" Lothrop merely added leaven to an already fermenting mix—and this at a time when and in a place where religious views dominated politics and society. Still, the accommodation achieved among residents of Oldtown, however uneasy, could well be a model for modern times, an exemplar of tolerance from an age of intolerance to twentieth century intolerances much in need of modification. Stowe's reminiscence—heavily reliant on her husband's New England experiences—is thus a timely study despite its seemingly antique air.

The only flaw in an otherwise admirably realistic novel is Stowe's sentimentality: her irresistible urge to marry Horace and Tina at the end of the novel—a "lived happily ever after" type of ending for two much-beleaguered people, and an inconsistency in an otherwise stark portrayal of real life. Even then, such a weakness is not anomalous, given Stowe's background. Reared by a strict Calvinist father, she was also strongly influenced by the liberal beliefs of her uncle, Samuel Foote. Under these ambivalent circumstances, Stowe ultimately abandoned her father's Calvinism without embracing her uncle's liberalism. Consequently, her loyalties and allegiances were divided, and that division is reflected in her resolution of the novel.

Bibliography

Adams, John R.   *Harriet Beecher Stowe.* New York: Twayne, 1963, pp. 93–95, 101–102.

Cowie, Alexander.   "Harriet Beecher Stowe," in *The Rise of the American Novel.* New York: American Book, 1948, pp. 456–457, 459–460.

Crozier, Alice C.   *The Novels of Harriet Beecher Stowe.* New York: Oxford University Press, 1969, pp. 102–103, 108–109, 111–114, 116, 125–128, 141–143.

Erskine, John.   "Harriet Beecher Stowe," in his *Leading American Novelists.* New York: Holt, 1910, pp. 320–321.

Foster, Charles H.   *The Rungless Ladder: Harriet Beecher Stowe and New England Puritanism.* Durham, N.C.: Duke University Press, 1954, pp. 161–165, 171–174, 176–182.

Gilbertson, Catherine.   *Harriet Beecher Stowe.* New York: Appleton-Century, 1937, pp. 248–259.

May, Henry F.   "Introduction," in *Oldtown Folks.* Cambridge, Mass.: Harvard University Press, 1966, pp. 3–43.

Parrington, Vernon.   "Harriet Beecher Stowe, A Daughter of Puritanism," in *Main Currents in American Thought,* Volume II. New York: Harcourt, Brace, 1927, pp. 371–374.

Rourke, Constance M.   "Harriet Beecher Stowe," in her *Trumpets of Jubilee.* New York: Harcourt, Brace, 1927, pp. 89–148.

Suckow, Ruth.   "An Almost Lost American Classic," in *College English.* XIV (March, 1953), pp. 314–325.

Wagenknecht, Edward.   *Harriet Beecher Stowe: The Known and the Unknown.* New York: Oxford University Press, 1965, pp. 17–18, 101–102, 111–112, 163–164.

Wendell, Barrett.   *A Literary History of America.* New York: Scribner's, 1925, pp. 352–356.

Wilson, Robert Forrest.   *Crusader in Crinoline: The Life of Harriet Beecher Stowe.* Philadelphia: Lippincott, 1941, pp. 529–531.

UNCLE TOM'S CABIN

Type of work: Novel
Author: Harriet Beecher Stowe (1811–1896)
Type of plot: Sentimental romance
Time of plot: Mid-nineteenth century
Locale: Kentucky and Mississippi
First published: 1852

A sentimental but powerful document in the controversy over slavery, Uncle Tom's Cabin, or, Life Among the Lowly *is a novel whose political and humanitarian pleading greatly influenced the cause for abolitionism.*

Principal Characters

Uncle Tom, a Negro slave. Good and unrebellious, he is sold by his owner. After serving a second kind but improvident master, he comes under the ownership of brutal Simon Legree and dies as a result of his beatings.

Eliza, a slave. Learning that her child is about to be sold away along with Tom, she takes the child and runs away, crossing the Ohio River by leaping from floating ice cake to floating ice cake.

George Harris, her husband, a slave on a neighboring plantation. He too escapes, passing as a Spaniard, and reaches Ohio, where he joins his wife and child. Together they go to freedom in Canada.

Harry, the child of Eliza and George.

Mr. Shelby, the original owner of Eliza, Harry, and Uncle Tom. Encumbered by debt, he plans to sell a slave to his chief creditor.

Haley, the buyer, a New Orleans slave dealer. He shrewdly selects Uncle Tom and persuades Mr. Shelby to part with Harry in spite of his better feelings.

George Shelby, Mr. Shelby's son. He promises to buy Tom back one day but

arrives at Legree's plantation as Tom is dying. When his father dies, he frees all his slaves in Uncle Tom's name.

Mrs. Shelby, Mr. Shelby's wife. She delays the pursuit of Eliza by serving a late breakfast.

**Marks and
Loker,** slave-catchers hired by Haley to track Eliza through Ohio. Loker, wounded by George Harris in a fight, is given medical treatment by the Quakers who are protecting the runaways.

Augustine St. Clare, the purchaser of Tom after Tom saves his daughter's life. He dies before making arrangements necessary to the freeing of his slaves.

Eva St. Clare, his saintly and frail daughter. Before her death she asks her father to free his slaves.

Mrs. St. Clare, an imaginary invalid. After her husband's death, she sends Tom to the slave market.

Miss Ophelia, St. Clare's cousin from the North. She comes to look after Eva and is unused to lavish Southern customs.

Topsy, a pixie-like Negro child bought by St. Clare for Miss Ophelia to educate;

UNCLE TOM'S CABIN by Harriet Beecher Stowe. Published by Hougton Mifflin Co.

later he makes the gift legal.

Simon Legree, the alcoholic and superstitious brute who purchases Tom and kills him. He is a Northerner by birth.

Cassy, Legree's slave. She uses his superstitions to advantage in her escape. Her young daughter, who was sold years ago, proves to be Eliza, and mother and daughter are reunited in Canada.

Emmeline, another of Legree's slaves. She escapes with Cassy.

Madame de Thoux, whom Cassy and

Emmeline meet on a northbound riverboat. She proves to be George Harris' sister.

Aunt Chloe, Uncle Tom's wife, left behind in Uncle Tom's cabin on the Shelby plantation.

Senator Bird, in whose house Eliza first finds shelter in Ohio.

Mrs. Bird, his wife.

Simeon Halliday and
Rachel Halliday, who give shelter to the fugitive slaves.

The Story

Because his Kentucky plantation was encumbered by debt, Mr. Shelby made plans to sell one of his slaves to his chief creditor, a New Orleans slave dealer named Haley. The dealer shrewdly selected Uncle Tom as part payment on Mr. Shelby's debt. While they were discussing the transaction, Eliza's child, Harry, came into the room. Haley wanted to buy Harry too, but at first Shelby was unwilling to part with the child. Eliza listened to enough of the conversation to be frightened. She confided her fears to George Harris, her husband, a slave on an adjoining plantation. George, who was already bitter because his master had put him to work in the fields when he was capable of doing better work, promised that some day he would have his revenge upon his hard masters. Eliza had been brought up more indulgently by the Shelbys and she begged him not to try anything rash.

After supper in the cabin of Uncle Tom and Aunt Chloe, his wife, the Shelby slaves gathered for a meeting. They sang songs, and young George Shelby, who had eaten his supper there, read from the Bible. In the big house Mr. Shelby signed the papers making Uncle Tom and little Harry the property of Haley. Eliza, learning her child's fate from some remarks of Mr. Shelby to his wife, fled with her child, hoping to reach Canada and safety. Uncle Tom, hearing of the sale, resigned himself to the wisdom of providence.

The next day, after Haley had discovered his loss, he set out to capture Eliza. However, she had a good start. Moreover, Mrs. Shelby purposely delayed the pursuit by serving a late breakfast. When her pursuers came in sight, Eliza escaped across the Ohio River by jumping from one floating ice cake to another, young Harry in her arms.

Haley hired two slave-catchers, Marks and Loker, to track Eliza through Ohio. For their trouble she was to be given to them. They set off that night.

Eliza found shelter in the home of Senator and Mrs. Bird. The senator took her to the house of a man known to aid fugitive slaves. Uncle Tom, however, was not so lucky. Haley made sure Tom would not escape by shackling his ankles before taking him to the boat bound for New Orleans. When young George Shelby heard Tom had been sold, he followed Haley on his horse. George gave Tom a dollar as a token of his sympathy and told him that he would buy him back one day.

At the same time George Harris began his escape. White enough to pass as a Spaniard, he appeared at a tavern as a gentleman and took a room there, hoping to find before long a station on the underground railway.

Eliza was resting at the home of Rachel and Simeon Halliday when George Harris arrived in the same Quaker settlement.

On board the boat bound for New Orleans, Uncle Tom saved the life of young Eva St. Clare, and in gratitude Eva's father purchased the slave. Eva told Tom he would now have a happy life, for her father was kind to everyone. Augustine St. Clare was married to a woman who imagined herself sick and therefore took no interest in her daughter Eva. He had gone north to bring back his cousin, Miss Ophelia, to provide care for the neglected and delicate Eva. When they arrived at the St. Clare plantation, Tom was made head coachman.

Meanwhile Loker and Marks were on the trail of Eliza and George. They caught up with the fugitives and there was a fight in which George wounded Loker. Marks fled, and so the Quakers who were protecting the runaways took Loker along with them and gave him medical treatment.

Unused to lavish Southern customs, Miss Ophelia tried to understand the South. Shocked at the extravagance of St. Clare's household, she attempted to bring order out of the chaos, but she received no encouragement because the slaves had been humored and petted too long. Indulgent in all things, St. Clare was indifferent to the affairs of his family and his property. Uncle Tom lived an easy life in the loft over the stable. He and little Eva became close friends with St. Clare's approval. Sometimes St. Clare had doubts regarding the institution of slavery, and in one of these moods he bought an odd pixie-like child, Topsy, for his prim New England cousin to educate.

Eva grew more frail. Knowing that she was about to die, she asked her father to free his slaves, as he had so often promised. After Eva's death St. Clare began to read his Bible and to make plans to free all his slaves. He gave Topsy to Miss Ophelia legally, so that the spinster might rear the child as she wished. Then one evening he tried to separate two quarreling men. He received a knife wound in the side and died shortly afterward. Mrs. St. Clare had no intention of freeing the slaves, and she ordered Tom sent to the slave market.

At a public auction he was sold to a brutal plantation owner named Simon Legree. Legree drank heavily, and his plantation house had fallen to ruin. He kept dogs for the purpose of tracking runaway slaves. At the slave quarters Tom was given his sack of corn for the week, told to grind it himself and bake the meal into cakes for his supper. At the mill he aided two women. In return they baked his cakes for him. He read selections from the Bible to them.

For a few weeks Tom quietly tried to please his harsh master. One day he helped a sick woman by putting cotton into her basket. For this act Legree ordered him to flog the woman. When Tom refused, his master had him flogged until he fainted. A slave named Cassy came to Tom's aid. She told Tom the story of her life with Legree and of a young daughter who had been sold years before.

Then she went to Legree's apartment and tormented him. She hated her master and she had power over him. Legree was superstitious. When she talked, letting her eyes flash over him, he felt as though she were casting an evil spell. Haunted by the secrets of his guilty past, he drank until he fell asleep. But he had forgotten his fears by the next morning, and he knocked Tom to the ground with his fist.

Meanwhile, far to the north, George and Eliza and young Harry were making their way slowly through the stations on the underground railway toward Canada. Cassy and Emmeline, another slave, determined to make their escape. Knowing the consequences if they should be caught, they tricked Legree into thinking they were hiding in the swamp. When Legree sent dogs and men after them, they sneaked back into the house and hid in the garret. Legree suspected that Tom knew where the women had gone and decided to beat the truth out of his slave. He had Tom beaten until the old man could neither speak nor stand.

Two days later George Shelby arrived to buy Tom back, but he came too late. Tom was dying. When George threatened to have Legree tried for murder, Legree mocked him. George struck Legree in the face and knocked him down.

Still hiding in the attic, Cassy and Emmeline pretended they were ghosts. Frightened, Legree drank harder than ever. George Shelby helped them to escape. Later, on a river boat headed north, the two women discovered a Madame de Thoux, who said she was George Harris' sister. With this disclosure, Cassy learned also that Eliza, her daughter, was the Eliza who had married George and with him and her child had escaped safely to Canada.

These relatives were reunited in Canada after many years. In Kentucky George Shelby freed all his slaves when his father died. He said he freed them in the name of Uncle Tom.

Critical Evaluation

It has been suggested that Mark Twain wrote the first book in the American idiom, but surely Mrs. Stowe's powerful novel introduces the reader to an in-depth use of a regional dialect from an earlier period. The author intentionally created the characters of Tom, Legree, Eva, and Sambo, all of whom subsequently became the stereotypes of white southern womanhood, the brutal slave owner, and various slave personalities, because these features were a part of the conventional wisdom of ante-bellum America. These characters were convenient, effective agencies to warn the Christians of the nation of an impending doom: "every nation that carries in its bosom great and unredressed injustice has in it the elements of this last convulsion." God would certainly punish such a nation.

First published in book form in 1852, this book attracted millions of readers then, and is now often required reading in high schools and colleges. This work will always provide an added dimension to our understanding of the spiritual crisis of pre-Civil War America. The human tragedy in the story symbolizes the moral decay of the country. Simon Legree becomes the manhood of white America that supported slavery, feared hell, yet was more concerned with the material world. Tom lost his wife, children, and life to the ravages of the "peculiar institution." The collective guilt of the nation could only be cleansed by the abolition of slavery.

The fate of the nation and the role of Christian churches in perpetuating slavery were topics of great concern to the author: "And yet, O my country, these things are done under the Shadow of thy laws! O Christ! Thy Church sees them, almost in silence." The author observed and wrote about the crisis that divided Protestantism into sectional churches, a spiritual antecedent of the war. Clearly, the moral regeneration of the individual would lead to the abolition of slavery. Seeking support for her cause, the author admonished the reader to pity "those mothers that are constantly made childless by the American slave trade."

The author was a colonizationist, but she believed deeply that white America must first pay reparations to the nation's enslaved blacks. Once freed, the author points out, blacks needed and desired education and skills. She hoped that her testimony might bring an end to man's inhumanity to man. Little wonder, then, that President Lincoln, upon meeting the author, remarked, "So you're the little lady who started the war."

Bibliography

Adams, John R.   *Harriet Beecher Stowe.* New York: Twayne, 1963, pp. 46–61, 64–65.

Ammons, Elizabeth.   "Heroines in *Uncle Tom's Cabin,*" in *American Literature.* XLIX (May, 1977), pp. 161–179.

Baldwin, James.   "Everybody's Protest Novel," in *Partisan Review.* XVI (June, 1949), pp. 578–585.

Brown, Herbert Ross.   "Uncle Tom's and Other Cabins," in his *The Sentimental Novel in America, 1789–1860.* Durham, N.C.: Duke University Press, 1940, pp. 241–280.

Cassara, Ernest.   "The Rehabilitation of Uncle Tom: Significant Themes in Mrs. Stowe's Antislavery Novel," in *College Language Association Journal.* XVII (December, 1973), pp. 230–240.

Crozier, Alice C.   *The Novels of Harriet Beecher Stowe.* New York: Oxford University Press, 1969, pp. 3–33, 55–73.

Davis, Richard Beale. "Mrs. Stowe's Characters in Situations and a Southern Literary Tradition," in *Essays on American Literature in Honor of Jay B. Hubbell.* Edited by Clarence Gohdes. Durham, N.C.: Duke University Press, 1967, pp. 108–125.

Erskine, John. "Harriet Beecher Stowe," in *Leading American Novelists.* New York: Holt, 1910, pp. 287–296.

Fiedler, Leslie A. *Love and Death in the American Novel.* Cleveland: World, 1960, pp. 261–267.

Foster, Charles H. *The Rungless Ladder: Harriet Beecher Stowe and New England Puritanism.* Durham, N.C.: Duke University Press, 1954, pp. 13–18.

Furnas, J.C. *Goodbye to Uncle Tom.* New York: William Sloane, 1956, pp. 1–64.

Gilbertson, Catherine. *Harriet Beecher Stowe.* New York: Appleton-Century, 1937, pp. 140–178.

Hubbell, Jay B. *The South in American Literature.* Durham, N.C.: Duke University Press, 1954, pp. 385–393.

Hudson, Benjamin F. "Another View of *Uncle Tom*," in *Phylon.* XXIV (1963), pp. 79–87.

Maxfield, E.K. " 'Goody-goody' Literature and Mrs. Stowe," in *American Speech.* IV (February, 1929), pp. 189–202.

Nelson, John Herbert. *The Negro Character in American Literature.* Lawrence: University of Kansas, Department of Journalism Press, 1926, pp. 73–81.

Papashvily, Helen W. *All the Happy Endings: A Study of the Domestic Novel in America, the Women Who Wrote It, the Women Who Read It, in the Nineteenth Century.* New York: Harper, 1956, pp. 64–74.

Pattee, Fred L. *The Feminine Fifties.* New York: Appleton-Century, 1940, pp. 130–145.

Phelps, Wilson. "*Uncle Tom's Cabin,*" in his *Howells, James, Bryant, and Other Essays.* New York: Macmillan, 1924, pp. 181–206.

Strout, Cushing. "*Uncle Tom's Cabin* and the Portent of Millennium," in *Yale Review.* LVII (Spring, 1968), pp. 375–385.

Taylor, W.R. "Whistling in the Dark," in his *Cavalier and Yankee.* New York: Braziller, 1961, pp. 299–313.

Wagenknecht, Edward. *Harriet Beecher Stowe: The Known and the Unknown.* New York: Oxford University Press, 1965.

Wilson, Edmund. "Harriet Beecher Stowe," in his *Patriotic Gore.* New York: Oxford University Press, 1962, pp. 3–58.

Wilson, Robert Forrest. *Crusader in Crinoline: The Life of Harriet Beecher*

Stowe. Philadelphia: Lippincott, 1941, pp. 259–278.

Yellin, Jean Fagan. "Harriet Beecher Stowe," in his *The Intricate Knot: Black Figures in American Literature.* New York: New York University Press, 1973, pp. 121–153.

MARK TWAIN
Samuel Langhorne Clemens

Born: Florida, Missouri (November 30, 1835)
Died: Redding, Connecticut (April 21, 1910)

Principal Works

NOVELS: *The Gilded Age,* 1873 (with Charles Dudley Warner); *The Adventures of Tom Sawyer,* 1876; *The Prince and the Pauper,* 1882; *The Adventures of Huckleberry Finn,* 1884; *A Connecticut Yankee at King Arthur's Court,* 1889; *The American Claimant,* 1892; *Tom Sawyer Abroad,* 1894; *The Tragedy of Pudd'nhead Wilson,* 1894; *Personal Recollections of Joan of Arc,* 1896.

SHORT STORIES: *The Celebrated Jumping Frog of Calaveras County and Other Sketches,* 1867; *Mark Twain's Sketches; New and Old,* 1875; *The Stolen White Elephant,* 1882; *The £1,000,000 Bank-Note,* 1893; *The Man That Corrupted Hadleyburg,* 1900; *A Double Barrelled Detective Story,* 1902; *The $30,000 Bequest,* 1906; *A Horse's Tale,* 1907; *The Mysterious Stranger,* 1916.

REMINISCENCES AND AUTOBIOGRAPHY: *Roughing It,* 1872; *Life on the Mississippi,* 1883; *Mark Twain's Autobiography,* 1924 (2 vols.).

TRAVEL SKETCHES AND IMPRESSIONS: *The Innocents Abroad,* 1869; *A Tramp Abroad,* 1880; *Following the Equator,* 1897.

ESSAYS AND HUMOROUS MISCELLANIES: *How to Tell a Story and Other Essays,* 1897; *My Debut as a Literary Person,* 1903; *Extracts from Adam's Diary,* 1904; *King Leopold's Soliloquy,* 1905; *What is Man?* 1906; *Eve's Diary,* 1906; *Christian Science,* 1907; *Is Shakespeare Dead?* 1909; *Extract from Captain Stormfield's Visit to Heaven,* 1909.

"Mark Twain" was the pen name of Samuel L(anghorne) Clemens, who was born in Florida, Missouri, on November 30, 1835. His father was a dreamy Virginia lawyer and experimenter who, in drifting westward in search of wealth through land speculation, married in Kentucky and settled finally in 1839 in Hannibal, Missouri. In this community, on the Mississippi River between Quincy and St. Louis, the boy grew up amid the scenery and in the atmosphere portrayed in *Tom Sawyer* and *Huckleberry Finn.* At twelve, following his father's death, Sam left school to become a printer; for ten years he set type as a roving journeyman as far east as New York City. In 1857 his plans to visit South America ended when Horace Bixby undertook to teach him to be a steamboat pilot. When the Civil War closed down navigation, Sam soldiered a few months with a Confederate volunteer company. With his brother Orion he went to Nevada as a clerk and then drifted into silver mining and journalism. In 1862 he adopted his pen name, a river term meaning "two fathoms deep." Fame came in 1865 with "The Jumping Frog of Calaveras County," a tall tale. Printed lectures about a journey to the

Sandwich—now Hawaiian—Islands increased his popularity, and *Innocents Abroad*, a hilarious book of fun-making at the expense of gawking American travelers in the Holy Land and in Italian art centers, solidified his position as America's leading humorist. Following his marriage in 1870 to Olivia Langdon, he settled in Hartford, Connecticut. Thereafter he alternated between periods of writing and lecturing in America and Europe. Ill-advised investments in a publishing firm and in the development of a mechanical typesetting machine—evidence of a lifelong dream of becoming a millionaire by a lucky turn of the wheel of chance—reduced him to bankruptcy in 1894, but in four years these debts were paid. A native vein of bitterness and pessimism deepened when his wife and two of their three daughters died; some of his last writings, at his wish, were issued several years after his death at his home in Redding, Connecticut, on April 21, 1910.

A humorist pokes fun at human shortcomings: Twain does so by exaggerating instances of gullibility, meanness, inexpertness, and unwise romanticism. His chief characters speak for him; the frontier humor tradition, which he inherited and which he carried to its greatest artistic successes, abetted his alternating moods of boylike playfulness and redheaded anger. His materials, though originating in anecdotes, wisecracks, and personal experience, entered like mosaics into large contexts and pictured—rather than explained in traditional essay form as did Hawthorne and Melville—the problems of his generation. Hidden behind the account of his "slothful, valueless, heedless career" in Nevada in *Roughing It* is a narrative of pioneers' "buffeting and hard striving" to establish civilization in an outpost. *The Gilded Age*, whose love story was written by Charles Dudley Warner, gave its name to, even as it half praised and half scowled on, an era of political and business dishonesty. *Tom Sawyer*, seemingly about a boy's high spirits, is a study of personal conscience set against a milieu characterized by "glaring insincerity." *Huckleberry Finn*, a first-person narrative in Missouri dialect, recounts a nature-loving boy's rebellion against an institution-ridden "sivilization" containing slavery, feuds, and fraud. *A Connecticut Yankee* flays the concept of the divine right of kings who enslave the common people and withhold from them the technological advances by which their lot might be improved; the masses of men, Twain said, can always produce "the material in abundance whereby to govern itself." A priest-led political league which betrayed "Patriotism embodied, concreted, made flesh" in the Maid of Orleans is excoriated in Twain's one biographical-historical novel, *Joan of Arc*. The posthumously published *The Mysterious Stranger* brings Satan in human form among Austrian villagers to ridicule religious and social concepts based upon an alleged "moral sense."

Twain's books reflect his view of man as an almost helpless and therefore comic free agent in a still incompletely formed society uncertain of its direction. Civilization seemed a vulgar parade of hypocrisy, scheming pretense, incompetence, bungling, pork-barrel politics, and boodlery. Yet Twain was not a thinker, not a philosopher as ordinarily fiction writers strove to be or to represent themselves.

He solved no problems in his stories, as Howells tried to do; rather, Twain was, like Henry James and Stephen Crane, a pictorial artist with insight into human psychological responses during climactic moments of decision. The ordinary boy-girl or man-woman romantic relationships seldom occur in Twain's books.

A man of feeling, Twain was a sensitive barometer. As with Tom Sawyer, Huck Finn, and Pudd'nhead Wilson, Twain's mental weather fluctuated with every cloud in the social sky. He yielded to self-pity, bragged about and scolded himself, roared defiance and whimpered despondently at fate's blows, curried favors of the great and snarled at co-workers like Bret Harte and G. W. Cable, minced like a spaniel and strutted in his white suit like a king beside the dons at Oxford and Yale, who conferred honorary doctor's degrees upon him. Yet it is exactly this mercurial quality—this unexpected flash of temperament, this alternation of favorable and negative response—which enlivens his writings.

A masterly control over the English language, in its standard and Western dialect forms, made many scenes memorable, like the uproarious visit of Scotty Briggs to the fledgling parson in *Roughing It* and Sherburn's successful defiance of the lynch-hungry mob in *Huckleberry Finn*. His stories move by scenes or episodes rather than by a tightly knit plot structure woven around a clearly stated theme; yet each picture plays its role in the painter's impressionistic manner to give a single effect. In artistic manner, as in language, Twain was wholly American, wholly a product of native forces. If he was, as Dixon Wecter has suggested, "a kind of pocket miner, stumbling like fortune's darling upon native ore of incredible richness and exploiting it with effortless skill—but often gleefully mistaking fool's gold for the genuine article," the gold he found and wrought into great art remains an imperishable possession for the world's enjoyment and enrichment.

Bibliography

The definitive edition, *The Writings of Mark Twain*, edited by Albert Bigelow Paine, 37 vols., 1922–1925, is now out of print. The best one-volume selections are *The Family Mark Twain*, with an Introduction by Albert Bigelow Paine, 1935, and *The Portable Mark Twain*, edited by Bernard DeVoto, 1946.

Mark Twain's Autobiography, edited by Albert Bigelow Paine, 2 vols., 1924, and *Mark Twain's Notebooks*, published by the same editor in 1935, provide valuable source material, though they are not always reliable. The *Autobiography* has been re-edited with previously unpublished chapters by Charles Neider, 1959. Bernard DeVoto, *Mark Twain in Eruption*, 1940, is an important addition to the autobiography. Two useful collections of correspondence are *Mark Twain's Letters*, edited by Albert Bigelow Paine, 2 vols., 1917, and *The Love Letters of Mark Twain*, edited by Dixon Wecter, 1949. The authorized biography is Albert Bigelow Paine, *Mark Twain: A Biography*, 3 vols., 1912 (reissued 1935); but an authoritative modern work is Maxwell Geismar, *Mark Twain: An American Prophet*, 1970. The best of the general Mark Twain studies are Bernard DeVoto,

Mark Twain's America, 1932; Edward Wagenknecht, *Mark Twain: The Man and His Work*, 1935; and Dixon Wecter, *Sam Clemens of Hannibal*, 1952. See also William Dean Howells, *My Mark Twain: Reminiscences and Criticisms*, 1910; Van Wyck Brooks, *The Ordeal of Mark Twain*, 1920; Clara Clemens, *My Father, Mark Twain*, 1931; Edgar Lee Masters, *Mark Twain: A Portrait*, 1938; Bernard DeVoto, *Mark Twain at Work*, 1940; DeLancey Ferguson, *Mark Twain: Man and Legend*, 1943; Samuel C. Webster, *Mark Twain, Business Man*, 1946; Dixon Wecter, "Mark Twain," in *The Literary History of the United States*, edited by Robert E. Spiller, Willard Thorp, Thomas H. Johnson, and Henry S. Canby, Vol. II, 1948; Kenneth R. Andrews, *Nook Farm: Mark Twain's Hartford Circle*, 1950; Walter Blair, *Mark Twain and Huck Finn*, 1960; Kenneth S. Lynn, *Mark Twain and Southwestern Humor*, 1960; and Henry Nash Smith, *Mark Twain: The Development of a Writer*, 1962.

For criticism and more specialized studies see the extensive bibliography in *The Literary History of the United States*, Vol. III, 1948, 442–450.

A CONNECTICUT YANKEE IN KING ARTHUR'S COURT

Type of work: Novel
Author: Mark Twain (Samuel L. Clemens, 1835–1910)
Type of plot: Social satire
Time of plot: Sixth century
Locale: England
First published: 1889

In this satirical chronicle, Twain exposes the glorified days of knight errantry as childish barbarism; instead of the legendary gallantry, the Yankee finds a cruel feudalistic system under which the common people are abused and impoverished. Through the Yankee, Twain transmits his belief that a government is only good if the bulk of the people benefit from it.

Principal Characters

The Connecticut Yankee, an ingenious man struck on the head during a quarrel in a New England arms factory. He awakes in Merrie England, in June, 528. About to be burned at the stake on the twenty-first of June, he remembers that history has recorded a solar eclipse for that day. By prophesying the eclipse, he saves his life and discredits Merlin. He gets the name of "The Boss" and determines to raise the status of the common people. He sets up public schools, installs a telephone system, introduces gunpowder, points out to Arthur the grave injustices of the feudal system while accompanying the King on a tour of his realm. He marries Alisande and when their little daughter becomes ill, he takes her to the seashore to recuperate. While he is away, the Church orders all his improvements in Camelot destroyed. When he returns, Merlin casts a spell on him that will cause him to sleep for thirteen hundred years.

Clarence, a foppish page who becomes "The Boss's" chief assistant in his efforts to modernize the land and improve the lot of the common people.

King Arthur, a kind and courageous ruler who does not realize the inequities that exist in the social structure of his kingdom. He is killed in a battle with Sir Lancelot over Queen Guinevere. His death is the signal for the Church to move against and destroy the social progress brought about by the Yankee's democratic innovations.

Sir Kay, who first captures the Yankee.

Sir Sagramor, who challenges the Yankee to a joust and is aided by Merlin.

Merlin, the sorcerer whose magic power cannot match the Yankee's nineteenth century knowledge.

Alisande (Sandy), a damsel in distress whom the Yankee helps and whom he finally marries.

Hello-Central, their daughter, whose illness gives Merlin a chance to unite feudal power and destroy "The Boss."

A CONNECTICUT YANKEE IN KING ARTHUR'S COURT by Mark Twain. Published by Harper & Brothers.

The Story

Struck on the head during a quarrel in a New England arms factory, a skilled mechanic awoke to find himself being prodded by the spear of an armored knight on horseback. The knight was Sir Kay of King Arthur's Round Table and the time was June, A.D. 528 in Merrie England, as a foppish young page named Clarence informed the incredulous Yankee, when his captor took him back to white-towered Camelot. The Yankee remembered that there had been a total eclipse of the sun on June 21, 528. If the eclipse took place, he was indeed a lost traveler in time turned backward to the days of chivalry.

At Camelot the Yankee listened to King Arthur's knights as they bragged of their mighty exploits. The magician, Merlin, told again of Arthur's coming. Finally Sir Kay told of his encounter with the Yankee, and Merlin advised that the prisoner be thrown into a dungeon to await burning at the stake on the twenty-first of June.

In prison the Yankee thought about the coming eclipse. Merlin, he told Clarence, was a humbug, and he sent the boy to the court with a message that on the day of his death the sun would darken and the kingdom would be destroyed. The eclipse came, and at the right time, for the Yankee was about to be burned when the sky began to dim. Awed, the king ordered the prisoner released. The people shouted that he was a greater magician than Merlin.

The court demanded another display of his powers. With the help of Clarence, the Yankee mined Merlin's tower with some crude explosives he had made and then told everyone he would cause the tower to crumble and fall. When the explosion took place, the Yankee was assured of his place as the new court magician. Merlin was thrown into prison.

The lack of mechanical devices in King Arthur's castle bothered the ingenious New Englander, and the illiteracy of the people hurt his American pride in education. He decided to make the commoners more than slaves to the nobility. He had a title of his own by this time, for the people called him the Boss. As the Boss, he intended to modernize the kingdom.

His first act was to set up schools in small communities throughout the country. He had to work in secret, for he feared the interference of the Church. He trained workmen in mechanical arts. Believing that a nation needed a free press, he instructed Clarence in the art of journalism. He had telephone wires stretched between hamlets, haphazardly, however, because there were no maps by which to be guided.

When Sir Sagramor challenged the Boss to a duel, the court decided that he should go upon some knightly quest to prepare himself for the encounter. His mission was to help a young girl named Alisande, whose story he could not get straight. With many misgivings he put on a burdensome coat of mail and on his heavy charger started off with Sandy, as he called her. Sandy was a talkative companion who told endless tall tales as they traveled through the land. Along the way the Boss marveled at the pitiable state of the people under the feudal system. Whenever he found a man of unusual spirit he sent him back to Clarence in Camelot, to be taught reading, writing, and a useful trade. He visited the dungeons of the castles at which he stayed and released prisoners unjustly held by their grim masters.

In the Valley of Holiness he found another opportunity to prove his magic skill. There a sacred well had gone dry because, according to legend, some sin had been committed. When he arrived, Merlin, now released from prison, was attempting magic to make the spring flow. With a great deal of pomp and flourish, the Boss repaired a leak in the masonry at the bottom of the well. As the well filled, Merlin went home in shame.

By chance the Boss came upon one of his telephone installations in a cave nearby. He talked to Clarence, who told him that King Arthur was on his way to the Valley of Holiness to see the flowing spring. He returned to the spring to find a fake magician assuring the gaping pilgrims that he could tell what anyone was doing at that moment. The Boss asked him about King Arthur. The magician said that he was asleep in his bed at Camelot. The Boss grandly predicted that the king was on his way to the Valley of Holiness. When the king did arrive, the people were again awed by the Boss's magic.

Anxious that King Arthur be convinced of the sufferings of his people, the Boss suggested that he and the king disguise themselves as commoners and travel as pilgrims through the country. The Boss knew that Arthur was not to blame for his own social doctrines; he was a victim of his place in society. On their journey the king proved to be courageous and kind.

Misfortune soon overtook them. They were seized by an earl and sold as slaves, because they were unable to prove themselves free men. The slaves were taken to London, where the Boss picked the lock that held him and escaped. The rest of the slaves were ordered to be hanged after his escape. But the Boss located one of his telephones and called Clarence in Camelot, ordering him to send Sir Lancelot and an army of knights to London to save their king from hanging.

The Boss came back to Camelot in glory, but not for long. He still had to fight a duel with Sir Sagramor—in reality a battle between Merlin and the Boss. Merlin professed to cover Sir Sagramor with an invisible shield, but the credulous knight was invisible to no one but himself. The Boss wore no armor, and so on the field of the tournament he was able to dodge the charging knight until Sir Sagramor grew tired. Then the Boss lassoed him and pulled him from his horse. When Sir Sagramor returned once again to the field, Merlin stole the Boss's lasso. There was no alternative; the Boss shot Sir Sagramor with his gun. Then he challenged all the knights of the Round Table. He had only twelve shots in his two revolvers, but fortunately, when he had killed nine of the charging knights, the line wavered and gave up.

Three years passed. By this time the Boss had married Sandy and they had a little girl. He and Clarence were planning to declare a republic after the death of Arthur, for the sixth century kingdom was now a nineteenth century land with schools, trains, factories, newspapers, the telephone and the telegraph. Although the code of chivalry had been abolished, the knights still insisted on wearing their armor. Then little Hello-Central, the Boss's daughter, became ill, and he and Sandy took the child to the seashore for recuperation. On their return, the Boss found Camelot in a shambles. Only Clarence remained to tell him the story. There had been a battle between King Arthur and Sir Lancelot over Queen Guinevere. The king was dead, and by interdict the Church had destroyed the work of the Boss. Clarence and the Boss built a fortress surrounded by an electrically charged barrier. In a battle with the surviving chivalry of England the Boss was stabbed. When an old woman came to the fortress from the enemy lines and offered to nurse him, no one recognized her as Merlin. The magician cast a spell on the Boss and declared that he would sleep for thirteen hundred years. And, indeed, the Yankee did awake once more in the nineteenth century.

Critical Evaluation

A Connecticut Yankee in King Arthur's Court should have offered Mark Twain one of his best opportunities to attack the repressive and anti-democratic forces which he saw in post-Civil War America as well as in sixth century England. That the attack becomes in large part an exposé of the very system Twain sought to vindicate reveals as much the deep division in Twain's own nature as any problem inherent in the material itself. Ironically, though, much of the interest the work holds for contemporary readers is based upon the complications resulting from Twain's inability to set up a neat conflict between the forces of progress and those of repression. Hank Morgan's visit to King Arthur's court discovers not only the greed and superstition Twain associates with the aristocracy and the established Church, it reveals some of the weaknesses in man himself which enable these oppressive parasites to exist, and it finally comes to the realization that the industrial Utopia Hank tries to establish in old England is nothing more than a hopeless dream.

As a character, Hank Morgan is, in many respects, a worthy successor to his predecessor, Huckleberry Finn. Like Huck, Hank is representative of the common people, and, at his best, he asserts the ideal qualities Twain associates with those who escape the corruption of hereditary wealth and power and the conditioning of tradition. Unlike Huck, however, who was largely an observer powerless to change the system, Hank is given the opportunity to make his values the basis of a Utopian society. While Huck saw the threat of being "civilized" as an infringement on his individuality and freedom, Hank is, in his own way, fully "civilized" according to the standards of the world he represents. The pragmatc wit which enabled Huck Finn to survive against all odds becomes for Hank the basis of his rise in the industrial system to a position of authority and success. He fully accepts the nineteenth century doctrines of *laisséz-faire* capitalism, progress, and technology as being expressive of the best social and human principles. Hank represents Twain's vision of technological man as a new social ideal: the greatest product of the greatest society.

Twain's choice of Arthur's court as the testing ground for Hank's ideas was not accidental. Most immediately, he was offended by Matthew Arnold's attacks upon the American glorification of the common man and the Englishman's view of America as a kind of cultural desert. Thus, in attacking the golden age of chivalry, Twain simultaneously sought to expose English history, culture, and traditions of aristocratic privilege. At the same time, Twain associates the age of Arthur with the sorts of romantic attitudes he had exposed in *Huckleberry Finn* as the ruin of the American South. Making his spokesman, Hank Morgan, a product of that society Arnold deplored, Twain mounts a two-pronged attack against Arnold's Europeanism and sophistication and, in his own view, the dangerously reactionary attitudes which asserted the superiority of the "romantic" past over the present.

What begins for Hank, with his prediction of the moment of the eclipse, a simple expedient for survival, quickly becomes open war between Merlin and the Church and the Machine Age represented by the Yankee. Hank sees himself as a Promethean bringer of new knowledge and a new order to the oppressed masses of old England. Hank's humanitarian values are pitted against the selfishness and greed of the aristocracy and Church, and his reason challenges their superstition. Based upon his own and Twain's view of technological man as the apex of human development, Hank naturally assumes that he is the rightful ruler of the world. Twain as well as Hank seems to assume that because he takes up the cause of the oppressed people against their oppressors, he necessarily has, in whatever he does, a moral superiority to those he fights against. Neither Hank nor Twain seems to give consideration to the question of ends and means.

It is particularly ironic that Hank, ostensibly the bringer of light to this benighted people, should rely no less than his arch enemy Merlin upon the power of superstition to gain ascendancy over the masses. From the moment he discovers the profound effect his prediction of the eclipse has upon the audience, Hank begins to challenge Merlin to ever greater miracles. Such episodes as the destruction of Merlin's tower or the restoring of the Holy Well represent Hank's use of technology to create fear and awe like that Merlin has commanded heretofore. Thus, recognizing that man is essentially base and weak, Hank, like Merlin, maintains his power through exploitation of ignorance and gullibility.

Thus, it is man rather than technology which finally fails Hank. With the exception of the fifty-two young men who have never been exposed to the teachings of the Church, the society Hank has constructed through his technology reverts to its former state the minute his guard is relaxed. Men are, as Hank perceives them, no more than conditioned animals, and all his modern miracles cannot change that fact. In the end, Hank's technology fails him and his companions. His dream of progress has become a nightmare—a sacrifice to the very ignorance it would replace. Promethean Hank Morgan, the bringer of light and knowledge, finally only vindicates Twain's pessimistic view of human nature.

The ending of *A Connecticut Yankee in King Arthur's Court* is as bleak as anything Twain was ever to write. The scenes of Hank's Utopia destroyed by perverse human nature, the destruction unleashed by the power of technology, and, finally, the prospect of Hank's forces being overcome by the pollution of the bodies piled in their trenches are frightening to contemplate. Twain, having apparently set out to affirm the nineteenth century doctrine of progress, finally comes full circle to suggest that something permanent within human nature makes such dreams hopeless. Clearly, there is here an anticipation of the later Twain who, having lost hope in the human potential of his Huck Finn, would become a misanthropic voice crying out against the "damned human race."

Bibliography

Allen, Gerald. "Mark Twain's Yankee," in *New England Quarterly.* XXXIX (December, 1966), pp. 435–446.

Anderson, Kenneth. "The Ending of *A Connecticut Yankee in King Arthur's Court*," in *Mark Twain Journal.* XIV (Summer, 1969), p. 21.

Baetzhold, Howard G. "Mark Twain: England's Advocate," in *American Literature.* XXVIII (November, 1956), pp. 328–346.

Baldanza, Frank. *Mark Twain: An Introduction and Interpretation.* New York: Barnes & Noble, 1961, pp. 74–79.

Bellamy, Gladys Carmen. *Mark Twain as a Literary Artist.* Norman: University of Oklahoma Press, 1950, pp. 311–316.

Canby, Henry Seidel. "Hero of the Great Know-How: Mark Twain's Machine-Age Yankee," in *Saturday Review of Literature.* XXXIV (October 20, 1951), pp. 7–8, 40–41.

Cox, James M. "*A Connecticut Yankee in King Arthur's Court*: The Machinery of Self-Preservation," in *Yale Review.* L (Autumn, 1960), pp. 89–102.

Fetterley, Judith. "Yankee Showman and Reformer: The Character of Mark Twain's Hank Morgan," in *Texas Studies in Literature and Language.* XIV (Winter, 1973), pp. 667–679.

Foner, Philip S. *Mark Twain: Social Critic.* New York: International Publishers, 1958, pp. 103–115.

Guttman, Allen. "Mark Twain's *Connecticut Yankee*: Affirmation of the Vernacular Tradition?," in *New England Quarterly.* XXXIII (June, 1960), pp. 232–237.

Hansen, Chadwick. "The Once and Future Boss: Mark Twain's Yankee," in *Nineteenth-Century Fiction.* XXVIII (June, 1973), pp. 62–73.

Henderson, Harry B., III. *Versions of the Past: The Historical Imagination in American Fiction.* New York: Oxford University Press, 1974, pp. 175–197.

Hoben, John B. "Mark Twain's *A Connecticut Yankee*: A Genetic Study," in *American Literature.* XVIII (November, 1946), pp. 197–218.

Holmes, Charles S. "*A Connecticut Yankee in King Arthur's Court*: Mark Twain's Fable of Uncertainty," in *South Atlantic Quarterly.* LXI (Autumn, 1962), pp. 462–472.

McKee, John Dewitt. "*A Connecticut Yankee* as a Revolutionary Document," in *Mark Twain Journal.* XI (Summer, 1960), pp. 18–20, 24.

Maynard, Reid. "Mark Twain's Ambivalent Yankee," in *Mark Twain Journal.* XIV (Winter, 1968), pp. 1–5.

Reiss, Edmund. "Afterword," in *A Connecticut Yankee in King Arthur's Court.* By Mark Twain. New York: New American Library, 1963, pp. 321–331.

Sanford, Charles. "Classics of American Reform Literature," in *American Quarterly.* X (Fall, 1958), pp. 302–305.

Simonson, Harold R. *The Closed Frontier: Studies in American Literary Tragedy.* New York: Holt, Rinehart and Winston, 1970, pp. 129–133.

Smith, Henry Nash. *Mark Twain's Fable of Progress: Political and Economic Ideas in* A Connecticut Yankee. New Brunswick, N.J.: Rutgers University Press, 1964.

Spofford, William K. "Mark Twain's Connecticut Yankee: An Ignoramus Nevertheless," in *Mark Twain Journal.* XV (Summer, 1970), pp. 15–18.

Towers, Tom H. "Mark Twain's *Connecticut Yankee*: The Trouble in Camelot," in *Challenges in American Culture.* Edited by Ray B. Browne, Larry N. Landrum and William K. Bottorff. Bowling Green, Oh.: Bowling Green University Popular Press, 1970, pp. 190–198.

Wiggins, Robert A. *Mark Twain: Jackleg Novelist.* Seattle: University of Washington Press, 1964, pp. 72–82.

Williams, James D. "Revision and Intention in Mark Twain's *A Connecticut Yankee*," in *American Literature.* XXXVI (November, 1964), pp. 288–297.

————. "The Use of History in Mark Twain's *A Connecticut Yankee*," in *PMLA.* LXXX (March, 1965), pp. 102–110.

HUCKLEBERRY FINN

Type of work: Novel
Author: Mark Twain (Samuel L. Clemens, 1835–1910)
Type of plot: Humorous satire
Time of plot: Nineteenth century
Locale: Along the Mississippi River
First published: 1884

The title character of this famous novel tells his own story with straightforward-ness laced with shrewd, sharp comment on human nature. The boy's adventures along the Mississippi form the framework of a series of moral lessons, revelations of a corrupt society, and contrasts of innocence and hypocrisy.

Principal Characters

Huckleberry Finn, a small-town boy living along the banks of the Mississippi in the 1800's before the American Civil War. Perhaps the best-known youthful character in world fiction, Huck has become the prototype of the boy who lives a life that all boys would like to live; he also helped to shape such diverse characters as Hemingway's Nick Adams and Salinger's Holden Caulfield. His adventurous voyage with the Negro slave Jim, when they drift down the Mississippi on a raft, is the trip every boy dreams of making, on his own, living by his adaptable wits and his unerring ingenuity. When he contrasts himself with his flamboyant and wildly imaginative friend, Tom Sawyer, Huck feels somewhat inadequate, but deep inside he has a triumphant reliance on the power of common sense. Thus the world of Huck's reality—his capture by and escape from old drunken Pap; the macabre pageant of his townsfolk searching the Mississippi for his supposedly drowned body; his encounters with the King and the Duke, two preposterous swindlers; his stay among the feuding Grangerfords and Shepherdsons; and his defense of the pure, benighted Wilks sisters—is proved to be far more imaginative than Tom Sawyer's imagination. Yet Huck is not some irresponsible wanderer through adolescence. He has a conscience. He knows it is wrong to be harboring a runaway slave, but his friendship with Jim makes him defy the law. His appreciation of the ridiculous allows him to go along with the lies and swindles of the King and the Duke until they seem ready to bring real harm to the Wilks sisters, and he himself will fib and steal to get food and comfort; but his code of boyhood rebels at oppression, injustice, hypocrisy. Mark Twain has created in Huckleberry Finn a magnificent American example of the romanticism that rolled like a great wave across the Atlantic in the nineteenth century.

Jim, the Negro slave of Miss Watson. Believing that he is about to be sold down the river for eight hundred dollars, he runs away and hides on Jackson's Island, where Huck also takes refuge after faking his own murder in order to escape from Pap. Jim has all the charm and the many inconsistencies of the Southern Negro. Ignorant, superstitious, gullible, Jim is nevertheless, in Huck's

HUCKLEBERRY FINN by Mark Twain. Published by Harper & Brothers.

words, "most always right; he had an uncommon level head, for a nigger." He will laugh at everything comical; but he suffers poignantly when he thinks of the family he has left in bondage. He protects Huck physically and emotionally, feeling that the boy is the one white person he can trust, never suspecting that Huck is struggling with his conscience about whether to turn Jim in. When the two companions encounter the King and the Duke, Jim is completely taken in by their fakery, though at one point he asks, "Don't it 'sprise you, de way dem kings carries on, Huck?" Typically, Jim is subservient to and patient with the white man. Even when Tom Sawyer arrives at the Phelpses, where Jim has been caught and held, the Negro goes through Tom's complicated and romantic ritual of escape with grumbling good nature. Jim is a sensitive, sincere man who seems to play his half-comic, half-tragic role in life because he is supposed to play it that way.

Tom Sawyer, Huck's friend, who can, with a lively imagination stimulated by excessive reading, turn a raid by his gang on a Sunday-School picnic into the highway robbery of "a whole parcel of Spanish merchants and rich A-rabs . . . with two hundred elephants, and six hundred camels, and over a thousand 'sumter' mules, all loaded down with di'monds. . . ." He is a foil to the practicality of Huck; he is the universal boy-leader in any small town who can sway his gang or his pal into any act of fancy, despite all grumbling and disbelief. His ritual for the rescue of the captured Jim (who he knows has already been set free by Miss Watson's last will) is a masterful selection of details from all the romantic rescues of fact and fiction.

Pap, Huck's father and the town drunkard. When he learns that Huck has been awarded in trust a share of the money derived from the box of gold found in the robber's cave, he shows up one night at Huck's room at the Widow Douglas's. He takes the pledge and stays in the widow's spare room. Finding that Huck's share of the money is legally beyond his reach, he breaks the pledge and creates such havoc in the room that "they had to take soundings before they could navigate it." Pap kidnaps his son, keeping him prisoner in an old cabin. He then proceeds to go on a classic drunk, followed by a monumental case of delirium tremens. Snakes in abundance crawl all over him and one bites his cheek, though Huck, of course, can see nothing. The boy finally makes his escape from Pap by killing a pig and leaving bloody evidence of a most convincing murder. Pap's end in life is discovered by Jim: a dead body in a flooded boat on the Mississippi.

The King and
The Duke, two rapscallions and confidence men with whom Huck and Jim join up on their trip down the Mississippi. Their so-called play, "The Royal Nonesuch," finally leads to their just deserts: tarring, feathering, riding out of town on a rail.

The Widow Douglas and
Miss Watson, unsuccessful reformers of Huck after he comes into his fortune.

Aunt Polly, Tom Sawyer's relative who at the end of the story sets straight the by-now complicated identities of Huck and Tom.

The Grangerfords and
The Shepherdsons, two feuding families. Huck spends some time with the Grangerfords, who renew the feud when a Grangerford daughter elopes with a young Shepherdson.

Mr. and Mrs. Phelps, at whose farm the captured Jim is confined until Tom arrives to effect his "rescue."

Mary Jane,
Susan, and
Joanna Wilks, three sisters whom the

King and the Duke set out to bilk; Huck   Judge Thatcher, "the law" who protects
thwarts the connivers.   Huck's interests.

The Story

Tom Sawyer and Huckleberry Finn had found a box of gold in a robber's cave. After Judge Thatcher had taken the money and invested it for the boys, each had a huge allowance of a dollar a day. The Widow Douglas and her sister, Miss Watson, had taken Huck home with them to try to reform him. At first Huck could not stand living in a tidy house where smoking and swearing were forbidden. Worse, he had to go to school and learn how to read. But he managed to drag himself to school almost every day, except for the times when he sneaked off for a smoke in the woods or to go fishing in the Mississippi.

Life was beginning to become bearable to him when one day he noticed some tracks in the snow. Examining them closely, he realized that they belonged to the worthless father whom Huck had not seen for over a year. Knowing that his father would be back hunting him when the old man learned about the six thousand dollars, Huck rushed over to Judge Thatcher and persuaded the judge to take the fortune for himself. The judge was puzzled, but he signed some papers, and Huck was satisfied that he no longer had any money for his father to take from him.

Huck's father finally showed up one night in Huck's room at Widow Douglas' home. Complaining that he had been cheated out of his money, the old drunkard took Huck away with him to a cabin in the woods, where he kept the boy a prisoner, beating him periodically and half starving him. Before long Huck began to wonder why he had ever liked living with the widow. With his father, he could smoke and swear all he wanted, and his life would have been pleasant if it had not been for the beatings. One night Huck sneaked away, leaving a bloodly trail from a pig he had killed in the woods. Huck wanted everyone to believe he was dead. He climbed into a boat and went to Jackson's Island to hide until all the excitement had blown over.

After three days of freedom, Huck wandered to another part of the island and there he discovered Jim, Miss Watson's Negro slave. Jim told Huck that he had run off because he had overheard Miss Watson planning to sell him down south for eight hundred dollars. Huck swore he would not report Jim. The two stayed on the island many days, Jim giving Huck an education in primitive superstition. One night, Huck rowed back to the mainland. Disguised as a girl, he called on a home near the shore. There he learned that his father had disappeared shortly after the people of the town had decided that Huck had been murdered. Since Jim's disappearance had occurred just after Huck's alleged death, there was now a three hundred dollar reward posted for Jim's capture, as most people believed that Jim had killed Huck.

Fearing that Jackson's Island would be searched, Huck hurried back to Jim and the two headed down the Mississippi. They planned to leave the raft at Cairo and then go on a steamboat up the Ohio into free territory. Jim told Huck that he would work hard in the North and then buy his wife and children from their masters in the South. Helping a runaway slave bothered Huck's conscience, but he reasoned that it would bother him more if he betrayed such a good friend as Jim. One night as they were drifting down the river on their raft, a large boat loomed before them, and Huck and Jim, knowing that the raft would be smashed under the hull of the ship, jumped into the water. Huck swam safely to shore, but Jim disappeared.

Huck found a home with a friendly family named Grangerford. The Grangerfords were feuding with the Shepherdsons, another family living nearby. The Grangerfords left Huck mostly to himself and gave him a young slave to wait on him. One day the slave asked him to come to the woods to see some snakes. Following the boy, Huck came across Jim, who had been hiding in the woods waiting for an opportunity to send for Huck. Jim had repaired the broken raft. That night one of the Grangerford daughters eloped with a young Shepherdson, and the feud broke out once more. Huck and Jim ran away during the shooting and set off down the river.

Shortly afterward, Jim and Huck met two men who pretended they were royalty and made all sorts of nonsensical demands on Huck and Jim. Huck was not taken in, but he reasoned that it would do no harm to humor the two men to prevent quarreling. The Duke and the King were clever schemers. In one of the small river towns they staged a fake show which lasted long enough to net them a few hundred dollars. Then they ran off before the angered townspeople could catch them.

The Duke and the King overheard some people talking about the death of a Peter Wilks, who had left considerable property and some cash to his three daughters. Wilks' two brothers, whom no one in the town had ever seen, were living in England. The King and the Duke went to the three daughters, Mary Jane, Susan, and Joanna, and presented themselves as the two uncles. They took a few thousand dollars of the inheritance and then put up the property for auction and sold the slaves. This high-handed deed caused great grief to the girls, and Huck could not bear to see them so unhappy. He decided to expose the two frauds, but he wanted to insure Jim's safety first. Jim had been hiding in the woods waiting for his companions to return to him. Employing a series of lies, subterfuges, and maneuverings that were worthy of his ingenious mind, Huck exposed the Duke and King. Huck fled back to Jim, and the two escaped on their raft. Just as Jim and Huck thought they were on their way and well rid of their former companions, the Duke and King came rowing down the river toward them.

The whole party set out again with their royal plots to hoodwink the public. In one town where they landed, Jim was captured, and Huck learned that the Duke had turned him in for the reward. Huck had quite a tussle with his conscience. He knew that he ought to help return a slave to the rightful owner, but, on the other hand, he thought of all the fine times he and Jim had had together and how loyal a friend Jim had been. Finally, Huck decided that he would help Jim to escape.

Learning that Mr. Phelps was holding Jim, he headed for the Phelps farm. There, Mrs. Phelps ran up and hugged him, mistaking him for the nephew whom she had been expecting to come for a visit. Huck wondered how he could keep Mrs. Phelps from learning that he was not her nephew. Then to his relief he learned they had mistaken him for Tom Sawyer. Huck rather liked being Tom for a while, and he was able to tell the Phelps all about Tom's Aunt Polly and Sid and Mary, Tom's brother and sister. Huck was feeling proud of himself for keeping up the deception. When Tom Sawyer really did arrive, he told his aunt that he was Sid.

At the first opportunity Huck told Tom about Jim's capture. To his surprise, Tom offered to help him set Jim free. Huck could not believe that Tom would be a slave stealer, but he kept his feelings to himself. Huck had intended merely to wait until there was a dark night and then break the padlock on the door of the shack where Jim was kept. But Tom said the rescue had to be done according to the books, and he laid out a most complicated plan with all kinds of story-book ramifications. It took fully three weeks of plotting, stealing, and deceit to let Jim out of the shack. Then the scheme failed. A chase began after Jim escaped, and Tom was shot in the leg. After Jim had been recaptured, Tom was brought back to Aunt Sally's house to recover from his wound. Then Tom revealed the fact that Miss Watson had died, giving Jim his freedom in her will. Huck was greatly relieved to learn that Tom was not really a slave stealer after all.

To complicate matters still more, Tom's Aunt Polly arrived. She quickly set straight the identities of the two boys. Jim was given his freedom and Tom gave him forty dollars. Tom told Huck that his money was still safely in the hands of Judge Thatcher, but Huck moaned that his father would likely be back to claim it again. Then Jim told Huck that his father was dead; Jim had seen him lying in an abandoned boat along the river.

Huck was ready to start out again because Aunt Sally said she thought she might adopt him and try to civilize him. Huck thought that he could not go through such a trial again after he had once tried to be civilized under the care of Widow Douglas.

Critical Evaluation

Little could Mark Twain have visualized in 1876 when he began a sequel to capitalize on the success of *Tom Sawyer* that *Huckleberry Finn* would evolve into his masterpiece and one of the most significant works in the American novel tradition. Twain's greatest contribution to the tradition occurred when, with an unerring instinct for American regional dialects, he elected to tell the story in Huck's own words. The skill with which Twain elevates the dialect of an illiterate village boy to the highest levels of poetry established the spoken American idiom as a literary language, and earned for

Twain his reputation—proclaimed by Ernest Hemingway, William Faulkner and others—as the father of the modern American novel. Twain also maintains an almost perfect fidelity to Huck's point of view in order to dramatize the conflict between Huck's own innate innocence and natural goodness and the dictates of a corrupt society.

As Huck's own story, the novel centers around several major themes, including death and rebirth, freedom and bondage, the search for a father, the individual versus society, and the all-pervasive theme of brotherhood. Huck's character reflects a point in Mark Twain's development when he still believed man to be innately good, but saw social forces as corrupting influences which replaced with the dictates of a socially determined "conscience" man's intuitive sense of right and wrong. This theme is explicity dramatized through Huck's conflict with his conscience over whether or not to turn Jim in as a runaway slave. Huck, on the one hand, accepts without question what he has been taught by church and society about slavery. In his own mind, as surely as in that of his southern contemporaries, aiding an escaped slave was clearly wrong both legally and morally. Thus, Huck's battle with his conscience is a real trauma for him, and his decision to "go to Hell" rather than give Jim up is made with a certainty that such a fate awaits him for breaking one of society's laws. It is ironic, of course, that Huck's "sin" against the social establishment affirms the best that is possible to the individual.

Among the many forms of bondage, ranging from the widow's attempt to "civilize" Huck to the code of "honor" which causes Sherburn to murder Boggs and the law of the vendetta which absolutely governs the lives of the Grangerfords and Shepherdsons, that permeate the novel, slavery provides Twain his largest metaphor for both social bondage and institutionalized injustice and inhumanity. Written well after the termination of the Civil War, *Huckleberry Finn* is not an anti-slavery novel in the limited sense that *Uncle Tom's Cabin* is. Rather than simply attacking an institution already legally dead, Twain uses the idea of slavery as a metaphor for all social bondage and injustice. Thus, Jim's search for freedom, like Huck's own need to escape both the Widow and Pap Finn, is as much a metaphorical search for an ideal state of freedom as mere flight from slavery into free-state sanctuary. Thus it is largely irrelevant that Twain has Huck and Jim running deeper into the South rather than north toward free soil. Freedom exists neither in the North nor the South, but in the ideal and idyllic world of the raft and river.

The special world of raft and river is at the very heart of the novel. In contrast to the restrictive and oppressive social world of the shore, the raft is a veritable Eden where the evils of civilization are escaped. It is here that Jim and Huck can allow their natural bond of love to develop without regard for the question of race. It is here on the raft that Jim can become a surrogate father to Huck, and Huck can develop the depth of feeling for Jim which eventually leads to his decision to "go to Hell." But, while the developing relationship between Huck and Jim determines the basic shape of the novel, the river works in other structural ways as well. The picaresque form of the novel and its structural rhythm are based upon a series of episodes on shore, after each of which Huck and Jim return to the peaceful sanctuary of the raft. It is on shore that Huck encounters the worst excesses of which "the damned human race" is capable, but with each return to the raft comes a renewal of spiritual hope and idealism.

The two major thrusts of Twain's attack on the "civilized" world in *Huckleberry Finn* are against institutionalized religion and the romanticism which he believed characterized the South. The former is easily illustrated by the irony of the Widow's attempt to teach Huck religious principles while she persists in holding slaves. As with her snuff taking—which was all right because she did it herself—there seems to be no relationship between a fundamental sense of humanity and justice and her religion. Huck's practical morality makes him more "Christian" than the Widow, though he takes no interest in her lifeless principles. Southern romanticism, which Twain blamed for the fall of the South, is particularly allegorized by the sinking of the Walter Scott, but it is also inherent in such episodes as the feud where Twain shows the real horror of the sort of vendetta traditionally glamorized by romantic authors. In both cases, Twain is attacking the mindless acceptance of values which he believed kept the South in its dark ages.

Many critics have argued that the ending hopelessly flaws *Huckleberry Finn* by reducing its final quarter to literary burlesque. Others have argued that the ending is in perfect accord with Twain's themes. But all agree that, flawed or not, the substance of Twain's masterpiece transcends the limits of literary formalism to explore those eternal verities upon which great literature rests. Through the adventures of an escaped slave and a runaway boy, both representatives of the ignorant and lowly of the earth, Twain affirms for us that true humanity is of men rather than institutions, and that we can all be aristocrats in the kingdom of the heart.

Bibliography

Adams, Richard P. "The Unity and Coherence of *Huckleberry Finn*," in *Tulane Studies in English*. VI (1956), pp. 87–103. Reprinted in *Samuel Langhorne Clemens:* Adventures of Huckleberry Finn, *An Annotated Text, Backgrounds and Sources, Essays in Criticism*. Edited by Sculley Bradley, Richmond Groom Beatty and E. Hudson Long. New York: Norton, 1962, pp. 436–443. Also reprinted in *Huck Finn and His Critics*. Edited by Richard Lettis, Robert F. McDonnell and William E. Morris. New York: Macmillan, 1962, pp. 420–428. Also reprinted in *Twentieth Century Interpretations of*

Adventures of Huckleberry Finn: *A Collection of Critical Essays.* Edited by Claude M. Simpson. Englewood Cliffs, N.J.: Prentice-Hall, 1968, pp. 26–40.

Altenbrand, Lynn. "Huck Finn, Emancipator," in *Criticism.* I (Fall, 1959), pp. 298–307.

Barchilon, Jose and Joel S. Kovel. *"Huckleberry Finn:* A Psychoanalytic Study," in *Journal of the American Psychoanalytic Association.* XIV (October, 1966), pp. 775–814.

Blair, Walter. *Mark Twain & Huck Finn.* Berkeley: University of California Press, 1960.

Brownell, Frances V. "The Role of Jim in *Huckleberry Finn,"* in *Boston University Studies in English.* I (Spring–Summer, 1955), pp. 74–83.

Burg, David F. "Another View of *Huckleberry Finn,"* in *Nineteenth-Century Fiction.* XXIX (December, 1974), pp. 299–319.

Cox, James M. "Remarks on the Sad Initiation of Huckleberry Finn," in *Sewanee Review.* LXII (July–September, 1954), pp. 389–405. Reprinted in *Problems in American Civilization.* Edited by Barry R. Marks. Boston: D.C. Heath, 1959, pp. 65–74.

Cummings, Sherwood. "What's in *Huckleberry Finn?,"* in *English Journal.* L (January, 1961), pp. 1–8.

Elliott, George P. "Wonder for *Huckleberry Finn,"* in *Twelve Original Essays on Great American Novels.* Edited by George P. Shapiro. Detroit: Wayne State University Press, 1958, pp. 69–95.

Fiedler, Leslie. "Come Back to the Raft Ag'in, Huck Honey," in *Partisan Review.* XV (June, 1948), pp. 664–671. Reprinted in *Discussions of Mark Twain.* Edited by Guy A. Cardwell. Boston: Heath, 1963, pp. 59–64. Also reprinted in *The Collected Essays of Leslie Fiedler,* Volume I. New York: Stein and Day, 1971, pp. 142–151.

Gullason, Thomas Arthur. "The 'Fatal' Ending of *Huckleberry Finn,"* in *American Literature.* XXIX (March, 1957), pp. 86–91.

Hansen, Chadwick. "The Character of Jim and the Ending of *Huckleberry Finn,"* in *Massachusetts Review.* V (Autumn, 1963), pp. 45–66.

Kaplan, Harold. *"Huckleberry Finn:* What It Means to Be Civilized," in *Democratic Humanism and American Literature.* Chicago: University of Chicago Press, 1972, pp. 225–252.

Lane, Lauriat, Jr. "Why *Huckleberry Finn* Is a Great World Novel," in *College English.* XVII (October, 1955), pp. 1–5. Reprinted in *Problems in American Civilization.* Edited by Barry R. Marks. Boston: Heath, 1959, pp. 95–100.

Levy, Leo B. "Society and Conscience in *Huckleberry Finn,"* in *Nineteenth-Century Fiction.* XVIII (March, 1964), pp. 383–391.

Lynn, Kenneth S. "Huck and Jim," in *Yale Review.* XLVII (March, 1958), pp. 421–431. Reprinted in *Mark Twain: A Profile.* Edited by Justin Kaplan. New York: Hill and Wang, 1967, pp. 123–133.

Marx, Leo. "Mr. Eliot, Mr. Trilling, and *Huckleberry Finn,*" in *American Scholar.* XXII (Autumn, 1953), pp. 423–440. Reprinted in *Discussions of Mark Twain.* Edited by Guy A. Cardwell. Boston: Heath, 1963, pp. 72–81. Also reprinted in *Huck Finn and His Critics.* Edited by Richard Lettis, Robert F. McDonnell and William E. Morris. New York: Macmillan, 1962, pp. 350–364. Also reprinted in *Twentieth Century Interpretations of* Adventures of Huckleberry Finn: *A Collection of Critical Essays.* Edited by Claude M. Simpson. Englewood Cliffs, N.J.: Prentice-Hall, 1968, pp. 26–40.

Metzger, Charles R. "*The Adventures of Huckleberry Finn* as Picaresque," in *Midwest Quarterly.* V (April, 1964), pp. 249–256.

O'Connor, William Van. "Why *Huckleberry Finn* Is Not the Great American Novel," in *College English.* XVII (October, 1955), pp. 6–10. Reprinted in *Huck Finn and His Critics.* Edited by Richard Lettis, Robert F. McDonnell and William E. Morris. New York: Macmillan, 1962, pp. 379–383.

Ornstein, Robert. "The Ending of *Huckleberry Finn,*" in *Modern Language Notes.* LXXIV (December, 1959), pp. 698–702.

Rubenstein, Gilbert M. "The Moral Structure of *Huckleberry Finn,*" in *College English.* XVIII (November, 1956), pp. 72–76. Reprinted in *Twentieth Century Interpretations of* Adventures of Huckleberry Finn: *A Collection of Critical Essays.* Edited by Claude M. Simpson. Englewood Cliffs, N.J.: Prentice-Hall, 1968, pp. 26–40.

Schwartz, Edward. "*Huckleberry Finn:* The Inward Thoughts of a Generation," in *Mark Twain Quarterly.* IX (Winter, 1952), pp. 11–16, 23–24.

Simonson, Harold R. "*Huckleberry Finn* as Tragedy," in *Yale Review.* LIX (Summer, 1970), pp. 532–548. Revised and reprinted in *The Closed Frontier: Studies in American Literary Tragedy.* New York: Holt, Rinehart and Winston, 1970, pp. 57–76.

Solomon, Eric. "*Huckleberry Finn* Once More," in *College English.* XXII (December, 1960), pp. 172–178. Reprinted in *Huck Finn and His Critics.* Edited by Richard Lettis, Robert F. McDonnell and William E. Morris. New York: Macmillan, 1962, pp. 420–428.

Trilling, Lionel. "Introduction," in *The Adventures of Huckleberry Finn.* By Mark Twain. New York: Rinehart, 1948, pp. v–xviii. Reprinted in *Discussions of Mark Twain.* Edited by Guy A. Cardwell. Boston: D.C. Heath, 1963, pp. 51–58. Also reprinted in *Huck Finn and His Critics.* Edited by Richard Lettis, Robert F. McDonnell and William E. Morris. New York: Macmillan,

1962, pp. 326–336. Revised and reprinted in *The Liberal Imagination: Essays of Literature and Society*. By Lionel Trilling. New York: Viking, 1950, pp. 104–117.

THE PRINCE AND THE PAUPER

Type of work: Novel
Author: Mark Twain (Samuel L. Clemens, 1835–1910)
Type of plot: Social criticism
Time of plot: Sixteenth century
Locale: England
First published: 1882

In this historical satire, Twain follows the twin adventures of the Prince of Wales and a street beggar, look-alikes who unwittingly trade identities. Besides the fascination of the storyline and the humor of many incidents, the novel is interesting in its scrutiny of the past from the point of view of modern morality, and for its satire of the foibles and injustices of the class system.

Principal Characters

Edward, Prince of Wales and son of Henry VIII. When a ragged waif named Tom Canty invades the royal grounds, Edward, curious about life outside the confines of the palace, invites the boy to his quarters. They change clothes as a prank and discover that they are identical in appearance. When the Prince appears in the courtyard dressed in Tom's rags, guards mistake him for the intruding waif and throw him into the streets. Protesting time and again that he is the real Prince of Wales, he is ridiculed and thought mad by skeptical London crowds. After many adventures and hardships that reveal to him the harsh lot of the common people, he appears as Tom Canty is about to be crowned king and proves that he himself is the rightful heir by disclosing the location of the Great Seal that his late father had entrusted to him.

King Henry VIII, his ailing father, who has entrusted to Edward the Great Seal.

Mary and

Elizabeth, daughters of the King, who think Tom is their brother.

Tom Canty, who was born the same day as the Prince of Wales and is his double in appearance. He trades places with Edward.

John Canty, his father, who treats Tom and Edward cruelly. When he becomes King, Edward wants to hang Canty but can never locate him.

Miles Hendon, the disinherited son of a baronet. He befriends the homeless Edward.

Hugh Hendon, his brother, who tricks Miles in order to marry Edith.

Edith, who loves Miles but is afraid Hugh will murder him if she identifies Miles.

Hugo, a thief who tries to teach Edward his tricks.

The Lord Protector, who identifies the real Prince.

The Story

On the same day, in London, Tom Canty and the Prince of Wales were born, the first unwanted and the second long awaited. While the prince, Edward Tudor, lay robed in silks, Tom Canty wallowed in the filth of Offal Court.

Tom's father forced him to beg during the day and he beat the boy at night; but Tom had private dreams of his own. Pretending that he was a prince, he gathered his ragtaggle court of street urchins around him. One day, hoping to see Prince Edward of England, he invaded the royal precincts, but when he tried to approach the prince he was cuffed by a guard and ordered away. Edward, witnessing the incident, protected Tom and took the young beggar into the palace. There, in the privacy of Edward's chamber, Tom confessed his longing to be a prince. When the two boys exchanged garments they discovered that they were identical in appearance. Unrecognized as the real prince and mistaken for the beggar boy, Edward was promptly thrown into the streets of London, where he wandered helplessly, mocked by people whom he approached with pleas that they pay homage to him as their rightful prince.

Meanwhile, in the palace, it was thought that the prince had gone mad because he could recall none of the royal matters which he was supposed to know. King Henry issued an edict that no one should discuss the royal lapse of memory, and the Princesses Mary and Elizabeth mercifully tried to aid their supposed brother, who by that time was too frightened to confess that he was Tom Canty, a beggar dressed in the prince's clothing.

King Henry VIII, sick in bed, had given the Great Seal of the kingdom to Prince Edward for safekeeping. When Henry demanded the return of his seal, Tom reported that he did not know where it was.

While the Prince of Wales, a homeless waif, wandered the streets under the crowd's mocking raillery, King Henry died. Edward was found by John Canty, Tom's father, and brought to Offal Court; but during the wild celebration of Tom's ascension to the throne Edward escaped from John Canty. Again tormented by skeptical crowds who laughed at his protests that he was now King of England, Edward was rescued by Miles Hendon, the disinherited son of a baronet. Thinking Edward was mad, Miles pitied the little waif and pretended to pay him the homage due to a monarch.

Miles had loved a girl named Edith, who was coveted by Miles' brother Hugh. By trickery, Hugh had gained his father's confidence and Miles was turned away from home. Edward declared that Miles had suffered unjustly and promised the adventurer any boon he might ask. Recalling the story of De Courcy, who, given a similar opportunity by King John, requested that he and all his descendants might be permitted to wear hats in the presence of the King of England, Miles wisely asked that he be permitted to sit down in Edward's presence, for the young king had been ordering Miles about like any other personal servant.

In the role of King of England, Tom was slowly learning to conduct himself royally. Regarded by his attendants as mad, he was able to display his lack of training, and his failure to recall events familiar to Edward, with no calamitous results. At the same time his gradual improvement offered hope that his derangement was only temporary.

John Canty lured Edward away from Miles' protection and took the boy to Southwark, there to join a pack of thieves. Still vainly declaring himself king, Edward was again the center of ridicule. One of the thieves, Hugo, undertook to teach Edward the tricks of his trade. Making his escape, Edward wandered to a farmhouse where a kind woman, pitying the poor, insane beggar boy who declared himself King of England, fed him. Edward wandered on to the hut of a hermit who accepted naïvely Edward's claim to royalty. In turn, the hermit revealed to Edward that he was an archangel; the hermit was really mad. While Edward slept, the hermit brooded over the wrongs done him by King Henry. Believing Edward really to be the king, and planning to murder him, the hermit managed to tie up the boy while he slept. John Canty and Hugo, following the trail of the escaped waif, rescued him and forced him to rejoin the band of rogues. Again he was compelled to aid Hugo in his dishonest trade. At last Miles found the boy and saved him.

Miles was on his way back to Hendon Hall to claim his heritage and Edith for a wife. Arriving at their destination, they learned that Miles' father was dead and Hugh, married to Edith, was master of Hendon Hall. Only five of the old servants were still living, and all of them, in addition to Hugh and Edith, pretended not to recognize Miles. Denounced as a pretender, Miles was sentenced to the stocks, where the abuse showered upon him by the mob so enraged Edward that he protested loudly. When the guards decided to whip the boy, Miles offered to bear the flogging instead. Grateful to his friend, Edward dubbed Miles an earl, but the imprisoned man sorrowed at the boy's display of insanity. Upon Miles' release from the stocks the two set out for London, where they arrived on the day before the coronation of King Edward VI.

In regal splendor, enjoying the adulation of his subjects, Tom Canty rode through the streets of London toward Westminster Abbey. There, just as the crown was about to be set on his head, a voice rang out demanding that the ceremony cease, and the real king, clothed in rags, stepped forth. As the guards moved to seize the troublemaker, Tom, recognizing Edward, ordered them to halt. The Lord Protector solved the mystery by asking the ragged king to locate the Great Seal that had been lost since King Henry's death. Edward, after much dramatic hesitation, managed to remember the exact location of the Seal. Tom admitted that he had innocently used it to crack nuts.

When Miles was brought before the rightful King Edward, he exercised his privilege of sitting in the king's presence. At first he had doubted that the waif was really the king, but when Edward ordered his outraged guards to permit that disrespectful act, Miles knew that his young friend had not been insane after all. Furthermore, Edward confirmed Miles' title of earl. Hugh was stripped of his titles and land. Later he died, whereupon Miles married Edith, whose earlier refusal to acknowledge his identity had been the result of Hugh's threat to kill his brother.

Tom returned to Offal Court with Edward's promise that he and his family would be honored for the rest of their lives. Edward righted many wrongs he had encountered during his adventures. John Canty, whom he wanted to hang, was never heard from again.

Critical Evaluation

The Prince and the Pauper was Mark Twain's earliest attempt to join his recent fascination for the romantic past of Europe with his natural bent for satirizing the injustices and social conventions of his own age. He was to do the same later, with far better effect, in *A Connecticut Yankee in King Arthur's Court* (1889), and with less success in *Personal Recollections of Joan of Arc* (1896). It is generally agreed that *The Prince and the Pauper* is a story mainly for children—though if that is wholly true, it must also be said that it is a children's story very rewarding for adults.

Twain employs in this novel many of the themes and devices which he may have exercised to better effect in other works, but which are nonetheless used well here also. There are, for example, all the usual techniques he learned so expertly as a teller of tall tales—tongue-in-cheek irony, ridiculous understatement, and exaggeration, to name a few. Miles Hendon's separation from Edward gives Twain the opportunity for soliloquy, a favorite literary device used with great success in *Huckleberry Finn*. The exchange of identities—as in *Huckleberry Finn* and *Pudd'nhead Wilson*—is another common occurrence in Twain's works, as is his use of coincidence.

Twain was also able in *The Prince and the Pauper* to underscore some of the social follies and injustices of his own age without actually having to attack them directly in the novel. He did this by satirically treating the social and legal conventions of Tudor England, and then assuming his readers would recognize for themselves the parallels with their own times. Hence, religious intolerance is the target of "In Prison," a chapter in which two women, who have kindly befriended Edward and Miles, are mercilessly burned at the stake because they are Baptists. Tom Canty, as king, labors to change laws which are unduly harsh or blatantly unjust; and Edward himself learns of the unnecessary cruelty of prisons, as well as the nature of the kind of life poor people must endure as a result of their poverty.

However, Twain's major criticism of society, both Tudor and his own, is of its mistaking the outward appearances of men or their circumstances as a final gauge of their true worth. The novel suggests that, under different circumstances, any man *could* be a king—just as Tom Canty, given the opportunity, learns to be one. Tom and Edward are equally intelligent and virtuous young boys, but each is born to a different kind of "court." Chance and circumstances alone determine much of our outward behavior and appearance. For Twain, this was as true for his own times as he felt it had been for Tudor England.

Bibliography

Baetzhold, Howard G. "Mark Twain's *The Prince and the Pauper*," in *Notes and Queries*. CXCIX (September, 1954), pp. 401–403.

Bailey, Elmer James. "The Essayists and the Humanists," in *A Manual of American Literature*. Edited by Theodore Stanton. New York: Putnam's, 1909, pp. 357–359.

Baldanza, Frank. *Mark Twain: An Introduction and Interpretation*. New York: Barnes & Noble, 1961, pp. 70–74.

Becker, Mary Lamberton. "Introduction," in *The Prince and the Pauper*. By Mark Twain. Cleveland: World, 1948, pp. i–xiv.

Blues, Thomas. "The Strategy of Compromise in Mark Twain's 'Boy Books,' " in *Modern Fiction Studies*. XIV (Spring, 1968), pp. 21–31.

Foner, Philip S. *Mark Twain: Social Critic*. New York: International Publishers, 1958, pp. 102–103.

Gale, Robert L. "*The Prince and the Pauper* and *King Lear*," in *Mark Twain Journal*. XII (Spring, 1963), pp. 14–17.

Paine, Albert Bigelow. "Introduction," in *The Prince and the Pauper*. By Mark Twain. New York: Harper, 1929, pp. xvii–xxi.

Quinn, Arthur Hobson. "Introduction," in *The Prince and the Pauper*. By Mark Twain. New York: Harper, 1920, pp. i–xxx.

Rogers, Franklin R. *Mark Twain's Burlesque Patterns as Seen in the Novels and Narratives, 1855–1885*. Dallas: Southern Methodist University Press, 1960, pp. 113–127.

Vogelback, Arthur Lawrence. "*The Prince and the Pauper*: A Study in Critical Standards," in *American Literature*. XIV (March, 1942), pp. 48–54.

Wiggin, Kate Douglas. "An Appreciation," in *The Prince and the Pauper*. By Mark Twain. New York: Harper, 1929, pp. xiii–xvi.

Wiggins, Robert A. *Mark Twain: Jackleg Novelist*. Seattle: University of Washington Press, 1964, pp. 72–82.

TOM SAWYER

Type of work: Novel
Author: Mark Twain (Samuel L. Clemens, 1835–1910)
Type of plot: Adventure romance
Time of plot: Nineteenth century
Locale: St. Petersburg on the Mississippi River
First published: 1876

More than a book for boys, The Adventures of Tom Sawyer, *with its rich native humor and shrewd observations of human character, is an idyl of American village life, of that quieter age that had already vanished when Mark Twain re-created St. Petersburg from memories of his own boyhood.*

Principal Characters

Tom Sawyer, the mischievous ringleader of countless boyish adventures, who almost drives his long-suffering aunt to distraction with his pranks. If not fighting with other village urchins, the indolent boy plans numerous romantic and impractical escapades, many of which cost him hours of conscience-stricken torment. If he is not planning misdemeanors on the high seas, he is looking for buried treasure. Although unthinking, he is not really a bad boy; he is capable of generosity; occasionally, he surprises even himself with magnanimous acts.

Aunt Polly, Tom's warm, tender-hearted aunt. Sometimes this simple scripture-quoting old soul does not understand her mischievous charge. Even though she uses Tom's brother Sid as an example of a model youth, her frequent admonitions, emphasized by repeated thumps on the head with a thimble, fail to have a lasting effect on Tom. Believing herself endowed with subtle guile, she often tries to trap the boy into admitting his pranks. Rarely, however, is she successful. Tom usually manages to outwit her if Sid does not call her attention to certain inexactnesses in Tom's excuses.

Huckleberry Finn, one of Tom's best friends and a social pariah to the village mothers, but not to their sons. In the self-sufficient outcast the boys see everything they want to be. They long for his freedom to do as he pleases. Sometimes, to their regret, the other boys try to emulate their individualistic hero. Carefully, they mark the way he smokes strong tobacco in smelly old pipes and sleeps in empty hogsheads. Although he is not accepted by the mothers, Huck, even if he is vulgar, is a decent, honest lad. Happy only when he can sleep and eat where he pleases, Huck feels uncomfortable when the Widow Douglas takes him into her home.

Becky Thatcher, Tom's sweetheart. With her blue eyes, golden hair, and winsome smile, she captures his rather fickle heart at their first meeting. A little coquette, she, like Tom, alternately suffers from and enjoys their innocent love. Tom proves his generosity and love for her when he admits to the schoolteacher a crime he did not commit, thus astound-

TOM SAWYER by Mark Twain. Published by Harper & Brothers.

ing the rest of the class by his incredible folly.

Injun Joe, a half-breed. A murderous, sinister figure who lurks mysteriously in the background, the savagely vindictive killer stabs young Dr. Robinson and is subsequently exposed by Tom. In a cave Injun Joe, who had leaped from the court room window during Muff Potter's trial, almost has his revenge against the boy. Finally he pays for his many crimes when he is trapped in the cave and dies of starvation.

Muff Potter, a local ne'er-do-well and, along with Pap Finn, the town drunk. After helping Injun Joe and Dr. Robinson rob a grave, Muff Potter is accused of killing the doctor and almost pays with his worthless life. Had Tom not belatedly intervened, he would have been hanged and Injun Joe would have gone free. When the boys see a stray dog howling at the newly released Potter, asleep in a drunken stupor, they know

that he is still doomed.

Sid, Tom's half brother and one of the model boys in the community. A quiet, rather calculating child, he exposes Tom's tricks whenever possible. However, when Tom is presumed drowned, Sid manages a few snuffles. To Tom, Sid's behavior is reprehensible; he keeps clean, goes to school regularly, and behaves well in church.

Mary, Tom's cousin. She is a sweet, lovable girl who often irritates him by insisting that he wash and dress carefully for church.

Judge Thatcher, Becky's pompous but kind-hearted father and the local celebrity.

Joe Harper, who runs away with Tom and Huck to Jackson's Island. Pretending to be pirates, they remain there for several days while the townspeople search for their bodies.

The Story

Tom Sawyer lived securely with the knowledge that his Aunt Polly loved him dearly. When she scolded him or whipped him, he knew that inside her breast lurked a hidden remorse. Often he deserved the punishment he received, but there were times when he was the victim of his tale-bearing half-brother, Sid. Tom's cousin, Mary, was kinder to him. Her worst duty toward him was to see to it that he washed and put on clean clothes, so that he would look respectable when Aunt Polly took Tom, Sid, and Mary to church on Sunday.

A new family had moved into the neighborhood. Investigating Tom saw a pretty, blue-eyed girl with lacy pantalets. She was Becky Thatcher. Instantly the fervent love he had felt for Amy Lawrence fled from his faithless bosom, to be replaced by devotion to the new girl he had just beheld.

She was in school the next day, sitting on the girls' side of the room with an empty seat beside her. Tom had come late to school that morning. When the schoolmaster asked Tom why he had been late, that empty seat beside Becky Thatcher caught Tom's eye. Recklessly he confessed he had stopped to talk with Huckleberry Finn, son of the town drunk. Huck wore castoff clothing, never attended school, smoked and fished as often as he pleased, and slept wherever he could. For associating with Huck, Tom was whipped by the schoolmaster and ordered to sit on the girls' side of the room. Amid the snickers of the entire class, he took the empty seat next to Becky.

Tom first attracted Becky's attention by a series of drawings on his slate. At length he wrote the words, "I love you," and Becky blushed. Tom urged her to meet him after school. Sitting with her on a fence, he explained to her the possibilities of an engagement between them. Innocently she accepted his proposal, which Tom insisted must be sealed by a kiss. In coy resistance she allowed Tom a brief chase before she yielded to his embrace. Tom's happiness was unbounded. But when he mentioned his previous tie with Amy Lawrence, the brief romance ended. Becky left her affianced with a haughty shrug of her pretty shoulders.

That night Tom heard Huck's whistle below his bedroom window. Sneaking out, Tom joined his friend, and the two went off to the cemetery, Huck dragging a dead cat behind him. They were about to try a new method for curing warts. The gloomy atmosphere of the burial ground filled the boys with apprehension, and their fears increased still more when they spied three figures stealing into the graveyard. They were Injun Joe, Muff Potter, and Doctor Robinson. Evidently they had come to rob a grave. When the two robbers had exhumed the body, they began to quarrel with the doctor about money, and in the quarrel Potter was knocked out. Then Injun Joe took Potter's knife and killed the doctor. When Potter recovered from his blow he thought he had killed Robinson, and Injun Joe allowed the poor old man to believe himself guilty.

Terrified, Tom and Huck slipped away from the scene they had just witnessed, afraid that if Injun Joe discovered them he would kill them too.

Tom brooded on what he and Huck had seen. Convinced that he was ill, Aunt Polly dosed him with Pain Killer and kept him in bed, but he did not seem to recover. Becky Thatcher had not come to school since she had broken Tom's heart. Rumor around town said that she was also ill. Coupled with this sad news was the fear of Injun Joe. When Becky finally returned to school, she cut Tom coldly. Feeling that there was nothing else for him to do, he decided to run away. He met Joe Harper and Huck Finn. Together they went to Jackson's Island and pretended to be pirates.

For a few days they stayed happily on the island and learned from Huck how to smoke and swear. One day they heard a boat on the river, firing cannon over the water. Then the boys realized that the townspeople were searching for their bodies. This discovery put a new aspect on their adventure; the people at home thought they were dead. Gleeful, Tom could not resist the temptation to see how Aunt Polly had reacted to his death. He slipped back to the mainland one night and into his aunt's house, where Mrs. Harper and Aunt Polly were mourning the death of their mischievous but good-hearted children. When Tom returned to the island, he found Joe and Huck tired of their game and ready to go home. Tom revealed to them an attractive plan which they immediately decided to carry out.

With a heavy gloom overhanging the town, funeral services were held for the deceased Thomas Sawyer, Joseph Harper, and Huckleberry Finn. The minister pronounced a lengthy eulogy about the respective good characters of the unfortunate boys. When the funeral procession was about to start, Tom, Joe, and Huck marched down the aisle of the church into the arms of the startled mourners.

For a while Tom was the hero of all the boys in the town. They whispered about him and eyed him with awe in the schoolyard. But Becky ignored him until the day she accidentally tore the schoolmaster's book. When the irate teacher demanded to know who had torn his book, Tom confessed. Becky's gratitude and forgiveness were his reward.

After Muff Potter had been put in jail for the murder of the doctor in the graveyard, Tom and Huck had sworn to each other they would never utter a word about what they had seen. Afraid Injun Joe would murder them for revenge, they furtively sneaked behind the prison and brought Muff food and other cheer. But Tom could not let an innocent man be condemned. At the trial he appeared to tell what he had seen on the night of the murder. While Tom spoke, Injun Joe, a witness at the trial, sprang from the window of the courtroom and escaped. For days Tom worried, convinced that Injun Joe would come back to murder him. But as time went by and nothing happened, he gradually lost his fears. With Becky looking upon him as a hero, his world was filled with sunshine.

Huck and Tom decided to hunt for pirates' treasures. One night, ransacking an old abandoned house, they watched, unseen, while Injun Joe and a companion unearthed a chest of money buried under the floorboards of the house. The two frightened boys fled before they were discovered. The next day they began a steady watch for Injun Joe and his accomplice, for Tom and Huck were bent on finding the lost treasure.

When Judge Thatcher gave a picnic for all the young people in town, Becky and Tom were supposed to spend the night with Mrs. Harper. One of the biggest excitements of the merrymaking came when the children went into a cave in the riverbank. The next day Mrs. Thatcher and Aunt Polly learned that Tom and Becky were missing, for Mrs. Harper said they had not come to spend the night with her. Then everyone remembered that Tom and Becky had not been seen since the picnickers had left the cave. Meanwhile the two, having lost their bearings, were wandering in the cavern. To add to Tom's terror, he discovered that Injun Joe was also in the cave. Miraculously, after spending five days in the dismal cave, Tom found an exit that was five miles from the place where they had entered. Again he was a hero.

Injun Joe starved to death in the cave. After searchers had located his body, Tom and Huck went back into the cavern to look for the chest which they believed Injun Joe had hidden there. They found it and the twelve thousand dollars it contained.

Adopted shortly afterward by the Widow Douglas, Huck planned to retire with an income of a dollar a day for the rest of his life. He never would have stayed with the widow or consented to learn her prim, tidy ways if Tom had not promised that he would form a pirates' gang and make Huck one of the bold buccaneers.

Critical Evaluation

Beginning his writing career as a frontier humorist and ending it as a bitter satirist, Mark Twain drew from his circus of experiences, as a child in a small Missouri town (who had little formal schooling), as a printer's apprentice, a journalist, a roving correspondent, a world traveler, silver prospector, Mississippi steamboat pilot, and lecturer. He was influenced, in turn, by Artemus Ward, Bret Harte, Longstreet, and G. W. Harris. Beginning with the publication of his first short story, "The Celebrated Jumping Frog of Calaveras County," in 1865, and proceeding through his best novels—*Innocents Abroad* (1869); *Roughing It* (1872); *The Gilded Age* (1873), brilliant in concept but a failure in design and execution; *Tom Sawyer* (1876); *Life on the Mississippi* (1883); *Huckleberry Finn* (1885); *A Connecticut Yankee in King Arthur's Court* (1889); and *The American Claimant* (1892)—Twain developed a characteristic style which, though uneven in its productions, made him the most important and most representative nineteenth century American writer. His service as delightful entertainment to generations of American youngsters is equaled, literarily, by his influence on such twentieth century admirers as Gertrude Stein, William Faulkner, and Ernest Hemingway.

Twain's generally careful and conscientious style was both a development of the southwestern humor tradition of Longstreet and Harris and a departure from the conventions of nineteenth century literary gentility. It is characterized by the adroit use of exaggeration, stalwart irreverence, deadpan seriousness, droll cynicism, and pungent commentary on the human situation. All of this is masked in an uncomplicated, straightforward narrative distinguished for its wholehearted introduction of the colloquial and vernacular into American fiction that was to have a profound impact on the development of American writing and also shape the world's view of America. Twain, according to Frank Baldanza, had a talent for "paring away the inessential and presenting the bare core of experience with devastating authenticity." The combination of childish rascality and innocence in his earlier writing gave way, in his later and posthumous works, to an ever darkening vision of man that left Twain bitter and disillusioned. But this darker vision is hardly present in the three Tom Sawyer books (1876, 1894, 1896) and in his masterpiece, *Huckleberry Finn.*

Twain's lifelong fascination with boyhood play led to the creation of *Tom Sawyer,* a book of nostalgic recollections of his own lost youth that has been dismissed too lightly by some sober-sided academics as "amusing but thin stuff" and taken too analytically and seriously by others who seek in it the complexities—of carefully controlled viewpoint, multiple irony, and social satire—found in *Huckleberry Finn,* begun in the year *Tom Sawyer* was published. Beyond noting that *Tom Sawyer* is a delicate balance of the romantic with the realistic, of humor and pathos, of innocence and evil, one must admit that the book defies analysis. In fact, Twain's opening statement in *Huckleberry Finn* is, ironically, more applicable to *Tom Sawyer*: "Persons attempting to find a motive in this narrative will be prosecuted; persons attempting to find a moral in it will be banished; persons attempting to find a plot in it will be shot." *Tom Sawyer* is purely, simply, and happily "the history of a boy," or as Twain also called it, "simply a hymn, put into prose form to give it a worldly air." It should be read first and last for pleasure, first by children, then by adults.

For *Tom Sawyer* is also, as even Twain admitted paradoxically, a book for those who have long since passed from boyhood: "It is *not* a boy's book at all. It will be read only by adults. It is written only for adults." Kenneth S. Lynn explicates the author's preface when he says that *Tom Sawyer* "confirms the profoundest wishes of the heart"; as does Christopher Morley, who calls the book "a panorama of happy memory" and who made a special visit to Hannibal because he wanted to see the town and house where Tom lived. During that visit, Morley and friends actually white-washed Aunt Polly's fence. Certainly there can be no greater testimony to the effectiveness of a literary work than its readers' desire to reenact the exploits of its hero.

Tom is the archetypal all-American boy, defining in himself the very concept of American boyhood, as he passes with equal seriousness from one obsession to another: whistling, glory, spying, sympathy, flirtation, exploration, piracy, shame, fear—always displaying to the utmost the child's ability to concentrate his entire energies on one thing at a time (as when he puts the treasure hunt out of his mind in favor of Becky's picnic). Tom is contrasted to both Sid, the sanctimonious "good boy" informant who loses the reader's sympathies as immediately as Tom gains them, and to Huck. As opposed to Huck's self-reliant, unschooled, parentless existence, his love of profanity, his passive preference for being a follower, his abhorrence of civilization, Tom is shrewd in the ways of civilization, adventurous and a leader. He comes from the respectable world of Aunt Polly, with a literary mind, with a conscious romantic desire for experience and for the hero's part, an insatiable egotism which assists him in his ingenious schematizations of life to achieve his heroic aspirations—and a general love of fame, money, attention, and "glory." The relationship between the two boys may be compared to that between the romantic Don Quixote and the realist Sancho Panza. It was Twain's genius to understand that the games Quixote played out of "madness" were, in fact, those played by children with deadly seriousness. Lionel Trilling summarizes Twain's achievement in this book when he says that "*Tom Sawyer* has the truth of honesty—what it says about things and feelings is never false and always both adequate and beautiful." Twain's book is an American classic, but a classic that travels well as an ambassador of American nostalgic idealism.

Bibliography

Baldanza, Frank. *Mark Twain: An Introduction and Interpretation.* New York: Barnes & Noble, 1961, pp. 103–111.

Bercovitch, Sacvan. "Huckleberry Bumppo: A Comparison of *Tom Sawyer* and *The Pioneers,*" in *Mark Twain Journal.* XIV (Summer, 1968), pp. 1–4.

Blair, Walter. *Mark Twain and Huck Finn.* Berkeley: University of California Press, 1960, pp. 50–70, 71–76.

————. "On the Structure of *Tom Sawyer,*" in *Modern Philology.* XXX-VII (August, 1939), pp. 75–88.

————. "Tom Sawyer," in *Mark Twain: A Collection of Critical Essays.* Edited by Henry Nash Smith. Englewood Cliffs, N.J.: Prentice-Hall, 1963, pp. 64–82.

Bratcher, James T. "Twain's *Tom Sawyer,*" in *Explicator.* XXII (January, 1964), item 40.

Cecil, L. Moffitt. "Tom Sawyer: Missouri Robin Hood," in *Western American Literature.* IV (Summer, 1969), pp. 125–131.

Coard, Robert L. "Tom Sawyer, Sturdy Centenarian," in *Midwest Quarterly.* XVII (1976), pp. 329–350.

Covici, Pascal. *Mark Twain's Humor: Image of the World.* Dallas: Southern Methodist University Press, 1962, pp. 78–80.

Cox, James M. *Mark Twain: The Fate of Humor.* Princeton, N.J.: Princeton University Press, 1966, pp. 127–149.

Dillingham, William B. "Setting and Theme in *Tom Sawyer,*" in *Mark Twain Journal.* XII (Spring, 1964), pp. 6–8.

Elliot, George P. "Afterword: Vacation into Boyhood," in *The Adventures of Tom Sawyer.* By Mark Twain. New York: New American Library, 1959.

Fetterley, Judith. "The Sanctioned Rebel," in *Studies in the Novel.* III (Fall, 1971), pp. 293–304.

Hill, Hamlin. "The Composition and Structure of *Tom Sawyer,*" in *American Literature.* XXXII (January, 1961), pp. 379–392.

Hoffman, Daniel G. *Form and Fable in American Fiction.* New York: Oxford University Press, 1961, pp. 321–330.

Howell, Elmo. "In Defense of *Tom Sawyer,*" in *Mark Twain Journal.* XV (Winter, 1970), pp. 17–19.

Karpowitz, Steven. "Tom Sawyer and Mark Twain: Fictional Women and Real in the Play of Consciousness with the Imagination," in *Literature and Psychology* XXIII (1973), pp. 5–12.

Rogers, Franklin R. *Mark Twain's Burlesque Patterns as Seen in the Novels and Narratives, 1855–1885.* Dallas: Southern Methodist University Press, 1960, pp. 101–113.

Rubin, Louis D., Jr.   "Mark Twain: *The Adventures of Tom Sawyer*," in *Landmarks of American Writing*. Edited by Hennig Cohen. New York: Basic Books, 1969, pp. 157–171.

————.   "*Tom Sawyer* and the Use of Novels," in *American Quarterly*. IX (Summer, 1957), pp. 209–216.

Smith, Henry Nash.   *Mark Twain: The Development of a Writer.* Cambridge, Mass.: Belknap Press of Harvard University Press, 1962, pp. 81–91. Reprinted in *Mark Twain: A Collection of Criticism*. Edited by Dean Morgan Schmitter. New York: McGraw-Hill, 1974, pp. 85–94.

Spengemann, William C.   "The Fallen Woman and the Bad Boy," in *Mark Twain and the Backwoods Angel*. Kent, Oh.: Kent State University Press, 1966, pp. 31–47.

Stone, Albert E., Jr.   *The Innocent Eye: Childhood in Mark Twain's Imagination*. New Haven, Conn.: Yale University Press, 1961, pp. 58–90.

Tracy, Robert.   "Myth and Reality in *The Adventures of Tom Sawyer*," in *Southern Review*. IV (April, 1968), pp. 530–541.

Wiggins, Robert A.   "Tom Sawyer: 'Seeming of Reality,' " in *Mark Twain: Jackleg Novelist*. Seattle: University of Washington Press, 1964, pp. 42–54.

ROYALL TYLER

Born: Boston, Massachusetts (July 18, 1757)
Died: Brattleboro, Vermont (August 16, 1826)

Principal Works

POETRY: *The Verse of Royall Tyler*, 1967
PLAYS: *The Contrast*, 1790; *The Island of Barrataria, The Origin of the Feast of Purim, Joseph and His Brethren,* and *The Judgement of Solomon,* published in *Four Plays*, 1941.
NOVELS: *The Algerine Captive*, 1797
MISCELLANEOUS WORKS: *The Prose of Royall Tyler*, 1971

Royall Tyler's father was a merchant and a man of some note in Boston politics prior to the Revolution. The son, born William Clark, legally assumed his father's name when Royall, Sr., died, and he also distinguished himself in a number of fields during the early years of the republic. He studied at the South Latin School in Boston and earned a law BA from Harvard between 1772 and 1776. Tyler received a fairly large inheritance at his father's death, and for a time after graduation he apparently indulged himself in much conversation and some drink with other prominent Harvard graduates. During this time he may have fathered an illegitimate child and did take a small part in the war, all the while pursuing his legal studies under a preceptor. He earned a master's in law from Harvard in 1779 and was admitted to the bar in 1780.

As a young lawyer, Tyler first practiced—unsuccessfully—in Fallmouth and then in Boston, where he became infatuated with Nabby Adams, John Adams' daughter. While Abagail encouraged the relationship, John Adams at first did not, but by the time mother and daughter left to join their father in Europe, Tyler had written to Adams vowing his sincerity and declaring his intent to marry Nabby. However, Tyler had a reputation for irresponsibility, and, despite evidence of his increasing financial stability, his failure to respond to some of Nabby's letters from Europe cooled the relationship, and she soon married her father's legation secretary, Colonel William Stevens Smith.

In 1787 Shays' Rebellion broke out in Western Massachusetts, and Tyler joined the forces organized to repress it. According to one legend, he converted a group of the rebels to the government cause by lecturing them at Sunday meeting. He also led troops, but was much more successful at persuading the Vermont legislature not to provide sanctuary for the rebels. This skill at diplomacy led to other missions, one of which took him to New York in 1787 where he launched his literary career.

Tyler stayed in New York for only about two months, but during that time managed to write and see performed two plays, including *The Contrast*, his best known work. Despite *The Contrast*'s success, including a revival in 1789, Tyler continued his legal career, first in Boston and then in Vermont, beginning in 1791 when he established himself at Guilford. In 1794, he married Mary Palmer, whom he had known for over ten years and who was the daughter of a prominent Boston family (one of Mary's nieces was Sophia Peabody Hawthorne, another was the wife of Park Benjamin, and a nephew was publisher George Putnam). Mary Tyler bore eleven children, and the struggle to maintain such a large family eventually created serious hardship for the Tylers. Between 1794 and 1813 Royall Tyler successfully held several public positions in Vermont including State's Attorney for Windham County, as well as Assistant Judge and Chief Justice of the Vermont Supreme Court, but when the regular income from these ended, Tyler had to rely on his private practice, his children's help, and, from 1822 on, public charity.

Despite the demands of his profession and family Tyler continued, at least sporadically, to write. In 1794 he and Joseph Dennie, as "Colon and Spondee," contributed satirical pieces to the *Eagle, or Dartmouth Centinel*, the *Farmer's Weekly Museum*, and the *Port Folio*. *The Algerine Captive* was published in 1797, *The Yankey in London* appeared in 1809, and numberous poems, plays, essays, orations, and sketches were written which have been collected and published since his death.

Tyler's major contribution, however, lies in *The Contrast* and *The Algerine Captive*, in both of which he reveals a sometimes sharp, sometimes subtle sense of humor, a keen insight into provincial manners and human foibles, and a Franklinian devotion to common sense. In *The Contrast* Tyler is credited with creating both "the first native comedy to be professionally produced" (according to his biographer, G. Thomas Tanselle) and the first stage Yankee, a provincial American whose artless rusticity is used to show up European affectations. Although this latter claim is not true, Tyler's Jonathan significantly embodies much of America's image of itself, its strengths and weaknesses in comparison with Europe. *The Contrast* is occasionally still performed, and *The Algerine Captive*, with its lucid style, stern indictment of slavery, and artful humor remains highly readable, perhaps the most delightful of early American novels. Thus, although his literary output was not large, Royall Tyler deserves wider recognition as one of America's more skillful satiric writers.

Bibliography

The main biographical study is G. Thomas Tanselle, *Royall Tyler*, 1967. For useful general commentary on Tyler see Alexander Cowie, *The Rise of the American Novel*, 1948; Arthur Hobson Quinn, *A History of American Drama from the Beginning to the Civil War*, 1943; and Constance Rourke, *The Roots of American Culture and Other Essays*, 1942. For more specialized studies see John Lauber, "*The Contrast*: A Study in the Concept of Innocence," *English Language Notes*, 1 (September 1963), 33–37; and Roger B. Stein, "Royall Tyler and The Question of Our Speech," *New England Quarterly*, XXXVIII (1965), 454–474.

THE ALGERINE CAPTIVE

Type of work: Novel
Author: Royall Tyler (1757–1826)
Type of plot: Satiric autobiography
Time of plot: Late eighteenth century
Locale: America and Algiers
First published: 1797

One of the first and best American satiric novels, The Algerine Captive *presents the experiences of a young man in America and Algeria, which expose not only the horrors of slavery, but also historical and cultural information in an episodic, readable style.*

Principal Characters

Updike Underhill, a young, rural New England doctor who spends six years as a slave in Algiers. Updike earns attention as a scholar because he recites poetry loudly. He acquires a useless scholarly education which he eventually channels more practically into medicine. Ill rewarded in America for his skill and knowledge, he goes to sea as ship's doctor on a slaver which acquaints him at first hand with the horrors of that practice. He learns these horrors even more intimately when he is captured by Algerine pirates. Thus, for most of his career Updike is out of place, either a dreamy scholar among rustics, a skillful physician among quacks and fools, or a stubborn Christian among devout Muslims. As the impractical classicist, Updike is either unconscious of the world around him or smugly superior to it, but in either case blind to his own folly. As a doctor, his sensitivity to the failings of others sharpens, but he is less smug than justifiably outraged. As a slave, he reflects the ways of his captors with less irony and more of the balanced view of the realist. But, unable to argue his faith with reason, he becomes mulish in defending it, as if it were the one way to preserve his sense of self. In the end

Updike is somewhat chastened by his experiences, and vows to settle down with a good woman and a more mature devotion to his practice.

Captain John Underhill, Updike's ancestor, a military man and somewhat of a rebel. Having joined Essex against Elizabeth I, Captain Underhill flees to the Netherlands and then to Massachusetts with John Winthrop. Although he serves the Puritans in the Pequod War, he is later banished to New Hampshire for lusting in his heart. As one repeatedly alienated despite his worthiness, he sets a pattern later followed by Updike.

A minister, Updike's first tutor. He is worldly enough to secure himself tutorial fees, but based on his own experiences at Harvard, he prepares Updike for nothing else but scholarship.

A renowned oculist, Updike's medical preceptor. Unlike the minister, he is both skilled and unpretentious. He teaches Updike the value of not intimidating patients with technical language.

A veterinarian, Updike's temporary medical associate. Somewhat of a con man, he bamboozles people with high-sounding terminology and medical theory, but he is less self-deceived than the other physicians. He often cures with common sense and a little whiskey.

The mollah, A Muslim priest who tries to convert Updike but ends up befriending him. The mollah has himself been converted and can defend Islam more successfully than Updike can defend Christianity. When Updike is near despairing unto death, the mollah discovers him and encourages him back to health.

Adonah Ben Benjamin, an ostensibly poor but secretly wealthy Jew living in Algiers. When Updike treats him,

Adonah gratefully agrees to help him accumulate funds which will be given to a third party and used to ransom him. Adonah even supplements the amount Updike raises. At the last minute Adonah dies, and the ransom plan dies with him because his son refuses to acknowledge the arrangements that have been made.

Adonah's son, reneges on his father's plan to help Updike. However, when he too requires medical treatment and is saved by Updike, he arranges for Updike to be rescued by boat. The plan turns out to be a double-cross, and Updike presents him as a stereotype of "Jewish" avarice and ingratitude.

The Story

Updike Underhill's ancestor, Captain John Underhill, came to America as part of the Puritan flight from persecution in England. He had been a renowned officer in the service first of the Earl of Leicester and then of the Earl of Essex. Having been involved in Essex's rebellion in 1601 Captain Underhill fled to Holland, eventually joined Governor Winthrop in Boston, and served in the Pequod wars. More tolerant than his Massachusetts contemporaries, Underhill was eventually banished from the colony for staring too intently at one Miriam Wilbore. Captain Underhill was charged with committing adultery in his heart, and he fled first to Dover, New Hampshire, where he was elected governor but was subsequently libeled by his Massachusetts persecutors and finally forced to remove to Albany. However the Captain's eldest son returned to New Hampshire some time after his father's death, and it is from him that Updike Underhill descended.

Young Updike early distinguished himself at school and was consequently called upon to recite a spelling lesson for the local minister who had come to inspect the schools. Updike's stentorian reading so impressed the minister that, when he later bargained with Updike's father over some cattle, he persuaded the senior Underhill that his son should be prepared for college. The cattle were swapped (to the minister's advantage), and Updike went weekly to study Latin and Greek with the enterprising clergyman (who was paid well enough for his instruction).

Updike's mastery of classical languages, in particular his memorizing some four hundred lines in Homer, was brought to the attention of other Cambridge educated clergymen who predicted grand careers for the young scholar. Updike's father began to plan more earnestly for sending his son to college, but these plans were soon halted, first when he discovered the cost of the education, and then when a traveling divine told him that Greek and Latin would fit Updike for nothing *but* college. Consequently, Updike was made to work on the farm for awhile, but this too failed since the would-be scholar spent more time dreaming Greek and Roman mythology than working in the fields and barn. The final blow came when he attempted to attract bees following Virgil's advice in *The Georgics* by killing a heifer (the family's planned winter beef) and leaving it to putrefy. As a result, Updike's father agreed that his son should continue his education career, and Updike became a school teacher.

Unfortunately Updike had no more success as pedagogue than he did as farmer. He began optimistically, relishing his role as *Master* but envisioning himself as a gentle despot, cheered by grateful parents, loved by dutiful children, and free to devote many hours in Homeric fantasies. Instead, the pupils were uninterested in learning and took advantage of his benevolence. When finally he resorted to the rod to discipline one of the older boys, he found himself confronted by an even larger, angrier parent who threatened him with a cart-whip. When he tried to fit in with the local tavern crowd, he discovered their interest in horse racing did not extend to Achilles' steed, Xanthus. The eligible young ladies at a neighborhood quilting party were equally baffled by his talk of Penelope at her loom and could only respond that the reason she took so long was that her yarn must have rotted. Strangely to Updike, these women and their buck-toothed beaus preferred square dancing to his declamations from the Odyssey, and since he knew no Homeric precedents for *bundling* or *getting the bag*, (Aeneas and Dido in the Latin were the best he could think of) he declined offers to accompany a Miss Mima home. The most he derived from the quilting was a reputation as a papist for having spoken French all evening. Updike finally forsook teaching when the children carelessly burned down the school house, but the townspeople held him responsible for it.

Thus, Updike returned to the farm still looking for a suitable profession. After reading some in theology, law, and medicine, he chose the last and began study with a prominent physician, noted for restoring sight to the blind, but ignorant of Greek. Updike learned readily from the physician, but persisted in displaying his knowledge of the classics, which in a number of instances, caused him trouble. On one occasion, he wrote an ode praising the ox-eyed, golden-haired beauty of a wall-eyed redhead who dyed her hair, and, as a result, he was challenged to a duel. The challenge was so cordially written that Updike agreed to it without knowing what it was, but he and his reputation were saved when authorities learned of the duel and stopped it. On another occasion, he was drawn to a young woman who expressed interest in his learning, and he responded by lending her his books. The relationship came to naught, however, when she told him she had twice read the pretty stories in Johnson's *Dictionary* and wished a copy of "Rolling Belly Lettres."

When Updike's medical education was complete, he began his search for a practice by riding through the countryside investigating the situations in various small communities. Most of these were as receptive to medicine as to classical learning, but he settled in one that already supported four other doctors: one who was learned; a second who prescribed by volume; a third who dealt in simples; and a fourth who attempted healing with entertainment and prayer. For a time his only patients were two love-sick country girls, but when his landlord, tiring of not receiving his rent, repeatedly had the young doctor paged during church service and recommended his skills to others, Updike's practice began to flourish.

Ironically, Updike entered in a loose partnership with another learned man, a veterinarian who frequently ministered to humans when the other physicians were unavailable. While Updike had learned from his preceptor to avoid medical jargon, the vet used that language to convince others of his knowledge. On one occasion a jockey was thrown from a horse, and all the medical men assembled to offer treatment. The learned doctor shut all the doors and windows, but could offer no cure since he had left "Pringle on Contusions" at home. The second doctor prescribed half a dose of crude opium and asked for trepanning tools. The simples doctor proposed brown paper dipped in rum and cobwebs, and the fourth doctor told a funny story and began praying. The vet then stepped forward and offered a convincing diagnosis laced with bogus terminology and a theory of medicine which located the jockey's soul in his heel. While the other four were arguing with one another and against the vet, he dosed the patient with urine and molasses which brought about an immediate and remarkable recovery.

Despite his association with the enterprising vet, Updike's practice earned him little, and he decided to head south where he hoped the citizenry would be more supportive of valuable, learned men. However, his hopes were not rewarded. While at an Anglican service, he observed the minister flog his black slave before mounting the pulpit to give his sermon. Afterwards, he saw the same minister at the race track, his robes stuffed with cash, and this man was admired by everyone, not despite, but because of this behavior. Even more dispiriting, he found the same coastal devotion to business and the same backwoods ignorance and prejudice that prevailed in the North, plus a reserve toward Yankees and a love of dissipation to which he was wholly unaccustomed. As a result, Updike signed on as ship's doctor on an English ship headed for London and then for the African coast to pick up slaves.

While in England the patriotic Updike was scornful of British presumptions to grandeur, but his experiences along the African coast were even more distasteful, for he discovered the slave trade to be truly monstrous. As ship's doctor, he was made to care for the hundreds of Africans made ill by close quarters, bad food, no sanitation, and the trauma of separation from home and family. When they set sail, seasickness worsened conditions and, in fact, threatened the loss of the entire slave cargo. Updike persuaded the Captain to return to shore and set up a kind of infirmary for the sick.

While Updike was on shore waiting for the last of the sick to heal, an Algerian ship entered the harbor, drove off the British slaver, and captured Updike and the few others left behind. His first taste of slavery aboard the Algerine ship confirmed by experience the horrors he had seen aboard the British ship, and only the kindness of one of his former black patients saved him from the worst kind of misery. Upon arrival in Algiers he was made to bow before the Dey, Vizier Hassen Bashan, and then was taken to the slave market, where he was ignominiously sold to Abdel Melic, a Turk.

With his general aversion to labor, Updike found the burden of slavery particularly onerous. The situation quickly worsened, however, when he was flogged and consigned to the quarry for striking the overseer. One day, a *renegado*, a European who had adopted Islam, spoke to Updike in the quarry and urged him likewise to give up his Christian faith in exchange for his freedom. Lured by at least temporary relief from his labors, Updike consented to meet with the Mollah (Muslim priest). He was taken to a sumptuous "college," where he was cleansed, clothed, and fed. For five days he debated religion with the Mollah, but while the priest was persuasive, Updike stubbornly resisted and was returned to the quarry.

Afterwards, Updike planned an escape and began hoarding provisions. On the day before the attempt, however, all the slaves were given a holiday to witness the gruesome execution of one who had previously attempted to flee. The sight of this man impaled on a high stake driven carefully along his backbone so as to keep him alive and wriggling like an insect delivered a clear message to Updike and he quickly hid the evidence of his plans. The signal was so devastating, in fact, that despair soon shattered his already labor-weakened health, and he was sent to the infirmary where, for a time, he lingered close to death.

Updike was saved by the Mollah, who visited him in the infirmary and instead of attempting a last-minute conversion had him transferred to another part of the hospital and recommended that the doctors employ Updike as an aide. Soon, Updike's health returned, and he acquired a wide reputation as the "learned slave," ministering not only to the lowly, but to the wealthy and powerful as well. These grateful, well-placed patients invariably offered him freedom if only he would adopt the true faith, but Updike doggedly resisted these allurements. Still, his renewed life as a physician was a vast improvement over the quarry, and for a time he was fairly comfortable. Updike's urge to escape was reinvigorated, however, when some American officers visited Algiers. He was temporarily placed under house arrest and then pledged not to speak to the officers. Thus feeling his alienation from home and friends, Updike befriended a wealthy Jew, Adonah Ben Benjamin, who offered to arrange ransom through a third party. The plan called for Updike to give Adonah all the money he could raise, and the Jew would supplement this from his own pocket. Before the deal could be completed, however, Adonah Ben Benjamin died, and his son claimed no knowledge of the prior arrangement. Moreover, the third party had spread the rumor that Updike was immensely wealthy, and this raised the ransom.

To restore Updike's newly deflated spirits, the hospital director sent him on a pilgrimage to Medina and Mecca. On the way back, Updike discovered the son of Adonah Ben Benjamin lying close to death in Alexandria. The son confessed knowledge of the ransom transaction with his father, and promised to help Updike if he recovered. However, no longer threatened by death, the son went back on his word and tricked Updike into a small boat which lead not to the promised freedom but to a new slavery among the Tunisians. But, before the ship reached Tunis, it was crippled by a storm and drifted near Sardinia where it was captured by a Portugese frigate. The Portugese released Updike, and he returned to the United States vowing to marry "some amiable woman" and pursue his medical practice with more diligence and success than he had as a youth.

Critical Evaluation

The Algerine Captive is one of the first and best American satiric novels. Presented as an autobiography, the structure of the work is episodic and, in the second volume, padded by historical and cultural information about the Algerians and about Muhammadanism generally. The two volumes, in fact, roughly divide between Updike Underhill's experiences in America and his adventures as a slave in Algeria, but the whole centers on the young man's maturing awareness of himself and of the world in which he lives. Tyler's insights into the manners and customs of the new republic are penetrating and remarkably relevant, and his analysis and indictment of slavery are equally effective. Moreover, unlike the novels of sensibility and terror written in America at about the same time, which were much more popular then and have been more thoroughly studied since, *The Algerine Captive* needs no apology for its style. Although the specific issue of protecting American citizens from Algerine pirates no longer exists, Tyler's novel remains eminently readable on many levels.

The most obvious issues in Tyler's novel are American manners and attitudes towards learning, the practice of slavery, and the need to protect American shipping from North African pirates. The primary vehicle for Tyler's commentary on these issues is the limited consciousness of the main character, Updike Underhill, who at each stage of the novel's development is out of step with the world around him. Therefore, beyond specific social and political issues of the 1790's the novel concerns the education of a young man, or, more exactly, the young man's need to discover in his education a practical and ethical basis for living. The depiction of American life in volume one exposes many weaknesses. In the account of Captain Underhill, Tyler attacks the narrow-mindedness and intolerance of the Puritans. The character of Updike's own education shows the Harvard educated clergy to be foolishly impractical, intellectually inbred, and even a bit venal insofar as the minister who first instructs Updike diverts his father with talk of the boy's promise and thereby not only bests the father in a cattle swap but also secures a well-paying tutorial job. However, just as in his better-known comedy, *The Contrast*, where the European fop is only by degrees more ridiculous than the Yankee bumpkin Jonathan, the satire in *The Algerine Captive* cuts two ways. Thus, while

Tyler sports with Updike's classicism, he also makes fun of the backwoods Americans' narrowmindedness, provinciality, and anti-intellectualism. The scenes at the rural school house, tavern, and quilting bee, seem to foreshadow Mark Twain's treatment of rural life in mid-nineteenth century Missouri. For Tom Sawyer's *Count of Monte Cristo* and *Don Quixote* we can substitute Updike's Homer, but the recalcitrant students, the indignant father who threatens the school teacher with a buggy whip, the "florid faced" young man "with two large prominent foreteeth," and the quilters who enjoy "bundling" would be at home in either New Hampshire or Missouri or, for that matter, in any of the locales of Southeastern humor from Longstreet's Georgia to Faulkner's Mississippi.

Furthermore, Tyler aims his satire south as well as north when Updike acquires a reputation for courage by merely accepting an invitation to duel, even though he only intends to be polite and the duel is stopped by the authorities to the great relief of both participants. Updike's second is from Carolina and is said, therefore, to be knowledgeable in such affairs. When Updike actually journeys south, he finds human failing not only in dueling, but also in the haughtiness of the Southern belles, a general hostility to strangers (especially Yankees) and in ministers who, with the enthusiastic support of their parishoners, beat their slaves before preaching and bet at the racetracks afterwards. The practice of slavery is more thoroughly and directly denounced when Updike discovers at first hand the horrors of a slave ship and when he becomes a slave himself in Algeria.

Of course, the medical profession is also examined and once again there is folly in doctors as well as in their patients. The American's willingness to understand and support the healing arts, to value skill and root out quackery is highly suspect. And, with the exceptions of Updike and his preceptor, the learned oculist, all the other physicians or pseudo-physicians are quacks: one is bound to his medical texts, another trusts everything to heavy doses, a third is more of an herb doctor, a fourth sings and prays like a witch doctor, and the most successful is a conning veterinarian, but all are quacks. As demonstrated in the injured jockey scene, the people's gullibility and the doctors' shams serve each other well.

For Updike, however, medicine is the means by which first he learns to translate his education into something useful, and then to survive and even prosper while a slave. It is important that Updike's preceptor is unpretentious in his knowledge, for, like him, Updike must learn to socialize his abilities before they can be useful. His is a history of alienation, beginning with the ancestor who is ostracized both from England and from Massachusetts. Updike follows that pattern in his career as pedagogue and backwoods doctor, in his flight to and then from the South, in his reaction to slavery which is not shared by the other ship's officers, and then in his years as a loyal Christian among the Muhammadans. This last is particularly interesting because Updike changes from one alienated by a stubborn orthodoxy.

Tyler's point in having Updike cling doggedly to his faith at the expense of both wealth and freedom may be to underline a need for courage and integrity in dealing with the Barbary pirates, but his perversity also signals the need to pre-serve his identity when custom, law, language, dress, diet, and faith are arrayed to blot it out. Unlike the European *renegado*, who expediently loses his self in Islam, Updike discovers a way for a time, to live within, to manipulate his environment but not lose himself in it. Thus, like Benjamin Franklin, whom he visited earlier on a trip to Philadelphia, Updike manages to exploit opportunities that keep him alive and eventually (with a touch of luck) lead to his release. Although we never finally see what Updike makes of himself, his avowal to settle down with a good woman and a solid practice when he returns to America suggests a success pat-tern similarly Franklinian. We sense now that Updike's knowledge has not only been directed to practical art, but also been socialized and humanized by his experience as a slave.

Bibliography

Cowie, Alexander. "Royall Tyler," in his *Rise of the American Novel*. New York: American Books, 1948, pp. 60–68.

Davidson, C.N. "Royall Tyler's *The Algerine Captive*: A Study in Contrasts," in *Ariel*. VII (July, 1976), pp. 436–439.

Leary, Lewis. "Royall Tyler: First Gentleman of the American Theater," in *Soundings*. Athens: University of Georgia Press, 1975, pp. 83–96.

Spiller, Robert. *Literary History of the United States*. New York: Macmillan, 1963, pp. 186–188.

Spingemann, William. "The Adventurous Muse: *The Algerine Captive*, and *Arthur Gordon Pym*," in his *The Adventurous Muse*. New Haven, Conn.: Yale University Press, 1977, pp. 119–150.

Tanselle, George T. "Early American Fiction in England: The Case of *The Algerine Captive*," in *Papers of the Bibliographical Society of America*. LIX (October–December, 1965), pp. 367–384.

————. *Royall Tyler*. Cambridge, Mass: Harvard University Press, 1967, pp. 140–180.

Van Doren, Carl. *American Novel*. New York: Macmillan, 1922, pp. 8–9.

OWEN WISTER

Born: Philadelphia, Pennsylvania (July 14, 1860)
Died: North Kingstown, Rhode Island (July 21, 1938)

Principal Works

NOVELS: *The Dragon of Wantley*, 1892; *The Virginian*, 1902; *Lady Baltimore*, 1906.

SHORT STORIES: *Red Men and White*, 1896; *Lin McLean*, 1898; *The Jimmyjohn Boss and Other Stories*, 1900; *Philosophy 4*, 1903; *Padre Ignacio*, 1911; *When West Was West*, 1928.

BIOGRAPHY: *Ulysses S. Grant*, 1900; *The Seven Ages of Washington*, 1907; *Roosevelt: The Story of a Friendship, 1880–1919*, 1930.

Owen Wister, born in Philadelphia, Pennsylvania, on July 14, 1860, began his career with a serious interest in music and only later became interested in writing. After being educated in private schools in the United States and abroad, he attended Harvard University, where he was graduated with highest honors in music in 1882. He then spent two years abroad, studying composition in Paris before ill health forced his return to the United States. Following a period as the employee of a bank in New York City, he suffered a nervous breakdown and traveled to Wyoming to recuperate in the healthful atmosphere of a Western cattle ranch. From 1885 to 1888 he attended the Harvard Law School. After graduation he was admitted to the bar and practiced law in Philadelphia.

Having grown extremely fond of the West while recuperating from his illness, Wister made frequent trips back to his favorite country. Two short stories based on western life, "Hank's Woman" (1891) and "How Lin McLean Went West" (1891), published in *Harper's Magazine*, were his first published literary works to gain recognition. Such volumes as *Red Men and White* and *The Jimmyjohn Boss* followed. In the meantime, Wister was married to Mary Channing, of Philadelphia, in 1898.

Wister's only well-known novel, *The Virginian*, was enough to make him famous. The book was a best seller for years, and succeeding generations have discovered this pioneer "Western" to their delight. The volume was dedicated to another outdoorsman and lover of the West, Theodore Roosevelt, who was a close friend of Owen Wister. One of the men who illustrated an edition of *The Virginian* was Frederic Remington, the famous painter of life in the West. Owen Wister continued to write, and he explored other themes than the West, but his other works were never widely accepted, largely because of their subject matter. *Philosophy 4*, for example, was a story about life at Harvard University, with limited appeal to general readers. *Lady Baltimore* is his one venture into the field of historical romance.

In the years after World War I, Wister wrote little. His last book was *Roosevelt: The Story of a Friendshipl* He died of a cerebral hemmorhage at North Kingstown, Rhode Island, July 21, 1938.

Bibliography

The collected edition is *The Writings of Owen Wister*, 11 vols., 1928, which includes writings previously unpublished in book form. There is also Fanny Kemble Wister, ed., *Owen Wister Out West: His Journals and Letters*, 1958. There is no full-scale study of Wister, but a fair and economical estimate is Jay B. Hubbell, "Owen Wister's Work," *South Atlantic Quarterly*, XXIX (1930), 440–443. Two opposing views of Wister's career are E. C. Marsh, "Representative American Story Tellers: Owen Wister," *Bookman*, XXVII (1908), 456–548; and H. W. Boynton, "A Word on the Genteel Critic: Owen Wister's Quack Novels and Democracy," *Dial*, LIX (1915), 303–306.

THE VIRGINIAN

Type of work: Novel
Author: Owen Wister (1860–1938)
Type of plot: Regional romance
Time of plot: Late nineteenth century
Locale: Wyoming
First published: 1902

The Virginian, *one of the classic novels of the American West, fashions a romantic myth of the cowboy hero. More than conventionally brave, the Virginian is idealized by Wister as the perfect specimen—a natural American whose moral superiority is seen as innate.*

Principal Characters

Vivian Grey, an ambitious young Englishman who desires a political career. His unscrupulous conduct ends that career. Traveling in Germany afterward, he learns how terrible politics can be and realizes how immoral his own conduct has been.

Mr. Dallas, proprietor of a school from which Vivian Grey is expelled.

Sidney Lorraine, the Marquess of Carabas, an incompetent who has been turned out of office. His support in politics is sought by Vivian because the man has a title and represents the aristocracy.

Mrs. Felix Lorraine, the fashionable sister-in-law of Sidney. Vivian attempts an affair with her, but she falls in love with Frederick Cleveland.

Frederick Cleveland, a retired minister of state. He gives his support for a time to Vivian. When he is insulted by Vivian, the two fight a duel, and Cleveland is killed.

Baron Eugene von Konigstein, a worldly German nobleman who becomes Vivian's friend for a time while the two are studying at Heidelberg. The Baron cheats at cards.

Essper George, a conjurer. He becomes Vivian's valet. He is killed during a storm, and his death has a sobering effect on Vivian.

Lady Madeleine Trevor, a friend of Vivian's father.

Mr. St. George, Lady Madeleine Trevor's brother.

Violet Fane, a friend of Lady Madeleine. She dies of natural causes in Vivian's arms, causing him to be grief-stricken.

Mr. Beckendorff, a recluse who is host to Vivian. He conspires to become prime minister of the Duchy of Reisenberg. When Vivian falls in love with Sybilla, Beckendorff plans to kill him but relents on condition that Vivian leave the duchy.

The Prince of Little Lilliput, a guest at Beckendorff's home. He becomes Vivian's friend and introduces the Englishman to court circles in Germany.

Sybilla, a beautiful young baroness. Vivian falls in love with her. But he is disillusioned when he learns that for political reasons the woman must marry a deformed, half-witted prince.

The Story

The Virginian had been sent by his employer to meet an Eastern guest at Medicine Bow and escort him the two hundred and sixty miles from the town to Sunk Creek Ranch. While the Virginian and the guest were awaiting the arrival of the Easterner's trunk on the following westbound train, the cowboy entered into a poker game. One of the players, a cowboy named Trampas, accused the Virginian of cheating. The man backed down, however, before the gun of the cowboy from Sunk Creek. It was apparent to everyone that the Virginian had made an implacable enemy.

A few months later, in the fall, a schoolmistress came West from Vermont to teach in the new school at Bear Creek, Wyoming. All the single men, and there were many of them in the territory, anxiously awaited the arrival of the new teacher, Molly Wood. The Virginian was fortunate in his first meeting with her. A drunken stage driver tried to ford a creek in high water and marooned his coach and passenger. The Virginian, passing by, rode to the stage, lifted out the young woman, and deposited her safely on the bank of the stream. After he had ridden away, Molly missed her handkerchief and realized the young cowboy had somehow contrived to take it.

The next time the Virginian saw Molly, she was a guest at a barbecue. The cowboy had ridden his horse for two days for an opportunity to see her, but she coquettishly refused to notice him. The Virginian and another cowboy, piqued by her attitude, got drunk and played a prank on all the people who had brought their children to the barbecue. They switched the babies and their clothing, so that when the barbecue was over many of the mothers carried off the wrong babies. Before he left for Sunk Creek, the Virginian warned Molly that she was going to love him eventually, no matter what she thought of him then.

During the next year the Virginian began to read books for the first time since he had left school in the sixth grade. He borrowed the books from Molly in order to ride to Bear Creek to see her at intervals. In the meantime he had risen high in the estimation of his employer. Judge Henry put him in charge of a party of men who were to escort two trainloads of steers to the Chicago market.

On the trip back to the ranch the Virginian's men threatened to desert the train to go prospecting for gold which had been discovered in the Black Hills. The ringleader of the insurgents was Trampas.

The Virginian saw that the best way to win over the men was to make a fool of Trampas. His chance came when the train stopped near a bridge that was being repaired. Since there was no food on the train, the Virginian went out and gathered a sackful of frogs to cook. Then he began a story about frogs, a tall story by which Trampas was completely taken in. As soon as the rest of the cowboys saw how foolish Trampas appeared, they were willing to return to the ranch, much to the discomfiture of their ringleader.

Back at Sunk Creek, the Virginian found a pleasant surprise awaiting him. The foreman of the ranch had been forced to leave because of an invalid wife, and the judge had made the Virginian his foreman.

Trampas had expected to be discharged from his job as soon as the Virginian became foreman at the Sunk Creek Ranch. The Virginian, however, decided it was better to have his enemy in sight, and so Trampas stayed on, sullen and defiant in his behavior.

The following spring the Virginian made a trip to a neighboring ranch. On the way back he was attacked by Indians and severely wounded. He managed to escape from the Indians and make his way to a spring. There he was found, half dead, by Molly Wood. The girl stayed with him at the risk of her life, for the Indians were still in the vicinity. She then bound his wounds and took him back to her cabin and called a doctor.

Molly, meanwhile, had packed her possessions, for she was preparing to leave for her home in the East. By the time the Virginian had recovered sufficiently to go back to work, she had decided not to leave Wyoming. She was sure by then that she was in love with the cowboy foreman. When the Virginian left her cabin for Sunk Creek, Molly had promised to marry him.

Upon returning to work, the Virginian found that his enemy, Trampas, had disappeared, taking another of the cowboys, Shorty, with him. About the same time the ranches in that territory began to lose cattle to rustlers, and a posse was formed to track down the cattle thieves. After several weeks of searching, two of the thieves were caught. Since the rustlers had somehow managed to gain control of the local courts and had already been freed on one charge, the posse hanged both of them. It was a terrible experience for the Virginian, because one of the men, Steve, had been a close friend. The Virginian hated to think he had hanged his friend, and the hurt was made worse by the fact that the condemned man had refused to say a word to his former companion.

On his way back to Sunk Creek, the Virginian came across the trail of the other two rustlers. They were Trampas and Shorty. Because they had only one horse between them, Trampas murdered Shorty in order to escape.

When Molly Wood heard of the lynching and the Virginian's part in it, she refused to marry him. But after a conversation with Judge Henry, she realized that the Virginian had done no more than his duty. She and the Virginian were reconciled and a date was set for their wedding.

On the day before their wedding, Molly and the Virginian started to ride to Medicine Bow. On the way they met Trampas, who galloped ahead of them into the town. Molly questioned the Virginian about the man and discovered the enmity between the two. When they arrived in town, they were warned that Trampas had said he would shoot the Virginian if he were not out of town by sunset. Molly told him that she could never marry him if he fought with Trampas and killed him. The Virginian, knowing that his honor was at stake, left her in the hotel and went out to face his enemy. Trampas fired first and missed. Then the Virginian fired and killed Trampas.

When the Virginian returned to the hotel, Molly was too glad to see him alive to remember her threat. Hearing the shots, she had been afraid that the Virginian had been killed. They were married the following day, as they had planned, and spent two months of their honeymoon high in the Rocky Mountains where no other humans ever went.

Critical Evaluation

This book appeared in 1902, some ten years after the closing of the frontier and shortly after Frederick Jackson Turner explained in his famous "safety-valve" thesis the function that the frontier had performed in American history. Perhaps *The Virginian* is an expression of the need, once the frontier was gone, to experience a frontier that never was. This book is one of the first serious novelistic treatments of the American cowboy, if one excludes the dime novels that had dismayed parents for almost the previous fifty years. When the open range was gone, the cowboy came into his own as a literary figure, and there seems to be more than coincidence in the two facts. The end of the frontier era and the beginning of the cowboy novel meld too closely for there to be much accident about it.

This book is not set in the American West so much as in a country called Cattle Land, where men are men and possess all the virtues and characteristics popularly associated with Horatio Alger. Wister associates one more element to this mythical character he is writing about—primal man. Wister very often describes the Virginian as "wild" or "natural" and the two words are seemingly interchangeable. The East is decadent and the American virtues have their last home in the West.

Tied up with this idea of primal innocence is the concept of an Americanism that is itself primal, free of the decadence of Europe. But decadence has swept westward, as Wister sees it, and has pushed Americanism in front of it. The only Vermonter, back in Molly's home state, to approve of her new husband is the great-aunt who sees in the Virginian the spirit of her own husband, a general in the Revolutionary War. This theme of Americanism being a primal, Adamic innocence and being found only in the West is brought out most forcefully when Judge Henry tries to explain to Molly why the Virginian and others had to lynch a cattle rustler. Molly objects that they took the law into their own hands. The Judge's reply is that the law came originally from people who delegated this responsibility to their representatives; in turn, they established in the Constitution machinery for administering the law. But in Wyoming the hands of the law were weak, and could not do the job that had been delegated them. So the Virginian had only been taking back what had been his own. The delegates to the Constitutional convention, then, were in spirit to be found in the far West, ironically at a Wyoming lynching party.

This is Wister's world and it is, as he said in his foreword to the novel, one that no longer exists. He was wrong when he said this in 1902, for men like the Virginian, although less romantic when seen in the flesh, are still spread over this country. They seem to be part of a dying breed. Many in America today would agree with much that the Virginian says and represents, and in that respect the cowboy has not vanished from the land any more than our belief in the primal innocence of America has lessened. He may have changed, perhaps become urbanized, but many contemporary Americans continue to live with the Virginian's values.

Bibliography

Barsness, John A. "Theodore Roosevelt as Cowboy: *The Virginian* as Jacksonian Man," in *American Quarterly.* XXI (Fall, 1969), pp. 609–619.

Cady, Edwin H. *"The Virginian,"* in *The Light of the Common Day: Realism in American Fiction.* Bloomington: Indiana University Press, 1971, pp. 182–192.

Cawelti, John G. "The Western: A Look at the Evolution of a Formula," in *Adventure, Mystery and Romance: Formula Stories as Art and Popular Culture.* Chicago: University of Chicago Press, 1976, pp. 192–259.

DeVoto, Bernard A. "A Birth of an Art," in *Western Writing.* Edited by Gerald W. Haslam. Albuquerque: University of New Mexico Press, 1974, pp. 8–15.

Downs, Robert Bingham. "Birth of the Western," in *Famous American Books.* New York: McGraw-Hill, 1971, pp. 213–219.

Gemme, Francis R. *Wister's* The Virginian. New York: Thor, 1966.

Houghton, Donald E. "Two Heroes in One: Reflections upon the Popularity of *The Virginian,*" in *Journal of Popular Culture.* IV (Fall, 1970), pp. 497–506.

Lambert, Neal. "Owen Wister's Virginian: The Genesis of a Cultural Hero," in *Western American Literature.* VI (Summer, 1971), pp. 99–107.

ALPHABETICAL LIST OF TITLES